The Mysteries of

Life & Death

The Mysteries of

Life & Death

An Illustrated Investigation into the Incredible World of Death

Consultant
Professor Keith Simpson, CBE, FRCP, FC Path

Leisure Books

Editor's Acknowledgements:

In the course of preparing this book for publication both Professor Keith Simpson and I have been fortunate in receiving assistance and information from a host of people and organizations. It is not possible to thank everyone individually here, but we would like to express our gratitude to all who contributed material for the book and who dealt patiently with persistent requests for information.

In particular, I would like to thank the following individuals: Mr P J Ball, Institute of Embalmers, Dr Douglas Chambers, coroner, N London, Gary Donovan, Dr John Gibben, Roger Planer, Nancy Tate, Churchill Fellowship, Professor John Taylor, King's College, London, and Dolores Taranko.

The following institutions were most generous in their assistance: ANPAT, Belgium, Association of Funeral Directors, Association of Life Insurance Medical Directors of America, British Academy of Forensic Sciences, BMA, Canadian High Commission, Catholic Enquiry Centre, Central Bureau of Statistics, Netherlands, Central Statistical Office of Finland, Daily Express, Friends of the Earth, HM Factory Inspectorate, Home Office, Justice Department, USA, Le Monde, Metropolitan Life Insurance Company, NY, Ministry of Justice, Denmark, Ministry of Labor, Brazil, Ministry of Labor, Spain, National Criminal Justice Reference Service, USA, National Foundation of Funeral Service, National Safety Council, UK, National Safety Council, USA, Office of Health Economics, Office of Population Censuses and Surveys (England and Wales), Royal Society for the Prevention of Accidents (RoSPA), Samaritans, Society of Actuaries, Swiss National Accident Insurance Fund, Thames TV.

In addition, I would like to thank Mark Smith, for his help in the preparation of the bulk of the statistical material, Helen Hill and Fiona Baird, for their valuable contributions to the Facing the Facts section, Dr Elie Cohen, for his essay on the Auschwitz Concentration camp, Mike Tregenza, for his advice in the preparation of material for the chapter on The Master Liquidator and Richard and Doreen O'Neill, for their work on chapter five, A Fatal Vision.

Martin Schultz

Leisure Books

Credits

Editor: Martin Schultz
Designers: Barry Savage/Rod Teasdale/Mark Holt
Picture Researchers: Barbara Peevor/Irene Reed

Colour and Line Drawings:
Oxford Illustrators Ltd
A Good Studio Ltd, England
© Salamander Books Ltd

Filmset: Modern Text Typesetting Ltd., England

Colour Reproduction:
Bantam Litho Ltd
Central Reproduction Ltd
Colour Craftsmen Ltd
Tenreck Ltd, England

Printed in Belgium: Henri Proost et Cie, Turnhout

Contents:

The Consultant

Professor Keith Simpson
Until recently Head of the Forensic Department at Guy's Hospital, and Consultant Pathologist to the Home Office

The Authors

Dr Stuart Brown, Senior Lecturer in Philosophy. Dr Brown has taken a special interest in an analysis of man's fears as they relate to death

Dr Peter Calow, Lecturer in Zoology at Glasgow University and author of two highly acclaimed books, Biological Machines and Life Cycles

Dr Jeremy Cherfas, Biological Sciences Editor of the New Scientist and author of several books on aspects of evolution and biology

Dr John Harcup, MRCP, is an advisor to several major pharmaceutical companies, the author of several medical reviews, and a GP with a particular interest in medical history

Paul Holberton, has had several works published on the history of fine art and is currently editing a four-volume encyclopedia on art, artists and sculptors for a leading London publisher

William Johnstone, radio broadcaster, journalist and author, has undertaken a number of sociological research projects for periodicals and other publications

Sidney Lightman is a Senior Editor and writer for the Jewish Chronicle

The Contributors

Dr Ann Bolton, FRCP, FRPsych (The Dying Child)
Child psychiatrist and author of several works on this theme

Professor Basil Mitchell (Euthanasia: Against)
One of the foremost authorities on the subject of euthanasia, Professor Mitchell is Nolloth Professor at Oriel College, Oxford

Dr Bernard H Pentney, MRCS, LRCP (Time of Crisis)
Clinical Director of the medical centre of a private medical insurance institution

Dr Cicely Saunders, OBE (Care of the Dying)
Foremost international authority on caring for the terminally ill and one of the originators of the concept of a hospice for the dying

Dr Eliott Slater, CBE (Euthanasia: For)
Former director of the Medical Research Council, Psychiatric Genetics Unit

Dr Michael Smith (The Case for Abortion)
Well-known author on medical matters, broadcaster and columnist

Michael Wallach (The Jewish Position)
Editor of the Jewish Year Book and a leading authority on Judaism and Rabbinical philosophy, and contributor to the Encyclopedia Judaica

Rev Norman Woods (The Protestant Conviction)
Vicar of St Leonard's, Hythe, Kent

Anthony Livesey, a specialist writer on military and political history, Mr Livesey has made a special study of military burial customs at different periods in Western history

Dr Malvern Lumsden, Research fellow at the Stockholm International Peace Research Institute, Dr Lumsden has been involved in work for the United Nations aimed at updating the Geneva conventions

Professor John Mason, CBE, former head of the Accident Reconstruction Unit of the RAF. Professor of Forensic Medicine, Edinburgh University

Malise Ruthven, specialist in Middle Eastern political affairs, author of the highly acclaimed book, Torture, A Grand Conspiracy, and regular contributor to newspapers and periodicals

Dr John Sparks, a BBC producer, has made about 250 programmes on nature subjects, and has also written a number of popular books on wildlife themes

Professor Keith Simpson Professor Emeritus and head of the Forensic Department at Guy's Hospital; Home Office Pathologist; President (1961) of the Medico-Legal Society; Harvard Associate in Police Science. 1927 Bacteriology Gold Medallist; author of several highly acclaimed medico-scientific works

Professor Trevor Gibbens, Professor of criminal psychiatry and international authority on the study of the criminal mind

Dr Cyril Wecht, MD, JD, Allegheny County Coroner, Clinical Associate, Professor of Pathology and Director, Pittsburgh Institute of Legal Medicine

Foreword

'It is as natural to die as to be born' wrote Francis Bacon in one of his seventeenth-century essays, and the words reflect a lawyer's calm appraisal of the fact. Death may indeed follow a common-place pattern in circumstances which occasion no surprise, often cause little sorrow, and hardly seem worth particular comment.

But death may also be a highly charged event, colourful, bizarre, mysterious, arousing suspicion or creating strong public feeling, a 'trigger' for new legislation, as in the famous McNaghten case. Equally, death may be a public disaster to be recorded in the pages of history like the Black Hole of Calcutta or the World War I slaughter in Flanders. Death has given rise to remarkable religious ceremonial in many parts of the world, to such profoundly moving music as Bach's Requiem Mass and to some memorable poetry. There is, however, remarkably little prose writing on the subject, and only comparatively short items describing the event in moving words, like those by Chekhov, himself a doctor.

Until now, no one has collected together into one encyclopedic work the beliefs, superstitions, plain and colourful facts, customs and statistics of this inevitable event. Search the shelves of the public libraries, thumb through the classics, pore over bulky tomes of both medicine and the law, and you will be struck by the paucity of interest shown in the subject of death. Why? Well might you ask. One would have thought that the subject must surely arouse at least the curiosity of everyone of all ages.

This modern, authoritative and superbly illustrated book covers every aspect of the subject. It has been written by a group of experts of acknowledged eminence, who have couched their contributions in readily understandable terms while, at the same time, taking care not to write down to the public for whom this outstanding work is intended. Every conceivable facet of the mysteries of life and death receive attention in counselling language, which is matched by striking illustrations – hundreds of them, mostly in colour.

It might well be felt that death is not a subject that can – or should – be popularized, and that any attempt in that direction would be in bad taste. However, a glance at any section of this magnificent book should be enough to convince even the most critical that its primary purpose is not to sensationalize, but to inform and educate a public which is increasingly demanding more knowledge about more subjects. The book fulfils its objective with taste and sensitivity, and it cannot offend anybody, even the most young and vulnerable. This volume does not have to be hidden away in a cupboard. It can and should be proudly displayed on the bookshelves of any home and valued for the remarkable and comprehensive work it is.

What is death? What happens – and when? Where does the soul go? Indeed, is there such a thing as a soul? Are doctors correct in their conception of 'brain death'? Should they switch off the equipment keeping a patient 'alive' when they have decided that all hope has gone? Was the famous Belgian artist, Wiertz, unduly anxious about being buried alive? What are the strange and exotic funerals like that are the custom in so many different parts of the world? Does mercy-killing occur – and what does the law have to say about this? Do many murders escape detection? Why do people commit suicide – or murder? What do psychiatrists have to say about it? Do we enjoy – or need – the church's elaborate ritual in the orderly disposal of the dead? What is there about mass disaster – air, rail, road, sea, fire or chemical, that excites such interest? Are accidents designed by fate? What are the statistics of death – in peace and war? Do we have any idea of how much money the powerful states of the world are spending on death-dealing weapons instead of on health, the fight against world famine and the struggle against population extinction? Do we really know the facts? Well, here they are, in profusion, tellingly illustrated, within the covers of a single volume – a remarkable achievement.

Keith Simpson

Professor Keith Simpson, CBE, FRCP, FCPath

Life Story

What is the connection between life and death? Did life originate by accident, without the intervention of any special forces? Was death indeed necessary for the evolution of life—can any living organism be immortal?

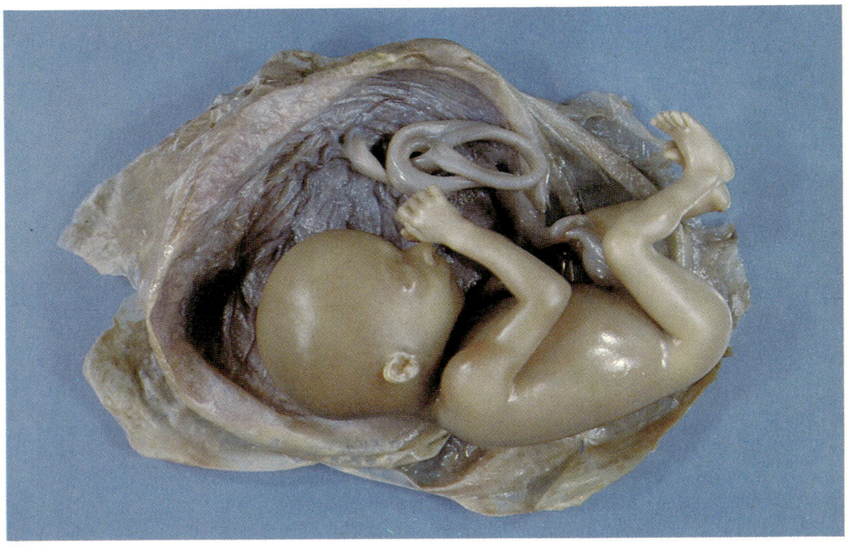

Above
A human foetus encased in the womb. The egg and sperm fuse to form a zygote and, by a process of sequential division, this is transformed into a complex, ordered and organized living being containing many millions of cells

Right
A consistent theme in the history of biological thought is the idea that the body is made up of matter plus some special organizing principle, often referred to as the soul. The soul was supposed to give form to matter, thus bringing into being those properties of organisms which we refer to as 'emergent'. This hypothesis can be traced back to Plato and even earlier thinkers. It proposes that the vitalizing principle enters the body at the beginning of life—as shown in this painting by William Blake of the soul, represented as Elohim, hovering over the body (Adam)—and makes its departure at the moment of death

A Late Arrival
The first signs of life in the form of living cells appeared on earth 3,200 million years ago. Man appeared only 3½ million years ago

A Grain in Time
If life on earth were depicted in the form of a clock face, the entire history of man's civilization would take up only one-tenth of a second

There are at least two ways in which things can be dead. Either they have never lived, like rocks, gases in the atmosphere or rays of sunshine, or they have lost the property of life like fallen leaves or fur coats. Actually the distinction is not so straightforward: dead things of the first class may become built into living things, while dead things of the second class may ultimately return to ash and dust. For example, any green plant in the garden can build minerals, water, carbon dioxide and the energy of sunlight into its own tissues in a process called photosynthesis (because it is light-powered), but once the plant is transferred to the garden incinerator it can quickly be completely converted back to water vapour, a mixture of simple gases including carbon dioxide, and ash.

Whole living organisms, then, are made up from and can be broken down into physical and chemical parts. However, it would be a mistake to suggest that, once incorporated into living organisms these parts themselves become alive, because 'being alive' is a property of the system as a whole. Life is, as Aristotle might have put it, a formal property resulting from the organization of the parts from which the system is built and the way they interact with each other. The same is true of the property of 'habitability' associated with the system of bricks and mortar found in houses—the bricks are not habitable but their intrinsic properties are such that they can be organized into something which is. We may say, therefore, that new properties *emerge* when the bricks are built into a house and when chemicals are built into an organism. Clearly, under appropriate conditions, the emergent properties of these systems may again disappear—as when a derelict house decays or an organism dies. In this book much attention will be paid to these degenerative processes and their consequences. To appreciate fully the kinds of changes that take place, however, we must first understand what is disappearing; in

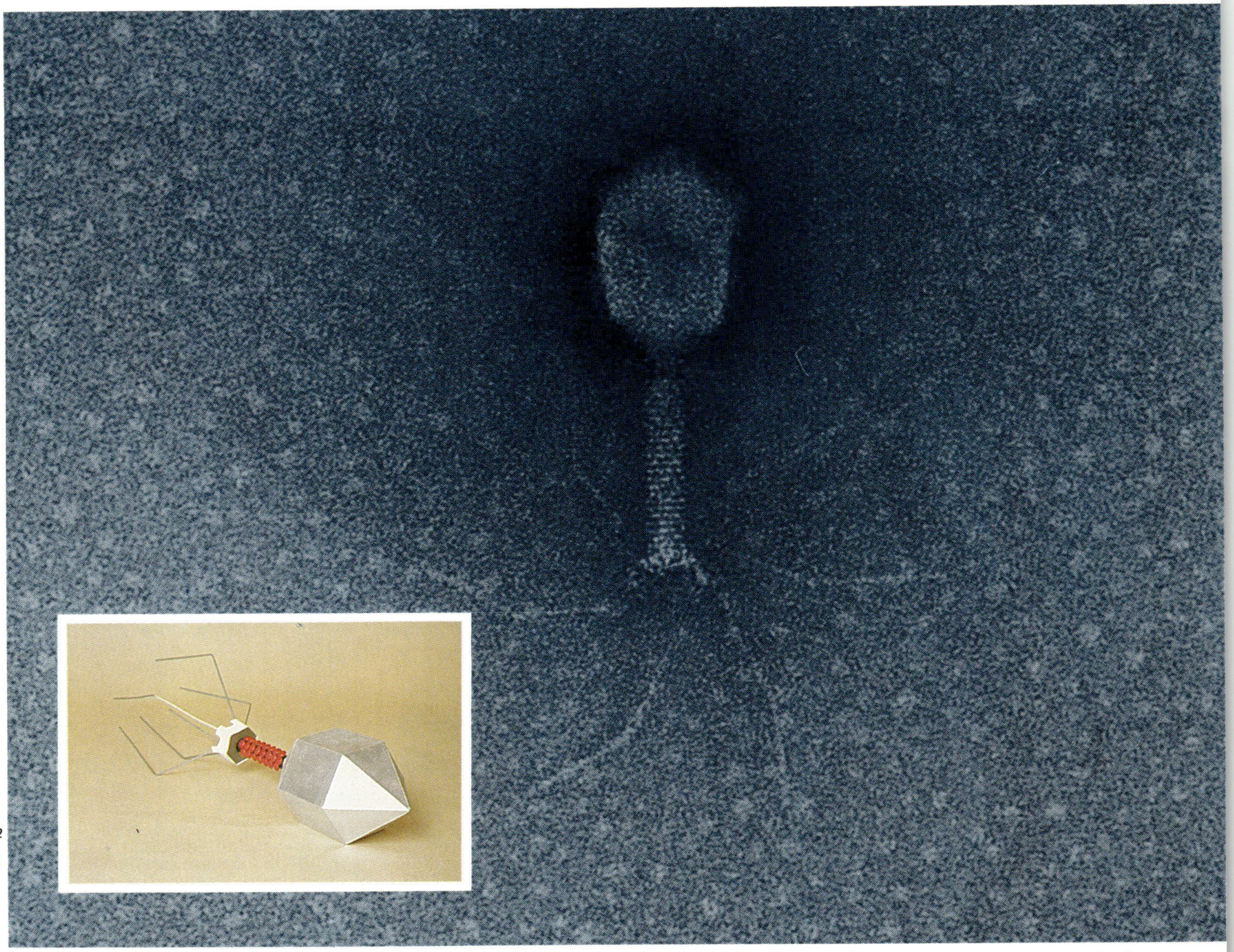

Right and Inset
An electron micrograph of a bacterial virus, magnified 108,000 times. The principal components of the virus – its head, stem and tail – can be clearly seen in this view. The genetic material (DNA) governing its activities is contained in the head. The kinked tail fibres are the structures by which the particle attaches itself to a bacterium. Note the high degree of regularity in the shape of the virus, which can be better appreciated from the model **(inset)**. A feature of living organisms which differentiates them from dead matter is their ordered nature and consequent predictability. One virus, for example, is essentially the same as all other viruses of the same species. But lumps of rock have a far more disordered, and hence random, structure

Time Span of the Earth
The 4.6 billion years of the earth's history are represented by the 12 hours on the clock face. At 4.00 the first life forms appear; not until 10.30 does invertebrate life evolve. 11.25 marks the age of dinosaurs. Hominids appear 30 seconds before noon and the history of civilization fits into the final tenth of a second

Information in Cells
There are 46 strands of DNA in each human cell. Every cell contains information equivalent to ten million books – the contents of 260 public libraries. A cell is about the size of a speck of dust

Microscopic Mysteries
Bacteria and viruses are the smallest living organisms on earth and, although very simple in structure, are not primitive. They have an astonishing ability to survive in the most inhospitable places, such as the oxygen-free atmosphere that exists on the summit of high mountains and in the extreme cold of the Antarctic. Bacteria are the smallest independent organisms, and can be either dangerous or beneficial to other living organisms. Viruses, which have been described as 'living chemicals', are very much smaller than bacteria. When they invade a host and cause disease they are extremely difficult to neutralize by most drugs

other words, we must know what the emergent properties of these systems are and how they relate to the properties of the chemical building blocks of organisms.

Thus, in this chapter we begin not with the dead and the dying, but with life itself. In particular, we must consider how the properties of living systems differ from physical and chemical ones which have never lived and how the properties of organisms can have emerged from those of non-living systems. Do these emergent properties depend for their formation on a rational force or agent, as do the emergent properties of a house which are put there by a builder and an architect? Why do organismic systems inevitably seem to degenerate, die and lose their emergent properties? Is death a necessary consequence of life and, alternatively, is death itself necessary for life?

What is the essential difference between living organisms and dead matter?

What is meant by being alive? One obvious characteristic separating even a simple life-form like a virus from a dead thing like a lump of rock is its *order* and consequent predictability. Once we describe the prominent features of one polio virus, for instance, we describe the essentials of all polio viruses and the same is true for any species of animal or plant, even our own. People differ in stature and in the fine details of their appearance – skin-colour, hair-colour, eye-colour and so on – but they all conform to a basic, recognizable and predictable pattern which enables us to identify them as human. On the other hand, non-living things are much more statistical and much less predictable in their form and are not as easily grouped into species. When we describe a single lump of rock, for example, we find that it is only roughly similar to others in shape and size.

There exists a group of entities which, though definitely dead, appear to possess some of the qualities and characteristics of living organisms

Having said this however, we must note that there is a group of non-living entities which does come close to and may even surpass organisms in terms of order and predictability. These are the crystals which, depending on the chemical involved, can take on remarkably consistent, complex and curious geometrical forms. Nevertheless, crystals differ from organisms in that they never contain as rich a variety of atomic, molecular and macromolecular subunits as living things, and are consequently never as *complex*. Furthermore, the building blocks of organisms are usually *organized* into complex and patterned arrangements 'designed' to carry out a particular job; in other words, the parts of organisms are organized for a *purpose*. More will be said about this purposefulness later. In the meantime let us concentrate on the attributes of order, complexity and organization. To begin with it should be understood that although we have an intuitive sense of what each of these properties entails they are surprisingly difficult to measure. On the other hand if it were possible to use some instrument to determine the extent to which a system is ordered and organized and to measure how complex it is, we would then be able to represent the state of this system as a point within a three-dimensional graph whose axes quantify the three primary properties. 'Families' of similar systems could then be depicted as spaces within the graph: and Figure 1 shows how we might expect such a graph to look for various kinds of familiar living and non-living systems. Gases, which are usually simple, disordered and disorganized, occupy one corner while living organisms reside in the opposite one.

In a world characterized essentially by chaos and death, how is it possible for living systems to evolve and continue to flourish?

It seems reasonable to assume that life must have originated from non-life and that complex molecular arrangements must ultimately have arisen from simple atomic systems; therefore, arrows representing this evolution should point upwards in the three-dimensional graph from the 'gas corner' to the 'organism corner'. Alternatively, personal experience teaches us that, left to themselves, ordered and organized systems ultimately become disordered and disorganized; organisms die and decay; old machines rust away; buildings collapse; civilizations and societies crumble. Every event in the world, whether of celestial or sub-atomic kind, seems to move relentlessly towards a state of chaos similar to what Milton describes in his *Paradise Lost* as 'that dark illimitable ocean, where length, breadth, height and time are lost', or what physicists refer to more prosaically as a world of maximum entropy (entropy = disorder). Thus, an arrow representing what has come to be called the *second law of thermodynamics* (ie, that all energy transactions proceed towards increased entropy) should point from the 'organism corner' to the 'gas corner' of the graph, in the opposite direction to the 'evolutionary arrow'.

How did ordered, complex and organized systems come into being and persist in this chaos-bent world? Many astronomers believe that the world before the creation of the present universe is best described as a kind of Miltonian chaos of radiations at trillions of degrees. If this is true how, given the second law of thermodynamics, did the processes of ordering and organization begin?

In the flash of a cosmic explosion the Universe is born—and within seconds it is flying apart at the speed of light

A widely-held theory postulates that in the beginning of the world as we know it there was a massive explosion, often referred to as the Big Bang. Within seconds of the explosion, the universe began to fly apart at the speed of light. In the first minutes of time, the basic units of atoms, the protons and electrons, came into existence and began to interact. They soon formed themselves into simple atomic systems consisting of one proton and one orbiting electron—what the chemist calls *hydrogen*. Then, as the temperature began to fall to a few hundred million degrees, the protons began to combine in pairs (a process called fusion, which still goes on in the sun and is the source of energy in the hydrogen bomb) to form another kind of gas called *helium*. This happened because under the conditions

Fig 1

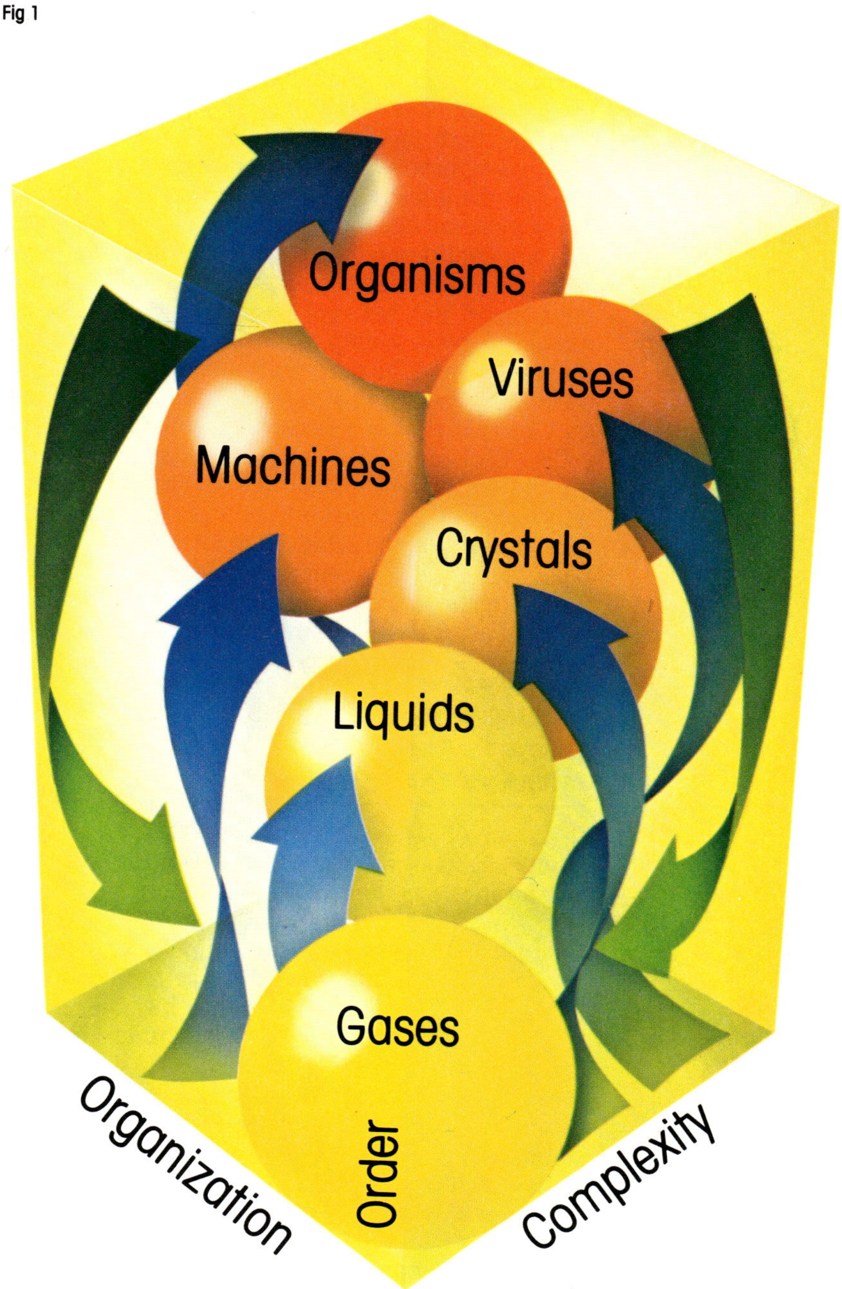

that prevailed at the beginning of time the 'helium organization' was more stable than any other configuration of protons, and through its stability was able to persist and 'survive'.

High temperatures favour fusion, so that this process could have continued at the unimaginably high temperatures of the early universe until all the available hydrogen had been swallowed up. Fortunately for us, however, the universe cooled rapidly to a temperature below which this process was no longer favoured—to a few million degrees. Under these new conditions fusion slowed down and the helium nuclei started to collide and interact. The resulting, pair-wise associations were very unstable and broke apart in less than a million-millionth of a second. Whenever a third helium nucleus collided with a pair during this micro-fraction of time, however, another extremely stable configuration representing the nucleus of carbon came into being. In this way, as conditions changed, progressively more complex and ordered atomic, molecular and, ultimately, planetary systems emerged. Atomic and molecular evolution thus proceeded like a man climbing a slippery path, moving cautiously from one stable resting place to

Chaos to Complexity
Shown here is a reasonable approximation of the relative positions of various familiar 'systems', in terms of their order, complexity and organization. The evolutionary force, propelling systems towards greater complexity, tends to move upwards. The entropic force, which propels living organisms towards decay and death, moves downwards, towards the 'gas corner'

Replaceable Rodents
In rats, 50 percent of the molecules in the brain, muscles and bones decay and are replaced every two weeks. The liver has an even higher turnover rate—50 percent every 10 days

Odds Against Existence
The chances against life evolving in any given part of the Universe are astronomical—billions of billions to one

Battle of the Beak
Hawaiian honeycreepers display a remarkable variety of adaptations, principally in their beak forms. Those with Finch-like bills, for example, are insect-, fruit- and seed-eaters. The thin-billed species are nectar-feeders, and there are several intermediate forms known

Seeds of Redundancy
The wastage of sperm cells in mammals is quite staggering – a human loses 350 million sperm cells with each ejaculation, a bull, 4000 million and a horse, 8000 million. These are quickly replaced, but only one of them, if any, will fertilize the female egg

another. Progressively more complex systems were built from each other, step-by-step, forming a ladder leading to greater complexity and, ultimately, to greater organization.

If we climb this ladder upward to its biological conclusion, however, we find a discontinuity – the rules of the game seem to have changed, because living systems depend not so much on stable states for their continuing existence, but on a rather more dynamic process. Living things persist in this chaos-bent world not because they are stable, but by virtue of their ability to *reproduce* and replace themselves and the parts from which they are made according to a set of instructions – the genes – which they carry in the nucleus of each of their constituent cells. Each fertilized egg cell carries genetic information on how to make another adult organism which, in turn, can make eggs and sperm. If, then, reproduction can be achieved before the reproducer falls foul of the 'agents' of the second law of thermodynamics, the organization of which it is part can persist even if particular individuals do not.

At every level of life it is the process of reproduction – not the ability to achieve balanced growth in itself – that ensures survival

Human development illustrates how the process of reproduction can preserve order, complexity and organization at several different levels. In humans, many adults pass on their genetic heritage to children before they die. This they do in gametes, the egg and sperm, which fuse at fertilization to form a minute zygote. From such humble, microscopic beginnings a new adult containing millions upon millions of cells is formed by a process of sequential division – the first cell divides into two, the two into four, the four into eight, the eight into sixteen, and so on. At each division, the original genetic material in the nucleus is faithfully replicated and passed on. However, not all this information is used in every cell and, indeed, the process of differential expression of genes leads to the formation of cells with different functions – skin cells, nerve cells, liver cells, kidney cells, and so on. Ultimately these come to occupy specific positions in the organism and to form tissues and organs. Thus, from a single cell, a complex conglomerate of cells becomes organized into a perfectly proportioned adult capable of reproduction.

Even at this stage in the process, however, the constituent cells may continue to divide, so that old and worn-out tissues can be replaced by new cells. This replacement is, of course, effected by the reproduction of one cell and its contents in accordance with the genetic instructions each cell carries. Cells in exposed sites, like the skin and lining of the intestine, for example, undergo a continuous sequence of turnover and replacement, whereas others, like those in the liver, begin to multiply only if the organ is injured, and still others, like those which make up our nervous system, do not divide at all. Within all cells, though, even non-dividing ones, there is another form of reproduction, since old molecular building blocks are continuously replaced by new, freshly formed molecules which, as explained later, are again synthesized according to genetic instructions. Old, worn-out molecules are thus replaced by new ones reproduced in accordance with the design of the organism. In fact, there is so much molecular turnover, that the body you have today is not quite the same as the one you had yesterday, from a molecular point of view, and is almost completely different from the body you had last year. It turns out therefore, that the external permanence of our bodies is as illusory as the external permanence of a flame, a waterfall, or a whirlpool. An adult body which neither grows nor shrinks is said to exist in a *dynamic steady state.*

In the words of an old Chinese philosopher, organisms have 'a wild obsession to multiply', to reproduce both themselves and their parts, and it is this which enables them to evade the consequences of the physicist's law of disorder – the Second Law of Thermodynamics. Old worn-out molecules and cells within organisms are replaced by means of reproduction and when this becomes inadequate, the whole organism can be reproduced. At least one puzzle remains, however: How did such a complex and organized system originate in the first place? Is there really a rung missing in the evolutionary ladder leading from the Big Bang to organisms, and can scientists begin to identify it and put it into its proper position?

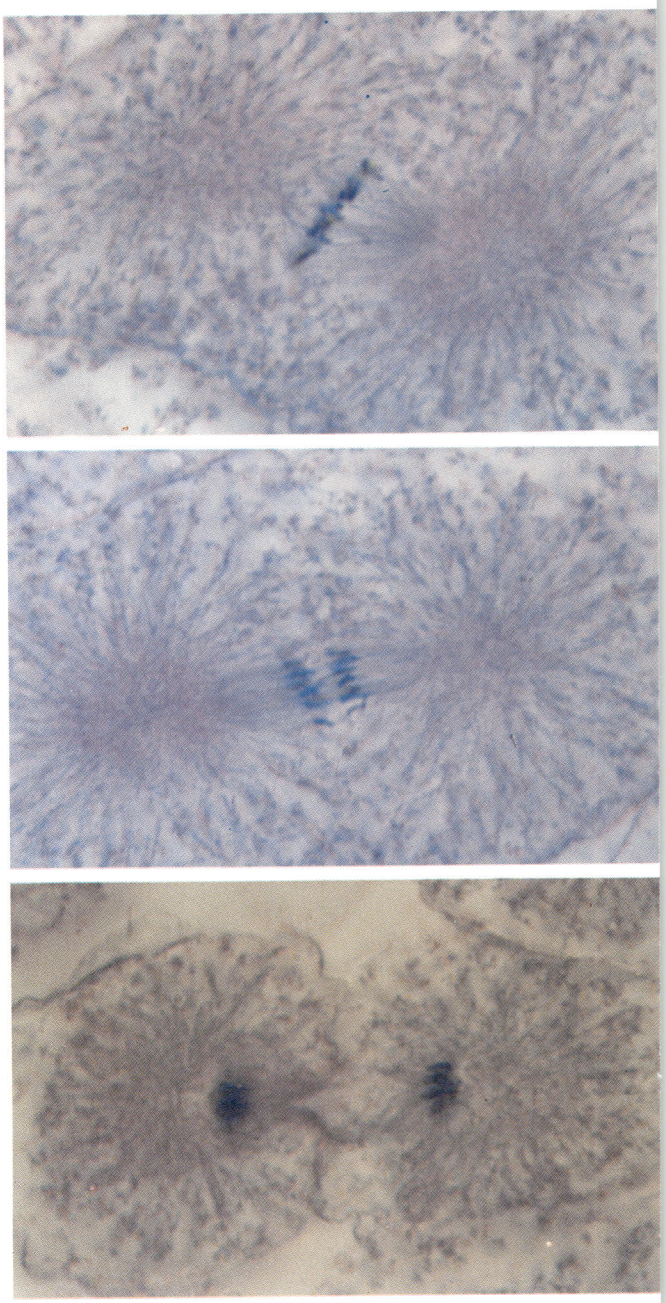

Right
The pulling apart of two cells. First **(top)** the chromosomal material is duplicated – the genetic instructions are copied – and the duplicate chromosomes are arranged along the equator of the cell. Next **(centre)** spindles pull the duplicate sets of chromosomes apart. Finally **(bottom)** the chromosomes are separated into two distinct cells. The membrane of the nucleus disappears during division, but will form again soon after the cells separate. This process continues until a complex assemblage of cells becomes organized into a perfectly proportioned adult capable of reproduction

Before the nineteenth century, biologists certainly believed that there was a very profound difference between the chemistry of the living and the chemistry of the dead (meaning things which have never been alive). The chemicals which make up living organisms (organic chemicals, as they are called) consist of large molecules with carbon backbones—carbohydrates, proteins, fats and nucleic acids—and these are so much more complex and organized than chemicals found naturally in the non-living world (the so-called inorganic chemicals), that it was thought that they could only have been made by living things. Hence, it was suggested, there must be some kind of special force in living organisms capable of converting inorganic to organic chemicals and, furthermore, that some very special force must have existed when life began on earth to carry out the necessary ordering and organizing.

In 1832 this Vitalistic Hypothesis was severely weakened, when Friedrich Wöhler, a German chemist, found that he could convert a simple inorganic molecule, ammonium cyanate, into a more complex organic one, urea (formed as an excretory product by many animals, including man), simply by heating it up in a test-tube. This was the first step on the road to demonstrating that the synthesis of organic molecules was possible without life. The next important step came in 1953, when Stanley Miller, then a student at the University of Chicago, demonstrated that it was possible to produce a rich variety of organic molecules simply by passing an electric discharge through an atmosphere containing methane, hydrogen and water. From this, and more recent work, we now know that, whenever a reducing mixture of gases containing carbon, hydrogen, nitrogen and oxygen is treated violently enough, more complex organic molecules are invariably formed. The atmosphere of the primitive earth is thought to have been of a reducing kind and to have contained the requisite atoms. In addition, there could have been electrical discharges by lightning, so the pre-biotic synthesis of organic molecules seems feasible, at least in principle. Another very important finding from Miller's experiments and those which followed is that, although many millions of organic chemicals can conceivably form under the conditions described above, only a few do so, and they happen to be precisely those molecules commonly found in all present-day living things—sugars, the building-blocks of carbohydrates; fatty acids, the building blocks of fats; amino acids, the building-blocks of proteins; nucleotides, the building-blocks of nucleic acids.

It has been established that the production of organic from inorganic chemicals is feasible without the intervention of special, vital forces, but a much more difficult problem, is how specific macromolecules were formed from the so-called *organic soup* which is thought to have concentrated in the oceans of the early earth and how these were organized further into the complex arrangement necessary for the self-replication discussed above.

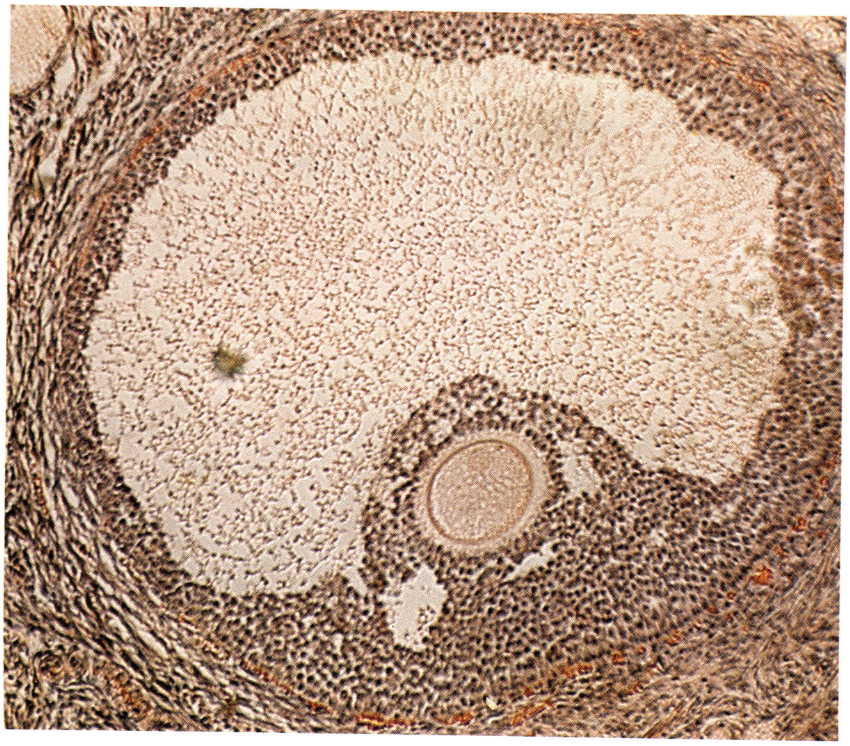

Above
A human egg—this is the circular structure in the centre of the picture. It is still lodged in the ovary and is surrounded by a Graafian follicle

Until 150 years ago it was strongly believed by biologists that the chemical composition of living things was radically and profoundly different from that of dead matter

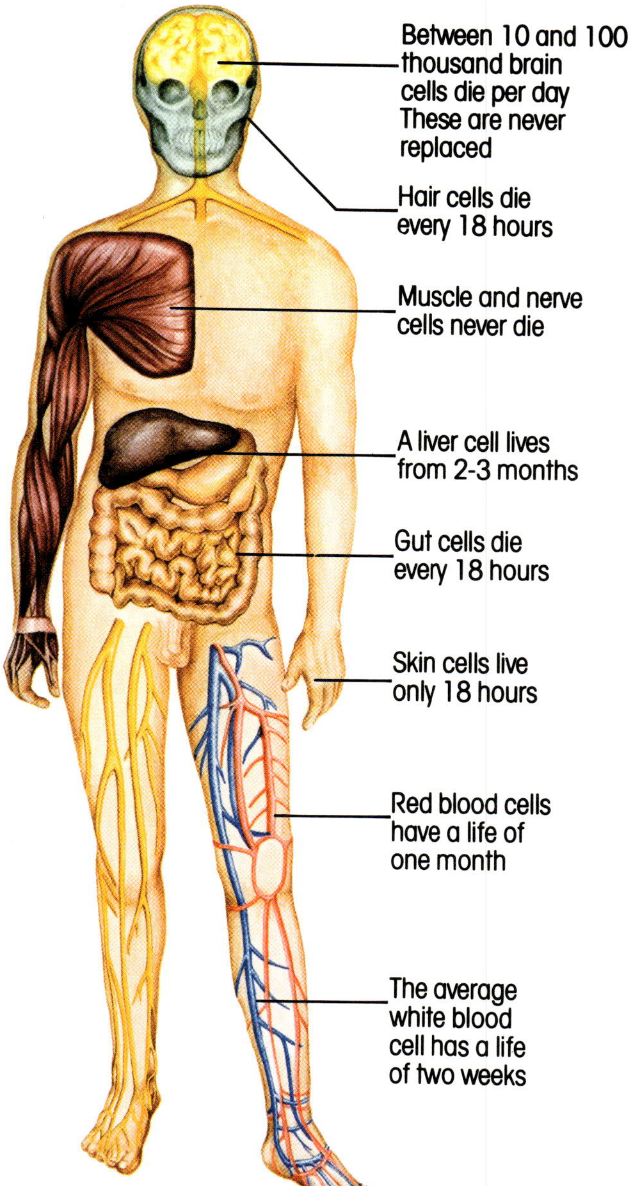

Body Count
Cells within the body are being replaced in some tissues with great rapidity and in others only very slowly

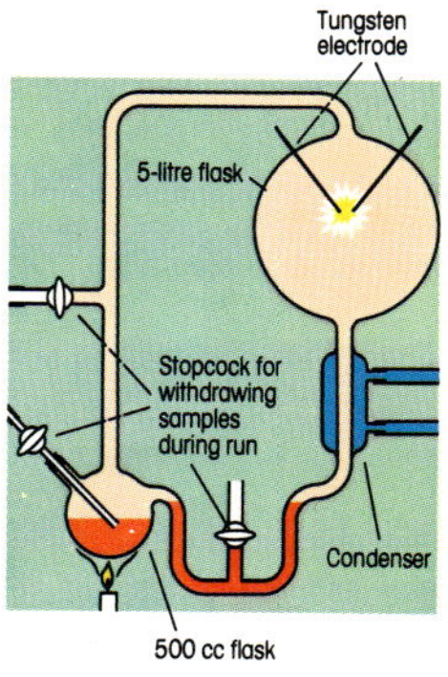

Experiment with Life
In 1953, Stanley Miller, a research chemist, demonstrated that organic molecules could be synthesized in a laboratory. In the Miller experiment, an electric discharge was passed through an atmosphere containing a mixture of methane, hydrogen and water. Subsequent tests established the presence of a rich variety of organic chemicals. In essence, what Miller did was to reproduce the conditions that are believed to have existed on earth before life appeared

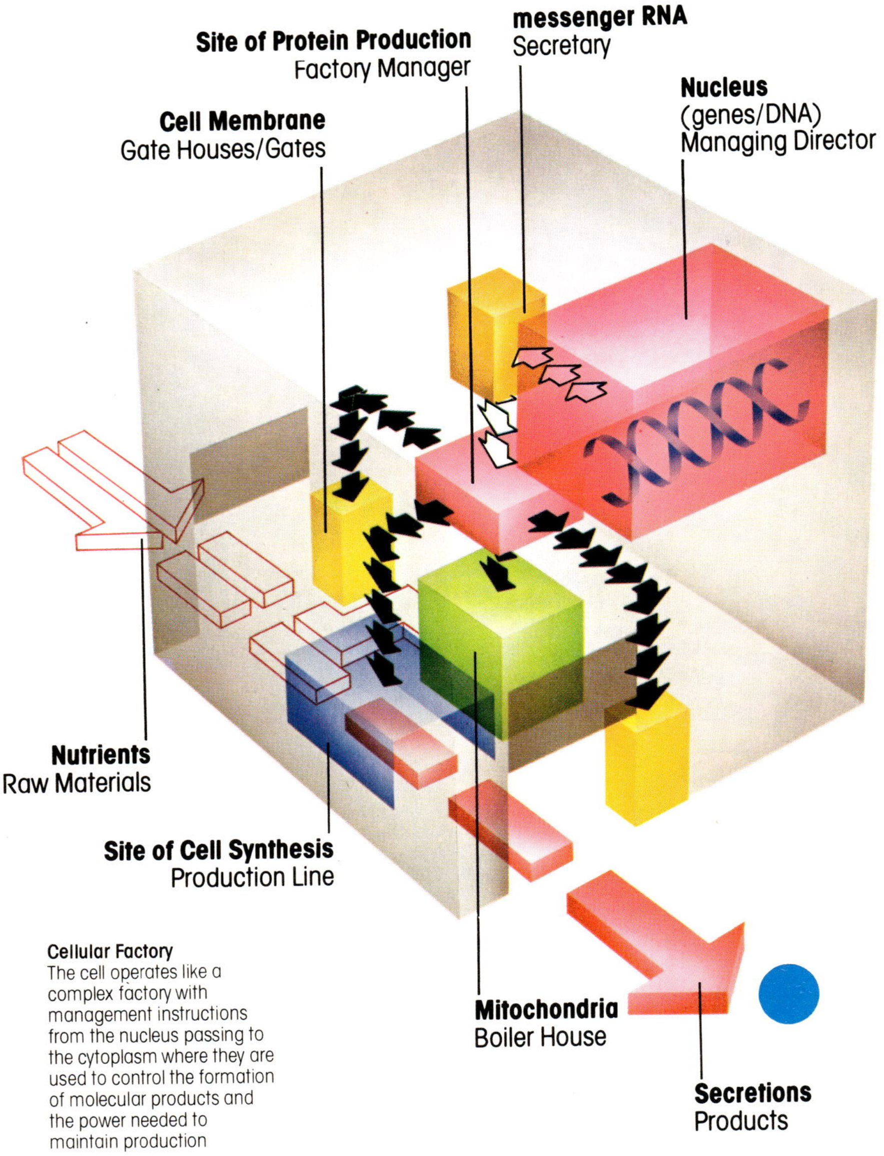

Cellular Factory
The cell operates like a complex factory with management instructions from the nucleus passing to the cytoplasm where they are used to control the formation of molecular products and the power needed to maintain production

To appreciate the immensity of this problem it is necessary only to consider the molecular organization and dynamics of individual cells, since the original life-form was almost certainly unicellular. Each cell is organized like a very complex and sophisticated factory, with executive control arising from the nucleus and with the production lines occurring in the cytoplasm. However, the central office is more like a library than an executive suite, since it contains a store of coded instructions sufficient to meet all contingencies in the normal day-to-day operation of the factory. When required these instructions are taken out of store, copied *(transcribed)*, and the copies are then passed to the shop-floor where a series of production managers *translates* them into terms that can be understood by the several departments of the firm.

There is little dispute today over how organic chemicals evolved. More difficult to understand is how exactly the next stage—the genetic code—originated

---

Instructions in the nucleus of the cell are not stored, of course, as words in a book or as the pattern of holes on a punched tape, but rather as a sequence of chemical building-blocks running along the length of a giant molecule called deoxyribonucleic acid (DNA). Middle-management of the cell is in the hands of other giant molecules—the proteins—which control the chemical reactions that do the work on the 'shop floor' in generating energy (needed to power the machinery of the cell) and in producing chemicals that may ultimately pass out of the cell to do a job for the organism as a whole; for example, the enzymes which are required in the digestion of food or the hormones which act as chemical messengers in the body.

A piece of information on the DNA is not passed to the cytoplasm directly, but is first *transcribed* on to another giant nucleotide called messenger ribonucleic acid (mRNA). This passes from nucleus to cytoplasm (hence the name) and the information it carries is there *translated* into a protein. In this process the mRNA acts as a kind of template upon which the building-blocks of proteins, the amino-acids, are assembled. These are transported from the body of the cytoplasm to the mRNA by another, smaller, RNA molecule called transfer, or simply t-RNA, which plugs it into the appropriate place on the template. The properties of a protein and how it manages metabolism in the different departments of the cell depends on the types of amino-acid it contains and on their sequence. Thus, the order of chemical building-blocks in DNA determines the sequence of building-blocks in mRNA, which in turn determines the sequence of amino-acids in the proteins. Which proteins are made determines how the cell should function. How the instructions are initially written into the DNA of the nucleus, the genetic material of the cell, will be considered in greater detail below.

The organization and complexity involved in this basic unit of replication is 'mind boggling'. How the requisite molecules could have formed spontaneously to make such a system from the soup of precursors in the primitive oceans remains very much a mystery. In fact the problem is even more profound,

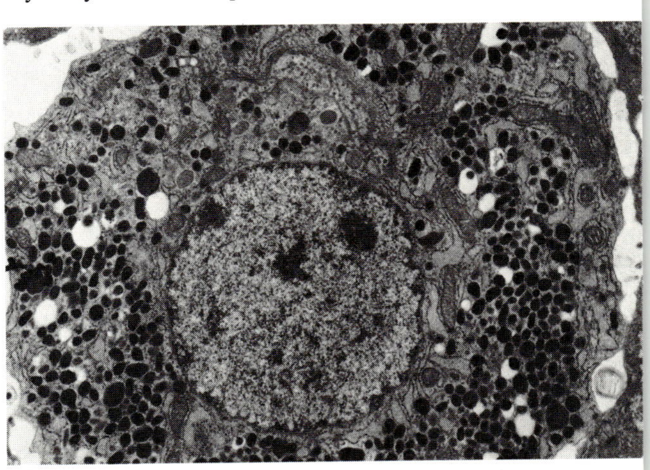

Right
An electron micrograph of an animal cell, magnified 12,500 times. The inner membrane-bound bag is the nucleus, surrounded by cytoplasm, rich here in secretions (black spots) and mitochondria (sausage-shaped structures).
The cytoplasm is itself bounded by a membrane

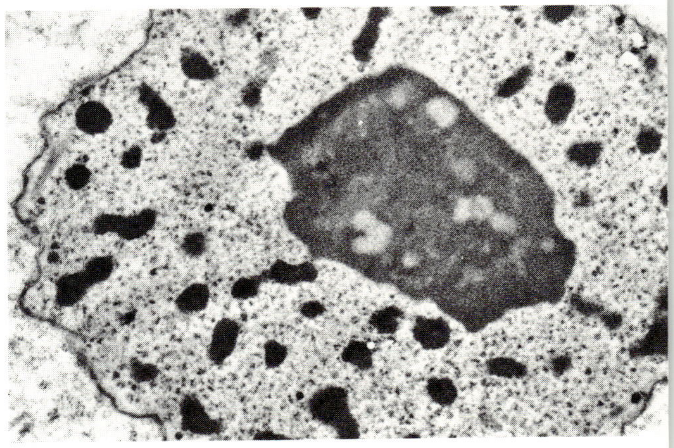

Bottom right
A cellular nucleus, magnified 23,000 times. The inner, dark area is the nucleolus, the function of which is still uncertain. The dark patches surrounding the nucleolus are sections through the chromosomes, which carry the genes. It is this genetic information which governs the type, appearance and activity of the cell

Molecular Millions
The human body contains about 10,000 million cells. Each cell is made up of 10,000 million molecules

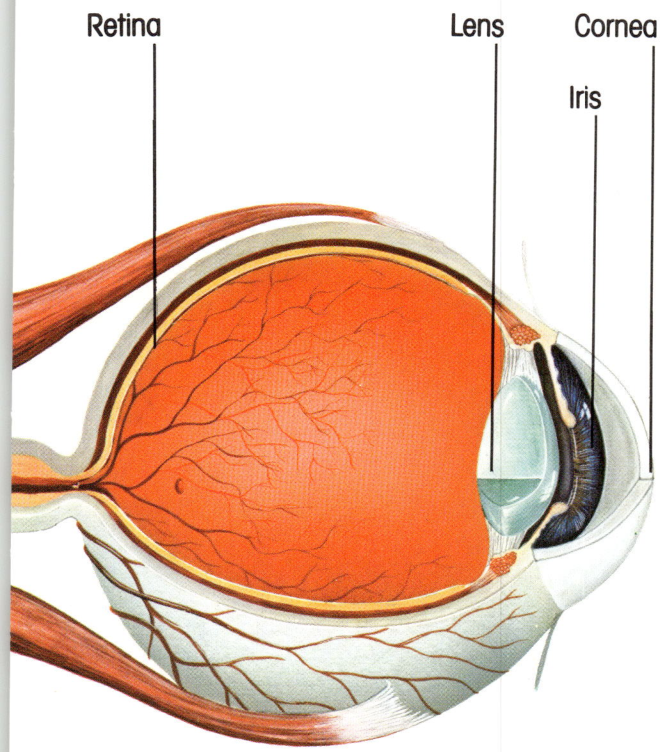

Left
A section through a human eye, which can focus an image on to a light-sensitive surface and then transmit the image to the brain via the optic nerve. The eye exemplifies the way in which organisms and their parts have developed, so as to do a particular job

because the transfer of information from DNA to RNA, the charging of transfer RNA with amino-acids and the assembly of amino-acids on the RNA template are themselves controlled by specific proteins which are also coded in the DNA. Which came first, then? How could all this molecular organization have been built up spontaneously, by chance? Some biologists still think that the only possible explanation is that special forces were at work. Others suggest that the organic soup may have been invaded by alien life-forms, brought to earth in meteorites and able to effect the initial ordering and organization on this planet. However, this explanation merely begs the question of how the aliens themselves originated.

Yet other biologists think that self-replicating systems originated by chance. They admit that the odds against this are enormous but maintain that it would have needed to happen only once to set the whole process of life in motion. On the other hand, others argue that the necessary associations are so unlikely that the chance of their occurring within even the five billion years of the earth's existence is unimaginably small. Finally, there are the proto-biologists, who believe that the ladder from the inorganic to the organic world must be a continuous one and are still searching for possible intermediaries between the organic precursors and a completely self-replicating cell.

Matters did not end with the origination of a self-replicating system: the replicators became more and more complex with the passage of time, and life evolved. There is ample evidence of these evolutionary changes in the fossil record and in the great diversity of life-forms that now inhabit the earth. Furthermore, it is quite clear that the changes which occurred were not haphazard but seem to have resulted in structures and systems with a *purpose*. Like man-made machines or buildings, organisms and their parts became 'designed' to do a particular job in particular circumstances. Think, for example, of obvious structures like eyes and ears—or the beautifully 'designed' jaw of snakes, which allows these reptiles to eat prey many times greater in circumference than themselves—or the flight mechanism of birds and insects. In fact, wherever we look in the biological world, we find evidence of purposiveness and 'design': in the organs comprising an organism; in the developmental process by which the organs are made and put together; and in the behavioural repertoire which enables the organism to avoid unpleasant things like predators and to find essential ones like food or mates.

It is tempting to ascribe such purposiveness to a purpose-giver—a designer or deity—something like the architect who decides how bricks should be organized to fulfil the purpose for which they are intended in a building, but modern biology has proposed an alternative non-vitalistic viewpoint dependent on the special ability of living things to reproduce themselves. This theory, first precisely formulated by Charles Darwin, is based upon the tension between the almost unlimited capacity for increase vested in organisms capable of self-reproduction and the definite limit to the resources of food and space upon which they depend. Consider, for example, a female fly, which may lay 100 eggs, each of them able to hatch and live through to a reproductive condition. If half of the resulting flies were female and were themselves able to produce 100 eggs before dying, then 5,000 flies or 2,500 pairs would be found in the next generation. Under favourable conditions, 15 generations could follow on each other in a year, leading to the production of more than a trillion flies. Assuming that each fly is about half an inch long and a quarter of an inch wide, this fly population would be more than enough to cover every square inch of land on the surface of the earth! Thankfully, there will never be such a quantity of flies, because most die from lack of food or living space, through being killed by predators like spiders, or in man-made fly traps

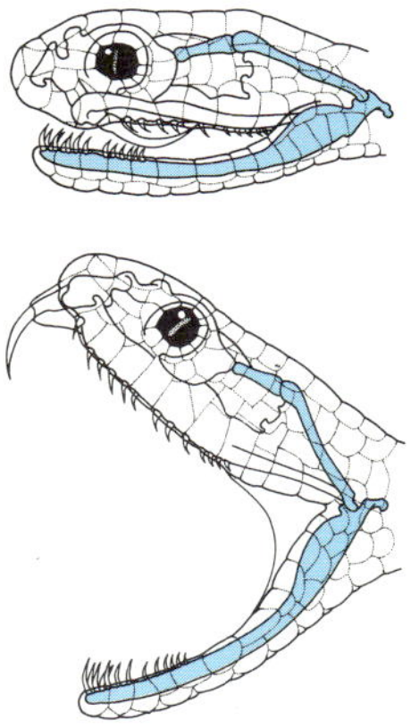

Giant Jaws
Another example of a part of an organism developing in such a way as to enable the organism to survive in its environment is the jaw of a snake. It is an elegant mechanism, which works on the principle of a hinge, providing the jaw with such an extension that certain snakes eat their prey whole

Below
Red-tipped herald snake consuming a toad whole

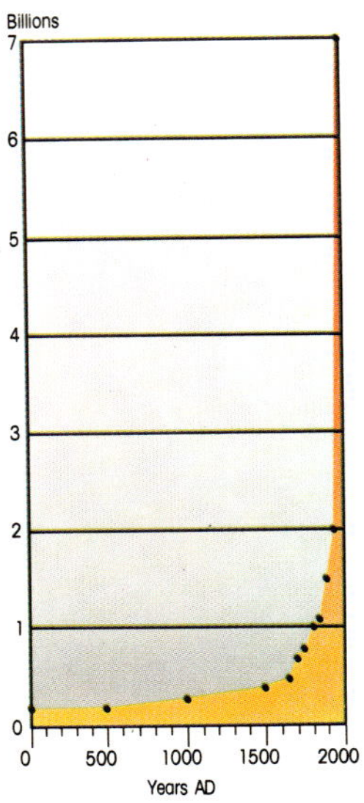

Population Time Bomb
For thousands of years the world population barely increased beyond a few hundred thousands. It was the arrival of the Industrial Revolution that sent it up to the billion mark and the coming of the atomic age that has seen it soar to beyond 4 billion. By the year 2000 AD, it could well reach 7 billion

before they mature. On average, out of each 100 eggs laid, only two are able to survive to parenthood, so there is an intense *struggle for existence*. Because some flies lay more eggs than others, or are better parents, or have offspring that are better able to escape spiders and fly killers (and for a host of other reasons), they will contribute proportionately more progeny to the next generation.

Does adaptation in animals and plants come about through the tug and pull of natural selection, or via the effective manipulation of life by 'outside' agents?

If these differences in character are heritable (genetically determined), the more advantageous traits will spread through the population. Given variations in character and heritability and the fact that only the 'fittest' can survive to exploit the limited resources available to them, all living organisms will become more and more adapted to coping with the problems posed by the environment in which they live (finding food, avoiding predators, and so on) and it is in this way, *through the natural selection of the fittest,* that instructions for survival become programmed into the genetic information store of organisms.

It might still be objected, of course, that evolution *is* planned, in that the genetic variation so crucial to the process of evolution might be 'put into a population' by some extraneous force or agent, or be acquired intentionally by organisms themselves. Jean-Pierre Antoine Baptiste de Monet, le Chevalier de Lamarck, was of this last opinion. He thought, for example, that a primitive, short-necked giraffe could acquire a long neck by continually stretching for leaves at the inaccessible tops of trees and that the information coding for a stretched neck might then be passed on to its offspring. Hence, a short-necked giraffe could have evolved into a long-necked species and this is referred to as Lamarckian, as opposed to Darwinian, evolution. Lamarck's ideas held great allure for many people since the theory that human beings are born equal, particularly in characteristics like intelligence and physical fitness has always been more attractive than Darwin's theory of evolution. Nevertheless, it must immediately be said that no mechanism has ever been discovered whereby the kind of information transfer needed for the Lamarckian process of evolution to occur (*i.e.,* from organism to genes, or cytoplasm to nucleus) could take place. In fact, all the available evidence suggests that genetic information travels *exclusively* in the opposite direction, from nucleus to cytoplasm. This makes good sense, for most of the changes occurring in an organism during its 'working life' are likely to be disadvantageous rather than advantageous—scars, wounds, broken limbs, even loss of limbs.

It would require a degree of selectivity quite outside the scope of the molecular replicating system to distinguish between good and bad acquired characters and to store information from the former rather than from the latter. Without such a mechanism Lamarckian evolution would be more likely to lead to maladapted rather than adapted characteristics, and this means that it would itself have been selectively excluded. There is in fact one—and only one—biological situation where a Lamarckian interpretation is acceptable, and that is in the evolution of human culture. Here ideas, concepts, rituals (for example, associated with the problems posed by death) are *acquired* by a population and are transmitted culturally. This is referred to as psychosocial, as compared with biological, evolution.

To summarize, then: It is now widely accepted that variation in characters between individuals in a population occurs through the random mixing of genetic information in the formation of gametes, in their fusion at fertilization and through the random modification (mutation) of genes by extraneous forces like radiation. There is no evidence to suggest that such informational changes are specifically directed by the organisms themselves, their environment, or anything else, for that matter. It is left to natural selection, in Darwin's words, 'to accumulate all profitable variation, however slight, to produce adaptations that are plainly developed and appreciable to us'. By these means it is supposed that adaptive mechanisms like eyes, ears and articulated jaws have evolved, that developmental programmes have acquired their goal-directedness, and that behavioural sequences have received their purpose.

Right
Jean-Baptiste de Monet, Chevalier de Lamarck contended that traits acquired by organisms in the course of their lives can be passed on to their offspring. This theory of heritability is rejected by most modern biologists and zoologists for the obvious reason that no mechanism has ever been found whereby the kind of information transfer needed for the Lamarckian process of evolution to occur could take place

The Body Controllers
The shape and function of a living body is under the control of 'genes'—packets of information stored within the nuclei of cells. The frequency of mutation in these genes, bringing about a change in the state of the body, is as low as one in 100,000

Biologists now believe that they can explain or describe most of the features of living organisms in terms of natural selection, but what about processes like ageing and death? Are suicide instructions, for example, programmed into living systems by natural selection?

Some think that 'suicide instructions' *are* 'designed' into living systems by natural selection for the purpose of dispensing with the old and worn-out and making way for the new and more virile. However, this hypothesis does not really solve the problem, because it uses the fact that organisms age (become worn out) to explain why they age. This is a little like explaining the wetness of water in terms of aqueousness! Furthermore, in Nature, most organisms die unnaturally by disease, accident or predation, so there would be no particular 'need' to 'write suicide instructions' into organisms to prevent over-population, or to provide space for new mutants to enter a population and enable evolution to proceed. As an alternative, therefore, some biologists suggest that ageing and death are not selected into the life-cycle at all, but occur because the forces of chaos progressively overcome those of order and organization as organisms get older; in other words, ageing is a statistical phenomenon. One of the major problems with this idea, however, is that ageing *looks as though it is selected* since it follows a predictable and fairly precise course of events. Thus, in the vast majority of people, greying hair, wrinkled skin, bent stature and other physical changes are signs of ageing and provide the visual clues which enable us to estimate reasonably accurately how old they are. In man, key physiological processes deteriorate after the age of 50 at a fixed and predictable rate of approximately 1 to 3 percent per annum and our vulnerability to certain kinds of disease rises continuously and predictably with time.

Both extreme theories of ageing appear to be incorrect. A more attractive hypothesis is that ageing is neither fully 'designed' nor fully accidental, but that certain features programmed into the organism to enhance its fitness allow the accumulation of accidental molecular damage.

It is now widely accepted that ageing is associated with internal wear and tear processes, leading to the accumulation of molecular damage. But repairing the damage might cost a great deal more than it is worth

It is now beyond doubt that ageing in the whole organism is associated with internal processes of wear and tear. These take place irrespective of environmental insult and lead to the accumulation of damage in the molecules, particularly the important proteins which make up the body. In fact, molecules are probably being damaged every minute of our lives through the 'action' of the 'agents' of the second law of thermodynamics, but the body is able to recognize and repair them. The extent of damage in the body can therefore be

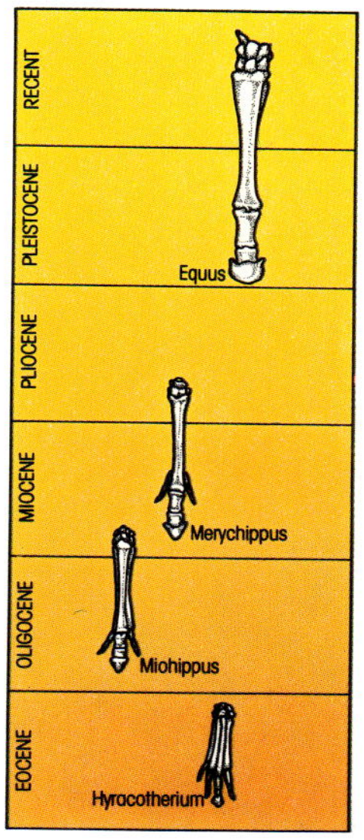

Structural Success
The source of variation in foot structure, which is illustrated here in the evolution of the horse's hoof, emerged by chance (random mutation of genes coded for feet and toes) and natural selection. These together ensured that the limbs best adapted for running in the circumstances which prevailed spread through the population

Left
Charles Darwin was often parodied by his contemporaries for the theory of evolution set forth in his book on Origin of Species. This suggests that all living things are related and that Man is descended from anthropoid ancestors

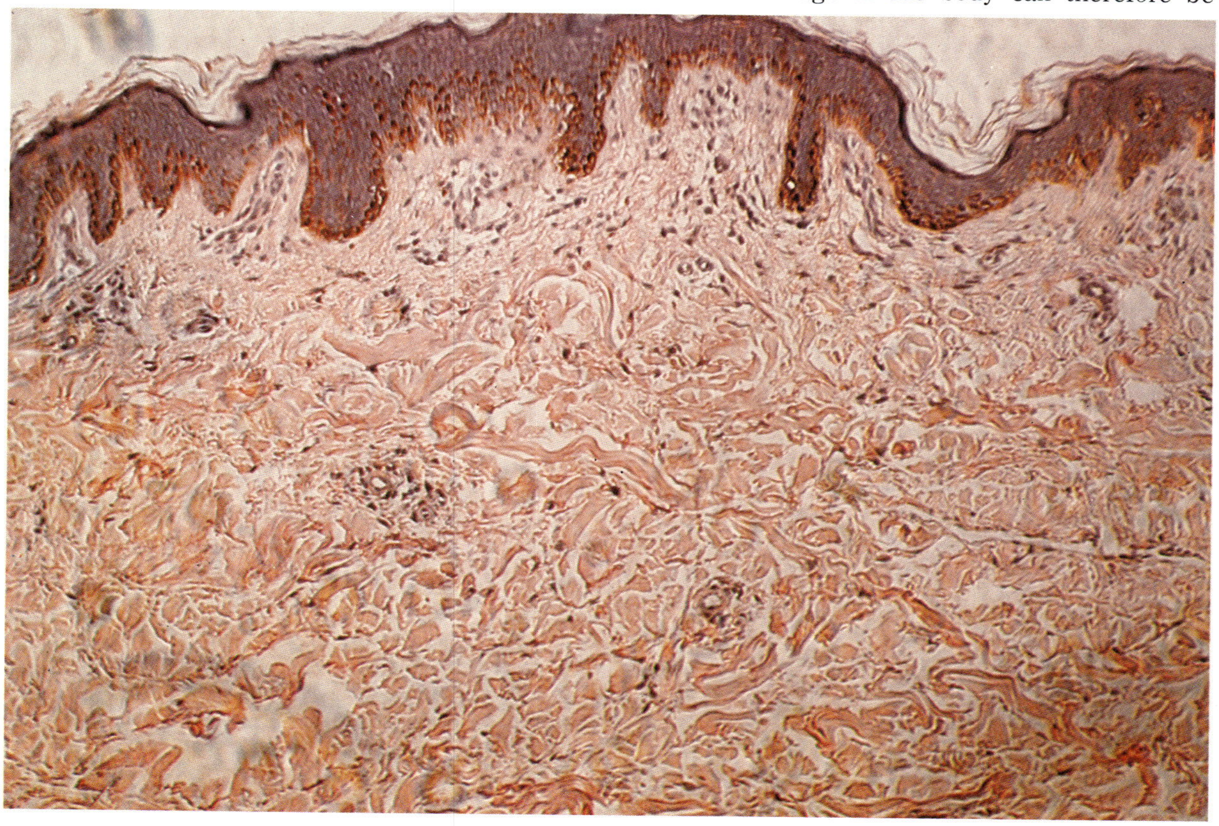

Left
A vertical section through skin, magnified 200 times. This covering of the body is many cells thick. Those at the surface (upper part of the picture) are dead and are sloughed away. Those underneath (darker region) are alive and divide and replace those that are lost. Cells in exposed locations, such as skin cells, are continuously replaced. Those within some internal organs only divide and multiply when the organ suffers injury. Others again, such as those in the nervous system, are never replaced

Divisions of Life
There are at least six easily identifiable types of cell in the human body. Within each type are a number of 'sub-divisions'– for instance, there are about 15 types of blood cell alone

Right
A Bristlecone pine, a member of the oldest tree species in the world. This one is estimated to be 5,000 years old. The reason it ages so slowly is possibly that it continually produces new cells at the tip of each twig

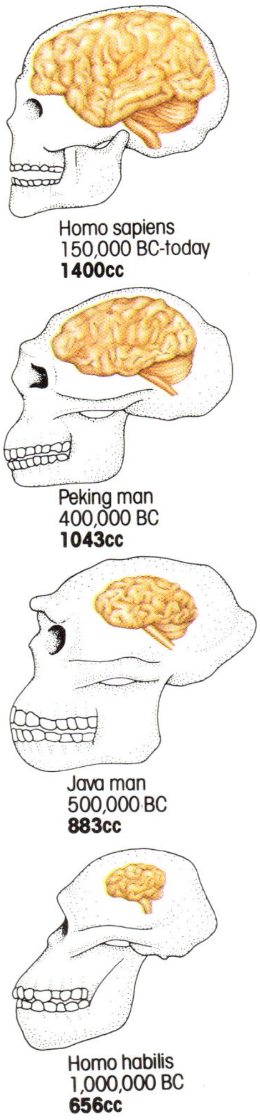

Ice-age Combat
Human evolution is characterized predominantly by increased brain size. Such changes occur over millions of years, but the four major ice ages, together with the intervening 'summers' seem to have given a strong 'evolutionary' kick to the process

Pattern of Survival
It may be said that we begin to die as soon as we are born. Our chances of dying certainly increase with age, but after our middle years, at a faster and faster pace

summarized extremely simply by the equation:

Extent of damage = Rate of production − Rate of repair

The repair process involves the active identification and modification or replacement of damaged molecules and cells—which is probably why the molecules and cells of the body are in a continuous state of turnover—and is likely to be very expensive in material and energy. Also, it should be remembered that, in Nature, most animals do not die naturally, but meet their end through the action of predators, accident, disease, war and murder. Hence, given that immunity from natural death would not protect an organism from death by unnatural causes, costly, high-fidelity repair may be a luxury that most organisms can do without. Material and energy saved in this way could obviously be used more directly in protecting the organism from predators, disease and accidents and in promoting reproduction. Moreover, because such a strategy would enhance fitness, it would be favoured by natural selection.

According to this view of ageing, organisms must compromise between using resources for repair and using them for other purposes. What they actually do will depend to a large extent on how long they 'expect' to avoid being killed. We face a similar sort of compromise when we buy a new car. Do we spend a lot of money on good rust-proofing to make the car last longer, or do we use the money to buy other things? If we expect to change the car quickly, we would probably decide against expensive rust-proofing on the grounds that we would be unlikely to have to suffer the consequences. Alternatively, if we expect to keep the car as long as possible, it would be foolish not to spend as much as we can afford on the best available rust-proofing.

Some organisms do appear to be immune from both ageing and predation. For example, turtles, which live within an armour-plated shell, have been known to live for years in zoos without showing any signs of ageing. Similarly, trees, once established, can usually withstand the ravages of most hungry herbivores and some are known (through tree-ring analysis) to have lived for more than a thousand years, again without showing any sign of ageing. Age-avoidance in plants is probably associated with a continuous turnover of tissues in the growing tips of stems and roots. Old cells are continuously replaced by new, with the old either left behind as dead vascular or supportive tissue, or lost in leaf-fall. Another group in which ageing is thought to be absent is the coelenterates (sea anemones, for example, one of which was kept for almost 100 years before it was inadvertently killed). These organisms, too, have a continuous turnover of cells within their bodies. As suggested above, therefore, cellular and molecular turnover are probably very important in ageing and its avoidance. In most organisms this turnover slows down with age.

If the avoidance of ageing is simply a matter of repair, would it be possible to extend the life of human beings by improving their repair processes? In principle, the answer to this question is 'Yes', but in practice, it is likely to be 'No'! The reason for saying this is that, in response to the potential diversity of damage-generating mechanisms and processes in organisms, there is likely to be great diversity in repair mechanisms as well. This being so, the system involved with ageing is not likely to be very amenable to manipulation and improvement unless one or two key processes can be isolated for treatment. In addition, there is the question of how wise it is morally, ethically and biologically to extend the human life-span by any significant amount. Most gerontologists see their main aim not as the extension of the life-span *per se,* but as the extension of *active* life. Even this carries profound biological and sociological implications in terms of the food and space requirements of our species, as well as in terms of when retirement should occur and how we should fill our active lives during old age. Perhaps there is the added individual, but nevertheless important, problem of how to face death with an active body and an active mind. Clearly, if gerontology is to go forward, *as it will,* it must do so hand in hand with theology, sociology, ecology, psychology and politics. That is why multi-disciplinary attacks on problems associated with ageing and death, as in this book, are so important and necessary.

To sum up: Living organisms are distinguished from things which have never lived by their order, organization and complexity and, more crucially, by the way they maintain these properties despite the entropic forces of the world. Living organisms are kept in existence by a process of copying, in which

A Gradual Process
Death is only a human concept of the cessation of functions. When one organ, the heart for instance, ceases to function, this does not mean that it is totally 'dead'—merely that there are no longer enough cells within it performing the functions necessary to keep the organ alive. This can be taken down to a cellular level. When a cell ceases functioning, only certain parts of it decay, while others remain living. From then on, total death is a gradual process, as the spread of damage due to more and more individual cells ceasing to function finally leads to total failure

Left
There are several groups of animals which appear to be immune to the ageing process. One such group is the coelenterates. These organisms, which include the sea anemone, have a continuous turnover of cells within their bodies. This is probably a key process in coelenterates' immunity to ageing. There is conclusive evidence proving that this process slows down with age in most other creatures

Below
Man and many other animals age. The fundamental answer to the question of why we grow old may be that, to stay young forever, as the sea anemones appear to do, would require us to invest resources in the maintenance of the body which, from the point of view of natural selection, would be better spent on reproduction

coded instructions on how they should be built and replicated are reproduced. Things that operate by instruction can be said to work according to a purpose in a more obvious way than non-living entities—another important distinguishing feature of living organisms. Darwin's great contribution was to show how this purposiveness could be explained without recourse to assuming the existence of a designer, deity or purpose-giver, but simply in terms of the great reproductive potential of organisms and their struggle for existence in a finite world.

Within organisms, replication is also important for the reproduction of damaged cells and molecules. This process seems to have been programmed by natural selection to keep the organism damage-free long enough for it to achieve maximum reproductive potential. Thereafter, damage is allowed to accumulate and, provided the organism is not killed by accident, disease or predators (as is, perhaps, only possible in farms, zoos and welfare states) the organism will die 'naturally' of old age.

This chapter could have opened with the question: What is life? The short answer seems to be: Nothing more than arises out of the property of self-reproduction. We should now be in a better position to answer the question: What is death?

Nature–A Merciless Murderess

For every species of animal and plant alive today, millions more have been sacrificed in the grim struggle for survival: they are the rejects of the constantly changing experiment with life

Above
The Gabon nightjar is so well camouflaged amid the leaves and twigs of the forest floor that it is almost impossible to notice its presence. Such concealment techniques enable animals to avoid discovery by predators

Right
A shoulder-striped carpet moth resting on some pine bark. This moth's defence against predators is concealment, others escape death by mimicking leaves, broken twigs, flowers and even inedible substances, such as bird droppings

Paradoxically, death has always been an essential part of life. Indeed, it is hardly possible to conceive of one without the other in the real world. Only in a dream world—a paradise where everything existed for eternity—could there be life without death, because nothing would ever change, so nothing would die. Living things as we know them could never have developed in such a perfect world, because the prodigious creativity of evolution is the inevitable result of a powerful process of differential mortality, whereby some privileged individuals live longer and breed better than those less fortunate. In fact few animals die of old age. Many fall prey to other animals, natural hunters, whose highly skilled and selective killing is one of the driving forces of evolution. Charles Darwin was the first person to realize that the immense riches of the living world were the outcome of a largely brutal struggle for existence in which violent and premature death was the lot of most individuals. The evidence is all around us.

Killers have been responsible for the development of many natural phenomena which we regard as beautiful and elegant. For example, animals whose shapes and markings contrast with the colours of the countryside are easily spotted by their predators, whereas those which match their surroundings have a much better chance of avoiding discovery. The camouflage patterns on the wings of some moths resemble to an astonishing degree the lichen-encrusted bark upon which they rest by day, helping them to escape the notice of keen-eyed birds. Scientific experiments have proved that those which match their background less well are quickly snapped up and thus prevented from breeding, and so handing on their faults. Other moths escape death for as long as possible by mimicking leaves, broken twigs, flowers and even inedible substances, such as bird droppings. Among

War without End
Throughout the period of man's tenure on earth, he has waged a long and bitter war on the insect for control of the world—yet, despite the expenditure of immense technical, financial and human resources, man has singularly failed to eradicate even a single insect species

The Killer Bite
Apart from man himself, our worst enemies are insects and snakes. It has been calculated that various kinds of snakes kill about 40,000 people every year

Primates of Death
Among the common killer diseases that non-human primates can transmit to man are tuberculosis (from monkeys and apes), shigella (a form of dysentery which can be fatal, from monkeys) and hepatitis (from chimpanzees)

Fatal Friends
More than 800 human deaths are caused every year by domestic animals, such as rabid dogs and nervous horses

Army of Dead Animals
During World War I some 480,000 horses, mules and bullocks died; in addition hundreds of dogs and carrier pigeons were made casualties by the four-year conflict

Right
Astoceras obtusum, a fossilized ammonoid which belonged to an extinct group of cephalopods, a class that today includes squids and molluscs. In the merciless struggle for survival that has been going on uninterrupted for billions of years uncountable numbers of animal and plant species have vanished. The only evidence we have that they existed at all are the impressions of their forms permanently recorded in ancient sea beds

Death Games
On one occasion the Roman Emperor Trajan staged a series of games that lasted 122 days. During this time, 10,000 animals were put to death. Another Emperor, Titus, had 5,000 wild animals killed during the games held to celebrate the opening of the Colosseum

Extermination for Pleasure
One result of the Roman Games was the extinction of hippopotamuses in the Egyptian Nile

Human Feast
The Romans, it seems, were never satisfied. According to the historian Pliny, games organizers arranged for slaves to be fed to starving eels, in order to provide entertainment for their bored patrons

birds, woodcocks and night hawks have evolved plumages which closely match the leaf-strewn woodland floor; only their big, lustrous eyes betray their presence. In the forest, the spotted coat of the chital deer makes it virtually invisible in the dancing, dappled light beneath the trees.

Of all the millions of species of animals and plants that have evolved since the first amoeba appeared 3,500 million years ago, fewer than one percent have survived to the present day

By their existence, predators have been responsible for the development of a wide variety of concealment techniques by some of their prey. Some moths have transparent wings; many planktonic organisms have translucent bodies and drift like ghosts in the blue surface waters of the sea; shoaling fish all but disappear from sight by virtue of their silver scales, which mirror the hue of the water in which they swim. On the other hand, highly inedible or venomous animals advertise themselves by means of their gaudy colourings. Certain praying mantises and hawk-moths warn off predators by displaying bold and colourful eyespots. The long, slim legs of gazelles, the wings of

birds, the needle-sharp spines of sea urchins and porcupines and the burnished scales of pangolins are all devices which enhance their owner's chances of survival. Unwittingly, then, killers are among the agents of evolution, promoting variety. As the hunters continue to refine techniques for discovering and dispatching their prey, the hunted develop ways and means of foiling them. However, the contest is not without its casualties.

Paleontology provides eloquent testimony to the huge scale of the obsolescence that accompanies the life game. The phenomenon of life – and death – was spawned in the sea nearly three and a half billion years ago. Since then, dynasties of living creatures have successively flourished and faded. The million or two species alive today are the distant descendants of those whose ancestors were winners in the life game and are still playing. For each winner, however, there were many losers at one stage or another, and these left no descendants. In fact, it is reckoned that more than 99.9 percent of all species are extinct.

In the fierce struggle for survival, whole classes of animals and plants have vanished. Immensely successful though they may have been in their heyday, the only sign that they existed at all is their fossilized remains in rocks. The further back we go, the stranger the forms of life appear. In the mud of ancient seas, nearly 650 million years ago, were entombed the frail bodies of creatures which can only be described as doomed 'experiments'. Today, we can see their fossilized forms in the rocks of Southern Australia and in the Burgess Shales, high in the Canadian Rockies. Such puzzling creatures have no known affinities with anything alive today. Trilobites, on the other hand, are clearly recognizable as the squat, segmented relatives of the horseshoe crab. Although once as common as crabs are today, they became extinct more than 250 million years ago. Eurypterid water scorpions, which were among the most rapacious predators of their era, vanished along with their armoured prey – primitive, jawless fishes. Blastoid feather stars have not adorned the shallow sea beds for perhaps 230 million years. Among land animals, the dinosaurs were hugely successful – yet their long-lived dynasty ended about 65 million years ago, when the last three-horned Triceratops expired in the forests which once covered northern Montana. Having failed to reproduce, this lonely old reptile ended its life as the last of its distinguished kind. Less well-known but almost as imposing were various groups of mammals like the Titanotheres and Amblypods, all of which failed to pass the test of time.

Basically, the extinction of a species is the result of individuals dying without offspring. Extinction is an inevitable property of evolution. Although we relish life, fight to preserve it, and regard its termination as the ultimate misfortune, there is every reason to believe that built-in obsolescence

Above
A herd of Thomson's gazelles on the move. As they speed along, they often make spectacular leaps, called 'stotting'. The victim of murderous attacks by packs of hyenas, the Thomson's gazelle's one means of escape is flight. Thus hyenas will usually hunt these graceful creatures on dark, overcast nights when the gazelle is unable to flee at high speed

Left
Huge land reptiles, some carnivorous but many herbivorous – the dinosaurs – flourished in all the continents of the world for 120 million years. The last of a long line of plant-eaters, the three-horned Triceratops died some 65 million years ago in the forests that once covered the northern part of Montana. This creature became extinct because it could not adapt to an environment that was inexorably changing

has been nurtured by natural selection. Put bluntly, individual organisms which readily age and die have proved to be more successful than those which have tended to cling over-zealously to life. The reason is not too difficult to discover: adaptability is often the key to success in the life game—and adaptability means making changes. There is a limit to the changes that can take place during an animal's lifetime, because its structure and behaviour are largely programmed by instructions 'written' into its genes, which are fixed at conception. Faults can, therefore, only be rectified and useful modifications created by going back to the drawing-board, as it were, and, with the help of the sexual process, producing fresh blueprints. In this way, new solutions can be found for the ever-changing problems of survival. Death sweeps away old and redundant models. The selection of Popes and Life Presidents is made with similar considerations in mind: in order to retain flexibility in policy, they are usually elected at a relatively advanced age, partly for their acquired wisdom, but also in the sure knowledge that they cannot rule for too long.

Life-spans have undoubtedly evolved in much the same way as the claws of a cat or the fangs of an adder. Of all life forms, some plants are the most successful in their ability to prolong life. Bristlecone pines in the western deserts of North America, for example, have reached the astounding age of 5,000 years. Many other kinds of trees survive for several centuries before wood-boring insects and fungi slowly kill them. The majority of plants, however, have strictly fixed terms of life; they are either annuals or biennials. By comparison with forest trees, most animals are very short-lived. The Methuselah of the animal world was a giant tortoise taken to Mauritius in 1766 and presented to the Port Louis army garrison as a mascot. It was

Mapping the Dangers
While Central Africa contains the greatest number of dangerous animals, Ireland is the world's safest country, with no more harmful wild creature than the bumble bee

Farmyard Murders
In a survey carried out for the West German health authorities in 1960, it was discovered that 169 people had died as a result of injuries caused by pigs, cattle and horses

accidentally killed 152 years later. Captive parrots can easily survive for half a century, if not twice as long, although the record for birds is held by an eagle owl, which survived into its 69th year. So did an Asiatic elephant. Even a sea-anemone in a tank outlived several human owners and survived to well over 90 years.

By human standards animals have an appalling death rate – in the wild few animals enjoy an old age. In the case of wild birds, most will survive for only one-tenth of their potential life-spans

Longevity records of animals cosseted in captivity have little bearing upon the age to which members of the same species normally live in the wild. Although a fair proportion of humans can hope to reach the biblically allotted span of three score years and ten – nearly three-quarters of our potential of a century – most animals die prematurely. Of course, there are exceptions, such as queen termites, which survive for perhaps 50 years, incarcerated in their royal chambers and pampered by their workers. A lion may live for more than 30 years in a zoo, but in the Serengeti National Park, it would be lucky to reach half that. Most wild birds survive for only 10 percent of their potential life-span. A pet herring gull once lived for 44 years, but on the coast its average expectancy would have been only three or four years. A captive blackbird has reached 20 years, but in the wild most die before they reach two. This reflects an appalling death rate by human standards. By comparison with birds, the annual mortality rate of larger mammals is correspondingly lower. In Tanzania, only 3 percent of adult zebras and 8 percent of adult wildebeeste die each year.

The life span of elephants and kangaroos is determined by their teeth. An elephant has six teeth in each side of its upper and lower jaws, making 24 in all. Only a few are in use at any one time, and as they become worn down they move forward, drop out, and are replaced by younger ones from the rear. After some 60 years of grinding coarse vegetation, the elephant wears down its last set of molars, can no longer feed properly, and starves to death. Of course, long before this happens, it may be killed by accident, possibly becoming hopelessly stuck in a swamp, falling into a ravine, or being crushed by a baobab tree. In the case of kangaroos, dental degeneration makes them ineffectual feeders when they are between 20 and 30 years old.

The business of breeding contributes greatly to mortality, especially among males, which become exhausted by the frenetic activity of fending off rivals and courting females. For this reason, they often tend to die younger than their mates. Stags, rams and buck Saiga antelope enter the winter after their autumn rut underweight, and often succumb to disease and starvation before the spring flush of grass arrives. Spawning completely exhausts salmon, which die after depositing their eggs and milt. However, their decomposing bodies release nutrients which encourage the growth of aquatic insects, providing food for their fry. Also, death removes the possibility that the adults may be tempted to cannibalize their offspring.

For a surprisingly large number of animals, copulation involves the male in an act of supreme danger – often one which he will not survive

The act of mating itself is lethal for many animals. Drone bees leave their penises behind in the queen's vagina. This so damages the males that they expire soon after their mating flight. Male marsupial mice also have short, passionate lives. The surge of cortico-steroids triggered by their summer sexual activity plays havoc with these primitive Australian opossums and, after intensive copulation for a week or so, they die of acute stress, liver failure, haemorrhages, ulcers and general infections. Their lives can be artificially extended by isolating them from females, but this, of course, prevents them from reproducing. By dying after ensuring the propagation of the species the males enhance the chance of survival of their offspring:

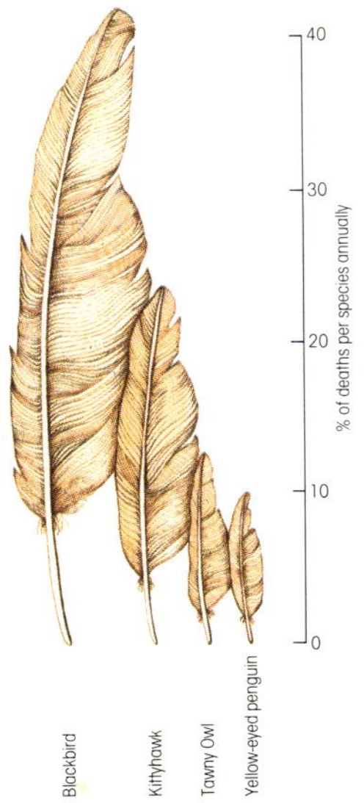

High Rate of Mortality
Few wild animals live out their full span, and birds perhaps more than most suffer enormous wastage. The vast majority of wild birds die while they are still young, victims of over-population and constant predation

Above right
Salmon spawning in a stream near Valdez, in Alaska Salmon spend their adult lives at sea, but return to rivers to spawn. Each adult makes a single spawning run, after which it dies. Salmon have been known to struggle against apparently insurmountable obstacles to reach their spawning grounds. The arduous journey leaves them exhausted, with just enough energy to deposit the eggs and milt

Right
This senile elephant is about 60 years old and will soon die. An elephant's life span is governed by its teeth, 24 in all, of which it uses only a few at a time. As they become worn, they move forward, drop out and are replaced. As the elephant ages, its teeth are no longer replaced; the last ones grind down, the elephant is unable to feed properly and it dies of starvation

they do not compete with their pregnant mates for the dwindling food supply. The reproductive strategy of 'mate and die' is widespread in insects. Indeed, the terminal stages of many are designed solely for propagation. Adult mayflies (Ephemeroptera) have aborted mouth parts and so cannot feed. They flutter on transparent wings, sometimes for as little as an hour, before breeding, and then die. Often, such a brief existence comes at the end of a long period spent as a grub: the North American cicada (*Megicica septemdecim*) has a life span of 17 years, of which all but a few weeks is spent underground as a burrowing grub.

The reproductive act takes on a macabre form for the many male spiders, flies and praying mantises: the females are literally *femmes fatales,* often turning on their mates and devouring them during or immediately after the act of copulation. Although the males lose their lives, they at least manage to fertilize the eggs and so pass on their genes. Sex also has its dangers for man. According to a survey of the causes of 5,500 sudden deaths in Japan, six women and 28 men died from heart attacks after sexual intercourse – mostly with partners to whom they were not married.

Occasionally, male animals experience a high mortality during the breeding season because of the nature of their role. They must often be flamboyant and noisy to attract and court a mate, and this sometimes also attracts predators. The song of the North American field cricket *(Gryllus integer)* enables a particularly unpleasant parasitic fly to locate it and

deposit its eggs. On hatching, the maggots eat their host alive.

The race to outbreed competitors has one important consequence: most young animals die sooner rather than later. The facts speak for themselves. A queen termite lays an egg a second. By comparison, the wood house toad, which can lay 25,650 eggs at a single spawning, is well down the league table. However, even slow breeders give birth to many young over the period of a life time, and their potential for increase is still enormous. A cow elephant can become pregnant ten times during its 40 years of reproductive life. A woman can have 20 children if she decides to breed relentlessly. Fortunately, few do so, but the potential for increase

Above
In the case of the praying mantis, the female of the species is certainly more deadly than the male. The female turns on its mate and devours it during the act of copulation. However, the male has ensured the perpetuation of his species by fertilizing the female's eggs and passing on its genes to the next generation

Left
Swainson's marsupial mouse, a primitive Australian opossum. Sex literally causes the death of the male. His summer sexual activity triggers a surge of cortico-steroids into his system, allowing him a week or so of intensive copulatory activity before he dies of acute stress, liver failure, haemorrhages, ulcers, or general infection

Deadly Fly
The insect most lethal to man is the common housefly, which is capable of infecting human beings with more than 25 diseases, including plague, cholera and even leprosy

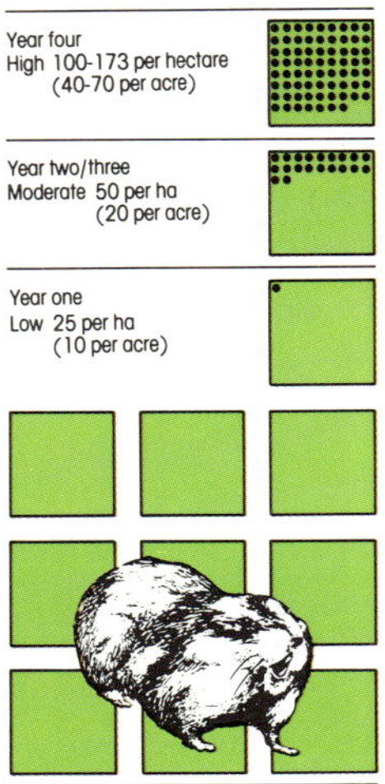

Mortal Journey
The lemmings have a four-year population cycle. In the final year the population reaches bursting-point and the lemmings break out of the tundra in search of fresh grazing lands. This journey ends in mass annihilation

Futile Slaughter
Every year something like 100,000 dolphins are uselessly slain through being trapped in the purse nets of tuna fishermen

Hunters of Humans
About 400 species of wild animals are considered to be the natural enemies of man

Acting Protector
To protect its young when threatened by a predator, the ringed plover feigns injury by flapping around helplessly as though its wings were broken. The predator will then follow what looks like the easier prey of the apparently injured bird instead of attacking the brood

is still there, and a centenarian may have twenty or more great-grandchildren.

In the wild, plagues of excess population are a rarity. The seas are not crowded with sunfish; the ponds are not brimming with toads; elephants do not stand shoulder to shoulder over the land. With few exceptions, animal populations are remarkably stable. On average, of each pair's offspring, only sufficient survive to replace the parents when they die. Surplus young die, and birth rates are balanced by death rates. In the case of spawners and egg layers, some young are killed before hatching. Almost half of all blackbird eggs are taken by jays, but even so, each pair usually manages to fledge about four young. By the end of summer, however, an average of under two are still alive. Since one parent will probably die or be killed during the winter, only one of the young will survive to breed the following summer. The high mortality rate among young animals is an inevitable consequence of high fecundity. Of the millions of fry produced by a pair of sunfish, only one or two escape starvation, disease or predators. Half the young of house mice living on the Welsh island of Skokholm are lost before weaning. Even in large mammals, the lives of the young can be pathetically brief and the killing wholesale. During the calving season, many young wildebeeste, still wet, feeble and bewildered, are seized and torn apart by jackals, hyenas and lions within minutes of emerging from their mothers' bellies. Three out of every four die violently within six months.

Whenever animal populations reach epidemic proportions, Nature steps in to restore the balance – with results that are tragically predictable

When conditions are exceptionally favourable, more young survive than usual, and populations quickly build up. Hosts of insect species, such as aphids, reach their peak numbers during the summer. Mice on Skokholm are ten times more numerous in the summer than in the winter months. Occasionally, populations reach plague proportions, as in the case of locusts, red-billed weavers and various species of rodents. But plagues do not continue indefinitely. When the food supply fails, as it ultimately does, mass emigration and starvation bring about a population slump. This happens periodically to lemmings, which normally live in the tundra. When their numbers are low, their distribution is about one individual to every 4 hectares (about 10 acres). During peak years, the population reaches a density of up to 173 animals a hectare – a 700-fold increase. At such concentrations the lemmings become highly stressed, over-graze the vegetation and break out from the tundra in search of fresh pastures. The ravenous animals are not daunted by water in their migratory path. In their eagerness, they do not distinguish between small streams and large lakes, and many drown. They are not, as popular belief holds, the victims of self-annihilation, but merely of accidents.

When lemmings and other plague species reach their population peaks, their predators also share in the success and breed unusually well. However, when the numbers decline again, the tundra and the surrounding forests are left with many starving Arctic foxes, stoats, snowy owls and various other birds of prey, all members of the killing trade.

To us, predators dispensing death may seem cruel and blood-thirsty. Although a peregrine falcon stooping on a wood pigeon kills instantly and painlessly, other hunters, like wild dogs and wolves hunting in packs, make no attempt to alleviate the suffering of their prey, which is often butchered alive. It must be remembered, though, that human

Right
The collared or snow lemming. Contrary to popular belief, these animals do not commit suicide on approaching a large body of water. They are simply unable to distinguish between a lake and the open sea. The further they swim out, the more tired they grow, eventually drowning. The periodic population changes are thought to be due to a reduction in the numbers of predators following a drop in the numbers of their prey, the lemmings, an increase in the numbers of lemmings which always follows a migration, and optimal conditions for breeding

notions of kindness, compassion and morality have no currency in the wild. A shrew tucking into the hind end of a writhing earthworm or a wild dog gnawing at the genitals of a kicking zebra are both procuring food in the only way of which they are capable. It is a matter of survival, and the fact that their victims are distressed or in dire pain – although unable to communicate it – is of no consequence to them. The technique of killing quickly has only developed if it is of benefit to the hunter. Solitary hunters, like cats and predatory insects, immobilize their prey rapidly, because a wildly struggling victim can sometimes inflict mortal injuries on its captor. Social hunters face different pressures. Each member of the pack is competing for a portion of the carcase and delivering the *coup de grâce* would be a waste of time, for the wounded prey cannot escape.

The tools and techniques of the killing trade reflect the marvellous enterprise of evolution, for nature abounds with killers of all kinds. Among the micronauts, predators are as voracious as elsewhere – gaping gullets lined with beating hairs sweep unsuspecting victims bodily to their doom. The *Amoeba* engulfs its prey; *Didinium* uses its snout to penetrate the victim which is then swallowed whole; the suctorian *Tokophrya* takes on prey many times its own size and, as its name suggests, sucks it dry within 15 minutes. Others, such as the minuscule foraminifers which live inside chalky shells in marine muds, capture their food on the end of sticky threads of protoplasm.

All predators, whether large or small, have had to solve a number of problems. They must *find* a victim, *seize* it, and *quieten* it or *kill* it before they can *feed* upon it. Some predators are so powerful in relation to their prey that they have little difficulty, like a robin with a small worm. Ladybirds seize aphids with their strong jaws and crunch them to death. Very often, killers are equipped to restrain or kill their victims in order to make the job of eating them easier. For example, the forelegs of the praying mantis are furnished with terrible spines and operate like a spring trap. Underwater, the jaws of the dragonfly larva are strong enough to hold a wriggling fish in a vice-like grip. The jaws of the ant lion, a larval form, are concealed at the bottom of a pit which it excavates in loose sand; small insects tumble down the sides into the deadly trap.

Many different kinds of animal have evolved venom, which is injected into the victim to quieten it and to soften its tissues to facilitate digestion. Bristle worms, shrews, and the gila monster – a

Above
Wild dogs with their zebra kill. Also known as African Hunting dogs, these animals can move extremely rapidly to corner game. When in pursuit they can outrun and overpower the swiftest and strongest antelope

Centre
These hyenas in Africa have just caught a wildebeeste which was in the act of giving birth and are eating it alive, easily avoiding being struck by the frenzied animal's kicking hooves. When they have eaten their fill, the hyenas will store the uneaten remains of their prey under water, to be devoured later, when they become hungry again. A hyena clan, usually numbering about 80, will fight viciously to defend its territory against another clan. One out of every five adult hyenas is killed in this way.

Left
Lunate ladybirds eating aphids. So powerful are they in relation to their prey, that they have no difficulty in overcoming them. They do not need to quieten or kill the aphids, but simply use their powerful jaws to crunch them to death. Their bright colouring advertises to other predators that they are inedible. They belong to the beetle family, which contains around 250,000 species, and is the largest order in the animal kingdom. Ladybirds lay their eggs inside leaves, the ends of which are folded over to protect the eggs

Right
This striped marine killer, the rare mantis shrimp, feeds on armoured creatures like crabs, smashing them to pieces with a pair of heavily reinforced appendages which strike with the force of a small-calibre bullet. The first blow stuns the crab, the next shatters its body

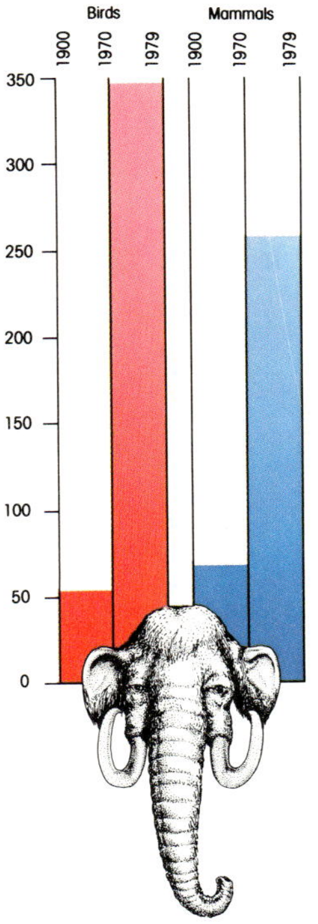

Doomed to Extinction
As man exerts an evergrowing influence over his environment, so more and more species of animals that fail to adapt will disappear. In the 1980s, for example, some 1,000 rare types of mammals and birds will be under a very grave threat

Right
Many different kinds of animal have evolved venom, which is injected into the victim to paralyze it. The tiny blue-ringed octopus is an especially vicious example

War aids the Scavenger
Tigers in Vietnam apparently learned to associate the sounds of gunfire with the presence of dead and wounded humans in the vicinity. This resulted in tigers moving quickly towards the zone of battle, where they consumed large numbers of casualties

Vanished Species
Since the beginning of the eighteenth century, 200 species of mammals and birds have vanished from the face of the earth

Threat to the Tiger
The total world tiger population is thought to be about 5,000. Two species are now extinct and there remain only a handful of the rare Javan tigers still alive

large lizard found in the Sonora Desert—have poisonous saliva which enters their prey through wounds. Spiders, many of which capture and restrain their prey in a web of gummy threads, inject a lethal blend of digestive juices when they bite, quickly reducing the flesh of their victims to a fluid which can be sucked out with ease. Octopuses and squids also introduce narcotic saliva into their prey when they bite with their parrot-like jaws. The tiny blue-ringed octopus of the Australian Barrier Reef secretes one of the most deadly nerve venoms known to man. Its bite is capable of killing a man within an hour, and when inflicted on its normal victims must cause almost immediate death. Assassin bugs are equipped with a proboscis like a hypodermic syringe. After stabbing this into their insect prey, they pump in a lethal dose of powerful venom. Among the vertebrates, some 800 out of 2,400 kinds of snake are accomplished poisoners. The vipers are the most advanced, with a pair of hollow fangs that swing forward during the final stages of the lightning-swift strike. A mixture of paralytic and digestive chemicals is forced through the fangs, and if—as is usually the case—the prey is a small mammal, death comes within a second or two of the fangs being withdrawn. Microscopic, stinging harpoons have been evolved by frail-bodied corals, sea anemones, hydroids and jellyfish. Batteries of these are often carried on long, trailing tentacles, into which fish and shrimp-like plankton blunder. This triggers off the harpoons, and salvoes of them pierce the bodies of the victims, rapidly inducing paralysis and death. The sea wasp (a jellyfish found

in the Pacific Ocean) also has harpoons. These contain an especially lethal toxin, which gives the sea wasp the dubious distinction of being the most venomous of all sea animals. A badly stung bather suffers excruciating pain and may die within minutes. Many molluscs are also surprisingly venomous. The Indo-Pacific cones, whose intricately patterned shells are highly prized by collectors, hunt fish with their minute, hollow, harpoon-like teeth, which are loosed through a proboscis. The fish succumbs after a few convulsive movements and is swallowed whole. New, needle-sharp harpoons are stored ready for future use.

Jaws capable of smashing backbones, venoms with the stunning power of our strongest narcotics, the range and complexity of weapons used by Nature's predators is a reflection of the constant war waged between hunter and hunted

Killers also use a variety of less subtle methods to subdue their victims. The mantis shrimp *(Hemisquilla ensigera)* feeds on armoured animals like crabs. It kills them by literally smashing them to pieces with a pair of heavily reinforced appendages, which strike with the force of a small-calibre bullet. The first blow invariably stuns the crab; and subsequent ones break up the body. Other kinds of mantis shrimp feed on fish. The shrimps are equipped with a pair of folded appendages like those of a praying mantis, but fashioned into forward-projecting spikes for impaling their prey. Their strike is one of the fastest animal movements known, attaining a velocity of more than 1,000cm (32.5ft) per second. Many fish- and frog-eating birds, such as herons and darters, also spear their prey. Some fish exploit electric stunning techniques. The electric ray and eel can project charges with a potential of several hundred volts—powerful enough to stun a horse. Nature also has its stranglers. One species of fungus lays nooses through which nematode worms crawl, become trapped, and are slowly digested. Even plants can be carnivores. Pitcher plants are acid-bath killers. Insects falling into the fluid contained in the pitcher are dissolved by digestive enzymes. Sundews lure, trap, and digest flies by means of glistening, sticky droplets on their leaves. The grotesque Venus fly-trap squashes its victims between the lobes of leaves hinged for the purpose. Death by suffocation is the fate awaiting the victims of many non-poisonous snakes, which gradually constrict their prey in ever-tightening coils.

Among the higher vertebrates, weaponry for dispatching prey is as advanced as anywhere else in the animal kingdom. Most birds of prey have a

Plants in Peril
Specialists estimate that some 30,000 out of a total of about 250,000 known species of flowering plants are threatened

Immortal Plants
In terms of longevity, plants are the most successful form of life; bristle-cone pines in the western deserts of North America have been known to reach the age of 5000 years

Left
Coiled round a hog deer, an Indian python squeezes the life out of it. One of the largest of all snakes, the Indian python has widely distensible jaws, which enable it to swallow even large prey whole. Before it begins to do so, however, it first crushes the bones of its victim and then compresses its carcase into the shape of a sausage. Pythons are highly mobile, and also climb well. The female often lays as many as a hundred eggs at a time

deadly grip. Their toes terminate in long, sharp talons which sink into the flesh of their victims, but they probably also squeeze the breath out of their prey. Generally, claws are used only for securing the prey. However, in *Deinonychus,* a long-extinct, 1.5m (4.9ft) tall dinosaur, a massive, pivoted claw was probably used to disembowel the victim with a kick of the foot. Usually, carnivores use their mouths, which are filled with teeth shaped like daggers and knives. The most spectacular killer of all time was undoubtedly *Tyrannosaurus,* which must have inflicted ghastly injuries on its giant victims by slashing them with its 15cm (5.85in) long teeth, serrated like steak knives. Most mammalian predators possess sharp, elongated canines—fangs—giving them a tenacious bite. With these fangs, they easily pierce the skin, tear blood vessels and rip nerves. Fairly primitive killers, such as opossums, civets and genets, kill their victims by delivering a series of frenetic bites wherever they can find a spot in which to sink their teeth. The more advanced cats kill cleanly, for they have perfected the deadly neck bite. By seizing the neck and squeezing it, their canines have a much greater chance of hitting something vital, such as the spinal cord or windpipe. The larger cats often kill by throttling. They hang

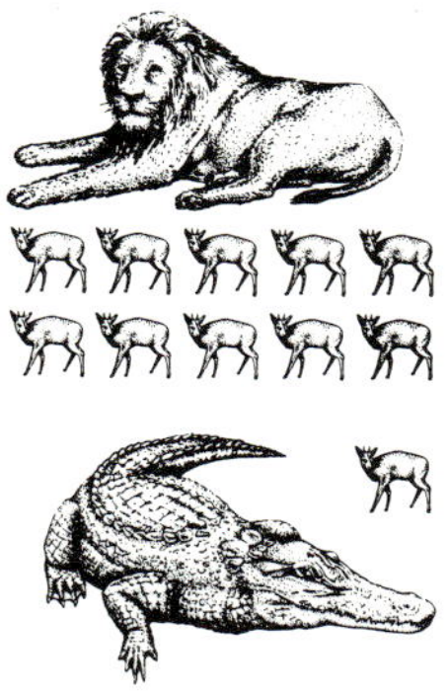

Hunters and Hunted
To sustain their high rate of metabolic activity, mammalian (warm-blooded) hunters, like lions and otters, require up to ten times as much food as the less active reptilian (cold-blooded) predators, like crocodiles and snakes

Left
Even plants can be carnivorous, like the Venus fly trap, shown here with a wasp caught between the lobes of one of its leaves. An open leaf, waiting to close on another victim, can be seen on the left. As the insect is slowly squeezed to death, the Venus fly trap leaf secretes a fluid containing an enzyme, which rapidly digests the soft parts of the creature

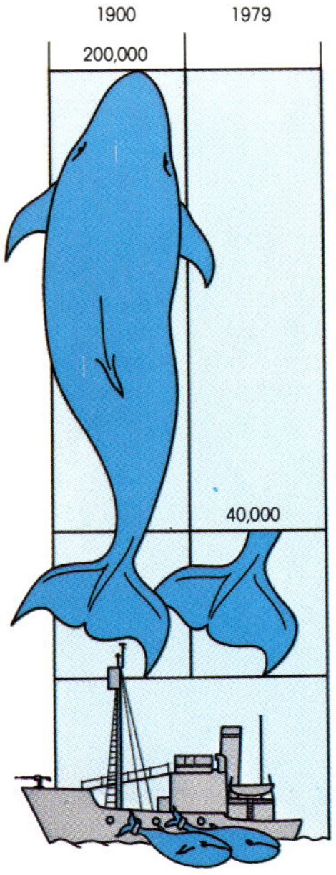

Disappearing Giants
Some 80 years or so ago, the seas were filled with the sight of the huge glistening bodies of the blue whale, the world's largest living creature. Today, due to the activities of fleets of whaling factories, this marine mammal is in danger of becoming extinct

on grimly to the neck or muzzle of a wildebeeste or zebra, which usually dies of asphyxiation within a few minutes. Once dead, or at least comatose, the carcase can be cut up with the help of the self-sharpening carnassial teeth at the back of the mouth. The extinct sabre-toothed 'cats', some of which were marsupial, employed quite a different technique. They fed on giant, thick-skinned mammals like ground sloths, and were in fact stabbing cats. Their lower jaws could open much wider than those of modern cats, exposing the full length of their serrated canines. Powered by massive neck muscles, the head was jerked up and down to drive the pair of 'sabres' deep into the flesh of the prey, which then died from a massive loss of blood.

Despite the mechanical efficiency of their killing apparatus and methods, it is worth bearing in mind that the larger cats have a high failure rate when hunting. Most hunts by lions are abortive. In Kana National Park, tigers may miss their prey some 30 times for every successful interception. Even feral farm cats catch mice with only about one third of their pounces. This is just as well, from the predators' point of view, for if they were 100 percent successful, they would quickly eliminate the sources of food upon which their survival depends.

Whether wild or domestic, apparently harmless or obviously very dangerous, a vast number of animal species will, if hungry or desperately frightened, attack humans

Humans occasionally fall prey to carnivores, although less frequently than is widely believed. A person floundering in a lake infested with crocodiles, or splashing around in the sea where sharks patrol, is inviting violent death, but such casualties are few and far between. Lightning kills many more people than these most feared animal killers. The same is true of other potentially dangerous members of the killing trade. Generally, leopards, lions and tigers are not a menace to man. However, when they do turn to man-hunting, they can terrorize wide areas

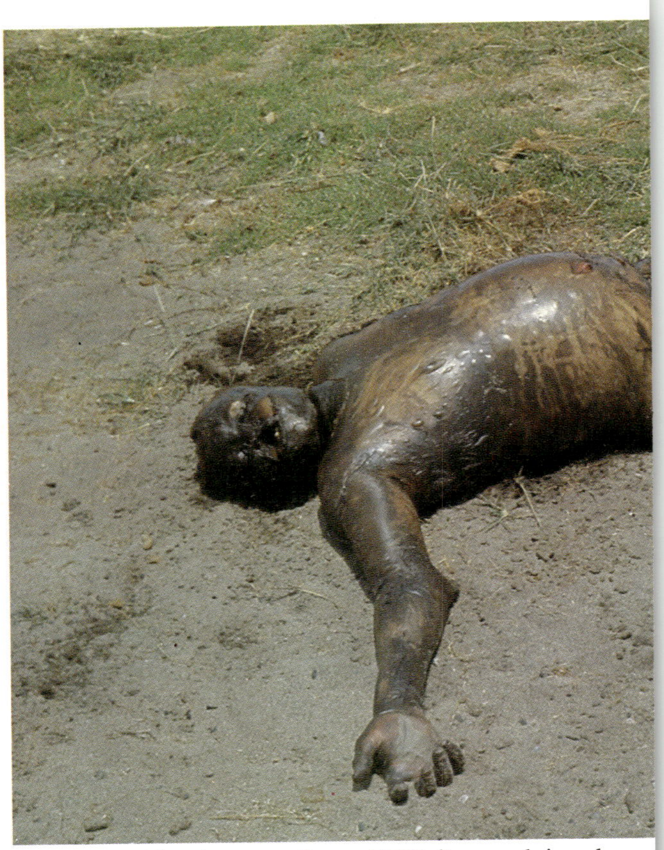

of countryside. As recently as 1962, it was claimed that leopards had taken the lives of about 350 people in Bhagalpur over a period of three years. True or not, this provoked massive retaliation—an attempt was made to liquidate all leopards over a 52 sq km (20 sq ml) area with guns, tear-gas and dynamite. Because most big cats are now far less numerous than they used to be, man-eaters were more prevalent in the past.

Colonel Jim Corbett, who made his name waging war on dangerous tigers and leopards, gives many accounts of their dastardly deeds in his books. During one wave of man-eating between 1918 and 1926, no fewer than 126 people were carried off by leopards. The man-eating tigers of Kumaon disrupted the day-to-day life of many villages until despatched by Corbett's gun. When examined, the tigers were invariably found to be old, crippled, or injured by porcupine spines, suggesting that they turned to human prey only when, because of their infirmities, they could no longer catch and kill their normal prey.

The same cannot be said of lions, which very occasionally turn to killing and eating people for no apparent reason. The man-eaters of Tsavo were perhaps the most infamous of all. In 1898 a pair of large, maneless males began hunting people with reckless abandon during the building of the railway which runs from Uganda to Mombasa, through the wide, rolling plains of Tsavo. Lieutenant-Colonel Patterson, an engineer employed on the project, finally brought the careers of these two man-eaters to an end, but only after they had killed and consumed 28 Indians and an unknown number of Africans, and had utterly unnerved the work force. Since then, a few individual lions have taken a fancy to human flesh but, considering the number of lions in the wild, this is an event of great rarity.

Pumas, jaguars, wolves and bears all have a claim to notoriety as man-killers. So have rogue elephants, cape buffalo and wild boar, which are extremely irascible and likely to charge without

Below.
A yawning lioness shows her fangs. The carnassial teeth at the back of the mouth are self-sharpening. They are used to cut up the carcase of the prey animal, once the fangs have done their work of killing it or rendering it unconscious

warning at the slightest provocation. In comparison, snakes are more lethal, because they use their venom in self-defence. Some 30,000 to 40,000 people die from snake-bite every year, with the king cobra and Russell's viper claiming more victims than any other species. However, no large animal can match the insects, which bring death indirectly to millions of people annually. The house fly is said to be the most dangerous of all insects. Its insanitary habits result in the spread of pathogens from dung and rotting flesh to food. Mosquitoes, which transmit yellow fever and malaria, certainly account for millions of deaths in under-developed countries. The tsetse fly, too, ranks as a major killer, carrying such diseases as sleeping sickness and filariasis. However, man is his own most dangerous adversary!

Ultimately, it is man, one of the most social of creatures, who is also the greatest exterminator of animals on this planet—yet it took millions of years before his murderous domination could make itself felt

We are by far the most efficient predators on this planet. Ever since our ancestral ape-man invented spears, clubs and bolas as a substitute for fangs and claws, we have been harassing wildlife on a scale unknown up to that time. For perhaps two or three million years, our hunting activities had little impact on the communities of game animals. Then, slowly, we improved our hunting methods and tools to the point where we steadily exterminated, first the large and vulnerable giants such as mammoths and, possibly, ground sloths, and then our competitors—wolves, cave bears and similar predators. Our ingenuity eventually turned us into undertakers. Since the invention of gunpowder, we have hunted without moderation and have eliminated species after species. Despite their enormous numbers, the North American passenger pigeon and South African quagga had no answer to lead shot. Nor have whales to the explosive harpoon, which is why they now face extinction.

Mass killing is not peculiar to man, however. Carnivores sometimes go on a rampage of slaughter which appears to be motivated solely by blood lust. Foxes attacking black-headed gull colonies often kill more birds than they can possibly consume. In one such attack, a single fox killed 230 gulls in one night. Much the same sort of situation occurs when a fox gets loose in a poultry run. Hyenas, too, leave a trail of carnage when they attack herds of gazelles. However, there is an explanation for this apparently wasteful slaughter. Survival is not easy for a hunter. Prey animals are usually few and far between, so predators must exploit every opportunity that comes their way. Thus, carnivores kill more than they actually need at any given moment, although they often make some use of meat surplus

Left
Some Africans living on the shores of Lake Rudolph, in the eastern part of the continent, make a living out of catching crocodiles. This African was unlucky; a crocodile caught him instead. Badly bitten, he managed to struggle free and reach land, only to die within minutes of coming ashore. Generally speaking, however, crocodiles do not kill many humans

Above
Remains of an elephant killed by poachers within the Samburu Game Reserve in Kenya. Most elephant-poaching involves the use of traps, and then shooting from close range

Bottom left
One of the most important factors in the decimation of the world's whale population is the explosive harpoon. In the photograph, a harpooned fin whale's blood stains the sea red as it tries in vain to escape its killers

Bottom
As a rule, the leopard is not a menace to man, but does occasionally turn to man-hunting. In the early 1960s, leopards were said to have killed some 350 people in the space of three years. A leopard usually drags its kill up into a tree and sleeps on it

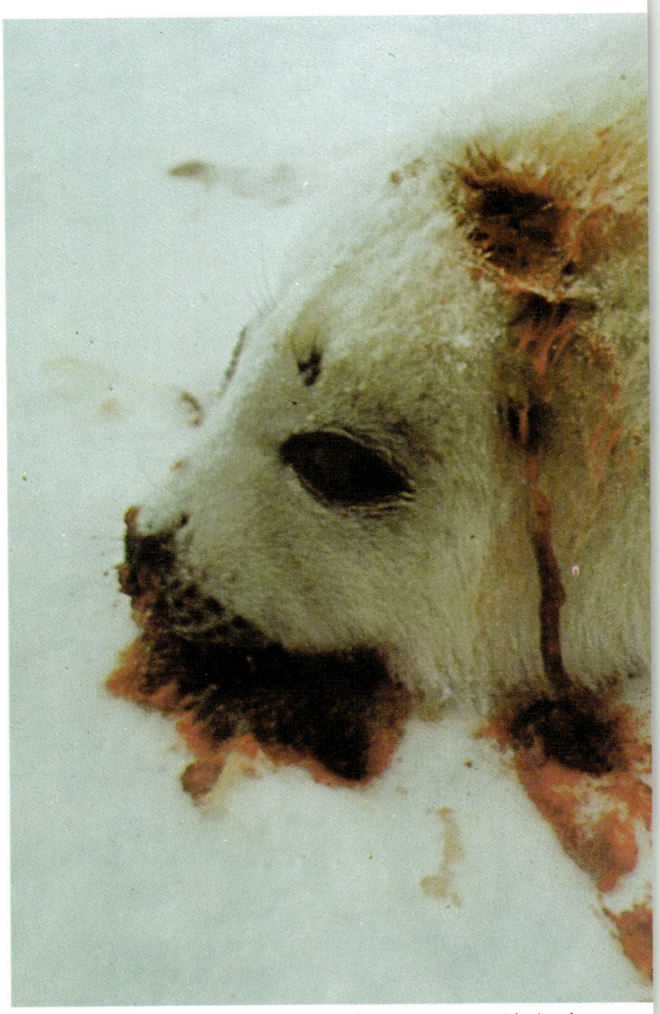

Nature's Killing Machine

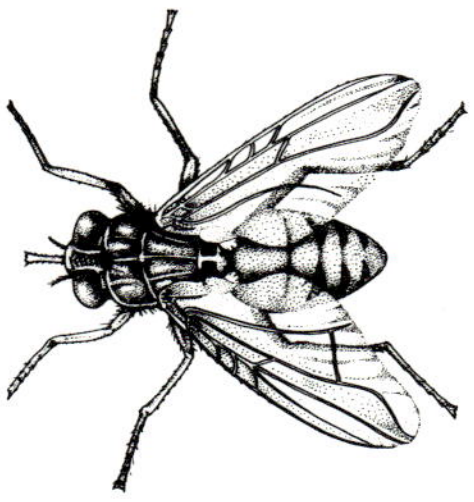

It has been estimated that insects cause the deaths of roughly 1,000,000 people a year

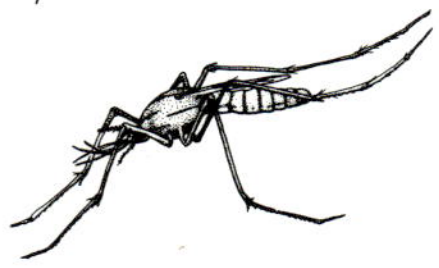

The anopheles (malaria-carrying) mosquito may have been responsible for one-half of all human deaths

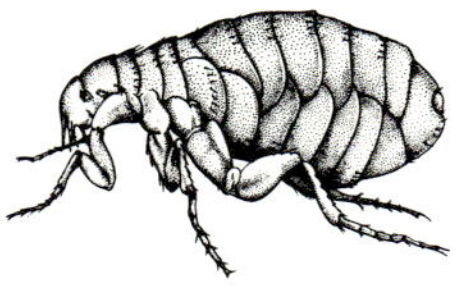

Plague fleas are thought to have killed 10,000,000 people in India alone in just a few decades

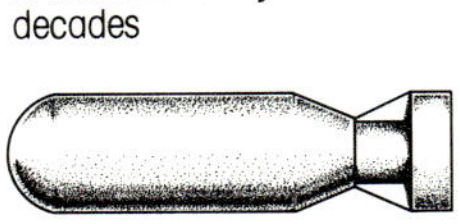

A single, medium-size nuclear bomb could kill about 100,000 people shortly after detonation

to their immediate requirements. Lions spend long hours guarding half-eaten carcases; leopards drag their kills into trees and sleep on them; hyenas store excess food under water; foxes cache their prey by burying it. Predators are likely to indulge in an orgy of killing only when, for some reason, their victims are unable to escape or defend themselves. The fault does not lie with the fox in the poultry house, so much as with the owner, for keeping large numbers of chickens in conditions which make it impossible for them to escape, thus providing unusually favourable conditions for the hunter. Similarly, the gulls live in densely populated colonies to which foxes have access, and the gazelles are handicapped by a dark, overcast night. In the same way, penguins and great auks were helpless against the onslaught of boat-loads of men armed with clubs, because they had not retained the power of flight.

The killing discussed above has been primarily for food, but there is a more sinister form of killing—murder. In conflicts involving territory, male animals occasionally fight to the death. In the case of octopuses, the victor eats its adversary. Combat between clans of hyenas takes the form of warfare. Each clan contains up to 80 animals, which defend their boundaries against neighbours with great ferocity. One out of every five adult hyenas is eventually killed on the battlefield. At Gombe Stream in Tanzania, a gang of marauding male chimpanzees initiated the systematic killing of members of a neighbouring troop, rather like Mafia hit-men eliminating the opposition. However, murder is usually related to the need to breed at almost any cost. For much of the time, male gorillas are gentle, unemotional animals, but when defending their females from rivals they become ferocious fighters, often inflicting dreadful and mortal injuries on their opponents. Male lions may also be killed while defending or taking over a pride. When a male is successful in acquiring a new set of mates, one of its first acts may be to commit infanticide, killing the former dominant male's cubs, so that the lionesses can start breeding afresh. In terms of evolution, tragedies like this make sense. Every lion must try to pass on its own genes, not foster another's. Infanticide is probably a widespread practice. In large colonies of lesser black-backed and herring gulls, there are individuals which specialize in cannibalism. The dominant bitch hunting dog will often not tolerate a subordinate giving birth to a litter and competing with her own offspring for valuable sources of meat, and so will kill the rival's pups if given half a chance: it is better for one litter to survive than for all to starve.

Infanticide, cannibalism, mass killings—these are acts of murder that we find particularly abhorrent, though among animals such practices may be necessary for the continued survival of the community

Such heartless acts are not confined to the animal world. The early history of many ruling families is disfigured by accounts of infamous murders, sometimes involving the elimination of defenseless children—and even today murder is rife. In the United States a murder occurs every 28 minutes. The scale on which man is capable of murdering his fellows is appalling. One of the most blood-thirsty societies ever to have existed was that of the Aztecs. Each year, an estimated 250,000 sacrificial

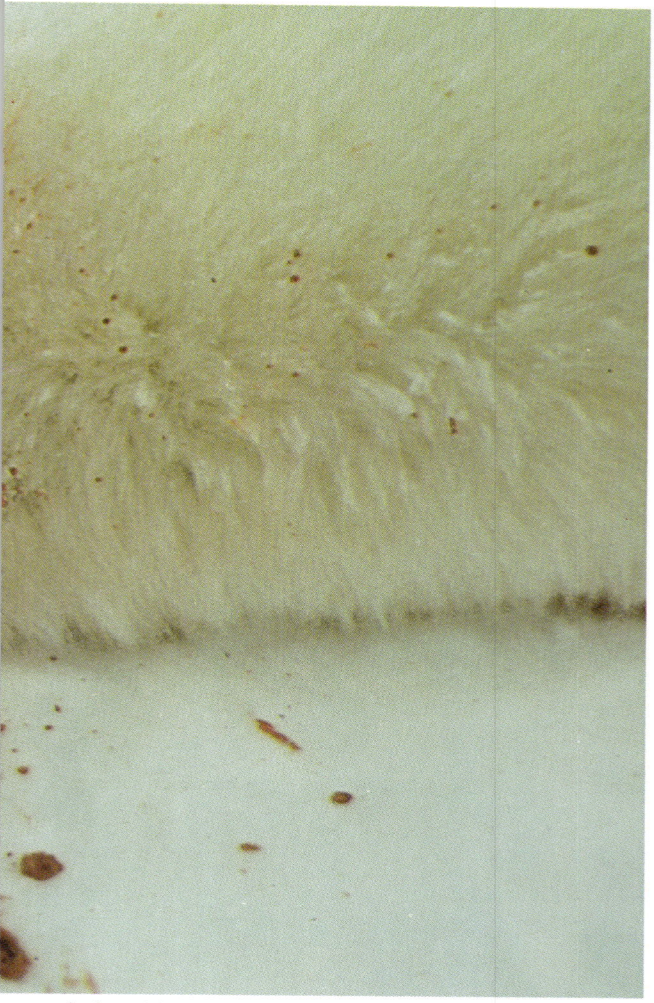

victims (1 percent of the population) were led up the steps of temples throughout what is now central Mexico, and their hearts ripped out. Modern research indicates that the purpose of this gruesome practice was cannibalism in response to failing food production, together with a dire over-population problem. Since then, the world has not lacked ruthless despots who have unhesitatingly put people to death on a monumental scale. Hitler's 'Final Solution', in which 6 million Jews were liquidated like vermin, took place in a relatively cultured and sophisticated country, the birthplace of such geniuses as Bach, Beethoven and Goethe. Unfortunately, the very technological ingenuity which made us super-hunters has also transformed us into terrifyingly efficient slaughterers during ideological or territorial conflicts. For example, some 50 million people died violently during World War II alone. Once, we simply hurled stones and spears at each other; today, the potential scale of an all-out nuclear war is at once terrifying and ridiculous. Every one of us has the equivalent of four tons of TNT reserved for us in the arsenals of the superpowers. Unleashing a destructive force of such magnitude would probably exterminate our species —and, of course, would be self-defeating.

Suicide may be a useful strategy to promote the survival of the genes of the victim. Male octopuses are programmed to lose their appetites and starve to death after mating. After tending the eggs, the female also languishes and dies. By not continuing to live, they may be promoting the survival of their young. There is an element of suicidal behaviour in the actions of human and animal parents who put their own lives at risk if this is necessary to defend their families. They are ready to die so that their children might live. The same self-sacrifice informs the action of worker social insects which attack a huge enemy and die in thousands. If their colony is saved, the queen, their mother, goes on reproducing.

The ultimate good fortune is to escape an untimely and violent death. Like all animals, we are endowed with a powerful will to live through every crisis, but we know that eventually, we shall all succumb to the final crisis, death, in view of the uncomfortable fact that our bodies are mortal. Religion is a cultural solution to this problem. It enables many people to cheat death by their conviction that the soul escapes into a spiritual world or, through reincarnation, returns to the mortal one in another guise.

Far left, top centre
Man is the most deadly and efficient predator on earth, killing animals without mercy and often exterminating entire species, however numerous. This wholesale slaughter is sometimes justified by the assertion that the animals killed compete with man for the diminishing supplies of food. Seals, for instance, are said to deplete the oceans' fish population, not only eating human beings' food, but depriving fishermen of a living. This is why the world's seal population is 'culled' every year by killing baby seals (as in these photographs) to keep the seal population down. Even this argument loses its significance, however, when baby seals are killed for their fur

Bottom left
Archeologists estimate that, during the peak of the Aztec civilization, some quarter of a million sacrificial murders were performed on the altars of the temples. The reason: to provide needed protein for a population desperately short of food

Bottom
Christians receiving communion at a Catholic Mission near Kavango, in Namibia – seeking escape from mortal death into an everlasting world of the spirit

Man and Death: The Funeral Complex

From the solemnity of a Victorian funeral to the uninhibited rejoicing at a Laotian mass cremation, the celebration of death has taken many forms through history—some of them extremely bizarre

Above
At the 'Iron Duke's' magnificent state funeral in 1852, his coffin, draped in black velvet, was carried on a massive funeral car drawn by 12 horses. It was followed by a procession of some 5,000 mourners

Right
At this funeral on the island of Bali, the pagoda containing the body is being carried to the cremation site. This form of disposal of the dead has been practised since antiquity in many parts of the world

Sociable Cemeteries
In France until the early eighteenth century, cemeteries were used as places of refuge and meeting-places, as well as burial grounds. Shops were common, merchants used to do business there, and gambling was rife. Burials and the reopening of tombs often had to be carried out among crowds of booksellers, second-hand clothes dealers and the general public. In the late eighteenth century, however, this began to change, as society came to abhor such close contact between the living and the dead

Primitive man's attitude to death was akin to that of the animal kingdom; a person was simply left where he or she had died. When man began to dwell in permanent settlements, however, the health of surviving members of the community demanded that bodies should be disposed of in some way or another.

Simple burial, or merely throwing a body into a ravine served at first, but man moved, inexorably if sluggishly, from the savage state. To lust and violence were added in time the gentler attributes of affection and love. With them, however, went a concomitant emotion—grief at the death of a companion.

The capacity to feel affection and grief led naturally to a desire to see the dead again, to believe in an after-life. This in turn induced a more respectful treatment of the dead. They were no longer disposed of casually, but were usually buried in a pit, often adorned with flowers and surrounded by their personal possessions.

No attempt can be made here to give an encyclopedic account of the myriad funeral customs of all cultures and peoples of the world. Nevertheless, it is precisely this great variety that seems at first view most striking. Two examples may illustrate this point. The English, it is often remarked, are particularly adept at organizing state functions. State funerals are perhaps the outstanding example. Although these are normally reserved for heads of state, exceptions have been made, most recently for Sir Winston Churchill. The Duke of Wellington was also given a state funeral, when he died in 1852. This ceremony, at the height of the Victorian religious revival, was both magnificent and of suitable solemnity. For five days before the funeral Wellington lay in state, and his coffin was seen by

Anthony Livesey

Right
The state funeral of Sir Winston Churchill, Prime Minister of Britain during World War II, was not as ornate as that of the Duke of Wellington a century or so earlier. Sailors of the Royal Navy draw the gun carriage bearing Sir Winston's coffin, draped with a Union Jack, through the City of London in 1965

Far right
Edward Kennedy kneels in silent homage at the grave of his brother, President John F. Kennedy

Preparing for Life
'There is no death! What seems so is transition,
This life of mortal breath
Is but a suburb of the life elysian
Whose portal we call Death'
(Longfellow)

Right
President Kennedy's widow (veiled) flanked by Edward and Robert Kennedy (right)

No Law for Disposal
In Britain, if a corpse can be sufficiently preserved to demonstrate that it does not constitute a public health hazard, there is no law requiring that it must be disposed of

Price of a Funeral
Since the 1950s, the cost of American funerals has nearly quadrupled, from a fairly low 500 to an astronomical 1950 dollars

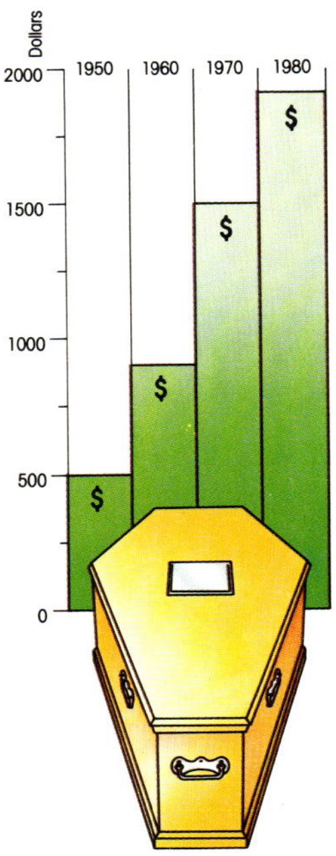

some 268,000 people. So great was public demand to enter Chelsea Hospital, where he lay, that on the first day a number of people sustained injuries. The funeral itself took place on November 18. The procession began at 7.30 a.m. and made its way from St. James's Park to St. Paul's Cathedral by way of Pall Mall, Piccadilly, the Strand and Temple Bar. The route was lined with spectators, many in funeral attire. The procession comprised some 5,000 mourners, about a third of them mounted. Among them were six battalions of infantry (each of 600 men) and eight squadrons of cavalry, as well as one soldier from every regiment in the Queen's service, 12 mourning coaches and 20 carriages. Also taking part were members of the Royal family, peers, members of the House of Commons and Lords and many of Wellington's friends and relations. The Duke's coffin, draped in black velvet decorated with escutcheons, headed the vast procession. It was borne on a massive funeral car drawn by 12 horses in mourning trappings and flanked by army officers on horseback. The funeral service was prolonged and music was provided by a vast orchestra hired for the occasion.

The funeral of President John F. Kennedy of the United States was almost as ornate, but was less successful. An estimated million people lined the processional route but the ceremony was marred by organization so poor that some world leaders were not allocated seats at the service. The intention, however, was identical—to mark the disposal of the remains of a greatly admired national leader with the utmost pomp and solemnity.

There could hardly be a greater contrast than the gaiety, dancing and feasting which form part of the funeral rites accorded to rich Laotians. In Laos death from natural causes is considered a joyous event because it marks the entry of the deceased

into Nirvana. The manner of death is crucial to the funeral rites. The law (originally promulgated as a royal edict) establishes six categories of death, which may seem arbitrary to Western minds—death from disease; from execution; from drowning or from being killed by a tiger; from falling from a tree, and from being struck by lightning. Those who die violently are subjected to the indignity of immediate cremation with a minimum of rituals, but those who die from natural causes, particularly if they happen to be rich, are accorded full ceremonial privileges.

For many Asians, including the Laotians, a person's death from natural causes is the signal for the start of joyous and energetic celebrations, marking the passing of a loved one into the realm of Nirvana

When a rich Laotian dies, his relatives close his eyes and wash his body in cool, perfumed water. A small piece of gold is placed in his mouth to symbolize the transitory and trivial nature of earthly possessions. After these and other ceremonies have been performed, the body is wrapped in a shroud and laid in a wooden coffin. A week of day and night parties and noisy celebrations follows in the house where the coffin is lying, for the dead person has attained a happier state, and everyone must therefore rejoice. To ensure that the spirit passes into Nirvana without hindrance, gifts and food are offered, lest it lack necessities for the journey. Everyone, not only relatives, contributes to the funeral preparations, which are accompanied by feasts and games.

At the end of one week, the coffin, protected by relatives against such parasites as wood lice, which would otherwise destroy it, is moved into a specially built shelter to await cremation. This cannot by law take place until the fourth month of the Laotian calendar. A great pavilion is built, and workmen erect a ceremonial canopy, a paper dome, under the roof. This will be the last resting place of the body before it is reduced to ashes. The joyous celebrations, with feasting and dancing, continue for a further six days and nights, culminating in the greatest feast of all on the night before cremation takes place. Finally, a priest lights the funeral pyre and the coffin is engulfed in flames. The celebrations continue while the fire is banked, and only when nothing remains save ashes is the ceremony at an end. Relatives then place the ashes in a jar and lodge it in a pagoda. Usually an elaborate monument is erected over the site of the cremation.

Left
Inside the pavilion, with its horned roof, reposes a wooden coffin containing the body of a rich Laotian on its way to cremation. Afterwards, relatives put the ashes in a jar, which is lodged in a special pagoda

Below left
Death from natural causes is considered a joyous event in Laos, because it marks the entry of the deceased into Nirvana. The funeral preparations are accompanied by feasts and games. The funeral rites include the killing of a bullock

Dining with Death
Wagner prepared his own grave in his garden and used to enjoy introducing the subject to his dinner guests, often taking them into the garden in the middle of a meal to show them his grave

Buried Upside-down
A certain eccentric named Richard Hull was buried upside down on horseback beneath the tower at Leith Hill, near London, some centuries ago. He believed this would give him an advantage on the Day of Judgement, when, according to legend, the world would be reversed

Profitable Respect
In the USA in 1961, 70 percent of the total revenue of the flower industry came from the sale of funeral flowers

Burial at the Crossroads
An Anglo-Saxon King of England laid down a law which stated that anyone who wilfully took his own life was to be denied a Christian burial. Suicides were commonly buried without ceremony at a crossroads, to lessen the possibility of the return of a vengeful spirit. People believed that the ghost would be confused by having to choose between four roads

Watcher of the Dead
In cemeteries in certain parts of Ireland it was believed that the ghost of the most recently buried person kept watch over the cemetery until another person was buried there. A gravedigger would often leave a pipe and tobacco on the grave of the 'watchman' to keep him happy while he was 'on duty'

Right
The Zoroastrians of Iran and the Parsees of India (who are descended from them) expose the bodies of the dead on the top of 'Towers of Silence', to be devoured by vultures. The towers, like this one at Yazd, in Iran, are usually on hilltops

Centre
Skeletons on the flagged top of the Yazd tower, after the vultures have done their work

Below
There are Neolithic caves throughout Europe, used both as homes and as tombs by the early races which invaded Europe from the East, bringing their flocks and herds with them. The remains of this Neolithic woman were found in a burial pit near the Brittany coast of France. Like so many peoples all over the world, Neolithic man buried his dead with their possessions

The contrast between the measured solemnity of the Duke of Wellington's funeral and the light-hearted indulgences of a rich Laotian's is striking. In considering the funeral rites of places far distant from each other it is easy to find such contrasts. Many are the result of differing local conditions and are dictated by the demands of hygiene. Others are the direct result of religious belief.

Of the many and varied methods of disposing of the dead around the world, few are as strange as the Parsee practice of exposing corpses in 'Towers of Silence'

The Parsees of India, for example, worship the natural elements. Thus, they cannot bury their dead, for this would contaminate the element earth. Nor can they bury bodies at sea or cremate them. Instead, they have devised an ingenious alternative method of disposal. Corpses are exposed in 'Towers of Silence', 20 feet high and open to the sky, where they are devoured by vultures within a few days.

A variation of this, called 'air burial', is common in Tibet, where every village has a special area set aside for the purpose. The body is taken to this deserted spot, where the men of the village burn sandalwood, whose aroma arouses the birds high up in the rock face. The white linen in which the corpse has been swathed is then unbound, and the men cut open the stomach and remove the intestines. During this process the birds start descending from the rock face in groups. After the body has been dismembered and the flesh stripped from the bones, the men grind them into small pieces and knead them with barley. The priest watches as the birds devour the remains. This usually takes no more than half an hour. If the birds do not consume all the remains, the priest regards this as a bad sign, because the highest attainment for a Tibetan is to give away everything. Once the soul has departed the body has no further significance for Tibetans, and they wish to leave no trace of it on earth.

Such funeral rites have their origin in profound religious belief but, as with so many customs, there are also practical reasons for them. In Tibet, burial is difficult, since the ground is frozen for much of the year. Cremation is no easier, for there is no coal and little wood, while consigning corpses to the rivers would pollute drinking water.

Before considering the funeral rituals of some of the great religions and cultures, both past and present, it is worth looking briefly at some of the numerous similarities in the methods man uses to dispose of his dead. These similarities are particularly striking, because they occur in diverse areas, often many miles apart and separated by originally uncrossable oceans or mountain ranges. In essence, the similarities stem from two factors. First, apart from groups like the Parsees, man has little choice in the disposal of his dead—they have to be either buried or cremated. Secondly, all human beings are subject to the same emotions, so many, if not most, funeral rites are designed both to pay respect to the dead and to alleviate the anguish of the bereaved. There is little difference save size between a Victorian gravestone and the Great Pyramids of the Pharaohs—both are intended to show respect to the dead, to perpetuate their memory, to record their achievements and to testify to man's belief in

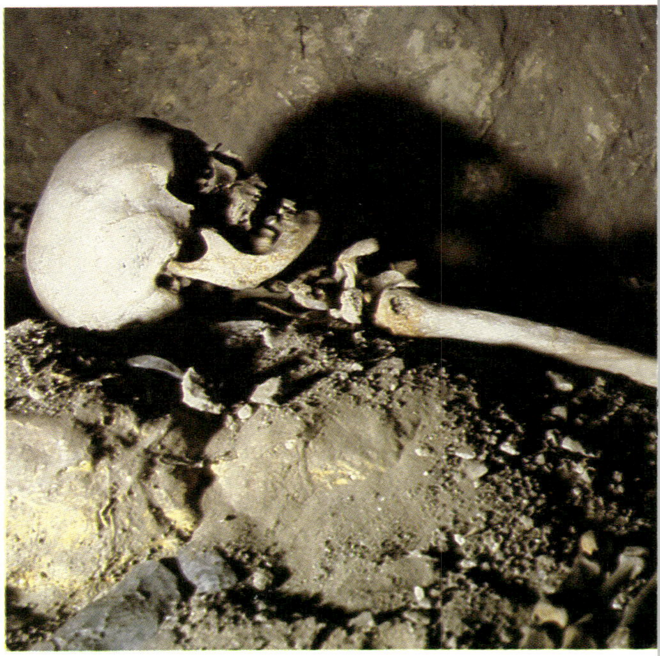

Eating of Ashes
Among the Indians of North America, several tribes practised the custom of eating the ashes of their dead relatives—in order to maintain close contact with the departed

Till Death Us Do Part
In the catacombs of Palermo, southern Italy stand row upon row of mummified Capuchin monks, many of them with expressions of wry amusement on their faces

Dragged to the Grave
The Baumana tribe in the French Sudan would abandon a dying man, wherever he was, for fear that he might drag one of them into the grave with him

Consumption of Brains
The oldest known example of ritualistic behaviour associated with death is from the Paleolithic Age. About 500,000 years ago, Peking Man practised ritual cannibalism, involving the drawing out of the dead person's brains and eating them

Far left
This method of disposing of their dead is practised by the Crow Indians, who live in the American state of Montana. They believe that burying a body in the ground makes it difficult for the spirit to reach the other world. Overhead burial and, thus, exposure to the elements, frees the spirit for its journey. One of the basic components of the Crow religious experience was the 'supernatural vision'. This could be induced by a series of rites, including fasting, and mutilating the flesh with skewers. Once a member of the tribe attained a 'vision', he was adopted by a supernatural guardian, who showed him certain magical powers

Left
This method of disposal is primitive in the extreme. The corpse is simply laid among the rocks and stones, which are considered holy. These Indonesian rock graves at Sulawesi are considered hallowed ground

Above
When an Egyptian Pharaoh died, he was embalmed and buried with elaborate ceremonies in a rock tomb underneath a pyramid. This one, the Great Pyramid at Gizeh, was built by Cheops and was one of the seven wonders of the ancient world.

Far left
The grave, with its fallen cross, symbolizes the sad state of this derelict English graveyard. The amount of land available for burials is inadequate, leading to a big increase in cremations

Left
The widow of the murdered black American civil rights leader, Dr. Martin Luther King, during the funeral service. Belief in an after-life is a logical result of man's capacity to feel affection and, hence, grief, when a loved one dies

Right
These elaborate Toraja burial caves in Indonesia have been carved out of solid rock. When the dead have been deposited there, together with one doll or figure representing each departed, the entrances are closed off. The custom of burying the dead in caves was widespread among Neolithic man all over the world

Consistent Mortality
In 1885, the population of England and Wales was 27,220,700. By 1970, this figure had risen to 48,680,100 – an increase of 78.8 percent. However, in the same period, the annual number of deaths rose by only 9.8 percent, from 522,750 in 1885 to 574,256 in 1970

Mass Graves
The wealthier early Christians held rights to plots of land which they shared with others of their faith and used for burial purposes. It was their custom to bury as many as ten people one above the other in a single grave, separated by stone slabs

Wrapping the Dead
A custom among the Moslems is to wrap their dead in a strip of matting to promote rapid decay, as they believe that everything which comes from the earth should return to it

Inseparable in Death
The mausoleum known as the Taj Mahal was built in 1643 by the Mughal emperor Shah Jahan in memory of his beloved wife, Mumtaz Mahal

Undertakers Unnecessary
When a Jew dies, the synagogue makes all the funeral arrangements, and an undertaker is not involved

Disposal of the Sick
At one time, among the tribes of the Northern Maidu, in the Pacific people lwho had been ill for a long time were tied up in a bearskin and buried alive

another life. All this applies with equal force to the ancestor cult of the Celebes Islanders, who display ritual effigies of their dead in niches on rock faces.

Rituals designed to relieve the distress of relatives and friends also have marked similarities. Cards and letters of condolence, so beloved of the Victorians, have precisely the same objective as the gifts of food brought to the house of a dead Laotian. Furthermore, although the period of mourning in Laos is passed in jollity, it is identical in purpose to the 'seemly' period of mourning prescribed in Christian countries, when black clothing or some other manifestation of respect must be worn and all entertainment eschewed.

Although funeral customs may differ quite dramatically from one culture to another, the underlying religious beliefs are often astonishingly similar—even when there could not have been any obvious contact between particular groups

Some further similarities deserve mention. In primitive societies, differences in funeral customs stem essentially from the dead person's class, sex, wealth and manner of death. Religious beliefs in these societies, on the other hand, are often remarkably similar. This is perhaps best illustrated by giving a few examples of man's explanation of what may be termed 'the origin of death', for, in a great number of societies, death is thought to be 'unnatural'. In the beginning, it is believed, man did not die, because he had the capacity, like the snake, to slough his skin and so renew himself. At a certain time, something went wrong and man was thereafter doomed to die. The only difference lies in the explanation of what it was that went wrong. Thus, in the Shortland Islands of Melanesia, it is believed that the original mother of the race did, indeed, slough her skin at regular intervals but was disturbed on one occasion by the crying of her child, from which moment man was doomed to eventual death. A similar belief is current in the Banks Islands in the Pacific. There, so the legend goes, when the mother returned to her child after sloughing her old skin the child did not recognize her. She therefore had to don her old skin again, and death came to the world. The legend that, in the beginning, there was no death recurs, with minor variations, throughout much of the world. It is found not only in the Pacific region, but also, for example,

among the Copper Eskimos of Victoria Island, north of the Arctic Circle. Their explanation for the advent of death in the world is in tune with the circumstances of their surroundings. One year, the legend goes, when the winter was more terrible than usual, a father and mother and their two sons ranged far and wide over the frozen land in search of food. Their efforts were in vain, and the family died, first the mother, then the sons and, finally, the father. They were changed into four hills and, thereafter, the Eskimos of Victoria Island knew death. There are many other examples, and it might not be thought too far-fetched to see parallels in Judaism and Christianity, which believe that the disaster (through the myth of the serpent, which sloughs its skin) occurred in the Garden of Eden.

There is a belief—universally shared by almost all religions, sects and creeds—in the efficacy of water to cleanse the body, purify the soul and wash away sin, thereby preparing a person for the approach of death

The human desire to be cleansed of sin as death approaches is not restricted to Christians. In much the same way as a dying Roman Catholic receives absolution from a priest, Hindus cleanse themselves of sin by bathing in the Ganges. Old people nearing the end of their days journey to Benares or to another holy city on the River Ganges—often covering considerable distances—and wash away their sins in its holy waters. They either sit on the banks or, with the help of relatives, stand erect in the water, so that they may die in its cleansing embrace. The use of water in some manner is almost universal. It is the custom of members of the Ashanti tribe in Ghana, for example, to put a few drops of water into a dying person's mouth, in order to refresh him as he climbs the hill leading to eternity. So vital is this rite, that elderly Ashantis always try to remain close to someone who could administer the water to them when they die.

Similarities also exist between methods of disposing of dead bodies. At the root of man's ceremonies in this connection lies the belief that, unless a corpse is disposed of ceremonially and with due respect, it will return as a ghost—usually a malicious one—to haunt the living. This belief is fortified by the fear that a returning ghost would almost certainly haunt the place where it used to live and would therefore be much more of a danger to relatives and friends than to others. It was thus not only their duty, but in their own interest, to conduct appropriate funeral rites. Failure to do so would have the same result as the death of any unhappy person—the dead person's ghost would walk. Incidentally, the belief in ghosts was once almost as common in the West as elsewhere.

Attitudes to the corpse itself also provide worldwide similarities. Human remains are believed by many societies to have the ability to ward off evil and protect a society from its enemies. Thus, a dead person's bones, or even his hair, are thought to give protection to their possessor. In much the same manner, Western man reveres the remains of his saints at the same time calling upon them for help and protection. The shock suffered by the living when they discover that someone close to them can no longer speak or move, see or hear, is universal and has conditioned the reactions of the living, engendering dread of the dead person's spirit (with a concomitant belief in the continued existence of the soul) and creating the necessity to hold mourning ceremonies. Human burial was seen at perhaps its most extravagant form under the Pharaohs of ancient Egypt. Few, if any religions, before or since, have placed so great an emphasis on burial rituals to ensure a favourable future. Morality played an essential role in the Egyptian religion, and truth, justice, humility, patience and wisdom were regarded as among the virtues. Funerary inscriptions often bear witness to a dead person's claim to these virtues. The chief part in the burial rites was taken by the priests. At first these were appointed by the Pharaoh, but later an independent, hereditary priesthood emerged. The role of women in the priesthood was restricted to dancing and providing music.

Egyptians were always buried, never cremated. Offerings were made to the corpse and acts of purification performed, together with the rite of touching the mouth with an adze, thereby, it was thought, renewing bodily faculties. The Egyptians were convinced that there was life after death, pointing to the fact that vegetation was renewed

Left
In parts of south-western Madagascar, skilfully carved wooden figures and other representations on timber posts take the place of the tombstones of the West. These carvings reflect some aspect of the deceased person's life or activities, and may depict anything from a football team to a farmer with his bullock, from a fisherman to a soldier. The posts, often scalloped, are also decorated, sometimes with the patterns picked out in red and white

Below left
Bundles of wood prepared for Hindu funeral pyres along the banks of the Ganges. The richer the man being cremated, the larger his funeral pyre will be. Old people nearing the end of their days often travel to Benares or another holy city on the River Ganges, so that they can properly cleanse themselves of sin in its holy waters before death

The Ultimate Achievement
Whereas Roman Catholics believe that life should consist of service to God and culminates in eternal happiness after one passes through death, the Buddhist religion believes that life is a continual search for Nirvana and extinction. Once Nirvana has been fully attained, one can go no further.

Extinct Civilization
Mayan temple of Chitchen Itza, with the sacred Jaguar in the foreground, a monument to a once-great civilization in central America

Solitary Mourners
When a Hindu husband dies, his wife becomes a social outcast, neither washing nor eating during the mourning period. Only when this has ended, and she has been washed and fed, can she resume any kind of social life

Determining Death
The tribes of Navitilevu, in Polynesia, often used to place a dying man in an open grave with supplies of food and water. When he was no longer able to eat or drink, they would close the grave

Right
Inlaid with blue and red enamel, this magnificent gold mask of the Pharaoh Tutenkhamen was found in his tomb in the Valley of the Kings. The mask, which covered the face of the mummified Pharaoh, is now in the State Museum in Cairo. Tutenkhamen's tomb was the only one in the area which had not been broken into and looted

Sight After Death
The practice of closing the eyes of a corpse originated in the belief that this would make the ghost unable to see and torment living people

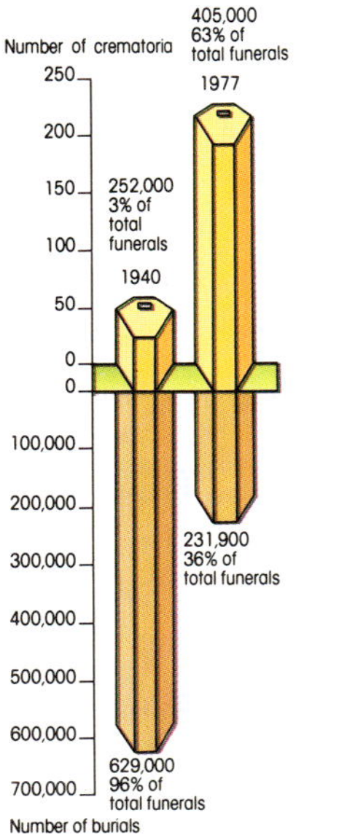

Burial on the Decrease
In the UK some 40 years ago, far more people were opting for burial than cremation. As fashions in funerals have changed there has been a dramatic swing towards cremation as the most popular form of disposal after death

Tomb Robbers
Looting tombs was a widely practised crime in ancient Egypt. After the collapse of the Old Kingdom at the end of the Sixth Dynasty, all the pyramids were looted. This behaviour continued into the Middle Kingdom. During the period of the New Kingdom, royal tombs were cut into the rock faces of the Valley of the Kings at Thebes and their entrances concealed in an effort to stop the looting. These measures succeeded in cutting down the tomb robberies to a great extent, but could not prevent them altogether

annually, and that, after setting, the sun always rose again. They believed that the soul would eventually return to inhabit the corpse once again, and that if the corpse should be found to have perished, the soul would perish also. They therefore put the greatest emphasis on preserving the corpse. The process they used, mummification, was elaborate, especially in the case of high-caste Egyptians. The brain and the intestines and, in the case of a male, frequently the sexual organs, were removed and preserved, usually in four jars. Natron (a native sesquicarbonate of soda) was applied to the body and also mixed with spices and oils, this mixture being poured into the holes left by the removal of the organs, which were then filled with wads of linen. After the application of aromatic oils, the entire body was bandaged with linen and laid in a coffin, which was then placed in a sealed tomb. As we shall see, embalming is again being practised in certain quarters today, but the high standard of preservation of Egyptian mummies, embalmed from about 2000 BC onwards, never ceases to arouse amazement. However, their impressive state of preservation is not, as is often supposed, the consequence of Egyptian embalming methods. Scientists now know that it is due to Egypt's climate and the absence of moisture in the sandy soil of the burial sites, as well as to the lack of bacteria in the sand and air.

While the ancient Egyptians went to fantastic lengths to preserve the body at death, the Greeks strongly preferred cremation, believing that fire alone had the power to release the soul

The ancient Greeks, on the other hand, generally favoured cremation, believing that the power of fire set the soul free. The mourners' hair was shorn

Far left
Tutenkhamen's sarcophagus in a corner of the burial chamber in his tomb, which was discovered less than 60 years ago – in 1922. When a Pharaoh died, he was embalmed and buried with elaborate ceremonies, in which male priests figured predominantly

Left
In ancient Egypt, the dead were always buried, never cremated. Before embalming was adopted, the body of a dead person was often placed in an earthen pot in the foetal position before burial

Far left below
Shown here is part of the gold frieze which forms one of the side panels of Tutenkhamen's sarcophagus. Ancient Egyptian burial rituals were designed to ensure a favourable future for the dead person's soul

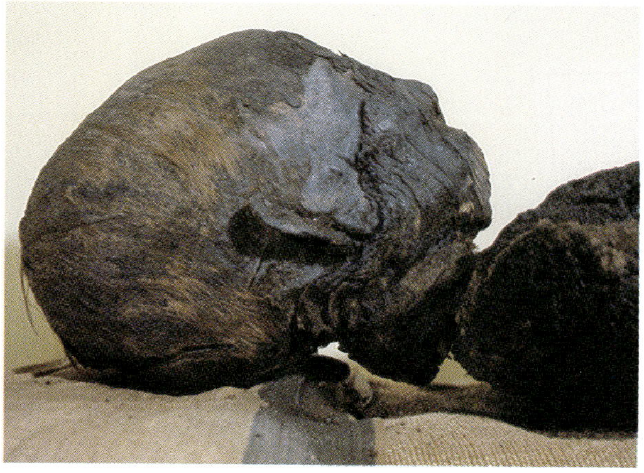

Left
When removed from their tombs, many mummies decay, as this one has. Up to that point they have been preserved by the Egyptian climate, the bacteria-free sand and air, and extreme desiccation of the sandy soil

and placed on the corpse, and the smouldering ashes quenched with wine. Great warriors were elaborately mourned with funeral games, races and athletic contests, but even a lowly man had the right to expect that his relatives and comrades would mourn him and cremate his body. It was thought that, if these rites were not carried out, the dead would find no rest in the other world and would remain for ever wretched. In the later period of classical Greece, both burial and cremation were practised. When Mycenae was excavated, it was found that the royal family of the city had been buried at death, together with many of their possessions, including weapons and regalia. The Greek ritual of disposal included washing the body and then clothing it in the garments worn in life. (Some philosophers were sceptical about these rites. When the time came for the sentence on Socrates to be implemented—to drink the poison hemlock—he took a bath to save the women the trouble of washing his corpse, and told his friends that they could do whatever they wished with his remains.) Some possessions of the dead person were usually thrown on to the pyre or buried with the body. Those who had attended the corpse ritually washed themselves, for contact with death was considered to be a defilement. Coffins, made of clay, stone or wood, were frequently placed in the tomb of the dead person's family; ashes were collected in an urn and deposited in the same way. Often, the tombs of the eminent became shrines.

In the Greek view, the proper disposal of a corpse was an inescapable concomitant of piety. Thus, after a battle the defeated survivors would ask the victors for permission to bury their dead (or at least scatter a few handfuls of earth on their bodies), and this request was seldom refused. To the Greeks, an unburied body was not only a source of human misery in the next world but an abomination to the gods. For this reason, criminals, especially traitors, were sometimes sentenced to be left unburied after execution. Even when the body had been properly disposed of, however, life in the next world was an unhappy affair, the Greeks thought, except for the few whose great merits in this life might be rewarded by transference to the Islands of the Blest. The Greek attitude to suicide was ambivalent. Ancient opinion never condoned it, although some Greeks thought that it could on occasion be the only honourable course. Some philosophic schools forbade it while others permitted it.

By the time of the early Christians, disposal was becoming a complicated choice between lavish cremation and simple burial—within 2000 years burial had become wildly extravagant, grandiose and wasteful

In Rome, the attitude towards the possibility of life after death was even more complicated than in other societies because as the empire expanded in the course of several centuries, it absorbed and modified the concepts of those whom it had overcome. Most notably, it absorbed the Etruscan and Greek apprehension of the possibility of punishment beyond the grave for wrongs committed in this life. Epitaphs testify to this although the commonest attitude seems to be a sense of impotence, showing neither hope nor fear. A recurring text reads: *Non fui fui non sum non curo*—'I was not. I was. I am not. I do not care.' The general assumption was, however, that another world did exist and that it might be pleasant or unpleasant to a greater or lesser degree. Certainly the Romans believed in ghosts, as the writings of Cicero and Pliny testify.

Reigning in Repose
Seated Buddha watching over a cemetery in a forest at Ryoanji, in Japan

Wages for Grief
Paid wailers and mourners have been used variously by the aborigines, the Christians, Romans, ancient Greeks, Welsh, Irish, Corsicans and Jews of Eastern Europe

A Coin for the Ferryman
An ancient Greek funeral custom was to place a coin in the mouth of the corpse. This was to enable the departing soul to pay the ferryman, Charon, to take it across the River Styx

Eternal Service
In Africa, it was an ancient tradition to put to death the wives and slaves of a king or chieftain when he died, so that their souls could continue to serve their master in the after-life

Right
When a Brahman priest dies on the Indonesian island of Bali, his purified body is placed inside a white-painted wooden effigy of a bull and cremated. Here, the bull is being carried to the cremation site

Below
The dead Brahman priest's body has been placed in the hollowed-out bull and a torch put to the funeral pyre. Soon, all that will remain will be a heap of glowing ashes

Immortal Union
Until the British banned the custom, Hindu wives used to throw themselves on the burning biers of their husbands and thus hope to remain at their sides throughout eternity

Death of a Chief
In the early 1800s, when a chief of the New Zealand Maoris died, his slaves were killed immediately and his wives were expected to commit suicide. Although it was not compulsory, the majority of wives did so

Holding Down the Spirit
The Melanesian and Polynesian inhabitants of Savage Island would throw heavy stones on to a grave to keep the spirit of the dead from rising

Face of Death
The death mask of Agamemnon, the legendary king of the Myceneans, who was brutally murdered by his wife's lover

Protected Funeral
Not until 1884 was cremation legalized, and even then, public opinion in Britain was so strongly against it that police protection was often necessary when a cremation was to take place

Varying Costs
In the UK, the average crematorium fee in April, 1978 was £23.42, ranging from £2 in the Channel Islands to £55 in Aberdeen

Increased Exhumation
In 1974, 241 exhumation certificates were granted in Britain. By 1977, this figure had risen to 292, an increase of just over 21 percent

As in so many societies, the main object of veneration in Rome for much of its history was the sun. For centuries, the sun had been the chief god of the Egyptians, while to the Greeks, Baalbek in Syria was Heliopolis, the City of the Sun. There are further examples in Persia and elsewhere. As the Roman Empire moved eastwards, it naturally absorbed many of these concepts and, in AD 274, Aurelian proclaimed the Sun-God to be the empire's pre-eminent deity. It has been argued that, if Christianity had not superseded other religions in Europe, sun-worship might well have been the norm for many centuries. However, the impact of Christianity, with its concept of love and message of hope was to prove irresistible. Until their conversion to Christianity, however, when burial became mandatory the Romans believed cremation to be the most honourable form of funeral. Burial was reserved for suicides and murderers, while in the case of a parricide, a particularly execrated criminal, a cock was sewn into the sack in which the body was buried as a sign of unpiousness.

Civilizations rise and fall, their structures change and, as with Rome under the impact of Christianity, their funeral customs change also. This may be brought about by other factors, however, including changes in the political situation. Perhaps the most notable example of this is Russia. Before the Revolution of 1917, the practice of holding elaborate funerals was so general that many poor families ruined themselves in their attempt to provide a suitably grandiose ceremony for the disposal of their dead. The rites would last an entire day (in the case of royalty often much longer) and would begin with a procession of great splendour. The leader, carrying a large cross, was followed by mourners bearing flaming candles, banners and icons. The number of people in the procession indicated the wealth of the family in question. The hearse, which was as elaborate as the family could afford, was drawn by six grey or black horses of identical size, each held at the bit by a groom. To add even greater splendour to the procession, a band of professional mourners would be hired. Dressed in cocked hats and black coats, they served as an advance party. All this changed completely soon after the advent of the Bolshevik regime. The Greek Orthodox ceremony virtually disappeared under pressure from the central government. Services, if they were held at all, became extremely simple. The state was now all-important, the individual of no importance.

Left
The elegant splendour of Frederick Chopin's shrine in Paris is in sharp contrast with the simpler and perhaps more sincere acceptance of death as expressed in the funeral rituals and processions of the East

Bottom
Behind the scenes at a modern crematorium, which is equipped with dual incinerators. The control panels enable the correct temperature setting to be obtained, and the viewing window allows the operator to see that matters are proceeding as they should

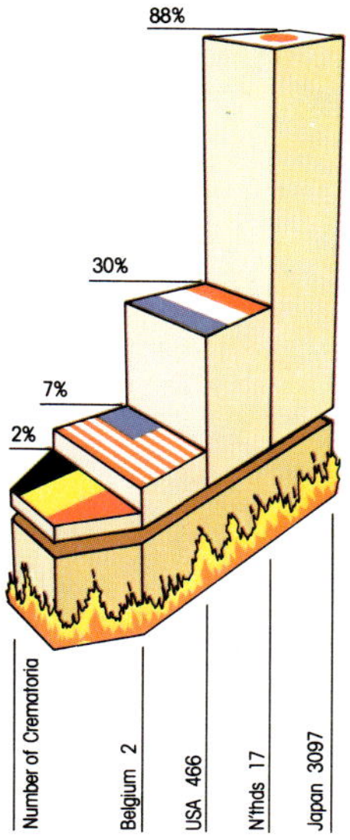

Cremation League Table in Four Countries
The figures on this chart represent the percentage of funerals carried out as cremations in each of the countries shown

Certificate for Ashes
Although the ashes of a person are not regarded by the law as a dead body, an exhumation certificate is still needed to retrieve them

A Rise in Popularity
In 1940 there were 56 crematoria in Britain. By 1977, this number had risen to 218

Thirst for Rebirth
In Oleai, one of the Caroline Islands in the Pacific, it was the custom to drink the water in which the corpses of children had been washed. This was thought to be a means of ensuring that the child would be born again

Digging up the Past
Reasons for Exhumation
Important documents buried with corpse.
Graveyard no longer used for burials (built over, etc.).
Identification of the body.
Suspicion of foul play.
Wrong grave – incorrectly buried.
Relatives leaving country and wishing to take body with them

From the decline of the Romans to the end of the 1800s cremation was generally outlawed. The breakthrough came when the Roman Church changed its attitude towards cremation, and today more people are opting for this form of disposal

Until recent years, Christian teaching held that burial was the proper form of disposal, following the example of the entombment of Christ. However, the manner of burial has varied over the centuries. For example, it was common practice at one time for the dead, especially if they were related, to be buried one above another, separated by horizontal stone slabs. It was no doubt for this reason that the grave-digger in Hamlet unearthed the skull of Yorick, for he was digging a grave on the site of an earlier one. Later, the system of individual graves was introduced, although relatives might still be buried in close proximity to one another. This, together with the increasing shortage of space for grave yards in modern, heavily industrialized societies, has brought further change in its train. Nowadays after an imprecise but seemly period of time, when all the relatives of the deceased have died too, it frequently happens that all their gravestones are discreetly removed and placed side by side at the edge of the graveyard. This compromise provides further burial space without hurting anybody's feelings. The growing shortage of conveniently sited burial space in cities has been accompanied by a dramatic rise in

the world's population. Even though advances in medical science and new concepts of hygiene have kept the percentage increase in deaths far below the increase in population, the amount of land available for burial has not kept pace with the demand, leading in recent years to an enormous increase in the number of Christians asking to be cremated.

Only in this century have Christians decided that the method of disposal of their remains is irrelevant to the hereafter. Roman Catholics resisted this trend the longest, but on July 5, 1963, the then Pope, John XXIII, finally approved cremation as a means of disposal acceptable to his faith. Many Catholics, although fewer than members of the other Christian denominations, now choose this form of disposal.

There has been a dramatic increase in the number of cremations in non-Catholic European countries. Between 1950 and 1970 the number of

Right
The jade-encased body of a Chinese princess of the Han dynasty. It dates from about 150 BC, or perhaps even earlier. The Chinese have always prized jade above all other stones, believing in ancient times that it conferred powers from heaven. They also looked upon jade as the symbol of virtue and held it to be of value for medicinal purposes, as did the people of Mexico in the sixteenth century

Bottom right
Sleeping the long sleep of death, Rameses II, founder of the XIXth dynasty, lies in his sarcophagus, his features preserved by the skill of his embalmers. He ascended the throne at an early age and ruled Egypt for 67 years. During his long reign, Rameses II, a man of very great courage, waged a series of wars – against the Hittites, the Nubians, the Libyans and the Syrians

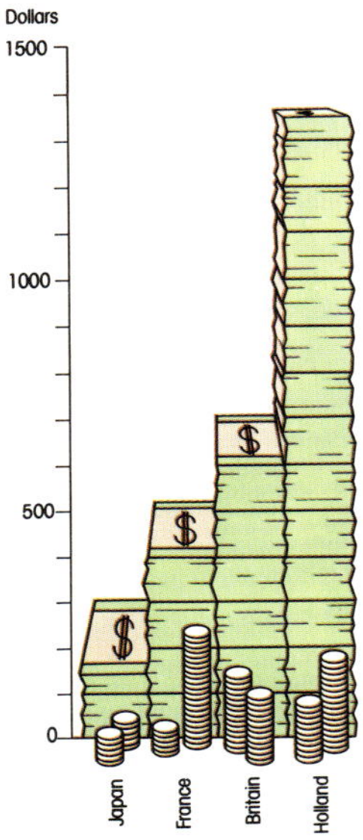

The Varying Costs of Death in Four Countries
Of the countries chosen for inclusion in this chart for the cost of a funeral, interestingly Holland comes out at the top and Japan, where more cremations are carried out than anywhere else, has the lowest funeral costs

A Watery Grave
In some cases, the Maoris disposed of corpses by throwing them into a swamp and trampling them under. In others, they were buried in sandhills. In some areas, corpses were weighted and dropped into a lagoon

Embalming for Everybody
In the United States, virtually every dead body ends up in the embalming room. In Britain, about a third of all corpses are embalmed

cremations in Czechoslovakia rose from 11.6 percent of all recorded deaths to 39 percent, in Denmark from 19.5 percent to 41 percent, in Switzerland from 19 percent to 33.6 percent, and in Britain from less than 16 percent to 57 percent. In Roman Catholic countries, notably Italy, the trend towards cremation is less evident, despite the Pope's edict validating cremation as a form of disposal. In Italy, the problem of burial space is being met in part by burying coffins in an upright position.

Another ancient means of disposal still in use today, although comparatively rarely, is burial at sea. Sailors still sometimes direct that their bodies or ashes should be disposed of in this way, and it is also necessary when a death occurs at sea. The practice can be traced back many centuries, and it is known to have been the choice of the ancient Norsemen. The corpse was placed on board a ship containing combustible material like tar or bitumen, and was then taken out to sea and set on fire. Even today, Hindu funeral rites include the scattering of ashes in the Ganges. Immediately after cremation, the ashes are buried near the river for ten days. They are then dug up and retained for several days before being cast into the river.

The ancient Egyptians embalmed the body to preserve the soul. Modern embalming preserves the body to safeguard its 'final' appearance for the benefit of the relatives

As we have seen, modern man continues to employ methods similar to those of ancient societies for disposing of his dead. Sometimes, he echoes the practice of the ancient Egyptians and embalms the dead, to preserve them. There have also been cases of accidental preservation, as in the case of bodies found in peat bogs. The first such corpses found in the 18th century, were not subjected to scientific investigation. Then in 1950, a body was found at a depth of seven feet at Tollund in central Jutland. The date of death was estimated by a Professor Glob at about 50 BC. The peat had turned the corpse's skin brown. The body was curled up with a leather belt round its waist, a leather cap on its head, and a rope of the same material round its neck. More bodies were found later. Some had halters around their necks, while others bore wounds, suggesting that they had either been executed or been offered up as human sacrifices. Bodies have also been found in bogs in Ireland and Scotland, some dating from as late as the 14th century. The reason these bodies were preserved is much the same as in Egypt – the absence of bacterial growth. However, while it was the dry climate and absence of moisture in the sandy soil which inhibited bacterial growth in Egypt, in Jutland and elsewhere it was cold and the acidity, the main characteristics of peat bogs.

The deliberate preservation of corpses is becoming more prevalent today. Embalming is the technique most commonly used, and it can be effective for up to a year or so. It is claimed that embalming, which makes a dead body look less corpse-like and more as it did in life, is a comfort to relatives and friends who wish to view it. The process performed by one person working alone, takes about one and a quarter hours on average. Basically, it consists of pumping preserving fluid into a main artery, thereby

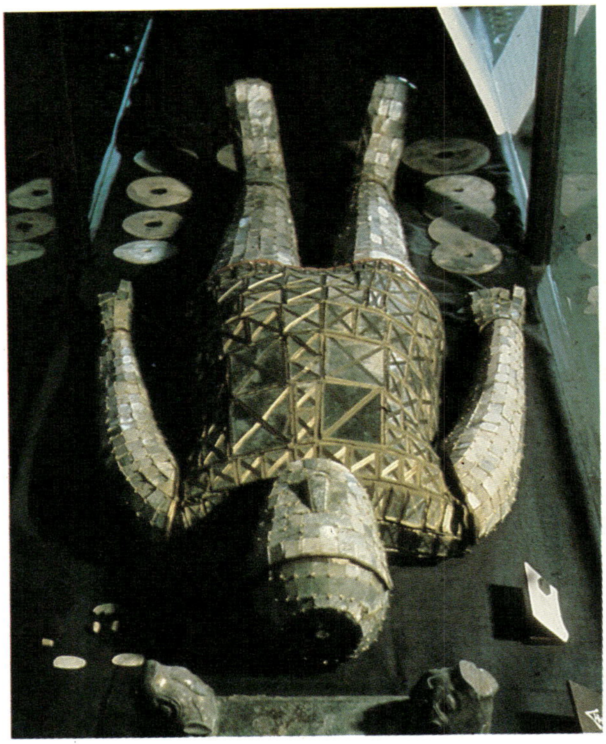

forcing the blood out of the body through a vein drainage tube connected to the heart. The preserving fluid most commonly used is made up of 60 percent formalin and 40 percent water, methyl alcohol (to modify the harsh action of the formalin on the body tissues), glycerin (to help the fluid penetrate into the tissues) several minor additives, such as magnesium sulphate to break up clots, and colouring agents in various shades of red. Whether or not the preserving fluid is diluted depends on the state of the body. If it has a low water content because of a dehydrating disease, a dilute preserving solution will be used, because otherwise it would cause wrinkles to form. Dilution does not affect the solution's preserving qualities. On the other hand, a more concentrated solution is required to overcome bacteria if the body has started to putrefy, although nothing can be done to improve the appearance of the corpse. In such cases, embalming is carried out solely in the interests of hygiene. Normally, cosmetics are applied to the face, neck, hands and other exposed parts of the corpse, care being taken to match the deceased's complexion in life. When embalming, which is widely practised in the United States, is performed by an expert, the contradictory result is a lifelike corpse.

This is not the only contradiction in present-day funeral rites. We have seen how certain societies opted for burial and condemned cremation, while

Left
Until recently at least, gypsies always cremated their dead. At a secret ceremony watched only by members of the clan the dead gypsy belonged to, his body, his possessions and his caravan were burnt to ashes. It may well be that this long-standing practice has died out in Western Europe but in the more remote parts of the continent as well as the United States, it is thought that secret gypsy cremations still take place

Far left
Part of a wall painting in the tomb of Seti I, a king of the XIXth dynasty. The funerary boat was used to carry the mummified body across the River Nile to the tomb on the west bank. At the door of the tomb, the last ceremonies were conducted by priests. These included the acting out of a drama telling the story of Osiris, the god with which every Egyptian king was closely identified from very early times

Above
The embalmed body of Chairman Mao Tse Tung reposes inside a specially constructed glass case. Some unusual chemical compounds were used in the embalming process, and the Chinese claim this will enable the body to remain in a high state of preservation for a thousand years

others did the reverse; how suicide was outlawed by some Greek philosophers, and advocated in certain circumstances by others. It is a curious contradiction that there exists in the Western world today, side by side with a general, reasoned acceptance of death as an inevitable part of life, two diametrically opposed views as to how death should be faced.

Early man believed that death occurred through the intervention of a 'divine' force. Modern man may soon be able to 'plan' the moment of his own dying —or even to delay it indefinitely

On the one hand, there is a growing movement of opinion in support of voluntary euthanasia, especially in cases of terminal illness. Why prolong suffering, so the argument goes, when the patient could be given a quick and painless release? The advocates of euthanasia readily concede that safeguards would be essential—the certificate authorizing the termination of a person's life would have to be signed by more than one doctor, and the person in question would have to have signed a document asking for euthanasia in certain circumstances while still well and of sound mind. There are signs that, in some countries euthanasia may be legalized in the reasonably near future.

At the other extreme there are those, particularly in the United States, who advocate scientific research into ways, not merely of preserving life, but of actually restoring it. In the hope that man will one day find a cure for all human illnesses, the body is frozen at death with a view to its being thawed out at some appropriate time in the future. It is thought that nearly 1,000 people in the United States have already asked for this treatment when they die, despite the prohibitive cost. One of the first was a Dr Bedford. Immediately after death, he was given an injection of hesparin, together with artificial respiration and cardiac massage. The massage and artificial respiration were continued until the corpse had been wrapped in aluminized plastic and its temperature reduced with dry ice. The corpse was then coated with a preserving solution and placed in a special capsule, which was immersed in liquid nitrogen and brought down to a temperature of −320°F. The capsule was then stored to await eventual thawing.

Whether a cure will ever be found for the disease from which Dr Bedford was suffering, whether he can be resuscitated, and, if so, whether the procedure would add to or detract from the sum of human happiness, must be left to speculation. What it demonstrates, however, is that, even in the last quarter of the 20th century, man is still seeking ways of facing—and overcoming—the awesomeness of mortal death.

A Last Wish Mislaid
Franklin D. Roosevelt hated the idea of being embalmed, and left explicit instructions forbidding it. Unfortunately, they were mislaid and were not found until a few days after he had been embalmed, placed in a sealed coffin and buried

Keeping Heroes Intact
Alexander the Great, after his death, was preserved in honey and wax. Nelson's body was sent home from Trafalgar in a barrel of brandy. Charlemagne was embalmed, dressed in robes and placed in a sitting position inside his royal tomb

In Search of the Soul

What does it mean to talk about 'the soul'? Is it right to believe in any such thing as a soul? These and similar questions have haunted man since time immemorial

Above
Hell was vividly real for Dante Alighieri, as he demonstrated in his 14th-century Divine Commedia. Part of it – the Inferno of Hell – was illustrated by Gustave Doré 550 years later. This is one of his illustrations, a sinner being devoured by a snake

Right
It seems unfair that Thomas, alone of all the disciples of Jesus, should have been singled out for the epithet 'Doubting', since all his fellow disciples refused to believe at first that Jesus had risen from the dead and escaped from the tomb 'hewn out of a rock' where his body had been placed after the Crucifixion. This fresco in the Church of St Mary of Zion, in Ethiopia, shows the body of Jesus being wrapped in a shroud and placed in a coffin

No kind of life with which we are familiar goes on for ever. In this respect a human life is no different from the life of any living thing. What is special about human beings is that they are able to recognize these facts. Only human beings have languages rich enough to express the thought that they will, at some time, die. Only human beings, therefore, are able to reflect on their lives as a whole or have fears about death when their lives are in no immediate danger. Whatever idea we have of the 'soul', it is intimately connected with such fears and reflections.

It is because of language that humans are able to plan ahead in the way they do. But for language, man would not have the knowledge which has made his mastery of his environment so much greater than that of any other animal. Yet an ability to plan for the future is associated with a tendency to worry about it. Concern about the fact that we will, sooner or later, die, is thus as natural to human beings as the fact itself. That we cannot avoid this concern entirely makes it seem to some like a curse. Their view is that we cannot help having certain fears and aspirations, even though they are a burden to us. Man, wrote Jean Paul Sartre, is a 'useless passion'.

Others take quite a different view and see in the human tendency to fear death evidence of a 'divine spark'. For these people, this fear is not an emotion to be suppressed the moment it makes itself apparent, but rather it is something to be overcome. They see it as a kind of blessing in the sense that it directs a person's attention away from the transient pleasures of life to a search for peace of mind. Fear, for a person with these ideas, can be the beginning of wisdom.

Such a positive reaction to the prospect of death is characteristic of a religious point of view. It is not, however, peculiar to religion. Nor is a religious view of the 'soul' necessarily one which represents it as some kind of entity which goes on existing after death. Here, for example, is a passage from the Old

Six Parts of Man
The ancient Egyptians believed that man was made of six elements; his name, his body and his shadow, and the three spirits Ka, Ba, and Akh

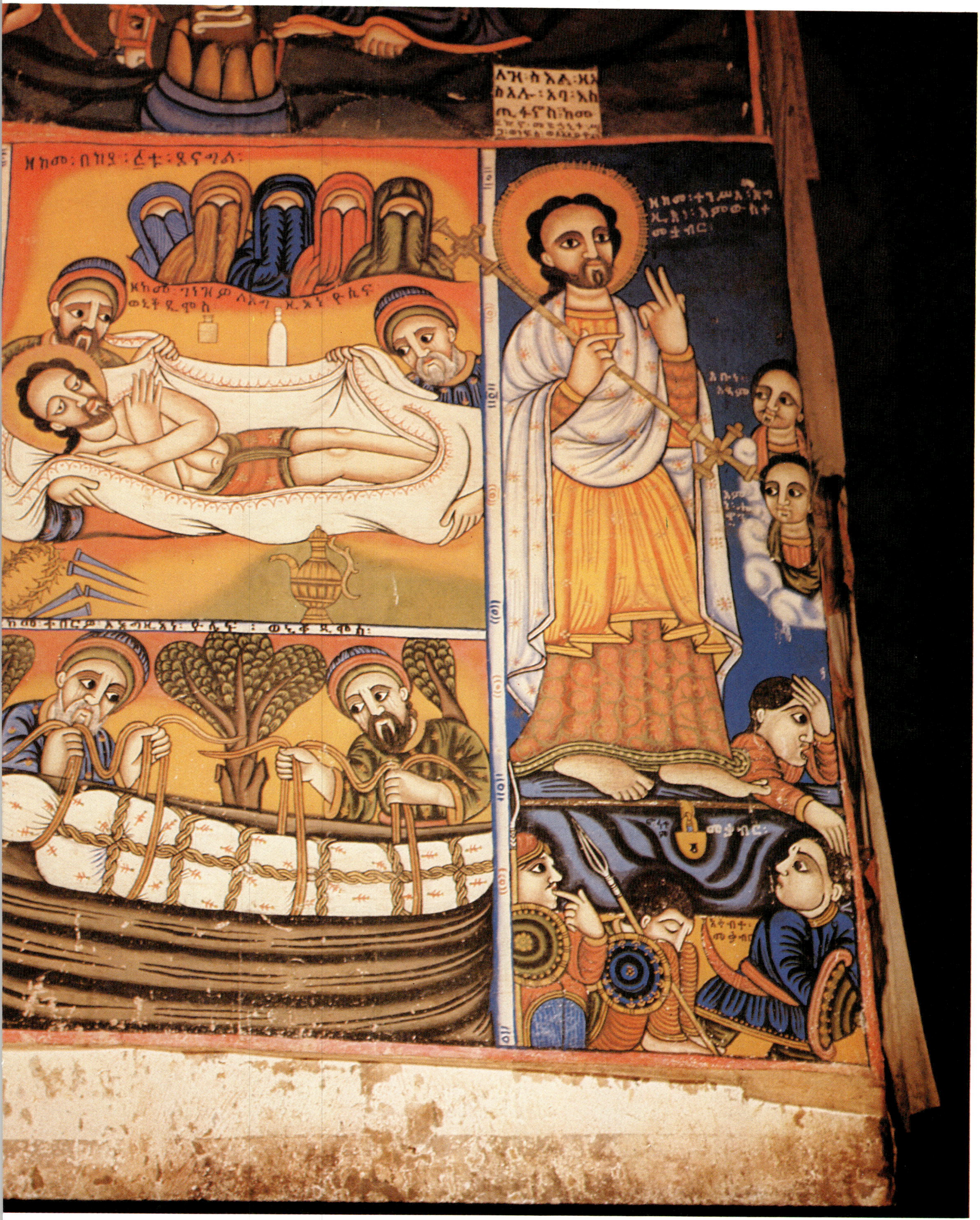

Right
Narcissus, detail from a painting by Moreau le Jeune. Narcissus, according to a Greek myth, pined to death after falling in love with his own reflection

Lower right
The Crossing of the Styx, detail from a painting by the 16th century artist, Joachim Patinir. It expresses the belief that the dead have a difficult journey ahead

TRANSLATION
Vision of Paradise
An experience of sublime ecstasy which apparently occurs either at the moment before death or during periods of meditation

NIRVANA
A Blissful Void
Theological term used by Buddhists, Hindus and Jainists to refer to an indescribable state of ecstasy achieved by enlightened beings upon their death

SATORI
The Gate of Perception
The 'enlightened experience' of Zen Buddhism – it is the goal of the Zen monk and may occur in a flash or in the fullness of Nirvana. It is considered as a state of absolute peace and harmony

DUALISM
The Divided Soul
In the Christian religion, the idea that mind and matter are distinct and equally real, and that with Christ Incarnate, there were two people and not just two natures

ESCHATOLOGY
Search for a Final Answer
The area of theology dealing with 'last things', such as the end of the world scenario, or of mankind, together with the second coming of Christ and other Messianic traditions

AURA
The Force of Life
A radiance which supposedly emanates from living organisms and which clairvoyants claim they can see as bands of colour

ECTOPLASM
A Matter of Communication
Substance out of which materialized forms are built by spiritualists

TELEKINESIS
Mind Over Matter
The apparent movement of objects without normal material connections to the cause

TELEPATHY
Minds in Communion
Transference of thoughts and ideas from one mind to another at a distance without the normal use of the senses. The great majority of scientists remain extremely sceptical about the validity of the claims made on behalf of these various parapsychological phenomena

Testament which emphasizes the transitory nature of the soul:

'Man that is born of woman is of few
days and full of trouble.
He comes forth like a flower, and withers;
he flees like a shadow, and continues not . . .
As waters fail from a lake,
and a river wastes away and dries up,
So man lies down and rises not again;
till the heavens are no more he will not awake,
or be roused out of his sleep.'
(Book of Job, Ch. 14, Verses 1-2, 10-12)

To think of a human death as resembling the death of a plant is to think only of its external meaning. It is an observed fact that all living organisms are subject to decay and death. In likening man to a flower, however, the author of the Book of Job is not merely comparing him with a piece of vegetation. A flower is something beautiful, even precious, perhaps, yet at the same time ephemeral. We confer an inner meaning on the death of a flower by seeing in it a symbol of our own deaths. Such symbolism is common in poetry and in painting. In Millais' painting, *Autumn Leaves,* the dead leaves which the bewildered girls are gathering symbolize grief.

The human sense of the inner meaning of death shows itself in the almost universal practice of rites marking respect for the dead

The author of the Book of Job is even more obviously referring to the inner meaning of death when he writes that 'man flees like a shadow, and continues not'. Shadows, reflections and even echoes are such powerful symbols of the inner meaning of death that it used to be widely believed that a man's soul was identified with his shadow or his reflection. Sir James G. Frazer, in his classic work, *The Golden Bough,* noted that, in many societies, the fear of death was expressed by the extreme care people took that no one should step on their shadows and that they should not see their own reflection. He suggested that the true meaning of the myth of Narcissus, who died on seeing his reflection, might have been that the ancient Greeks identified a person's soul with his reflection.

These symbols have not altogether lost their power for us. Our conception of a ghost, for instance, is of an inverted shadow, that is to say, something white which fades at daybreak, as opposed to something black which fades with the loss of light. Painters who make extensive use of symbolism, like the Surrealists, often use shadows to symbolize the proximity of death. A production of *Hamlet* can be expected to give the voice of the ghost of Hamlet's father the far-away quality of an echo. The power that such symbols have for us is not diminished by trying to explain away claims to have seen a ghost by saying that the place is frequented by barn owls, and it is one of these that was mistaken for a ghost. But for the symbolism, no one could ever mistake a barn owl for a ghost. We can understand the symbolism and therefore the point of believing in ghosts even if we are too guarded in our opinions to describe anything we see as a ghost.

It is commonly taken for granted that all religious practice must be founded on some belief about the results of engaging in it. No reasonable person, it is

assumed, would engage in a religious practice without holding certain opinions. It is not difficult to think of examples which seem to fit in with this assumption. The ancient Greeks, for instance, believed that the dead had to cross the River Styx by a ferry, and that the ferryman (Charon) would only take them across if they could pay the fare. If not, they would be condemned to wander along the river bank forever, without finding rest. Accordingly, it was the custom in ancient Greece to bury the dead with coins in their mouths.

To assume that all religious practices are founded on opinions of this sort is seriously to misunderstand the place of religious ritual, since certain attitudes and practices are independent of any such opinions. A man can believe in showing respect for the dead without holding any opinion about the possible effect on them of the way they are treated. It is a remarkable fact that human beings rarely view the disposal of the dead with indifference. Those who do are regarded as extremely callous, or even sub-human. It is easier to understand those societies which treat the bodies of their slain enemies with the utmost contempt. For to subject a dead person to ritual expressions of contempt is still to acknowledge his humanity, if only in a backhanded way. On the other hand, those who dispose of the dead without

Left
Death and its inevitability; the brevity of life; the dying year; the idea that, in the midst of life, we are in death; the contrast between vibrant youth and sere old age; the thought that life goes on, despite death; the realization that death is a part of life – all this is symbolized in Autumn Leaves, by the Victorian painter, Sir John Everett Millais, which was painted near Perth, in Scotland. John Ruskin said that it was 'the first instance of a perfect twilight'. Sir John Millais was the initiator, along with W. Holman Hunt, of the pre-Raphaelite movement in 1848

any such acknowledgement, as they might dispose of rubbish, make themselves monsters in our eyes. Moreover, rituals expressing contempt for the dead appear to derive from those showing respect, much as the Black Mass derives from the Christian rite. Mockery gains its point by being directed where others think respect is due.

Rituals involved in disposing of the dead vary from one culture to another. In ancient Greece, for example, burial was for a long time regarded as essential. Indeed, Sophocles' play, *Antigone,* hinges on the dilemma with which the heroine is faced by her uncle's edict that her brother's slain body must be left unburied. In other societies burial is a form of disgrace. But, for all the sharp differences there are as to how respect for the dead should be marked, some ceremony or other is almost universal. Such practices reflect a sense of what has here been called the 'inner' aspect of death. It reflects, in other words, the fact that our attitude to the death of

METEMPSYCHOSIS
Roving Spirits
Metempsychosis means literally the passing of the soul, after death, into another body. Historically, the concept has been derived from certain of the great religions and is more concerned with the upward journey of the soul, possibly through countless numbers of lives, towards its ultimate purification

PALINGENESIS
Past Lives
This is the theological term for reincarnation, a belief in the rebirth of the soul through several possible existences, which may be human, animal or even vegetable. The word 'palingenesis' means: 'Origin again'

TRANSMIGRATION
Eternal Journey
The third of the terms used to describe the condition of the soul after death. In transmigration the soul, having already passed through innumerable lives, will continue its own path towards absolute perfection in yet another material body

LIMBO
Suspended between States
Part of Roman Catholic theological tradition, limbo was supposed to be the dwelling-place of souls who are not given the privilege to enjoy the full vision of God in Heaven, although they do not suffer any torment or other punishment

TRANSUBSTANTIATION
The Divine Union
A change of substance. This refers to the Christian doctrine of the eucharist – that, after consecration, the body and blood of Christ and the bread and wine exist together in union

OBIT
Devotion for the Dead
A mass for a dead person celebrated on the anniversary of the death

PLACEBO
Holy Requests
A name given by the Christian church to the practice of holding evening prayers for the dead

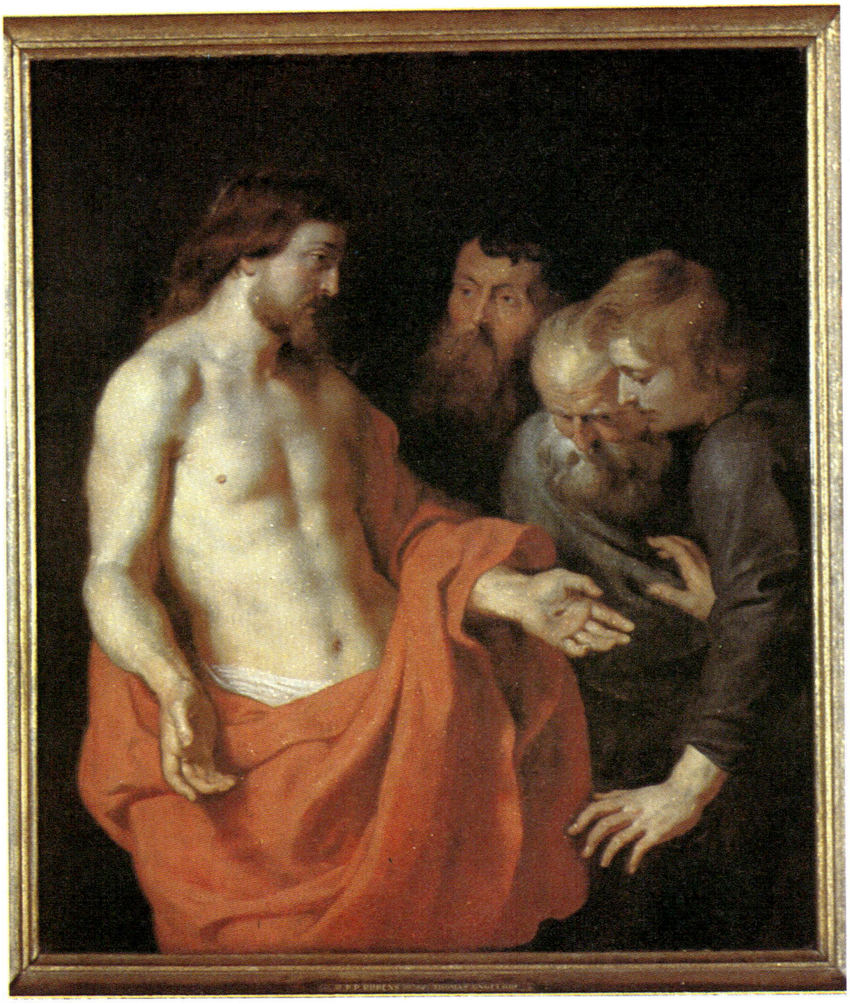

Above
The Incredulity of St Thomas, a triptych by Sir Peter Paul Rubens (1577-1640). As the title of the painting implies St Thomas – 'Doubting Thomas' – was not incapable of believing in the Resurrection, but refused to do so without proof. He would better be called 'Faithless Thomas'. Indeed, Jesus says to him '... and be not faithless but believing... Because thou hast seen me, thou hast believed; blessed are they that have not seen and yet have believed'

Above right
This fourteenth-century Italian painting, The Last Judgement, depicts the myth of the three-tier Universe, with heaven above, hell below, and earth in the centre. The resurrected righteous, the elite, are ranged in orderly rows, their haloes gleaming, waiting patiently for their imminent translation to heaven, that paradise where they will join the Father, the Son and the Virgin Mary, with their attendant host of angels, the seraphim and the cherubim, together with all the lower angelic orders. It is a paradise of eternal bliss, where the sight of God is sufficient reason for perfect contentment. Down below in hell, meanwhile, Satan eats a sinner alive, while other devils torment the damned – in perpetuity

another person, even of a complete stranger, cannot be separated from our attitude to ourselves and to our own deaths. To deny someone a ceremony appropriate to the fact of his being dead would be to deny the humanity we have in common with him. A denial of the 'soul' of another person is at the same time a denial of our own. That is why we regard it as monstrous to dispose of a human corpse as if it were so much rubbish, or surplus cargo being jettisoned to lighten a ship.

We are taught from our earliest youth to be discriminating about what we believe. If someone 'can believe anything', his education has been a failure by our standards. Such is the influence of science on our culture, that honest doubt – if not outright scepticism – is socially valued. We would think it a waste of time to listen to the opinions of anyone not inclined to scepticism. That is why we find it difficult to believe in myths. Myths flourish only where there are no sceptics. In the face of sustained scepticism some myths wither and die, while others become transformed into theology or metaphysics and are passed on in that way. Sceptics do appear in myths, but as villains rather than heroes. Significantly, it is in St John's Gospel – the latest and most theological of the four Gospels – that the story of so-called 'doubting Thomas' occurs. He is presented, not as someone *unable* to believe that Jesus had risen from the dead – an idea quite foreign to the Bible – but as someone who *refused* to believe. The point of the story is plain enough: 'Blessed are those who have not seen and yet believe'. It would thus be more accurate to call Thomas 'faithless Thomas'. Some versions of St Mark's Gospel conclude with a similar story about the refusal of the remaining Disciples to believe those who claimed to have seen Jesus 'alive'.

Myths about the dead can enrich our understanding of the soul, even though we sometimes find it hard to believe them

The idea that belief is a virtue reflects the way certain communities regard adherence to certain myths. Adherence to a common set of beliefs may be necessary for a community to preserve its identity or may be socially desirable in some other way. This accounts for the prevalence of certain kinds of myth about the after-life.

There are, for instance, many myths in which the after-life is portrayed as a paradise peopled by a perfectly harmonious and happy, though highly select group of beings. The elite character of this society is confirmed symbolically by the presence of a guard or guards whose function it is to restrict entry to souls of a particular earthly group. These souls rarely qualify for automatic entry. During the Crusades, for example, assurances of a place in Heaven were given to Christian knights who died in battle. But heavenly societies are usually doubly selective, being restricted to souls from a particular earthly group who also have shown the right moral qualities. No doubt it was held to be sufficient proof of the faith of a Christian knight that he was prepared to die for his religion. There has always been some tendency in Christianity for the moral qualities to be seen as paramount. There are indeed Christians who have denied that membership of any earthly group, as symbolized by baptism for

example, is necessary to gain entry to Heaven. But select society myths commonly do require membership of an earthly community.

Such myths may reflect in large measure the social order which gave them birth. A constantly repeated theme in the text found on the wall inside the Pyramids is the opening of the double doors of the horizon to admit a dead Pharaoh to the company of the gods. The fact that their retinues and their valuables were buried with them, indicates the Egyptian belief that the Pharaohs would continue to enjoy in the after-life the privileges to which they had been born and which they had enjoyed on earth. Such myths may reasonably be thought to reflect a belief in the continuity of the prevailing social order. However, there is usually more to such myths than that. Even though the double doors of the horizon are unlocked automatically to admit a dead Pharaoh and his retinue, it is significant that they are locked at all. The idea that entrance to heaven is subject to strict conditions took firm root in later Egyptian mythology, and moral considerations became prominent. This was sometimes symbolized by, for example, weighing a dead man's heart in a balance. Such myths may owe their prevalence to a common experience of the inner meaning of death.

Myths about an after-life which contain such a moral content express a sense of the inner meaning of death. Death, as a limiting factor of all life, puts human existence into perspective. In the myth of a day of judgement it is a moral perspective. But other perspectives are possible too. It may not be too fanciful to suggest that Chirico's *Mystery and Melancholy of a Street* expresses the emptiness of human life when viewed from such a perspective.

The idea that death may involve final condemnation is a more traditional one. The popularized forms cater to man's fear of dying. Thus, Christian representations of Hell have tended to embody fantasies derived from various gruesome methods used to torture people to death. These ideas become intelligible only on the basis of highly extravagant

Above
Originally a local Egyptian god, Osiris, shown here holding the emblems of his power – a shepherd's crook and a whip – later became one of the country's cosmic gods. Osiris reigned as king of the dead in the nether world, and was also the judge of their souls. In the Osiris legend, he was killed by his evil brother, Seth, and brought back to life by his devoted wife, Isis, who used her magical powers to join his limbs together after they had been severed by Seth. Osiris is thus a potent symbol of resurrection

Left
Seth, depicted here in a stone carving, was considered the author and root of all evil, in contrast to Osiris, who was known as 'Onnophris' – 'the good Being'. Seth is always shown in paintings in red – the colour of evil. He was so abominated that his figure was often obliterated on monuments. His bitter conflict with Osiris was regarded as symbolizing the never-ending battle between life and death. Where Osiris was blessed with fertility, Seth was cursed with sterility. When Horus, the son of Osiris and Isis, grew up, he avenged his father, eventually conquering and dispossessing Seth after terrible struggles. Another version of the legend holds that Horus and Seth were made to divide Egypt between them

Above
When an ancient Egyptian died he was identified with Osiris and regarded as having undergone all the indignities inflicted upon the god. It was also believed that every dead man would have to face a judgement – the weighing of his heart (symbolizing his conscience) against the feather of truth on a balance – before his fate in the after-life was decided. If his heart balanced truth, he was admitted to the other world to lead a life of bliss, but if his conscience was found wanting, he was devoured by the creature Amenuit. Anubis, the jackal-headed god, is seen here weighing the heart, while Thoth inscribes the result of the judgement on a tablet

Above centre
Vishnu is a member of Hinduism's supreme trinity, together with Brahma and Siva. The Vishnu myth holds that the god, in his character of the preserver of men, became incarnate on a number of occasions, in order to rid the world of some great evil

Plato, whose writings in the fifth century BC did much to help transform mythology into metaphysics

assumptions. How, for instance, can the flesh of the damned burn continuously for eternity? A Moslem theologian once proposed that Allah constantly renewed it.

Myths about death can be seen as allegories of life. In Bunyan's *Pilgrim's Progress,* for instance, the distinction between death and life is blurred. The pilgrim is clearly in ordinary society at the beginning of the book, and in heaven by the end of it. However, he does not die in the meantime. The difficulties confronting him represent the obstacles man faces as he goes through life. In life, however, the obstacles have to be faced many times. In the *Pilgrim's Progress* they are faced only once, as with the Slough of Despond, for example.

In the face of great doubt, myths either disappear or become transformed into metaphysics. This is how the doctrine of the immortality of the soul arose

A similar allegory of the Christian life as a difficult journey is portrayed in Dürer's *Knight, Death and Devil.* The hourglass held up by Death symbolizes the shortness of life. The Christian soul, on his way to Paradise (located here at the top of the hill), has followed the Biblical injunction to shield himself with 'the armour of God'. He is able to turn his back on the Devil and pass Death without fear.

Dürer's engraving is a visual elaboration of a metaphor – that of the 'soldier'. It is one which has been developed in many different ways in Christian hymns. The metaphor was curiously popular in the nineteenth century in the hymns written by Protestant revivalists. Part of one of them goes as follows:

'Soldiers of Christ! arise,
And put your armour on,
Strong in the strength which God supplies
Through his eternal Son!
To keep your armour bright
Attend with constant care,
Still walking in your Captain's sight,
And watching unto prayer.'

The writer of that hymn did not, of course, intend his words to be taken literally. Anyone who inferred, from this hymn (or, for that matter, from the Dürer engraving) that wearing armour was essential to the Christian life would have misunderstood what the 'armour' symbolism was meant to convey.

It is tempting to say that talk of 'armour' is a *mere* metaphor, but that the Christian life *really is* a 'journey'. There may be some truth in this, but the myth of a difficult journey still involves metaphor – and metaphor which is, arguably, basic to how Christians think of their lives. A Christian can talk about temptation without using the 'armour' metaphor, or talk about faith without using the 'soldier' metaphor. However, if he were asked to describe the Christian life without using the 'journey' metaphor, he might be reduced to silence. Indeed, it may be that religious beliefs can be expressed only in metaphorical terms, that mythology is an integral part of religion.

In recent years, there has been much discussion between thinking Christians as to whether or not myth is essential to their religion. Many people, whatever their religious persuasion, are inclined to insist that whatever truth there is in a metaphor must be capable of being stated in literal terms. When someone tells us that something is weighing on his mind, what he says is informative, because we know what factual truth might lie behind the metaphor. Instead of saying: 'Something is weighing on my mind' he might equally have said, without the metaphor: 'Something is worrying me'. Some theologians have tried to remove the element of myth from certain traditional beliefs, eg about 'resurrection', and restate the truths behind them in an idiom more suited to modern ways of thinking. Nevertheless, the orthodox have often felt uneasy

Left
In many myths about the after-life, only an elite group can enter paradise – reflecting the social order in which these myths evolved. In Sweden, warriors constituted such an elite group, as did the Crusader knights in Britain. This stone, from the town of Hammar, in Gotland, Sweden, shows a warrior being received by a woman holding a horn. Such scenes, representing the dead warrior's membership of a select social group, are common on these Swedish stones

Above
In the Roman Catholic Church, the sacrament of penance secures for those already baptized the forgiveness of post-baptismal sins and ensures that their souls are not excluded from salvation at death. Penance also refers to the disciplinary punishment imposed on a penitent by the priest in earlier times. For many centuries, penitents had to do penance in public, and in the Middle Ages, this was often a terrible and humiliating process. Penance is depicted here on a fifteenth-century sacramental font in St Bartholomew's Church at Sloley, on Britain's east coast. Public penance was abolished hundreds of years ago, however, and the disciplinary penance imposed by Roman Catholic priests today usually consists of the recitation of a psalm or prayer

about how far one could go in this direction without, so to speak, letting the baby out with the bath-water. Their feeling has been that nothing is left to them if they are expected to think of the Christian 'journey', the last 'judgement', eternal 'punishment', and so on, as mere metaphors.

Although the existence of an afterlife cannot be justified by a process of deduction, is there any other way to prove that a conscious part of us survives death?

A completely different approach is to say that such myths may contain truths, but not in the same way as statements of fact. Myths do not, on this view, describe an objective realm of fact, but present possible ways of conferring significance on human life and death. This approach may help in explaining why it is that people think there is some truth in certain myths, but are unable to accept others. Such diverse reactions are not unlike those inspired by religious ideas when they are expressed in common language. There is something of a gulf between those who think that 'Virtue is its own reward' is simply bad grammar, and those who think it expresses a profound insight. Seeing the point of the saying: 'Virtue is its own reward' is part and parcel of learning to see one's own life in a different way. It is a way of looking at injustice from the perspective of eternity.

In the same way, the Dürer engraving of *Knight, Death and Devil,* or any other representation of mythical ideas, might strike us as strange, even bizarre. Grasping its inner meaning means that we have a way of looking at our lives. The easier it is to do this, the less of a change is involved. The more a myth has to teach us, the less easy it is to grasp on first acquaintance.

This way of regarding myth, though in one way sympathetic, concedes, in effect, that myths are grounded in human realities, rather than in anything transcending human life. It is one way of interpreting myths in the face of scepticism. There are, however, approaches which make fewer concessions.

A sceptical attitude and one which can accept myths, as understood here, exclude one another like oil and water. The spread of scepticism may be expected to bring about a decline in adherence to myths. The process may go the other way too, of course, and myths can even reappear. On the whole, though, scepticism will gain ground so long as it can promise knowledge in place of traditional belief. Many myths, like that of the three-tier Universe, with heaven above and hell below, are unlikely to be revived for this reason. Other myths survive by being transformed into metaphysical doctrines which are offered as contributions to knowledge rather than received as traditional beliefs.

Metaphysics itself has undergone development and transformation. But its roots appear to lie in mythology. A striking example of a transformation

Above
Fear of death is natural to human beings, suppressed by some and actively challenged and overcome by others. However, the message of this highly symbolic 1513 engraving by the German master, Albrecht Dürer, entitled Knight, Death and the Devil, seems to be that the soul (the knight) has more to fear from the leering, goat-headed Devil–seen approaching from behind–than from death

from myth into metaphysics is that of the Christian myth of resurrection of the body into the metaphysical doctrine of the immortality of the soul. No one pretends that the 'orthodox' belief in the resurrection of the body is anything more than an exercise of faith—the acceptance of a principle laid down by authority. The invocation of authority in matters of belief is one response to scepticism. The search for metaphysical justification is another. The metaphysical doctrine of the immortality of the soul is one for which numerous arguments have been produced, with the result that many Christian apologists have turned to it as a doctrine that can be believed in the face of scepticism.

The rise in importance within Christendom of belief in the immortality of the soul owes much to the influence of Greek thought, that of Plato in particular. His writings represent an interesting and important stage in the transformation of mythology into metaphysics. Plato assumed that scepticism about a great deal of Greek mythology was widespread among the intellectual élite in Athens in the fifth century BC, but that the mass of the people would continue to believe in myths. He thought it proper for the philosopher to act as a censor of mythology.

Plato objected to myths about Hades portraying all men as being condemned to a shadowy existence after death, irrespective of their lives on earth. He adopted, and sought to give some substance to, myths deriving from the Orphic poets, describing the body as the prison of the soul and death as its liberator. According to such myths, a soul remaining attached to a body at death would be reborn as an animal of a species appropriate to the life lived in that body. The myth of the transmigration of souls is fundamentally a moral one, promising those who cultivate detachment from their bodies an eventual release into the company of the gods. This myth, which is still adhered to in certain Indian religions, is one which Plato seems to have accepted. He gave various accounts of the details of it, although he did not claim that they were accurate.

In Plato's view, the life of a philosopher was a preparation for death. This was based on the idea that the soul is entirely separate from the body, and that while the body would die and decay, the soul would be freed to continue its immortal existence

Plato effectively identified the soul with the human mind, conceiving it as an entity quite distinct from the body. Accepting this view, a saintly man would despise the pleasures of the body and look forward to being freed from them—in other words, to dying. Plato considered the life of the philosopher to be a preparation for death. The fact that people are capable of feeling detached from their bodies made this way of thinking about the soul so popular, that it is still current today among many people. The metaphysical arguments for the immortality of the soul are largely elaborations of this intuitively plausible idea, and they survived the encroachments of the 'new science' in the seventeenth century. Human bodies came to be seen as among the objects of a material world whose behaviour could increasingly be explained by science. The decay of the human body was seen as the breaking down of an organized spatial entity into parts. The soul, however, was not spatial or divisible. How, then, could it perish, it was argued, unless by a special miracle?

The psychological state of detachment from the body has not been shown to be entirely illusory. On the other hand, increased knowledge of physiology has made it less and less plausible to build much on it. Closer and closer correlations have been found between brain states and states of mind. Also, while there is much that is not yet known, it is quite foreign to modern brain science to conceive of the mind as a totally separate entity. Many philosophers are inclined to speculate that the mind is either identical with the brain, or, at least, that mental states are no more than a by-product of brain states.

Philosophers who believe that there are substantial entities called 'souls' or 'minds' are now very much in a minority. Many would agree with at least the main thesis of the late Professor Gilbert Ryle, in his *The Concept of Mind,* that talk about the 'mind' does not require us to believe that there is any such entity. I believe the same is true of talk about 'souls'. Ryle's argument is directed in particular against a way of thinking associated above all with the seventeenth century philosopher, Descartes. He had been struck by the fact that human beings were not mere machines, but then went on to infer from this—wrongly—that they were essentially something over and above machines. This is the same sort of mistake as a person would make if he were anxious to reject the idea that a work of art is nothing but paint on canvas and went on to

The Revenge of God
The Nubian peoples of East Sudan used the following myth to explain Man's mortality. After a man had died, God would tell his relatives that he was merely asleep, and that he would bring the man back to life the next morning. For this reason, He would instruct them to put the corpse aside for the night. Then one day a man died, and a hare told the relatives to bury him or they would face the anger of God. They did this, and when God found out, he was so angry that they had listened to the hare and ignored him that he proclaimed that from then on no man would ever be brought back to life again

conclude that a work of art is essentially something other than paint on canvas.

If myths about the after-life cannot be substantiated by metaphysical reasoning, it remains to be considered whether there could be any other kind of backing for them. The advantage of metaphysical reasoning in relation to the soul is that, if successful, it would offer grounds for believing that the conscious part of us survives death, even in the absence of any evidence about what happens to that conscious part. As things stand, however, belief in continued existence after death must be founded on less ambitious reasoning which does not depend upon there being a detachable part of us that is known as 'the soul'.

Beliefs about immortality have commonly been based on the authority of men. Their claim to authority has often rested on the evidence of miracles performed by them or their disciples

There are two possible strategies here, both of which appeal to the evidence of the senses. Both direct our attention to the fact, readily conceded by scientists, that there are more things in heaven and earth than are dreamt of in our philosophy. The first strategy is to maintain that anomalous events occur in the universe which cannot be explained by science, and which it is appropriate to describe as 'miraculous'. The existence of such events can then be used to defend the retention of a system of beliefs which can make them intelligible. This kind of strategy has been popular during periods, like the eighteenth century, when the fundamental body of scientific theory has appeared to be relatively stable. Today, when people have grown accustomed to expecting large changes in scientific theory, an alternative strategy seems more appropriate: to propose that the anomalous events occurring in the Universe—called 'paranormal'—should be investigated by a new science, such as parapsychology.

The failure of metaphysical arguments to give substance to myths about an after-life has in some degree restored belief in a miraculous resurrection of the body. Christianity has traditionally been supported by miracles and has a miracle—the resurrection of Jesus—at its centre. 'If Christ be not risen, your faith is in vain,' wrote St Paul in the First Letter to the Corinthians. The idea of resurrection is free of the difficulties connected with the metaphysical belief in continued consciousness after death, but it involves an appeal to evidence of a kind which cannot readily command acceptance from sceptics—testimony. To the sceptic it always seems easier to believe that the testimony is mistaken or fraudulent than that the events occurred.

Particular religions have their own traditions of miracles. The tradition of stigmata in Catholicism is an example. Spontaneous bleeding from the palms of the hands is at once evidence of divine grace in the person who shows this symptom, as well as of a power at work in the world to transform matter in ways unknown to science. The tradition of stigmata goes back at least as far as St Francis of Assisi and

Above
Human life is put into moral perspective by the Christian belief that there will be a day of judgement at the end of the world, when all men will be brought to account for the way they have lived. This is William Blake's conception of the scene, The Last Judgement, painted in the late eighteenth or early nineteenth century

Left
Some myths survive by becoming transformed into metaphysics, like the Christian myth of the resurrection of the body, which has developed into the metaphysical doctrine of the immortality of the soul. This engraving by the Italian, Giorgio Ghisi (1550-1582), La Resurrection des Morts (Resurrection of the Dead), illustrates the Christian myth, not the metaphysical doctrine

Far left
La Grande Danse (The Great Dance), by an anonymous eighteenth-century French engraver. Death (again the conventional skull symbolism, although death's body is fully fleshed) rides out to claim his own, while the dragon of hell, his head alone almost as big as death's horse, devours a sinner alive and watches death's horse gallop away

alleged cases are not unknown even in the twentieth century. The case of Teresa Neumann has been backed by purported photographic evidence, but it does not even prove bleeding, still less 'spontaneous' bleeding, and has been alleged to be fraudulent. Many alleged cases of miracles have, of course, been proved to be frauds, but most are shrouded in such obscurity that it is no more possible to prove it is a fraud than it is to prove the miracle itself.

The sceptic's position is likely to be based on a few frauds and on general difficulties he feels about the other cases. Among the general difficulties is the fact that the evidence of miracles claimed by a particular religion is granted only to adherents of that religion. If non-Christians were to manifest the symptoms of stigmata, this would support the view that there are psychosomatic phenomena which science cannot yet adequately explain. It would not, except in a person of saintly character, be any evidence of divine grace. However, faced with Moslem miracles claimed for Islam and Christian ones for Christianity, the sceptic will think himself justified in rejecting them all. They cannot all be true, but they could all be false. Moreover, there is *no more reason* for believing the miracles of one religion than for believing the miracles of another.

Many people now believe in the existence of psychic phenomena. This reflects a desire to turn away from established science and recreate a mythology of the soul

There is a way out of this predicament. It is to say that there are anomalous 'psychic' phenomena in the world, but that these do not lend support to any particular religion.

'Psychic phenomena' are phenomena which are thought to suggest extraordinary powers of communication (telepathy), of bringing about events (telekinesis) or of foreknowledge (precognition). Psychic powers are conceived as not requiring the usual physical means of communication or of making things move and indeed as not being explicable by reference to such means. For example, a man fighting on a battlefront is, to any ordinary way of thinking, quite out of touch with his family. Nevertheless, wives of soldiers have often claimed to have had a premonition that their husbands have been killed or wounded at the very moment when, as was later confirmed, they fell in action. Is this sudden feeling of anxiety at just the right time to be regarded as merely a coincidence, or is it to be regarded as evidence of psychic powers, such as precognition?

This sort of case is not regarded very seriously by those who approach such claims scientifically. From a scientific point of view, it would be necessary to know how often such premonitions were experienced and to be able to correlate a large number of such cases with what was happening to individual soldiers at the relevant times. Only then would it be possible to decide whether there was any significance other than coincidence to be attached to those cases where the premonition turned out to be right. As things stand, we hear nothing at all about the many cases where such fears bear no relation to any misfortune a husband might be suffering.

Those who write books suggesting that there is something in psychic phenomena which establishment science refuses to take seriously tend to focus on cases of this kind. They assume that there is an onus on the sceptic to discredit or explain away such phenomena. They even pretend to be sceptics themselves, who have been forced with due reluctance to accept that there really are such phenomena. Yet they put forward these phenomena as being on the margin of human experience.

The fact is that, if psychic powers really existed, they would not be marginal to human life but would

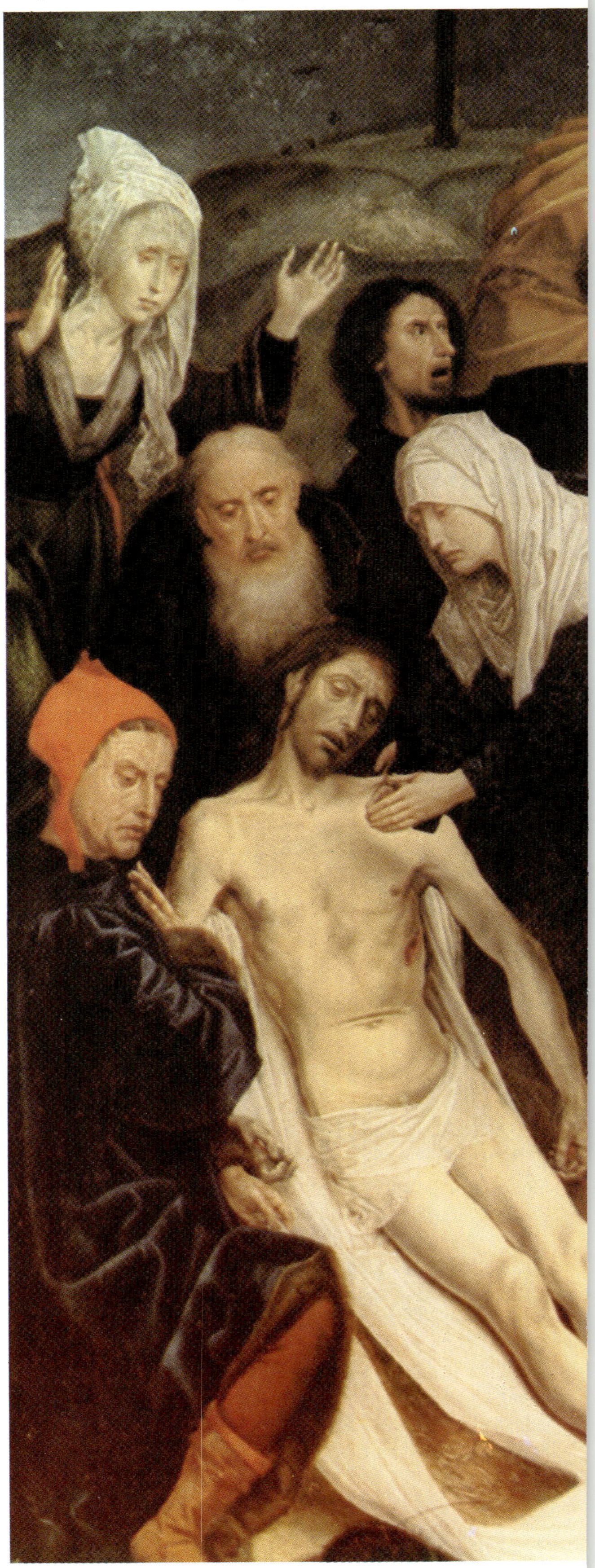

Judgement by the Scales
The ancient Egyptians believed that before it was decided whether a man should be sent to Heaven or Hell, he was first judged in the Great Court of the Gods

Assessment in Heaven
In ancient India it was thought that man would serve his time in Heaven (determined by the quantity of his virtues) before entering Hell

STIGMATA
Bleeding for Christ
An abnormal physical state which often produces pain or bleeding in areas of the human body in imitation of the wounds of Christ – a phenomenon regarded with suspicion by all churches

Eternal Life
Death as we know it did not exist for the ancient Egyptians. To them, it was a superior extension of their earthly life, but unlike our idea of life it was eternal

Cleansing the Soul
The ancient Egyptians did not fear death. They saw it as a purification of the soul; a state in which a man could be purged of his passions – 'the excreta of his heart'

Right
The prelude to the resurrection of Jesus – the removal of his body from the Cross – as seen by the sixteenth-century Flemish painter, Jan Gossart, also known as Jan Mabuse. Painted in about 1520 and acclaimed by Dürer, it is a replica of an altar-piece by Gossart for St Michael's Monastery in Tangerloo, which was destroyed by fire in 1568

radically alter how we conducted our affairs. No one but a fool would put a penny on the football pools if there were any reason to suspect that someone with powers of precognition was also entering. Anyone who actually possessed such powers would enjoy a position of wealth and power in society beyond the nightmares of science fiction.

No one believes in psychic powers in the same way as in say, electricity. Those who profess belief in them think of them as exercised only in very special circumstances and not in a systematic way in relation to everyday affairs. A variety of reasons might be given for why this is so. However, the simplest explanation is that, only by confining the supposed manifestations of psychic powers to the margins of human experience, can belief in such manifestations be protected against being proved false. That is not to say that there cannot be a science of parapsychology. Any class of phenomena which can be reproduced under experimental con-

A Guided Flame
Those in ancient India who had lived particularly virtuous lives were believed to turn into flames on their funeral pyre; they were then guided into the realm of Brahman, a state of timelessness, and there they achieved immortal happiness

ditions is open to scientific investigation. But so long as alleged psychic phenomena are unique, peripheral or elusive, there will remain good grounds for doubting whether research in this area will ever be very fruitful.

The existence of widespread interest in psychic phenomena is symptomatic of the way in which science dominates our thought. It is also symptomatic of a certain rejection of this domination. I believe that the source of this interest is a desire to recreate a mythology of the soul which will help people, in the way such mythologies have in the past, to live with their sense of the inner meaning of death. It is, to be sure, a mythology in modern guise, as science fiction often is. But, if it is mythology, then it is not the kind of belief to be hazarded in the tough and sceptical arena of scientific debate. It is at bottom a modern equivalent of those mythologies of the soul by which men have always sought to accommodate themselves to their sense of the inner meaning of death.

Above
It is difficult to see anything comic in this nineteenth-century engraving after Redolphe Bresdin (1825-1885), Comedie de la Mort (Comedy of Death). The artist has used the time-honoured symbolism of skulls and skeletons to portray death, but appears not to have attempted to depict the souls of the dead

Fate of the Sinners
The ancient Indians believed that after death sinners went to one of the seven hells of Yama, the King of the Dead, and were then reincarnated as worms or snakes

A Fatal Vision

The moment of dying, the confrontation with death, is both the most moving and possibly the most difficult of all the themes dealt with by artists since prehistoric men first painted hunting scenes on their cave walls

Above
Few nations respected their dead as much as the Chinese, whose major religions – until the Communist revolution – enjoined ancestor worship. This glazed pottery figure dating from the T'ang dynasty was set up as guardian of a tomb in Ch'ung-p'u, Shensi, in the early 8th century AD

Top right
The Maya people, who dominated Central America from the 3rd to the 16th centuries AD, buried their potentates in massive vaults, along with their valuables, during the classic period (3rd-9th centuries), but later turned to cremation

Right
The Triumph of Death by Pieter Brueghel the Elder. Death on his pale horse leads his ghastly army against the living. Neither love nor chivalry can prevail against him: the fond lovers (bottom right) will perish and the nobleman who bravely draws his sword will be struck down before he can wield it

Exposing Death Myths
Da Vinci was perhaps one of the first Europeans who used art to demystify death. In those days, the study of anatomy was not allowed and it is thought that da Vinci performed illegal post-mortems to further his knowledge

One of the most forceful and pungent statements ever made about the transience of life can be found in the graveyard in Pisa known as the Campo Santo (Sacred Field), 150 metres from the Leaning Tower. It is a cycle of frescoes by a nameless artist best known as the 'Master of the Triumph of Death', who worked round about 1360-70, in the wake of the Black Death. The central feature of the frescoes is a large representation of the Last Judgement. On one side are ranged the patient pious in orderly rows, while on the other, devils and angels fight over the tormented damned, dragging at them in opposing directions. The torments of the damned are continued on another wall, itemized according to each cardinal sin, while a third bears an allegorical depiction of the delights of Heaven—a group of stately virgins in a trellised rose-garden.

The modern viewer will find little relevance in these main parts of the fresco, although he may wince at the torments of Hell portrayed there, or chuckle at the sight of a friar making for the ranks of the elect, but being pulled back to Hell by some of the devils. His reaction to the scene of the courtly hunting party would almost certainly be much stronger. He would be upset, as if, in holiday mood, he had suddenly come upon a gory road accident.

A medieval viewer would have reacted differently, however. He would have recognized in the scene the familiar theme of 'The Three Living and Three Dead', which usually shows three kings in their trappings and finery meeting their similarly attired doubles—doubles, that is, in dress, but not in appearance, since they are not living men of flesh and blood, but skeletons. He would also recognize the bearded hermit tendering the scroll as St Macarius, from whose name the word 'macabre', as in 'danse macabre', or 'Dance of Death', was supposedly derived. Frescoes of it were painted on the walls of many churches. Death was not only a visitant of the old, or very young; nor did it appear

Above
The desire to live on in stone was not limited to the great and powerful: in an English parish church, the country gentleman Thomas Selwyn and his wife are realistically portrayed at prayer. Below them, in a tradition deriving from medieval funerary sculpture, kneel their six daughters. The monument dates from 1630

Top right
A medieval congregation might well be too unsophisticated to understand a preacher's words – or perhaps too weary to listen – but they could hardly escape the warning message of this stained-glass panel, in an English parish church, showing a horned devil carrying off a female sinner to everlasting torment

An Immortal Record
The ancient Egyptians regarded art as primarily functional – they believed that depicting a human being would ensure his immortality

Haunted by War
The work of the German artist, Max Beckmann, was strongly influenced by the horror of war and the torture that accompanied it. It haunted him so much, in fact, that it became the motif in several of his pictures, among them The Night and Deposition

only as a consequence of war: the plague which had periodically ravaged Europe since the mid-fourteenth century—the Black Death—could strike at anyone, regardless of age, station or condition. The towns bore the brunt of its onset, but the countryside did not remain unscathed. There are frequent portrayals of death as a huntsman, pouncing on travellers or hunting parties like an ambushing bandit.

The Dance of Death was performed in the streets by mummers, each representing a different trade or class, since death, in the Middle Ages as now, came to all

The most famous sculptured representation of 'The Three Living and the Three Dead' (now destroyed) was above the portals of the Church of the Holy Innocents in Paris, while inside, in the cloisters, there was an abundance of charnel-houses and emblems and representations of death. At the same time, the church was one of the most popular meeting-places in Paris. There was small evidence of any feeling of reverence or grief, and the atmosphere seems to have been more suited to a fairground than a church. At the same time manifestations of grief were more violent, more extreme, though the gloom of a funeral might suddenly be transformed into the exuberance of a wake.

Because he could find a ready emotional response, in the Middle Ages, death was a prime subject for the artist. And it was a subject that in time became more sombre. A synthesis of many of these medieval images of death was later achieved in Pieter Brueghel the Elder's *Triumph of Death* painted round about 1562, which now hangs in the Prado, in Madrid. Here the Dance of Death and other images from the medieval repertoire are given new expression. A huge figure of Death on a red charger leads an army of corpses and skeletons against the living. One man is drawing his sword against the ghastly host, but he will never strike a single blow for he is about to be struck down from behind. Death is the ultimate victor.

A medieval visitor would not only have been much more prepared for the shock of coming upon *The Triumph of Death* than his modern counterpart, but would also have been taught how to react to it. The moral to be drawn from it was, no doubt, inscribed on the now obliterated scroll borne by St Macarius—repent and come to terms with death. The means of coming to terms with death was there to see, in the accompanying images of God and Heaven. Art was, of course, in the service of this moral, and another of the forms it took to convey its message was the *Ars Moriendi* (Art of Dying)—a usually crude woodcut of a deathbed scene. These woodcuts provided the most explicit instruction on how to compose oneself for death and decomposition—Repent!

The medieval obsession with Hell seems to be one and the same as the obsession with death. The images used to depict Hell derive either from the destruction of the body, in the grave—worms devouring it—or from violent death—unchaste women being attacked and bitten by snakes; criminals and traitors being executed by hanging and quartering or disembowelling; heretics being burned at the stake, disembowelled or quartered. Executions were very common in the Middle Ages and were, of course, public. The physical torture was sometimes accompanied by mental torture—the denying to the victim of the consolation of confession and the administering of the last sacraments. It was considered almost impossible for anyone who had not received the last sacraments to gain entry to Heaven. To medieval man, Heaven meant the literal resurrection of the body, not simply the eternal life of the soul. To a large degree, medieval man saw the decomposition of the body after death as the consequence of his own sin and as the opening stage of the tortures of Hell.

Above
There is no trace of sentimental piety in Rogier van der Weyden's The Descent from the Cross (c 1435). The dead Christ is at peace, but his mourners, confined by the artist to a shrine-like space, graphically express the wide range of human emotions in the face of death

Far left
Man has long sought after better ways of killing his enemies. This scene of battle in a Mesolithic rock painting from the Valltorta gorge, Spain, dating from c 6,000 BC, was probably intended to invoke the death of the enemy, or perhaps to bring luck to the warriors depicted, by sympathetic magic

Left
Strikingly similar in intent to the prehistoric rock painting (to the left) is this contemporary, bilingual 'curse' in spray-can graffiti from a Middle Eastern state: a malediction on what radicals term 'dollar imperialism', obviously aimed at an oil company. Social scientists see in the proliferation of elaborate graffiti a modern expression of the wish for personal immortality that inspired the pyramids

There was rather less scope for the artist's imagination when his task was to picture the positive benefits of Heaven. To us, certainly, it must seem that the strongest argument for getting to Heaven was the horror of Hell. Typically, medieval tombs show painted or sculpted representations of the decayed or decaying body, surmounted by images of rescue—the Crucifixion, the Salvation, or the interceding Virgin Mary. In some tombs, however, the resurrection is shown as already taking place. This dream of the body's resurrection encouraged the more optimistic to envisage their resurrection as essentially taking the form of an idealized version of this life. Hence the double tomb of the late Middle Ages, with the worms' food beneath and the man himself proud and intact, above. One can interpret the image of an ecclesiastic comfortably stretched out above not only as a memorial to his earthly pastorship, but also as a pious depiction of what he regarded as his due in Heaven.

The Renaissance saw the revival of the Greek and Roman idea that some kind of immortality could be earned by a man's actions or status in this life

The unmitigated triumph of death in the Pisa fresco had already been placed in perspective by Petrarch in his *Trionfi*. Here, chastity overcame love, death overcame chastity, and fame overcame death, only to be itself overcome by time, which was

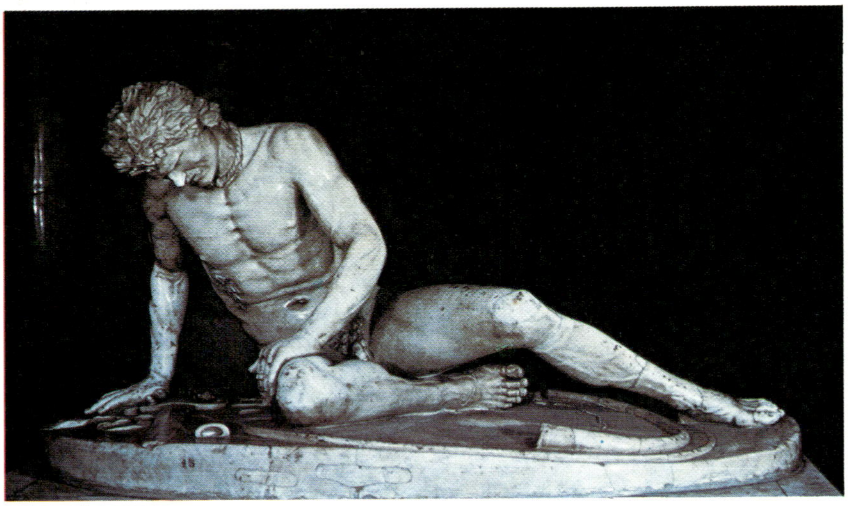

Above
Lacking the Judaeo-Christian belief in divine retribution, the artists of classical antiquity had a very different approach to death from those of the medieval period. Pain, sadness and, above all, resignation, are depicted in this marble figure of The Dying Gaul, dating from the 3rd century BC, but not fear or horror. The medieval attitude to death was expressed in Dunbar's famous line: Timor mortis conturbat me (Fear of death troubles me)

Right
Et in Arcadia Ego by Nicolas Poussin: the Arcadian shepherds, tracing the inscription on a tomb, are reminded that, 'I, too, lived in Arcadia'. Poussin evokes both the classically stoic approach to death and, in his statuesque figures, the forms of classic art. The modern viewer may also read into the work a comment on the element of naivety, even of guilty curiosity, in contemporary attitudes towards death

Purging of the Futurists
The Futurists, a strongly patriotic movement, believed that war was the only way of purging the system of redundant ideas. This belief contributed to the downfall of the movement, because so many of its followers fought and met their deaths in World War I. The Futurists disliked and distrusted women, and their political beliefs verged on Fascism. One Futurist artist, Boccioni, with an excellent war record, ironically died after falling off a horse

Skeleton in the Cupboard
The Belgian painter, James Ensor, has been described as having a 'peculiarly macabre outlook'. He frequently used grotesque masks and skeletons in his pictures for expressionist purposes. For instance, Spectral Cupboard, an otherwise cosy domestic scene contains the image of a skeleton

in turn overcome by eternity. Renaissance tombs follow the medieval scheme, substituting classical for Gothic forms, but the dead body beneath soon disappears. For example, the mid-fifteenth century tomb of Leonardo Bruni in the Church of Santa Croce, in Florence, is a memorial, a cenotaph, to Bruni's earthly being. In the Church of San Andrea in Mantua, designed by Alberti and deliberately evoking classical antiquity on a grand scale, is the tomb of a much less important man, dated 1490. In very low relief closely imitating Roman reliefs, it shows arms, trophies and books, for he was a scholarly soldier. This tomb celebrates the man's life without celebrating his fame. During the same period, Antonio Pollaiuolo was working on the bronze tomb of Pope Sixtus IV, which discourses allegorically on humanistic culture.

Art could now be used against death. It could perpetuate a man's memory by recording his deeds or his likeness, or by being so magnificent and beautiful that it brought the man who commissioned it eternal glory. Nowhere is this purpose more transparent than when the work of art to be created is a tomb and is undertaken when the man who is to lie in it is still alive. Julius II and Leo X, the two High Renaissance Popes, who successively monopolized the services of Michelangelo, must have followed the example of King Mausolos and his Mausoleum. Julius II commissioned a vast cenotaph, of which only a few fragments were ever completed, most notably *Moses* and the frame he sits in, in the Church of San Pietro in Vincoli, in Rome, and the *Slaves* in the Louvre, in Paris. Leo X took Michelangelo from that tomb and set him to work on the cenotaph of his own family, the Medici chapel in the Church of San Lorenzo, in Florence. Michelangelo spent most of his life on these works: the Sistine Chapel was a mere interlude.

These and other High Renaissance and later tombs are richly decorated with a huge variety of figures and motifs, symbolizing resurrection and the after-life. The multitudinous sarcophagi, busts, vaults, chambers, Pyramids, towers and even man-made hills the Romans left behind them have none of this decoration, except for a few early Christian symbols. This can be explained by the fact that the Romans and the Greeks visualized the after-life, either as a weakened, shadowy, bloodless version of the earthly one, or as some form of transmigration of the soul. They did not believe in the resurrection of the body or, it seems, the survival of the ego. Thus, even the most optimistic pagan would not quarrel with the typical Roman epitaph: 'I was what you are; you will be what I am'. The moral drawn from this was the Epicurean one: 'Eat, drink and be merry'. There are endless epigrammatic variations on this dual theme, of which Horace's *Carpe diem,* 'Seize the day', is only one. Their range, variety and pungency have never been matched in any body of literature since.

The Etruscans and Romans were frightened by ghosts, and mourning among the Greeks was a violent business. Nevertheless, it was accepted calmly and with composure that life had to end eventually

Fear of death, whether explicit in the horrific representations of the Middle Ages, or implicit in the insistence on an after-life during the Renaissance and after, does not appear in classical art. Perhaps not every ancient was as rational in the face of death as Socrates in Plato's *Phaedrus,* but there is everywhere a quality of resignation and acceptance which the Middle Ages rejected. This can be seen as well in *The Dying Gaul* in the museum on the Campidoglio in Rome—showing grief, pain and sadness, but not fear—as in the most beautiful expression of classical resignation in the face of

Above
In The Death of Sardanapalus, Eugene Delacroix achieves a splendidly-orchestrated Romantic equivalent to a scene from a modern movie epic: the sybaritic king of Assyria witnesses the deaths of his favourite women and horses before himself perishing by fire. This theme also inspired a tragedy by the poet Byron

Left
Depicted here by Gerard Honthorst, the ordeal of St Sebastian (who did not, in fact, die in this manner) was a favourite subject with artists who, at a time when most commissions were for religious works, welcomed an opportunity to depict a male nude

death: Greek stelae of the fifth century BC. These, utterly composed and utterly sad, are understated to the point of total silence.

Most Roman tombs are, like ours, little more than name-plates, but there is one significant difference: modern tombs merely record, whereas Roman tombs were probably felt to preserve something of their occupants' *persona*. The centre of a Roman household was a room containing busts and death masks of deceased members of the family, which were the object of a daily ritual of devotion. This implies that the Romans felt some form of their ancestors' original being to reside in them, and explains the strong Roman bent towards realistic portraiture, especially on tombs, in terms of ancestor-worship. It links the Classical Age with the Stone Age, from which red-painted bones—an early appearance of death in art, and almost the earliest appearance of art—survive, showing that some form of life was felt to persist in them. The Classical Age is also linked with the art of the earliest known civilizations, such as the decorated skulls, with cowrie-shells for eyes, from Jericho, dating from about 7000 BC. These resemble decorated skulls produced in New Guinea, perhaps even today. It seems that, in every culture except those produced by the great monotheisms, death is seen as a continuation of life in a changed and reduced form—either in the same place, or transferred to some other place—but always in this one Universe. In the case of Christianity, death is regarded as superseding life, stepping outside the rhythm of life, becoming a threat to life.

The figure of death which had stalked through so many prints and books and gestured from so many walls, that attenuated skeleton with a skull for a head, reappears with unimpaired vigour in Bernini's tombs and chapels in the baroque era

Death was a personification invented by the Middle Ages and, once it had been brought to life, as it were, it was not going to be suppressed. Crowning Bernini's tomb of Pope Alexander VII in St Peter's is the imposing, solid figure of the Pope himself, stretching out his hands in papal blessing. Below, struggling through the massive marble curtain, as if he had leapt out of the door beneath, the gesturing, threatening figure of Death rears up, waving an hour-glass in one hand and a scythe in the other. Similar skeletons are inlaid in the floor of Bernini's Cornaro Chapel in the Church of Santa

Heart in the Head
Plato's inaccuracies in anatomy were such that he believed that the heart was located inside the skull. This was due to the fact that in his day, as in da Vinci's, anatomy and dissection were illegal. However, unlike da Vinci, Plato remained on the right side of the law

Memento Mori
There are several paintings that contain a reminder of death, such as Holbein's 'Two Merchants'. The painting was commissioned by its subjects, who probably paid generously; Holbein, clearly wishing to prove to himself that he was not totally prostituting his art, painted a skull between the two figures in such a way that it can only be seen from a certain angle—he also used this technique in 'Dance of Death'

Winged Obsession
When the modern German painter Max Ernst was a child, he had a pet bird which died in rather unpleasant circumstances. This seemingly minor tragedy caused him to have a nervous breakdown and obsessed him for the rest of his life. It also made a deep impression on his work – most of his paintings contained birds, and one of his favourite images was that of the head of a bird superimposed onto the body of a man. The painting which most vividly depicts this obsession is 'Bird in a Forest' – it shows a huge, menacing forest with a bird in a tiny cage in the middle of it

Maria della Vittoria in Rome, in which the famous vision of St Theresa is represented, as well as in other chapels, almost audibly rattling their bones and dancing a mad jig. Bernini's new concept of the tomb as a sort of battleground between the person commemorated by it and death, was seized upon by many of the sculptors who followed him and retained something of his drama, even while they revised his style. There is a most splendid example in Westminster Abbey, Roubiliac's Nightingale tomb (1761): here, the husband tries in vain to fend off the hideous spectre rushing up from below to lay his foul hands on the poor man's departed wife.

However, sculptors of the rationalist eighteenth century soon lost Bernini's ardent faith. He had portrayed death as being vanquished by the piety of the victim, but, in neo-classical tombs, one feels that death is the victor. If monuments are meant to be unforgettable, surely one of the most effective anywhere is Canova's tomb of Maria Christina of Austria, in the Augustinerkirche in Vienna. Its pyramidal shape is supposed to signify eternal life, as is the serpent biting its own tail, which encircles the medallion of the Duchess. The procession of allegorical figures entering the tomb leaves the viewer with the impression of a funeral procession delivering the unfortunate Duchess into a prison. The hope of an after-life seems dim. The medieval conception of death has faded. All it is now is what happens in the tomb, the putrefaction of the body. That the grave is an eternal prison for the body, which will go nowhere after death, is explicit in the tomb of Jean-Jacques Rousseau in the crypt of the Panthéon in Paris. Here, however, the idea that fame is immortality re-emerges, and a hand holding a torch forces its way out of the double-leaved door at the end of the sarcophagus.

Right
Cezanne called Claude Monet 'only an eye, but what an eye'; and there can be few more striking instances of painterly objectivity than Monet's record of how he painted Camille on her Deathbed. Gazing on his newly-dead wife, he found himself 'analyzing the succession of appropriate colour gradations which death was imposing' and he 'automatically reacted to the colour stimuli'

Below
The fearful atrocities committed by both sides during the Napoleonic campaigns in Spain inspired Francisco Goya's series of works depicting the miseries of war. In The Executions of the Third of May, 1808, he translated a single incident into a universal image of death for all men in all times, with a sharply-lit central figure who is, at one and the same time, Christ recrucified and Everyman in extremis. In his own life, however, Goya showed little patriotic feeling, working with equal dedication for the Spanish Court and for the usurper Bonaparte

In painting, the most striking image of death produced in the Age of Reason, is Jacques Louis David's *The Dead Marat* (1793; Musée Royal des Beaux-Arts de Belgique). The grief and emotion associated in the Middle Ages and Renaissance with the dead Christ, of which there are countless examples from Giotto to Michelangelo's *Piètà* in St Peter's, are taken over and reworked in a contemporary setting to produce a secular, classicized *Piètà* whose realistic details (faithfully recorded within a short time of Marat's murder) serve to reinforce its dramatic and propagandist impact as an image of a revolutionary martyr. The rigid realism of David's approach in this painting is paralleled in the Romantic period in such works as Géricault's series of *Decapitated Heads*.

Mantegna's famous foreshortened *Piètà* has been re-used in a similar way—not only because of its associations, perhaps, but because that is how a dead body looks to us when viewed from the feet or from the head. Manet, for instance, echoed Mantegna to show the aftermath of civil war. So, too, as has frequently been pointed out, did the creator of a famous photograph of the dead Che Guevara. Probably the most famous realistic image of death in nineteenth century painting (as well as the largest—314cm x 663cm) is Gustave Courbet's *Burial at Ornans* (1849; Louvre, Paris). Rejecting the traditional depictions of death, Courbet concentrates on its effect on his own family and village community in his native Franche-Comté. Courbet succeeds in his intention to *'faire l'art vivant'*, to record faithfully the customs, ideas and appearance of his own time. The members of the whole community are rendered equal in the face of death, with the gravedigger as the central figure and the pall-bearers averting their faces from the corpse. The painting's 'brutality' created a contemporary scandal.

Women and death were depicted by painters like Millais as virgins surrounded by flowers, which epitomized the beauty that ultimately fades

Women in death were romanticized rather differently, in a manner that bore no specific connotation of death. They were depicted as virgins surrounded by flowers, which epitomized perishable beauty. Millais established a type with his Ophelia, and it is interesting to see it taken up by Van Herkomer, the official painter at Queen Victoria's funeral, and to compare both of them with Monet's portrait of his wife, Camille, on her deathbed, where the impressionistic brush strokes reproduce the effect of flowers. We have Monet's own extraordinary account of this event: 'I caught myself, my eyes fixed on her tragic forehead, in the act of mechanically analyzing the succession of appropriate colour gradations which death was imposing on her immobile face . . . Even before I had the idea of setting down the features to which I was so deeply attached, my organism automatically reacted to the colour stimuli, and my reflexes caught me up in spite of myself'.

In striking contrast to such amazing objectivity in the face of death are the sentimental or grotesque images which appear at much the same time and often seem to hark back to earlier sources. Claus Sluter, for example, working at the very beginning of the fifteenth century, carved the most emotionally affecting mourners in painted wood for his tomb of Duke Philip the Bold of Burgundy. They are as faceless as death, mere empty, sack-like monkish forms, as if they had no bodies, but were only phantasms symbolic of horror and grief. Perhaps the most famous example of these mourning monks is the tomb of Philippe Pot, Grand Seneschall of Burgundy in the Louvre. An artist called C.E. de Beaumont used the entire structure in *In the Sun* (1875) to signify death striking, even on a summer's day. This incorporeal monkish figure reappears in early nineteenth-century Gothic novels by – 'Monk' Lewis for instance – whence it has passed into the vocabulary of the horror film. Even on Sluter's monument, if you tore away the cowl, you would expect to see the face of death itself.

The taste for the horrific or grotesque was as much a part of the 'romantic' temperament as the tendency to sentimentality – the Benjamin West of *The Death of Wolfe,* directly comparable to David's *Marat,* produced *Death on a Pale Horse* in 1802. However, a new moralism begins to appear in the many similar examples, from Goya to Géricault. It is not the moralism of the Middle Ages, or of Beaumont's picture, but a humanistic moralism, which sees death as part of man's inhumanity to man. Into this class fall all the anti-war pictures which have proliferated since Goya produced his *Third of May, 1808,* transforming the conventions of patriotic prints engraved by British artists during Wellington's Peninsular War.

Left centre
Edvard Munch was an artist who showed himself obsessed by suffering and death, which had for him strong sexual connotations. In Death in the Sickroom he does not show the corpse, but harshly highlights the reactions of the living. The spectator is directly involved in an eye-to-eye confrontation with the disturbingly ambiguous central female figure

Below
Commissioned to paint the murdered French Revolutionary leader, David produced in The Dead Marat a secularized pièta, stressing Marat's ascetic life-style by turning the packing-case on which he worked (from the bath to which a skin disease confined him) into a memorial tablet. David made his preliminary studies for this painting while the corpse was still in situ

Left
Another secular pièta, from the Victorian painter Henry Wallis. In The Death of Chatterton, Wallis takes as his subject the early Romantic poet (and literary forger) Thomas Chatterton who, starving and unrecognized, killed himself at the age of 18. A narrative painting packed with 'clues', it 'reads' like a novel

A Last Pose
When he knew he was about to die, John Donne reclined on his bed and posed for his death statue

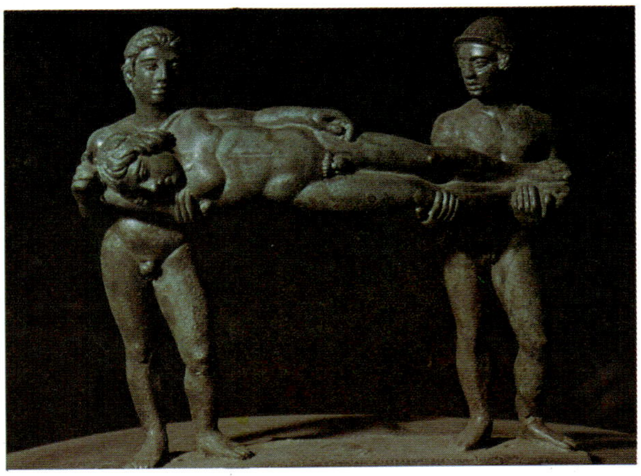

Above
Duncan Edwards, captain of the Manchester United soccer team, who died with several of his team-mates in the Munich air crash of 1958, is here commemorated in a stained-glass window that echoes the Victorian era in sentiment

Above centre
This stone angel on a grave in London is characteristic of Victorian funerary sculpture and of a time when death was surrounded by an elaborate, comforting – and expensive – ritual

Above right
Some 24 centuries before the memorialization of the other sportsmen shown on these pages, an Etruscan craftsman produced this bronze handle for a funerary urn to mark the death of an athlete

Right
In Mexico, All Souls' Day, November 2, is both a solemn religious festival and a day of celebrations in honour of the dead. The graves of relatives and friends are decorated and, for the children, there are appropriate sweetmeats – like the sugar skull

Right centre
Mount Rushmore National Memorial, Southwest Dakota, USA. Each some 18 metres (59ft) high, Presidents George Washington, Thomas Jefferson, Abraham Lincoln and Theodore Roosevelt symbolize the nation's founding, political philosophy, preservation, and expansion

Of these two trends in romantic art, the grotesque rather than the sentimental seems to have prevailed. Death is regarded as the dead person's own fault. The message of one piece of modern commercial art, for instance, is that death can and should be remedied. What kind of thought might run through a modern viewer's mind in the Campo Santo in Pisa? That everything portrayed in the frescoes was the result of poor sanitation?

It is no longer heroic to die. Death, on the contrary, has become an unnatural mistake – it is murder and it is now grotesquely ironic: Little Nell died through a failure of the Social Services

Expressionist works from Rouault to Bacon emphasize the grotesque element of death. So now, perhaps, whenever art takes death as its subject – if it has a subject – it will be dismissed or revelled in only as something morbid. It is ironic that, in Poussin's *Et in Arcadia Ego,* one can see not only a superbly realized example of classical stoicism and resignation revived, but also the naivety and unpreparedness – even the guilty curiosity – of modern people in the face of death.

The way in which artists have approached the subject of death has, of course, been considerably influenced by photography and, later, cinematography. At first, some thought that the invention of photography presaged the end of art. 'From today, painting is dead!' exclaimed Paul Delaroche, after seeing an exhibition of daguerrotypes in 1839. As we know, this was an exaggerated reaction. Nevertheless, it was obvious that no painter could match the immediacy and impact of, for example, Mathew Brady's photographs of the carnage in the War between the States or, in the twentieth century, the panoramic photographs of the destruction of Hiroshima. It is significant that, possibly, the most moving evocation of the shattered cities of Germany in World War II should occur not in painting or literature, but in music, in the *Metamorphosen* of Richard Strauss. No painters of cosmic disaster, like John Martin and Washington Allston in the early nineteenth century, attempted to portray the nuclear holocaust – although Max Ernst produced striking images of 'dead cities' and a ravaged Europe 'after the rains'. Generally, modern artists have chosen to emphasize the grotesque (as we have noted) and 'personal' elements of death, leaving larger statements to photographers, cinematographers and some writers.

Death in literature is an immense subject, which can hardly be satisfactorily summarized here. From the earliest times, writers have been – as T. S. Eliott said of the Jacobean dramatist, John Webster – 'much possessed by death'. Homer's *Iliad* centres

Dreams of Cannibalism
Dali, as a child, had vivid dreams of being eaten alive. These led to an obsession with this image in later life, and inspired a number of his well-known paintings, perhaps the most famous being 'Autumn Cannibalism'

Disbelief in Death
The artist Andy Warhol once said about death:
'I don't believe in it, because you're not around to know that it's happened.'

Top Left
The complex ritual of mourning during the Victorian era involved the dress of the bereaved. Widows were expected to wear 'weeds' (sombre clothing) for up to one year and many also wore commemorative jewellery – brooches and sometimes entire parures – in which the hair of the departed loved one was woven into ornamental designs, as seen here.

Top
The Mahafaly tomb carvings of Madagascar are not unlike those of the great potentates of Renaissance Europe in their complexity – and in their strange dignity. This painted wooden monument, in which the funeral rites are themselves recorded, obviously honours a local sportsman, whose team-mates carry his coffin in solemn procession. In all cultures, monuments commemorating the subject's major activity are common

Above Left
Although the modern trend is towards simple funerals – and undertakers have been denounced by some writers for making death 'big business' – expensive ritual is still a comfort to some families, as this display in a London cemetery proves

on the death of Achilles. Like their contemporaries in painting, medieval writers often personified death. Chaucer's *Pardoner's Tale* and the morality play, *Everyman*—in which the eponymous protagonist greets the image of mortality with the piteous cry: 'Oh, Death, thou comest when I had thee least in mind!'—are notable examples. Dante Alighieri portrayed the after-life in a manner which has profoundly influenced artists for six centuries. John Donne apostrophized death in poems and sermons: 'Any man's death diminishes me, because I am involved in Mankind; and therefore never send to know for whom the bell tolls; it tolls for thee'. Sir Thomas Browne analyzed man's attitude to death in some of the finest English prose ever written. Daniel Defoe documented death in his *Journal of the Plague Year.* John Bunyan charted man's journey through life to death and to eternal life beyond.

The sentimental literature of death reached its zenith (or its nadir) in the nineteenth century, most famously in Charles Dickens' description of the death of Little Nell in *The Old Curiosity Shop* which, Oscar Wilde claimed, it was impossible to read without tears (of laughter), and in the dramatization of Mrs Henry Wood's novel, *East Lynne* ('Dead! and . . . never called me mother'.) At the end of the century, the realism of such writers as Ibsen and Zola heralded a grimmer attitude, which found full expression in the literature inspired by World War I. The comfortable fatalism manifested at the war's outset by such writers as Rupert Brooke soon gave way to the savage irony and bleak despair expressed in the poetry of Wilfred Owen and Siegfried Sassoon, and in such novels as Erich Maria Remarque's *All Quiet on the Western Front.* One of the most disturbing polemicists of modern literature, the French right-wing author Louis-Ferdinand Céline, was provoked into writing by his experiences on the Western Front. His *Journey to the End of Night* and *Death on the Instalment Plan* are major contributions to the literature of death. Yet the sentimental attitude to death persisted into the twentieth century in such writers as Sir James Barrie, whose *Peter Pan* exclaims: 'To die will be an awfully big adventure'.

World War II made death a commonplace. In the face of the 'Final Solution', Stalingrad and the destruction of Dresden and Hiroshima, it was difficult for any writer to produce a coherent or convincing statement concerning the death of the individual. Thus, the most striking evocations of death in modern literature occur not in panoramic and strident war novels like Norman Mailer's *The Naked and the Dead* and its many imitators, but in grotesque parables like Joseph Heller's *Catch 22,* Gunter Grass's *Dog Years* and Kurt Vonnegut, Jr's *Slaughterhouse V,* as well as in 'decadent' comedies of manners like the novels of Yukio Mishima.

Ecstatic Death
The French believed death and sex to be closely linked – one of their terms for orgasm is 'petit mort' ('little death')

As the ultimate in endings, death, exploited in ways ranging from the cynical to the clinical, has been a staple ingredient of movie plots since bioscope days

Right
Seconds away from death, the gangster Clyde Barrow (Warren Beatty) stumbles from his automobile under the guns of federal lawmen, in a scene from Arthur Penn's Bonnie and Clyde (1967). The movie was in many ways typical of the mood of the 'sixties, portraying the killers Clyde Barrow and Bonnie Parker as 'beautiful people', free and untrammelled by convention, robbing the rich and being hero-worshipped by the poor in America during the Depression, until they are cut down in a welter of blood by the hated representatives of law and order. It was nothing new for a movie to glorify the exploits of vicious criminals: the famous Little Caesar of 1930 was similarly criticized

Far right
There is irony in this shot of Judy Garland clinking glasses with Dirk Bogarde in I Could Go On Singing (1963), her last movie. Six years later, the star was to die from the effects of drink and drugs, the abuse of which had permeated her turbulent career. Pushed into stardom as a child of 14, her whole life was lived in a glare of sensational publicity with which she found herself unable to cope

The All-American Artist
The abstract expressionist, Jackson Pollock, revolutionized American art by his method of 'drip-painting'. An alcoholic, hypersensitive and self-obsessed, he was nevertheless seen as the personification of the 'All-American male'. He killed himself in 1956 by crashing his car

Bonnie Parker (also known as Gun Molly) and Clyde Barrow, the original Bonnie and Clyde, who terrorized the Mid-West during the Depression

Death has been used in the cinema for dramatic and emotional effects almost from the birth of cinematography. *The Great Train Robbery* of 1903, often considered the first narrative film, features a scene in which bandits shoot an innocent man in cold blood. In the first fifty years of films, the portrayal of the moment of dying, while often horrific and moving, was rarely graphic. Since the 1950s, however, death scenes have become more and more realistic, and film-makers increasingly preoccupied with them. The nadir was reached in the 1970s, when a cheap South American film called *Snuff* achieved commercial success because it was rumoured that a scene showing the killing of a girl was not simulated but real. (This turned out to be a hoax in the worst possible taste.) It was the mirror reflection of the television news broadcasts showing real deaths in the Vietnam War, which people had begun to treat almost like fiction.

Most cinema deaths occur in action films, the Western, the gangster film, the horror film, the swashbuckling adventure film and the war film. All five types originated in the silent era, but it was not until the arrival of sound that the verism of bangs and screams could be added. Such films tend to occur in cycles with, for example, gangster and horror films more common in the 1930s and war films in the 1940s. Despite the large number of deaths in these films, blood was very rarely shown. Deaths were 'clean', whether they were caused by James Cagney's gun, Errol Flynn's sword or King Kong's strength.

As Hollywood films became more realistic in the 1950s, so did the portrayal of dying. One of the first major films to show the obscenity of death was Stanley Kubrick's graphic anti-war film, *The Paths of Glory*. Even more disturbing was Alfred Hitchcock's *Psycho* (1960) in which Janet Leigh is seen being stabbed to death in a shower, with her blood pouring down the drain. The 1960s saw the maximization of violent death on the screen in blood horror films like *Witchfinder General,* violent Westerns like *The Wild Bunch,* and disturbing gangster movies like *Bonnie and Clyde* (which goes into great detail in showing Faye Dunaway and Warren Beatty being riddled with bullets). The Italian 'Spaghetti Western' of the 1960s and 70s added even more gory realism.

The most memorable and beautiful death figure in the cinema was Maria Casares in Jean Cocteau's Orphée, made in 1949. Glamorous, almost a vamp, she tempts the modern Orpheus of the film to love her

In the 1970s, the brutal depiction of death in frightening close-up had become the principal *raison d'etre* of some films, like *The Texas Chain Saw Massacre.* Directors like Sam Peckinpah and Robert Aldrich are notorious for the violent deaths in their films. The idea of death as pleasure reached its chilling peak in *Salo or the 120 Days of Sodom,* an adaptation from the Marquis de Sade by the Italian director, Pier Paolo Pasolini. This was an enormously upsetting film, which gained even more notoriety when its director was murdered shortly after it was completed.

Strangely, the few films which have made a serious treatment of death and dying their central subject have rarely been popular. Whether John Wayne dying of cancer in the Western, *The Shootist,* or an elderly Japanese man in Akira Kurosawa's *Living,* trying to find a meaning for his life in his last months, audiences did not want this kind of realism. In the same way, the mass deaths of millions in the Nazi concentration camps have rarely been treated in the cinema. Cinema goers do not object to gallons of fake blood being shed in action films, but they do not want to see death depicted in too believable a form. This may explain why personifications of death in films are so readily acceptable. There have been many, by stars as famous as Fredric March, Jack Benny and Richard Burton, but the most memorable death figures appear in the French film, *Orpheé,* and the Swedish film *The Seventh Seal. Orpheé,* made by Jean Cocteau in 1949 features the most beautiful personification of death to have appeared on the screen—Maria Casares. Cocteau said of the film: 'Death is a spy who falls in love with the man on whom she is spying. She condemns herself, in order to help the man she is duty bound to destroy. The man is saved but death dies; it is the myth of immortality'. The messengers of death in this film are also memorable, garbed in black leather and riding motor-cycles. In Ingmar Bergman's *The Seventh Seal,* death, white-faced and wearing a black hood and cloak, meets a knight returning from the Crusades and agrees to play a game of chess with him. This scene, one of the most famous in world cinema, is only a brief diversion for death (Bengt Ekerot), and he eventually takes the knight (Max von Sydow) and his companions off to the other world.

Death stalks through another plague film to great effect—Roger Corman's 1964 British picture *The*

Masque of the Red Death. Here, death is dressed all in red, first appearing stalking through the land and then spreading terror at an evil prince's masked ball. In his final horrific confrontation death removes his mask to reveal to the astonished prince nothing other than his own face.

The most likeable and sophisticated death personified in the cinema was Fredric March's, in the classic 1934 American film, *Death Takes a Holiday*. He comes to earth to find out why people fear him so much and to see what the attractions of life are. During his three-day stay, disguised as a prince, no human being, animal or plant dies, and he falls in love with a woman who does not fear him. When he discovers that the world actually needs his services, he leaves for the other world with his new love.

One of the first film-makers to feature death on the screen was the great German director, Fritz Lang, in the 1917 *Hilde Warren and Death* (in which he himself portrays death) and in the 1931 *The Weary Death (Destiny)*. Lang's *The Weary Death* concerns a young woman trying to save her lover from death (Bernhard Gotzke). During their continuing dialogue, he shows her three scenes from the distant past proving that her task is impossible. He lives in the Crypt of a Thousand Candles in a house surrounded by walls so high that it is impossible to see where they end. He is weary of killing and offers to spare her lover's life if she will give him someone else's. She cannot find anyone willing to die, so she eventually joins her lover in death.

Other notable death figures in the cinema (though they might better be described as Angels of Death) are Jack Benny in *The Horn Blows at Midnight* (set to destroy the world), Richard Burton in *Boom* (in which a dying millionairess, Elizabeth Taylor, wants him as her last lover) and George Jessel in *Hieronymus Merkin*. The most disconcerted death figure in films was Cedric Hardwicke in *On Borrowed Time*. When he comes to collect an old man (Lionel Barrymore), his intended victim chases him up an apple tree and refuses to die.

Left
Warren Oates slumps over his Maxim gun while William Holden, leader of The Wild Bunch, prepares to make his last stand. Made in 1969, Sam Peckinpah's movie set new standards – lower ones, according to some critics – in cinematic violence and death, littering the screen with bodies. In his later films, notably Straw Dogs (1971), the director extended the frontiers of screen violence even farther. Sadistic violence is a commonplace of the contemporary cinema and protest is now muted

Left
The death of Marilyn Monroe in 1962 from an overdose of barbiturates rounded out the substance of a myth: that of the 'sex goddess', unable to find happiness with any husband or lover, dying as a sacrifice to the hang-ups of modern society. She was the creation of that society; its symbol; and its victim. Touchingly vulnerable and tragically unsure of her very real talent, she has become a cult figure. Her potent myth was reinforced by Norman Mailer's 'faction' (fact plus fiction) biography of 1975

Left
Just as Marilyn Monroe was a sex symbol for Everyman, so James Dean – seen here in a frame from The James Dean Story (1957) – was a symbol of revolt for Everyman's teenage children in the 'fifties. His status as the archetypal 'outsider' was fostered in such movies as East of Eden and Rebel Without a Cause and irrevocably established when he died in his Porsche sports car in 1956, aged 25. His myth is paralleled by that of the earlier 'sex idol' Rudolph Valentino, who died in 1926

The Nature of Death

Death is seldom of short and painless duration. It usually involves a slow and agonizing dissolution of mind and body. The crucial question is: Do we have the moral right to sustain life at any cost?

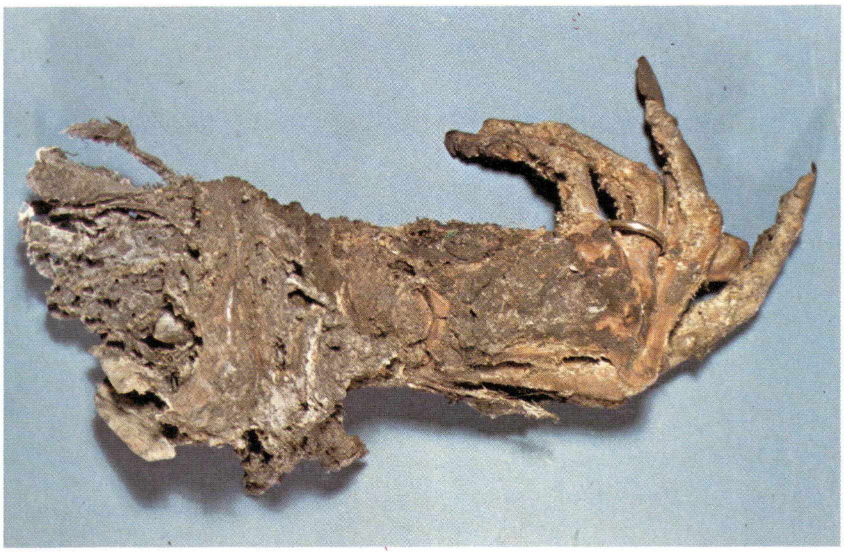

Above
A bomb which destroyed a house in Brighton, southern England, in 1943 blew one victim to pieces. The only part of the body ever recovered was this hand, hurled by the blast into the roof of a house opposite. When discovered 13 years later, the hand had become mummified. It was identified by the ring

Right
A carrier bag containing the corpse of a new-born baby, found in a telephone booth in a London underground station. The post-mortem showed that it had been born only a very short time before and that no attempt had been made to deal with the umbilical cord or afterbirth. The nose and mouth were still blocked by birth fluids, which had prevented the baby from breathing. There was no prosecution, since no criminal act had taken place and the body had not been disposed of secretly

The Final Definition
The Oxford English Dictionary defines death as 'The final cessation of the vital functions'

The Last 40 Winks
According to researchers at the Veterans Administration Centre in Florida, more people die around 6 a.m. than at any other hour. The cause is believed to be linked with an interruption in the normal breathing pattern

One of the few comments made by Boswell, in his life of Samuel Johnson, that lack his usual perception was:

> 'It matters not how a man dies, but how he lives. The act of dying is not of importance *it lasts so short a time.*'

The italics are not Boswell's, for indeed no one would question the first part of the generalization—it is a part of what André Maurois wrote so charmingly about in his 'Art of Living'; but only a poet or a philospher could think of death as an event of short duration.

It may be comforting to hope with Tennessee Williams that 'Death is one moment and life is so many of them', but such a conception is false, even in its physical sense. To many, death comes only at the end of an agonizingly protracted illness, the outcome of which has been written clearly on the wall for years. The slow erosion of mind and then body resulting from dread diseases of the nervous system like multiple sclerosis or Parkinson's disease is no 'short-time' passing, either for the victims or for those who have the responsibility of caring for them. There is, too, the slow grinding down of fine intellects that is the fate of 'dissidents' taken to mental hospitals for 'treatment' for their political beliefs, and of those who have their defences against illness undermined by privation, malnutrition and despair.

What constitutes death, actually, now that intensive care can sustain a body in a 'living state' artificially for an indefinite period, even when the brain has become dead as a result of a road accident? How long, indeed, can it take to die? And who can assume the moral right to determine the hour of death—using clinical observations which have proved fallible often enough in the past? The law has had to make certain rules in connection with the taking of life, but has, in its wisdom, never made a determined attempt to define death.

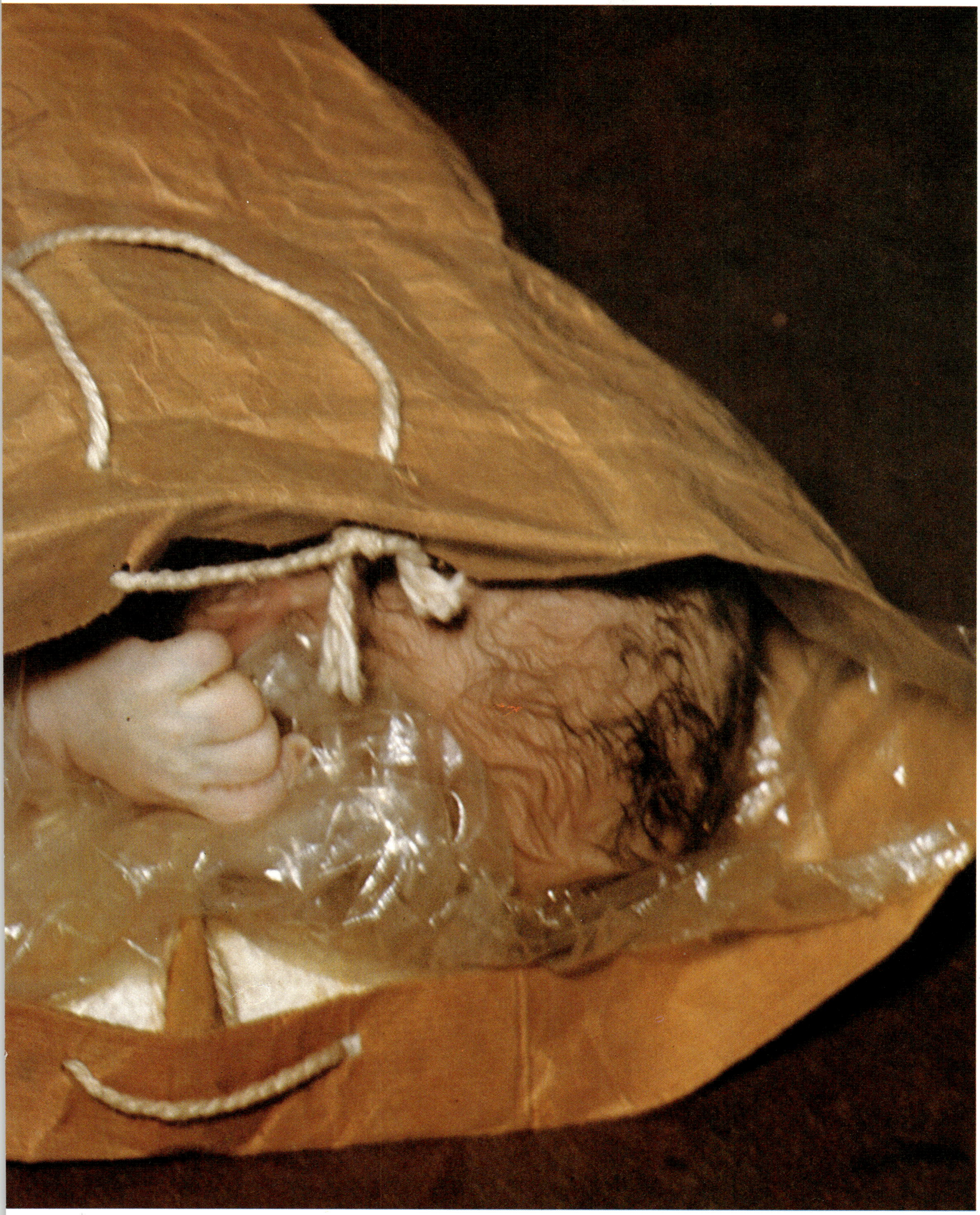

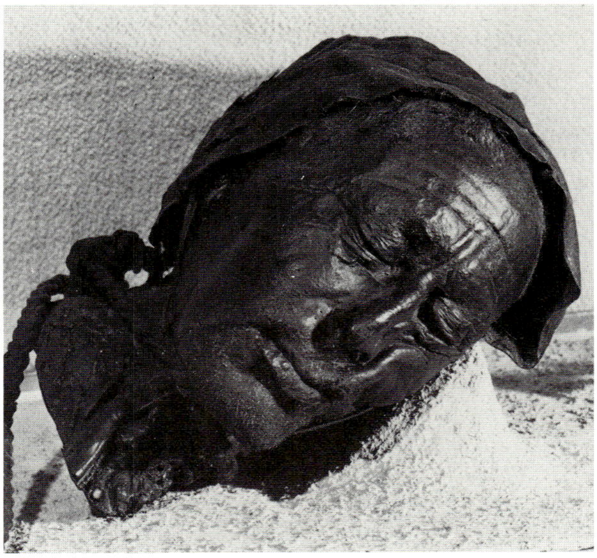

Above
Coroners were held in low esteem in Britain during the last century, as this contemporary cartoon makes clear. It was the coroner's job to inspect the body before issuing a death certificate, but the inspection was too cursory to ensure that death had really taken place

Above right
Still perfectly preserved, this head of an Iron Age man was found in a Jutland peat bog some thirty years ago. He was strangled with the leather rope which remains round his neck, but his features are surprisingly peaceful. For more than 2,000 years, he had lain undisturbed, his leather hood on his head, and a day's growth of beard on his chin

Life Sentence
White blood cells live for only 13 days. Red blood cells exist for about 120 days. Nerve cells can survive for 100 years

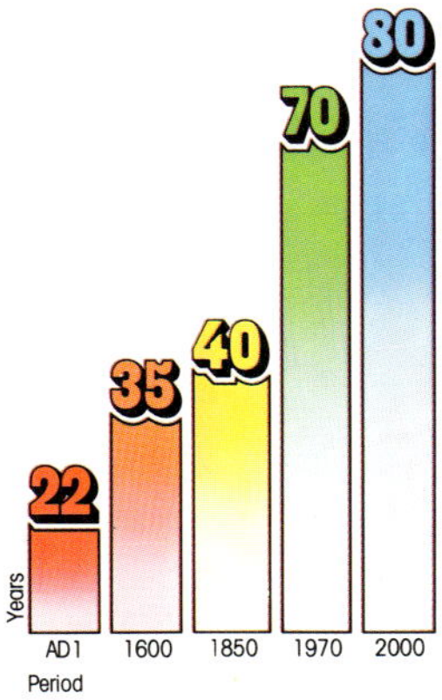

The Trend Towards A Longer Life
More and better-quality food, generally improved hygiene and living conditions and, more recently, higher standards of health care have all helped to contribute towards longer lifespans in human beings

The Oxford English Dictionary was curiously wise when it defined death as: 'The final cessation of the vital functions'. Changing views, and the availability of the means to sustain life artificially, have given Milton's words: 'Over them triumphant Death his dart shook, but delayed to strike', a meaning the poet can never have envisaged. The stillness of death, with non-existent pulse and breathing, unresponsive reflexes in the eyes or limbs, and even an electrocardiogram (ECG) or encephalogram (EEG) showing nothing, no longer mean that there is not even a tiny spark of life in this 'electrocuted' boy, that 'drowned' swimmer, or that rejected lover who has taken an overdose of drugs. On the contrary, they have become a warning of the dire consequences of overlooking the most minute such spark. The majority of deaths are obvious of course, but most countries insist that a death must be certified by a doctor before the body is committed to a mortuary. Even then, mistakes can happen, as the Brussels artist, Wiertz, so graphically reminds us in his picture of the hand of a 'corpse' raising the lid of a coffin from the inside, while on it can clearly be seen the premature legend: 'mort du choléra; Certifie par nos docteurs' ('Died of Cholera. Certified by our doctors').

Pressures are mounting to force doctors, lawyers and politicians to define medically and legally the moment of death. But should such judgements be left to ordinary mortals, however qualified they may be?

In 1957, the 78-year-old widow of a lawyer was found with suicide notes and an empty box of sleeping tablets by her side. She was removed by undertakers to the public mortuary and certified dead by a doctor. Six hours later a young police officer, called to identify the body, found her to be breathing. A year earlier, this time in Melbourne, a woman sat up and spoke to the police officer detailed to search the body in the mortuary! A similarly bizarre experience befell a pathologist at a London hospital shortly after World War II. A woman certified dead by a casualty officer was seen to swallow shortly after being placed naked on the mortuary slab for an autopsy to be performed. She lived for a further nine hours.

How can such frightening things happen? The pulse may be impalpable in those shocked by injury or loss of blood, the breathing imperceptibly shallow in drug overdoses, the ECG and EEG a mere flicker in cases of gross head injury. It would hardly be practicable to admit all such cases to hospital for observation—'just to be on the safe side'. The conclusion must be that life will never be without its risks, even the rare risk of premature certification. In legal terms, death has taken place when it is certified to have done so by a doctor—after he has assessed the physical signs, the clinical features he has been taught to search for with care before certifying. In metaphysical terms, however, the conception of the end of life is not so clearly defined. We do not know what happens after spontaneous, self-supported physical existence has ceased. We can only hold beliefs.

Living to a good old age and remaining strong in mind and body are as dependent on the quality of our genes as they are on eating properly and refraining from smoking and heavy drinking

In Elizabethan times, the expectation of life was a little over 35. By Queen Victoria's time it was about 65. Today, thanks to modern surgery and therapeutics, antibiotics and newer concepts of public health, it is nearly 75. The toll taken by measles, diptheria and tuberculosis has been reduced to nothing. Only cancer remains the scourge it has always been, as do man's own follies: obesity, arterial disease and associated hypertension. We are thus faced with geriatric overpopulation, which has been brought about by medicine. The biblical 'three score years and ten' have crept up nearly half a decade and we shall soon 'expect' to live to 80. Our end will be the same, however—death, 'his dart delay'd' a little, while the state attempts to care for the ageing population.

Ageing is not simply a physical process in which the body tissues mature and then deteriorate at a rate commensurate with the passage of the years. Some people last noticeably better than others—either in mind or body—and the fortunate in both. Actuarial experts and geriatric physicians agree that one's chances, generally speaking, lie not so much in the lap of the gods as in the quality of the genes provided by one's parents, together with adequate nutrition and wise and effective treatment of any illnesses which may come one's way. Longevity does not favour those who take liberties

Left
Wiertz, a nineteenth-century artist working in Brussels, was terrified that he might be pronounced dead and put in a coffin while still alive or, even more nightmarish, that he might actually be buried alive. So fearful was he that he might be wrongly certified dead by some slipshod doctor, that he painted a number of pictures on this macabre theme, in an effort to draw public attention to the possibility. 'Mort du choléra. Certifié par nos docteurs' – 'Died of cholera. Certified by our doctors' reads the legend on the coffin lid being pushed up by the desperate man in the picture. Fear of being buried alive induces many people to opt for cremation

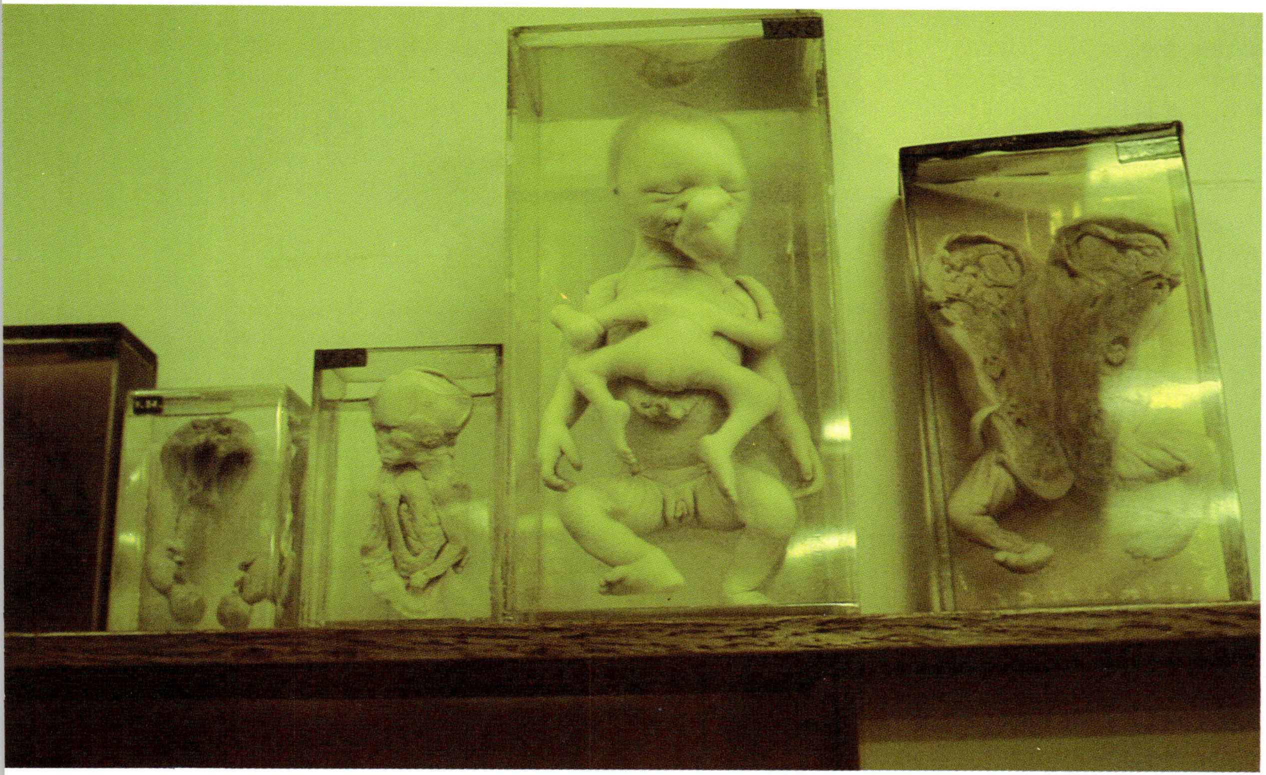

Left
Advances in medicine, new techniques in cosmetic surgery, can often repair the disfiguring effects of man-inflicted injury. But when a baby is as terribly deformed as these, which are preserved in King's Cross Hospital, London, even modern medicine can do nothing for them. It is as well that they are usually born dead, or else survive for only a brief span of time. Those that do survive into infancy and middle age may lead rather miserable lives, especially those with severe handicaps

Below left
Uprooting a tree in Hampshire, in England, in 1967, workers found these human remains. The roots of the tree had grown right through the body of a man lying dead in a ditch. From the bits of clothing still adhering to the remains, it was possible for investigators to identify them as being of an inmate of a mental hospital in the area, who had disappeared some seven years earlier

with their bodies: over-eating, drinking alcohol, smoking, drug-taking or refusing to take any exercise at all. They reap what they sow, and regrets usually come too late. We know that a diet high in tri-glycerol encourages the 'furring-up' of the vital coronary and cerebral arteries, which can lead to deterioration in the functional efficiency of heart and brain: we accept the US Surgeon-General's statistics and those of Sir Richard Doll in Britain, showing how much the risk of lung cancer increases with heavy cigarette smoking. Just the same, many people accept that a high tri-glycerol diet and heavy cigarette smoking are dangerous and still continue to indulge in them.

As we age, the heart muscle shrivels, the liver and kidneys shrink and the brain loses weight, its ventricles enlarging to fill the vacant space in the skull vault. The remarkable skills displayed by the mind deteriorate, and the sensible among us learn to adapt themselves to their limitations. This adaptation, plus increased experience and time deliberately allowed for thought, decision and action, is regarded in many as wisdom. Man would do well to face the process of ageing with

Freezing for Survival
In some cases, it is an advantage to live in extremely cold conditions. The lower the body's temperature, the less energy is required to sustain life

Evidence Unseen
Legally, the doctor who signs a death certificate need not have seen the patient either before or after death. If he has not attended the dead person professionally in the 14 days preceding the death, the Registrar of Births and Deaths will refer the certificate to the coroner

Radiating Deterioration
Severe radiation poisoning stops cell division. It also results in the disintegration of the gut lining and inside of the mouth, and the falling out of the hair, as well as having other extremely unpleasant effects

Outwardly Dead
In cases of hypothermia or severe drug-induced coma, the heartbeat can be so weak as to be indistinguishable, although the victim is alive. Barely perceptible signs of life may also exist in near-fatal drowning and in electrocution

Weight Loss
When a person dies, the body always loses a certain amount of weight. No one has discovered why

equanimity, calmly and deliberately seeking out and savouring its particular pleasures, denied to youth. Senescence and final decay may never be reached, while physical decay and loss of faculties, which are more trying to others than to the ageing person concerned, are nowadays often met with understanding and affectionate tolerance.

More and more insistently it is being asked whether it is worth making use of scarce and expensive resources to keep alive people who are merely 'vegetating'

The physical changes which take place in the body and organs where 'life' is being artificially maintained are, in fact, post-mortem changes. The delicate cells of the brain, the conduction system, the renal parenchyma, cannot survive the initial disaster of circulatory failure and suboxia, and suffer irreversible change. This is followed by softening of the brain, cytolysis, necrobiosis and swelling of the liver and kidney, as well as of other cells in tissues with more complex functions. Organs like the brain become semi-liquid—a slime which it would be foolish to expect to function again. 'Brain death' is the popular term for this. The public readily understands it and has come to accept that it justifies switching off the life support system.

In the case of what might be called 'normal deaths', which form the great majority, the doctor accepts the fact of death, but *only when he has made absolutely sure* that life has departed. He can be sure of death if he hears no heartbeat through his stethoscope after listening for several minutes, coupled with the cessation of breathing and the 'stillness' of death. In rare cases, EEG and ECG records showing a total lack of brain and heart activity decide the matter. Muscles may still twitch if pricked or pinched, but do not contract spontaneously. In the elderly, *cooling* often starts before death, and, after a short plateau, develops the steep incline that results in the loss of two to three degrees an hour at the beginning. Later, the rate of heat loss falls to one to two degrees an hour, and finally to only a small fraction of a degree an hour.

The body often *feels* cold at death, but it is not finally cold (the temperature of the surroundings) for 20 to 24 hours. Body temperature is the only really helpful source of information regarding the lapse of time since death, and must be recorded whenever this information is needed, ie in cases of suspect and criminal deaths.

Death is inevitable and few seem to approach it in any anguish of spirit when it derives from natural disease, for the ability to feel pain has been lowered by sickness or the clouding of consciousness. In those under medical and nursing care, the added balm of pain-killing drugs or the remarkable euphoria that comes from the famous 'Brompton Mixture'—a cocktail made up of heroin, cocaine and gin—ease the way out. The peace of mind that the wise and humane use of drugs can create is a relief both to the dying and to their saddened relatives.

Right
This measures brain waves. If the line appears flat, this indicates that there is no electrical activity in the brain, and to all intents and purposes, the patient is considered to be dead—unless he is a victim of electrocution

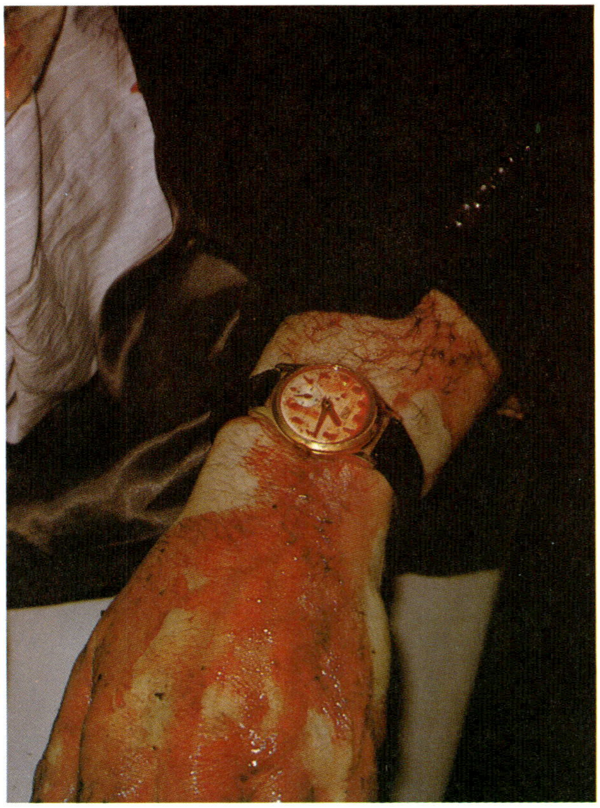

Bottom right
The hands of this battered wrist watch stopped at 1.15, almost certainly the time of death. It must have been in the very early morning, as well, since the man had last been seen at 1.00 am, leaving a drunken party. His body was found at the foot of a flight of concrete stairs some six hours later

Rate of Decay
As soon as death occurs a number of chemical processes are initiated which cause the body to decay

Time elapsed	Changes
Immediately	Muscles relax
Immediately	Brain begins to liquefy
10 minutes	Eyes cloud over
3-5 hours	Onset of lividity (colouration of skin due to draining of blood)
6 hours	Rigor mortis begins (in face)
12-18 hours	Rigor mortis completely established
12 hours	Body temperature down to approx. 25°C (77°F)

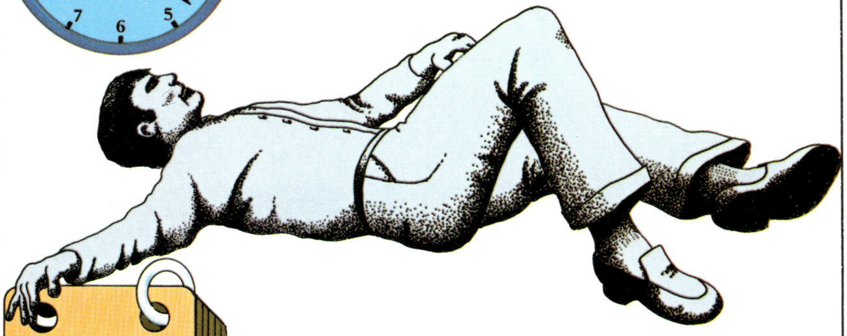

Time elapsed	Changes
24 hours	Body temperature down to that of environment
24 hours	Process of decomposition begins
24 hours	Rigor mortis begins to disappear
36 hours	Rigor mortis disappears altogether
2 days	Green and purple stains on abdomen
3 days	'Marbling' of veins due to presence of gases
5 days	Distended appearance

Euthanasia, however, is a different matter. Can there be anything but anguish in the act of killing those loved ones whose lives are doomed by the dread diseases that cripple the nervous system, such as Parkinson's disease, multiple sclerosis, the progressive destruction wrought by repeated strokes, or the brain damage that can sometimes result from using certain vaccines or drugs? Has euthanasia a defensible place in an intelligent, humane society? It is, after all, wilful killing, even though it cannot be equated with the inexcusable crime of murder, which is punishable by law, and is often enough defensible on humanitarian grounds. Medicine has gradually convinced an anxious public that, when life has become a mere vegetable existence, as after irreparable brain injury, the time may come for a firm hand to switch off the system that is merely maintaining a 'living state' in tissues which are biologically dead.

On the other hand, the plight of those deformed by thalidomide or irreparably damaged by drug addiction, or who are dyslexic or epileptic, is a challenge to medicine, not an argument for euthanasia. Medicine only has responded to the thalidomide challenge—tardily in the event—by developing a remarkably efficient artificial hand, thus sweeping away many of the clouds that seemed to hang for life over thalidomide victims.

So what of death? Is it just an incident, an unavoidable event that marks the final running down of the machinery and spirit whose creative days have come to an end? Leaving aside the physical aspects, is death simply a quiet fade-out, or is it an agonizing struggle to survive? Is there a sense of the metaphysical? Can man see himself existentially when what Saurin called the 'long torment' of life comes to an end? We do not and cannot know. Even those who have been snatched back from a disaster on the operating table and have survived with a conscious mind can recall only a series of confused dream-like 'events'. Some of these have even been recorded in correspondence in medical journals such as *The Lancet* by doctors who have themselves come near to death. It would, however, be more instructive to examine the various reactions to *approaching* death. As is well-known, when the mind is in a state of high tension, reactions to physical stimuli tend to be exaggerated. A frightened woman, roused by shouts of 'fire', got out of bed and went to the door of her bedroom, while her daughter looked on from her own bed. Opening the door, the old lady was confronted with a 'wall of flame shooting up the stairway' some 20 feet away. Clutching her chest, she gave a scream of terror and dropped dead. The subsequent post-mortem revealed nothing more than the normal physical changes of old age, for the physiological reflexes which slow—or, sometimes even stop—the heart rhythm are not detectable in the dead body.

This reflex arrest of the heart action, and often of the rhythm of breathing, comes from stimulation of the vagus nerve 'receptors'—in the eyes, the skin and the viscera, the danger-receptor and the areas of the brain which react to danger—and is well-

Stress in the Sky
Scientists in California have suggested that people who live close to an airport have a 20 percent higher death rate than people who live farther away. Most of the deaths are related to stress-induced diseases, such as strokes and cirrhosis of the liver

Great Expectations
In Elizabethan times, life expectation was just over 35. In the Victorian age, it was around 65, now it is nearer to 70

Shock Treatment
With electrical stimulation, human muscles will contract for between one and two hours after death

Vital Liquid
Normally, brain cells deprived of blood die within three to four minutes . . . five or six at the outside if deprived of oxygen to a lesser degree

Slim Chance of Survival
About 80 percent of victims of severe drug overdoses are dead when found

Above
An elderly woman used this cup for the drink she took to wash down the overdose of pills with which she committed suicide. She was found dead in bed by her daughter, who removed the cup and threw it in the dustbin before reporting her mother dead. She hoped that this would enable her mother to avoid the stigma of suicide

Left
The body of this coloured woman was found in a flat which she shared with her husband. The couple were known to be on bad terms. After she had been killed by blows to the head with a bottle and her body left slumped in the armchair, it was set on fire, after having been doused with paraffin. The body later slid off the armchair onto the floor. The post-mortem revealed a split in the scalp and a fracture of the skull. Often a post-mortem reveals crucial evidence of death which may not be apparent during the initial investigation

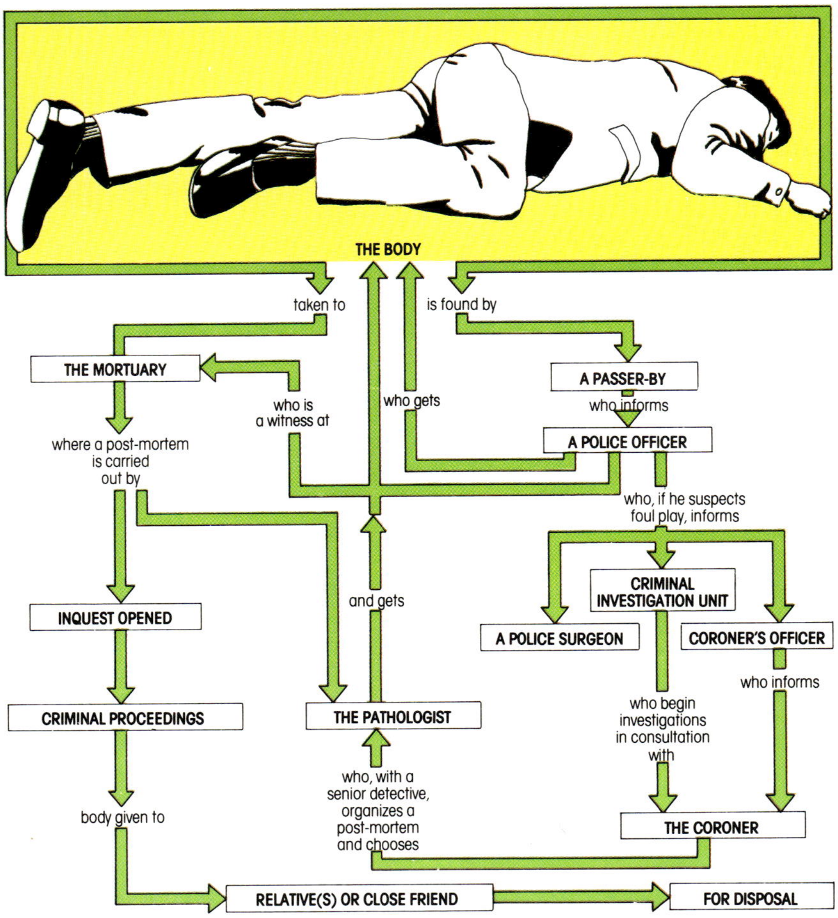

Due Process
Whenever a death occurs in unusual circumstances a number of legal arrangements have to be gone through, such as a coroner's inquest, before the body is released for disposal. If the death is accompanied by suspicious circumstances, the police, the criminal investigation unit, the police surgeon and a pathologist will be called in

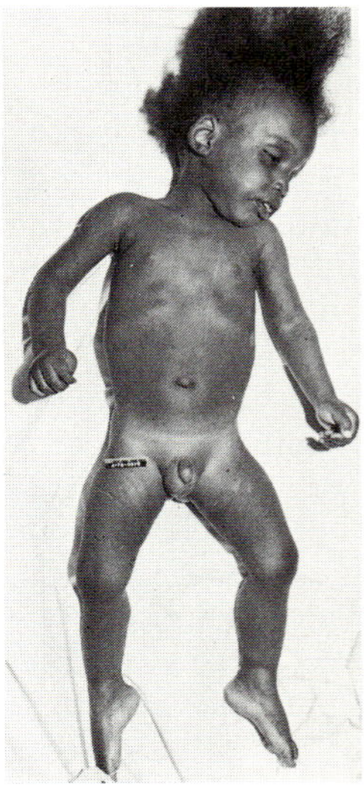

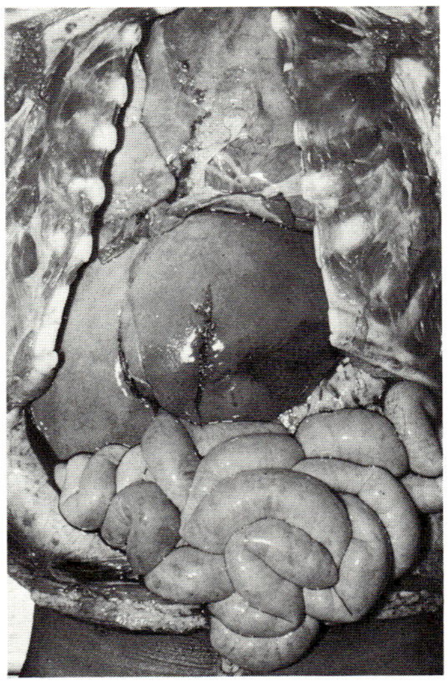

Top right
This boy was killed by his father, whose defense at his trial in Pittsburgh, Pennsylvania, was that the child had fallen off a chair (shown here with a rule, to indicate its height from the floor). In fact, the father had hit the 18-month-old baby repeatedly in the abdomen. As the photograph centre right shows, the liver was ruptured by the blows, and the child died in minutes.

Above centre
A casual 'pick-up' on the promenade had a tragic sequel – rape and murder. The photograph on the left shows a red purse and a knotted piece of material lying in the angle of a wall and the bottom step of a concrete stairway. Bloodstains can be clearly seen. The next photograph shows articles of clothing torn off the woman lying on the sand. As she was dragged along the beach to meet her grim end, the woman's sunglasses, belt and another scrap of material were left behind. She was then raped and strangled

known to doctors dealing with anxious patients. Dentists know that some apprehensive patients will faint at the first prick of the needle, before any injection, and in a recorded hospital death a young man died in similar circumstances. 'If they do that again', he said, after a painful needling of his chest for the withdrawal of fluid, 'I'll die'. And he did, the instant the needle reached the sensitive inner lining of his chest on the next occasion, three days later.

How slender the thread on which may hang the life of anybody whose emotional tension runs high! 'In the midst of life we are in death', the burial service declares, and indeed it is so. Death may strike so quickly that the victim may not even have time to ask: 'Where is thy sting?' Every pathologist accepts the fact that in some cases of sudden death – from 'vagal inhibition' or other functional reactions like the instant anaphylactic reaction to unacceptable protein, for instance – the cause of death is not going to be demonstrable in the dead body. Physical happenings do not necessarily leave discernible signs: an electric current can arrest heart action without any visible sign after death.

How strong is the motive to murder? Is it the product of boredom or feelings of vengeance, or does it spring from some far deeper psychotic frustration?

Violent and unnatural death has always troubled the ordered, disciplined world, and like other evils, has become the subject of both statistical and causal study. State-organized restraining measures are essential. Suicidal inclinations can be redirected through psychiatric advice and treatment, and aggressive behaviour curbed, or confined to the institutions all states have had to create to deal with behavioural disorders. The purpose of statistical study is to direct corrective measures effectively, but government statistics, in this field at least, tend to appear some two years after the year to which they refer. It may thus be more purposeful to look at the constant causes of crimes of violence. The Marquis de Sade believed that boredom is a prime factor in the attitude of indifference to death, either suffering it or inflicting it. In his view, sexual perversion, violence, the act of killing, relieve boredom and create an excitement that makes the possibility of death of little or no importance. The appetite for mugging, robbery, rape and, if it happens, killing, often nourished by slum poverty and degradation or the lack of any kind of opportunity to show even a glimmer of talent, is so strong because violence offers an opportunity to put some colour into life, or death. Statistics would appear to show that this is a major cause of the increase in crimes of violence during the past decade.

Thoughts of violence take root in the mind for a variety of reasons. Ten of what he regarded as the most common ones were listed by David Abrahamson in 1973, in his book, *The Murdering Mind*. The list begins with 'extreme feelings of revenge and fantasies of grandiose accomplishments, which may result in the acting out of hateful impulses'. It continues with 'loneliness, withdrawal, feelings of distrust, helplessness, fears, insignifi-

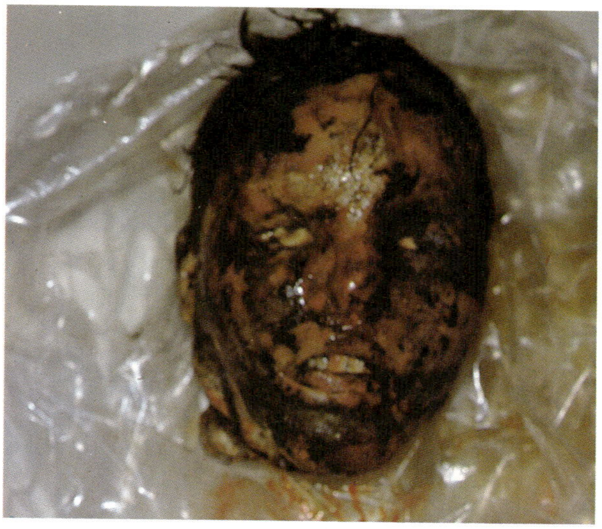

Left
The mummified, darkened head of a Pakistani girl of 15. It was found on the London to Manchester rail track, having been thrown from a moving train. The girl's father, enraged because she wanted to marry someone he regarded as unsuitable, had seized his daughter by the hair and hacked off her head with a carving knife. Wrapping it in plastic and putting it in a carrier bag, he left the girl's body in London and boarded a train to Manchester, throwing the head out of a carriage window when a suitable opportunity presented itself. Such crimes are usually the work of psychotic or extremely unstable personalities

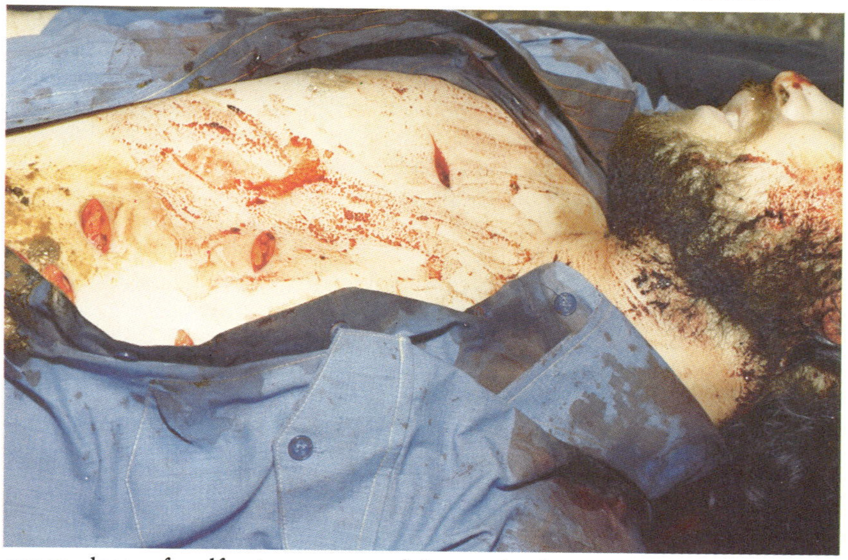

Above
Multiple stab wounds in a youth killed in an affray outside a London club. The absence of cuts on his hands indicated that his arms had been pinioned to his sides, while a number of people stabbed him repeatedly in the chest and abdomen. The sharpness of the knives which were used is evident from the very acute mouths of the slit-entry wounds about the body

Left
Still clutching the rifle with which she had shot herself, a housewife lies on the living room floor of her home in a pool of blood. Her hand was stiff from cadaveric spasm, and the fingers were curled so tightly round the trigger guard, that they had to be prised free in order to remove the rifle

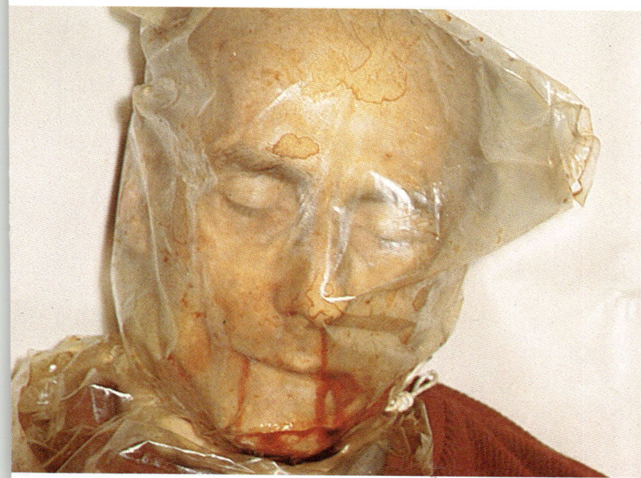

Bottom left
The elderly man with a plastic bag over his head did not mean to commit suicide. He used the bag in the course of the masochistic practices in which he often indulged. His aim was to bring about fading consciousness, but the bag suffocated him, causing asphyxial bleeding from the nose. It is apparent from the records kept by coroners that such 'accidents' occur all too frequently

cance, loss of self-esteem caused by early (pre-Oedipal) childhood experiences'; 'sexually over-stimulating family situation because of primal-scene experiences'; 'errors of spelling or speed related to emotional disturbances in early (pre-Oedipal) childhood'; 'tendency towards transforming identification. Blurred self-image, suggestible, impressionable'; 'inability to withstand frustration and to find sufficient gratification for expressing hostile, aggressive feelings through constructive outlets'; 'inability to change persistent egocentricity, self-centredness (primitive narcissism) into elements of healthy ideals and conscience (ego ideals and superego elements) resulting in dependency on and contempt for authority'; 'suicidal tendencies, with depression'; 'seeing the victim as the composite picture of the murderer's self-image'; and 'history of previous antisocial or criminal acts associated with threatening, or committing, murder'.

This list, compiled in psychiatric terms and language, reflects the more inaugurative attitude of the psychiatrist, usually the result of study of those accused of crime. It does indicate how varied the roots of violence may be, but it bears little relationship to the experience of the police or the pathologist. A pathologist would take a more practical viewpoint and use more down-to-earth terms. He sees the victim—not the perpetrator nor the event, far less its background—and he has to set out his views in words which are intelligible to a jury. As far as the pathologist is concerned, killing by violence (except for war) usually falls into one of the following categories:

Right
Ambushed and shot in broad daylight by terrorists of the Red Brigades, a bodyguard lies spread-eagled on a Rome road, a short distance from the white car in which he had been travelling with the Italian politician Aldo Moro. After shooting the guard, the terrorists kidnapped Moro, later killing him as well. Terrorist killings for political or ideological ends have become almost an everyday occurrence, not only in Italy, but in many other countries as well. They are also becoming more desperate, as security services step up their own activities

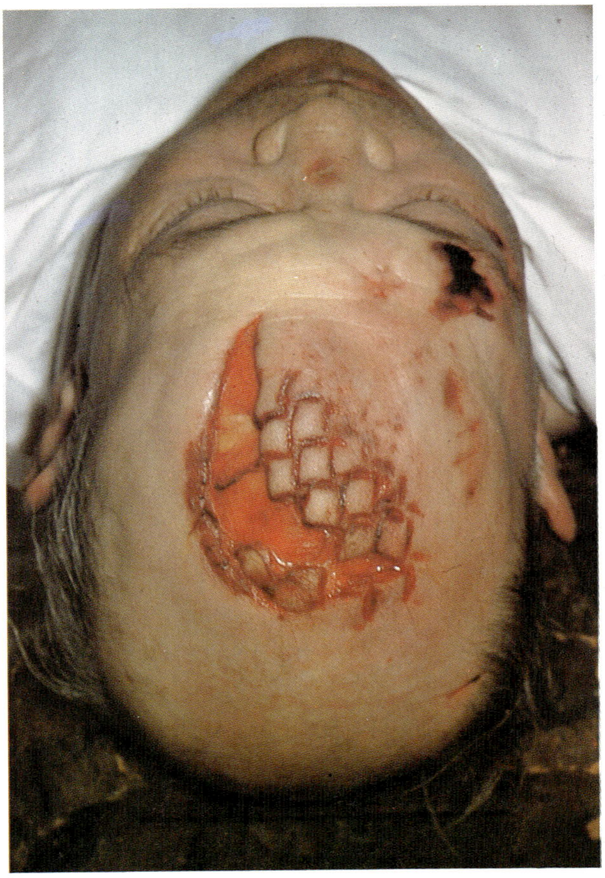

Top right
It was thought at first that this man had been murdered. However, when the body was moved from the bottom of the cellar stairs in a public house where it was lying, the police found that the diamond pattern on the cranium matched that of a wire mat at the foot of the stairs. This showed that the man had fallen down the stairs and landed on his head, and the cause of death was ultimately recorded as misadventure

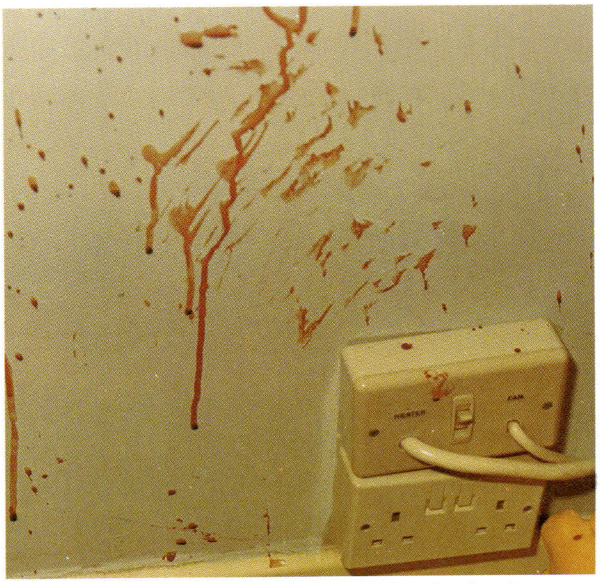

Centre right
Bloodstains on the wall of a house in which a man had been stabbed to death by his wife. The spattering on the wall indicates that the man coughed up blood before collapsing onto the floor, where his body was found. The fact that some of the blood has run down the wall also points to the man having coughed up blood when he was stabbed. The smearing of some of the stains was probably caused by the husband's clothing brushing against the wall as he collapsed onto the floor. Since the blood splashes are finely distributed and the smears are superficial, it is almost certain that the stabbing did not take place against a wall. Sometimes it is extremely difficult to pinpoint accurately how the person has died

Laying a Clue
If a body has remained undiscovered for some time, it may be possible to determine the time of death from the development of maggots hatching from eggs laid on the corpse by flies or, where the time of the last meal is known, from the rate of the emptying of the stomach into the small bowel

A Flaccid Mind
The sign that death ('brain death') has taken place is the general softening of the brain that follows when the blood, or oxygen, supply fails

1. The outcome of domestic quarrelling or infelicity, in which bickering and tension end in an outburst of violence. If blunt instruments are used, they tend to be such things as a kitchen pastry roller, a chair, or a mantelpiece clock. Often, the victim is not battered to death, but strangled. Murder as such may not, initially, have been intended.
2. The result of a quarrel, usually between men and often after drinking. Even nowadays, fists are more common than knives, and fatal results are more likely from the victim being knocked to the pavement than from a knife blade accidentally piercing the heart. Deliberate, intentional murder by knifing is uncommon.
3. Uncontrolled sex urges in which rape, if met with opposition, ends in the attacker overpowering the victim—and, often enough, stifling her cries by putting his hand over her mouth or round her neck. Some of these incidents involve children, who are lured into woods or to a river-side by promises of sweets or some other trifle. Some rapes are also the outcome of an uncontrolled, often sadistic, sex drive. Killing may not have been intended.
4. Baby battering—a relatively recent crime in which a background of domestic tensions, often in crowded and relatively poor homes, ends in one or both parents assaulting the child. This is a sinister outcome of the pressures of modern times. It did not exist before World War II.
5. Killings accompanying another crime, such as robbery, mugging, or breaking and entering.
6. Planned murder—usually for personal gain, or for convenience.
7. Motiveless killings. Where little girls are abducted and killed, usually after a not always perverted sexual assault, the motive, if not the mental state, seems apparent, but this is not always so. A lust to hurt, a kind of sadism, is apparent in some of the injuries which are inflicted by attackers.
8. Assassination. To the carefully planned assassinations of kings and political figures in earlier years, where nothing more complex than the removal of a prominent figure was involved, must now be added the terrorist killings of ordinary people by bombing, shooting or other violent methods, in furtherance of the aims of such groups as the Provisional Irish Republican Army or the Palestinian El Fatah. Massacres by shooting and threats to kill hostages have introduced an element that has so far escaped psychiatric classification.

There can be almost no room for doubt that war provides an outlet for violence, and a legalized one, at that. When authority transfers thousands of men to the battlefield, the incidence of violent crime at home tends to fall. In time of war there is unification of effort and an almost euphoric uplift, which, to a great extent, relieve frustration with the boredom of day-to-day life. Death itself becomes an everyday event, and armies of men seek relief in camaraderie and song: only, as history shows, to revert to their customary behaviour on return to civilian life. More significantly, the former fighting man brings back into civilian life the aggressiveness and rough masculine attitude he has been trained to cultivate. He does not talk things out, but settles them with a karate chop, as he has learnt to do in warfare, where there is no place for tolerance.

To many whose lot is constant physical suffering, who face illness for which there is no cure, who are crushed by poverty, misery or the loss of a loved

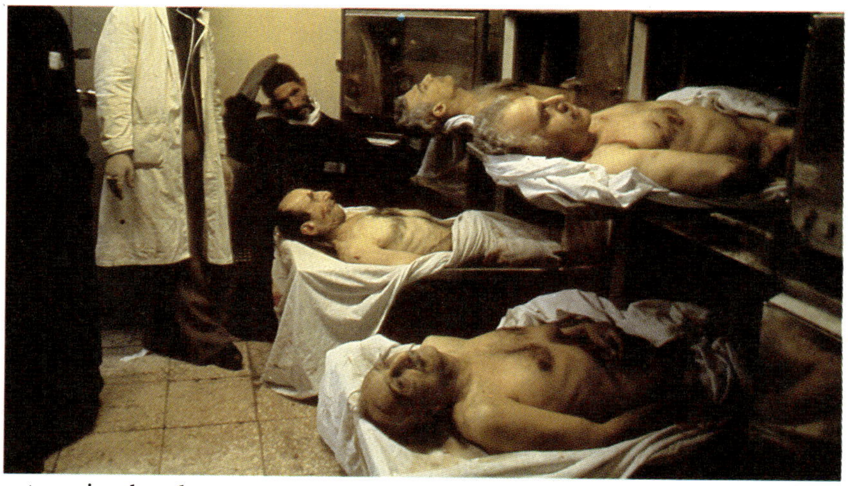

partner, death by suicide is a matter of personal choice, a way out always available to those who have lost hope.

Self-killing, whether for the reasons mentioned above or for ritualistic motives (such as the Hindu widow casting herself on her husband's funeral pyre, or the Japanese committing hara kiri for the sake of honour), has been part of the life of every society since the dawn of civilization. Suicide rates fluctuate, rising in times of suffering, depression and anxiety, and falling in times of prosperity, and war. During the anxious period before World War II, when Hitler was severely oppressing the Jews of Germany and threatening to unleash war in Central Europe, the suicide rate rose dramatically, but as soon as war actually broke out, it returned to normal.

The methods adopted by those who commit suicide stem partly from considerations of simple practicality—drowning, hanging, cutting some vital artery in the throat or wrist, stabbing, shooting, jumping from a great height or self-precipitation underneath some moving vehicle like a train. All, one would think, require more than a little determination. An easier way is to take an overdose of drugs, usually combined with drinking alcohol. The days of drinking corrosives like strong acid or lysol have long since passed. Placing one's head in a gas oven is no longer a suicide method in most countries, principally because of the substitution of natural gas for 'town' gas.

Suicide, in some particularly tragic way, could be taken as a useful barometer of the state of world affairs—a low suicide rate indicating a pattern of relative normality, a high rate showing abnormal stress in international relations

However, a suicide attempt may be nothing more than what psychiatrists call 'a plea for help', a trial-run aimed at bringing back an erring husband or persuading creditors to re-schedule a debt. It can also look very like suicide when a youth is found trussed and hanging from an attic beam. Only the knowledge that adolescent youths often 'experiment' with ties and slings and nooses, intentionally courting danger, sometimes with sexual overtones—they dress up in female clothing or arouse themselves with titillating photographs—tells us that 'accidental death' would be a preferable verdict and that suicide was never intended. The masochist likes to be tied up and reduced to helplessness, even to having a close brush with death, but he does not actually wish to die.

The classical methods of suicide have been repeated by generations of sick and depressed people: few choose any method other than a single bullet through the head or the heart, cuts across the throat, quiet self-suspension in some secluded room or an excess of pills or capsules, usually with a farewell note of regret. Curiously, suicide notes are often affectionate but seldom ask for sympathy. Apologies for causing distress or trouble are far more common. Directions for disposal of the body never seem to come to mind, though the victims of deliberate suicide usually seem to have remained calm. Relatives giving evidence at coroners' courts frequently say that the suicide victim, though depressed and worried, and, perhaps, showing suicidal tendencies for many weeks or months, had changed a few days before the incident and had shown all the signs of relief and a new contentment. This would seem to result from having taken the

Above
Once generals in the army of the Shah of Iran, these men were shot after being summarily tried by the revolutionary courts set up after the Shah had left the country and the Ayatollah Khomeini had seized power. The courts did not restrict their activities to military men. A number of civilians were shot as well, and for a time the government was helpless to prevent such retribution from running its full course

Top left
Aftermath of the bombing of the Hilton Hotel in London in 1974. Two women were killed and many other people injured, when a parcel left in the crowded lounge exploded. One of the women had come to the wrong hotel to meet a friend, while the other had arrived 20 minutes late for an appointment. The bombing was the work of the Irish Republican Army

Centre left
In addition to the normal hazards which confront commercial aircraft, they are also at risk from hijackers. In September, 1970, Arab terrorists hijacked four airliners to Jordan, taking their passengers hostage. One plane was flown to Cairo and blown up there. The other three were destroyed in Jordan. Two of them can be seen here, burning

Cost Assessment
Long before inflation became a way of life, the value of the chemical constituents of a human body left to a medical school in America was about one dollar. Today, the value is nearer to six dollars

Death without Warning
In a survey conducted among 178 psychiatric patients in a clinic in Scandinavia, over two-thirds apparently preferred sudden to protracted death. The proportion favouring instant death was highest among the young and middle-aged

Right
This bloody footprint was found on the stairs of a house where a man had been murdered in a first-floor room. The man whose print it was denied any link with the crime. He told the police that he had not known that the man on the first floor was dead, and had been going upstairs to try to patch up an earlier quarrel with him. He was proved to be lying

Bottom right
Handprints in blood on the wall near a settee where a homosexual victim was stabbed while lying on his face. He had managed to rise to his knees and clutch at the wall before sinking to the floor. His hands were covered with blood because he had tried to staunch the flow from his wounds

Centre
After tying up his own arms sufficiently to stop himself from struggling later, this man committed suicide by hanging himself from a tree in a quiet wood. Suicide notes are often affectionate, but seldom ask for sympathy. Apologies for causing distress or trouble are far more common

Coming to Terms
Terminal patients often go through a series of five stages in accepting the reality of their approaching death:

1. Rejection of diagnosis
2. Anger, in the form of 'Why me?'
3. Submission to God, i.e., prayers
4. Depression
5. Acceptance, often aided by 'terminal' drugs

Examining Doubt
About 30 years ago in the USA, nearly half of all hospital deaths were followed by autopsy. Today, the figure is below 20 percent. One reason is the increasing cost of the examination. Another is doubt among doctors over the usefulness of autopsies

Unique Evidence
One infallible proof of drowning as a cause of death is the presence of diatoms – multi-cellular organisms found in water – in the bone marrow of the brain, which it can only have reached in a 'live circulation'

City of Suspicion
In London, about 30 percent of all deaths are treated as obscure or suspicious and reported to the coroner. In the rest of England and Wales, this figure is nearer to 20 percent

Proof by Procrastination
It is often wise to delay reporting the injuries found in a post-mortem for 24 to 36 hours; during this time, bruises may 'show up', after spreading from deeper regions in the body

final decision—to commit suicide. Many suicides are at peace with themselves once they have been able to make up their minds to act on their impulse.

Whereas suicide appears to involve a high degree of preparedness, murder is much more likely to be the result of a fortuitous series of events coinciding with an abnormal level of stress or provocation

Most deliberate killings are, in a sense, chance happenings. Remarkably few murders are planned. Under provocation, self-restraint gives way to violence, and harsh words turn to blows. What the law so often refers to as a *mens rea*—the calculating, evil intent to kill—is absent. Nevertheless, violent death behind which there has been the intent to hurt 'grievously', as the law says, is murder, for there is an important element of carelessness as to what happens—or callous indifference to the need for help, treatment, an ambulance, or indeed admission to hospital.

Some murder victims have been quite unaware of the finger beckoning them to their fate, especially when poison has been used. Indeed, one wonders how often the victims of deliberate homicidal killing see death approaching. Do those who lie trussed semi-conscious in a sack about to be dumped, or those about to be shot for belonging to the wrong gang have coherent thoughts of any kind? Or does fear blot out everything else? Does the sharp pain of the first stab or the first bludgeoning blow to the head supersede the perception of fast approaching doom? Happily for the victim, strangling, bludgeoning and the like bring early loss of consciousness. The same cannot be said of savage beatings or the callous muggings of elderly citizens, who are then left to their fate in a deserted alley or country lane.

Violent death resulting from accidental causes, such as when disastrous air crashes occur, can tax the organizational powers of local authorities to the very utmost

Air crashes, in which scores or even hundreds of people are killed, can present the police with tests of organization for which plans have to be formulated in advance. Local forces are well aware of the expert help at their disposal, but during the hours that must pass before the experts arrive at the scene, the chances of a successful investigation may be completely nullified by untrained handling of the wreckage.

The first major tasks: identifying the dismembered or burned dead and their belongings, and collecting the debris that may furnish vital clues to the cause of the disaster, can be seriously hampered—or even rendered impossible—by ill-informed and premature action.

An example is the air disaster at Tenerife, in the Canary Islands, in March, 1977. Two 'Jumbo' jets (belonging to Pan Am and KLM) collided on the take-off strip in poor visibility and burst into flames. Sixty passengers managed to escape from the shattered fuselage of one airliner, but 577 others perished. The Spanish authorities put a tight cordon round the wreckage, largely to prevent looting and keep press photographers away. However, before

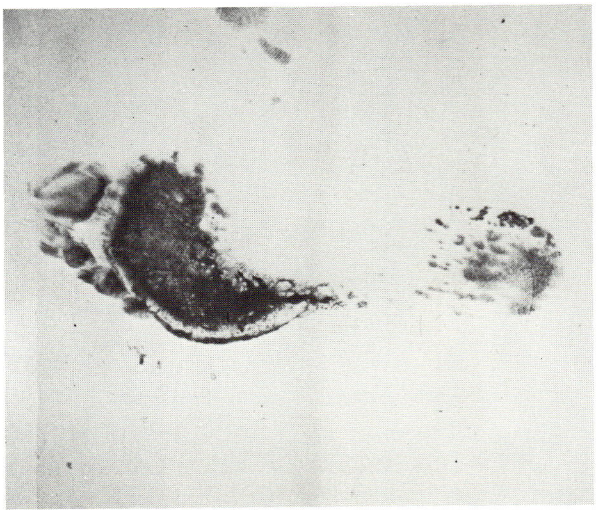

experts (immediately summoned from the USA and Holland) could arrive, the Spanish authorities had collected all the bodies either from the remains of the aircraft or from the ground where the collision had thrown them—*without marking* where they were recovered from—and dumped them in airport sheds to be numbered. No effort was made to preserve the bodies and, as no official (international) identity or property forms were available, local police forms were used. Local pathologists without medico-legal or disaster training and unaccompanied by odontological experts (for identity purposes) were allowed to start the mammoth task of performing autopsies. There were no facilities for technical photography, toxicology (for drugs, carbon

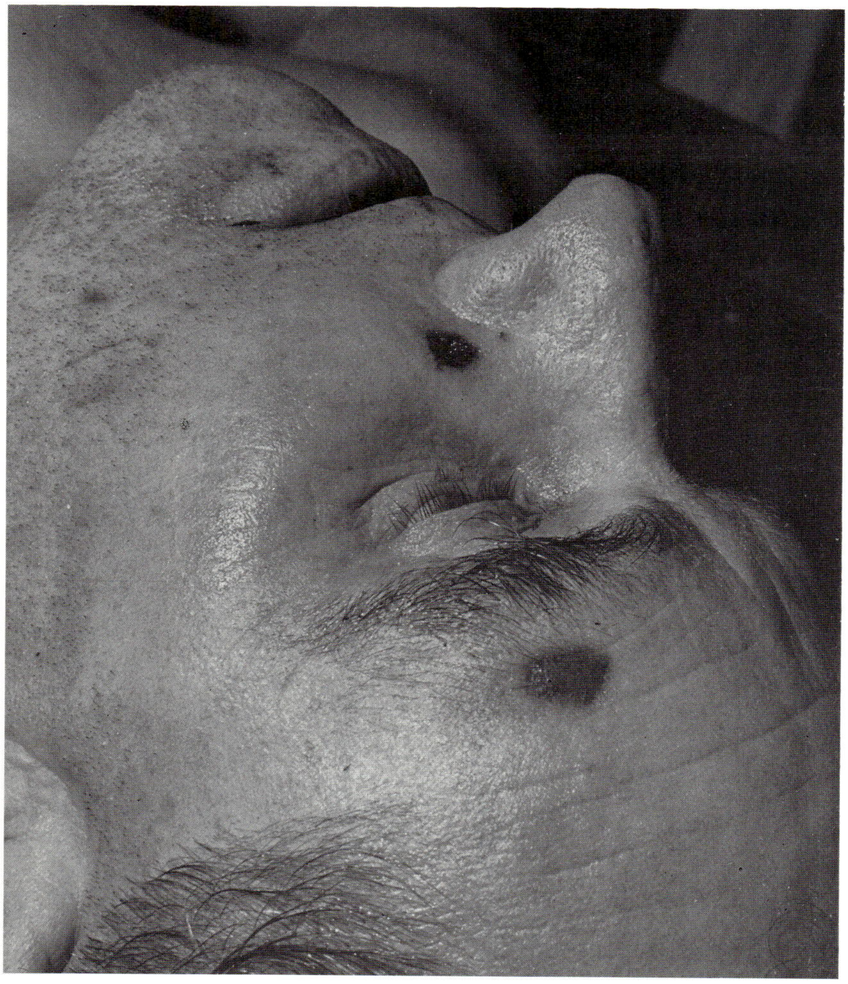

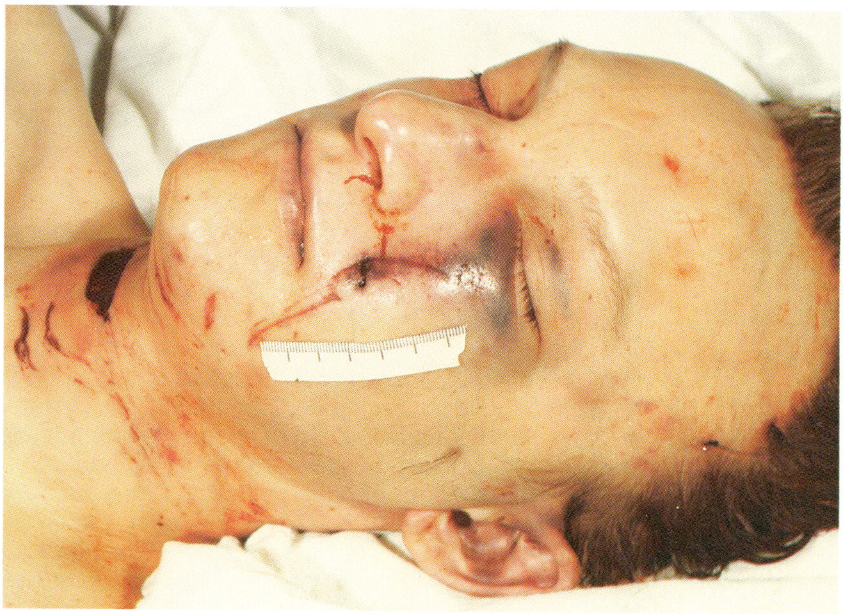

monoxide or alcohol) or serology (for matching blood groups or dismembered bodies). It emerged later that a local law specified embalming and burial within 48 hours of death—irrespective of the nature of the accident, the need to investigate its cause, or the insurance problems that would certainly follow.

In contrast, so carefully was the investigation of the 1962 Comet disaster in the Middle East handled, that all the dead—air crew and passengers—were precisely identified, and the captain of the aircraft was shown to have been suffering from serious and previously undetected heart disease. More significantly, a defect in the 'horizon indicator' of the Comet (after indifferent maintenance) was also found. This had resulted in the airliner rising too steeply on take-off and stall-crashing. All these details were vital when a civil action followed in the London High Court in connection with the payment of insurance and compensation.

The first people with training in the organization and integrated handling of the teams investigating air, rail, mining or other mass disasters to arrive on the scene will usually be the local police, summoned together with ambulance teams, nurses and doctors. Also immediately involved are: the International Civil Aviation Organization (ICAO); the regional commission appointed to enquire into the accident; the local legal authority—medical examiner, coroner, magistrate—in whose jurisdiction (for disposal of the dead) the accident occurred; the medical and

Top
There are two marks on the face. That above the left eyebrow is simply a graze, but the mark near the nose is a neat hole where the bullet entered the cheek penetrating the brain

Above
This man had his face cut about with a knife after a fist fight. His assailant then cut his throat. The throat wounds could have been suicidal, but not the face wounds, for suicides do not cut their faces, possibly because unconsciously they wish to appear composed and undamaged

Above
Violent death came to some 570 passengers when a Pan American 'Jumbo' jet collided with a KLM 'Jumbo' on the runway at Tenerife Airport, in the Canary Islands, in 1977. Investigators comb through the charred wreckage of the American airliner, searching for crash clues

Right
Airport workers haul away part of the fuselage of the wrecked KLM airliner. Although the Spanish authorities moved quickly to prevent looting after the collision occurred, they bungled the other arrangements, destroying valuable evidence

Top right
The remains of a Lufthansa Boeing 747 which crashed at Nairobi Airport, Kenya, in 1974

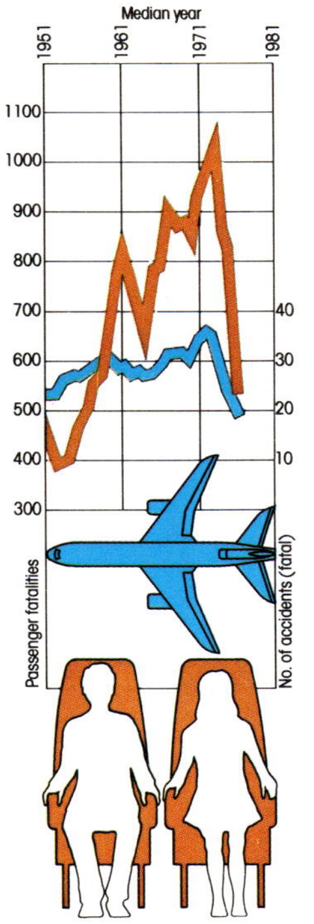

Air Safety Improves
Until the mid-1970s, there was a steady increase in the number of fatal accidents and fatalities. Thereafter the situation steadily improved

scientific team employed to examine the dead; the airline or airlines concerned, for technical matters. Since the airlines have passenger lists, they may be in the best position to inform relatives, but this duty often falls to the lot of the police or other local authority.

The ICAO is responsible for drawing up the conventions governing civil aviation. It has recommended that investigation of an accident should be the responsibility of the state where it occurs, but that observers from other countries whose aircraft are involved must be given the opportunity of attending and participating in the investigation. This gives them the right to visit the scene of the accident; examine the wreckage; question witnesses; obtain full access to all relevant evidence and documents, and make various legal and medical submissions about the steps to be taken in the subsequent enquiry.

The police must do their best to facilitate the communication of information and to ensure that ambulance, first aid and intensive care teams have unimpeded access. At the same time, the police—just as they do at the scene of a crime—ensure that nothing is disturbed and that only the injured or those endangered by fire, gas or debris are moved. Wherever possible, notes and a plan, together with a marked bag or a photograph, should record the position from which anything—a body, documents, or burning (or exploding) debris—is removed.

The ICAO has prepared a manual detailing the procedure to be followed in aircraft accident investigations. It incorporates recommendations from the International Criminal Police Organization (Interpol), and should be available at all regional police headquarters.

In the first few hours after an accident, the police should concentrate on:

(a) Ensuring a quick access for ambulance teams, as well as Red Cross and hospital nurses—and doctors, who alone are entitled to certify the fact of death. Marked posts to which cards have been attached, must be placed in the exact position from which first the injured and, later, the dead are removed, and must also be provided for personal belongings; wallets; papers; jewellery; handbags; personal baggage, and so on—and occasionally, for valuable freight. Calls for fire services, the search for the tell-tale black box, aircraft papers and any more significant parts of a crashed plane may safely be left to the more experienced air-accident investigators;

(b) sealing off the area, mainly against those who will quickly be drawn to the scene by the possibility of looting. The press may be marshalled at an information post to be set up near by.

(c) leaving the dead untouched, while ensuring that they have been marked (with numbers on waterproof labels), on certification, and are not removed until phases (a) and (b) have been completed, preferably after the arrival of the team of trained pathologists and odontologists, together with their laboratory liaison staff;

(d) supervizing the organization of reception sheds, schools or halls, where the dead may be laid out, clothed (even when the clothing is torn, partially missing or burnt) and with jewellery still in place—later to be sealed in labelled bags, so that relatives can look for papers and other means of identification. Cardboard boxes should be marked in indelible ink, not have labels tied to them. The box lids should be similarly marked;

(e) arranging waiting rooms, relatives' toilets, and so on. The Red Cross and Salvation Army will be found to function remarkably well, usually without waiting for an official request. Ministers of religion and priests whose services are likely to be needed should be properly warned at an early stage of the proceedings.

Coroners vary in their attitudes. Some arrive on the scene with their officers at an early stage, while others prefer to be called by telephone 'if required'. However, they must be informed, for they are required by law to deal with the dead—to certify the causes of death and to issue burial orders. They will also have to hold an inquest, and it is for them to decide how far to go into the various relevant technical matters.

In the 1975 underground train disaster at Moorgate in London, the City of London coroner decided to make a full technical enquiry, using his standing team of experts with laboratory services, based on the capital's university medical schools. The police and underground engineers who worked with teams of local hospital doctors and nurses to free passengers (living and dead) trapped in the concertinaed coaches were careful to record (and photograph) all stages. Data on temperatures, air samples, track information, signal connections, track mechanisms, and so on were matched by a full physical, odontological and serological record, analyses for alcohol and drugs, and bacteriological tests, all of which was collated with painstaking care.

Unless such needs are foreseen, the opportunity for recording details that might *later become important* is lost. The police and ancillary teams investigating mass disasters never have a second chance. They must do everything right first time. If they do not, vital evidence may be lost forever.

Above
This British European Airways Trident crashed at Staines, outside London Airport, in June, 1972. It sometimes happens that an airliner crashes because the pilot is suffering from a disease which has gone undetected, despite regular and exhaustive medical examination. This was the case with a British Comet, which crashed in 1962. The pilot was found to have a serious heart condition. In addition, the aircraft's 'horizon indicator' had a major defect. Today, routine maintenance checks on aircraft, and regular medical examinations of pilots help to reduce accidents

Left
Spanish Civil Guards sift through the belongings of 105 British tourists and seven aircrew, killed when their chartered Comet crashed near Barcelona in July, 1970, en route to a Costa Brava holiday resort. Collecting the dead and their belongings is one of the first major tasks of expert teams investigating an air disaster. They must also collect every scrap of debris and find the crashed aircraft's flight recorder, the 'black box', which may hold the key to the crash

The Scythe of Sickness

Down the ages man has sought ways to resist the onslaught of his most lethal enemy—disease. Most of the time he fails, and the resultant toll, as during the Black Death epidemics, can reach staggering proportions. Occasionally he succeeds in suppressing a particular disease, only to find it reappearing later in a possibly even more virulent form. Sometimes, he unwittingly causes the appearance of a killer disease for which there is no known cure

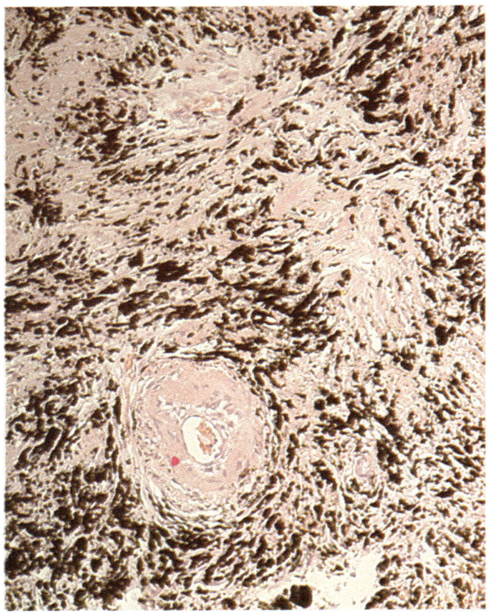

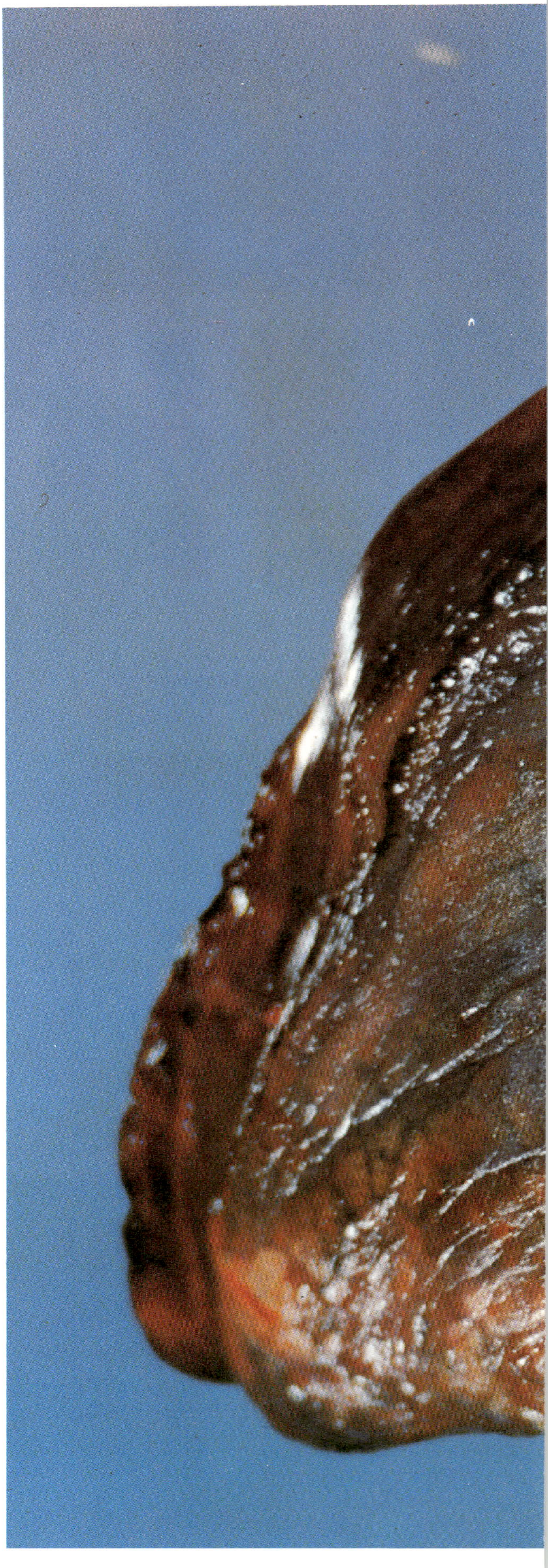

Above
When embalming a body, the ancient Egyptians used to remove the internal organs and place them in canopic jars buried alongside the mummified body. This jar once contained the organs of '1770', an Egyptian mummy which was completely dissected at Manchester University in Britain, in 1975

Above right
Anthracosis, coal-miner's lung, is the result of breathing in coal dust. This photograph shows part of the cells lining the inner membrane of a diseased lung, with the particles of coal dust showing up as irregularly shaped black patches. Such lung ailments are of very ancient origin

Far right
Cancer of the lung. Like tuberculosis and leprosy, lung cancer is an ancient disease. Today, the two main causes of lung cancer, which kills more people in the West than any other malignant disease, are cigarette-smoking and carcinogenic agents of pollution

Deceptive killer
The bacillus that caused the Black Death manufactures a protein that appears to kill some animals, while remaining harmless to others

On June 10th 1975, at Manchester University Medical School, England, under the recording eye of television cameras, a series of postmortems was performed on some of the oldest preserved human remains on earth. An Egyptian mummy known anonymously as '1770' was completely dissected; another 16 human mummies were thoroughly examined by modern, non-destructive methods such as radiography, tissue biopsy and electron microscopy.

During the initial process of mummification, internal organs (lungs, liver, stomach, kidneys and intestines) were removed, via an incision in the left side of the body, and placed in canopic jars buried alongside the mummy. Occasionally, the preserved organs were replaced inside the body.

Lung tissue from one of these canopic jars at Manchester revealed damage similar to that seen in the lungs of stone workers and coal miners who have been inhaling silica over long periods of time. The silica causes inflammation of the lungs with scarring and permanent inefficiency. '1770' was not a stone mason, but the particles found in the lung resembled sand and it seems apparent she was suffering from sand pneumokoniosis.

Other human remains were found to contain a type of liver fluke and a nematode worm—strongyloides—in the stomach and intestines, while '1770' carried about in her abdominal wall the calcified remains of a parasite, a guinea worm, *Dracunculus medininsis.*

These investigations reveal that the peoples of ancient civilizations suffered from diseases that are

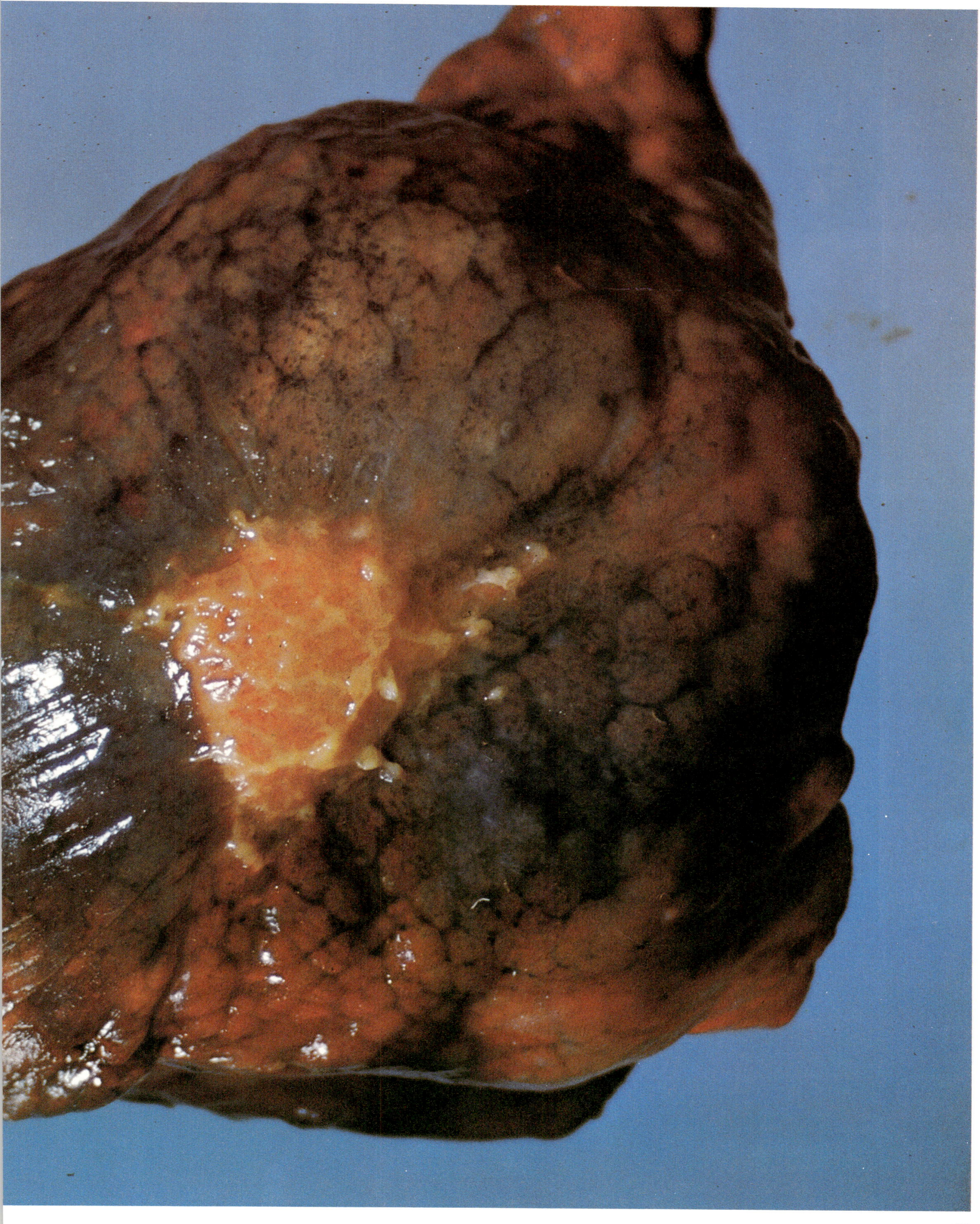

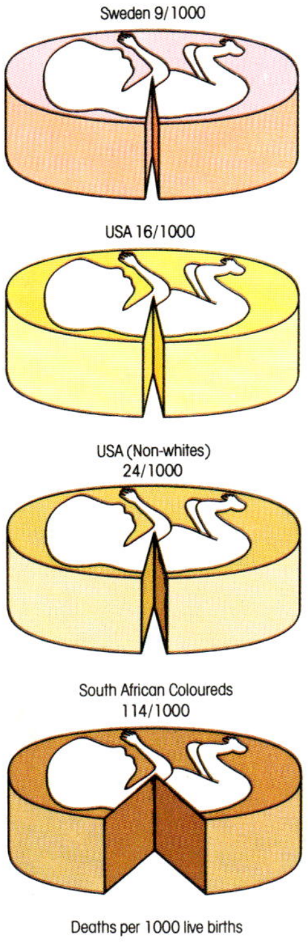

Death in the Cot
In the poor countries of the world, and among certain depressed minority groups in the industrialized West, the combination of poor medical facilities, an inadequate diet of low nutritive value and inferior living conditions all conspire to ensure that infant mortality in such circumstances will be high

prevalent even in tropical countries today. Parasitic infections appear to have been especially common in earlier centuries.

One mummified head in the Manchester series, for example, was shown to have a portion of damaged brain tissue where the blood supply had been cut off due to narrowing of the blood vessels and the formation of blood clots. This condition, known as cerebral thrombosis, has been noticed by a number of researchers. Other investigators have found mummies suffering from tuberculosis of the spine with abscess formation, arthritis, appendicitis, leprosy, poliomyelitis, smallpox and pleurisy. Even Java man, one of the earliest of human remains (and the skeleton only) was found to have a tumour of the thigh bone.

Two scrolls of medical interest were found on the river Nile at Thebes last century. Named after their finders, the 'Edwin Smith papyrus' and the 'Ebers papyrus', each was written around 1500 BC, but it is believed that some of their contents date back as far as 4,000 BC. The Ebers papyrus describes the diseases then known to man and their treatment: the Edwin Smith papyrus deals with various surgical conditions.

Some of the best descriptions of recognizable medical conditions are to be found in the Hippocratic writings. These are texts composed by the father of Greek medicine himself (tradition dates his life 460-377 BC), and by his pupils and may comprise the remains of his library on the island of Cos. Though some of his books are called Epidemics, the word then meant 'visits to places'.

Hippocratic writings describe a disease (mumps) visitation on the island of Thasos. Descriptions of three- or four-day fevers must have been tertian and quartan malaria. Some modern medical historians have identified diphtheria, tuberculosis and influenza among his accounts, though these symptoms are less obvious. There are some surprising omissions, among them measles, smallpox and bubonic plague. Were these diseases never encountered by Hippocrates and his pupils?

What archeological and written evidence there is on the subject of disease among ancient civilizations suggests that our ancestors were afflicted by much the same sicknesses as we are today, though some have now been eradicated, while several new diseases have emerged. But, judging from the Ebers papyrus, the chances of finding cures and relieving suffering in the days before Christ was practically impossible.

Down the ages, the scythe of sickness has swung in uneven strokes to affect the life of mankind. Different diseases have had different effects over the centuries, and the battle between man and disease has been an uneven one, with man often losing, though he has sometimes won in certain areas. Biologically, disease and the sweep of death-dealing epidemics can be seen as one of nature's many mechanisms to control population growth, although advances in medicine since the last century have considerably lessened the incidence of epidemics and reduced their toll when they do occur.

The effect of epidemic disease on populations is graphically described in the Bible, in Deuteronomy: '. . . He will bring upon you once again all the diseases of Egypt which you dread, and they will cling to you. The Lord will bring upon you sickness

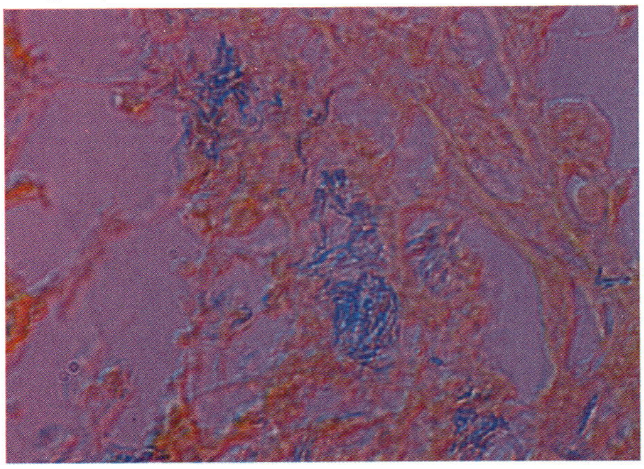

Above right
Tuberculosis bacilli (dark blue areas) invade a human lung. They are among the oldest and most widespread of all. Wherever white men have settled, they have taken tuberculosis with them, and it is as rife in Africa and the East as it used to be in Europe centuries ago. Today, it is no longer a killer in Europe or America. It has been brought under control by the use of antibiotics and vaccines, and by improved hygiene

Right
Achilles binding up the wounds of Patroclus. A contemporary Greek copy of a sconce dating from the fifth century BC, the period of Hippocrates, the father of Greek medicine. But, despite the progress he made in medicine, it was virtually impossible then – and for centuries afterwards – to find cures or relieve suffering

Right centre
The mummy of an Egyptian princess embalmed during the Roman period. Disease played a major role in the decline and fall of the Roman Empire. First of all, malaria, with its chronic, relapsing nature, was endemic. In addition, there were three major epidemics – smallpox, bubonic plague and measles

and plagues of every kind . . . until you are destroyed. Then you who were countless as the stars in the sky will be left few in number . . .' The diseases of Egypt included malaria, blindness due to trachoma—which is still a problem today—tuberculosis, and 'leprosy called elephantiasis which is peculiar to this country', according to Pliny.

Measles, smallpox, bubonic plague and malaria played a major role in the decline and fall of the Roman Empire. It is also widely accepted that the plague of the Philistines referred to in the Bible was, in fact, bubonic plague

In England, the Black Death wrought terrible slaughter on the population during the fourteenth century. From 1.1 million in 1086, the population had risen to 3.7 million by 1348, when the Black Death struck. During the plague years the numbers fell to 2.2 million and did not reach the pre-plague total again until 1601.

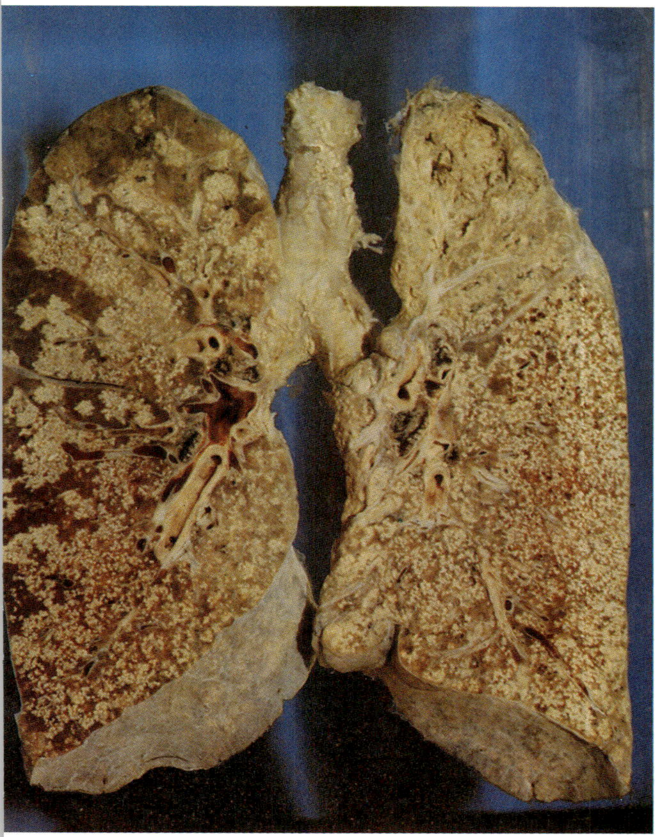

Diseases and epidemics have played a large part in changing the course of history. The invading Mongol army which laid siege to the trading city of Caffa, on the Black Sea, brought with it the black rat and bubonic plague, which spread to the Mediterranean via the trade routes and thence to northern and western Europe. So many people died—about a third of the whole population of Europe—that the effects lasted for six generations, and the progress of civilization was retarded for several centuries.

A mystery illness toppled the city state of Athens at the zenith of its influence—during the age of Pericles and Sophocles. According to Thucydides, the symptoms were raging fever, a red throat and skin ulcers. It has never been explained or identified and has no counterpart among modern diseases. A quarter of the Athenian army died from this sickness in one year—430-429 BC—and then the causal agent burnt itself out completely, never to reappear. Athenian society never fully recovered, however, and the Spartans gained the ascendancy.

The Roman Empire was similarly affected by disease but it was a slow, debilitating and cumulative process spread over centuries, rather than one catastrophic sweep of sickness. It must be borne in mind, however, that the area and population involved were vastly greater than in the case of Athens. It is possible to make informed guesses about the individual organisms which played a major role in the decline and fall of the Roman Empire. There were numerous minor epidemics of uncertain origin, but three major outbreaks stand out: the Antonine Plague of 65-80 AD, an even worse pestilence which lasted from 251-266, and the so-called Plague of Justinian (542-543). At the height of the pestilence, 5000 deaths a day were said to have occurred in Rome. Tacitus recorded that 'houses were filled with dead bodies and the streets with funerals'. These outbreaks could have been caused by measles or small pox. According to some scholars, the literary record points to the second and third centuries as the period when these diseases emerged. Certainly, the interval between their occurrence in Rome is consistent with the recirculation of a disease to which there was little immunity. It is also known that malaria was endemic

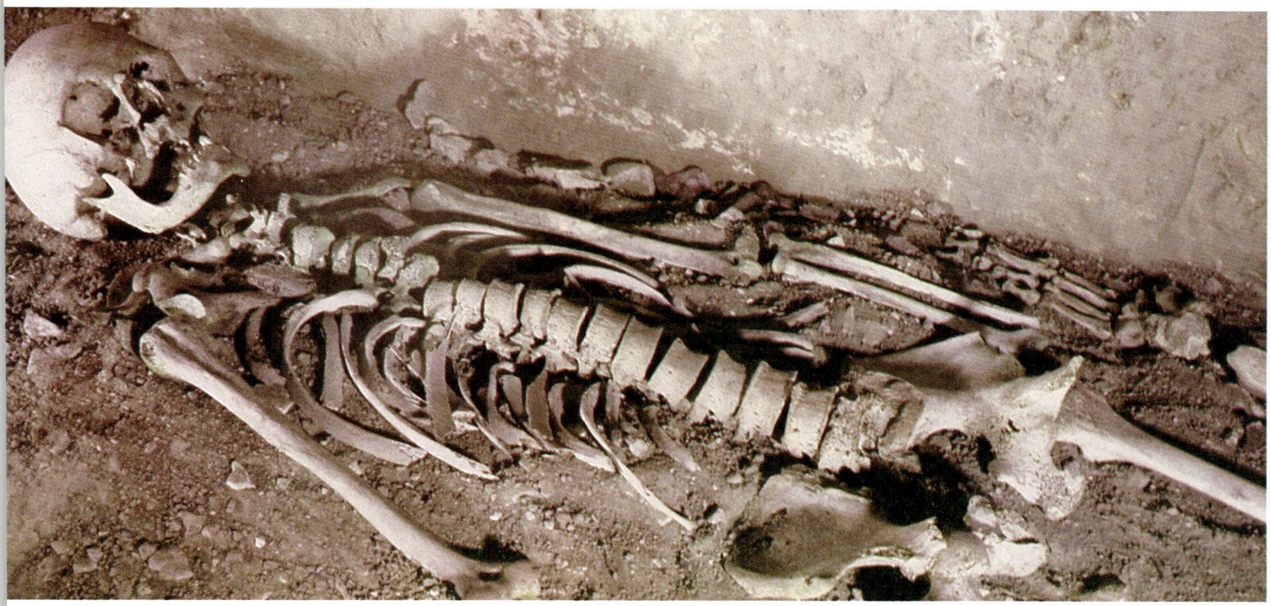

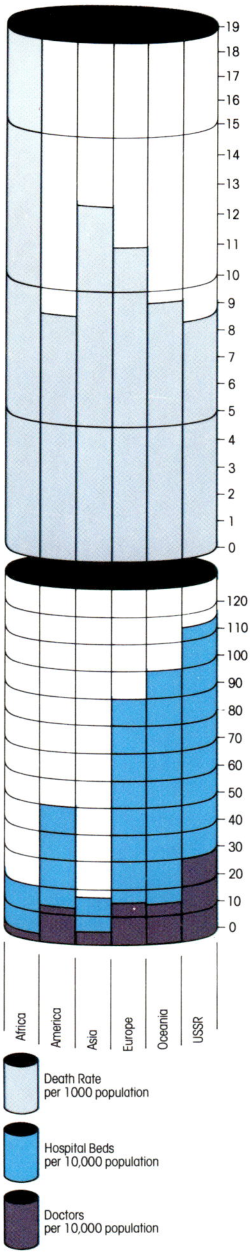

The Link Between Death Rates and Medical Care
In the six major demographic areas of the world, there is a strong and obvious ratio of death rates, and the number of doctors and hospital beds available

Above left
Calcified lungs. Physical factors like dust can cause lung disease, as can bacteria and viruses, as well as sensitivity phenomena like those which cause asthma. Disorders in the circulating blood can also cause lung disease. In addition, the lungs may be involved in malignant disease

Left
Primitive man suffered to a tremendous degree from diseases like rheumatism and arthritis, but he did not usually live long enough to be crippled by them. Skeletons like this one in a burial pit have been investigated by scientists and show that primitive man was also liable to such diseases as bone tumours

Above
Since the cause of bubonic plague was unknown until early in this century, all attempts to stop it from spreading were based on guesswork. In Portugal as this 1899 coloured Sunday supplement shows, houses thought to be contaminated by the plague were burnt down

throughout the Roman Empire. The chronic, relapsing nature of malarial disease, added to the intermittent shocks of the other epidemics, weakened the whole structure of the Empire and Roman society. From the clear description by Procopius, the Plague of Justinian can be identified as bubonic plague—caused by *Pesturella pestis.* Its undoubtedly true that this and other epidemics also seriously weakened the military strength of the Empire.

Not until 1905 was it discovered that the black rat flea was the carrier of bubonic plague. In the seventeenth century, it was thought that dogs carried the disease, and many were slaughtered by special dog-killing patrols

According to some students of history, there is no evidence that the disease occurred at any time during the pre-Christian era. Nevertheless, the idea that the plague of the Philistines referred to in Chapter Five of the First Book of Samuel was the bubonic variety is widely accepted. The 'emerods in secret parts' mentioned there could mean the swellings in the groin, which are symptoms of the disease, since—although the original Hebrew is not easily translatable—'emerod' is thought to be synonymous with 'haemorrhoid'. This means a swelling or 'tumour'—the word used in the New English Bible. The coincidental rise in the quantity of tumours and the excessive numbers of rodents is clear from a reading of the biblical text. For centuries, the relationship between rats and bubonic plague remained undiscovered. It was not until 1905 that the life cycle of the black rat flea was finally understood.

In fact, surprisingly few of the bacteria and viruses whose normal hosts are insects or wild animals cause human disease. However, these few, of which the plague bacillus, *Pesturella pestis,* is the most important, are wholesale killers. Bubonic plague waxes and wanes, depending on many factors. These include not only the temperature and climate, but also the movement of infected rats and the size of the population.

No one knows when this microbe first came to inhabit the black rat and its fleas. In ancient times there were probably two disease pools and, judging by the spread of the illness, one was in the region of the Asiatic steppes. From these reservoirs of infection the disease travelled along the trade routes, or followed in the wake of advancing armies. Ships remained the best of all means of distribution. The black rat is a skilled climber and would have had no difficulty in running up the mooring ropes of vessels waiting in port. Moreover, a ship's hold provided a relatively safe, food-laden 'burrow'. On land, coastal ports, with their food stores, slums and street garbage formed an ideal habitat in which the rat could breed, almost completely free of natural competition.

By the time of Justinian, the infected fleas and their hosts had spread all over northern Africa, southern Europe and the Near East. Cities became deserted and civilized societies disappeared almost overnight. Europe sank into the Dark Ages. Then bubonic plague disappeared as mysteriously as it had arrived, and returned to a remote disease pool until 1347. In December of that year, it crossed the Black Sea and re-entered the Mediterranean basin, having earlier broken out among the invading armies of a Mongol prince. So rapidly did it spread across Europe that it had literally leapt across the English Channel and infected inhabitants of a south England coastal district by July, 1348.

The symptoms of plague appear swiftly, and without warning—fever, delirium, headache, vertigo and severe thirst, together with swollen glands (plague buboes) and purpura (purple areas caused

Right
As this print shows, when the Black Death struck in England in 1348, doctors donned leather gowns, wore masks with a spice-filled nosepiece and carried a wand, so as to be able to feel the pulse without touching the patient

Scourge of the Black Death
The Black Death, which appeared in London in 1348, wiped out over half of England's population, which was then approximately 3½ million. World-wide, the Black Death claimed approximately 20 million victims

Killing en masse
The plague bacillus generates a particularly virulent infection. During the Black Death epidemic, it caused the deaths of an estimated 25 percent of the entire population of Europe. Of those infected during the Hong Kong outbreak in 1899, 95 percent succumbed to the effects of the disease

by broken blood vessels called plague tokens). Mortality was very high: in the region of 90 percent. Doctors could do nothing for their patients. In dread of the disease, they were garbed in leather gowns and wore masks with a spice-filled nose-piece, designed to purify the inhaled air. They carried a wand to enable them to feel the pulse without having to come into personal contact with the patient.

Vapours were supposed to spread the disease, so bathing was prohibited lest the skin pores opened up and received the disease! At every sixth house, fires burned aromatic substances to cleanse the air. Perfumed water was liberally sprinkled on skin, clothing and furniture. Eau de Cologne is a lone survivor of these plague waters and essences.

In fear, people fled from the towns and those suspected of spreading the disease, such as the Jews, were then burnt to death.

Dr Sydenham, the 'English Hippocrates', viewed the Great Plague of London in 1665 from outside the city. He noted that it 'seldom rages violently in England above once in thirty or forty years' and 'sometimes the disease, tho' rarely, is not preceded by any perceptible fever and proves suddenly mortal: the purple spots, which denote immediate death, coming out, even whilst the persons are abroad about their business'.

According to other sources and the plague posters of the day, dead carts rumbled first by night, then by day. 'Searchers', each carrying a staff of office, traversed the city. They were accompanied by dog-killers who slaughtered every dog in sight, as it was thought that the animals carried the disease. 'Churchyards were filled; to this day they stand high above the streets; when they no longer sufficed, huge pits were dug in the fields for the dead', recorded one observer.

The plague ravaged England for 300 years. In the course of the seventeenth century, cramped wooden homes with thatched roofs, where man and rat were in close proximity, gave way to spacious brick and tile. As a result, it became less easy for a flea to change hosts from a dying rat to a fit man.

Many attempts were made to curb the spread of the plague. The most effective was quarantine, which became standard practice after being tried out at Ragusa, in 1465, and in Venice, in 1485. The quarantine period of 40 days was long enough to enable the infection to burn itself out within a ship's company and stop the disease from spreading inland from the coastal ports. The last important

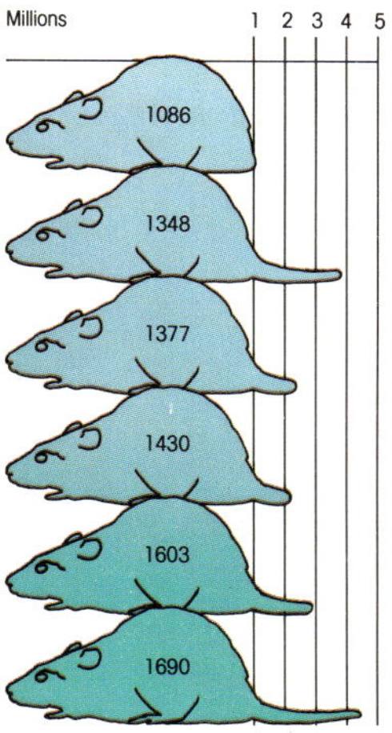

A Plague of Darkness
The Black Death, or bubonic plague had periodically visited Europe for hundreds of years before it reached epidemic proportions during the Middle Ages

Left centre
The macabre title page of Ainsworth's Old St Paul's depicting the Great Plague in London in 1665

Left and below
Medieval operations as depicted in prints in the Bodleian Library, Oxford University. Until 1163, when the Council of Tours issued an order banning the clergy from practising surgery, a considerable proportion of both medical and surgical practice was in the hands of members of the religious orders, the Benedictines in particular. By the time the Council of Tours issued its order, the medical school at Salerno, in Italy, had already been in existence for more than 250 years and had gained much knowledge of disease

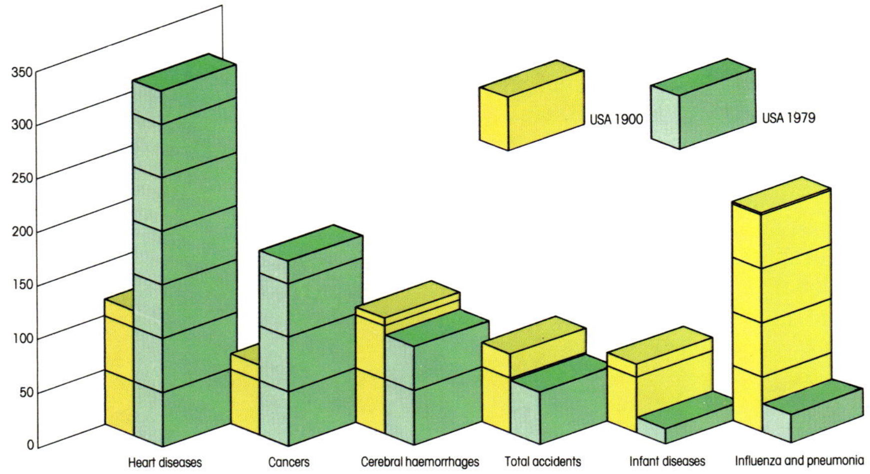

Changing Disease Patterns in the USA, 1900 to 1979
Some 80 years ago people in the USA were dying from such common diseases as influenza, tuberculosis and pneumonia. Today, the pattern has changed dramatically

Top Right
The bubonic plague microbe can be carried by a variety of rodents and their fleas, including even the common brown rat

Right
Quarantine became standard practice during plague outbreaks. It was first tried in Ragus in 1465, and again in Venice 20 years later. It was found that a quarantine period of 40 days was enough for the infection to die down among a ship's company and to prevent it from spreading inland from the coastal ports

Dying Young
As expected, the infant mortality rate is highest in the Third World, and relatively low in the affluent West, and the industrialized East

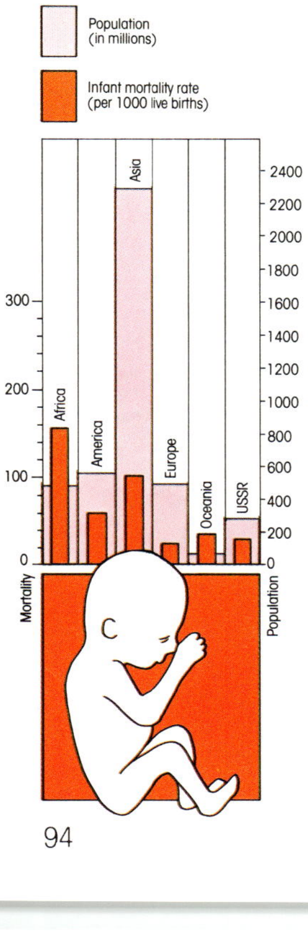

outbreak in the Mediterranean was at Marseilles in 1720, when half the population perished.

The world was relatively free from plague from 1720 until 1834, when there was an outbreak in Alexandria. Then, in the 1870s the disease raged in China, culminating in the Canton epidemic of 1894 and the crucial research work of the Plague Commission. Its members proved by experiment that it was the *Xenopsylla cheopsis* flea which was the culprit.

Bubonic plague is one of the most fascinating diseases of history, showing dramatically the effect of sickness on the world. William McNeill, in his book *Plagues and Peoples,* argues that, before Christ, disease pockets occurred throughout the world and acted as invisible barriers to invading forces. The inhabitants became immune to diseases within their environment and a delicate equilibrium between illness and man evolved. Some diseases required an intermediate host, as in malaria; other organisms were spread from domesticated animal sources, such as tuberculosis (eg dog and man share 65 diseases, cow 50, horse 35 and chicken 26).

Illnesses which grow and multiply only in man need a reservoir of non-immune members of the community in which to survive. When man congregated into large groups, involving the formation of cities, with the attendant problems of overcrowding, shared water supply and food chain, and disposal of waste products, these conditions were fulfilled. Then, diseases distributed by human skin contact, water and insects, could spread and propagate freely.

McNeill estimates that cities and the surrounding areas would need to number at least half a million before there were enough non-immune individuals for diseases such as measles, smallpox, influenza, or the water borne infections of typhoid and dysentery to survive. These so called 'civilized diseases' could not have established themselves much before 3000 BC as there were no large urban areas until after that time. A gradual development of urban life in ancient empires occurred down to 500 BC. By now, in heavily urbanized population centres, human chains of infection were enabling diseases to be permanently established in patterns that have continued down to modern times.

The empires of the world ebbed and flowed over the years with peripheral incursions by barbarians. This mixing of cultures and peoples by trade and war enabled disease to spread to new hosts. When entering a non-immune group the new infection had a catastrophic effect, picking off the very old and very young in large numbers. Furthermore, disease presentations were more dramatic than in an immune community.

Malaria has probably killed more people in the world than any other disease. It is spread by 24 of the approximately 200 species of Anopheles mosquito, and has still not been conquered, despite advances in medicine

Where a group was very susceptible to the new infection, either because of poor nutrition, or the presence of debilitating illnesses such as malaria and tuberculosis, all but the strongest members succumbed. Even today, three quarters of the world's population suffer, in varying degrees, from diseases associated with malnutrition; there is a great deal of truth in the saying 'Famine kills, but malnutrition kills more'.

The disease which has probably killed more people in the world than any other is malaria. The huge mortality is principally due to the long-term debilitating effects of repeated attacks. Before present-day prevention and control, the world-wide incidence was one in ten, or three hundred million cases annually, of which one percent died.

Malaria is an ancient disease. It was already common in India, China and around the Mediterranean two thousand years ago. In 400 BC Hippocrates noted that 'the intermittent fevers' were associated with swamps, and occurred mostly in the heat of summer. The name of the disease means 'bad air' in Italian and for centuries it was thought to be due to 'miasmas'—noxious exhalations rising from swamps. Until comparatively recently, it was

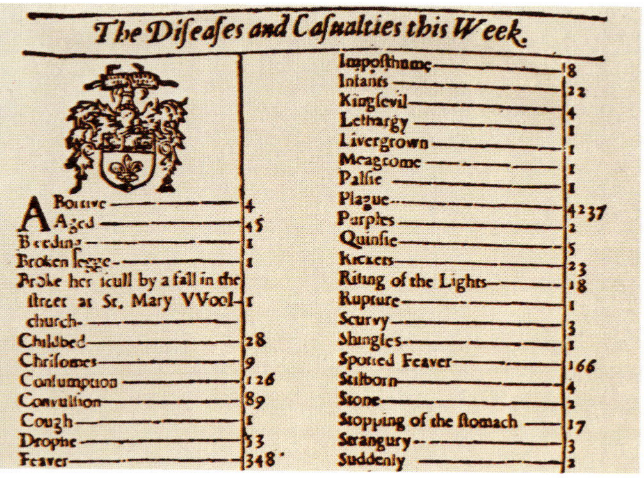

The Diseases and Casualties this Week.

Abortive	4	Impostume	8
Aged	45	Infants	22
Beeding	1	Kingsevil	4
Broken legge	1	Lethargy	1
Broke her scull by a fall in the street at St. Mary Wool-church	1	Livergrown	1
Childbed	28	Meagrome	1
Chrisomes	9	Palsie	1
Consumption	126	Plague	4237
Convulsion	89	Purples	2
Cough	1	Quinsie	5
Dropsie	53	Rickets	23
Feaver	348	Rising of the Lights	18
		Rupture	1
		Scurvy	3
		Shingles	1
		Spotted Feaver	166
		Stilborn	4
		Stone	2
		Stopping of the stomach	17
		Strangury	3
		Suddenly	2

prevalent in Holland and England, where in the seventeenth century, the symptoms were known as 'the ague'.

People afflicted with diseases like the plague and typhus either die very soon after the onset of infection, or else recover virtually completely. Malaria is different. It can be a chronic relapsing disease, which the sufferer has to endure, with its attendant weakness, apathy and ill-health. The origins of malaria reach down to the beginnings of man's struggle for survival, when he cleared portions of the forest for agriculture and dwellings, thus letting sunlight reach stagnant pools of water, where mosquitoes like to breed.

Malaria is spread by 24 of the 200 or so species of the Anopheles mosquito, which breed on the surface of bodies of water, most often quite small, shallow, sunlit pools, although some species prefer lakes and the backwaters of sluggish rivers. Down the centuries man has been responsible for improving the breeding conditions of the Anopheles mosquito by damming streams for water supplies, forming artificial lakes by his mining and quarrying activities, and flooding large areas of land for rice production. As with bubonic plague, typhus, cholera and the epidemics of the nineteenth century, so with malaria —man has helped to create his own disease conditions. Colonization of the world area by area altered the environment in favour of diseases in the nineteenth century.

During the past 50 or 60 years, the picture has slowly changed, as agriculture has become more intensive, with improved and increased land drainage. However, even as recently as the end of World War II, in the second half of the 1940s, malaria was still a problem, even though the parasite and its life cycle had by then been known for 40 years. It has still not been conquered. Efforts to control the disease by destroying the Anopheles mosquitoes have been only partially successful. So, too, have

Above
Mangrove swamps like these along the coast of Kenya provide ideal breeding grounds for the Anopheles mosquito, of which 24 species spread malaria. More people have died from malaria than from any other disease

Left
As people died in their thousands from the plague, irrational fears gripped the population. They began seeking scapegoats, and turned on the Jews and the Gypsies, accusing them of spreading the disease. Many were burned to death

Above left
The mortality bill for the week August 15 to 22, 1665, showed that 4,237 people died of the plague. It is likely that the figure was even higher, since many of those shown as dying of fever may well have been plague victims

Panic at the Plague
One of the rumours that helped to throw the medieval population into panic was that more than thirteen million people had died as a result of the plague since 1348. It was said that the entire population of Cyprus had perished, and that more than 15,000 people a day were dying in Cairo (which then had a population approaching 500,000)

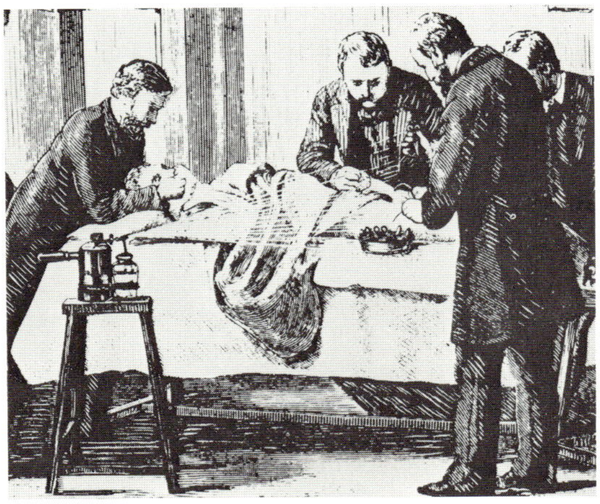

Above
It was Joseph (later Lord) Lister who realized that the frightful mortality rate after surgery in the nineteenth century was due to bacteria. In the 1870s, he introduced his spray, designed to ensure antiseptic surgery, with considerable success

Right
A Dutch barber-surgeon at work at the end of the seventeenth century. In Britain, barber-surgeons were restricted by law to blood-letting and the pulling of teeth

Far right
Operation at Charing Cross Hospital in 1901. By then, better ways than Lister s spray had been introduced to ensure that all operations continued to be antiseptic

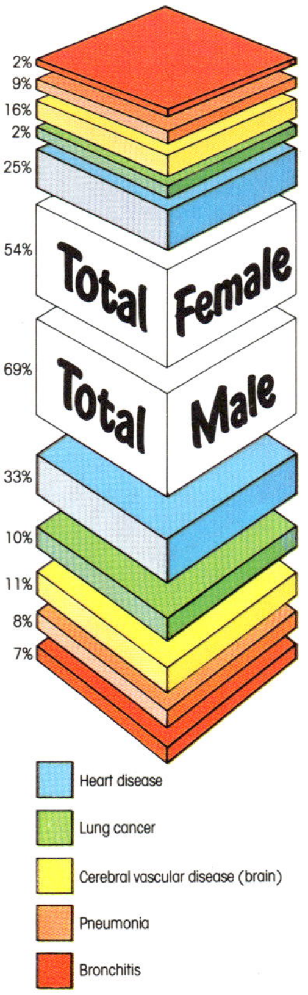

Fatal Illnesses of the Western World
54 percent of female, and 69 percent of male deaths are attributable to the diseases listed above

mosquito nets, insect-repellant sprays, insecticides and the anti-malarial drugs developed in World War II. These had largely replaced quinine, the basic drug therapy for decades, but quinine has made a come-back because the malaria microbes have developed a powerful and growing resistance to a number of the newer drugs.

Tuberculosis is a disease of urban living. The white races of the world have carried it to wherever they have settled, and it is now as widespread in Africa and the East today as it was in Europe in earlier centuries

The bacilli of tuberculosis are among the oldest and most widespread on earth. There is archeological evidence of tuberculosis of the skeleton going back to the Stone Age. This, as well as tuberculosis of the lymph glands and abdomen, is often spread by mycobacterium tuberculosis which is transmitted in the milk of domestic cows. Dairy herds have been infected with it since before Christ, but it has never been found in wild animals or become established as a human parasite. Pulmonary tuberculosis, known colloquially in the last century as 'consumption', is usually caused by the human bacillus, which is propagated in slums, factories and schools. It is, in short, a disease of urban living, which began to affect Europe seriously with the spread of the Industrial Revolution. The white races of the world have taken tuberculosis to wherever they have settled and, today, it is as widespread among the peoples of Africa and the East as it used to be in Europe in earlier centuries. During the nineteenth century, it undoubtedly killed more people in the western world than any other disease—some three million a year out of the approximately 50 million people throughout the world suffering from it at any one time. Chopin, the Bronte sisters, Elizabeth Barrett Browning, Goethe, Keats, Paganini, Washington Irving, were all victims of tuberculosis. The disease was gradually brought under control by improving working and living conditions, isolating active cases in sanatoria, pasteurizing milk and eliminating infected herds. Today, antibiotics cut short the course of the disease and vaccination using an attenuated bovine strain (BCG) has helped to reduce its incidence to such an extent that it is no longer the killer disease it once was in North America and Europe.

Man's greatest achievement in the battle against infectious diseases has been the conquest of smallpox, which has ravaged man for at least 2000 years. It contributed to the ill health of the Roman empire. Gregory of Tours described a European outbreak in 581 AD and four hundred years later there were records of isolation hospitals in Japan, where the treatment was 'hangings of red cloth'!

The disease had increased in virulence by the eighteenth and nineteenth centuries, though diagnosis was so uncertain that the double pathology of 'smallpox and measles' was often made. Throughout these centuries smallpox killed more young children than any other disease, more than 80 percent were under 5, and decimated the population of several European countries, just as, 200 years before, it had affected the Aztecs, following the Spanish invasion of Mexico.

By the eleventh century, the Chinese were inoculating people against smallpox by scratching pus from a smallpox sufferer into the skin. This

method later came to be used in the Mediterranean as well. However, it was not always successful as the patient could develop a severe attack instead of a mild one in the process of developing immunity to the disease.

It was an English physician, Dr Edward Jenner, who discovered a safe way to immunize people against smallpox. In his country practice, he noticed that milk-maids who had caught cowpox through their work did not contract smallpox. Immunity to cowpox helped to give immunity to smallpox—the virus which caused it was a variant of the same group. Vaccination against smallpox, developed by Jenner, gradually spread throughout the world. Today, except for a few isolated pockets of the virus in Ethiopia, the world is free of the disease. One battle has been won.

Dr Jenner was the father of immunology, which became a potent weapon against diseases such as tetanus, whooping cough, diphtheria and tuberculosis, with attendant improvement in the mortality of the diseases. However, the results have not been as striking as would be expected. In whooping cough and tuberculosis, the incidence of the diseases was already decreasing. Immunization has only accelerated the decline. Similarly, antibiotics have altered the course of these illnesses and prevented complications by invading secondary bacilli; but there again, decline had already begun. The current theory on this phenomenon is that the incidence of infectious diseases began to drop during the first half of this century, due to improvements in nutrition, water supply and with less overcrowding in homes and factories. The lessons concerning hygiene, taught by Lister, Pasteur and Semmelweis were also being put into practice.

Cholera bacilli have developed strains resistant to some antibiotics, notably penicillin, but alternative drugs have been developed which are extremely effective. Viruses, however, have so far defied all attempts to curb them, and a number of new virus diseases have made their appearance

Another battle is on the way to being won—against person-to-person infectious diseases caused by bacilli. Thanks to the discovery of antibiotics in the 1930s and their subsequent development, most bacilli no longer constitute a serious problem. Strains resistant to some antibiotics—especially penicillin—have developed, but this has been dealt with by the discovery of alternative drugs. With insect carriers of disease, control of the environment is important, as it is in the case of water-borne diseases like cholera. This frightening disease, which dehydrates its victims and often kills them within 24 hours, is a major problem in India, even today. The foci of infection are the sacred rivers like the Ganges, in which thousands of pilgrims immerse themselves every year, polluting them on a large scale. Where river pollution occurs in countries from which cholera has been almost totally eliminated—after an earthquake, flood or other natural catastrophe—it rapidly returns in the wake of the calamity.

Modern technology has still not produced an adequate answer to viruses, the existence of which was discovered a century ago. There are now known to be many hundreds of different types, causing a wide variety of human diseases, ranging

Above
Like all pioneers, the discoverer of vaccination, Dr Edward Jenner, had to face initial scepticism, not only from some fellow doctors, but also from the public. This famous James Gillray cartoon satirizes Dr Jenner's discovery

Left
Dr Edward Jenner found that vaccination with cowpox virus resulted in immunity from smallpox, leading to almost complete eradication of the disease

Far left
Green monkey disease gets its name from this animal, also known as the vervet monkey. Interferon has been successfully used against this and other viral diseases. The entire world production of this drug is one fifth of a gramme a year—enough to treat 200 patients

1938	2,800
1939	2,150
1940	2,400
1941	2,650
1943	1,300
1945	700
1947	250
1948	150
1949	100
1950	75
1951	56

Conquest of Diphtheria
The controversy continues to rage over the reasons for the declining death rate from diphtheria. Did it decrease because of mass inoculation, or was it going down in any case?

from pneumonia and meningitis to influenza, poliomyelitis, gastro-intestinal upsets and colds. Human body cells have to fight their battle with viruses unaided, since antibiotics have no effect on them, and the diseases they cause take their natural course, either by burning themselves out or by killing their human hosts.

In 1979, an internationally renowned Professor of Virology was asked whether there were more viruses now than before antibiotics had taken care of bacilli. His reply was: 'most viruses have been with us for centuries, only recently have we become aware of them. The worry is not so much the viruses we know, but the ones latent within us'. Ominous evidence of this are the virus diseases which have only recently made their appearance: Lassa fever, isolated in Nigeria in 1969, and Marburg or green monkey disease, which first occurred among German laboratory staff who had been in contact with this monkey. In 1976, there were outbreaks in southern Sudan and Zaire. Also in 1976, there was an outbreak of a mysterious disease among delegates attending an American Legion convention in Philadelphia. Now known as legionaire's disease —a germ infection—it affected nearly 200 people on that occasion, and has since caused temporary disability, and even death, in such other, widely separated parts of the world as Scotland and Spain, where tourists spread the infection.

Viruses have the disturbing ability to change their antigenic character slightly which confuses the host's antibody mechanism, so that the disease may re-infect members of the community. This happens frequently in the case of the influenza virus. New types which are slightly different from existing ones continually sweep across the world. Their names are taken from their area of origin, such as Asian (1957), Hong Kong influenza (1968), Victoria (1975), and Texan influenza (1978).

Influenza epidemics are almost annual events. Pandemics occur approximately every 30 or 40 years as in 1918 and 1957. In 1918 there were 200 million cases. Now, the World Health Organization Epidemiological Service tries to isolate new strains as they occur, and forecast when and where they will spread. Given time (the preparation of vaccine

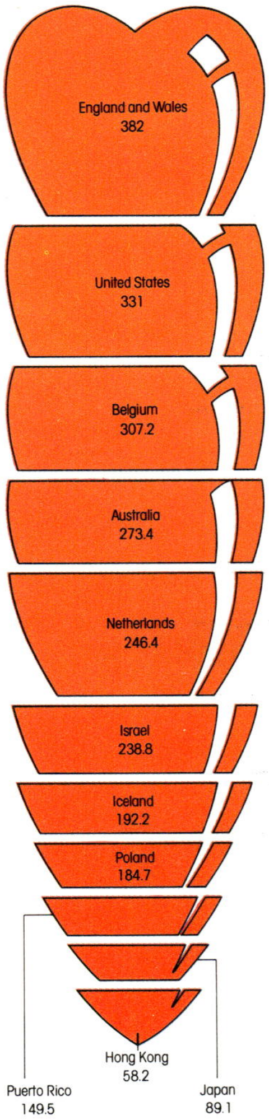

Death Strike
An international league table of numbers of people killed by heart disease (per 100,000) shows fairly conclusively that fatal coronary attack and the level of affluence are strongly correlated

Right
The tsetse fly, carrier of Trypanosomiasis, or as it is better known, sleeping sickness. It is the scourge of the third world, particularly Africa, for it infects man and cattle alike with its bite

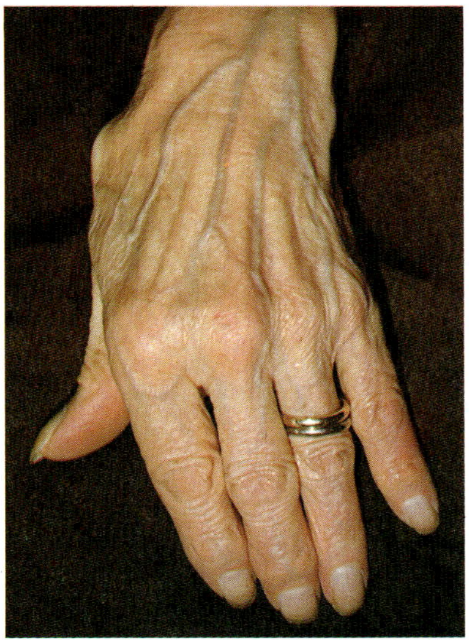

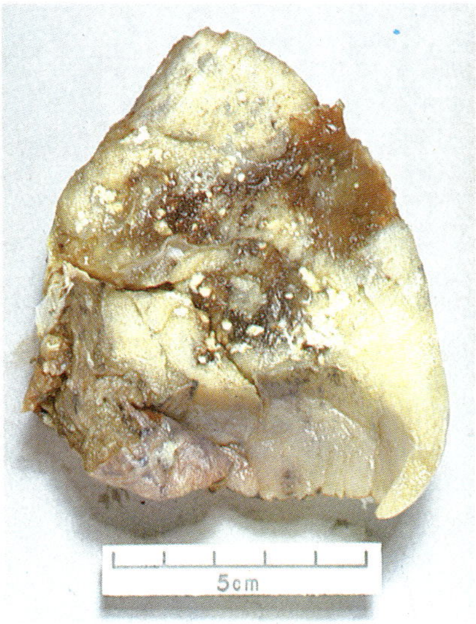

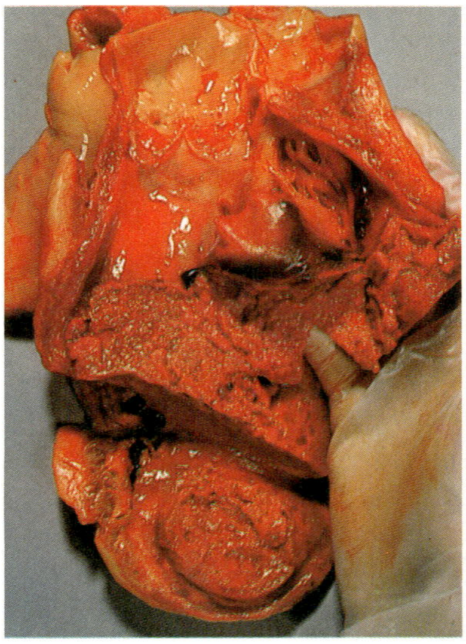

Right
Arthritis is one of the degenerative and deforming diseases which constitute a serious and growing problem in the West. The photograph shows the arthritic hand of a woman aged 87

Centre and far right
Cancer-filled alveoli – the air sacs at the end of the bronchia inside the lungs. In addition to becoming cancerous, they can also become blocked with fluid or dust.
The interior of a heart after a massive heart attack. The incidence of heart disease is rising in Western countries for a variety of reasons, which include diet and strain

in commercial quantities takes more than six months), susceptible members of the population and those at risk can be partially protected, but only for a limited period of time.

Chemotherapy is another form of treatment, although most agents have still not been proved. One promising substance is interferon, first isolated from infected cells in 1957. This can affect the reduplication of viruses, but there is a fair degree of host specificity, so that for example, only monkey or human interferon is effective in man. Derived from human white cells it has been used successfully against leukaemia, smallpox and green monkey disease, but the world output is a mere one fifth of a gramme a year, although this is enough to treat 200 cases, since successful treatments require doses no larger than one thousandth of a gramme.

Unfortunately, modern medical technology has brought in its train iatrogenic disease (disease caused by doctors), with accompanying disability and death on occasions. Certain drugs, developed to aid the quality of life, have been shown by extensive use to produce serious side effects, such as Practolol, for instance, used for angina in heart disease and the tranquillizer, Thalidomide.

Man himself undermines medical advances because of his way of life. Western man must pay heed to the epidemiological evidence, so as to improve his health still further, ensuring at the same time that the Third World is enabled to raise nutritional and hygienic standards and thus take full advantage of the progress made by medicine

There is a school of thought gathering momentum in the 1970s with the philosophy that: 'Health depends, not on what doctors do to us, but what we do to ourselves.' This is graphically illustrated by the examples of killer diseases which are of recent origin—the so-called non-infectious diseases of the 20th century. The medical problems related to these diseases have proliferated, despite improvements in living standards which have brought increased life expectancy. Out of every 1,000 boys born in 1841, only 230 reached the age of 70. By 1975, more than double survived to the same age. This has been due principally to improvements in infant mortality. Though pneumonia, 'the old man's friend,' kills one in seven over the age of 75, cancer kills one in six males and one in nine females. In younger age groups, the cancer figures are even higher; as with all diseases, age and sex take different death tolls. In early middle age (25-45 years), accidents, poisoning and violence account for the same number of deaths, in males and females, as diseases of the circulatory system. By middle age (45-65 years) coronary heart disease is the foremost cause of death in males in almost every western society. Though increases in average life expectancy have brought an associated higher incidence of degenerative disease, such as osteoarthritis, the real problem is the dramatic rise of the so-called 'diseases of affluence' which have appreciably changed the character of the scythe of sickness. These diseases of modern living—coronary artery disease, strokes, hypertension, appendicitis, late-onset diabetes and diverticulosis and cancer of the bowel—are all found in the richer countries of the world, in contrast to the incidence in earlier centuries and poorer countries today.

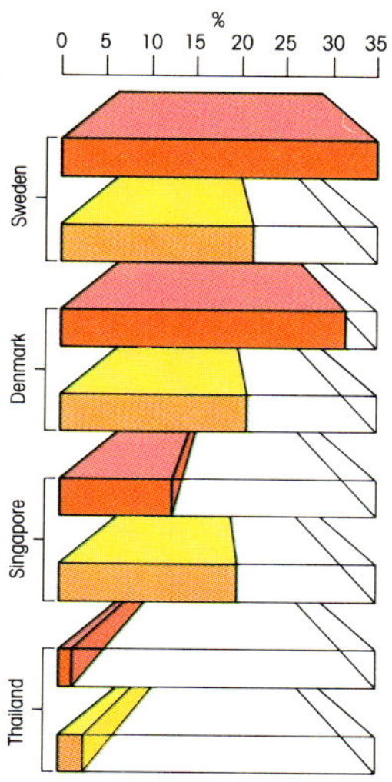

Risks of Affluence
In highly industrialized countries, the diseases of affluence, coronary attacks and various fatal tumours reach correspondingly lethal levels. Ironically, countries which have remained under-industrialized and, more important, under-urbanized, appear still to show low levels of fatalities from heart diseases and cancers

Waiting for the Dead
The study of anatomy in America in the seventeenth century was a laborious affair, because so much time had to be spent waiting for a corpse; however, there was no objection to the dissection of the bodies of Indians

Origins of Syphilis
In Tudor times, communal bathing was believed to lead to the spread of syphilis and plague. Because of this it was virtually abolished by the end of the sixteenth century. There is a widely held belief that syphilis was first brought to Europe by Columbus's sailors on their return from the West Indies

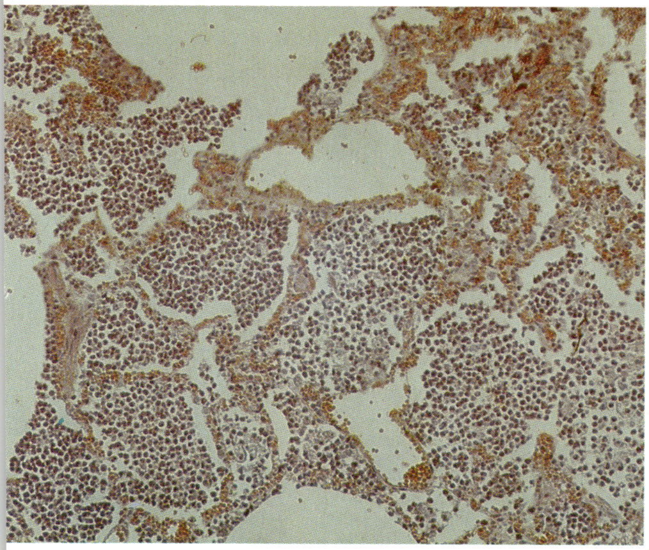

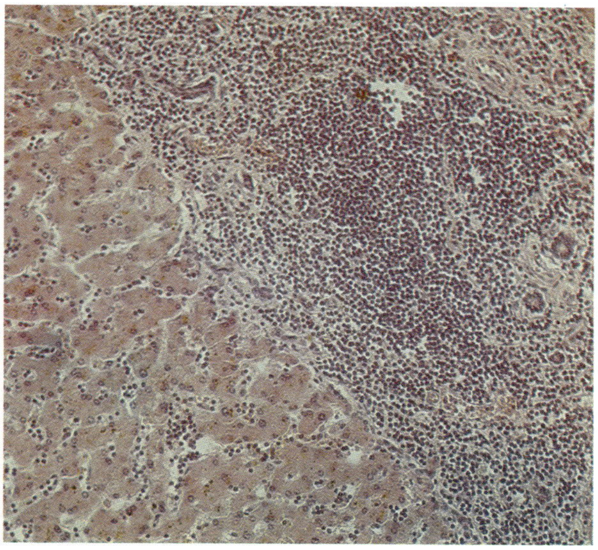

Top left
A woman in the Central African Empire, only minutes after giving birth in a hut. The rate of infant mortality is high in the country, as medical and health care are far from adequate. Diet is also a problem. This baby will probably not survive long

Far left and left
Acute broncho-pneumonia. The dark areas of the lung are filled with bacteria. Antibiotics have neutralized the disease, but it still kills one in seven over the age of 75. Leukaemia in liver cells. Interferon has been used successfully to treat it

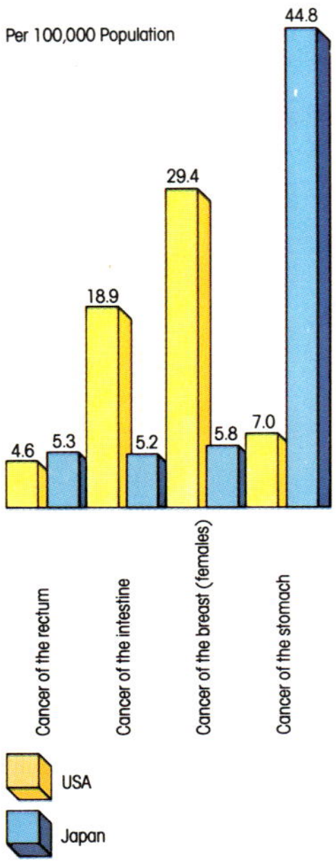

Cancer Risk
Certain types of malignant cancer may be linked fairly closely with diet. Americans eat a great deal of fatty foods, for example, and seem to suffer disproportionately from various lethal cancers of the intestine and the breast. The high level of nitrates in the diets of most Japanese may account for the high rates of stomach cancer observed in Japan

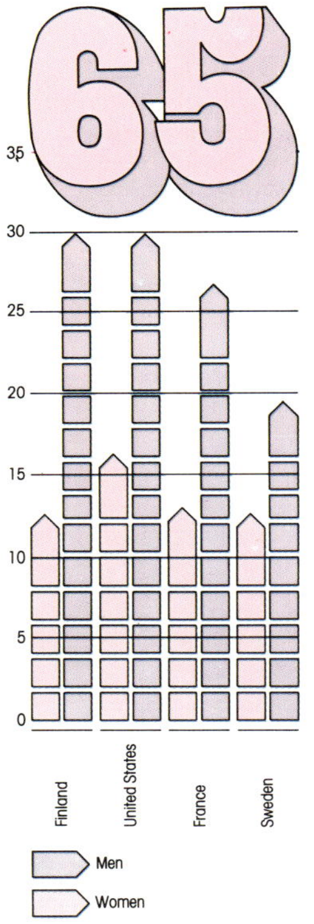

The Fatal Years
An increasing concern among health experts today is the growing risk of early death in the middle-aged. Stress, inadequate exercise, high cholesterol diets and high blood pressure collectively lead to high levels of coronary heart disease among the middle-aged, with attendant fatalities before retirement age is reached. Interestingly, this syndrome is more prevalent among men than women

The study of the influences on disease has become more urgent than ever before as a basic cause for these killer diseases is sought. What is clear, however, is that there are a number of inter-related contributory factors, such as dietary fats, fibre and sugar, together with high blood pressure, obesity and cigarette smoking.

Among the mass of epidemiological evidence gathered in recent years, the following stand out: Finland, Scotland and the U.S.A. have the highest incidence of coronary heart disease (C.H.D.) in the world, with England and Wales not far behind. In Japan, where the traditional diet of low fat and high fibre is eaten, the C.H.D. figures are one-tenth that of Finland. However, if Japanese migrate to Hawaii or the U.S.A. and change to a western-style diet, with high fat and sugar and low fibre content, their disease patterns alter to match those of the Americans.

Similar changes are seen in the disease patterns of the rural African if he adopts an urban lifestyle and a western diet, or emigrates to the U.S.A. These changes appear to date from the late nineteenth century and result partly from such factors as the modern methods of milling. Western diets now have 80 per cent less fibre than those of the 1870s. Flour, for example, has lost its brown husk. Less vegetables are eaten, and rice is finely polished, compared to that consumed with rural African diets. Fibre fills the gut and lessens hunger, stools are larger and passed more frequently, so that there is a smaller uptake of fats. Bacteria in the bowel of people eating a Western type of diet, break down bile into substances which can cause cancer. Where fibre is deficient these agents are in contact with the bowel for longer periods of time.

The average European consumes almost a hundredweight of sugar annually, compared with four pounds two centuries ago. One-sixth of his calorie intake is in sugar. Besides damaging teeth, high sugar intake affects the metabolism of sugar and the number of late onset—or maturity diabetics—is increasing in the Western world. Cane sugar forms a non-filling, unnecessary source of energy and the result is a tendency to impared glucose tolerance and obesity. Diabetic men have three times and diabetic women five to six times more C.H.D. than non-diabetics.

The cigarette smoker is twice as likely to suffer from C.H.D. than the non-smoker, but under the age of 45 the risk is even higher—a ten to fifteen fold increase if more than 25 cigarettes are smoked daily. These factors appear to be cumulative; the Japanese, on his traditional diet, smokes heavily but has a very low C.H.D. rate and a low blood cholesterol level.

Obesity, lack of exercise, high blood pressure and fat intake all make a significant contribution. The cholesterol controversy will rage for decades to come as there are many different fats in our diet, some of which actually appear to have a benign affect. Serum cholesterol levels rise when fibre is removed from the diet. The conclusions, so far, are: that total fat intake should be reduced; saturated fats (butter, eggs and milk) should be partially replaced by polyunsaturated fats (e.g. corn oil and sunflower seed oil) and olive oil. The use of poly-unsaturated fats aids the lowering of cholesterol in the blood. Many scientists suggest that unrefined carbohydrate should be increased and sugar intake

reduced to a much more moderate level.

The role of fibre is being increasingly appreciated as bowel disease rises and now occurs in one-third of the population. Gall bladder disease or cancer, while rare in a high fibre diet, are dramatically increasing. Now, cancer of the colon is second to lung cancer in the malignant disease league in the Western world.

Many of the factors are inter-related; obesity is associated with low fibre, high saturated fat intake, diabetes and high blood pressure. The latter predisposes to strokes and coronary heart disease. These form a vicious circle of cause and event, affected by smoking and low physical activity. Many of our present medical problems can be avoided by control of the environment and personal pollution and habits.

However, medical science destroys more lethal

Left
People who take exercise, eat low-fat foods, cut their sugar intake, make sure that their diet contains adequate fibre, do not smoke or drink alcohol heavily and have an optimistic outlook and positive attitude to life, have a far better chance of not falling victim to CHD than those who do the opposite. However, although medical science destroys more lethal agents than it creates, man himself undermines many of the advances made by medicine. Modern means of treatment and the body's natural defence mechanisms form a powerful combination against disease and death. But twentieth-century living hinders rather than helps. Many of our present-day medical problems could be avoided by control of the environment and of personal pollution and habits

Left
High blood pressure, diet, obesity and cigarette-smoking are factors in coronary heart disease (CHD). Finland, Scotland and the United States have the highest CHD rates, with England and Wales not far behind. The average European consumes almost a hundredweight of sugar a year. Apart from damaging the teeth, this high sugar intake affects metabolism. The number of late-onset diabetics in the West is increasing

Bottom
The indulgences we allow ourselves in our youth might all too easily result in an early demise

agents than it creates. It is man himself who undermines the advances in medicine. Modern methods of treatment and the body's natural defence mechanisms form a powerful combination against disease and death. However, twentieth-century living hinders rather than helps, just as, in the eighteenth and nineteenth centuries overcrowding and lack of hygiene actively promoted the spread of diseases like cholera, typhus and tuberculosis.

By paying heed to the epidemiological evidence, the Western world can improve its health still further, while raising standards of nutrition and hygiene will bring its own rewards in the Third World. We have begun to blunt the scythe of sickness and lessen the swathe of death it has cut in the world over the millennia. Continuing medical research will enable us to make even more progress towards our goal of vanquishing disease.

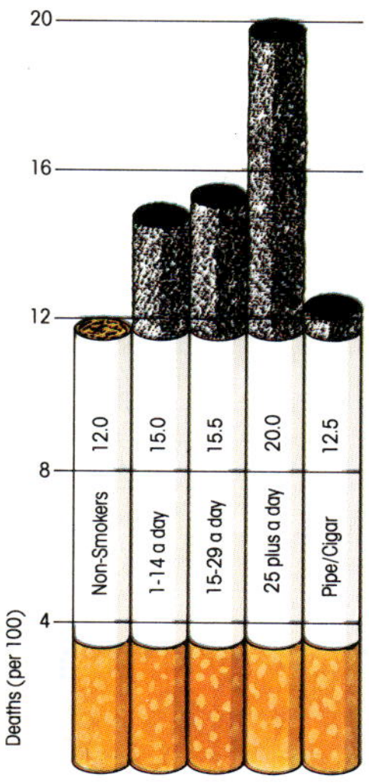

Going Up in Smoke
The controversy over the link between heavy cigarette smoking and lung cancer continues to rage. Shown here are the death rates per 100 which appear to be related to non-smokers, cigarette smokers according to number of cigarettes smoked per day, and cigar and pipe smokers

Death by Misadventure

Man is continually developing new technologies, many of which are extremely hazardous. Unless we learn quickly how to control these processes, we shall be forced to accept the probability that a disaster may soon occur – with far-reaching consequences

Above
Apart from ships, trains are probably the safest method of passenger transport today. Nevertheless, railway accidents do occur from time to time. Every railway accident is the result of a conjunction of improbable occurrences. Either operating instructions are disobeyed, or several apparently fool-proof automatic processes fail at the same time, or else nature intervenes

Far right
Two racing cars, one of them driven by the Belgian ace, Jackie Ickx, explode into flames after colliding on the race track. Racing drivers have virtually no chance of escaping from their vehicles when something like this happens. Although racing cars are open, not enclosed, their cockpits are so cramped that the drivers have to be dragged out after an accident

A Safer Journey
The number of fatal road accidents a year in Britain has remained almost static since 1929. However, the number of cars on the road has increased tenfold. There could be several reasons for this proportional drop in road deaths – better road conditions, better street lighting and the increased use of seat belts are some of them

'Every death which is not gradually brought on by the miseries of age, or when life is extinguished for any other reason than that it is burnt out, is the effect of accident; he that dies before 60, of a cold or consumption, dies, in reality, by a violent death'.

Samuel Johnson 1758

There is much to commend Johnson's panoramic view of death by misadventure but to accept it here would be to embark on a text book of medicine. Those who died in the medieval pandemics of smallpox, typhus or the humble measles or who, today, are respiratory casualties of atmospheric pollution could certainly be said to have died from misadventure. However, although it may be semantically incorrect to do so, most people regard misadventure as being synonymous with accident —and this being generally associated with some degree of violence.

Even when so limited, 'accidental death' is not clearly defined. Very few accidents are strictly 'unforeseen'. Indeed, in most cases, considerable foresight had been put into the prevention of just such contingencies. How is it, then, that accidental death is still so much a part of our lives? There would seem to be three main factors involved.

Firstly, there is very commonly some degree of contributory negligence. This can range from the absence of an adequate warning system or failure to heed one which does exist—the reason for the massive death toll at Pompeii—to frank incompetence, the cause of the most disastrous mid-air collision in history, over Yugoslavia in 1976. What constitutes negligence depends very much on the circumstances prevailing at the time. The conditions

DUNLOP
10

Right
Many areas of the world are known to be prone to earthquakes. Seismologists are gradually learning to predict when and where they will occur, but the science is still in its infancy, and earthquake deaths can be prodigious. Most deaths during earthquakes result from crushing or asphyxia

Bottom right
A tornado spirals in on a country town in the USA. Tornadoes, local whirlwinds of extreme violence, can cause a tremendous amount of damage and destruction in a matter of minutes

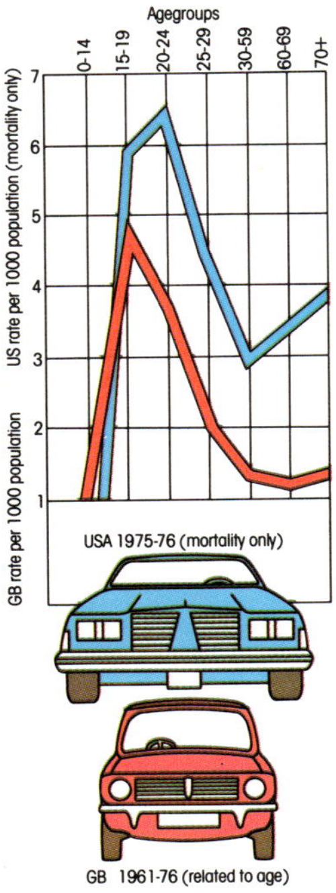

Death on the Road (Fig 1)
The rates of fatal and serious injury in various agegroups, averaged over 15 years for Britain. The peak in young adulthood is clearer in the USA curve. Note the rising curve for the old aged in both countries

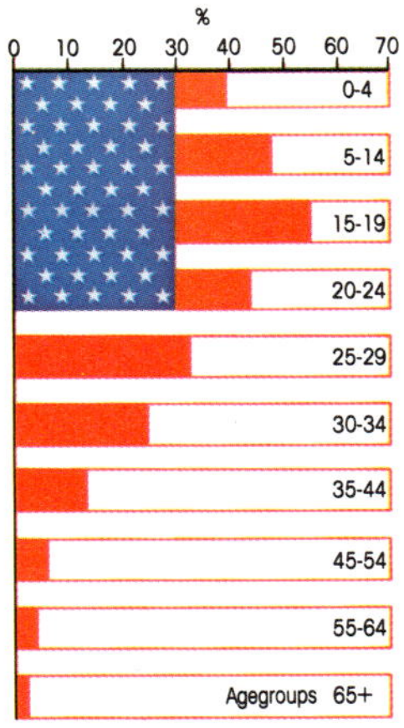

One Throw of the Dice
Accidental deaths as a percentage of total deaths, divided into various agegroups, in the USA during the 1970s. Most at risk are the 15-19 year-olds

in which the Great Fire of London started in 1666 may have been acceptable in the social climate of that time, but would certainly have led to a criminal prosecution today. No one thought of safety precautions in the factories of the Industrial Revolution—workers were to all intents expendable. Today, most modern countries have social security legislation, under which compensation is payable to an injured employee—even if he has been guilty of ignoring safety regulations.

More often than not, there is contributory negligence in cases of accidental death. These cases do not have one single cause, but result from an improbable combination of events

Secondly, most accidents do not have one single cause which can be anticipated, but result from an improbable combination of events. It is possible to make reasonable safety regulations governing the bulk transport by road of inflammable liquids, and adequate safety standards can be ensured within a camping site. However, disaster ensues when, as happened in Spain in 1978, a tanker laden with propylene overturns into a holiday camp. Again, General 'Stonewall' Jackson must certainly have strayed from his lines on many occasions, and his army must have included many trigger-happy sentries, but the conjunction of these two conditions may well have affected the whole course of the American Civil War.

Thirdly, man is continually developing new technologies and, at each point, is probably slightly over-estimating his ability to compensate for the added hazards. Henry Ford can hardly have anticipated that his brain-child would kill many thousands of people on the world's roads every year. It is this type of anticipatory thinking which activates those who are concerned to limit the use of nuclear power.

Earthquakes frequently account for a staggeringly high toll of human fatalities. The Kanto earthquake of 1923, for example, with the huge fires and tidal waves that followed it, destroyed two of the world's largest cities, Tokyo and Yokohama. They experienced a devastation that exceeds the atomic damage at Hiroshima and Nagasaki

Accidental death may strike either at an individual or at a group. The latter may attain the proportions of a major disaster. Earthquake, hurricane and flood produce mass casualties on a scale unsurpassed by human invention save, perhaps, in the context of modern warfare. It is estimated that 125,000 people died in the Allied fire bomb attack on Dresden in 1945, and some 78,000 people died when the first atomic bomb was dropped on Hiroshima. Modern nuclear weapons could, in effect, reproduce the consequences of a composite natural disaster. Earthquake mortality—which results from a combination of crushing, asphyxia and, most particularly, fire—is sometimes staggeringly high. There were nearly 150,000 casualties in Tokyo and Yokohama in the 1923 great Kanto earthquake. Some 15,000 fatal casualties occurred at Agadir in 1960, while an estimated 650,000 people died at Tangshan, in northern China in 1976. Much depends on the precautions taken in a particular area. One can only hope, for example, that the stringent building regulations enforced in San Francisco will never be put to the test.

By contrast, man seems better able to cope with the hazards of hurricane and flood. These generally repeat themselves sufficiently often for 'cost effective' preventive measures to be taken. In 1900, the city of Galveston, in Texas, was struck by high winds gusting up to 176 kph (110 mph). The resulting death toll was at least 6,000. Subsequently, a protective wall was built, and when a similar hurricane stuck 15 years later, the total death toll

Above
The awesome power of destruction unleashed by earthquakes can be seen in this photograph of a small area of the Sicilian town of Gibellina, hit by a series of tremors in 1968

Far left
A tornado-damaged house. In addition to its whirling motion, a tornado advances at between 32 and 64 kph (20 and 40 mph), carrying destruction along its narrow path

Left
For all his progress in every field of human endeavour, man has not yet succeeded in taming nature, and natural disasters like earthquakes, floods, volcanic eruptions, hurricanes and snowstorms remind us of this fact with sickening frequency. Natural disasters generally result in casualties on a scale unparalleled by any man-made disaster, with the possible exception of modern war

fell to 108. In 1961, when winds up to 240 kph (150 mph) were recorded, only six people were killed. The mortality from floods is usually less dramatic, except in very primitive communities or when the flood results from the failure of a man-made project (such as when a dam bursts), where the suddenness of the catastrophe can cause many casualties. In 1972, 125 people were drowned in this way at Buffalo Creek, West Virginia.

The dangers of natural disaster do not end with the original emergency. The possibility of epidemic disease is always present, and some degree of civil disturbance is almost inevitable. Study of some recent catastrophes has also demonstrated the existence of what has come to be called 'the disaster syndrome', where the survivors appear to lose the will to live—they are overwhelmed and can accept no more. In general, panic and consequent stampede are rare, unless those in danger see their way of escape suddenly cut off. This happened during the bombing of London in 1942, when an orderly retreat to an air raid shelter in an underground station turned into a rout, and more than 170 people were killed in the resultant panic.

Despite a variety of protective measures, wind and water take an appreciable toll of human life. About 8,200 such deaths were recorded in the United States between 1941 and 1975. These emanated from 335 'accidents', 19 of them resulting in 100 or more fatalities. During the same period there were 15 major disasters resulting from a combination of unnatural causes.

Disastrous Days
The most likely time to die in a motor vehicle accident in the United States is on a Saturday in July; the least likely is on either a Monday or a Tuesday in the month of January

Top row
A girl plunges to her death from the upper storey of a blazing building in New York City, while a fireman makes an unavailing attempt to catch her as she falls. When a high-rise building catches fire, many people, finding their escape cut off, panic and jump from the nearest window, only to die from their injuries when they hit the ground. Not all those who wait for the fire brigade to rescue them escape either. Some are asphyxiated by smoke and fumes before help can reach them

Bottom right
Once the pride of Britain's passenger fleet, the 'Queen Elizabeth' ablaze from stem to stern in Hong Kong harbour in 1972. She was completely gutted, though fortunately casualties were few

Water also claims life by way of shipwreck. Apart from wartime, catastrophic loss of life is now largely caused by blatant incompetence or over-confidence, of which the sinking of the *Titanic* in 1912, with the loss of 1,500 lives, is a prime example. On a smaller scale, it should be noted that, generally speaking, deep-sea fishing is a more hazardous occupation than mining.

A hazard much feared by golfers and farmers is being struck by lightning. More than half the fairly rare accidents of this kind occur in open fields, but the mortality rate is lower than might be expected—some 40 percent of people actually struck by lightning die as a result.

Few people realize how serious is the extent of the domestic accident problem. In the United States, for example, more than twice as many people are killed in their homes as at their places of work. The fatality rate in both the USA and Great Britain is about 12 per 100,000. In Britain up to 1970, more people were killed in the home than on the roads. Even now, the figures are very comparable. Falls account for 60 percent of all such deaths (as shown in Fig. 10), and this figure would be higher, were it not for the improved treatment of such conditions as fractures of the femur.

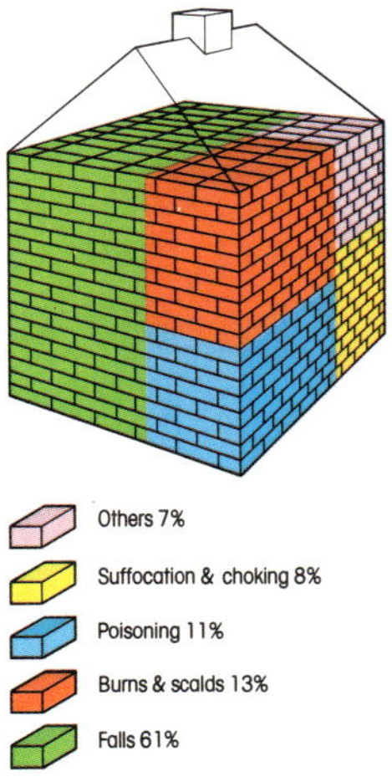

House of Death
Fatal accidents in the home, divided by cause, in the UK, during the mid-1970s. It is notable that falls account for the highest percentage of deaths in the home

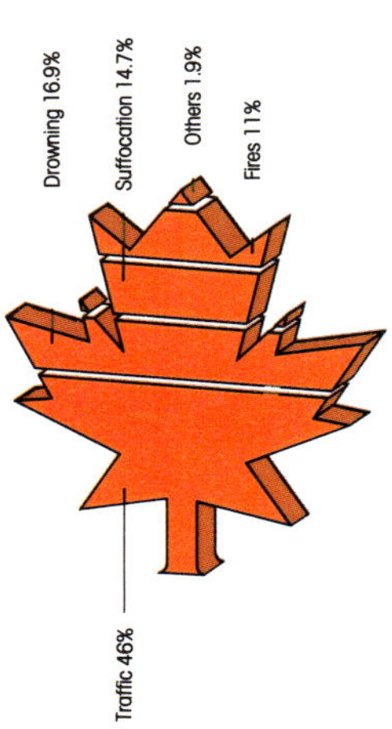

Youth at Risk
Fatal accidents among the under 15 agegroup in Canada, with the figures averaged out for the 1970s. Not too surprisingly, traffic accidents by far account for the majority of deaths

The number of home accidents due to burning is now only surpassed by fatal falls. The excess of females affected is also demonstrable in the young persons' age group. the fact that this is now far less marked than it was 25 years ago can be attributed to the introduction of flame-resistant nightdresses and frocks, and particularly of regulations concerning fire guards.

A remarkable feature is the incidence of drowning, particularly in home swimming pools. In 1971, 12.7 percent of all drownings in the USA were in swimming pools. Of these, two-fifths were in private pools, and 68 percent of them involved children under the age of five.

Industry's improved safety record is impressive. Between 1967 and 1976, coal-mining death rates in the USA and Britain fell by an average of 38.5 percent. Mining procedures may now be safer than before, but the risks from underground explosions can never be entirely eliminated

No matter what safety precautions are taken—and current legislation throughout the industrialized world tends to err on the side of over-protection—accidents at work will continue to occur. The precise part played by negligence is difficult to assess, because of changing regulations, but it is a significant one. There were 231 fatalities in British factories in 1975. Just over half resulted from a breach of statutory regulations on the part of employers. In a further 12 percent of cases, members of the work force were at fault.

Nevertheless, the improved safety record of industry is impressive. Following the outrageous era of the Industrial Revolution, a real beginning was made with effective industrial legislation in the late nineteenth century. Since then, the trend towards safer working conditions has been more or less progressive, particularly in the traditionally dangerous occupations. Thus, between 1901 and 1910, an average of 1,269 people were killed in British mines each year. This yearly average fell to 184 in the ten years from 1961 to 1970, and to 58 in 1976. Both Britain and the United States can boast an average 38.5 percent reduction in coal-mining death rates per man-hours worked between 1967 and 1976. Much of this reduction is due to a decrease in deaths caused by roof falls, following the introduction of powered hydraulic supports to replace individually inserted pit props.

Although underground fires are still frequent,

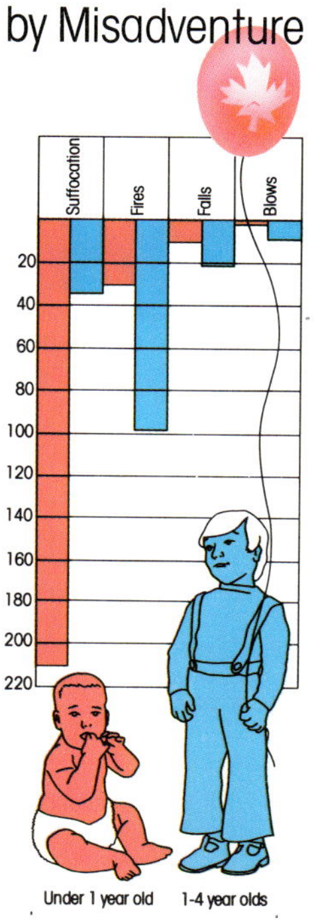

Dangerous Time of Life
Accidental death in the first four years of life, split into two agegroups, in Canada, mid-1970s. Note high rate of suffocations

mining disasters due to explosion and fire are rare nowadays. The biggest one in Britain occurred in South Wales in 1913, when 439 men died. In the United States during the last 35 years, only one mining accident has killed more than 100 persons—in Illinois in 1947. The biggest mining catastrophe ever reported occurred in China in 1942, when 1,572 men died. Explosions are particularly serious when a mixture of methane, air and coal dust is ignited, while electrical sparking is a major hazard. A mixture of air and coal dust is less explosive than one containing methane as well, but it is especially dangerous because a self-propagating flame travels ahead of the blast wave. Death is caused by injury, burning or asphyxia.

Almost all other occupations show a fall in total mortality over the years, but this improvement is largely—if not wholly—the result of a decrease in the dangerousness of many industrial processes. In the United States, as in Britain, the rate of fatality related to man hours worked in the manufacturing industries has shown no fall at all during the last decade.

In the construction industry on the other hand, total fatalities in Britain increased steadily every decade from 1900 to 1970. It must be assumed that construction projects have become more complex and dangerous to complete. The recent drop in fatalities is as likely to be associated with economic depression as with increased safety awareness. The effect of changes in the industrial scene is well illustrated in Britain, where oil exploration and production have become significant only recently. Although only about 10,000 people are employed off shore, it is currently Britain's most dangerous occupation.

Death in industry is not always caused by violent injury, however. Many industries leave a lingering residue of chronic, and often fatal, ill-health. This is particularly true of the mining industry. Some 500 new cases of coal miners' pneumoconiosis are reported annually in Britain. While it is true that, thanks to modern surveillance and disposal methods, few of these cases will be fatal, it is to be noted that 30 years have elapsed since a comparable number of miners were killed because of accidents. Current observations on the prevalence of asbestosis highlight the problem. We almost certainly do not yet know the toll of life from the use of asbestos, and it is now apparent that sufferers from asbestosis may not be confined to workers in the industry.

Above
Negligence, both by employers and, to a markedly lesser extent, by workers, is a significant factor in fatal industrial accidents. However, these have continued to decline as legislation throughout the industrialized world has made the taking of an increasing number of safety precautions mandatory

Sports like boxing, which are essentially legalized assaults, are now rarely associated with death. More deaths occur during cricket matches and on golf courses than happen in the ring

Sports have become progressively less dangerous through the years, as governments and sporting associations have tightened regulations, and as new and improved safety devices have become available. These days, those sports which are essentially

Investing in Safety
Public awareness of the need for effective safety precautions has increased greatly over the past few hundred years. Conditions when the Fire of London started in 1666 were perfectly acceptable then, but would certainly lead to a criminal prosecution today

Stroke of Doom
In 1971, nearly 13 percent of all drownings in the USA occurred in swimming pools

Drilling for an Accident
In terms of death by misadventure, off-shore oil installations are now the most dangerous places of work in the British Isles

No Risk in the Ring
'Violent' sports are in reality safer than they look. Boxing has caused only ten deaths in Britain in the last 30 years, and all-in wrestling a mere two, one of which was due to natural causes

Right
Bull-fighting is one of the very few sports in the civilized world which involve the degradation and killing of animals to provide a spectacle for mass audiences. It is certainly a risk sport; one error of judgement, and the toreador can find himself being tossed by the bull and gored repeatedly, sometimes fatally. An average of four toreadors are killed in Spanish bull rings every year

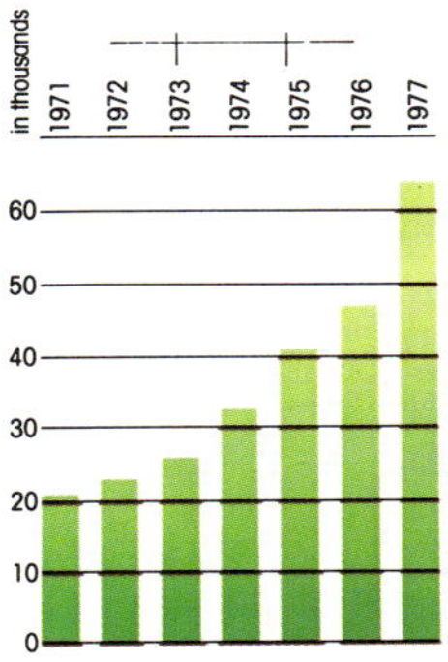

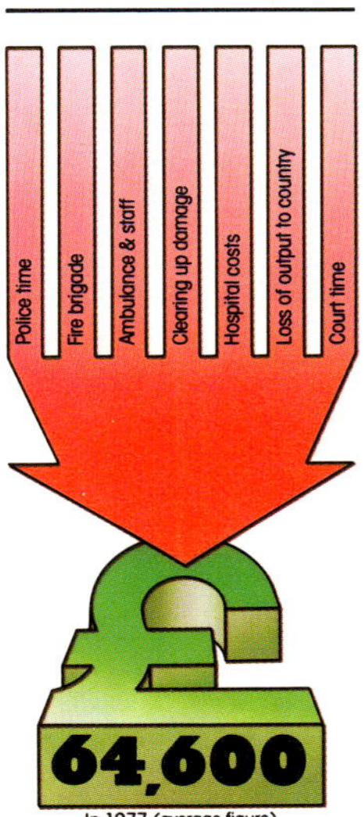

In 1977 (average figure)

Putting a Cost on Death
In Britain, in 1977, each fatal accident on average cost the nation roughly £64,000. This figure, due to inflation and other incidentals, is expected to rise in the years to come

legalized assaults are now rarely associated with death. Professional boxing has accounted for only ten deaths in Britain in 30 years. Even in the case of all-in wrestling there have been only two deaths in Britain in 40 years, and one of these was due to natural causes. Amateur wrestling is quite safe in Western Europe, because the rules have been changed to eliminate the more dangerous holds, but it causes a significant number of deaths in Eastern Europe. There are more deaths during cricket matches in England than there are in the boxing ring, although the bald statistics may be misleading. Were they to be taken at face value, golf would appear as the most dangerous sport in the world. In point of fact, virtually all deaths on the golf course are natural in origin—the jest that 'poor old X took his stroke at the fourteenth' describes a true situation

that occurs very often. Contact sports are responsible for a large number of injuries but, again, surprisingly, few deaths. In American football, some 20 percent of players will be carried off the field during the playing season, but few indeed are killed, thanks to the sophisticated preventive clothing worn and the high standard of fitness and selection. In both Rugby Union and American football it is the cervical spine which is at greatest risk, and deaths attributable to the game may, therefore, be rather long delayed.

Where men crowd together during leisure activity, there are two major hazards of misadventure—stampede and fire. Few persons are fatally crushed at sports events in normal circumstances, but once the crowd moves—particularly if the movement is urgent—a minor blockage may lead to rapidly increasing panic, which creates a disaster situation. This is at its worst when there is danger to be avoided, but it can occur in apparently ordinary circumstances. In Glasgow in 1971, 66 people died when a goal was scored in the last moments of a somewhat frustrating football match.

While multiple fire deaths may occur in hotels—119 people died in Atlanta, Georgia, in 1946—it is the dance hall which seems to provide the prime fire hazard of the twentieth century. Elegant establishments can be affected—there were 492 deaths in a Boston night club in 1942—but major concern today is, perhaps, concentrated on the often makeshift discotheque like the one burnt out in France in 1971. Only the strictest enforcement of modern fire precautions and the ruthless closing down of all premises which are fire traps can prevent such catastrophes.

Whether facing an enraged bull in a ring or tackling an ice-field in the Alps, the possibility of death is a risk that has to be accepted as an intrinsic part of the sport

In his love-hate sporting relationship with animals, man may go to great lengths to enjoy their destruction or forge intense emotional bonds with them. In either case, human beings put themselves at varying risk. Very few sports in the civilized world now involve the deliberate destruction or degradation of animals for the benefit of spectators. Only bull-fighting remains as a risk sport *par excellence*. Some four toreadors are killed every year, although apprentices may be at greater risk.

The horse has always been man's companion, initially from necessity and, later, as his partner in recreational activity. Inevitably, there are casualties, particularly in fox hunting, or when the hazards are deliberately increased, as in steeple-chasing. However, while the injury rate is high, mortality is surprisingly low.

Man inevitably places himself in some jeopardy when he sets out to kill animals for sport, whether he acts as beater in an Indian tiger shoot or, more probably, as a member of a weekend rabbit shoot. Despite all warnings, some people will be either so ill-trained or so lax as to put their companions at grave risk.

Little need be said concerning man's sporting instinct to prove his superiority. Indeed, it could be argued that, since most situations of this kind result from a conscious exposure to unnecessary and, at times, unreasonable risk, death is not strictly due to misadventure—unless this is defined as an adventure gone wrong. This happened when Sivel and Croche-Spinelli took their balloon into a relatively unexplored situation and, in 1874, became the first aviation fatalities since Icarus fell out of the sky.

Perhaps mountaineering provides the most outstanding example of this type of death, when so much depends upon the correlation of motivation and experience—is one out for a simple bout of healthy exercise or is one deliberately stretching one's ability to its limits or beyond? Many mountain ranges acquire a possibly spurious reputation for safety or danger, because of their relative accessibility to the tyro. Even so, nature, in the form of avalanche or sudden storm, may destroy the most experienced and dedicated climber.

Experience, or the lack of it, also plays a part in the water. 71 percent of recreational swimming deaths in the United States have been attributed to exhaustion. Over-estimation of ability was listed as a contributory cause in 31 percent of cases.

The overwhelming majority of road accident casualties are in the 15-24 age group. Very flat countries like Holland and Denmark have an exceptionally high number of deaths among pedal cyclists. Great Britain and Ireland are outstanding for the high proportion of pedestrians killed on the roads

With regard to the accidental deaths for which man himself is wholly responsible, road traffic accidents attract the greatest attention. This is, perhaps, not so much because of the number of deaths—which is very considerable (as Fig. 2 shows)—as because of the horrifying results of being injured in such accidents and surviving to tell the tale. After years of safety propaganda, some 80,000 people will still be severely injured on British roads every year. The overwhelming majority

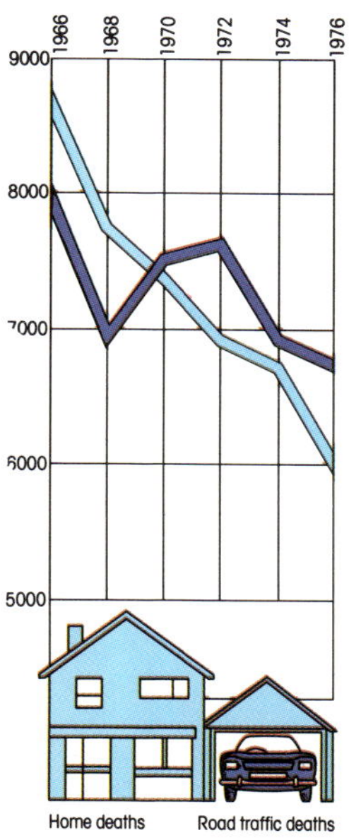

Safety Pays (Fig 2)
Trends of fatal accidents in Britain. Similar numbers are killed in the home and on the roads, but there is a great difference in the age and sex incidence

Left
Potholing, mountaineering in reverse, can be as dangerous as climbing, with the added hazard of darkness

Below left
Mountaineering is an outstanding example of conscious exposure to unnecessary and, at times, unreasonable risk. Nor does experience count for much when an avalanche strikes. This photograph shows rescue workers still searching for victims after an avalanche at Plateau d'Assy, in France, in 1970

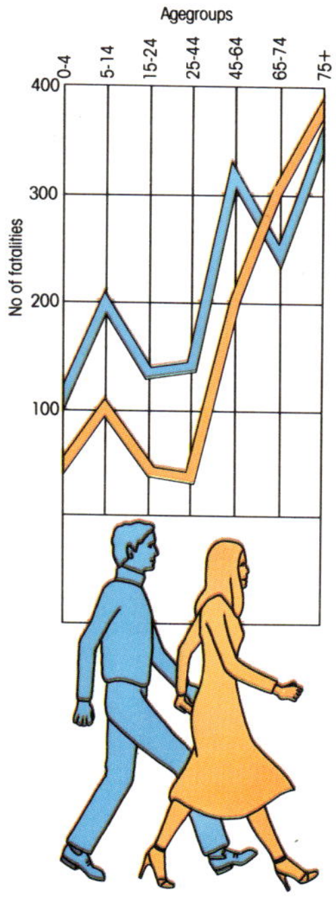

Pedestrian Peril (Fig 3)
Fatal pedestrian accidents. The mean total number of pedestrian deaths is shown. The escalation in old age is clearly demonstrated

Right
When cars involved in accidents catch fire, they do so within seconds, engulfing the occupants in a sea of flames

Below right
Bicycles, like motor-cycles, offer their riders no protection whatever in the event of an accident. In the photograph the cyclist had been riding close to the kerb when a lorry travelling along side him turned to the left

Transport to Danger
Travelling by rail or air carries much the same risk of death through accident

Hazardous Households
In the United States, more than twice as many people die in accidents in the home as in accidents at work

Killer 'Quake
The earthquake that claimed the greatest number of human lives occurred in Shansi, in China, in 1556, where the death toll reached 800,000

Stroke of Distortion
Statistics can be extremely misleading. It has been observed that more people die while playing golf than any other sport. Statistically, this could be seen to prove that golf is extremely dangerous, but in fact, nearly all golf course deaths result from natural causes, i.e. strokes and heart attacks

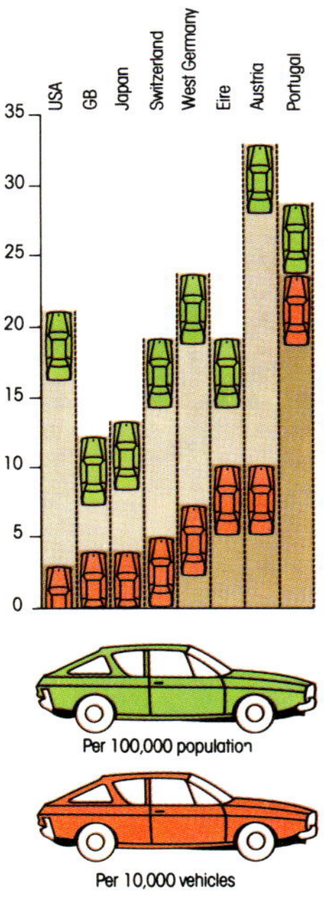

Menace of the Car (Fig. 4)
The association between vehicle density and deaths per vehicle for a selected number of countries. There is a tendency for the death rate to increase as the density decreases

of casualties occur in the 15-24 age group, with a very definite preponderance of males (Fig. 1).

A significant number of deaths among this 'young group' is attributable to the motor-cycle, a form of transport that is particularly European (Fig. 7), but which is becoming increasingly popular in the USA. Some 3,000 motor-cycle deaths a year are now reported from there. In 1976 there were more than 300 serious motor-cycle casualties per 100 million vehicle kilometres, compared with 10 for drivers of cars and taxis in England and Wales. The motor-cycle (and scooter) are even more destructive in Italy, where one-third of road casualties involve two-wheeled vehicles. Inevitably, the very flat countries—such as Denmark and Holland—have an exceptional number of deaths among pedal cyclists.

Britain and Ireland are outstanding for the high proportion of pedestrians killed on the roads. This is not only due to the ratio of pedestrians to other road users, but also to the virtual absence of legislation governing pedestrian behaviour. As Fig. 3 shows, the number of casualties among pedestrians increases with age. Also, the number of women involved is appreciably greater than that of men among the elderly—a reversal of the situation in the case of the 'young group'.

The comparative significance of road traffic deaths in various countries is difficult to judge. Much depends on the method of assessment. For instance, in proportion to its population, Britain seems to have a very good safety record as compared with, say, the United States. If the number of vehicles involved is taken as the parameter, however, the USA is shown to have a much higher standard of safety than Britain. It has been suggested that, the fewer cars there are in relation to the total population, the more dangerously they are driven, although factors such as the concomitant lack of good roads must also be taken into account. If the line computed in Fig. 4 expresses this hypothesis fairly, it must be accepted that some countries, such as France and Austria, have outstandingly poor safety records. Some specific circumstances must be responsible for this.

There has been much research into the prevention of road traffic accidents. A great deal can be done by improving road configurations, surfaces and lighting, and intensifying tests for vehicle road-worthiness and the like, but there is little doubt that speed is one of the principal factors in accidents and governs their severity (the problem of alcohol is discussed later). On the other hand, it is the function of the motor car to transport people from place to place as efficiently and as fast as possible, which means that some accidents are inevitable. The problem then becomes not simply how to prevent accidents, but how to prevent fatal accidents and those causing severe injury. Much could be done as regards

Left
There is very little avoiding action that train drivers can take in an attempt to minimize an impending railway accident, particularly where two trains suddenly find themselves travelling towards each other on the same stretch of track. In this particular case, more than 160 people were killed instantly, both locomotives were wrecked, the trains were derailed and the first few carriages disintegrated completely on impact

Below
This crumpled mass of scrap metal was all that remained of the sports car in which the film star, James Dean, met his death, when he collided with another car at high speed. There is little doubt that speed is one of the main factors in road accidents and may govern how serious they are. Another important factor is alcohol

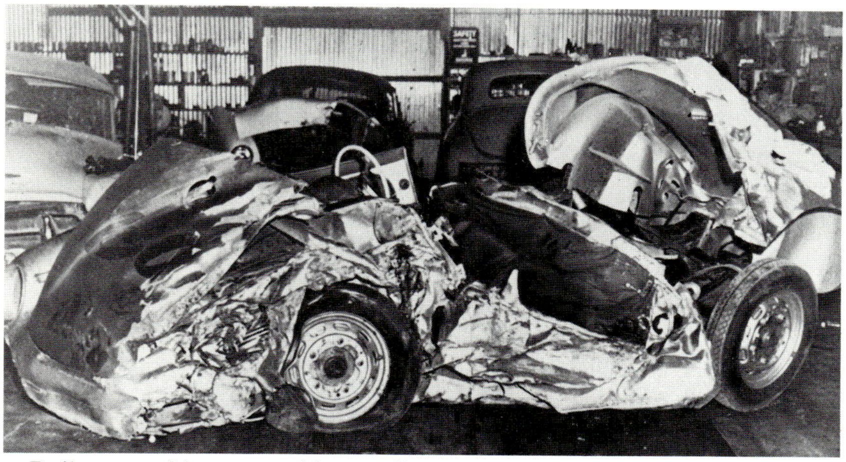

pedestrian deaths by improved car exterior design.

Most preventable deaths among motor-cyclists result from head injury. Wearing a crash helmet considerably reduces the risk of such injury. In Britain, it is compulsory, but the law varies from state to state in the USA, providing an opportunity for comparison. In some states where the wearing of a crash helmet is not compulsory, there are three times as many cases of severe head injury in motorcycle accidents as in states where a crash helmet must be worn by law.

Major attention has focused on the compulsory use of seat harnesses in cars. The Australian experience is pre-eminent in this respect. Following legislation compelling their use, there was a reduction in the predicted number of fatal casualties of 15 to 20 percent in Victoria and 25 percent in New South Wales. The incidence of hospitalization for head and facial injuries was reduced from 79 percent to 23 percent. Restraining harnesses must be efficient to be of value. The simple lap belt offers little or no advantage in the head-on crash situation. One can extrapolate from the British experience in light aircraft, where lap belts have long been compulsory, though shoulder harnesses were only rarely used prior to regulations introduced in 1978. It has been estimated that 40 percent of those killed in light aircraft would have survived—often without injury—had they been using an efficient and reliable shoulder restraint system.

The safest form of passenger transport is railway travel, although commercial air transport runs it a close second. Private flying is a different matter. The number of fatalities in the private sector exceeds that in both commercial and peace-time military flying

---

It is generally accepted that, excluding the largely leisure activity of sea voyaging, railway travel is about the safest form of passenger transport, although there is little to choose between it and scheduled air transport today (Fig. 5).

Railway accidents provide excellent examples of how the conjunction of improbabilities can bring about an unpredictable crisis. Either there is a flagrant abuse of regulations, or a number of apparently fool-proof automatic processes fail simultaneously or, characteristically, nature intervenes. When the last happens, railway bridges become very vulnerable. Two examples are the Tay Bridge, in Scotland, which collapsed in a high wind in 1897 as a main line express was crossing it, and the bridge over the Wangaehu River, in New Zealand, which was swept away by the eruption of Mount Ruapehu in 1953. This disaster almost certainly instigated a change in the New Zealand laws concerning the disposal of estates in the event of a husband and wife dying simultaneously.

Apart from major accidents, there is a steady trickle of deaths at railway level crossings, particularly when these are of the automatic type. Pedestrians are mainly involved, but tragedies occur when motor cars attempt to 'beat the bell'.

Fatal aircraft accidents are unique in many respects. In the first place, aircraft are a comparatively recent invention, so the regulations covering their manufacture and operation, as well as accident investigation, have been drawn up in the light of modern knowledge rather than evolving from the practices of the past. Also, the international nature of air travel has dictated the adoption of universally

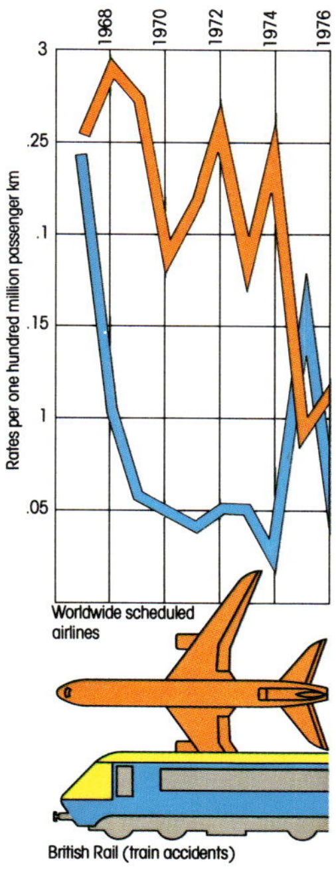

Dangerous Departure (Fig 5)
Fatality rates derived from passenger distances travelled. The rates shown are so low that a single severe accident in one year can dramatically distort the pattern

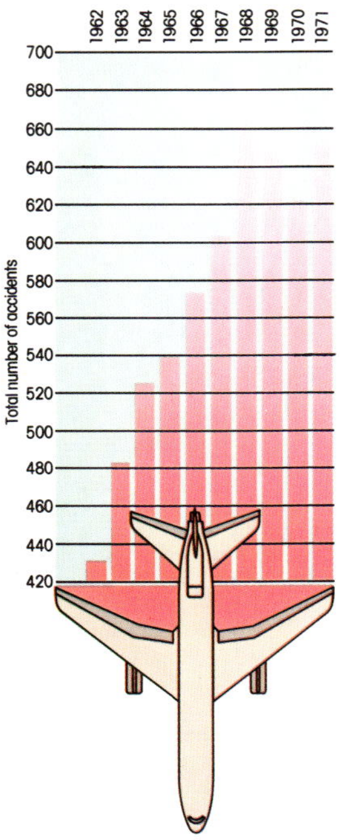

Air Disasters (Fig 6a)
The number of US private general aviation accidents which occurred in the ten years up to 1972

high standards and close co-operation between national authorities. Secondly, aircraft operate in an alien and hostile environment which is unforgiving of minor defects or errors which might pass unnoticed elsewhere. Thirdly, in a commercial airliner, the safety of a large number of people is effectively in the hands of one man. If he is suffering from disease and this prevents him from doing his job properly or he dies during a flight, his illness or natural death may cause a large number of accidental deaths.

Aviation deaths do not constitute a homogeneous group. The conditions of military, private and commercial flying are dissimilar, and different populations are involved.

Accidents may be due to either extraneous causes (weather conditions), or structural failure, system failures (eg electrical faults), or human error. This last, so far as the pilot is concerned, may be the result of frank incompetence, physiological causes (associated with altitude or with rotational forces, for example), toxicological effects (eg intoxication by carbon monoxide, therapeutic drugs or alcohol) or pathological processes (ie, disease). It is interesting that this kind of analysis of 'pilot error' received scant attention before the early 1950s.

Not only will these factors interact, but their influence will differ according to the type of flying involved. In private flying, by far the most important cause of accidents is human error. Significantly, the loss of life in the private sector exceeds that in both commercial and peace-time military aviation. It is probably worth noting that the effect of all adverse factors will be greatly exaggerated in the inherently dangerous military environment, where even a relatively minor disease may precipitate a fatal spatial disorientation.

Emotionally, however, it is the commercial airline disaster which attracts most interest. The largest number of passengers ever killed in a year of world-wide scheduled operations was 1,299 in 1974.

It is commonly stated that most airline accidents are due to human error. This may be true of non-fatal accidents, which tend to be associated with take-off and landing—that is, with moments of maximum human involvement, but less than half of those accidents with a large number of fatalities involve human error.

The trend of aviation fatalities is very interesting. There was a steady rise in the number of fatal air accidents up to the early 1970s and a corresponding increase in the number of fatalities. These trends might represent no more than an increase in the level of activity, but, at the same time, the fatal accident *rate* was actually falling exponentially. Clearly, improved aviation technology is largely responsible for this improvement in flight safety, although some of the success must be attributed to intensive accident investigation.

As already stated, pre-existing disease in the

Above right
One of the causes of Britain's worst air disaster, the crash of a BEA Trident at Staines, near London Airport in 1972, was an abnormal heart condition from which the pilot had been suffering

Below
Air accident at Nairobi airport, 1974. Remains of a Lufthansa Boeing 747

pilot has a special significance in commercial aviation. Its precise contribution to fatal accidents is uncertain. In the worst disaster occurring in Britain, which involved a Trident aircraft taking off from London Airport in 1972, the public inquiry found that an abnormal heart condition discovered in the pilot at autopsy was only one of seven underlying causes of a catastrophic handling error. In general, it is unlikely that more than one percent of fatal commercial aircraft accidents are due to pilot disease. The comparable figure in private aviation has been assessed at between five and ten percent, but this may be a gross over-estimate.

Accidental deaths are invariably investigated by the responsible medico-legal authority—coroner, procurator fiscal, medical examiner etc. Very often, these inquiries are publicized. In addition, there is often a statutory requirement in many countries for the relevant government department to conduct its own technical investigation. The findings can be fed into the medico-legal system, enabling not only the cause of the death or deaths but also the reason for them to be established in a relatively academic environment. Such a system contributes greatly to the general understanding and prevention of man-made accidents.

When an accident is of particular severity, these procedures are often replaced by a public inquiry, in which evidence is led, in the main, by legal counsel representing interested parties. It is arguable whether the quasi-judicial nature of the proceedings provides the ideal environment for the solution of difficult technical problems, particularly when these are of a medical nature. Too often one hears experts expressing diametrically opposed views, say, as to the origin of ethanol discovered in the blood of a dead train driver or even as to the retrospective analysis of an electrocardiogram. The impression is left that such matters would have been better debated with scientific detachment in private. Public exposure is, however, a now-entrenched condition of the Western way of life.

The more sophisticated the processing of food, the more likely it is to poison the person who eats it. Food may also be accidentally contaminated by insecticides and other substances

Natural poisoning results from either ingestion or inoculation. Not surprisingly, the majority of cases of 'food poisoning' stem from conditions in which the food is unaltered by the toxic principle—few people will eat obviously rotten meat. Paradoxically, therefore, it is the more sophisticated treatment of food which poses danger to man—mass pre-packaging of meals for air travel, canning, bottling and long-term preservation in the cold have all been implicated. The food-handler is a potent source of infection by virulent staphylococci or by the organisms causing dysentery and typhoid fever. Also poisonous foods may be eaten in error—the highly toxic Amanita may be mistaken for the edible mushroom, Agaricus, while children, particularly, may eat poisonous wild berries in mistake for those they have seen in the greengrocer's store.

In addition, foodstuffs may be accidentally contaminated by insecticides, herbicides or other substances. In 1959, 10,000 Arabs were poisoned because olive oil was adulterated with lubricating oil containing three percent of tri-ortho-cresyl phosphate. Almost incredibly, tragedies still occur because toxic substances like Paraquat are stored in whisky bottles still bearing their original labels.

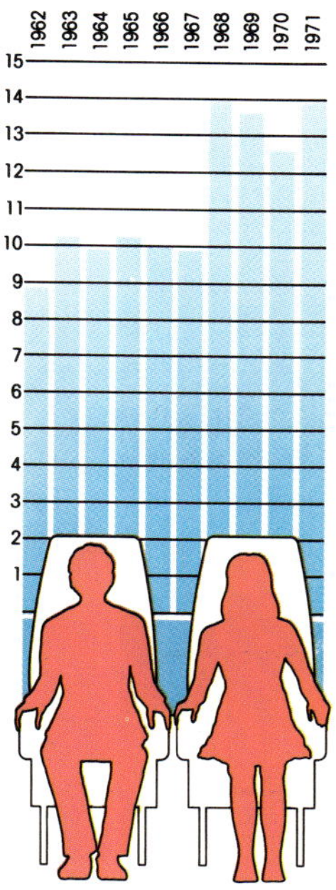

Air Disasters (Fig 6b)
The percentage of US private general aviation accidents involving fatalities which occurred in the 10 years up to 1972

Below
The international nature of air travel has resulted in the adoption of universally high standards. Just the same, however strict and all-embracing the regulations may be, they cannot obviate accidents due to bad weather conditions, structure or system failures, or human error. The result is that there will always be accidents like this one at Nairobi, 1974

Right
This photograph, taken after the widespread floods in Pakistan in 1970, shows the drowned bodies of people and dead animals, left behind by the receding flood waters

Mortal Danger (Fig 7)
Percentage of fatalities by class of road user. A significant loss of life in the 'young group' is due to the use of the motor cycle, particularly in Europe

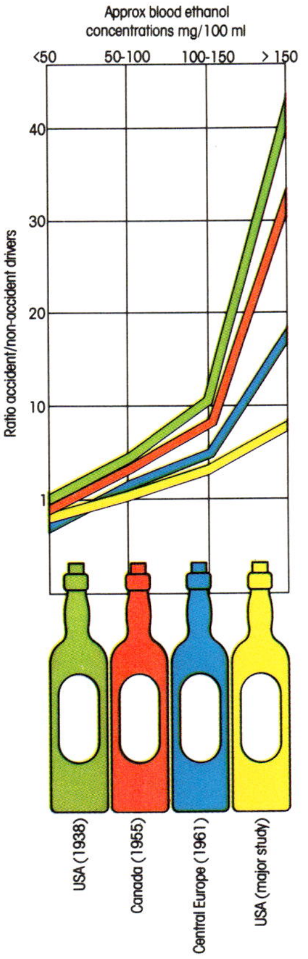

Death via Alcohol (Fig 8)
A simplified analysis showing the steadily increasing chances of having an accident as the blood ethanol level rises

Although its fatal incidence may be exaggerated, snake bite is a common cause of death in many areas of the world—in particular, India and Pakistan where some 10,000 deaths are reported annually, mainly from cobra bites. In the Americas and Australia, a considerable number of people die from snake bite. Members of the Viperidae family are largely responsible, particularly Crotalinae, or rattlesnakes. Many tropical fish inject venom when touched, particularly during the spawning period. Death as a result of shark bite, although misadventurous, is due to injury, not poisoning. Death from spider bite is rare. Only Latrodectus, the Black Widow, has any practical significance. The ratio of the victim's body weight to the quantity of venom is important in all types of natural poisoning by injection. The prognosis is thus always worse in children than in adults.

In Britain, thanks to legislation and the increasing efficiency of doctors in industry, industrial poisoning—other than that due to dust—has now fallen to the comparatively low figure of 497 cases (1976 total). Five of these were fatal, three being due to gassing. The importance of vigilance, is, however, emphasized by the discovery of new hazards, particularly in the form of long-term effects. The association of cancer of the liver with the processing of vinyl chloride monomer is a recent example. Microbiological infection remains a possibility, and the medical profession may be at significant risk here—the contraction of fatal hepatitis, for example, is a very real hazard for pathology laboratory workers.

The growing complexity and increasing use of drug therapy heighten the danger of accidental iatrogenic poisoning—poisoning occurring through the medium of medical practice

This brings us to the question of iatrogenic death—accidental death occurring by or through the medium of medical practice.

A surgical operation or the administration of an

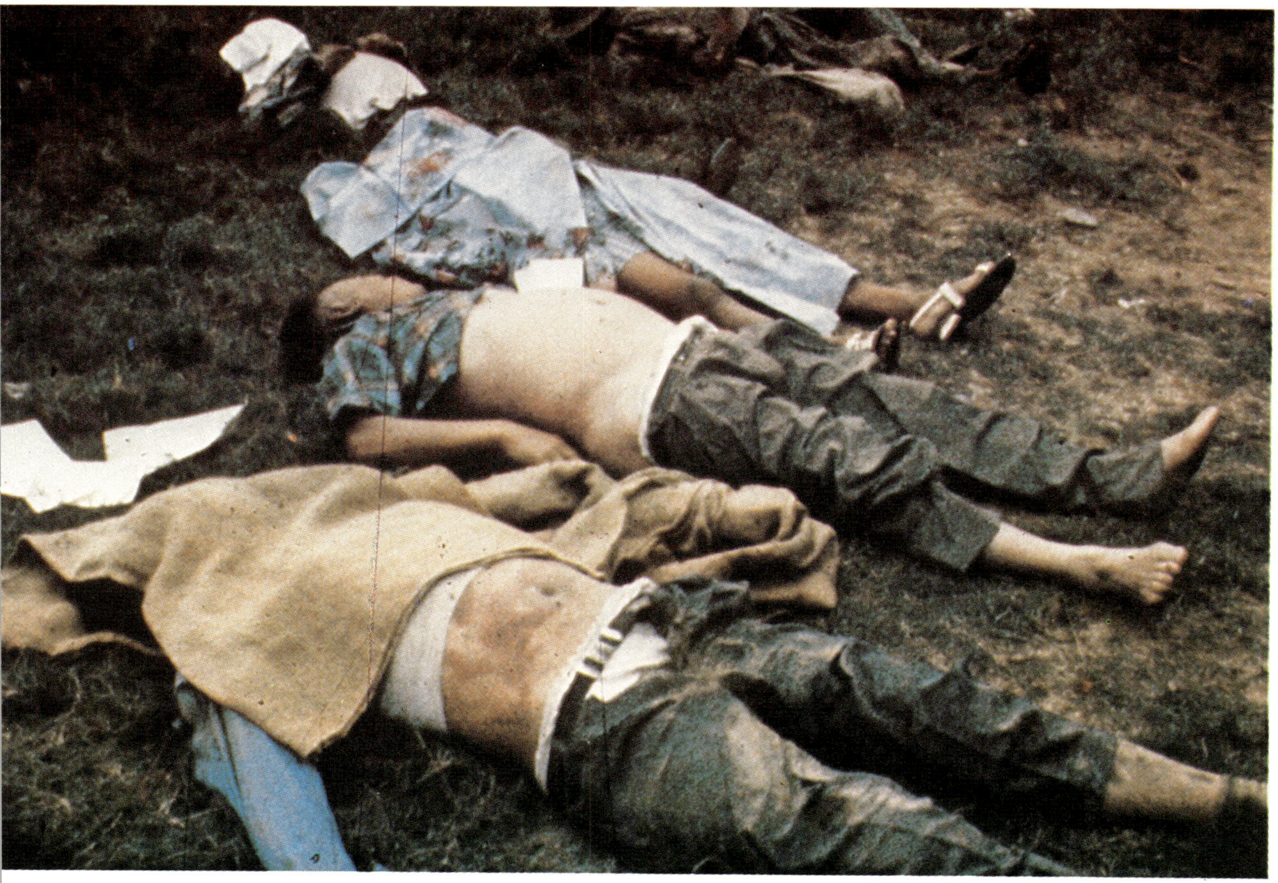

Left
Bodies of earthquake victims in Huarez, Peru, in 1970. Most countries in earthquake zones appear to have taken few precautions against casualties or damage

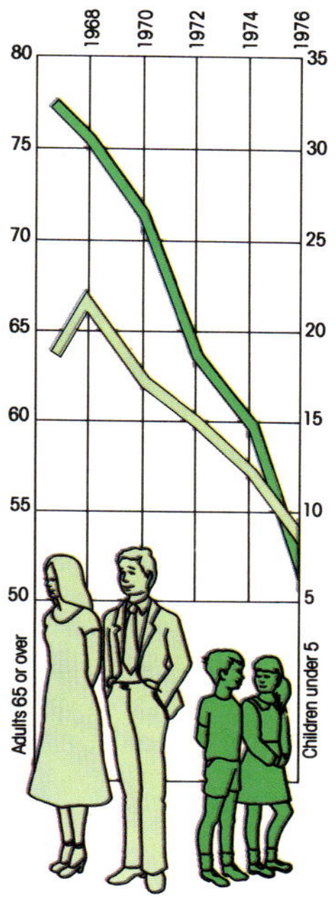

Residential Death (Fig 9)
Fatal accidents in the home. There has been a 53 percent reduction in the death rate (per 100,000 population) for the infant group, as opposed to a 32 percent improvement among the aged

anaesthetic may result in death (there are between 50 and 70 incidents a year in England and Wales), but this is not always the result of negligence. Modern techniques allow increasingly severe procedures to be offered to increasingly high-risk patients who would otherwise be left without hope. At the same time, improved scientific understanding of the basis of disease dictates the more widespread use of invasive investigatory techniques. The inherent risks grow as these become more complicated. The problem is one of balancing the advantages to the community as a whole against an occasional failure.

The hazard of accidental iatrogenic poisoning becomes greater with the growing complexity and increasing use of drug therapy. There are two main reasons for this. In the first place, there are many drugs which either have a cumulative effect or have an adverse effect on body systems which are not being treated. For instance, many drugs prescribed for abnormalities of the nervous system are positively dangerous to a diseased cardiovascular system. Although cases of this nature do still occur, the growth of the problem has been halted by propaganda. Secondly, and of far greater importance, is the fact that, generally speaking, potent and expensive drugs are more readily available than, say, forty years ago, and large quantities are retained in the home. As a result, adults may take larger doses in circumstances or combinations which are different from those envisaged by their doctors. Furthermore, unless such drugs are stored securely, children may poison themselves through curiosity or by mistaking tablets for sweets. Above all, the effect of many drugs, particularly those affecting the central nervous system, will be enhanced and their toxic threshold reduced by the action of alcohol, itself a drug.

Of all drugs available to man, alcohol has the greatest effect on accidental death. A drunken man is more likely to fall off a quayside than a sober one; he is more likely to handle a shotgun injudiciously; he will even die more easily from cold when 'sleeping it off'.

Much has been written on the relationship of alcohol and vehicular accidents. It is not widely appreciated that, both in the United States and United Kingdom, some seven percent of fatal private aviation accidents are alcohol-associated. Astonishingly, nearly half (42 percent) of cases in the USA show ethanol levels in the pilot in excess of 150 mg/100 ml blood. The greatest interest, however, centres on the road accidents. Fig. 8 shows results obtained in four well-known and well-controlled studies—the positive relationship between alcohol and accident susceptibility is well demonstrated. The constant 'negative' association below the value of 50 mg/100 ml does not necessarily indicate that small doses of alcohol actually improve perceptivity and reactivity. It is far more probable that drivers who are aware they may be approaching the legal limits for driving are at particular pains to ensure that they are not put to the test. A drunken pedestrian is also more vulnerable than one who is sober. The association between driving accidents and alcohol also holds for those on foot.

Another major area of interest lies in the delicate relationship between alcohol, homicide and death by misadventure. A high proportion of homicides today are alcohol-associated, and most of them relate to scuffles or stabbing affrays outside drinking establishments. It is tempting to regard such deaths as misadventure rather than murder, since there is minimal premeditation. It is, however, a clear principle of law that drunkenness cannot excuse or mitigate homicide, except when the accused was so drunk as to be incapable of forming an intention to kill or do serious injury. As one judge expressed it—the concept of diminished responsibility due to abnormality of the mind was neither intended to be, nor was it, a charter for drunkards.

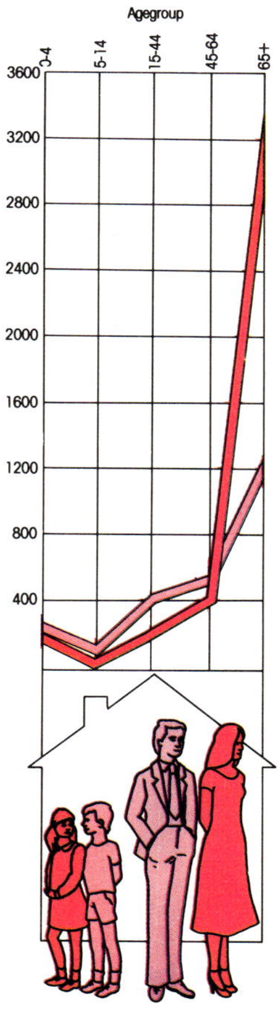

Fatal Falls (Fig 10)
Over a ten-year span an aged person is 35 times more likely to have a fatal fall than is an infant below the age of five years

Strategy of Suicide

What makes one man commit suicide while, in an equally desperate situation, another decides to go on living? What are the psychological stresses and environmental pressures that induce so many men, women and children to take their own lives?

Above
Nero had been Emperor of Rome for 14 years when he killed himself in 68 AD at the age of 31. When he saw the horsemen sent by the Senate approaching to drag him to his execution he stabbed himself to death

Right
A Buddhist monk in Saigon burns himself to death in 1963 in protest against the Vietnam War. In contrast to Islam, which regards suicide as a worse crime than murder, Zen Buddhism considers it a virtue, in certain circumstances, for a person to take his or her own life

World-wide Death Wish
About 2000 people a week kill themselves around the world

Notes for a Death
A certain proportion of those who kill themselves leave suicide notes. Here are three which are quoted in J. Maxwell Anderson's book 'Discovering Suicide':
'You can't very well go, so I guess it will have to be me. I don't think I could stay here anyway after today'.
'Tell the train driver not to worry. It's my doing, not his'. (In an extract from a letter to a girlfriend)
'. . . things are getting me down a bit lately, so this evening I am going to commit suicide

Suicide is not a recent or a rare phenomenon. Considerably more than 100,000 people throughout the world kill themselves every year, for a variety of reasons and using a variety of methods, ranging from the unremarkable to the bizarre. However, despite the statistical and other information available today, our understanding of the psychology of suicide has not greatly advanced, and many questions remain unanswered. Indeed, it is true to say that the greater the flow of information and the more detailed it is, the less successful are our efforts to understand suicide.

Of course, some progress has been made, and the contemporary attitude to suicide is more tolerant than in the past. For centuries, suicide was considered to be the work of Satan, and was surrounded by superstition, as well as religious dogmatism. This has been largely swept aside, but modern sociologists and psychologists like Adler, Freud and Durkheim, for instance, have come no nearer than Aristotle or Plato to developing a generally acceptable theory about the forces that induce suicide. There are as many conflicting theories on the subject as there ever were, and this situation seems unlikely to change in the near future.

From the time of the Ancient Greeks to the late Middle Ages, suicide—at least when committed by those other than the privileged—was condemned by many societies. In Europe until the Middle Ages, the corpses of suicides were severely mutilated if not torn limb from limb and, in many cases, surviving members of the family were attacked. In Ancient Greece it was standard practice to cut off the hand of a suicide which had held the death weapon. Eminent Greeks, like Pythagoras and Plato, abhorred suicide. In their writings they urged that the corpses of suicides should be buried in unmarked graves, away from those used by ordinary

One Man's Earth
'The man who kills a man kills a man.
The man who kills himself kills all men.
As far as he is concerned, he wipes out the world.'
(G. K. Chesterton)

people. However, as in so many aspects of life, there was one law for the rich and another for the poor. The Greeks, as hundreds of classical tragedies demonstrate, encouraged the artistocracy to regard suicide as an act of noble sacrifice. As far as the lower orders of society were concerned, suicide was seriously frowned upon, although not prohibited. A convicted Greek criminal had the option of killing himself rather than face public execution. The magistrate kept a quantity of poison available specifically for this purpose.

For almost one thousand years Western civilization regarded the practice of suicide with fascination and loathing. While the nobility were largely applauded for choosing to kill themselves rather than face 'dishonour', the lower classes were resolutely condemned for seeking to avail themselves of the means to end their own lives, for example to escape the suffering of a public execution

The Romans were equally hypocritical. While the ruling classes were praised in their acts of ritual suicide, every effort was made to deter slaves, and soldiers, by laws which were not moral in tone, but principally designed to protect the Empire and its property. Thus, any transaction involving the sale of a slave could be declared null and void if he killed himself within six months of the deal. The dead slave's property and possessions were forfeited to the state, and his body was ignominiously cast into a pit with those of common criminals. No punishment was meted out to any slave failing in a suicide attempt, but any soldier attempting suicide and failing was executed, since attempting to kill himself was regarded as desertion. On the other hand, the history of the Roman Empire includes a number of highly fashionable and lauded suicides. Cato, the Stoic philosopher, spent several hours ironically reading Phaedo—Plato's assertion of the immortality of the soul—before killing himself with his own sword. The double suicide of Anthony and Cleopatra is another example, although it was not the romantic symbol of rapturous love that some would have us believe, but a rather more sinister affair. Mark Anthony did not develop an overt intimate relationship with Cleopatra until after the death of Julius Caesar, with whom she had been living in Rome. Fearing for her own life after Caesar had been assassinated, Cleopatra returned with Anthony to Egypt. Not long after his flight and already depressed when his army was routed at sea, Mark Anthony's mental endurance was stretched to the limit on hearing a rumour (false as it turned out), that Cleopatra had committed suicide. He weakened and soon after killed himself with his own sword. Cleopatra, for her part, followed suit mainly, if not entirely, to avoid the humiliation of being led through the streets of Rome a defeated captive. How much, if at all, Anthony's suicide influenced Cleopatra's decision is a matter for conjecture.

Almost as significant for Rome, though far less sensational, was the death of Seneca. A powerful Senator who had enjoyed the patronage of more than one Roman Emperor, Seneca ultimately fell out of favour with the Emperor Nero. He resolved to save his honour by killing himself, and made a suicide pact with his wife. She died soon after stabbing herself, but Seneca bungled his suicide. He began by opening his veins with his dagger, but being old and feeble, did not cut deeply enough to bring about a speedy death. Instead, he suffered agonizing pain, which so distressed his servants that they gave him poison to drink. This did not work either, so the servants carried Seneca to a

Right
Christian martyrs being slaughtered by wild animals in the Colosseum in Rome—a romanticized drawing by a nineteenth-century German artist. Early Christians preferred this agonizing but relatively quick way of committing suicide to enduring a lifetime of slavery, believing that it guaranteed them immediate entry to paradise

Centre right
The martyrdom of Ignatius, Bishop of Antioch, in Rome in the second century, AD. While being taken to Rome by a group of soldiers, he wrote: 'Let it be known that I die for God of my own free will . . . Let me be given to the wild beasts, for through them I can attain to God'

Bottom right
Socrates—a bust in the Naples Museum. In ancient Athens, even criminals were given the choice of killing themselves instead of being publicly executed. When Socrates, the philosopher, was condemned to death in 399 BC, he drank hemlock

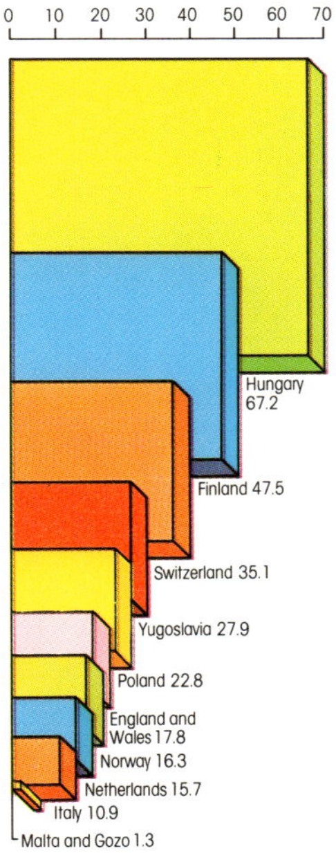

North-South Divide
Suicide rates in ten selected European countries, both male and female, per 100,000 population. Not surprisingly, the north European countries have a very definite lead over those in the Mediterranean basin

steam bath, where he died a lingering, intensely painful death by suffocation.

The fear and hostility of European society towards suicide were reactions strongly influenced by the Church, which had long banned the practice of self-destruction even though it had been the preferred death of the early Christian Martyrs. By contrast, various communities in the East strongly encouraged individuals to take their own lives

In medieval Europe, the attitude towards suicide was generally extremely hostile, strongly influenced, no doubt, by the attitude of the Church. The Roman practice of confiscating the property of those of the lower orders who killed themselves was incorporated into most European codes of law, and remained in force in several European countries until well into the middle of the eighteenth century. The ill-treatment of suicides' corpses was widely practised, even though the Church later condemned it. In France, for example, such corpses were beaten, dragged through the streets and then hung from a gibbet. In Switzerland, people who killed themselves by jumping from a mountain were buried at its foot, while in other countries, those who drowned themselves were buried on the shore. These practices were based on the belief that the mode of burial should be related to the mode of death, and would help to prevent a disturbed soul from 'wandering abroad'. There is a connection here with a practice observed in many parts of England for centuries. The corpse of a suicide could not be removed from a house until nightfall, when it was lifted through a window, not a doorway. The body was then buried at a crossroads with a stake through its heart, the idea being that the soul of the suicide would be unable to decide which road to take and would therefore be deterred from wandering. The last burial of this kind took place in the King's Road, London, as recently as 1823. Sometimes, permission was given for a suicide to be buried in a churchyard, in which case the body was bundled over the cemetery wall and interred between the hours of nine and midnight without benefit of religious rites or service.

However, by no means did all societies adopt a hostile attitude towards the act of suicide. Many, such as the ancient Greeks, encouraged individuals to take their own lives. In India, it was the practice, until stopped by the ruling British authorities, for a widow to immolate herself on her husband's funeral pyre. This reached its peak in 1821, when more than 2000 killed themselves in this way. In parts of North America and among the Maoris of New Zealand, widows were put to death by strangulation. The custom of putting widows to death was particularly widespread among tribes facing a constant struggle to survive. Among the Eskimos and the peoples of Siberia, the weak, the old and the

Death before Dishonour
In ancient days, virgins killed themselves to protect their virtue

According to the Book
There are several Biblical examples of suicide. They include Samson destroying himself and the Philistines by pulling down a temple; Saul falling on his sword to avoid imminent defeat at the hands of the Philistines, and Judas hanging himself for betraying Christ

Below
Scene III, Act V of 'Romeo and Juliet', by William Shakespeare. Juliet, in a drugged sleep, has been taken for dead and laid in the Capulet family tomb. Waking, she asks Friar Laurence, who has earlier married her in secret to Romeo, a Montagu, where he is. She has not yet seen him lying dead at her feet. He has taken poison, after killing Paris, her father's choice to marry her

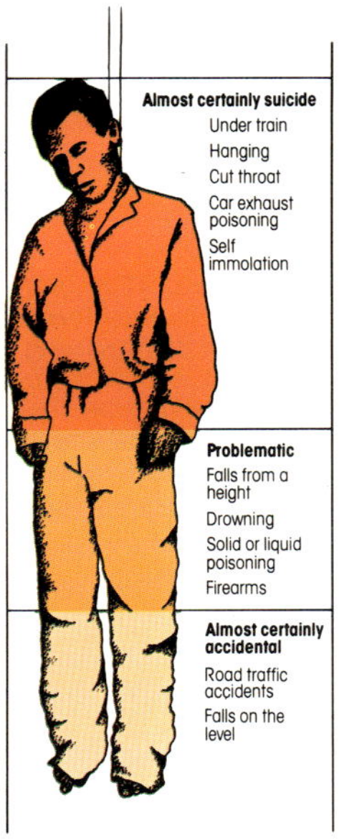

Doubts and Certainties
Most attempted and actual suicides can be placed under the classification which includes falling under trains and hangings. These are fairly definitely suicide acts. More problematic are those deaths which result from falls and the use of firearms

Conflicting Concepts
The Koran, the sacred text of Islam, looks upon suicide as a more serious crime than murder. In direct contrast, Zen Buddhists believe that, in some circumstances, it can be positively virtuous

Following the Path
In the early nineteenth century, when a Maori chief died, it was the custom for his wives to commit suicide, usually by hanging themselves from a tree

sick voluntarily killed themselves to give the remainder of the community a better chance of survival.

Of all the countries where suicide was tolerated or even encouraged, Japan alone raised the act of self-destruction to the level of transcendental ritual. For a warrior to die by the sword, whether an enemy's or his own, was considered to imbue him with supreme honour

Nowhere has suicide become more ritualized and refined than in Japan, where the first recorded act of ritual suicide by a Japanese warrior (samurai) took place in 1170. The samurai, a great and famous archer called Tametomo Minamoto, surrounded by enemies, ripped open his belly with a sword, in the conviction that he was thereby setting his spirit free. The Japanese have believed for centuries that a man's spirit, the source of the will and the deepest emotions, resides in the belly (*hara*). Hence the term *Hara-kiri* ('belly-cutting') commonly used in the West to refer to Japanese ritual suicide, although the Japanese themselves prefer to use the word *seppuku*. For 700 years, until the abolition of the samurai caste in the late nineteenth century, seppuku was established as an honourable death for a Japanese warrior—ever since, in fact, Yoshitsune Minamoto, the foremost hero of Japan's age of chivalry, had disembowelled himself to avoid capture in 1189. The act was confined by law to the warrior caste. Other classes, from the nobility to the peasantry, had to use other means of self-destruction. Seppuku is still practised in Japan, not only by the successors of the samurai.

For a warrior to kill himself by hanging, drowning, poison or shooting was regarded as shameful, yet even these were preferable to the dishonour of being captured. However, the avoidance of dishonour was not the sole reason for seppuku. Another was a mark of respect on the death of one's feudal lord. A third was in protest at the decision of a superior. Finally, suicide could be imposed as a punishment. In 1912, General Maresuke Nogi, the victor of Port Arthur, committed suicide with his wife following the death of Emperor Meiji. (The wife of a warrior committing seppuku was allowed to die with her husband by stabbing herself in the throat with a dagger). In 1933, Lieutenant-Commander Kusuhara disembowelled himself on a train because of the Government's refusal to make funds available for new battle-cruisers. In 1867, a band of samurai who had attacked some French sailors were sentenced by the Government to self-destruction in the presence of the French Ambassador—who begged for pardon for the survivors after seeing eleven men die.

Death after disembowelling could take several hours, but it was usual for the agony to be terminated by a close friend appointed to stand behind the samurai with a sword and decapitate him at a given signal. This was the practice followed by the novelist and Nobel Prize nominee, Yukio Mishima, in November 1970. After haranguing men of the

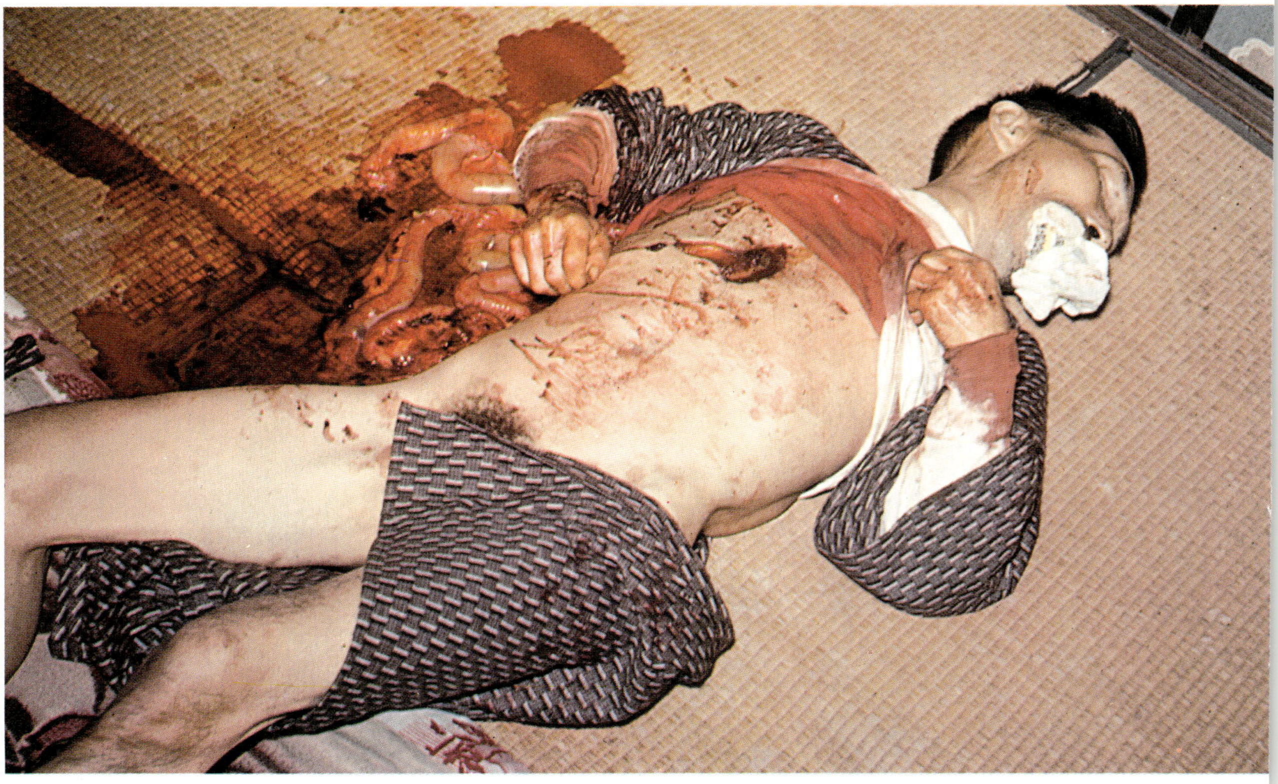

Right
Ritual suicide in present-day Japan, committed in the traditional manner. The Japanese believe that the belly ('hara') is the site of the spirit, hence the term 'hara-kiri' ('belly-cutting') used in the West to refer to Japanese ritual suicide. The Japanese themselves, however, prefer to use the word 'seppuku'. Until the abolition of the samurai (warrior) caste in the last century, seppuku had been regarded for 700 years as an honourable way for a samurai to die

Top right
A Japanese print of a man about to commit seppuku. Death could take several hours, but a close friend usually stood behind the samurai and decapitated him with a sword at a given signal. Avoiding dishonour was not the only reason for a man to commit seppuku. It was also a mark of respect on the death of a feudal lord, and a protest against a superior's decision. In addition, suicide could be imposed as a punishment

Army Self-Defence Force about what he saw as the decadence of modern Japan, he slit open his stomach and was beheaded by one of his disciples at the third attempt. A more spectacular suicide was that of the actor, Mitsuyasu Saeno, who crashed his light aircraft on the Tokyo home of a millionaire called Yoshio Kodama, in protest against Kodama's involvement in the Lockheed bribes scandal.

The armed forces of several of the principal powers involved in the 1939-45 conflict built up suicide groups to further their war aims. For example, during the Battle of Stalingrad, the final stages of which took place in the winter of 1942-43, groups of Russian infantrymen, dressed in black, were sent forward to draw enemy gunfire and thus give away the German positions

During World War II, the Japanese used suicide as a form of warfare. So did the Nazi and Soviet (Red) Air Forces, although to a far smaller extent. In addition to the suicide aircraft squadrons known as *kamikaze*, the Japanese used purpose-designed midget submarines, manned torpedoes, explosive motor-boats and frogmen. The kamikaze squadrons were the best-known and most effective Japanese suicide weapon. The first successful kamikaze mission was flown in October, 1944, and the squadrons reached their peak of activity at Okinawa in the Pacific, between March and August, 1945, when 2,571 suicide sorties were flown. During this period, 26 ships were sunk and 164 damaged. By the time Japan surrendered, on August 15, 1945, 4,615 kamikaze pilots had been killed. Vice-Admiral Takijiro Onishi, the prime mover in the formation of the kamikaze squadrons, committed seppuku in 1945, prolonging his death agony for a full day.

The Nazi Air Force included squadrons of Focke-Wulf 190A-6s specially armoured for ramming attacks, while the Red Air Force's Komsomoltsi (Young Communists) 'Do-or-Die' squadrons flew similarly equipped I-16 fighters. After World War II ended in Japan's defeat, the number of civilian suicides reached unprecedented heights, and although it fell heavily during the ensuing ten years, it is still running at the rate of 20,000 a year—nearly seven percent of the world total.

Historically, there has been confusion about the morality of suicide. Initially, the Roman Catholic Church tolerated it, but the enthusiasm of the early Christians for dying as martyrs—many felt that immediate entry into paradise after a few minutes of agony in the arena was undoubtedly preferable to a lifetime of slavery—became increasingly difficult to control. By 452, the Church declared that suicide was inspired by Satan and, 100 years later, it issued a decree refusing Christian burial to suicides. In the East, China and India, suicide for religious reasons was looked on as socially acceptable, sometimes even desirable. Every year, Chinese Buddhists volunteered to set fire to themselves on Mount Tien-toi, in exchange for a blessing protecting their communities from evil. In India, many Hindus, whose belief is that life is merely an interlude in eternity, put themselves into an extreme state of hypnotism before allowing themselves to be buried alive. Suicide is referred to in the Bible only four times, the two most famous incidents being those of Samson and King Saul, but nowhere does the Bible actually make an ethical judgement on the acts. This omission gave rise to an intense debate on the morality of suicide which continued for many centuries. St Augustine, one of the leading theologians of the Church, condemned suicide as 'utterly damnable'. Several hundred years later one of the most formidable opponents of the Church's denunciation of suicide, the German philosopher, Arthur Schopenhauer, took issue with the Church. He wrote: 'I am of the opinion that the clergy should once and for all be challenged to explain by what right they, without being able to show any biblical authority or any valid philosophical arguments, stigmatize in the pulpit and in their writings an action committed by many'. The controversy continued with growing intensity into the nineteenth century, when proponents of the principle of free choice asserted that a man had the right to choose whether to continue living or take his own life. As

TOP TEN

1. Pharmacists
2. Chiropodists
3. Labourers and unskilled workers
4. Qualified medical practitioners
5. Housekeepers, Stewards, Matrons and Housemothers
6. Medical Workers
7. Bricklayers and semi-skilled Labourers
8. Nurses
9. Maids, Valets and other service workers
10. Telegraph and Radio Operators

Means and Ends
Listed above in order of magnitude are the ten vocational groups with the highest rates of suicide in the UK. Obviously, because of their access to drugs, pharmacists come out on top

Left
A British manned torpedo under way—a World War II photograph. Unlike the British, the Japanese did not attempt to swim to safety after approaching as closely to the target as they could and then aiming the torpedo at it. Instead, the Japanese stayed astride their weapon, knowing that they would be killed when it hit home

Left
Suicide aircraft squadrons known as 'kamikaze' were the best-known and most effective suicide weapon in World War II. Between March and August, 1945, more than 2,550 suicide sorties were flown, sinking 26 ships and damaging 164. In the last eleven months of the war, 1,615 kamikaze pilots were killed. Here, an officer briefs a group of pilots before they take off

Left
A Japanese plane plummets towards the sea in flames after receiving a direct hit from a US carrier's anti-aircraft guns. This photograph was taken from the carrier during World War II operations near Saipan, in the Mariana Islands, in the Pacific

Sentenced to Suicide
Compulsory self-disembowelling (seppuku) could be ordered by a feudal chief in Japan until 1868, when it was made illegal

Four Roads to the Grave
Until about 150 years ago, suicides in Britain were buried at a crossroads with a stake through their heart

Customs and Attitudes
Among certain East African tribes, the attitude to suicide is such that a tree on which a person has hanged himself must be cut down and burnt. Other tribes kill a sheep or other animal to pacify the suicide's troubled spirit

the controversy raged, Emile Durkheim, the French sociologist, published *Suicide*, the first major work on the subject, in 1897. His book expounded the theory that the forces producing suicide were largely generated by the structure and type of society in which it occurred. Earlier, Quetelet had expressed a similar view in his *Treatise on Man*, in which he wrote: 'it is the social state, in some measure, which prepares these crimes. The criminal is merely the instrument to execute them'. Sigmund Freud's view was the opposite to Durkheim's. Freud considered that the subconscious, not external factors, was responsible for the drive towards suicide. His contemporary, the Austrian psychiatrist, Alfred Adler, took yet another view: he emphasized the need for strong personal relationships as a means of combating suicide. The controversy continues today, with many kinds of theories proposed, in an attempt to explain the act, and justified with copious use of statistics. Of these there is no shortage, since both the United Nations and one of its agencies, the World Health Organization, collect and collate data in co-operation with the central statistical bureaux of all UN member-states. The resulting statistical tables analyze suicides all over the world by sex, social class, race, income group, age and population.

Although the world total of suicides is increasing in proportion to the growth in population, the frequency rate in individual countries has fluctuated very little. Potential suicides are more likely to be male than female, professional men with a high standard of education, and single

Examination of these statistics and the result of other research show that the world total of suicides is increasing in proportion to the growth in world population, but that the frequency rate in individual countries has fluctuated very little over the past 20 years with the exception of Japan. Looking at the number of deaths, Hungary tops the list, with Sweden, Denmark, Finland and the USA not far behind. Indeed, the figure in the USA is rapidly approaching 30,000 a year. At the bottom of the list are Norway, Scotland and Italy. The most suicidal city in the world is West Berlin.

Irrespective of which country is studied the incidence of suicide is highest among those above the age of 55, who are more likely than any other age group to suffer from chronic illness, immobility, loneliness and depression. Far more men than women die in their attempts at suicide: because, many psychiatrists believe most men who attempt to kill themselves really intend to do so, while the overwhelming majority of apparent suicide attempts by women are not so much genuine efforts to do away with themselves as cries for help. Psychiatrists call them 'parasuicides'. It is certainly a fact that only ten percent of women apparently trying to kill themselves, usually with poison, actually succeed in doing so. As we have already stated potential suicides are more likely to be male than female. A potential male suicide victim is more likely than not to be single, divorced, or a widower; childless; a city-dweller, and strongly dependent on alcohol or drugs. He may also come from a broken home, have a history of mental or physical illness and have a high level of education. If he is a professional, he is likely to be a medical worker. However, the foregoing is merely a stereotype, based on the findings of research, but this same research has demonstrated that the number of variables reputed to contribute to a suicide are infinite and are equalled only by the number of theories adduced to explain them.

No satisfactory hypothesis has yet been put forward to account for the high suicide rate in the United States and Sweden, both stable democracies with a high standard of living. The high suicide rate in the United States in particular is puzzling, because its population includes groups, principally religious in origin, which have traditionally been characterized by a high level of stability and an accompanying low rate of suicide. Two such groups are the Roman Catholics and the Jews. Both have strong family units, reinforced by a highly structured, disciplined religion, which provides members of each community with an identity, thus helping the

Right
A French periodical of 1900 carried this illustration of an American banker about to commit suicide by detonating some dynamite he had placed on his abdomen. In America, the suicide rate is rapidly approaching 30,000 a year, which puts it among the top five countries in the world

Below right
Alfred Adler, the Austrian psychologist, 1870-1937. He stressed the necessity to build up strong personal relationships as a means of combating suicide, although he came no nearer than other modern psychologists – or ancient philosophers – to developing a generally acceptable theory about the forces inducing suicide

A Cry for Help
The majority of suicides often speak of their intentions to someone beforehand, or at least obliquely indicate them. A recent study showed that about a third of all suicides see a doctor on the day they kill themselves

A Cure for Frustration
Insincere suicide attempts – parasuicides' – are particularly common among women in the 25-34 age group

Trying Again
People who attempt suicide on impulse and fail are more likely to repeat the attempt than those who plan the act – and still do not succeed

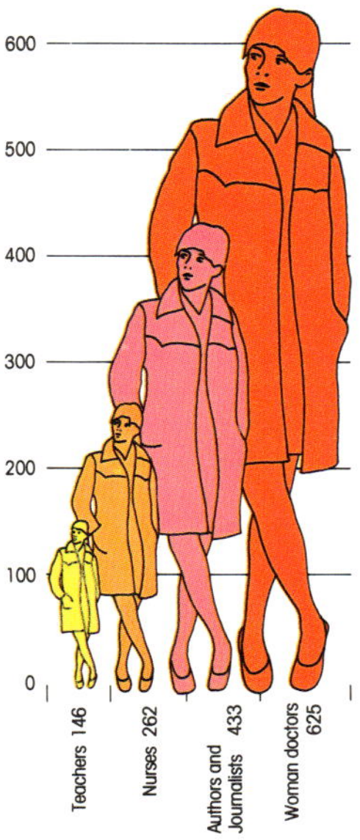

Women at Risk
The actual numbers of women, in four professions, who committed suicide in the UK in 1972. The figures and proportions for each group have barely altered in each year since

Far left and left
Salvatore Patti, 61, falls from the roof of a block of flats in Milan in May, 1972. He had climbed up there thinking that his wife was dead, after he had attacked her and rendered her unconscious following a fierce quarrel. Neighbours called the police and fire brigade, who tried to persuade Patti to leave the roof, explaining to him that his wife was not dead. However, Patti was startled when two firemen tried to approach him. He fell off the roof, landing on some railings. He was still alive after being freed **(left)** and was taken to hospital, but died later

Bottom far left
Sigmund Freud, 1856-1939 (centre), in London a year before his death. With him are his daughter and Dr Ernest Jones, his leading British disciple and his biographer. Freud, the father of psycho-analysis, believed sub-conscious, not external, factors to be responsible for the urge to suicide in some people

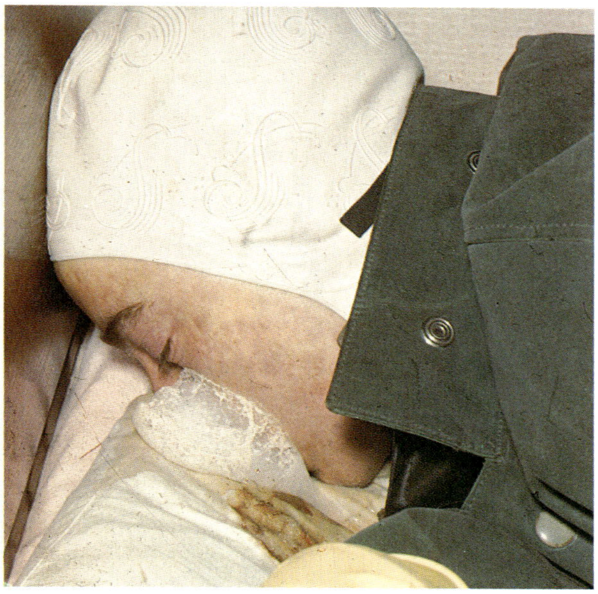

Left
An obsession with rubber led to the death of this British youth, who killed himself from irrational, sexual motives. Until 1961, suicide was a criminal act under British law, and today, assisting a person to take his or her own life remains an offence

formation of substantial personal relationships. Yet, even here, there is no hard and fast rule, for while there are certainly some Catholic countries with low suicide rates (Ireland, Spain and Italy, for instance), others, like France and Austria, have high suicide rates, while Hungary has the highest rate of all.

Suicide is most frequent among doctors and others working in the medical field. Most kill themselves with drugs. Contrary to the generally held view, the film industry does not suffer from a high rate of suicide, although film stars who kill themselves receive an inordinate amount of publicity. George Sanders' suicide note in 1972 said that he was taking his life because he was bored

The belief that the increasing incidence of suicide is directly proportional to a higher level of education is supported by the fact that the frequency of the act is greatest among professional people, particularly doctors and others working in the medical field. More members of this group commit suicide, especially with drugs, than any other. Doctors have the knowledge to make their suicide attempts succeed, but above everything else, they also have access to the means. This question of the availability of the means is a fundamental one and has a definite bearing on the increased rate of suicide among certain professional groups. In the United States, for instance, firearms are abundantly available and do not have to be licensed. As a result, 40 percent of American suicides are committed with a gun. In Britain, on the other hand, firearms are not readily available, whereas coal gas was until about ten years ago, when it was replaced by natural gas, which is far less toxic. Before the changeover, some 1,400 people a year asphyxiated themselves in Britain—60 times as many as in the United States. Today, far fewer people in Britain choose to commit suicide in this way.

A Case for Perseverance
In a study made in 1972, it was shown that 27 percent of male and 36 percent of female suicides had made at least one previous attempt

Firearm Fatalities
In the USA, guns account for 56 percent of all male suicides, and 25 percent of female suicides

Road Safety
Suicides are 50 percent more frequent in Sweden than fatal road accidents

The Last Operation
Doctors are two and a half times more likely to kill themselves than the average person. In Britain, six percent of all doctors under 65 meet their death through suicide

Planting a Suicide
In a recent report, two American psychiatrists came to the conclusion that 'seeds' leading to suicide are sown in infancy, and that rejection by one's mother can influence suicidal tendencies later in life

Fatal Education
More than 500 schoolchildren shot, hanged or poisoned themselves in West Germany in 1977, because they feared they would fail at school or get poor exam results

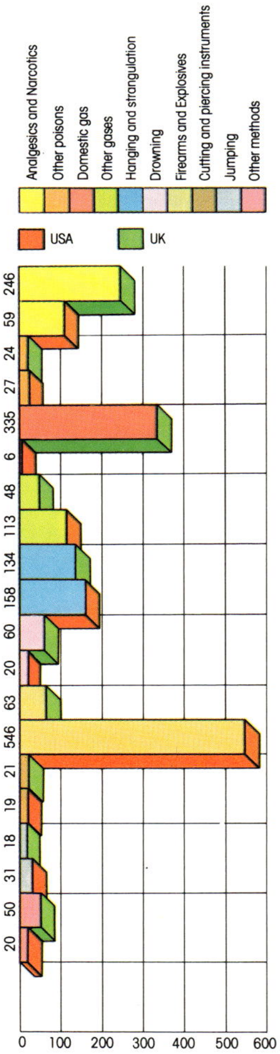

Suicide Methods
This chart gives a comparison of the different numbers of males who kill themselves (per 1000 suicide deaths) in the USA and UK, under the classification system adopted by the World Health Organization. While drugs and domestic gas account for a large proportion of deaths in the UK, it is firearms and, to a lesser extent, narcotics, which cause the greatest number of suicides in the USA

Right
Availability of the means to commit suicide is a fundamental factor in the increase in some kinds of self-killing. In the case of this office cleaner, he was able to hang himself from some overhead piping with a short length of cord because he had a ladder as part of his equipment

Generally, although the film industry is reputed to have a very high suicide rate, this is actually not true. The reason for the film industry's undeserved reputation in this respect is the inordinate publicity —the banner headlines and saturation television coverage—accorded to anyone connected with films who commits suicide. The first American film star to take her own life was Florence Lawrence, in 1938, after her career had been prematurely ruined. The first European to do the same was Max Linder, who made a death pact with his wife in 1925. Two of the greatest stars of the silent film era, John Barrymore and John Gilbert, unable to sustain their stardom when sound took over, drank themselves to death. Soon after Paul Bern, a leading executive of Metro-Goldwyn-Meyer, married Jean Harlow, a film star of the 1930s, he killed himself. In the 1960s, three of Hollywood's most famous stars all died after taking an overdose of sleeping pills—Marilyn Munroe in 1962, Alan Ladd in 1964 and Judy Garland in 1969. George Sanders killed himself in 1972, leaving a note saying that he was bored.

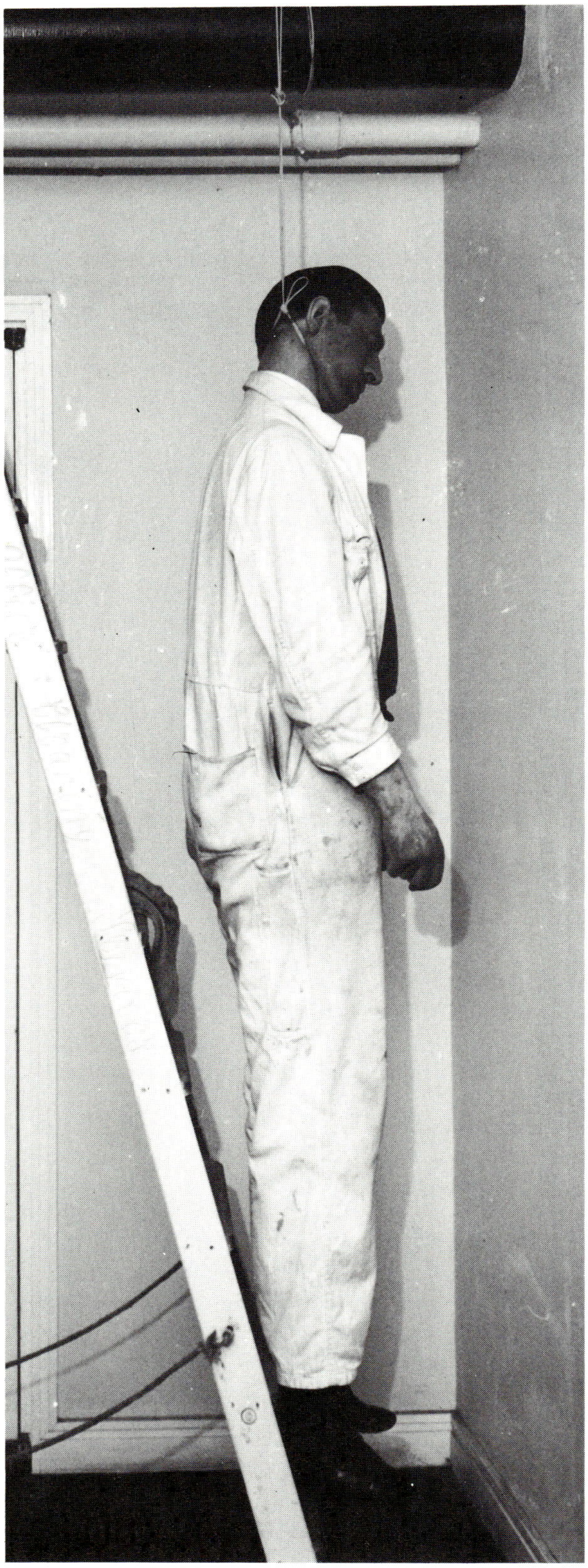

It is not only the availability of the means of suicide which governs the method most frequently used, but also its social acceptability. It was Durkheim who said that no one would employ a method regarded as ignominious by society, and research carried out at the Westminster Medical School in London into global suicide trends over the past 100 years has produced strong evidence to support his contention. For example, the number of suicides by hanging in Germany, France, Denmark and Sweden is conspicuously higher than in Britain, Holland, Australia and the United States, where hanging has been used in the past as a method of capital punishment. The Westminster researchers have also found that, if they 'weight' their statistics to take account of availability and acceptability with a particular community, there is a correlation between the suicide rates in many countries, something which has not been noted before.

Changed circumstances can render suicide acceptable, as with the case at Masada, a Jewish Zealot fortress in Israel besieged by the Romans in AD 73, when the garrison killed themselves rather than fall into Roman hands. The Jews of York killed themselves in 1190 to escape a Christian mob

Of course, what has previously been unacceptable can be rendered acceptable by extreme circumstances which can rock the very base on which a society may be founded. For example, Judaism has always been uncompromising in its condemnation of suicide, regarding deliberate self-destruction as equivalent to murder, but when hundreds of Jewish Zealots committed suicide in AD 73, this was condoned. The mass suicide took place at Masada, a mountain-top fortress in the south-east of Israel. A group of about 1,000 Zealots, with their wives and children, captured it from the occupying Romans after the destruction of the Temple in AD 70, and defied all attempts to dislodge them. The Romans brought up an army of 15,000 men with accompanying armour to besiege Masada. The Zealots withstood the siege for two years, during which time the Romans built a huge ramp from the foot of the mountain almost to the base of the fortress, enabling them to scale the walls. When the Jews saw that the end was near, they took their own lives rather than be captured by the Romans and forced into slavery. At York, in Britain, the Jews of the city killed themselves in 1190, rather than fall into the hands of a Christian mob. In more modern times, and on a far smaller scale, the Dadaist movement in art and literature also impelled people—mainly artists—to kill themselves, this time as a protest at bourgeois values and in despair at World War. I. A nihilist movement founded in 1916, Dadaism spread rapidly from its base in Zurich to Berlin, New York

Far left
Suicidal film star. Judy Garland, who killed herself in 1969 at the age of 47. Contrary to general belief, the film industry does not have a high suicide rate. It only seems to, because of the intense publicity given to film star suicides

Left
Masada. View from the top, showing the old walls. It was here, in AD 73, that hundreds of Jewish Zealots who had resisted two years of siege by the Romans committed suicide, rather than be captured and forced into a life of slavery

Left
Agonizing suicide by fire. In Geneva, in February, 1978, a young woman is consumed by the flames she herself has lit. A member of the small, fanatical Ananda Marga sect, she set herself on fire in front of the Palace of the Nations, in protest at the United Nations which, she felt, had betrayed its trust

and other cities. Some of its adherents took their own lives as a final expression of their nihilism.

Suicide rates appear to fall in wartime, but this may be simply because many suicides are not recognized as such, since the victims of air raids, for instance, may deliberately have exposed themselves to death. In the final analysis, the ordinary person's attitude to suicide is mainly conditioned by religion

Medical opinion differs over whether the suicide rate falls in wartime, as the statistics appear to indicate. Many believe that the figures are correct, and suggest that reasons for there being fewer suicides in wartime are the unusual close personal relationships people develop, together with the feeling of communal purpose and involvement. Equally strongly supported is the view that the suicide rate does not fall in wartime, since would-be suicides have many opportunities for quick death which they rarely have to employ themselves. Thus, it is not possible to tell how many air raid victims for example died accidentally or how many courted death. Military personnel, particularly in war, have infinite opportunities to die, not least as members of official suicide units, as we have previously mentioned (see discussion on page 121).

In the final analysis, the ordinary person's attitude to suicide is conditioned by a combination of law and religion. But as the centuries have passed so attitudes to suicide have changed, usually reflecting the new social conditions of the time. For example, within a year of the French Revolution in 1789, France had repealed her anti-suicide legislation. Prussia followed suit within a decade, and Austria in 1860. In Britain, it was not until 1961 that suicide ceased to be a criminal act, although it remains an offence to assist anyone in the act. Generally, the laws relating to suicide have been liberalized throughout Europe, as well as in the United States. A Bill to allow voluntary euthanasia, which was debated in the British Parliament, and legal battles in the USA over the permissibility of switching off life-support systems are beacons of the adapting social climate. Sympathy and understanding are increasing in many countries, and such energies have been channelled into voluntary organizations helping potential suicides to resist the urge. One of the largest of such organizations is the Samaritans, founded in London by clergyman Chad Varah in 1953. The Samaritans, now totalling more than 20,000 volunteers, have branched out from Britain to the USA, Australia, New Zealand, Hong Kong and India, in the process helping many hundreds of thousands, if not millions, of people to prevent them from becoming just another suicide statistic.

The End of the Road
It has been estimated that up to 15 percent of single vehicle crashes in the USA are suicidal

Stop Press
Attempted suicide is often a way of seeking attention and sympathy. Recently, during a 270-day news blackout in Detroit, the suicide rate was 20 percent lower than when newspapers were being published normally

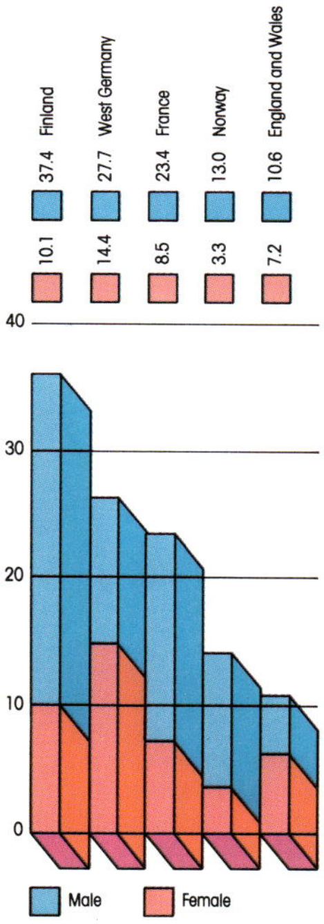

Suicidal Sex War
Comparison of male and female suicide rates, per 100,000 population, in five selected European countries. It is generally thought that women make far more attempts at suicide, but that men are more likely to successfully carry out their intentions

The 'Reverend' Jim Jones was able by the force of his personality to persuade hundreds of people to poison their children and then drink poison themselves

Psychopathic Priest
Jim Jones, the leader of the People's Temple, 900 of whose followers committed suicide at his behest in their commune in Guyana in November, 1978. Jones was later found dead with a bullet through his head

Top
Some of the Jonestown dead. Most were poor American blacks. After giving their children a drink consisting of fruit juice laced with poison, they drank some of the lethal mixture, too, dying within minutes

Drunken Demise
Up to half of all suicides are found to have a large quantity of alcohol in their blood at the time of death

On November 17, 1978, one of the most horrifying events in recent years took place in a remote jungle settlement called Jonestown, on the coast of Guyana, in South America.

In the early evening of the third Friday of November, 900 men, women and children, mostly poor American blacks, took part in a self-imposed orgy of suicide and murder. Under the influence and supervision of their leader, the 'Reverend' Jim Jones, the adults calmly administered to their children a fruit-juice cocktail laced with potassium chloride and potassium cyanide and then drank some of the mixture themselves.

The victims of this bizarre act of mass suicide were members of the People's Temple, an obscure religious cult originally established by Jones in Indiana, USA, which had subsequently moved on to California in search of the uninhibited freedom for which that state is known. Still driven by a consuming obsession with the need for isolation, the group—numbering several hundred—moved into the jungle-clad hinterland of the northern Guyana coast. There the People's Temple set up a commune.

However, the church's rigid policy of total isolation from the outside world alarmed many of its members' relatives, who began to complain openly about the cult's violent behaviour towards some of its members. It was in response to such complaints that an American Congressman, Leo Ryan, began an investigation which not only ended in the mass suicide, but also cost him and a number of journalists their lives. Congressman Ryan had taken account of the results of a previous enquiry, conducted by the American embassy in Georgetown, Guyana. This had reported favourably on the Jonestown community. When the visiting Congressman arrived at Jonestown with eight newsmen and a number of complainants, there seemed at first sight little justification for the accusations of coercion, an impression strengthened by the hospitality of the commune members and the entertainment they staged for the visiting group. However, the atmosphere soon changed dramatically. Questioned about the rumours of armed guards and the forced internment of his church's followers, Jones became dangerously hostile. When he learned that 14 of his followers intended to leave with the Ryan party and return to the United States, Jones's self-control weakened and he began planning the assassination of the whole group, to be carried out in conjunction with the ceremonial mass suicide of all the People's Temple members in Jamestown.

The Congressman, who had already been unsuccessfully attacked in the colony, was gunned down together with three newsmen and a defector as they prepared to board a waiting plane. Ten other people intending to leave with Mr Ryan were badly wounded. By the time the news of the killings was reported to Jones, he had already begun persuading his followers to drink the poisoned fruit juice prepared by the commune's doctor and some assistants. He wanted everybody to drink the fruit juice and give it to their children to demonstrate their loyalty to his church and their desire to take part in its act of 'revolutionary suicide'. Parents used syringes to drop the deadly brew into the mouths of unsuspecting babies, and then drank their share from paper cups.

Everybody who was there from beginning to end died. The only people to survive were a few who took advantage of the chaos reigning at the beginning of the ritual to slip away. It was they, still terrified several months later, who were to bear witness to the hardships imposed on members by the church and the sinister behaviour of its leaders. The loyal suicide toast, they disclosed, had been rehearsed many times before. These rehearsals according to the survivors, took place on what were termed 'white nights', during which the sleeping commune would be woken by loudspeakers and everybody summoned to the settlement's central pavilion. After a sermon by Jones on the attractions of death, everyone was given a glass of 'poison' to drink. On these occasions, the drink was not really contaminated, although everybody thought that it was until they had drunk it. Jones held these rehearsals fairly frequently as a demonstration of the loyalty his church demanded—and received—from its members.

Not until many days after the massacre did the full extent of the death toll become apparent. The sight and the stench of hundreds of corpses in the humid Guyanese jungle were enough to turn the stomachs of the hardiest among the troops whose ultimate task it was to deal with the aftermath of this human carnage. Mothers lay dead with their lifeless babies in their arms, families huddled together, and lovers were locked in their last embrace, their bodies rigid with the stiffness of death. The first count revealed 409 corpses. Then, many more passports were found, giving rise to the belief that several hundred people had taken to the jungle in a desperate attempt to escape the holocaust. The troops spent three days combing the jungle looking for the supposed survivors, before the gruesome truth was discovered—the owners of the passports were also dead, their bodies and those of their children piled in heaps. There were some 500 in all,

bringing the tally to the staggering total of 900.

The sinister aspects of the case were far from over, even then. Several months later, during a press conference in Modesto, California a 32-year-old former aide of the 'Reverend' Jim Jones shot himself. He had been arrested after the massacre and found to have in his possession a suitcase containing $100,000. Jones, he maintained, had instructed him to take the money to the Soviet Embassy in Georgetown. Shortly after his death, NBC television in America obtained, and broadcast, a two-minute extract of a tape recording made at the time of the Jonestown death rite. The full tape, 43 minutes long, is in the possession of the FBI and Guyanese Government. On the tape, the voice of Jones can be clearly heard, persuading his flock to drink the cyanide, interspersed at times with the screams and cries of his followers. It is evident from the recording that not everyone was a willing victim. One woman in particular took a stand against Jones, but was shouted down by her confused and frenzied fellow members, who turned a deaf ear to her urgings that: 'As long as there's life, there's hope'. They were completely under Jones's spell, slavishly obeying his exhortations to drink the poison, even as they swallowed it agreeing with his shouted claim: 'We didn't commit suicide. We committed an act of revolutionary suicide, protesting the conditions of an inhuman world'.

A shocked world and a stunned America are still trying to understand how a man like Jones could gain such power over so many people and what depths of social deprivation drove so many to follow him. Those same disciples who died with him had gone into the streets of America and sold photographs of him to raise money for the People's Temple, to which they also turned over their savings and earnings, enabling Jones to amass a fortune estimated at some $15 million. It was no coincidence that those who joined Jones's church, searching for a purpose in life, were predominantly black, socially deprived and victims of discrimination. Jones professed to hate 'racists and fascists', and his social work among blacks in parts of the United States seemed to bear this out, as did the adoption by him and his wife of eight children, who included Koreans and blacks. Because of his views and actions he was subjected to considerable personal abuse, Jones claimed. He certainly became increasingly bitter and hostile. It is also possible that the break-up of his parents' marriage when he was 14 years old could have contributed to his later mental instability, since such circumstances are a feature of many—if not most—suicide cases. At the end he was undoubtedly deranged, raving about his affinity with God and his personal suffering from cancer. Many believe that his church had sinister political undertones, although no evidence has so far been found to substantiate such an allegation. In the end, Jones died not from cyanide as had his flock, but from a bullet through the head. It has never been established whether the wound was self-inflicted or Jones was murdered. A post mortem revealed that Jones was not suffering from cancer, as he had frequently declared.

Many psychiatrists believe that the vulnerability of his followers stemmed largely from their loneliness and lack of self-confidence as individuals, and that membership of the sect reinforced them as a group and generated a collective inner strength which they could only feel as part of a group. The corollary was that most of them lost their sense of personal identity and, with it, the mental strength and decisiveness to withstand and reject Jones's insane commands to kill themselves and their children.

Above
Jonestown seen from the air after the mass suicide. The bodies were all flown back to the United States for burial. As his followers began to drink the poisoned fruit juice, Jones shouted: 'We didn't commit suicide. We committed an act of revolutionary suicide, protesting the conditions of an inhuman world'. There is no doubt that Jones was deranged at the end, raving about his affinity with God and his suffering from cancer —which, a post-mortem revealed, he did not have

Varied Techniques
In the USA, jumping from a high place as a method of suicide is far more common among non-whites than among whites. A greater percentage of whites kill themselves by taking pills, whereas a larger proportion of non-whites poison themselves with solid or liquid substances, like rat poison

Merchants of Death

Despite the welter of information on homicide available to sociologists and psychiatrists, it remains true that society is unable to contend effectively with the man who, in a raging fit, suddenly picks up a knife and plunges it through his neighbour's heart

Above
In the back bedroom in an apartment on Chicago's Southside, Richard Franklin Speck, 24 (whose photograph is being displayed by an official, right), killed eight nurses in July, 1966. He tied their wrists, made them lie on the floor and knifed them to death. Speck, who had been in prison for burglary and assault, was obsessed with 'wine, women and knives'

Right
Hoisted aloft by a pulley, the body of an executed former Iranian leader is silhouetted against the dawn sky in Teheran, the capital. Despite protests from inside the country and abroad, the revolutionary courts set up in Iran by the Ayatollah Khomeini when he seized power early in 1979 continued to conduct summary trials of high-ranking army officers and others who had held high office under the Shah. Few escaped death

A Life for a Life
It has been suggested that capital punishment may act as a stimulant to murder rather than a deterrent: A prisoner serving a life sentence for murder in Oklahoma strangled a cell-mate in 1966 and was sentenced to die in the electric chair. Just before his death, he told a prison psychiatrist that he had committed the murder because he had been disappointed with the sentence for his first crime and wished to be executed

In considering criminal homicide—murder and manslaughter, as well as the relatively desultory killing which continues in societies which are not at war—it should be borne in mind that wartime killing and the relative ease with which people can be brought to believe it necessary constitute a facet of fundamental psychological importance in all homicides. Men are most frequently led to kill when they have a strong feeling of self justification and feel they have a need and, especially, a right to kill. The element of justification is particularly strong in civil wars, which are exceptionally bloody, because the warring parties feel that religious or political principles are at stake. In the religious civil wars of the sixteenth century and the heretical wars of the Middle Ages whole populations of cities were exterminated.

Patterns of homicide in different countries are the result of many years—and even centuries—of cultural history, and vary very widely. In Arab and some Mediterranean countries, homicide carried out from a sense of social duty is still quite common. For instance, a wife who has committed adultery, or a sister who has been dishonoured, must be killed, by custom if not by current law. Not many years ago when I visited a Lebanese prison, I saw a boy of 14 who was serving a life sentence for the murder of his 15-year-old unmarried sister. It appeared that she had allowed herself to be seduced, and when this was discovered, a family conclave decided that the boy, as the youngest male, should have the honour and duty of killing her. He proudly put on a red apron, took the girl behind a barn and cut her throat. He could not understand why he had been arrested, let alone jailed, for the killing since there had been no other way to save his family's honour. In Greece, a brother, with the agreement of his parents, took his pregnant, unmarried sister to a nearby stream and held her head under the water until she drowned. In southern Italy and Sicily, family feuds and vendettas still exist, while it was

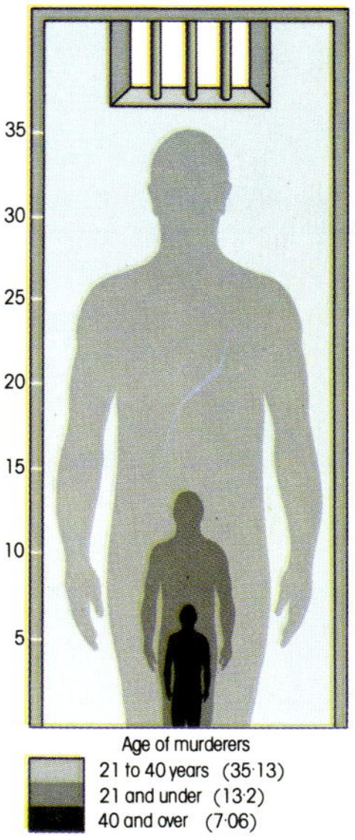

Men of Murder
The number of murderers in the UK, per 100,000 male population, divided into age-groups. Inevitably, it is the 21 to 40-year band which contains the most killers

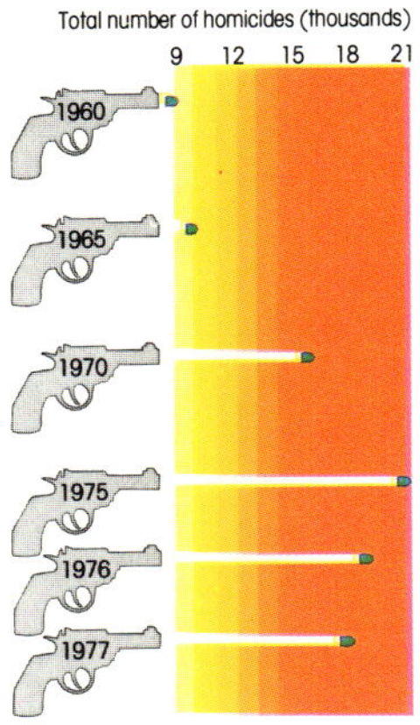

History of Homicide
The number of people murdered in the USA between 1960 and 1977. 1975 was the peak year, while the second half of the 1970s has seen consistently and worryingly high rates of murder for each year since 1975

the custom in some southern states of the USA until recently for a white man to shoot dead any black he suspected of having raped his wife, or face social ostracism. Thus, in many countries all over the world, murder from a sense of social or family duty is not only accepted as the norm, but is usually regarded as an inevitable course of action.

Not only do patterns of homicide vary widely, but so does the murder rate and its corollary, suicide. In southern Europe, for example, the murder rate is relatively high, while the suicide rate is fairly low; in northern Europe, the reverse holds true

One of the interesting aspects of the wide variations in the murder rate in different parts of the world—some countries have a rate up to 15 times higher than others—is that, generally speaking, the countries which are 15 degrees of latitude north or south of the Equator have the highest rates. To be more accurate, since the world population is concentrated more in the north, the countries lying between 15 and 30 degrees of latitude north of the Equator and those between 35 and 45 degrees to the south have exceptionally high homicide rates. The first group includes India, while the second includes the Mediterranean countries, most of China and Japan, and most of the heavily populated areas of the USA. All these countries have a homicide rate which is about ten times as high as in countries 45 degrees of latitude or more north of the Equator—Canada, the northern part of Western Europe and Britain, Scandinavia and the Soviet Union. The high temperatures in the first group of countries are certainly an important factor (the stifling heat of New York's over-populated, deprived areas in summer, for example, certainly leads to excessive irritability), but there is a religious dimension. Throughout the world, and especially Europe, there is an inverse relation between the rate of homicide and suicide. In Sweden and most other north European countries the suicide rate is higher than the homicide rate. The reverse is true in most of the countries bordering the Mediterranean, which are predominantly Roman Catholic. For their populations, suicide is a mortal sin, while one can obtain absolution for homicide. During the Middle Ages in Germany it became so frequent an occurrence for Catholics contemplating suicide to murder some helpless invalid or imbecile and then be hanged in a state of grace after receiving confession, that the authorities abolished the death penalty for some years in an effort to deter suicide-motivated homicide.

In the Western world the two main factors which profoundly affect the extent of homicide are the spread of car ownership and the possession of weapons, especially firearms. The car is far more dangerous than any other weapon. In Britain in 1977, 6,600 people (drivers, passengers and pedestrians) were killed in road accidents of all kinds. This compares with approximately 500 cases of suspected murder during the same period. Carrying knives is common in most of the countries with a high homicide rate and also in some northern countries, Scotland and Finland among them, where homicide in general is rather frequent.

However, firearms are enormously important in the United States and some other countries. Where a knife is used to commit a killing, there may be some doubt as to whether anything more serious than a cut was intended, but when a pistol is fired at point-blank range, even impulsively, one can hardly claim that serious injury, if not death, was not intended.

Regardless of cultural and other differences human nature varies little from country to country, so that the patterns of murder with regard to personality, motivation and victim are very similar everywhere, especially in the United States and Western Europe. What does vary is the frequency of the different types of murder. Twenty years ago I was given permission to study the very full records of the 120 people convicted of homicide (first and second degree murder and manslaughter) in the state of New Jersey, in the USA, in the three years

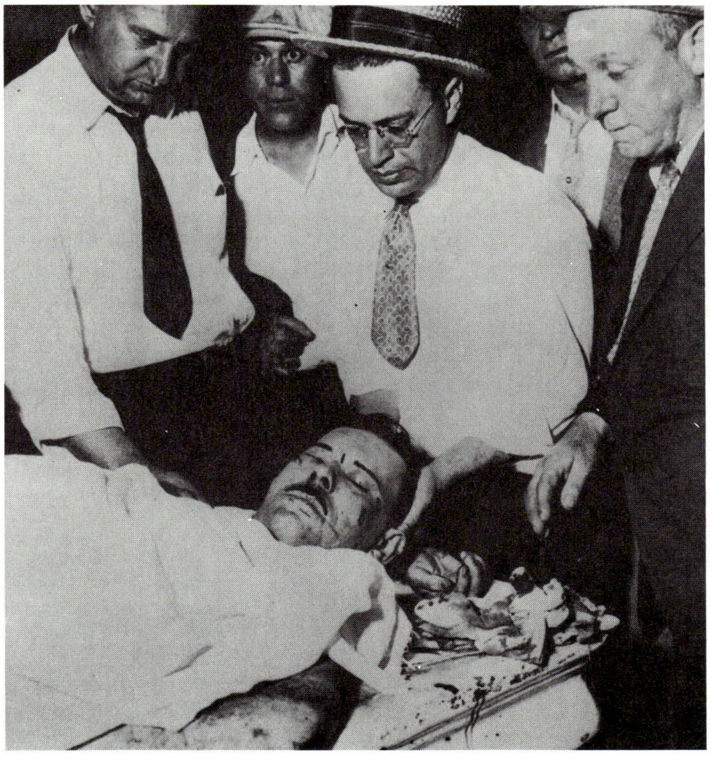

Right
December, 1934. America's Public Enemy Number One, John Dillinger, lies on a slab in the Chicago county morgue, after being shot by Government agents and police lying in wait for him outside a cinema in the city

Far right
Murder in Cheshire. One July night in 1971, this French girl, Claudine Liebert, 20, her sister Monique, 22, and Monique's fiancé Daniel Berland, 20, on a camping holiday in Britain, were shot by a frenzied killer while asleep in their tent

1947 to 1949, and compare them with the equally full records of the 115 individuals convicted of homicide and committed to the state mental hospital as irresponsible. This total included everyone committed since 1938, whether they had died or been discharged in the meantime or were still patients there, together with a few survivors from earlier times, the eldest being a man who had committed murder in 1921.

Of the 147 male homicides in New Jersey in 1947-49 (including 15 sentenced to death and not studied) only nine were committed to the state hospital as insane, though a few more had a murder charge reduced to manslaughter on the ground of mental disorder. Three committed suicide after committing homicide. The position is totally different in England and Wales. During the period 1967 to 1971, 20 percent of murder suspects committed suicide after the crime, while 32 percent were mentally disordered and were regarded as partially or totally irresponsible.

Considering the fierce emotions which often culminate in murder, it is a remarkably rare crime. Those who commit it come from the two extremes of normality—they are either aggressive and uncontrolledly impulsive, or inhibited and abnormally over-controlled

Wherever committed, homicide has three main characteristics. First, it involves the strong murdering the less strong—men threaten and kill women, while they, in turn, threaten and kill their children. (The pistol has altered this to some extent however.) Secondly, because of the extreme passions with which murder is frequently connected, it is very largely a crime in which the victim is a member of the murderer's immediate family, has developed an intimate personal relationship with the murderer or is a close acquaintance. Because of this, murder does not generally represent a threat to society, although killings which do not hinge on personal relationships do represent such a threat and must be regarded very seriously. Thirdly, murder is a crime which is committed because of the murderer's past history and development, as well as his or her perception of what society regards as customary behaviour. In some cases, there is a clear dominance of either individual or social factors, but they are often very difficult to disentangle. Considering the universality of these fierce emotions and frustrations, homicide is a remarkably rare crime everywhere.

Those who do kill come from the two extremes of normality—they are either aggressive, uncontrolledly, impulsive, unsympathetic and, perhaps, callous, or else over-controlled, inhibited and unag-

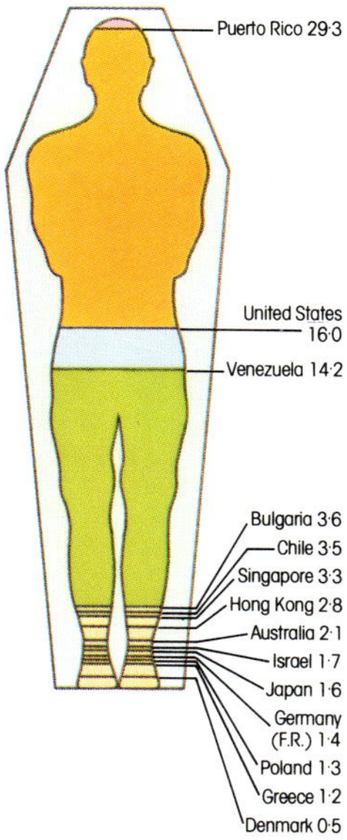

World of Killing
The murder rate in a number of selected countries, per 100,000 male population. Topping the list is Puerto Rico, while Denmark remains the least murderous state

Left
Psychotic murderer, David Berkowitz, a 24-year-old postal worker known as 'Son of Sam', who shot six people with a .44 calibre revolver and wounded eight others in 1976. He was traced by means of a parking ticket

Below
Fatal escape. Francois Besse, serving 15 years in La Santé Prison for armed hold-ups, lies dying in a Paris street. Escaping over the stone wall of the prison with two other convicts early one May morning in 1978, he was shot by a patrolling gendarme. His companions got away on foot

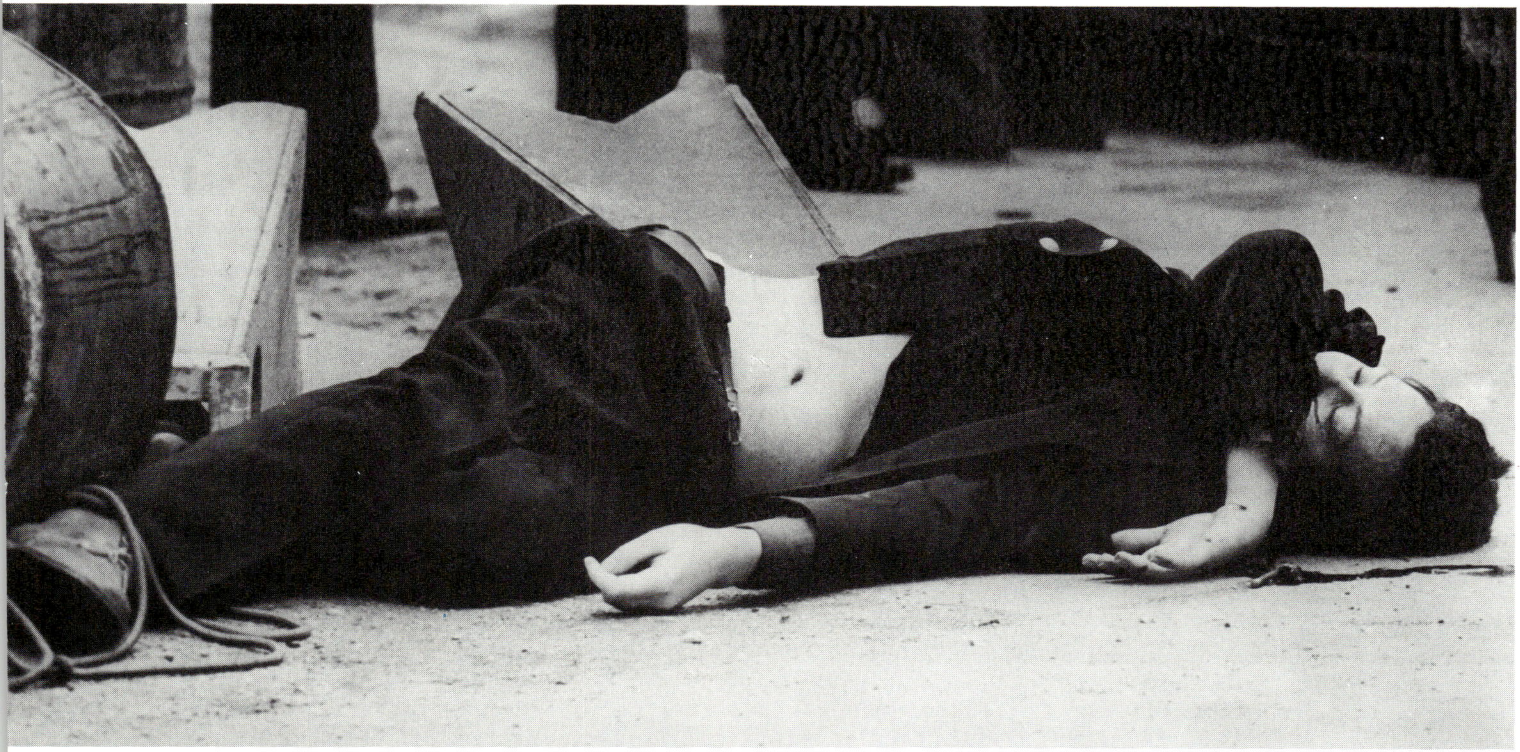

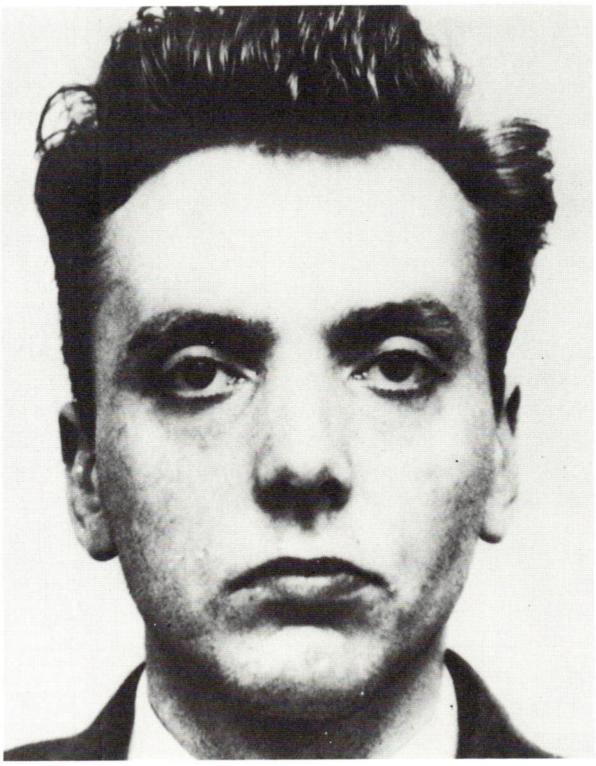

Right
John Christie, seen here in 1953, when he was 55, looked harmless enough, but he was a sadistic murderer. He strangled his wife and three young women, hiding the bodies under the floorboards of his West London home

Far right
'Moors murderer' Ian Brady as he looked in 1961. With Myra Hindley, he was found guilty in 1966 of torturing and murdering a boy of 14 on the Yorkshire moors. Brady and Hindley were gaoled for life

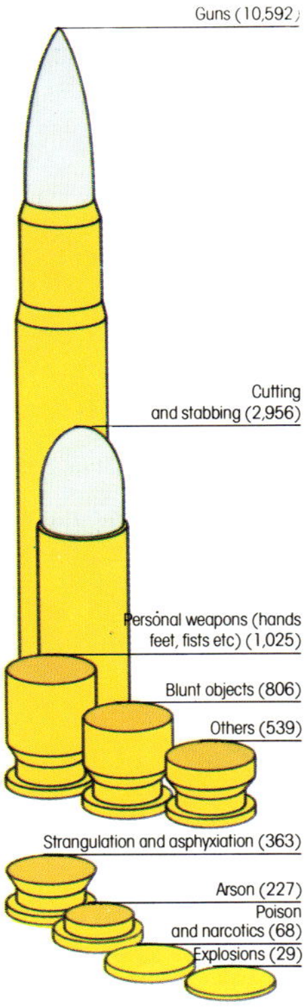

Weapons of Death
The number of people murdered in the USA, divided into groups according to weapons used, 1976. Firearms, and particularly guns, have a substantial lead over the second most common group of weapons used, stabbing implements

gressive, but with a very deep, but suppressed, sense of hostility and resentment. It is the latter who, perhaps surprisingly, are rather more likely to commit murder than the former. The uninhibited tend to express their aggressiveness often and relatively 'mildly' in pub quarrels and assaults on the police, while the over-inhibited boil with resentment until there is finally a violent and lethal explosion. Many of the aggressive group, perhaps 50 percent, become badly drunk, which reduces their ability to control their aggressiveness.

An example of an over-inhibited man eventually bursting the bonds of his inhibitedness and giving vent to his bottled-up anger is afforded by the following case—a highly respected and respectable office worker in his forties, and a man of very rigid and regular habits. He had married a woman much younger than himself and, at the time of which we are writing, the two sons of the marriage were aged about 10 and 12. For about five years, the wife had been engaging in a series of extra-marital affairs with young men aged between 18 and 20 who were much the social inferiors of both her and her husband. He was very attached to his wife and protested violently about her affairs, although they managed not to quarrel in front of the children. They had lived for some years in a state of bitter truce, sleeping apart from each other, the husband hoping his wife's habits would change. One day, he found her packing a suitcase, and tried to take it from her in the entrance hall. As the couple struggled with one another, they banged into the hall cupboard and a Japanese bayonet, a memento of the war which was hanging there, fell to the ground. The husband picked it up impulsively and stabbed his wife three times, killing her. He was deeply contrite about what he had done, but his main concern was about who would look after the two boys, who were getting on exceptionally well at school. At the trial, the judge told the jury that he would not allow them to find the accused guilty of manslaughter. He must be convicted of murder or nothing. The jury decided that it would have to be nothing, and acquitted him. This apparently simple and straightforward case, and others like it, demonstrates the essential fact that men like the husband will hang on until something breaks. Thousands of men leave their wives, perhaps because they have come to despise them or no longer have any feelings for them. Thousands of women walk out of their homes, leaving the care of their children to the state. The men who beat and maltreat their women—and sometimes even kill them—have at least a perverted love for or attachment to them.

Official statistics generally divide the motives of murder into six categories—rage or quarrel, jealousy or revenge, sexual motive, furtherance of theft or other gain, feud and escaping arrest. There is also the apparently motiveless category.

The structure of the law naturally affects the motive, type of victim and offender to some extent. Murder implies the intention to kill or do grievous bodily harm. This is most clearly established where there is premeditation or a 'long-acting' motive like jealousy or revenge. In 'rage and quarrel' murders, the intention to kill is often shown by the aggressor breaking off the immediate quarrel, going away and obtaining a weapon or lying in wait until an opportunity presents itself to get the victim on his or her own. The physical provocation during the quarrels which might have reduced the charge from murder to manslaughter has been dissipated. Homicide in the course of crime against property is the most threatening to the general public, since it involves totally innocent strangers. Although classed as murder, unless there are highly extenuating circumstances, homicides of this type are due more to stupidity, callousness, thoughtlessness and lack of imagination than to any intention to kill or seriously injure. An example is the increasingly common type of murder in which two or three youths or men break into a house, and when surprised by the householder, often an elderly woman living alone, tie her up and gag her so inexpertly that she either suffocates, or soon after dies of shock or exposure.

The murderer's basic personality and the extent

The Killing Trade
There is only one state executioner in France. He receives a salary of 25,000 francs (just under £3,000) per annum, plus a bonus of 8,000 francs (about £950) for each execution carried out. His bonus payments, however, have been few and far between over the past ten years. In that time, only seven people have been guillotined, out of a total of 27 sentenced to death. The remaining 20 were reprieved. The job of executioner in France is a lifetime appointment

Left
Now in a London museum, this gate led to the execution courtyard in Newgate Prison, London, demolished in 1902. From 1763 to 1868–when they were stopped–all public executions in London took place at Newgate

Far left
After delaying his execution in California for 12 years, Caryl Chessman lost the fight and was executed in May, 1960, only minutes before the news of a reprieve reached the prison governor

to which he may be mentally ill profoundly affect the motive and choice of victim. Most people realize today that there are degrees of mental illness, some mild and transitory like many depressions, others compatible with normal social life, such as obsessions and irrational fears. The law exonerates only those suffering from acute mental illness–a psychosis (insanity) or a condition bordering on psychosis. It must be emphasized that psychotic individuals do not commit more murders than normal people.

Signs of a Killer
Late in the nineteenth century, the Italian criminologist, Cesare Lombroso, put forward the rather fanciful theory that a typical violent criminal could be identified by a sloping forehead, either very pronounced ear lobes or none at all, a chinless jaw, and either profuse amounts of body hair or none at all

---

Depression, when severe, is one of the three main types of acute mental illness which impel people to commit homicide. Everyone, without exception, has suffered from depression, although it is not usually lasting or serious enough to merit treatment

---

There are broadly three types of acute mental illness. Schizophrenia is the commonest and is most often associated with murder. In the full form, the patient has delusions (false beliefs which cannot be shaken by argument) and hallucinations, either seeing or feeling things not there, or hearing voices and feeling under the direction of others. The important feature of schizophrenia is that feeling tends to be detached from thinking and acting. Terrible actions arouse no emotion, and great importance is given to trivialities. About a third of schizophrenics recover, but the rest remain ill to a greater or lesser extent, although their illness is usually controlled by drugs if they are taken regularly. Those who kill have usually been out of contact with doctors for months or years, or have forgotten to take their tablets. There are many forms of the disease, of which the most common is paranoid schizophrenia, where the sufferer has delusions of being persecuted or mysteriously influenced.

The second type of acute mental illness is severe depression. This is accompanied by delusions of

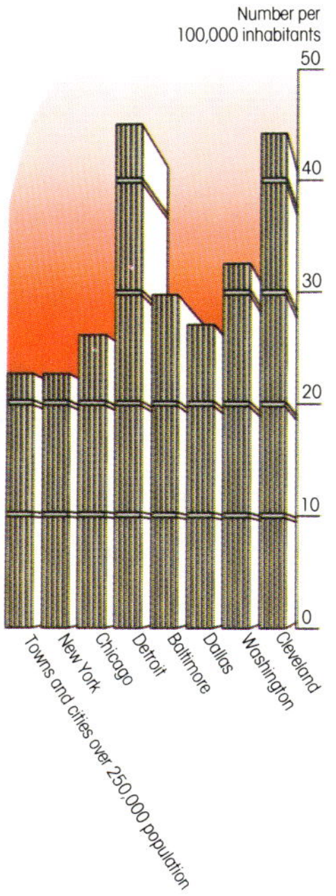

Murder Cities of the USA
Cleveland and Detroit far outstrip other American cities in the urban homicide league and, as this chart shows fairly conclusively, New York is a rather safe city

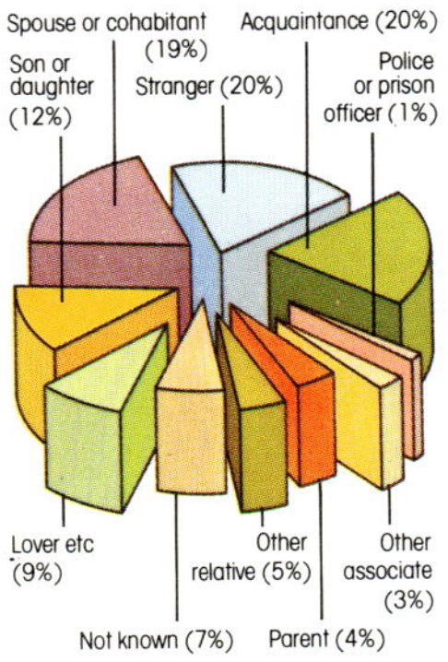

Related by Death
Relationship of murder victim to principal suspect, in England and Wales. Random killing of strangers only makes up one-fifth of known murders, while the slaying of a wife or husband, together with that of a son or daughter, comprises nearly one-third of all reported murders

worthlessness and hopelessness, a determination to commit suicide and the slowing of all functions, physical and mental. Patients usually recover completely, although depression fairly often recurs or alternates with its opposite, euphoria—patients become excessively cheerful and over-active, thinking so fast that they lose track of their thoughts, or have delusions of grandeur: that they are great artists or multi-millionaires. Those in the over-cheerful, over-active manic phase almost never commit homicide. However some schizophrenics also get grandiose delusions and show signs of over-activity.

Finally, there is 'organic' mental illness, caused by, among other things, deterioration of the brain, arterial sclerosis (hardening of the arteries), tumours, some infections like chronic syphilis and encephalitis after whooping cough, and severe head injuries. People afflicted by this third type of mental illness are forgetful, cannot concentrate and lose ordinary hygienic habits. Their poor memory makes them suspicious and fearful (of being robbed, for example) and they can be irritable and impulsive. Similar symptoms appear in old age and senility, but at a later stage in life and more gradually.

Less severe forms of all three conditions summarized above are seen in many people with behavioural problems, including those who commit homicide. Depression, however, has afflicted or will afflict everyone, whether suffering from behavioural problems or not. No one can claim with truth never to have been even mildly depressed. Many people have friends or relatives who have had definite mental illnesses and have had to spend some time in hospital as a result. Most of us know people whose reaction to stress or frustration is to become withdrawn, blame themselves and feel that they are failures. We also know others who react with angry complaints of being hard done by, misunderstood and victimized. In most cases, a high proportion of convicted murderers are found to be distinctly ill. Normal murder or manslaughter tend to be concentrated in the 20-35 age group, but there are 'abnormal' murderers included even among adolescents, children and the elderly.

Furtherance of theft and other gain is the least likely motive of grossly abnormal killers, although statistics for England and Wales show that it is the motive of 25 percent of 'normal' murderers. However, it will be recalled that murder committed in the furtherance of theft and other gain is sometimes almost accidental, as in the case of some house break-ins. Such murders also include armed bank robberies in which bystanders are killed, but not professional gangland killings or the murder of a wife by her husband, who hopes to inherit her property.

'Rage or quarrel' is the commonest motive in murder and manslaughter. In contrast to the United States, murder in Britain most commonly involves knives or strangulation/asphyxia. Shooting is quite rare (10 percent of 'normal' murders) and is actually highest in murder followed by suicide.

Jealousy and revenge are often long lasting emotions leading to premeditated and logically planned murder. However, murders from this twin motive are sometimes sudden and impulsive, as when a husband comes home unexpectedly, finds his wife in bed with a lover, and kills one or both of them. In some countries, such a murder, the 'crime passionel' of France, is not considered a crime at all.

In most cases where a killer is mentally ill, the mental illness reduces his or her capacity to control a normal emotion. One of the most famous of such cases involved a retired judge of the Australian High Court

Only about a third of mentally ill killers are recorded as 'apparently motiveless' or dominated by delusions. In most cases, illness does no more than reduce the murderer's capacity to control a normal emotion, so that the motive is perfectly clear. The most obvious examples are provided by people suffering from physical deterioration of the brain due to arterial sclerosis. A New Jersey

Bitter End
In the Middle Ages, decapitation was seen as a dignified way to be executed. Hanging was considered degrading and an insult. The really unfortunate were hanged, drawn and quartered

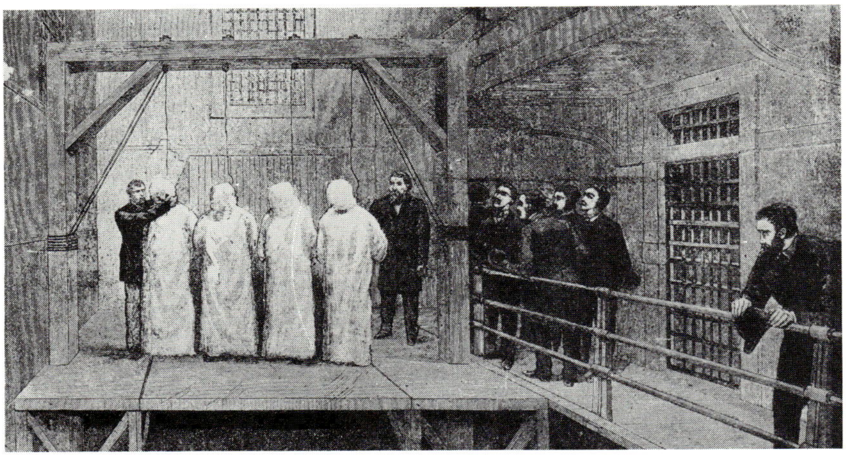

Above
Four anarchists being hanged in Chicago in 1886, after a bomb had killed seven police and injured others trying to disperse their meeting. Four other anarchists were also arrested. Three were gaoled and one killed himself

Above right
Before and after. A Dutch print of the guillotine in action in Paris **Right** An executioner about to release the deadly blade. **Left** His colleague proudly holds up a severed head

Right
A child-murderess in Germany in the sixteenth century about to be thrown off a bridge to drown. In England at one time, many children were killed for the burial money paid by benefit clubs

businessman, a forceful member of the board of directors of a successful company, failed to realize that his management powers were deteriorating. When his fellow directors combined to demand his resignation, he bitterly resented it. Later, he decided to settle the matter by calling a board meeting and shooting the other directors dead with a revolver. He fired six shots, but most missed their targets, although one man was killed. How many directors have felt like doing the same, but have controlled their anger?

One of the most famous cases of mental deterioration due to arterial sclerosis was that of Thomas Ley, a former justice minister and judge of the Australian High Court. He had always been a somewhat ruthless and aggressive man. On one occasion, his political opponent in an election was found dead in mysterious circumstances which were never cleared up. When he retired, Ley settled in England, where he fell victim to the delusion that his middle-aged wife was being unfaithful with his young gardener-chauffeur. Hiring two criminals to overcome the young man, Ley tied him to a chair. Then either the two criminals or Ley himself killed him and buried the body in a lonely chalk pit in the country. Ley was tried in the late 1940s, convicted and sentenced to death, but was reprieved.

Murder with an overtly sexual motive is much rarer than might be supposed from the great publicity such murders receive. In Britain they amount to only seven percent of all murders. Most sexual murders are grossly perverse and sadistic, and those responsible display an acutely psychopathic personality, although not suffering from any defined illness.

Most murders which appear to have no motive are committed by young men under 21. Contrary to appearances, these murders are not the result of schizophrenia, but actually pre-empt its development. Some sexual murders come into this category

Apparently 'motiveless' murders are not uncommon. They are most often committed by young men under 21, although there are occasionally instances of older individuals being involved. A New Jersey case is typical. A young man of 20 was adopted by a kindly farmer and his wife. He showed no abnormality, although somewhat solitary and unapproachable. His adopted father bought him a horse, to which he became very deeply attached, training the animal with great care. One day his father asked if he could ride the horse. The son became very upset and refused, but the father insisted in a robust way that there could be no harm in having just one ride. The boy went up to his room and later went out and hid the horse in a shelter in the forest. When his father again asked to ride the horse, the son killed father and mother with a shotgun. He was sentenced to life imprisonment. He showed no sign of remorse during his sentence, but otherwise appeared to be normal, although remaining extremely unapproachable. His sole concern was whether the horse was being well-treated. In such

A Point of Honour
In southern Italy and north Africa, it is still customary for a wife who has been unfaithful to be killed! Similarly, a daughter who loses her virginity before marriage is ceremoniously murdered, usually by the youngest son in the family

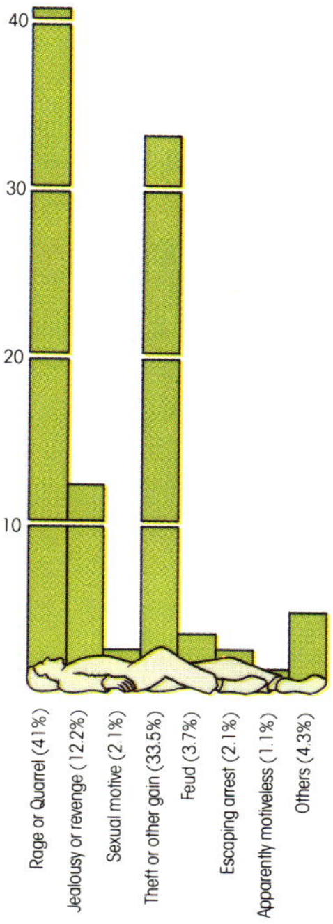

Motivated to Kill
Male murder victims in England and Wales, divided into groups according to motivation, as a percentage of total murders

Death Chair
The first person to meet his death in the electric chair, William Kemmler, in the USA in 1890, took over eleven minutes to die

Justice without Mercy
In ancient Egypt, the punishment for perjury was embalming alive. In ancient India, perpetrating a false rumour, slaughtering a cow and stealing an elephant were all capital offences. In Britain in 1800, a person could be put to death for over 200 crimes, including the theft of a loaf of bread

Left
Saudi Arabian execution. In the first photograph, the condemned man, an alleged murderer and rapist, dressed in white, has been brought to the place of execution, a Jeddah car park. He does not have long to wait. The charges are read out, and the executioner beheads him with a sword, afterwards inflicting a wound on the body (second photograph)

Right
Public execution in France. The guillotine blade has just fallen, decapitating the executed man. The last public execution in France occurred as recently as 1939

Origins of the Guillotine
A decapitating machine was used by the ancient Persians and the ancient Chinese, and engravings have been found depicting the use of a machine similar to a guillotine in Europe before the middle of the sixteenth century. Dr Guillotin, in fact, recommended the use of a decapitating machine as a swift and painless form of capital punishment in 1789. The first execution was carried out on April 25, 1792. The machine was initially called the 'Louison', after a certain Dr Louis, but the popular nickname 'guillotine' soon replaced it

Bite of Execution
In the ancient Orient and in the Roman Empire, a method of capital punishment was to sew the offender inside a sack with a venomous snake

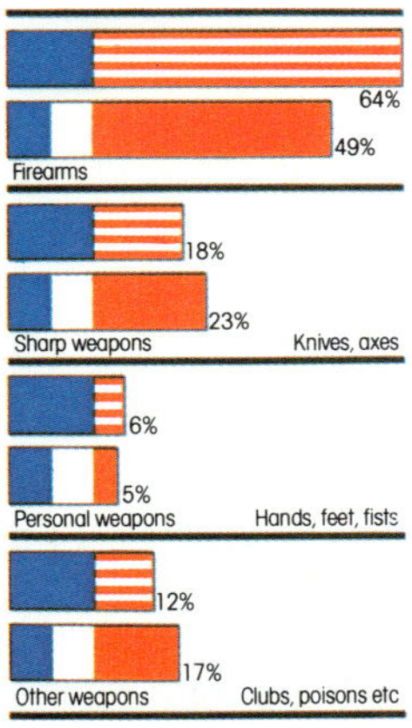

From Firearms to Poison
A comparison of murder by type of weapon used, in the USA and France. America, apparently the world's most gun-happy nation, surprisingly only just manages to stay ahead of France for the number of murders involving the use of firearms

Killers at Bay
Psychologists believe that we all have a killing instinct, but it is controlled by a 'safety-mechanism' evolved in us from inherited and environmental influences

cases, it might be thought that the murderer is suffering from a sort of schizophrenia. In practice, however, this is rarely so, and it has been suggested that an outburst of abnormal violence pre-empts the development of this mental illness. In the USA it has been called the 'catathymic crisis', in which a young person, in intolerable conflict, forms an intention to kill. This seems to resolve the conflict and bring mental calm, and the murder may be planned with considerable care. Some sexual murders are of this sort.

As long ago as 2000 BC, the legal code of the Babylonian Empire made it mandatory to prove criminal intent or criminal recklessness before the death sentence could be imposed for murder

Judicial homicide—the death penalty—seems to have existed ever since laws were first devised. The Hammurabi code of the Babylonian Empire (about 2000 BC), discovered in 1902, included burning or stoning to death for murder if criminal intent or criminal recklessness was proved. The ancient Israelites imposed the death penalty not only for homicide, but also for adultery, bestiality, blasphemy, cursing father or mother, idolatry, incest, rape, Sabbath-breaking and witchcraft. The Roman Empire imposed capital punishment for murder, treason, adultery and sodomy, forgery by slaves, rape and, in some cases, corruption and kidnapping.

It is probable that capital punishment has very often been more rarely imposed than the law allows, becoming to some extent a deterrent rather than a practice. The early settlers in the United States, especially the Quakers and other religious sects restricted the death penalty to wilful murder only, in Ohio in 1788 and in Pennsylvania in 1794. A federal law made it obligatory for treason, murder and rape. In Britain, it was theoretically maintained for more than 200 felonies until the early nineteenth century, although the vast majority of death sentences were commuted to transportation, at first to the American colonies and later to Australia. Apart from a few cases of wartime treason, no one was hanged in Britain between 1838 and the abolition of capital punishment in 1967 for any crime but murder. The death penalty is gradually being abolished throughout the western world, on the ground that, since it cannot be shown to be an effective deterrent, it is unethical.

Methods of capital punishment have varied through the ages. Burning, as already mentioned, was used by the Babylonians and ancient Israelites. The latter also employed stoning, while the Assyrians favoured impaling with a stake. The Romans threw offenders from a cliff or crucified them if they were not Roman citizens. The Romans

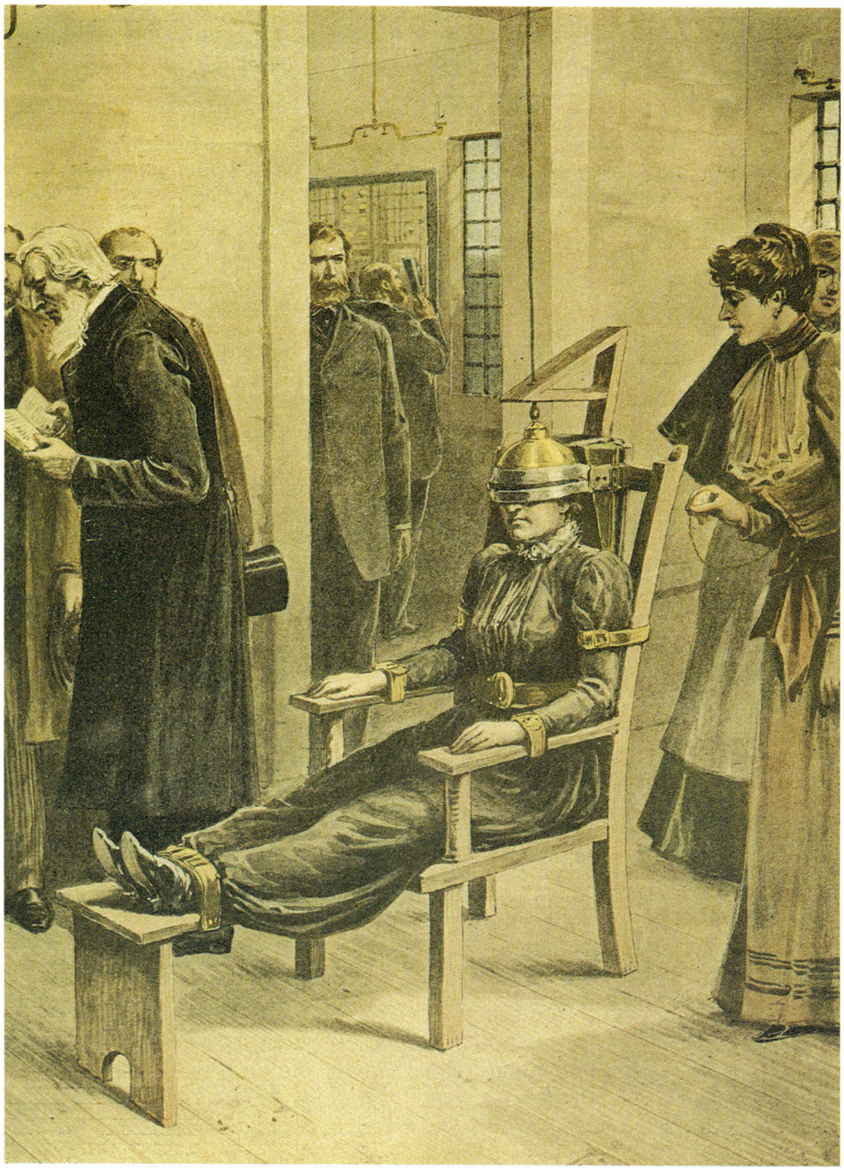

had a particular horror of parricide and it is said that the punishment for this crime consisted of being sewn inside a sack with a dog, a cock, a viper and an ape, and then thrown into water. Another Roman method of execution was starvation. The offender was either placed in a pit and left there without food and water until he died, or walled up inside a confined space with a pot of water.

In the Middle Ages beheading was an honourable method of execution for aristocrats, while traitors, for example, were hanged, drawn and quartered. Heretics were burnt, unless they repented before going to the stake.

In recent times some countries have remained faithful to old methods. Garrotting (from *garrote*—a stick twisted to tighten a loop) was long used in Spain, probably introduced by the Moors, who strangled murderers and unfaithful wives with a bowstring. In later times, the loop was replaced by a collar, through which a spike was driven from behind until it reached the spinal cord. France has remained faithful to the guillotine, which, contrary to popular supposition, was not invented during the French Revolution, although named after a Dr Guillotin, who recommended it as efficient, quick and humane. The guillotine consists of a weighted blade falling downwards between two posts and operates by decapitating the person being executed. It was used in Germany in the thirteenth century and was known as the 'diele', or dolabra, and in Italy as 'the mannaia'. In Scotland the original guillotine used to behead the Regent Morton in 1581 was still in a museum in 1930; known as 'the maiden', such a device was last used in Scotland to behead the Earl of Argyll in 1685. Shooting by firing squad became common especially in military offences.

The method favoured in Britain before the abolition of capital punishment was hanging. Expertly used, it breaks the neck, and death is instantaneous but it is easily bungled, leading to strangulation. Hanging can be slow, but if expertly performed it is extremely rapid and humane. Only 9 to 25 seconds elapse from the appearance of the executioner to death.

Electrocution, used in many states of the USA, (2,000 volts repeated four times for three seconds, with 500 volts in between) is no doubt instantaneous, but takes from three to six minutes before the first shock. It is the least disfiguring method of execution, leaving no sign except an occasional small burn on the ankle. Gassing, in which sulphuric acid is poured on to sodium cyanide tablets, requires elaborate equipment and takes five to six minutes.

Above left
In this 1857 illustration of the garrotting of a Chinese criminal, a cord round his neck is being tightened with a stick, leading to death by strangulation

Left
A French paper pictures Dr Crippen's hanging in 1910 at Pentonville Prison, London. A wife-poisoner, he was the first criminal caught through a radio message

Above
Mrs Place in the electric chair in New York in 1899, as seen by a French-language newspaper. She was sentenced to death for murdering her daughter-in-law

Toll of the Gallows
The reign of Henry VIII was marked by extreme severity in the execution of criminals. During that period, 7,200 people were publicly hanged

Charles Manson wielded such power over his followers that he was able to 'programme' them to kill with savage bestiality, feeling not a vestige of remorse

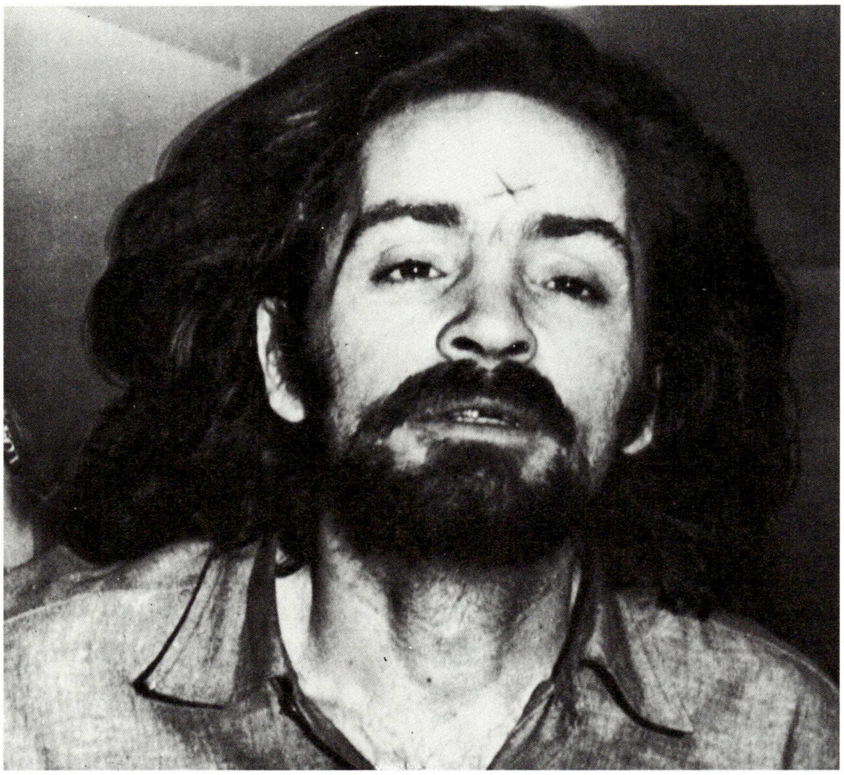

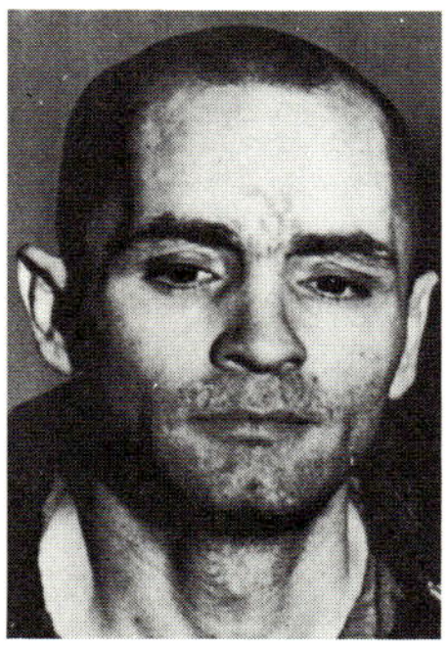

Above
Charles Manson on trial in 1970, bearded and with long hair, a cross scratched on his forehead. A year later, the cross had healed and a swastika had been painted on in its place. The hair and beard had been shaved off

Right
Sharon Tate – a publicity photograph. She pleaded with the Manson 'Family' not to kill her, because she was pregnant, but her plea fell on deaf ears. Manson, who had an almost hypnotic influence on the 'Family', had ordered that everyone in the house must die. As always, he was obeyed to the letter

On March 29, 1971, the Tate-La Bianca case, the longest murder trial in American history, ended in Los Angeles. During the nine and a half months the trial lasted, the bizarre story of the Charles Manson 'Family' and the brutal murders of seven innocent people were described in lurid detail and reported around the world.

Murder is a common way of death in the USA, but this case was very unusual for the number of murderers and known victims. Manson stood out as a macabre, twisted personality.

Charles Manson started early in crime. At 13 he was sent to reform school for armed robbery and spent the next 19 years in and out of penal institutions for offences such as stealing cars, robbing petrol stations, fraud and pimping.

He was 32 years old when he came out of prison, and before long he landed up in Haight Ashbury, San Francisco, the centre of the hippy, counter-culture world. There he spent time gathering 'flower children' round him and recruiting the first members of his 'Family'. He had a magnetic and persuasive way with him and attracted followers easily. 'I'm a very positive force—I collect negatives', he later told a friend.

One evening in August, 1969, when the 'Family' were camping out at a run-down ranch near Hollywood, Manson suddenly ordered four of them—three girls and a man—to prepare themselves for a big night's work. Their target was an isolated house in Beverly Hills which symbolized the rich establishment world they so despised.

Manson instructed Charles 'Tex' Watson to kill everyone in the house as gruesomely as possible. One possible plan was to hang the 'rich piggies' and then cut them to pieces. To the girls, Susan (Sadie) Atkins, Linda Kasabian and Patricia (Katie) Krenwinkel, he said 'Leave a sign—something witchy!'

The group did not know or care whom they would find in the house. They were simply instructed to kill everyone they found there. Their weapons were three knives, a gun and 43 feet of nylon rope. When they arrived at the entrance gate, Watson parked the car out of the way and cut the telephone wires. The group then climbed the fence round the grounds and saw 18-year-old Steve Parent, who had been visiting the caretaker at the back of the grounds, driving towards them. Watson yelled at him to stop, jammed the gun against his head and fired, point blank, four times.

The four continued to the house, and Linda Kasabian was posted as a look-out, while the other three climbed in through a window. Voytek Frykowski was dozing on the living-room couch. He opened his eyes to see a man standing over him, pointing a revolver at his head. 'Who are you?' Frykowski asked. He was told: 'I'm the Devil, here to do the Devil's business. Give me all your money'. Watson and the two girls tied his hands with a towel and made him lie on his back. Then, the other three people in the house: Abigail Folger, Jay Sebring and Sharon Tate, who was eight months pregnant, were ordered out of the bedrooms at knife-point and told to lie on their stomachs, on the floor.

The most incredible butchery then took place, as each victim was beaten, hanged, shot and viciously stabbed dozens of times. The last to die was Sharon Tate, who begged the intruders not to kill her because she was soon going to have a baby. Mercilessly, she was stabbed some 16 times. Susan Atkins, who had got some blood on her hand, licked it off. She said later that, if she and her companions had had enough time, they would have gouged out the eyes of their victims and mutilated the bodies

still further. Before they left, Atkins wrote the word 'PIG' in blood on the front door.

The next night, Charles Manson himself led a murder mission to the home of a Mr and Mrs LaBianca. The gang's weapons were four bayonets and a sword. Manson went in alone and tied up the couple, then told three of his followers to go in and kill them. Mr LaBianca was brutally stabbed with a kitchen knife, a cord was tied tightly around his neck, and a carving knife left protruding from his stomach. The word 'WAR' was carved into the flesh on his abdomen. Mrs LaBianca was throttled by a cord attached to a heavy lamp and stabbed no fewer than 41 times. This time, 'DEATH TO PIGS' and 'RISE' were scrawled in blood on the wall and 'HEALTER SKELTER' across the refrigerator door. The mis-spelling of 'Helter Skelter' was the key to the killings. It was the title of a popular Beatles song of the time which had a special message for Manson. It told him that the Day of Judgement was coming, when there would be a black revolution and the blacks would kill all the whites except Manson's 'Family'.

Atkins was arrested in 1969 on suspicion of involvement in the murder of one Gary Hinman, who had run foul of the group, possibly trying to expose their criminal activities, which included theft, fraud, drugs, and so on. He had been stabbed to death the previous July and the words 'POLITICAL PIGGY' daubed on the wall above his head. Atkins' naive bragging to a cell-mate led the police to connect the Manson 'Family' with the Tate killings. Manson, Atkins, Kasabian and Krenwinkel were put on trial in Los Angeles.

The prosecution had the unnerving task of convincing the jury that the bizarre belief in the message of *Helter Skelter* was the real motive for the apparently senseless murders, and that Manson's powers of indoctrination were so strong that his 'children' would savagely kill on his instructions. Manson's influence was uncanny. 'He does nothing himself: all the women have been programmed to do exactly as he says, and they all have knives', the prosecution declared.

Drugs were one of Manson's weapons. Newcomers to the group were initiated with an LSD 'trip', although it was not this which caused them to kill. None of the murderers was under the influence of drugs when they went on their savage missions.

Open and group sex was a more potent influence in conditioning them. Manson 'had a talent for sensing and capitalizing on a person's hang-ups and/or desires'. By breaking down his 'Family's' inherent middle-class morality, he led them to abandon all the other rules of civilized society.

Manson himself was totally amoral—'Death to Charlie was no more important than eating an ice-cream cone'. He was opposed to killing animals, but not people. When Watson was brought to trial later on, he admitted that he thought of the victims as 'just blobs'.

Manson's influence was almost totally hypnotic. He represented God to his 'slave-girls' and, although he never said in so many words that he was Christ come down to earth a second time, he implied it, pronouncing his surname as 'Man Son' and convincing his 'Family' that he had divine powers.

At the end of the long-drawn out trial, Manson and the three girls were found guilty and sentenced to die in the gas chamber at San Quentin. The man convicted of the Hinman murder, Bobby Beausoleil was also sentenced to death. So was Charles Watson, for his part in the Tate-LaBianca killings. However, all were saved from execution when the death penalty was abolished in California on February 18, 1972.

Above
Manson returns to his cell after sentence. He escaped death because California abolished the death penalty

Below
Peter Hurkos sitting in the room where Sharon Tate and her friends were murdered. A clairvoyant, Hurkos was engaged to work on the Tate-LaBianca case. In 1969, he worked with police on the Boston Strangler case

League of Assassins

'If it were done when 'tis done, then 'twere well It were done quickly'

Assassination strikes terror in the hearts of us all. It is murder for political reasons, and the pages of history books are spattered with the blood of leaders spilled in the cause of revolution

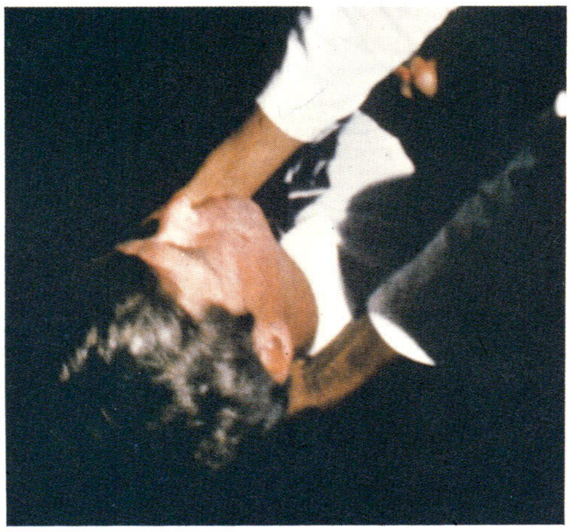

Above
Wounded twice in the back and once in the head by a gunman, Robert F. Kennedy lies dying on the floor in the Ambassador Hotel, in Los Angeles, in June, 1968. His brother, President John F. Kennedy, was assassinated in Dallas, Texas, in November, 1963, and died in 30 minutes

Above right
Dr Martin Luther King, the American black civil rights leader, shot in the neck in April, 1968, while on the balcony of his motel room in Memphis, Tennessee. He died an hour later. His assassin escaped, but was caught in Britain in June of that year

Far right
Mount Almut, in the north of Persia, the site of the 'Eagle's Nest', where the hashasheen, the original 'League of Assassins', took refuge from persecution at the very end of the eleventh century. The hashasheen were an ancient secret fraternity of members of the Mohammedan Ismaili sect

Historically Prominent Assassinations
Julius Caesar
March 15, 44 BC
Roman general and dictator, stabbed to death in Roman Senate by Brutus, Cimber, Cassius, Casca, and others
Gustavus II
March 16, 1792
King of Sweden, shot at masked ball by assassin hired by nobles
Jean Marat
July 13, 1793
French Revolutionary leader, stabbed by Charlotte Corday

Assassination—a fairly simple word, yet one that evokes thoughts of the most cataclysmic and complex social phenomena in man's experience: terrorism, political upheaval, even global warfare. A single assassination can precipitate such events—or end them. In its 'pure' form, assassination always represents the ultimate tool for bringing about sudden and violent change. Although more than mere murder, it is not always easily distinguished from it. What then differentiates the assassination of a political figure from the murder of someone who may be equally prominent, but is not connected with politics? Why is the victim of a terrorist attack usually considered to have been 'murdered', rather than 'assassinated'? Analysis of the term 'assassination', together with some examples of historic assassinations, should help to explain the essential difference between murder and assassination.

We begin with the word itself. 'Assassination' comes from the Arabic 'hashasheen' (literally, 'drinkers of hashish'), the name given to the members of an ancient secret fraternity of fanatical adherents of the Mohammedan Ismaili sect. The sect had been persecuted for many years in northern Persia, Iraq and Syria, when Hsan ibn-al-Sabbah formed the secret fraternity in 1090 to protect the faithful and propagate the order. By a ruse Hsan seized an impregnable castle on Mount Almut in northern Persia, using it as a base from which to protect the Ismailis. Also, by the systematic use of assassination, he began to eliminate or 'convert' the sect's former persecutors. The name given to Hsan's followers stemmed from the way in which he commanded their fanatical obedience. Novitiates were first given hashish to drink, and then taken to special parts of the mountain fortress, where, for five days and nights, they experienced every imaginable earthly delight. At the end of this period, the young men were again drugged and

Paul I
March 4, 1801
Czar of Russia, slain by Russian nobles after he refused to abdicate
Abraham Lincoln
April 14, 1865
16th US President, shot by John Wilkes Booth in Ford's Theater in Washington, D.C. Died next day.
Alexander II
March 13, 1881
Czar of Russia, assassinated by Russian terrorists
James A. Garfield
July 2, 1881
20th US President, shot by disappointed job seeker Charles J. Guiteau. Died September 19, 1881
Elizabeth
September 10, 1898
Empress of Austria, assassinated in Geneva by Italian anarchist
Humberte I
July 29, 1900
King of Italy, killed by Gaetano Bresci at Monza, Italy
William McKinley
September 6, 1901
25th US President, shot by anarchist Leon Czolgosz at Buffalo, New York. Died eight days later
Alexander I
June 11, 1903
King of Serbia, and his wife, assassinated in Belgrade.
Carlos I
February 1, 1908
King of Portugal, and his son, the crown prince, shot in Lisbon
Francisco I. Madero
February 22, 1913
President of Mexico, shot by guard after being imprisoned by General Victoriano Huerta.
George I
March 18, 1913
King of Greece, assassinated during the second Balkan War
Franz Ferdinand
June 28, 1914
Archduke of Austria-Hungary, and his wife, shot by Serbian nationalist in Sarajevo, starting World War I
Grigori Rasputin
December 30, 1916
Russian monk, poisoned, stabbed and shot by nobles who hated his influence on Czar Nicholas
Nicholas II
July 16, 1918
Czar of Russia, his wife and children, shot in Ekaterinburg
Emiliano Zapata
April 10, 1919
Mexican revolutionary and reformer, killed in ambush by agents of President Venustiano Carranza
Pancho Villa
July 29, 1923
Mexican revolutionary, assassinated at his estate in Durango

then brought before Hsan. He promised them that they would later return permanently to the paradise they had just visited on condition that they offered him blind and total obedience. Thus motivated, the hashasheen, armed with daggers of solid gold, terrorized their part of the world.

The essential element of assassination is its political motivation. Repressive dictatorships and democratic societies have suffered less from assassination than other types of régime—with the two notable exceptions of America and El Salvador

Having determined the derivation of the word 'assassination', we shall now proceed to formulate a workable definition of the act. The essential element of assassination is its *political* motivation—the desire to produce precipitous political change. An assassin perceives that the death of a specific individual will cripple or eliminate some political movement, and/or advance his own cause. Assassins rarely know their victims, or even have strong feelings about them. What incites an assassin to act is the political system or ideology personified by the victim. Thus, a terrorist cannot be said to have assassinated his victims, since they have rarely been specifically selected with the thought in mind that their death will directly affect political conditions. Terrorists exploit the cumulative effect of mindless murder, the crippling fear it generates, to bring pressure to bear on political leaders to make major policy changes.

Mere murder clearly falls outside our assassination definition. Hate, greed, passion, etc. motivate the murderer. There is no particular desire to change the course of history. The murderer simply wants to precipitate a change in circumstances that will be beneficial to his own immediate ends.

Not surprisingly, most assassinations occur in the less sophisticated and more politically volatile countries of the world, although it is interesting to note that repressive dictatorships and permissive democracies have historically suffered less from assassination than other types of regime. (Two notable exceptions are the United States and El Salvador.) Assassination thrives in areas where there are numerous, organized nationalistic groups; where the external expression of aggression is common and accepted; where there are suppressed and frustrated minority factions; where the homicide rate is generally high, and where frequent political upheaval is commonplace. It is, therefore, not surprising that more than half of the successful assassinations in the past 50 years have occurred in Latin America and the Middle East.

Let us now examine two European and four American assassinations and explore their effects.

The Ides of March of 44 BC marked the end of one of the most famous rulers in history: Julius Caesar. He practically invited his assassination by his insensitive subjugation of even those individuals closest to him. It was, in fact, Caesar's 'loyal friends' in the Roman Senate who first plotted and then carried out his assassination.

Julius Caesar had triumphantly led the Roman legions to a long succession of victories. As his fame and power grew, so, too, did his appetite for them. He finally assumed absolute control of the Roman Empire by turning the hitherto democratic Senate from a genuine ruling body into a mere puppet organization. Many members of the Senate had spent their lives serving Rome, and they believed fervently in democratic representation. Caesar's actions not only affronted them personally, but also flew in the face of their strongest beliefs and ideals. Truly believing that they were acting in the best

Right
Murder in the cathedral. In December, 1170, four knights took at their face value some angry and violent words spoken by King Henry II of England and put to the sword Thomas Becket, Archbishop of Canterbury, on the altar steps of his own cathedral

interests of Rome, 60 of Caesar's friends, led by Cassius, plotted his death. On March 15, 44 BC, Caesar was induced to attend a session of the Roman Senate, where Brutus, his best friend, Cimber, Cassius, Casca, and others leapt upon him with knives and swords, stabbing him 23 times. Caesar's death touched off thirteen assassination- and murder-ridden years of political turmoil, as various factions fought for control of the Empire. Finally, his primary heir, Augustus, asserted himself as sole ruler.

By Greek and Roman standards of the time, Caesar's assassins had committed a laudable act—tyrannicide. This is a variant of assassination, in which the assassin or assassins are striking at the tyrant himself, as well as what he represents, and are willing to sacrifice themselves for the wider political good. Clearly, the senators sought to remove Caesar because of the enormous power he had assumed, and because he had effectively eliminated democratic representation in Roman politics. The bitter irony of Caesar's assassination was that the old democracy sought by the assassins never again returned to the Roman Empire.

The men who plotted the assassination of Archduke Franz Ferdinand in Sarajevo in 1914 bungled the attempt. By pure mischance, they were given a second opportunity only hours later, when the Archduke's chauffeur took a wrong turning.

In recent history, the assassination which had the most far-reaching effects was that of Archduke Franz Ferdinand, of the Austro-Hungarian Empire, on June 28, 1914. On July 28 that same year, Austria declared war on Serbia, whereupon Russia began to mobilize. Three days later, on August 1, 1914, Germany declared war on Russia. On August 3 and 4, France and Britain declared war on Germany. World War I had begun. Ferdinand's assassination also led directly to the fall of four royal empires: the Hapsburgs, Romanovs, Hohenzollerns and Ottomans.

The killing of Ferdinand graphically illustrates how political instability and, particularly, strong nationalist movements breed such murders. At the time, Europe was a hot-bed of political activity. Many countries were experiencing their first taste of democracy, or were fighting for it. The small cluster of countries known as the Balkans exemplified the political unrest of the times. These states were frequently the scene of assassinations, because they had been under foreign rule for hundreds of years. With total insensitivity to the feelings and aspirations of nationalist groups, the area was arbitrarily divided up by various empires. Bosnia was annexed by the Austro-Hungarian Empire and ruled by it. Nearby Serbia was independent and democratic. The seeds of Ferdinand's assassination grew from the unrest created among the Bosnians because statehood had been taken away from them, while the Serbs, who belonged to the same 'people', had remained free.

In an attempt to placate the people of Bosnia, the Hapsburg Emperor of Austria-Hungary sent his nephew, Archduke Ferdinand, on an official public relations visit to the Bosnian provincial capital of Sarajevo. A group of students led by Gavrilo

Left
Julius Caesar, Roman Emperor and victorious general, one of the most famous victims of assassination

Centre
The conspirators stab Julius Caesar to death – a print after a painting by Gérôme. So hungry was he for power, that he finally made himself dictator of the Roman Empire, turning the Senate from a democratic ruling body into a mere puppet Chamber

Bottom
Archduke Franz Ferdinand, of the Austro-Hungarian Empire, whose assassination in June, 1914, had easily the most far-reaching effects in recent history. When Gavrilo Princip killed the Archduke, he set in train a series of events culminating in World War I and the fall of four royal empires

Alvaro Obregon
July 17, 1928
President of Mexico, killed by Roman Catholic fanatic
Anton Cermak
February 15, 1933
Mayor of Chicago, killed in Miami by Joseph Zangara, who was trying to assassinate President-elect Franklin D. Roosevelt
Engelbert Dollfuss
July 25, 1934
Austrian chancellor, assassinated by Nazis
Alexander I
October 9, 1934
King of Yugoslavia, killed by terrorist in Marseille, France
Huey P. Long
September 8, 1935
U.S. Senator from Louisiana and candidate for Democratic presidential nomination, shot by Dr Carl A. Weiss. Died two days later
Leon Trotsky
August 20, 1940
Russian revolutionary exile, stabbed by Stalinist agent

Above
Fourth time lucky. Russian Nihilists had already tried to shoot Czar Alexander II, derail his train and blow up the Winter Palace in Petrograd, when they threw some bombs at him in the city in 1881 and killed him

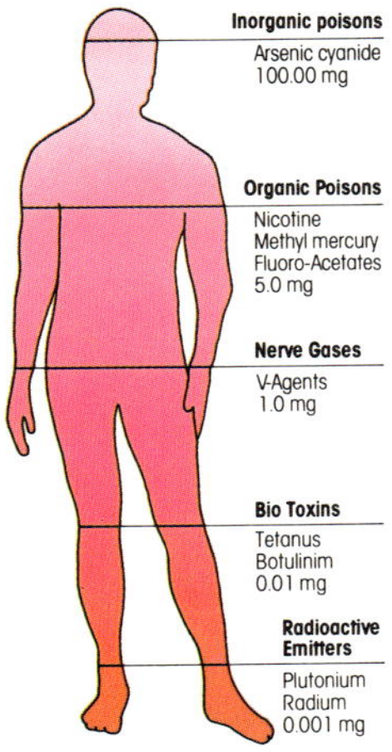

Technology of Death
The quantity of various toxic chemicals and other substances that could be introduced into an assassin's bullet to ensure the death of his intended victim. Note the very minute amounts of radium required, compared with, say, arsenic cyanide

Princip, Nedeljko Cabrinovic and Trifko Grabez decided to use the opportunity of close contact with a Hapsburg to strike a blow for freedom. With the help of a secret society, 'Smrt ili Zivot' ('Death or Life'), they procured revolvers and bombs for their attempt.

The security in Sarajevo on June 28, 1914, was surprisingly lax, especially in view of the open political unrest in Bosnia. The Archduke and his wife began their tour of Sarajevo in an open car. At half-past ten in the morning, as the vehicle was travelling down the Appel Quai, Cabrinovic tossed a bomb at it. The bomb bounced off the royal car, rolled under the following car and exploded. The royal car sped away to a reception at the town hall, where Archduke Ferdinand, infuriated by the assassination attempt and the obvious lack of security, strongly upbraided the provincial governor. On learning that a passenger in the following car had been injured by the exploding bomb, Ferdinand felt compelled to rush to the hospital to visit him. The driver began to retrace the route he had taken in the morning, but took a wrong turning. Realizing his mistake, he stopped the car and prepared to turn round. Incredible as it may seem, Gavrilo Princip was standing only six feet away. The failure of the bomb-throwing attempt had convinced Princip that there was no hope of realizing the plan to assassinate Ferdinand, yet here he was, a sitting target in a stationary motor car. Princip drew an automatic pistol and fired wildly at the royal couple. His first shot passed through the car door and struck the Archduchess. The second shot hit Ferdinand in the neck, severing his jugular vein and then lodging in his cervical spine. By half-past eleven, only an hour after the initial, abortive assassination attempt, Archduke Franz Ferdinand and his wife were dead.

Twenty-two people were tried in connection with the assassination. Since none of the principals in the plot was more than 20 years of age, their lives were spared, but they were all sentenced to long prison terms with hard labour. Only two survived the ordeal. The other defendants involved were all hanged. At the trial, Gavrilo Princip stated the classical political motivation behind his act, 'I am not a criminal' he declared, 'for I have suppressed a harmful man . . . I am a South Slav nationalist. My aim is the union of all Slavs . . . and their liberation from Austria.'

Both assassinations described here were sparked off by subjugation. The killing of Julius Caesar was applauded by many Romans, but the political goal of the assassins was never achieved. Ferdinand's death, on the other hand, did result—at least indirectly—in the political upheaval sought by the conspirators.

We now turn to America. Many hypotheses have been put forward to explain why that country is an exception to the rule that permissive democracies (like repressive dictatorships) suffer less from assassination than other types of regime. Some people say that Americans are a generally hostile, aggressive and violent people, others that the frontier tradition is still strong in the United States. These hypotheses, like others that have been put forward, are unconvincing, and further speculation would be profitless. The plain fact is that, whatever the reasons, America is definitely assassination-prone. Also, the four most infamous assassinations in America, described on the following pages, were apparently the result of conspiracies, yet only one was officially revealed, and even then, not completely. Why? We do not know, and we may never be given the chance to find out.

There were more than 80 abortive plots on the life of Abraham Lincoln. And there is very strong evidence implicating his Secretary of War in the conspiracy which led to Lincoln's assassination by John Wilkes Booth in 1865 and Lincoln's canonization in America

Now canonized by the American people, Abraham Lincoln was one of the most hated United States Presidents in history. During his Presidency, there were more than 80 abortive plots against him or attempts on his life. To thwart one such plot, President Lincoln had to sneak into Washington in disguise before he even officially took office! The hatred many felt for Lincoln stemmed from the fierce controversy at the time over the slavery issue. Contrary to popular belief, Lincoln was not in favour of freeing the slaves when he first took office. He had pledged himself to peace and to preserving the Union. The White House's early official stance was to allow slavery to continue where it already existed, but to prevent the custom from spreading. The Civil War and other events, however, finally forced Lincoln to declare the emancipation of all slaves in America. Because of this, and also as the leader of the Union forces,

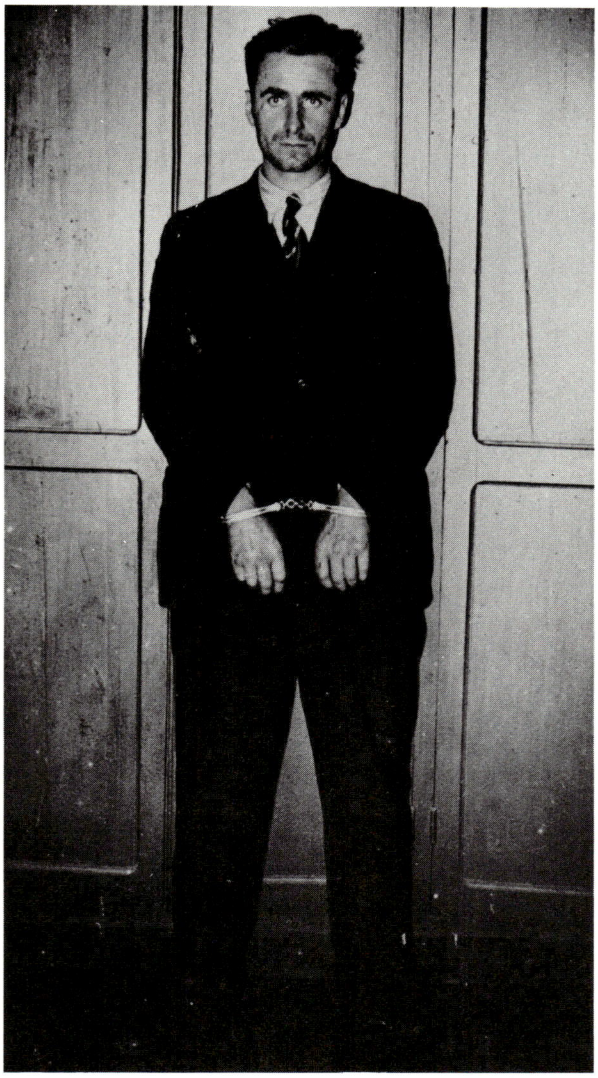

Far left
Czar Alexander II, who came to the Russian throne in 1855, succeeding his father, Nicholas I. Alexander II was a great reformer. In 1861 he emancipated 23 million serfs throughout the Russian Empire, and had signed a ukase for further reforms on March 13, 1881, the day of his assassination

Left
King Alexander of Yugoslavia failed to replace Serbian and Croatian nationalism by loyalty to the country as a whole. While on a visit to Marseille in 1934, he was assassinated by Croatian terrorists. This one, Malny, was gaoled for life by a French court

Lincoln was despised by Southerners. John Wilkes Booth was one such Southerner.

Born in Maryland and a fervent Confederate supporter, Booth hatched a scheme in late 1864 or early 1865 to kidnap President Lincoln. The Confederacy was then in desperate straits, and Booth hoped to exchange the President for 100,000 Confederate soldiers who were prisoners-of-war in Northern hands, thus revitalizing the Confederate forces.

Booth recruited five accomplices to aid him in his scheme: John Harrison Surratt, Jr, 21, also born in Maryland; David E. Herold, 23; George Andrew Atzerodt; Samuel Bland Arnold, and Lewis Paine. Surratt was a Confederate spy, based in Washington, DC, and an underground courier for the Confederacy. He persuaded his mother, Mrs Mary E. Surratt, to put her boarding-house at Booth's disposal for a meeting place and staging area for the conspiracy. Herold was selected because of his intimate familiarity with the Maryland countryside. Atzerodt, an illiterate Prussian immigrant who occasionally worked as a boatman for the Confederate underground, was so lacking in worthwhile attributes, that it has been speculated that he was to have been made the 'fall guy' for the plot. Arnold was an old friend of Booth's. His was the primary responsibility for the procurement of weapons. Paine was to provide the 'muscle' for the conspiracy. He had been involved in some of the bloodiest confrontations of the Civil War, and had developed a near-paranoid hatred of Northerners as a result.

Booth and his co-conspirators began meeting frequently at Mary Surratt's boarding-house to practise their 'kidnapping skills' and lay plans for their deed. Then, on April 9, 1865, General Robert E. Lee, of the Confederacy, surrendered to the Union, ending the Civil War. There was no longer any point in attempting to kidnap Lincoln. Embittered by the defeat of his beloved South, Booth decided to assassinate him instead.

It had been well reported that the President and Mrs. Lincoln were to attend a performance of 'Our American Cousin' at Ford's Theater in Washington on the evening of April 14, 1865; Booth decided to kill Lincoln there. During the afternoon of the 14th, he went to the theatre to make his preparations. He first drilled a peephole in the panelling of the Presidential box, so that he would be able to see any security personnel with the President, and then concealed a board in the box, so that he would be able to wedge the door shut once he had entered, so that nobody would be able to get in. That evening, dressed in dark clothes and wearing a false beard, Booth made his way silently to the Presidential box. Amazingly, there was no guard at the door, so Booth entered and hid behind some curtains to await his 'cue'—a certain point during the play when the audience invariably laughed. This was when he planned to strike. At precisely the planned moment, Booth leapt from behind the curtains, levelled a derringer at President's Lincoln's head, and fired at point blank range. Lincoln's security guard for the evening, Major Henry Rathbone, who was in the box, grappled with Booth, but was overpowered. Leaping onto the stage, Booth ran out

Jean Francois Darlan
December 24, 1942
Commander of French Navy and pro-Nazi governor of French Africa, assassinated in Algiers
Gualverto Villarroel
July 21, 1946
President of Bolivia, killed during coup d'etat
U. Aung San
July 19, 1947
Premier of Burma, and five associates, killed by opponents
Mohandas Gandhi
January 30, 1948
Leader of India, shot by Nathuram Godse, Hindu who blamed Gandhi for partition of India
Count Folke Bernadotte
September 17, 1948
Swedish UN mediator, slain by Israeli terrorists
Abdullah ibn Hussein
July 20, 1951
King of Jordan, assassinated in Jerusalem
José Antonio Remón
January 2, 1955
President of Panama, killed by machine-gunner
Anastasio Somoza
September 21, 1956
President of Nicaragua, shot during election campaign dance. Died eight days later
Carlos Castillo Armas
July 26, 1957
President of Guatemala, shot by a palace guard
Faisal II
July 14, 1958
King of Iraq, killed in revolt by Abdul Karim Kassem
Solomon Bandaranaike
September 25, 1959
Prime minister of Ceylon, shot by Buddhist monk
Hazza Majali
August 29, 1960
Premier of Jordan, killed by time bomb in his office
Rafael L. Trujillo
May 30, 1961
Dictator and president of the Dominican Republic, slain
Sylvanus Olympio
January 13, 1963
President of Togo, killed by former soldiers in Lomé
Ngo Dinh Diem
November 1-2, 1963
President of South Vietnam, and his brother, slain

Above
President Abraham Lincoln is assassinated by John Wilkes Booth in a Washington theatre box in April, 1864. Lincoln was one of the most hated American Presidents

Right
The death of John Wilkes Booth. Shot and captured by pursuing troops in Virginia, Booth lived for more than five hours, but no attempt was made to interrogate him

Far right
There were more than 80 attempts on the life of President Abraham Lincoln and plots against him, many hatched by Southerners, who hated and despised Lincoln. Lincoln was assassinated just a few days after the Union victory in 1865, and he came to be seen among later generations of Americans as something of a martyred hero. Yet the principal reason for this hero-worship, Lincoln's espousal of the cause to emancipate black slaves, was not an issue with which he was originally linked

of the theatre through a stage door, and was joined by Herold shortly afterwards. The two men fled into the Maryland countryside. Eleven days later, they were brought to ground in a tobacco barn in Bowling Green, Virginia. Booth was shot before he and Herold were captured. A further six people were arrested soon afterwards in connection with the assassination. Together with Herold, three of them—Paine, Atzerodt and Mary Surratt—were sentenced to the gallows. A sad chapter in American history had ended.

It may be argued that the killing of President Lincoln was not assassination but simple murder. From the account above, it appears that Booth was motivated purely by hate, and had no political objective. However, recent discoveries by historical scholars indicate strongly that the conspiracy behind the killing of President Lincoln was not only much more widespread than originally thought, but was also politically motivated.

Among those apparently implicated in the assassination plot was Edwin M. Stanton, Lincoln's Secretary of War. A staunch Unionist and Northern supporter, Stanton was opposed to Lincoln's plan to aid the South after the Civil War to help heal the wounds left by the bitter conflict. Stanton wanted to strip the Southern states of their statehood, eliminate—or, at least, reduce—Southern representation in Congress, and generally disfranchise the South. In other words, Stanton wanted to make the South a colony of the North, to be plundered and exploited at will. Strong circumstantial evidence shows that, at the very least, Stanton knew about the conspiracy and acquiesced in Lincoln's assassination—and he may even have facilitated it. War Department records make it clear that Stanton was aware of Booth's plot as early as January, 1865. The information reached Stanton from a Captain D. H. L. Gleason, one of whose subordinates in the War Department, a clerk called Louis Weichmann, boarded with Mary Surratt. Weichmann noticed the strange goings-on in the boarding-house and reported his suspicions to Captain Gleason, together with the name and description of each conspirator.

Both Stanton and General Grant had been invited by President Lincoln to join him at Ford's Theater on April 14. Stanton declined the invitation and persuaded General Grant, whose superior he was, to do so as well. If General Grant had gone to the theatre, he would have been accompanied by a heavily armed military escort.

Edwin M. Stanton, Lincoln's Secretary of War, was in charge of the forces which chased and caught Booth after the killing of the President. Instead of capturing him unwounded, they shot him, but although he remained alive for five hours, no attempt was made to interrogate him. Some other conspirators escaped scot-free

On the afternoon of April 14, President Lincoln personally requested that Major Thomas L. Eckert, a physically powerful and fearless man, be assigned

A Lingering Death
Although shot at point-blank range by Charles Guiteau in Washington in July, 1881, President James A. Garfield lingered on until September

Right
President Garfield was in a Washington railway station on his way to Ohio for the commencement exercises at Williams College, his alma mater, when he was shot by a disappointed office-seeker

as his bodyguard for the evening. Secretary Stanton (who was in charge of the President's safety) said that this was not possible, because Eckert had important telegraphic duties to perform that evening. Instead, Major Henry Rathbone, a competent but not particularly robust man, was detailed for the job. Investigations have revealed that Stanton did not keep Eckert in the office that evening, and that no telegraphic messages of any consequence were sent or received. The man assigned to guard duty at the door of the Presidential box was one John F. Parker, of the Metropolitan Police Force, a known chronic drunk and malingerer. True to form, Parker left his post outside the box on the evening of April 14, to go to a saloon. Parker was not dismissed for this grave dereliction of duty.

Immediately after the assassination, all the telegraph wires into Washington went dead—except those of the War Department. As a result Stanton's handpicked pursuit forces had a substantial lead over the others who were pursuing Booth.

Reason would suggest that every conceivable effort should have been made to take Booth without harming him and to interrogate him to the fullest degree. However, he was shot at the very earliest opportunity, and although he did not die for more than five hours, no attempt whatever was made to question him.

Some of the conspirators whose identity, it will be recalled, was known to the War Department, escaped scot-free. No attempt was made to apprehend them. John H. Surratt left the United States altogether.

Those who did stand trial faced a military court, whose members were hand-picked by Stanton—he would have had no standing in the matter if a non-military court had dealt with it. The members of the court initially wanted to sentence Mary Surratt to life imprisonment, but a deal was worked out, under which she would be sentenced to death and President Johnson would commute this to life imprisonment. When the court members and other groups sought to see President Johnson about the commutation, they were blocked by two senators loyal to Stanton.

The Secretary of War was also implicated in the suppression of evidence—Booth's diary. When Booth was captured, his diary was taken from his coat by a Lieutenant Colonel Everton Conger and handed over to a Colonel Lafayette C. Baker. He, in turn, gave it to Stanton. The diary was never presented as evidence at the trial. When it was finally released to the public, 18 pages of entries leading up to the eve of the assassination were found to have been removed.

In 1960 a man called Roy Neff came across a coded message written in the margin of a bound volume of the 1864 issues of *United Services Magazine*. Purportedly written by Colonel Baker the message accused Stanton of being behind the assassination plot; noted that Baker had brought the plot to Stanton's attention on April 10, 1865; alleged that Major Thomas J. Eckert made the arrangements for the assassination, and claimed that Baker had been blackmailed into silence by Stanton. The last paragraph of the message read: 'There were at least eleven members of Congress involved in the plot, no less than twelve Army officers, three Naval officers, and at least 24 civilians, one of whom was a governor . . .'

Not all the evidence presented here has been officially documented, but enough exists to establish that Secretary of War Stanton at least allowed the plot to come to fruition. The apparent motive of the conspirators was to block aid to the South and allow Stanton's 'colony plan' to become US policy. This was the first conspiracy in connection with an American assassination not to be officially uncovered.

Mystery still surrounds the assassination of President John F. Kennedy in 1963. Although the Warren Commission found that a single bullet caused the wounds suffered by both President Kennedy and Governor Connally, this theory is untenable. There must have been more than one assassin

The most investigated, disputed and written about assassination in recent history has been that of US President John F. Kennedy in 1963. Mystery and confusion still surround it. The official account is that he was cut down by a lone assassin, Lee Harvey Oswald, but evidence to be presented here will show that this is not, in fact, the case.

Irony of Death
William McKinley was the 25th President of the United States. He was born in Ohio and trained as a lawyer before entering politics. He was an orthodox Republican who was associated with such policies as trade and tariff protectionism. Ironically, he was in the process of adopting a more liberal attitude on protectionism when he was killed

Below centre
President McKinley is shot at point-blank range. His assailant, Leon Csolgosz, was an anarchist of Polish origin. He fired twice at McKinley with a revolver

Below
Leon Csolgosz about to die in the electric chair for assassinating President William McKinley in New York, in September, 1901

John F. Kennedy
November 22, 1963
US President, shot by Lee Harvey Oswald, in Dallas
Hendrik F. Verwoerd
September 6, 1966
Prime Minister of South Africa, stabbed in parliament in Pretoria by Dimitrio Stifanos
Martin Luther King, Jr
April 4, 1968
US Civil Rights leader, shot by ex-convict James Earl Ray in Memphis, Tennessee
Robert F. Kennedy
June 5, 1968
US Senator from New York, shot by Sirhan Sirhan in Los Angeles while celebrating California presidential primary victory. Died next day
A. A. Shermarke
October 15, 1969
President of Somalia, assassinated at Las Anos, Somalia
Cleo A. Noel, Jr.
March 2, 1973
US ambassador, slain in Khartoum, Sudan, by Arab terrorists
Rodger P. Davies
August 19, 1974
US ambassador, slain by Green Cypriots in embassy at Nicosia, Cyprus
Col. Richard Ratsimandrava
February 11, 1975
Madagascar head of state, slain in ambush
King Faisal
March 25, 1975
Of Saudi Arabia, shot by nephew during palace reception
N'Garta Tombalbaye
April 13, 1975
President of Chad, slain in military coup
Mujibur Rahman
August 15, 1975
Bangladesh president killed by army officer in coup
Gen. Murtala Ramat Muhammed
February 13, 1976
Nigeria's head of state, killed in unsuccessful coup attempt
Francis Meloy, Jr.
June 16, 1976
US ambassador to Lebanon, assassinated by terrorists
Christopher Biggs
July 21, 1976
British ambassador to Ireland slain in Ireland
Gen. Teferi Bante
February 3, 1977
Ethiopia's head of state, assassinated in coup by associates
Marien Ngouabi
March 18, 1977
Congo's president assassinated in Brazzaville
Ibrahim al-Hamdi
October 11, 1977
Yemen's president, and his brother assassinated in Sana
Aldo Moro
May 9, 1978
Italy's ex-Prime Minister and senior statesman, shot eleven times in the chest. Shot by members of the anarchist Red Brigade, Moro had come to be associated with the Liberal wing of the Christian Democrat party, favouring a more conciliatory approach to Italy's second most powerful political entity, the Communists

On November 22, 1963, President Kennedy visited Dallas, Texas. The local population was decidedly hostile to him, because of his liberal political attitude. Mrs Kennedy and the Governor of Texas, John Connally, accompanied the President on a tour of Dallas in an open car. As the vehicle was passing the Texas School Book Depository, three shots rang out. President Kennedy was seen to clutch at his throat, jerk forward and then collapse as Mrs Kennedy threw herself across him in an attempt to shield him from the unseen assassin. Governor Connally also went down with severe wounds in the chest, arm and thigh.

The Presidential car sped away to the nearby Parkland Memorial Hospital, where every effort was made to save Kennedy's life, but he was wounded so seriously in the head that there was no hope. By 1 pm, just 30 minutes after the shooting, President Kennedy was dead.

Immediately after the shooting, security forces threw a giant cordon round the area of the assassination. Roughly sixty minutes later, Patrolman J. D. Tippett supposedly challenged a man who was walking along a street some distance away from the surrounded area. The man was Lee Harvey Oswald, and he allegedly answered the challenge with pistol fire, shooting Tippett dead. Oswald then darted into a cinema, where he was later cornered and arrested.

Police rushed him to Dallas police headquarters for two days of intensive interrogation. The questioning over, Oswald was being escorted through the police headquarters basement preparatory to being transferred to the county jail on Sunday morning, November 24, when Jack Ruby stepped out among a crowd of newsmen, photographers, TV cameramen and onlookers, and shot Oswald dead.

These events led to a special federal investigation of President Kennedy's assassination—by the Warren Commission, appointed by President Lyndon B. Johnson and named after Earl Warren, Chief Justice of the United States Supreme Court. The Commission spent several months developing the official version of the assassination. The Commission members concluded that two of the three shots fired had caused all the wounds suffered by both President Kennedy and Governor Connally: Kennedy—head wound, back wound, and throat wound: Connally—back wound, arm wound, and thigh wound. The bullet that caused President Kennedy's throat wound was also responsible for *all* of Governor Connally's wounds. The shots were fired from a sixth floor window of the Texas School Book Depository by a lone assassin: Lee Harvey Oswald. The weapon used was a 6.5 mm Mannlicher-Carcano rifle. This conclusion has recently been 'supported' by another US Government investigation, in spite of devastating evidence to the contrary.

I was personally involved with the Kennedy assassination dispute, and could produce enormous amounts of evidence disputing the Warren Commission's conclusions. However, only the salient points will be presented here.

A problem arises immediately with the rifle allegedly used by Oswald. It is theoretically possible to hit a moving target once with a non-automatic rifle with a defective telescopic sight at the range at which President Kennedy was shot (approximately 60 metres [200 feet]), but in practice it would need a near-miracle. To do it twice is virtually impossible.

Admittedly, this does not constitute scientific counter-evidence to the Warren Commission conclusion, but what follows certainly does.

Films taken of the assassination prove that Kennedy's initial wound and Connally's wounds occurred within 1½ seconds. It is physically impossible to fire Oswald's rifle twice in less than 2.3 seconds, much less reaim it after the first shot. This being so, the Warren Commission was forced to conclude that the bullet that struck Kennedy's throat also entered Connally's back, shattered one of his ribs, passed through his chest, hit his wrist (fracturing the large bone in his right lower forearm) and finally embedded itself in his left thigh. Only by accepting this single bullet theory is it possible to conclude that Oswald was operating on his own. A bullet and two fragments that matched Oswald's rifle were found in the Presidential car, but the whole bullet that allegedly caused all the damage listed above was found, quite 'fortuitously', under a stretcher at the Parkland Memorial Hospital a few hours after the shooting.

The discovered bullet could not possibly have caused the wounds sustained by Kennedy and Connally. It was copper-jacketed and weighed 158.6 grains, compared with 161 grains when unfired. Except for a very slight deformity at its base, the

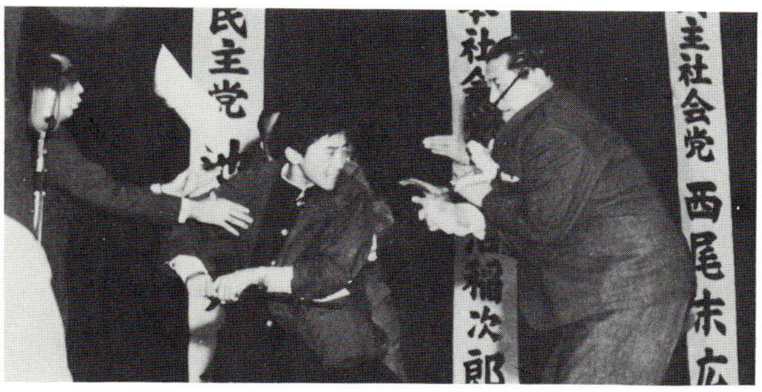

Top row, left to right: Robert F. Kennedy, brother of President John F. Kennedy; Leon Trotsky, former Bolshevik leader; President John F. Kennedy; assassination of Inejiro Afanum, leader of Japan's Socialist Party; Count Folke Bernadotte, United Nations mediator in Palestine, 1947; body of Aldo Moro, former Italian Premier, left in a car in Rome

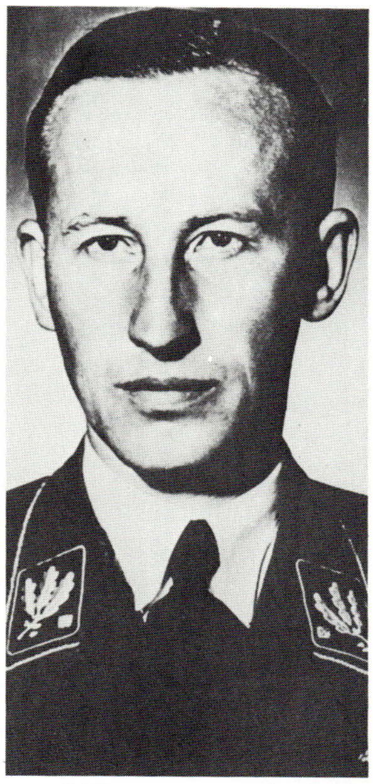

Bottom row, left to right: Adolf Hitler after unsuccessful 1944 assassination attempt; Dr Martin Luther King, Jr; Indian leader, Mohandas Gandhi; Pancho Villa, Mexican revolutionary; Ngo Din Nhu, Vietnamese strong man; Reinhard Heydrich, Nazi governor of Czechoslovakia; General Rafael Trujillo, President, Dominican Republic

bullet was perfect. Photos and X-rays of Kennedy and Connally, however, show metal (lead) particles in all their wounds, totalling more than 2.4 grains. How could a copper-jacketed bullet leave any lead behind at all? More importantly, how could the fired bullet leave metal behind, but show a weight loss of only 2.4 grains?

More serious questions come to mind when the fired bullet is compared with test-fired bullets. According to the Warren Commission report, 'Oswald's bullet' passed through a man's neck and chest, shattered a rib, and broke a large arm bone, yet it showed no more distortion than a bullet fired into cotton wadding. Bullets fired at a rib of a goat carcase or the wrist of a human corpse during research tests showed significantly greater distortion than the 'Oswald bullet' and they hit only one bone each! The conclusion that this one bullet did not do all the damage is inescapable.

To return to the subject of the films, they show that Governor Connally's reaction to the impact of the bullet followed President Kennedy's by at least 1½ seconds. Connally was, in fact, still holding his hat in the hand below his shattered wrist and a partially severed nerve, 1½ seconds after President Kennedy had been hit. This indicates quite clearly that Connally was hit by a different bullet. If not he would have reacted within milliseconds, not seconds. Because of the already discussed firing limitations of Oswald's rifle, two bullets mean more than one assassin.

A 'newly discovered' tape recording of a motorcycle policeman's radio transmission from the scene of the assassination has clearly revealed that four, not three, shots were fired. Extremely sophisticated electronic analysis of the tape also indicates that one of the four shots was fired from the famous 'grassy knoll'. (From the beginning, eye-witnesses have maintained that they observed an assassin on a grassy knoll near the assassination site. Their claim was dismissed, however.)

Finally, the trajectories required to sustain the single bullet theory are ballistically impossible. Governor Connally was sitting directly in front of President Kennedy, and with his back to him. The 'miracle' bullet supposedly emerged from the left side of Kennedy's throat (the left side of his tie knot was singed), and entered Connally's back on the right-hand side. To accomplish this, the bullet would have had to make a sharp mid-air turn. Bullets do strange things sometimes, but they do not make mid-air turns. Again, we are inexorably drawn to the conclusion that the single bullet theory simply does not stand up to examination.

The Plot that Failed
During the late stages of the war, senior German military officers were becoming increasingly frustrated as they tried to prosecute a war policy that was based more on Hitler's paranoid instincts than on logical strategic aims.
In July 1944, an army colonel, Count Stauffenberg, acting in concert with a number of other officers, succeeded in placing a bomb in Hitler's headquarters. Hidden inside a briefcase, Stauffenberg left it beside a conference table. Hitler unwittingly kicked it aside, and in the resultant explosion, was badly wounded

Above
The Dallas building – the Texas School Book Depository – from which the shots were fired that killed President John F. Kennedy in 1963, according to the Warren Commission. But there was one more shot fired from a nearby grassy knoll

Above right
An investigator holds the rifle supposedly used by Lee Oswald to assassinate John Kennedy. Since it was non-automatic, there were limits on the speed with which it could be fired, re-aimed and fired again. This means that there was a second assassin, as maintained at the time by a number of eye-witnesses

A postscript to the John F. Kennedy assassination came in a relatively recently discovered letter from J. Edgar Hoover (then Director of the FBI) to J. Lee Rankin (then general counsel to the Warren Commission). The July 8, 1964 letter stated that a neutron activation analysis test on the 'miracle' bullet did not clearly match bullet fragments found in the Presidential automobile! If true, this represents indisputable evidence that more than one weapon was used in the Kennedy assassination.

Was there a conspiracy behind President Kennedy's assassination? The scientific facts, cited above, together with much more evidence, establish that more than one weapon was used. Circumstantial evidence and inexplicable subsequent events lend additional credence to the theory that a conspiracy was involved. Who were the conspirators? Why did they choose President Kennedy as their target? How have they managed to cover their tracks? These questions will remain unanswered until the hard scientific evidence refuting the single bullet theory, the kingpin of the Warren Commission's conclusion that there was only one assassin, is accepted and a new inquiry ordered.

The 1968 killing of the Reverend Martin Luther King touched off large-scale disturbances in at least 125 United States cities. It also led to the passing of the Civil Rights Act, over which Congress had been dragging its feet up to that time. There is evidence of an assassination conspiracy against the black civil rights leader

The Reverend Martin Luther King, Jr, epitomized the black struggle for equality of blacks in America. There is no doubt whatever that, as the moral leader of America's black population, and its brilliant spokesman, he was the object of intense hatred by many white racists. It was ostensibly because of the hatred for the movement that King led and the objectives that he supported, that he was cut down by rifle fire on April 4, 1968.

King criss-crossed America in the 1960s, leading non-violent demonstrations aimed at improving the plight of blacks. On April 4, 1968, he was in Memphis, Tennessee to lend his support to striking black refuse collectors. At 6 pm that evening, he left his motel room to go to dinner. He paused on the motel balcony to talk to someone on the ground below, when there was the sound of a single rifle shot. Dr King was hit in the neck and died less than an hour later.

The assassin had fired the fatal shot from the window of a boarding-house just 200 feet away from the motel balcony. According to the FBI investigative report, within a period of two minutes, the assassin fired the shot, ran from his room, hid the rifle, and drove off in a white Ford Mustang. Nine minutes after the shot was fired, police had the rifle, knew from which room the shot was fired, and had a detailed description of the suspect and his vehicle. Yet the assassin escaped. Not until June 8, 1968, was James Earl Ray apprehended at Heathrow Airport in Britain.

King's assassination set off large-scale public disturbances in at least 125 United States cities, many of which had never experienced racial problems. In Baltimore, Chicago and Washington, 21,000 regular army troops were needed to control the several days of rioting, looting, sniping and arson. A further 21,000 regular troops were on ready alert, and 34,000 National Guard Troops were deployed. Excluding the Civil War, this was the largest military force ever used in the United States to control civil disturbances. Property damage totalled $45,000,000; 46 people died; 2,600 people were injured and 21,270 arrests were made.

King's death also had a political impact. After having been stalled in Congress for months, the Civil Rights Act of 1968 was swiftly passed by the House of Representatives and the Senate. More interesting was the backlash among voters in the 1968 elections. Many voted for candidates con-

THE ASSASSINATION OF FOUR AMERICAN PRESIDENTS

Abraham Lincoln

Assassination	April 14, 1865
Date of death	April 15 1864
Place	Washington DC
Assassin	John Wilkes Booth
Method	Pistol at point blank range
Motives	Partly political

– Booth was a fanatical supporter of the Southern cause, and saw Lincoln as a threat. It has been suggested that he was encouraged by extremists on both political sides. Another possible motive could have been Booth's search for immortality enhanced because of his relative failure as an actor (his father, Junius Brutus Booth, was known as the greatest Shakespearean actor of his time, and Booth dearly wished to emulate his success). The assassination was altogether a very theatrical operation – Booth shot Lincoln in a box at the theatre, and then leaped onto the stage yelling Sic semper tyrannis (Thus perish all tyrants)

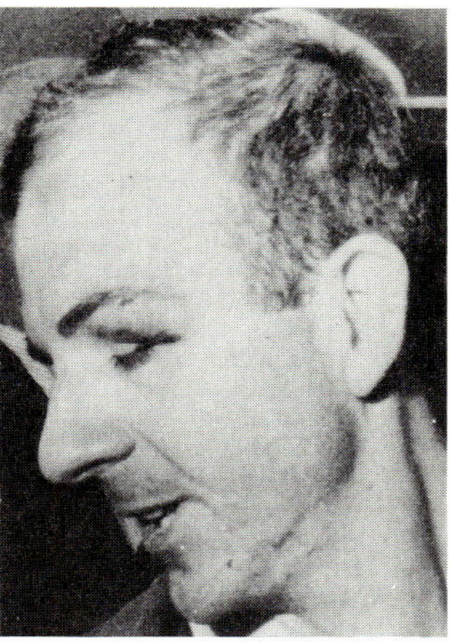

sidered less sympathetic to minorities. George Wallace's strong showing in the Presidential election graphically illustrates this point.

Of the three 1960s assassinations (King, John F. Kennedy and Robert F. Kennedy), it seems that King's had the most widespread—and certainly the most violent—impact. James Earl Ray's professed motive was primarily racism and a desire to stop the black equality movement. The King murder, therefore, fits the definition of assassination, because the political component of the assassination concept need not be directly related to government. In other words, the movement for black equality clearly qualifies as 'political', within the context of the Civil Rights struggle in the United States at that time.

As in the other two 1960s assassinations, the local and federal authorities concluded within 24 hours that there had been only one assassin. Serious doubts have recently been raised about this, however. Only a matter of days after his confession, Ray began talking about a mysterious man called 'Raoul'. Ray claims that 'Raoul' framed him in the King assassination. In November, 1978, Mark Lane, Ray's counsel, appeared before the House Select Committee on Assassinations in Washington, DC and claimed to have evidence directly linking King's assassination to the FBI. Lane went so far as to say that the FBI actually committed the murder. Evidence has been presented that at least one man, Russell G. Buyers, was offered $50,000 to procure the assassination of King. Very recently, strong circumstantial evidence has been revealed that implicates Ray's two brothers in a conspiracy with Ray in the King assassination. So far, no changes have been made in the official version of the assassination, but investigative staff of the House Select Committee on Assassinations have made it very clear that their review and evaluation of all the evidence strongly suggests that others were involved together with James Earl Ray.

During the year preceding King's assassination, Ray wandered from city to city after having escaped from prison. The question is: How did a man with apparently limited funds and background plan and finance the escape route followed by Ray? In the course of his flight after the assassination, Ray went to Mexico, Canada, Portugal and England, using masterfully forged documents. When apprehended, Ray was on his way to Belgium and thence to Africa. Along the way, he purchased and abandoned two cars, and used three different passports.

Above
As President Kennedy slumps down in the rear seat of the Presidential car, his wife crawls towards an aide who has rushed forward to see if he can offer any help

Top left
Lee Harvey Oswald, 24 years old at the time, seen just before he was charged with the murder of President Kennedy. About an hour after the assassination, Oswald was reportedly challenged by a policeman. Oswald shot him dead and then ran into a cinema, where he was later cornered and arrested. The police then interrogated him intensively for two days

Left
After questioning, Oswald was being transferred to Dallas city goal, when a man with a revolver stepped out of a crowd of newsmen and onlookers. The man, Jack Ruby, a night-club owner, fired one shot, hitting Oswald in the stomach. He died several hours later. This photograph was taken a split second before Ruby pulled the trigger

Mad Assassins
According to a report by the German psychologist, Perlman, of all the people who either succeeded in assassinating political leaders, or attempted the act, up to 1940, almost 90 percent of them would be judged insane

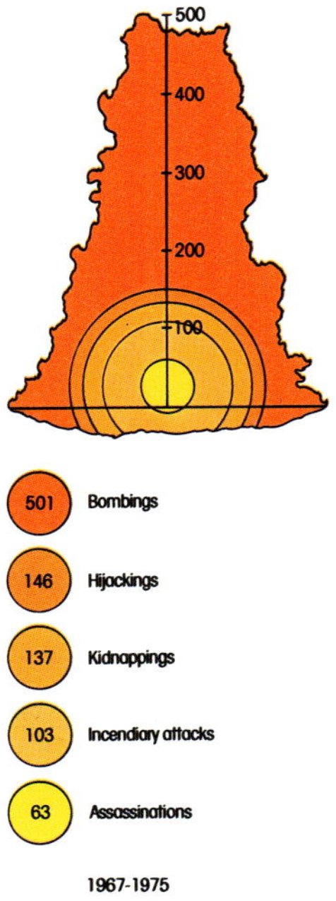

Mathematics of Murder
A list compiled by the Central Intelligence Agency of the number of attacks launched against government individuals in five major categories of crime

James Garfield
Assassination July 2, 1881
Date of death September 19, 1881
Place Washington DC
Assassin Charles Guiteau
Method Pistol at point blank range
Motives As he shot Garfield, Guiteau shouted out that he wanted Garfield's rival, Chester A. Arthur, to be president. Despite this, he had campaigned vigorously for Garfield to be elected, and thought he should be offered a diplomatic post with the Government. When this was not forthcoming, he believed Garfield had treated him badly, and would deal with America in the same way; he felt Garfield should be disposed of for the good of the country

William McKinley
Assassination September 6, 1901
Date of death September 14, 1901
Place Buffalo, N.Y.
Assassin Leon Czolgosz
Method Pistol at point blank range
Motives Czolgosz was known to be an anarchist, but the assassination was apparently motiveless

John Kennedy
Assassination November 22, 1963
Date of death November 22, 1963
Place Dallas, Texas
Assassin Lee Harvey Oswald
Method Rifle at long range
Motives Not fully understood

Obviously, this escape plan cost thousands of dollars and required detailed advance planning. All official evidence shows Ray to have been penniless and incapable of such sophisticated planning. What was the source of Ray's funds, and who planned his escape? Raoul?

The capture of James Earl Ray was overshadowed by the brutal and apparently useless killing of Robert F. Kennedy three days earlier.

In 1968, Robert F. Kennedy was attempting to secure the Democratic Presidential nomination. After a tough election campaign throughout California, he decided to stay at the Ambassador Hotel in Los Angeles to watch the primary election returns. By the end of the evening of June 5, 1968, he had won the valuable support of the State of California, and seemed almost certain to gain the forthcoming Democratic nomination. He left his room and went down to a ballroom in the hotel to make a victory speech, after which he was due to meet the press in an adjoining room. However, the ballroom was so crowded that he could not walk across the floor to the 'press room', so Kennedy and his entourage left the ballroom intending to reach the 'press room' via a kitchen pantry. As the group were passing through the pantry, a gunman leapt out of the crowd and began firing wildly at Kennedy. He reeled backwards, flung his right arm over his face in a gesture of protection, and fell to the ground on his back. He had sustained three wounds, two in the back, and one in the head. He was rushed to hospital, and died there several hours later.

The gunman, Sirhan Bishara Sirhan, attempted to escape, but was immediately overpowered by several of Kennedy's friends and bodyguards. He was accused and convicted of being the sole assassin of Robert F. Kennedy, but eye-witness accounts and physical and scientific evidence have established with compelling clarity that Sirhan Sirhan did not act alone, and may very well not even have fired the fatal shot to Kennedy's head.

The Los Angeles County medical examiner/coroner, Dr Thomas T. Noguchi, a forensic pathologist of world-wide reputation, established that Robert Kennedy suffered three .22 calibre bullet wounds. Each wound was caused by the bullet entering from the rear, with a forward and slightly downward trajectory. The fatal head wound was caused by a shot fired from a range of only one inch. These findings are not especially remarkable, until compared with the numerous eye-witness accounts of the events of June 5, 1968. Every eye-witness said that Sirhan Sirhan had been in front of Robert Kennedy at all times, and no witness recalled Sirhan ever being any closer to Kennedy than three feet. These accounts obviously do not square with the range, rear entrance, and trajectory of the wounds. The official (post-trial) rebuttal of these facts was that Kennedy's head twisted during the confusion. This ignores Dr Noguchi's findings, about the distance from which the fatal shot was fired, and no witness saw Kennedy do anything but fall straight backwards and away from Sirhan Sirhan.

Only minutes after the gunfire, Donald Schulman, a CBS news employee, told a radio reporter that he had seen a *security guard* fire at Robert Kennedy and hit him three times. One of the accompanying photographs shows a clip-on tie by Kennedy's right hand. That tie belonged to a guard, Thane Eugene Cesar. Cesar stated that he had not fired his gun at all that evening. Amazingly, it was not confiscated by the police that evening for ballistic tests. He also said that he had owned a .22 calibre pistol similar to Sirhan's weapon, but had sold it three months earlier. However, a signed receipt showed that the pistol was sold by Cesar three months *after* June 5, 1968. Officials checked up on the story and visited the purchaser of the pistol at his home in Arkansas. The very next night, the purchaser's home was broken into and the pistol stolen. Ballistic evidence also militates against Sirhan having acted alone. Firearms experts were unable to confirm that a number of bullets which injured various bystanders, and those that killed Kennedy came from the same gun. All the experts stated that significant differences existed between the various bullets recovered from the victims and the pantry.

The bullets allegedly used by Sirhan, known as 'minimags', are copper-jacketed. When fired, they leave no lead deposits in the barrel of the weapon, and are in fact often used to clean out a gun barrel. These facts sharply conflict with the fact that, although it was not fired between the time of the Robert Kennedy shooting and the time it was inspected, officials noted heavy leading of the barrel of Sirhan's pistol. This demonstrates that the bullets inflicting wounds that night came from a gun other than Sirhan's.

The question immediately arises: Where, then, did Sirhan's bullets go? It would be foolish to suggest that not one of Sirhan's bullets found their mark. A possible answer is provided by the following

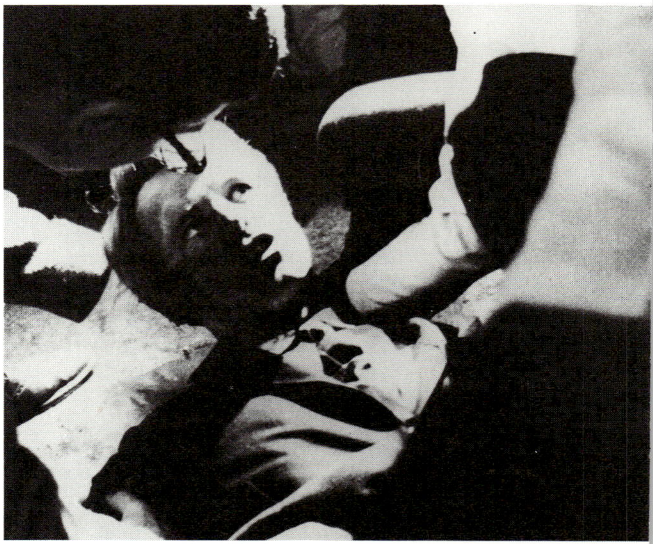

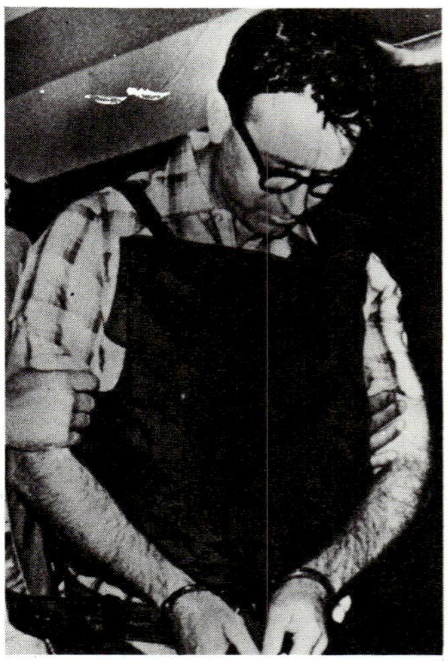

evidence. Eye-witnesses of the event consistently stated that the tongue of flame emitted from Sirhan's pistol was between six and 12 inches in length. 'Minimag' bullets do not discharge more than a one-inch flame. Flames of the length described by the eye-witnesses are consistent with blanks! Sirhan may well have been 'firing' bulletless cartridges. Indeed, a live cartridge from which the bullet had been removed by hand was found in the pocket of the coat Sirhan was wearing on the night of the assassination.

The gun that Sirhan carried held eight shots. The Los Angeles police department accounted for all of them: seven bullets in the victims, and one fired into the ceiling. Witnesses in the pantry during the investigation, however, noted at least one bullet embedded in a door jamb. When eye-witness accounts and various official reports are reviewed, the conclusion is that anywhere from 13 to 15 bullets were found at the scene or in victims. This tallies with numerous accounts by witnesses who described the gunfire that night as sounding like 'firecrackers'. Now, one gun, even if fired rapidly, emits a regulated series of explosions, not the irregular, staccato sound of firecrackers. In any event, it was impossible for Sirhan to have fired more than eight shots that evening. Physical proof of the extra bullets is lost forever, because the Los Angeles police removed and later destroyed the various parts of the pantry where the witnesses saw the extra bullets.

Much more exists to dispute the official conclusion that Sirhan Sirhan acted alone. Why the available evidence of conspiracy has been ignored mystifies many. The only logical conclusion, however, is that someone has orchestrated a clever cover-up.

The assassinations described above cover the whole spectrum of this 'political crime'. Caesar's death was tyrranicide; Ferdinand's precipitated a world war; Lincoln's probably delayed the healing of the wounds left by the Civil War; John F. Kennedy's shattered an American dream of liberalism; King's touched off civil violence, and a racial backlash, and eventually led to a giant step forward for the blacks of America; and Robert F. Kennedy's apparently led to a massive cover-up. In each case, the results were violent and far-reaching. All were political acts aimed at achieving some particular end. The American assassinations smack of conspiracy and cover-up. We may never know the real truth, but observers must continue to dig for evidence. To allow possible conspiracies in these American assassinations not to be uncovered would be a national disgrace. Even worse, it would allow the true villains to go unscathed, and perhaps repeat their deed.

In each case presented here the death of a man was intended to have some sort of political impact. Sometimes the intended objective was obvious, and in others not so obvious. It was, however, the desire to bring about political change that made these particular deaths true assassinations. In the study of the murder of a prominent figure, it should now be obvious that the perpetrator's objectives must be discerned in order to properly label a death as murder or assassination. And note carefully, that it is the perpetrator's objectives, not the actual result, that are determinative.

High Risk Areas
Well over half of the successful assassinations carried out during the past 50 years have taken place in just two areas of the world: Latin America and the Middle East

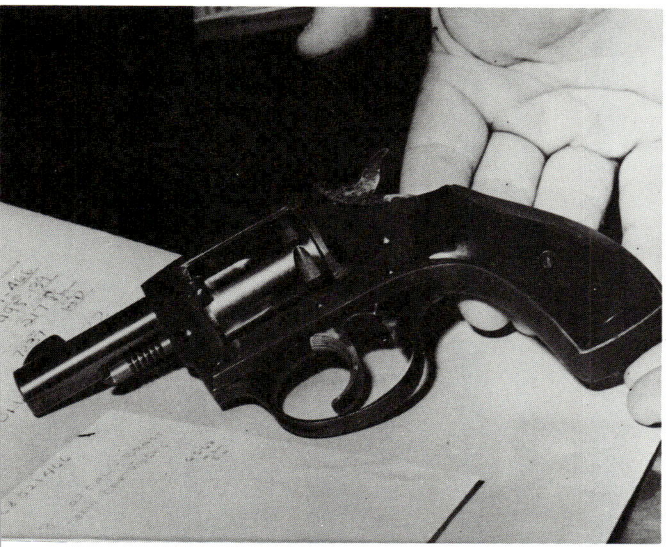

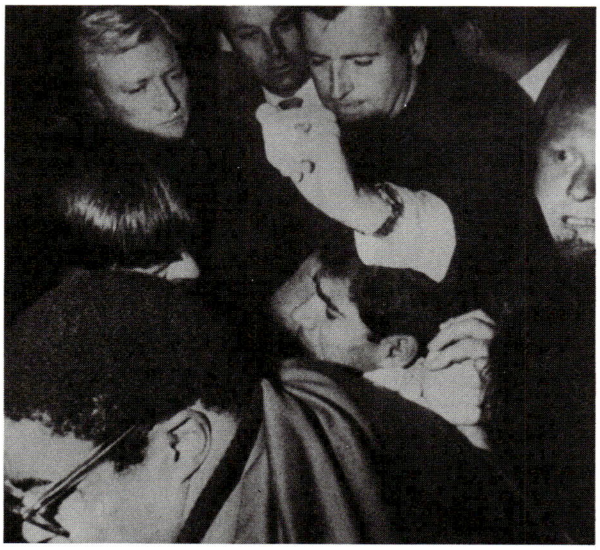

Left
Before losing consciousness, Senator Robert F. Kennedy looks up at people assisting him after he had been shot in a Los Angeles hotel on June 5, 1968. Hit by three bullets, two in the back and one in the head, he died the following day. The man later convicted of assassinating Robert Kennedy was Sirhan Sirhan, seen in the second photograph, with a man's fist about to strike him after the shooting. Sirhan's revolver is shown in the third photograph. Eight shots had been fired from it. Ballistic evidence seems to indicate that Sirhan did not act alone. Indeed, a man present at the shooting said that he had seen a security guard fire at Robert Kennedy and hit him three times

Below left
The first photograph, left, shows James Earl Ray, convicted of assassinating Dr Martin Luther King, being brought, handcuffed, into a Memphis, Tennessee, gaol after being sent back to the United States from Britain, to which he had fled via Mexico, Canada and Portugal, following the assassination. The next photograph shows the assassin's view through the telescopic sight of the murder weapon. In the third photograph, the wounded Dr King can be seen, lying on the balcony where he was shot

Below
The scene at the motel after the shooting. The balcony in the left foreground is where Dr King was assassinated

The Master Liquidators

The twentieth century has seen the worst examples of mass murder in history, but the phenomenon is far from being confined to modern totalitarian régimes. Indeed, terror and genocide as systems of control seem to have evolved thousands of years ago

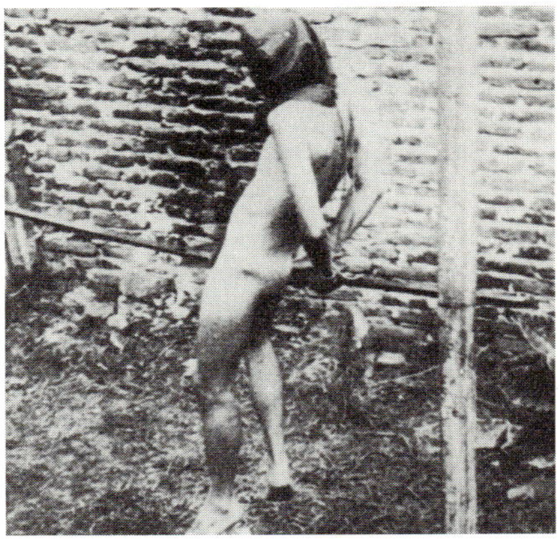

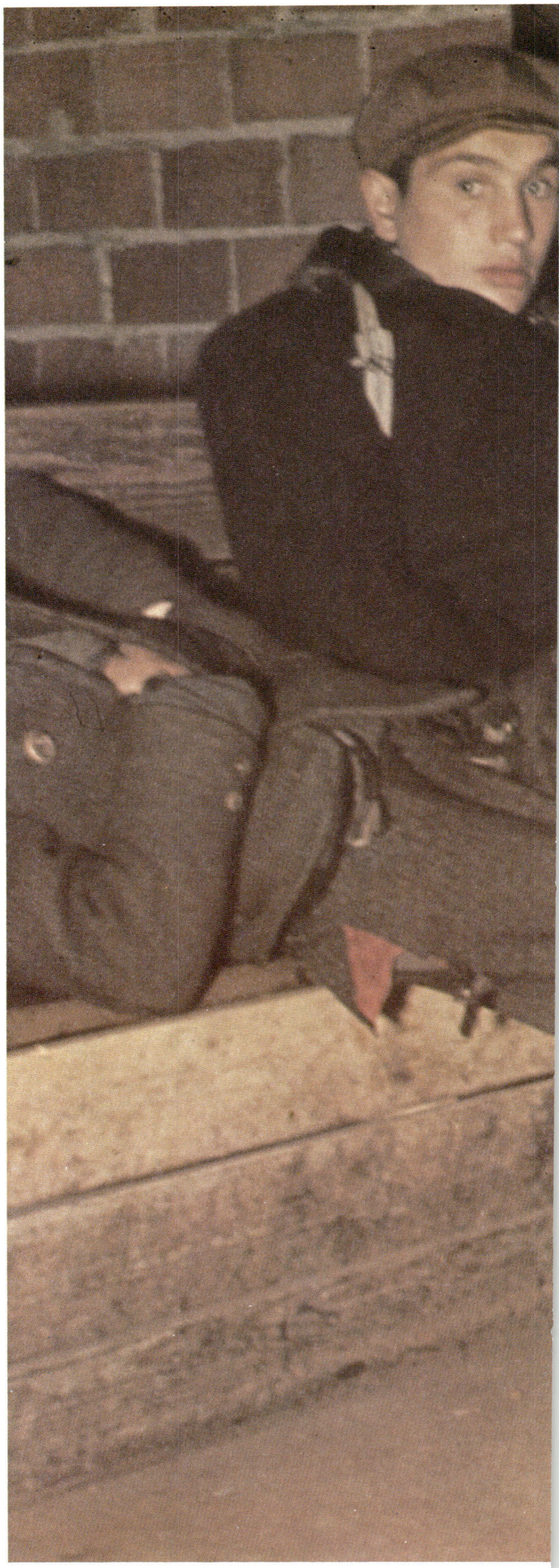

Above
Torture in Uruguay, 1976. A naked man, his head covered with a hood and his wrists handcuffed behind his back, is forced to sit for hours astride an edged metal bar, which is too high for him to be able to put his feet on the ground

Above right
Jews in the Kutno ghetto early in World War II. At that time, special Nazi killing squads used to take them outside the towns and shoot them. When this proved too slow, killing centres were established

Right
A group of young Jews at Warsaw railway station. Millions of Jews from all over Europe were deported in cattletruck trains to the killing centres, which worked quickly and with great efficiency, using assembly line methods. At Auschwitz alone, 20,000 Jews and others were gassed every day

Tribal Genocide
The Zulu king Chaka was known to practise genocide in the context of tribal warfare. An English trader called Nathaniel Isaacs, who was forced to fight in one of Chaka's battles, was ordered 'not to leave alive a child, but exterminate the whole tribe'. When he argued that these 'poor offending innocents' could do no harm, Chaka told him: 'Yes they can – they can propagate and bring children who may become my enemies. It is my custom not to give quarter to my enemies'

Liquidation and mass murder are as old as human history, possibly older, and it is hard to avoid the conclusion that killing is a characteristically human activity. Animals, faced by circumstances such as competition over territory or food, which often lead to war among men, usually stop short of killing their own species. The defeated individual makes a gesture of submission, which has the effect of inducing the winner to desist from further attack.

Not that all wars have led to mass killings. There is an ancient tradition of limiting warfare, which has existed among primitive and more civilized peoples alike. In pre-Islamic Arabia, for instance, tribal raiding was conducted according to a more or less strictly observed code. The aim was to detach the enemy from his camels, rather than to kill him. The ritual practices of hospitality were normally extended even to members of hostile tribes while, in the holy month of Muharram, the pilgrimage season, all hostilities were suspended. Similarly, under the rules of medieval warfare, captured knights were shown the greatest possible courtesies. Many of these self-limiting customs survive in the conventions governing the treatment and custody of prisoners-of-war.

However, the concept and practice of total war, intimately connected with genocide and the perpetuation of a 'regime of terror', are far from being, as is sometimes suggested, a purely modern phenomenon; Attila the Hun, Ghengiz Khan and the Zulu Emperor, Chaka, practised 'total war' long before the expression gained currency during World War I. Classically, the aim of war is to destroy the enemy's fighting capacity and to gain control of his territory and population, either for use as a bargaining counter in peace negotiations or, in the case of permanent conquest, as a source of labour and revenue. In these conditions, little advantage is to be gained by wholesale massacre. In the ancient world, captives were usually sold into slavery, a more merciful fate than execution, and one with definite economic advantage for the victor.

Right
Roman law regarded rebels as objects without legal personality. When the Jews rebelled against the Romans in 4 BC, the governor of the province of Syria, Publius Quintilius Varus, had many of them crucified

Centre right
Overworked and brutally mistreated by their Spanish conquerors, the Indians of South America were ravaged by disease as well. In New Spain, there were 25 million Indians in 1519. By 1605, there were only a million

Bottom right
When Francisco Pizarro and his brothers landed in Peru in 1531, they eventually made their way to the Inca city of Cajamarca, where they received a friendly welcome from Atahualpa, the Inca ruler. Pizarro repaid him by having him murdered in 1533

Ironic Contrast
In his diary, SS doctor Johann Kremer wrote: 'In comparison with the mass killings at Auschwitz, Dante's Inferno seems almost a comedy . . .'

Close to Extinction
By the end of 1942, three-quarters of all Polish Jews had been exterminated by the Nazis

Murderous Conquests
One of the more horrifying consequences of military invasions is the brutal suppression of the indigenous population. The examples below represent possibly the most sustained attempts at the complete eradication of the native peoples of conquered lands

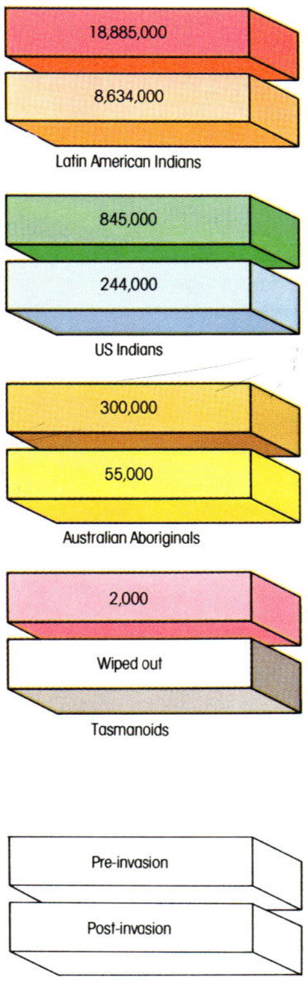

Why, then, has large-scale massacre been a feature of so many wars? Notions of 'bloodlust' or 'primitive barbarism' are clearly inadequate to explain what has been a recurring phenomenon in human history. In our own day, otherwise civilized modern states like Germany and the Soviet Union have developed mass murder and liquidation into systematic policies. In attempting to explain this phenomenon, it may be useful to distinguish between the two main categories into which wars of conquest fall—the consolidation of power, and genocide. Inevitably, however, where terror is employed in the one case, its practitioners will normally be unable to resist succumbing to the temptation of using it in the other.

The practice of total war has existed side by side with a tradition of limiting warfare from ancient times. The Assyrians destroyed whole peoples. So did the Huns and, later, the Mongols. Chaka's Zulu Empire, too, was based on the rule of terror

Among the nations of antiquity, none was held in greater terror than the Assyrians, who destroyed whole peoples by slaughtering their leaders, deporting their urban populations and reducing the rest to serfdom. A similar reputation is borne by the Scythians, horseback riders from the steppes of Central Asia, who tugged at the fringes of the Roman Empire in Anatolia and western Asia. In the fifth century AD, the Empire trembled before the depredations of a probably related people, the Huns, who swept into Europe under their leader Atilla, the 'Scourge of God'. Originally pastoral nomads from southern Russia, the Huns brought about a vast displacement of peoples in Central and Eastern Europe. In 437 AD, they attacked the Burgundians, a Germanic tribe which had established itself on the west bank of the Rhine, massacring as many as 20,000 people, according to contemporary chroniclers. In 447 they invaded the Eastern Empire, but an attack on Italy lost impetus through depletions in their ranks caused by plague and famine. Like other pastoral nomads, the Huns used their prowess in horsemanship and archery to become a parasitical community of marauders. Their main interest was the acquisition of gold and slaves, but they also traded these commodities for furs, meat and horses. However, the depredations of the Huns cannot be compared with the horrors of the Mongol invasion eight centuries later, and most modern authorities think that accounts of the atrocities committed by the Huns are exaggerated.

There is enough historical data surrounding the Mongol invasions of the thirteenth century to make it clear that a policy of conquest by terror was systematically thought out. The Mongols were not as 'barbarous' as their Scythian and Hunnic predecessors. In order to subdue the walled cities of central and western Asia (the centres of political power and the only places of refuge for the population), they constructed sophisticated and devastatingly effective siege machinery. When the cities surrendered, the Mongols practised a policy of systematic, cold-blooded massacre. Once a city had been stormed, the surviving population would be taken outside the walls and the skilled male workers, who would be useful as slaves, formed into a separate group and ordered to stand to one side.

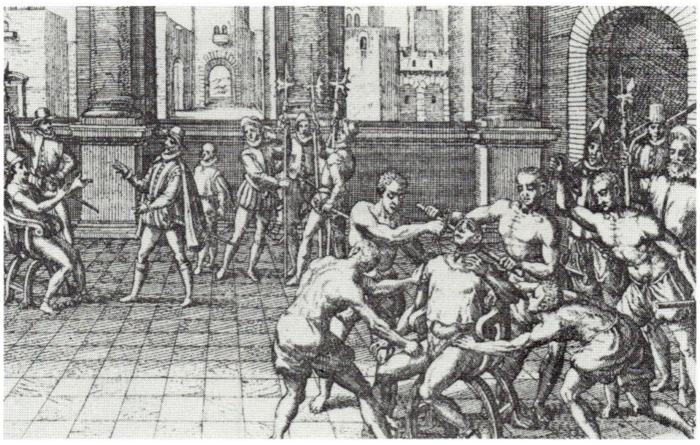

Then the soldiers would go through the rest of the population, methodically killing them with their swords and hand-axes. Each Mongol trooper was required to kill a given quota of people—ten, 20 or 50. Sometimes the soldiers cut off their victims' ears, to furnish proof that they had carried out their orders. The effects of the Mongol terror were devastating. According to the Persian historian, Ibn al Athir, 700,000 people were slaughtered in this way in the city of Merv in February, 1221. The story was repeated at Nishapur, where the heads of men, women and children were piled into separate pyramids. At Herat (in modern Afghanistan) a full week was devoted to killing the population. A modern writer estimates that along the once rich belt of Arab-Iranian civilization, four-fifths of the population were eradicated. The Mongol emperor, Ghengiz Khan, deliberately turned the area into a no man's-land, putting an end to farming and creating an artificial steppe—where the Mongols, presumably, would feel at home.

The Zulu Empire founded by Chaka in the 1820s, like the Mongol Empire, was also based on the rule of terror. It remained the dominant native power in southern Africa until the British conquest in 1879. It has been estimated that, during his wars of conquest, Chaka had as many as one million people put to

death. Chaka's state grew like a vast amoeba, either displacing or destroying the people in its path, or absorbing them within its internal structure. After one engagement which lasted less than two hours, an English eye-witness, R. F. Fynn, estimated that the Zulus massacred a whole tribe numbering at least 40,000. Any remnants of the defeated armies who were not massacred were absorbed into Chaka's impi regiments. Their women and children were usually slaughtered, although some of the nubile girls were spared for the royal seraglios.

Chaka's system was built on the use of the death penalty to uphold his omnipotence. His own Zulu warriors were driven by fear. After each battle the regiments were required to 'bring forth the cowards', who were summarily executed, usually by impalement. When a regiment was defeated or forced to retreat before superior numbers, all its warriors would be massacred, together with their families. To be fully effective, Chaka's rule of terror had to bear as hard on those nearest to him as on the rest of his subjects. Anyone who coughed or sneezed in his presence or otherwise caused offence was immediately taken away and executed. Chaka had only to point his finger at someone, for the unfortunate to be seized immediately and beaten to death with sticks or taken to the place of execution. This was a small hill near the royal kraal, a veritable Golgotha, where vultures swarmed round the bodies of impaled victims. As a political scientist, E. V. Walter, has pointed out in his study of the Zulu state, the system was based to a remarkable degree on a form of consent. People would voluntarily 'report' for execution. Parents would murder their own children without complaining. On the death of Chaka's mother, some 7,000 people were massacred to create sympathy for the leader's sorrow. 'Many of them' wrote Fynn, 'received the blow of death while inflicting it on others'. After Chaka's assassination by his half-brothers in 1828, his successor, Dingane, tried to liberalize the system by abolishing arbitrary executions and doing away with various restrictions. However, the result was a series of tribal rebellions which threatened to tear the state apart, and Dingane was obliged to restore the terror, though in a modified form.

Although the actions of Chaka and his successors often appeared arbitrary and whimsical, this was in fact the essence of the system. Constant obedience to the tyrant's 'irrational' orders kept the Zulus fused into a single unit, in which each individual became an active and seemingly willing instrument of the ruler's will—in other words, a voluntary extension of his nervous system.

Above
Rorke's Drift, 1879. Two British lieutenants and 120 men repulsed an attack by 4,000 Zulus, killing 350 for the loss of 17 killed and 10 wounded. Six times during their attack, the Zulus reached the Rorke's Drift trenches, and each time they were driven back at bayonet point. The Zulu Empire created by Chaka was finally broken by Britain in 1879. In the same way as the Mongol Empire, it had been founded on genocide and the rule of terror

Bitter Fruits
After the Soviet army liberated Auschwitz in 1945 and extinguished the fires started in the camp warehouses by the SS to cover up their crimes, they managed to salvage: 348,820 suits of men's clothes; 836,525 suits of women's clothes; 5,255 pairs of women's shoes; 38,000 pairs of men's shoes; 13,694 carpets

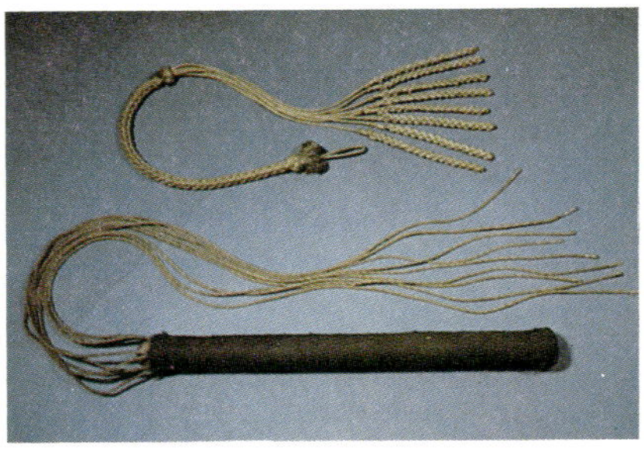

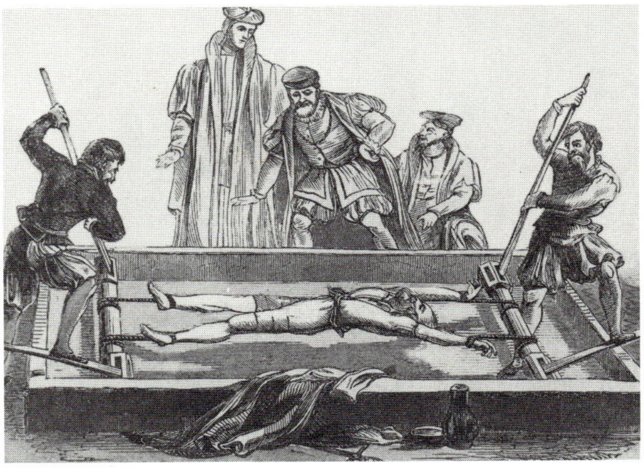

Top
A nineteenth-century 'cat o' nine tails' – a handle of wood or rope with nine knotted cords or thongs, used in the British army and navy for floggings until the last century

Top right
This multi-thonged whip, the scourge, was already ancient in Roman times, when it was known as a 'flagellum'. In fact, it is depicted on Pharaonic monuments as one of the two symbols of power held by the Egyptian god, Osiris

Above
Manacles were used either as a punishment or, like today's handcuffs, to secure the hands of a person under arrest. The bottom manacles were much more restricting than the top ones

Above right
This is a Mexican chain scourge, dating from the seventeenth or eighteenth century. Unlike the Roman 'flagellum' and the 'cat o' nine tails', it is circular and has 12 'tails', but the principle is the same

Bottom
The rack was widely used to torture suspected heretics, in order to force them to confess. As the ropes were tightened, they dislocated the joints of the victim. John Holland, the fourth Duke of Exeter, is said to have been the first to use the rack in England, in the mid-fifteenth century

Centre right
In England, it used to be the custom to hang the body of an executed murderer in chains from a gibbet as a warning to evil-doers. Sometimes, gibbet irons, like those shown here, were used instead of chains. The body was often smeared with pitch to prevent too rapid decomposition. The last gibbetting in England took place in Leicester in 1832

In more sophisticated societies, the régime of terror may operate within a framework of laws and decrees designed to place the dissident or potential dissident beyond the boundaries of protection afforded by customary law. In Greek and Roman law – the fount of much modern jurisprudence – the use of torture was usually confined to slaves, who were regarded as 'objects' without legal personalities. The same applied to those who by an act of rebellion had renounced their status as subjects. Rebels or 'traitors' were subject to torture, and a variety of other punishments, from which freedmen were normally exempt. In times of persecution, Christians were treated as rebels, because they refused to recognize the deification of the pagan Emperors. They were tortured to make them renounce the claims of Christ and accept those of the Emperor. Later the Church and the medieval rulers assimilated the notion of spiritual dissent into the laws against treason. Heretics – those who wilfully persisted in religious doctrines or practices forbidden by the Church – became 'traitors against God's Majesty'. In suppressing the most formidable heresy of the Middle Ages, that of the Cathars or Albigensians in the Languedoc, Pope Innocent III was obliged to rely on the crusading armies of Simon de Montfort and the Kings of France. The knights and their troops (recruited from the roughest elements in the urban population) were granted spiritual indemnities against any excesses committed in the name of Christ. The results were predictable. When the city of Beziers refused to deliver up its heretics in 1209, the walls were breached and the whole population – numbering several thousand – was slaughtered. When asked how the troops could possibly distinguish between heretics and true believers, the papal delegate is supposed to have uttered the famous remark: 'God will recognize his own.' The laws against heresy were too useful to be suspended after the collapse of the Cathar rebellion. Secular rulers found them an effective means of extending their jurisdiction – even into areas of Church supremacy.

The mass murder of heretics by the Catholic Church in Europe was a feature of the Middle Ages. The activities of the Inquisition foreshadowed the witch hunts which took place from the fifteenth to the seventeenth centuries. As with modern persecutions in totalitarian states, the killings were partly inspired by propagandists

In the fourteenth century, the Inquisition was set up to seek out any hidden heretics who might have survived in France or Italy. The widespread use of torture ensured that almost everyone arrested on suspicion would end by confessing. Contemporary witnesses testify that many orthodox Catholics perished at the hands of the Inquisition. The Inquisitorial procedure, which was adopted by the secular courts on the Continent, laid the groundwork for the great witch hunts between the fifteenth and seventeenth centuries. The crime of witchcraft was assimilated to heresy, and many thousands of people accused of witchcraft – most of them women – were burned at the stake. Estimates of the

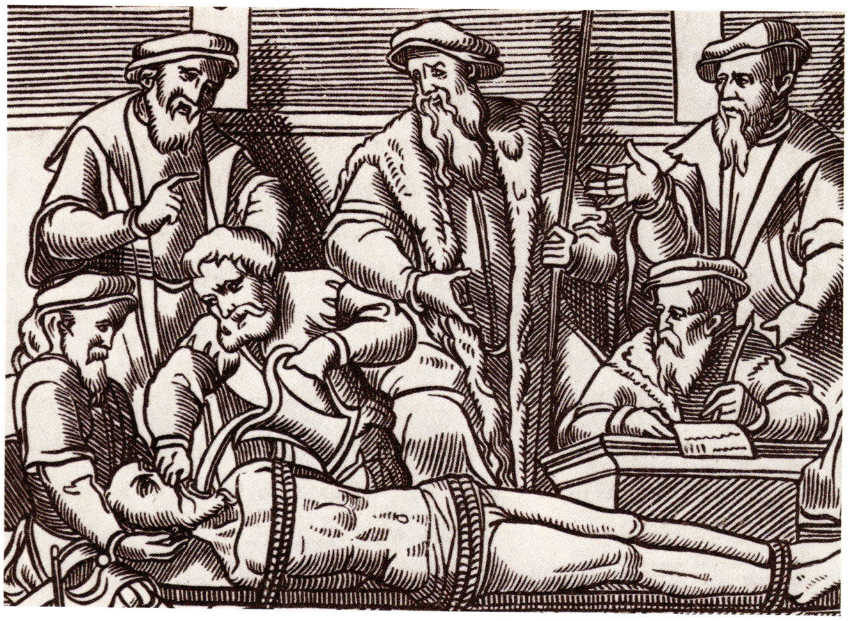

Above
A sixteenth-century Antwerp woodcut of a man undergoing the water torture. The book containing the woodcut is concerned with criminal matters, so the victim is not a heretic, but a common criminal. The three elderly bystanders seem to be urging him to confess, and the man at the desk, quill poised, is ready to take down his confession

Left
Torture, like the ability to reason and the capacity to tell right from wrong, is one of the things that differentiates man from animals. Secret police have always used torture, often for its own sake. The Nazi secret police, the Gestapo, were no exception. One of the more primitive methods employed by the Gestapo was to crush a victim's fingers

number who died in the witch burnings during this period range between 200,000 and a million. The terror was not continuous, but reached peaks of intensity at certain times in certain areas. For example, in the diocese of Como in Italy, 1,000 witches were burned in one year; at Quendlingberg, in Saxony, 133 were burned in a single day in 1589. As with modern persecutions in totalitarian states, the killings were partly inspired by propagandists like the lawyers, Jean Bodin and Nicholas Remy, in France and the Inquisitors, Sprenger and Kramer, in Germany. However, contemporary legal procedures constituted the crucial factor. They included torture, and not only guaranteed forced (and false) conviction, but ensured that denunciations would be made against the innocent. The system was self-fulfilling and self-extending to the point where magistrates and even rulers themselves often fell under suspicion. In England, where the crime of witchcraft was very difficult to prove under common law procedures, the scale of persecution was very much smaller than on the Continent. A survey of court records between 1558 and 1736 revealed that only 19 percent of those charged with witchcraft were executed. This would give a probable figure of 1,000 hangings for witchcraft in England and Wales for the whole period.

The religious dimension in the European wars of the sixteenth and seventeenth centuries accounts in part for their peculiar ferocity. As far as the Catholics were concerned, all Protestants were heretics. While the theoretical aim of these wars may have been to bring the Protestants back into the fold of true religion, the political fact that this might not be a practical possibility often led to repression by massacre. The St Bartholomew's Day massacre in August, 1572 is one example, where 3,000 Protestants were killed in Paris alone and, according to contemporary Huguenot accounts, a further 60,000 or more in the provinces.

Popular pressure, fanned by religious fanatacism, accounts for the ferocity of the European wars of the sixteenth and seventeenth centuries. In revolutionary times, when the barriers of legal authority have been swept away, power usually falls into the hands of those willing to carry out popular demands for vengeance

This notorious episode, and the fearsome way in which Protestants were treated by the Inquisition in Spain and the Netherlands ensured that, when Protestant rulers feared rebellion by their Catholic subjects, no quarter was given. In 1580, Lord Deputy Grey slaughtered some 600 Italian and Spanish soldiers who surrendered the fort of Smerwick to him in Kerry, in Ireland. During the following century, when the religious conflict in Ireland had developed even further, Oliver Cromwell committed similar atrocities at Drogheda, where the whole garrison was put to the sword, and at Wexford, where about 1,800 Catholic troops, priests and civilians were butchered.

The French Revolution of 1789 was accompanied by 'jacqueries' in the countryside, when the peasants turned on their landlords, sometimes slaughtering them, often burning their property. However, the revolutionary terror found its most concentrated expression in Paris. After the fall of Langwy in 1792, when France's enemies crossed into French territory for the first time to suppress the revolution, priests who had been arrested were slaughtered in the prisons, and there were demands in the National Assembly for a massacre of aristocrats, as the only way of saving the revolution. Fears of invasion were compounded by fears of an uprising by the thousands of aristocrats held in prison, culminating in the September Massacres, when a group of prisoners was attacked and murdered by a mob while being transferred to the Abbaye prison. Later, popular tribunals sentenced about half the Paris prison population of 2,500 to summary

Above
There is no end to the ingenuity of man in devising instruments with which to inflict pain. This torture chair, said to be Spanish and to date from the seventeenth century, was featured in 'The Devils', a film directed by Ken Russell

Above
This picture of 'Liberty at the Barricades' was painted by Ferdinand Delacroix, who was born in 1793, the first year of the Reign of Terror that began with Robespierre and the Jacobins. During the terror, there were more than 16,500 registered death penalties, and well over 10,000 rebels were shot without trial after giving up their weapons, or were drowned in the River Loire. Robespierre himself fell victim to the terror

Sentenced to Die
It has been estimated that 90 percent of those arrested before World War II and condemned to labour in the Gulag camps did not survive the experience

Fatal Moves
In the three years from 1975 to 1978, two million Kampucheans died as a direct result of the Pol Pot regime, mainly due to purges or the 'resettlement programme'. This represents 30 percent of the entire Cambodian population

execution. These killings were not the work of cut-throats or hardened killers, but of respectable tradesmen and artisans. (Similar murders of imprisoned royalists and clergy occurred in Madrid and Bilbao in the beleaguered Spanish Republic during the Civil War in the mid-1930s.)

The Reign of Terror in Paris began after the accession of Robespierre and the Jacobins in 1793. Laws were passed prescribing the death penalty for the slightest expression of royalist sentiment, resulting in a daily procession of tumbrils taking prisoners to the guillotine. After the French victory at Fleurus in June, 1794, the crisis passed, but the terror continued under its own momentum until Robespierre himself fell victim to it. The executions were mostly conducted according to legal forms, though justice was summary and the defendants were often denied the right to say anything at their trials. A modern historian maintains that most of those executed were in fact guilty of the political activities attributed to them. The charges were often supported by documents and witnesses. There were no squads of special political police, the trials were conducted in public, and torture—a notable feature of the old régime—was not used in interrogations. The number of registered death penalties has been put at 16,594. In addition, some 10,000 to 12,000 rebels in the Vendée were shot without trial after surrendering their weapons, or drowned in the Loire. Many also died in the prisons, which were badly overcrowded, with poor sanitation and inadequate food. A recent estimate puts the total number of non-combatant victims of the French revolution at between 35,000 and 40,000.

There is a certain spontaneity about revolutionary terror, whereas counter-revolutionary terror is more organized and tends to be centrally directed. The Spanish Civil War in the 1930s exemplified this. In its later phases the Russian Revolution laid the foundations of a system of terror organized and controlled by a vast, self-perpetuating bureaucracy

Revolutionary terror in moderate societies usually originates in the more or less spontaneous actions of the under-privileged—fanned, if not controlled, by demagogic leaders. Counter-revolutionary terror, however, is the response of more organized, centrally directed forces like the army or police. After Napoleon's accession, the French army put down the peasant rebellions in Brittany and the Vendée with a savagery that cost some 600,000 lives. In Spain, where the French found themselves fighting a guerrilla campaign against such partisans as Francisco Mina, they retaliated by terrorizing the population, burning villages and executing prisoners.

In the nineteenth century, armies suppressed unsuccessful rebellions, especially among colonized peoples, with unprecedented ferocity. In India, after the Mutiny of 1857, Colonel Neill, commander of the Madras Fusiliers, burned down scores of villages and allowed his native troops to torture their captives before killing them. In Bulgaria, the massacre of about 15,000 Christian villagers by the Ottoman 'bashi-bazooks' after the collapse of a nationalist rebellion in 1876 caused an outcry in Britain against Disraeli's eastern policies. However, nothing in the European experience compared with the savagery with which the French troops of Marshall MacMahon, fresh from their defeat by the Prussians, unleashed their desire for revenge against the people of Paris after the fall of the Commune in 1871. The military courts-martial held in the Châtelet Theatre each lasted on average a quarter of a minute. Those who were condemned were taken to the nearest garden or courtyard, where the gendarmes simply opened fire, without even arranging them in groups. 'There were so many victims', wrote an eye-witness, 'that the soldiers, tired out, were obliged to rest their guns against them. The wall of the terrace was covered with brains; the executioners waded through pools of blood. Women with children who followed their husbands cried: 'Shoot us with them!' and were shot. In a single week in May, 17,000 people are estimated to have been shot. The repression was quite out of scale with the provocation: the execution of 60 prisoners by the Communards. A similar situation occurred in China after the suppression of the Communist rising in 1927. During the rising, the Canton commune, for example, had killed 210 'capitalists' and imprisoned 71. The death toll among the Communists after the rising had been put down by the Nationalists totalled 5,700.

Perhaps the clearest illustration of the distinction between spontaneous revolutionary violence and organized counter-revolutionary repression comes from the Spanish Civil War. During the revolutionary period in the Republic, from July to September 1936, about 55,000 people were murdered. Many were members of the middle classes, like the victims described in Hemingway's novel, 'For Whom The Bell Tolls', who were beaten with flails by villagers before being flung over a cliff. About 6,000 were priests, including 13 bishops, whose former spiritual authority made them objects of special hatred to rebelling workers and peasants. Nearly all these murders were illegal, and occurred during the first weeks after the outbreak of civil war. Nationalist repression, on the other hand, followed a quite different pattern. Mass executions —of all former Republican officers and people merely suspected of having Republican sympathies or of having voted for the Popular Front in elections—were a matter of official policy. 'It is necessary' General Mola declared, 'to spread an atmosphere of terror. We have to create an impression of mastery. Anyone who is overtly or secretly a supporter of the Popular Front must be shot'. About 50,000 non-combatants were shot by the Nationalists in the course of the war, and a further 100,000 or so in the repression that followed the collapse of the Republic.

In the French Revolution, the policy of terror was initiated by a régime unsure of its legality and uncertain of its chances of survival. Once the danger to the Republic had passed, the terror abated and the leading 'terrorists', Robespierre and St Juste, fell victim to their own weapon. The Russian Revolution, by contrast, initiated the infinitely more devastating phenomenon of terror by bureaucracy. In its revolutionary phase, the Red Terror in Russia (1918-1921) claimed about 50,000 victims—proportionately fewer than the French Revolution, given the size of Russia's population. However, it took place under conditions and in forms which made possible the execution of millions during Stalin's despotic rule 20 years later.

Instead of suppressing counter-revolutionaries by popular tribunals on the French model, the Bolsheviks entrusted the internal defence of the revolution to a terrorist élite—the Cheka—answerable for its actions only to the highest party leadership. Lenin himself allowed the taking of hostages to ensure grain supplies to the Reds during the Civil War. In 1918, there were mass shootings of some of them after the murder of Commissar Uritsky and the attempt on Lenin's life by the left-wing socialist revolutionaries. The shooting of suspected counter-revolutionaries was justified by Trotsky as a necessary repressive measure, since the Whites had to be convinced that the Revolution would last. However, once the external threat to the Revolution had receded with the defeat of the White armies and the end of foreign intervention, instead of abating as in France,

Top
A Japanese officer, his head covered with a hood, stands ready to draw his sword and decapitate three Chinese soldiers captured in a village in civilian clothes by his unit. There were many such incidents in the bloody Sino-Japanese War of 1937-1945, which was preceded by the Japanese conquest of Manchuria from China without formally declaring war in 1931

Above
Revolutionary China, 1949. A land-owner, regarded as 'a dangerous enemy of the people', about to be shot in the back by a Communist soldier. Between 1949 and 1952, the years of the Chinese campaign against counter-revolutionaries, fewer than a million are estimated to have been killed, although the true figure could well be rather higher than this

Murderous Response
During the post-Stalin era in the early 1950s, prisoners in several Gulag camps revolted —the authorities responded by sending in aircraft to bomb the camps and even tanks to level them

Right
Josef Stalin, ruler of the Soviet Union from 1924 until his death in 1953 and the man who institutionalized terror in the country. Many millions of people were killed in Stalin's purges, including many old comrades

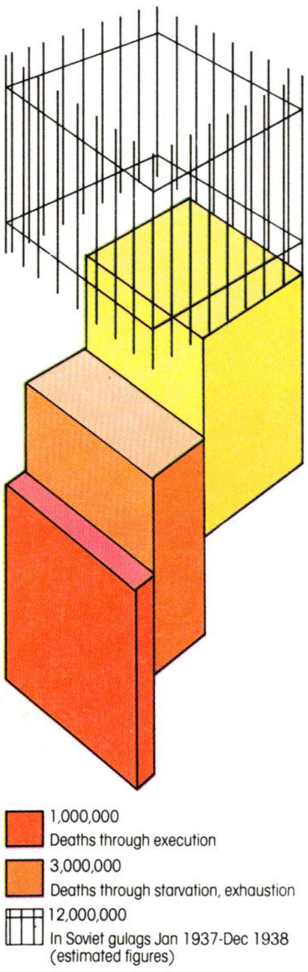

Gulag Genocide
At the height of Stalin's campaign of terror directed at Communist Party officials, the Red Army hierarchy, and other officials, 12 million people were being held in the prison camps of the Gulag system

the repressive terror continued. This was partly, no doubt, because the Bolsheviks remained suspicious of the peasants, on whom they depended for food.

Stalin admitted that ten million kulaks had been executed by firing squad or exiled to Siberia during his forced collectivization of Soviet agriculture. In 1936, he ordered the NKVD (secret police) to arrange the first great political show trial of Soviet Communist Party members

Although the administrative independence of the Cheka and its successor organizations: the OGPU, GPU and NKVD, was sometimes criticized by party leaders, they were too divided among themselves to make a concerted effort to combat its powers and restore a measure of party democracy. After the death of Felix Dzerzhinsky (the chief of the secret police) in 1926, Stalin, who had gradually extended his personal control over the party apparatus, managed increasingly to staff the OGPU with his own nominees. In 1928, he embarked on the radical collectivization of Soviet agriculture, using terror squads from the cities to shoot or deport the dispossessed kulaks (rich peasants) and anyone else who resisted incorporation into the collective farms. Many peasants—by no means all of them kulaks—retaliated by slaughtering livestock and destroying farm machinery. The result was a famine in which five to six million people died, more than half of them in the Ukraine. Later, during World War II, Stalin told Winston Churchill that ten million kulaks had been 'dealt with' in the upheaval—that is, either executed by firing squad, or deported to Siberia. At the same time, to silence the growing opposition within the Communist Party, Stalin perfected his control over the repressive apparatus. In 1934, he used Yagoda, the head of the NKVD, and a number of operatives to 'arrange' for a young fanatic to murder his principal rival, Sergei Kirov. In 1936 he ordered the NKVD to arrange the first great political show trial of Communist Party members. Witnesses were produced whose testimony, some of it concocted under torture, implicated Stalin's principal left-wing rivals in the party, Zinoviev and Kamenev, in Kirov's murder. The following year, a group of industrialists and senior party officials, headed by Yuri Piatakov, were put on trial for allegedly conspiring with the exiled Trotsky and foreign capitalists to sabotage the Soviet economy and assassinate Stalin and his colleagues. As in the previous trial, most were found guilty and shot. Next came the turn of the Soviet officer corps, which was decimated in the secret trial of Marshal Tukhachevsky and the 'Red Army Group'. Finally, in 1938, the most distinguished Old Bolshevik of all, Bukharin, was put on trial, together with Rykov, Krestinsky, Yagoda and a number of other former party leaders, on similar charges of conspiring to wreck the Soviet economy and overthrow Stalin. The defendants who appeared in public were only the visible tip of a vast system of repression extending throughout Soviet society. For, it was claimed, the 'Trotskyite-Bukharinite' conspiracies had spread to every *oblast* (region) and *raion* (district), every factory and commune in the country. 'Trials' were held in every district, most of them *in camera*. The charges were based on

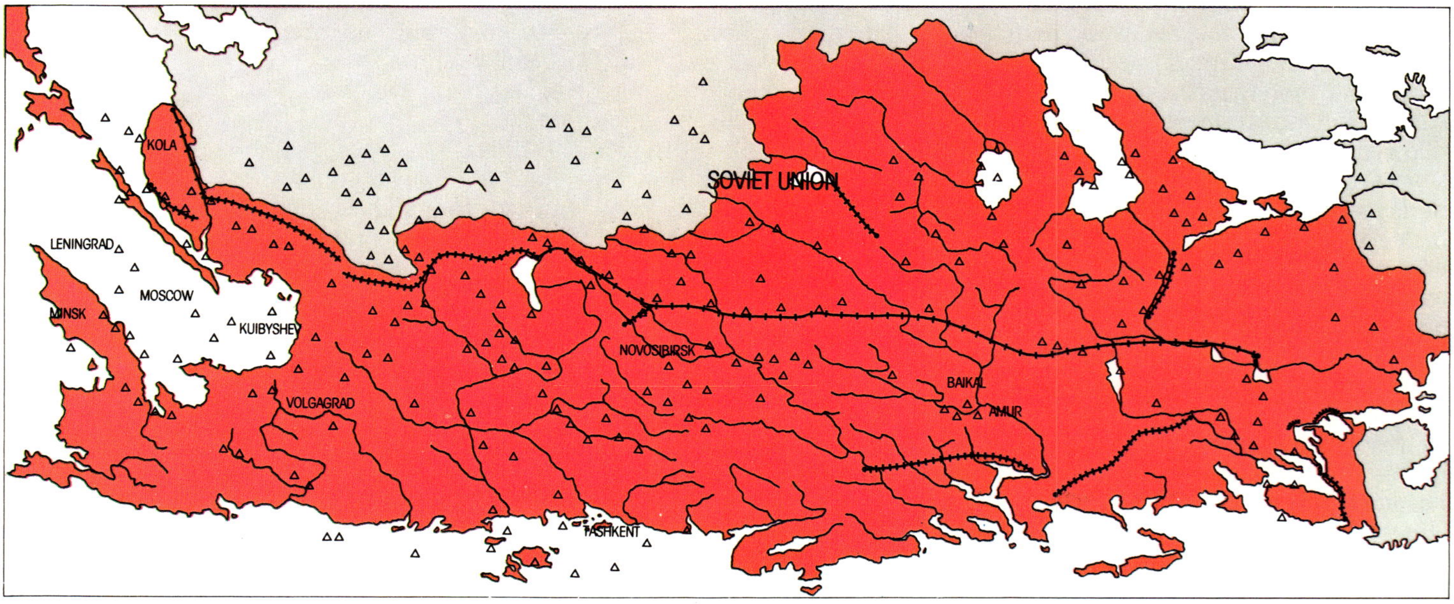

Below
According to the reports of various Soviet dissidents, and respected Western historians, a vast network of concentration camps, known as the Gulag Archipelago, covers the Soviet Union. Its purpose is to isolate from society those elements the government considers 'harmful'

denunciations, many of them at party meetings. Once arrested, defendants were under pressure to denounce as many others as possible. In Odessa, a single Communist denounced 230 people; in Poltava a party member denounced his entire organization. The party itself was decimated. Between 1936 and 1939 about half its membership of 2.4 million had been arrested, and for every party member, there were perhaps eight or ten ordinary citizens under arrest. The historian, Robert Conquest, estimates that, by mid-1937, practically the entire urban population of the Soviet Union had become little else than 'purge fodder'.

The number of victims will never be known with certainty. Roy Medvedev, the dissident Communist historian, believes that Stalin personally signed 40,000 death warrants. 'Official' executions have been estimated at between half a million and 700,000. A former NKVD officer estimated that there were one million 'liquidations' between 1937 and 1938 alone. An official Yugoslav estimate put the total as high as 3 million. In addition, there was a huge population in the prison camps (Solzhenitsyn's famous 'Gulag Archipelago'), whose inmates numbered on average eight million between 1936 and 1950. With about ten percent dying of hunger, disease, overwork or exposure each year, the total of purge victims who died could be as high as 12 million, and some sources even mention 15 million.

The dynamics of Stalin's purges were, at the local level, not unlike those of the sixteenth- and seventeenth-century witch hunts, although, of course, on a vastly greater scale. The NKVD was under pressure from its superiors to uncover 'Trotskyite spies and saboteurs', but it did not necessarily initiate the charges. Originally, many denunciations were made at party meetings, some of them in good faith. In the regions, the level of education and basic literacy was low, even among party members. Accusations of sabotage which sounded fantastic or impossible to Western ears in a Moscow court were not necessarily so to peasants bemused by the rapid changes happening around them. Ambitious party men used the charges in order to displace their superiors, only to find themselves eventually caught up in the maelstrom. Under the snowballing pressure of denunciations, the NKVD adopted 'physical methods' (usually beatings) during interrogation, thus speeding up the rate of confessions and swelling the ranks of the prison camp populations. A favourite method of interrogation also used by the NKVD, was the so-called 'conveyor system'. This involved a non-stop process of sleep deprivation and constant questioning undertaken by relays of NKVD men.

In the astronomical figures of the victims of Stalinist persecution we can see how terror, originally a revolutionary phenomenon, can be built up through the bureaucracy into a system of government. Having established terror in the Soviet Union, Stalin succeeded in exporting it—for a period, at least—to Eastern Europe. Terror in subsequent Communist revolutions (for example in

Above
Death of a quisling. Ferenc Szalasi, the wartime Nazi puppet Premier of Hungary, is executed in Budapest in March, 1946. **Left** Szalasi kisses a cross held up to him by a Catholic priest **Centre** The hangman places the rope round Szalasi's neck. The ex-premier was wearing a green skirt, the emblem of Hungary's Nazis **Right** The execution over the hangman closes the dead man's eyes

Below
The bodies of Ferenc Szalasi and three former members of his Government after they had been publicly hanged as traitors. The three Nazi ex-Ministers – Gabriel Vajas, Karoly Beregffy and Joseph Gera – were hanged within a few minutes of Szalasi's execution

Above
Mass burial of the dead on the battlefield at Wounded Knee, South Dakota, on January 1, 1891, after the defeat by General Miles of Sioux Indians who had gone on the warpath. When some Indians resisted an attempt to disarm them, 200 Sioux men, women and children were massacred

China or, more recently, Cambodia) has shared some of the Soviet features, although there is little evidence that it reached Stalinist proportions in China. The number of victims executed in the Chinese campaign against counter-revolutionaries from 1949 to 1952 has been conservatively estimated at fewer than one million, although the true figure may be of much greater magnitude.

Having instituted an era of terror in the Soviet Union, Stalin succeeded in exporting it to Eastern Europe. Terror in Asia (China and Cambodia, for example) also shared some of the Soviet features, although it did not reach the proportions of a Stalinist-type purge in China

As we have seen, the policy of systematically seeking to exterminate whole peoples or races is certainly not an exclusively modern—or European—phenomenon, although Europeans have tended to practise it more efficiently than other peoples. Indeed, in the context of tribal warfare, Chaka the Zulu practised genocide and was perfectly aware of it. Nathaniel Isaacs, an English trader who was forced to fight in one of Chaka's battles, was ordered 'not to leave alive even a child, but exterminate the whole tribe'. When he remonstrated that these 'poor offending innocents' could do no harm, Chaka told him: 'Yes they could: they can propagate and bring children who may become my enemies. It is my custom not to give quarter to my enemies'.

Nevertheless, the superiority of firearms over native weapons made genocide—international or otherwise—the inevitable by-product of white colonization in the less developed regions of the world. If the natives acquiesced in white settlement, their culture was liable to be destroyed by traders and missionaries. If they tried to resist, the colonists declared 'open season' on them. The superiority of the white man's weapons usually showed itself in the first campaigns of conquest. At Iztapalan, in Mexico, Hernando Cortez, with a column of 200 infantry and 18 cavalry, slaughtered some 6,000 Aztecs. In New England, the colonists virtually exterminated the native population in the sixteenth century. Sometimes there were straightforward massacres, like the killing of 200 Sioux men, women and children at Wounded Knee, in South Dakota, in 1890, but more often it was a matter of sporadic murder, a consequence of the fact that, in the remoter regions, white men could kill natives with impunity. In Australia, in the safe isolation of the bush, white settlers shot down Aboriginals, poisoned their water-holes or presented them with packages of flour laced with arsenic. The statement by a group of settlers before they were hanged in 1837 for the murder of 28 Aboriginal men and women was probably quite sincere: 'We were not aware that, in killing the blacks, we were violating the law . . . as it had been so frequently done before'. Similar pleas might have been made by white colonists in any of four continents, almost up to the present. As recently as 1967, the Brazilian Government shocked the world with a report that its own Indian Protection Service had been directly and indirectly involved in the widespread destruction of the native Brazilian Indians with whose welfare it had been entrusted. A total of 134 functionaries, including a number of top government officials, were charged with more than 1,000 crimes, ranging from murder and torture to the theft of Indian lands.

Frequently, the natives themselves became

Survival Statistics
Conditions in Soviet labour camps at the time of Stalin's purges were so grim that about one third of the prisoners died within a year, mainly from exhaustion. Starvation was another factor. So small and poor in quality were the camp rations that prisoners unable to supplement them almost always died within two years

Russian Roulette
Of the 33 members of the Soviet Politburo in office from 1919 to 1938, just under 50 percent were assassinated

Criminal Neglect
A conservative estimate of the number of people who perished as a result of the Stalin regime is 15 million. The vast majority of these deaths resulted from starvation, exhaustion, exposure and disease in the Gulag camps

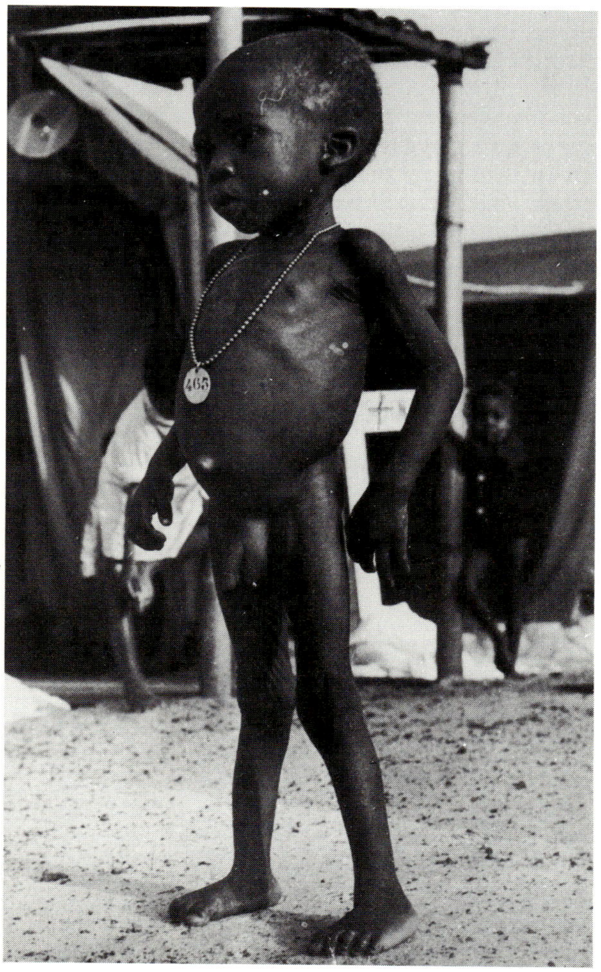

agents of their own destruction—through being made 'allies' of the whites and acquiring training in the use of firearms. Thus, in North America, the English-backed Iroquois practically annihilated the Huron allies of the French Canadians. In Louisiana the pro-English Chikasaws fought the French-backed Chocksaws. The French Governor congratulated himself on arranging for the 'self-destruction' of these 'barbarians', which he saw as the 'sole efficacious way of ensuring tranquillity in the colony'. In the Congo Free State, where King Leopold II of the Belgians ruled as an absolute monarch, his native levies, working for the white rubber exporters, succeeded in reducing the population from about 30 million in 1890 to 8.5 million in 1911. As a Belgian official told the British Consul, Roger Casement, in the fight for rubber the quantity gained depended on the number of guns—ten tons per gun per month. Whole villages which failed to produce enough rubber were wiped out. The authorities prevented the native troops from wasting bullets, ordering them to produce a human hand for each round of ammunition issued. If they missed their targets—or happened to take a pot shot at game—they generally made good the shortfall by cutting off the hands of living people.

The effect of introducing modern weapons and systems of controls into the traditional framework of African society may be gauged from two notorious recent examples. In Uganda, according to a report by the International Commission of Jurists in 1977, about 100,000 executions had occurred since President Amin came to power in 1971. The victims are believed to include some 50,000 members of two Christian tribes, the Lango and Acholi, as well as an Archbishop and several Cabinet Ministers. Amin is said to have assisted personally in some of the murders, most of which were carried out by the Cheka-type State Research Bureau, staffed by members of his own Kakwa tribe, as well as Nubian and Arab mercenaries. In the former Belgian protectorate of Burundi, the ruling Tutsi élite have completely exterminated the upper social strata of their Hutu subjects, in what has been described as 'selective genocide'. A rebellion by the Hutu against the dominant Tutsi in 1969, in which about 1,500 Tutsi were killed, provoked a massive reprisal by the military Government of President Micambero. Belgian teachers watched helplessly as Hutu pupils were dragged from their classes to be taken to places of execution, sometimes, with savage irony, in vehicles belonging to the United Nations Children's Fund (UNICEF). An English journalist who reported the massacre saw mass graves and open trenches awaiting bodies, as well as scores of burnt-out villages, where nothing remained but blackened cooking-pots and the bleaching and swollen bodies of those who had tried to escape along the shores of Lake Tanganyika. The Government claimed that the victims were Tutsi, who had been killed by the rebels, but from the evidence of foreign missionaries and other dependable sources, it is clear that the vast majority—about 80,000—were Hutu. African governments have in general sought to avoid giving publicity to these large-scale massacres, since this would tend to diminish the propaganda impact of atrocities committed by colonialists at Wiryamu in Portuguese Mozambique (about 400 victims) and Sharpeville, in South Africa (about 100).

However, genocide is far from being a purely colonial or post-colonial phenomenon. In at least one case in this century it provided a radical solution to the problem of sharing power in a multi-national

Far left top
When part of Nigeria tried to secede in the mid-1960s, calling itself Biafra, it was encircled and blockaded by Nigerian troops. Biafra soon faced starvation. In the photograph, taken in July, 1968, a group of mothers and their babies wait at the Enugu civilian hospital in Kwasikor, where 1,300 women and children were reported to be suffering from malnutrition

Left
One of the many Biafran children suffering from malnutrition. This small boy was one of the lucky few. Still alive when the civil war in Nigeria ended with the collapse of Biafra, he was rescued by one of the international organizations. Many other Biafran children died of starvation

Far left below
The officer in command of the firing squad which shot these two men, administers the coup de grâce to one of them. Convicted of attacks on women, Encarnacion and Nieves Hernandez were sentenced to be executed in February, 1944, under emergency legislation. The sentence was carried out in front of a sand-bagged wall in the Venta military camp near Pachuca, in Mexico

No Space in the Stable
The conditions at the Birkenau 'quarantine camp' were appalling—originally based on a design for stables, they were used to accommodate up to 1,200 prisoners

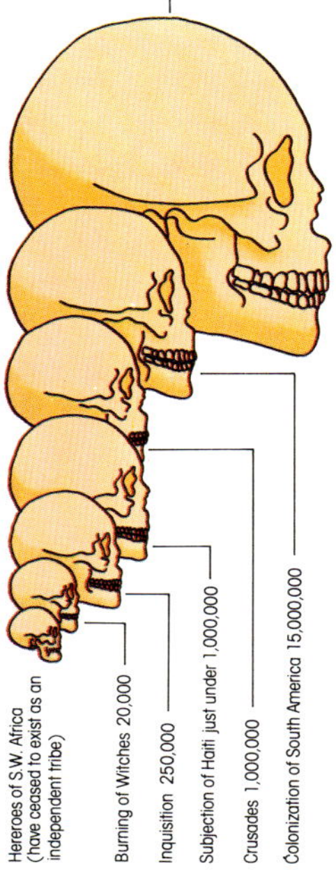

The Cruelty of Colonization
Political and military colonization policies, and religious conversion movements, have at different times taken a horrifying toll of human life, and permanently damaged local cultures

Right
Anti-semitism is as old as Christianity, and there are few Christian countries where Jews have not been massacred. In Russia in 1648, the Cossacks murdered hundreds of thousands of Jews. Only those accepting baptism were spared. More attacks followed over the centuries, like this one at Konnovino, near Novgorod, in June, 1884

Below right
Anti-semitism in Lithuania was reinforced when the country became part of Czarist Russia in 1795. (It was ruled by Russia until 1918.) In addition to persecuting the Jews, the Lithuanians also expelled them from time to time, and the Russians did the same in the 1840s, as this print shows. During World War I, many thousands of Jewish families were forced to leave Lithuania

Final Solution?
Dr Carl Clauberg, an Auschwitz SS doctor, performed numerous 'medical experiments' on prisoners with the object of discovering an effective method of liquidating entire peoples and races—notably Jews, Poles, Czechs and Russians. In a letter to Himmler, Clauberg wrote: 'The method is almost ready . . . a properly trained surgeon . . . would, most probably, be able to perform the sterilization of up to 1,000 persons in a day'

Cost Conscious
The principal Nazi method of mass killing was particularly economical in its use of resources: to kill 1,500 people in a gas chamber, only six kilos of the prussic acid crystals, known as Zyklon B, were required

Six Years of Genocide
It has been estimated that one and a half million children died in Nazi concentration camps between 1939 and 1945

From Farmer to Police Chief
Before joining the Nazis, and subsequently being appointed head of the SS in 1929, Heinrich Himmler ran a chicken farm

Web of Secrecy
The Nazis were careful not to let the details of their killing operations leak out. There were cases of unsuspecting Germans boarding trains reserved for the transportation of German Jews to death camps, believing them to be normal, scheduled trains. When they arrived at the destination, no matter what proof of identity they possessed, they were shot in order to maintain secrecy

state. In 1908, the Ottoman Empire fell into the hands of radical Turkish nationalists. During World War I, they found that the Armenians of northeastern Turkey were an obstacle to their ambitious plans for a drive to the east to reach the oil wells of Baku. After two successive defeats on the Russian front, the Government of Enver Pasha set up a special organization—mainly consisting of former criminals—with the task of exterminating the Armenians with the help of the Turkish army. Special squads rounded up the men in each Armenian village and led them off to be shot, while the women and children were deported to the Syrian desert, where most of them died of thirst and starvation. About a million and a half Armenians died in the holocaust 1915-1916.

Turkey's genocide of the Armenians was dwarfed by Nazi Germany's genocide of the Jews during World War II. It should be borne in mind, however, that the Nazis were not the first Germans systematically to adopt a policy of genocide in their conquered territories, although the scale of their genocide of the Jews has never been equalled, either before the 1940s or since. In South-West Africa, after the collapse of a rebellion by the Hereros some years before World War I, the German Governor, von Trotha, ordered that all the survivors—men, women and children—should be massacred. With their

In 1915-1916, the Turks massacred a million and a half Armenians, shooting the men and deporting the women and children to the Syrian desert to die of thirst and starvation. In World War II, in the most systematic murder operation ever conceived, the Nazis exterminated six million Jews and many millions of Russians, Poles and others

usual efficiency, the Germans—according to their own official figures—had reduced the Herero population from about 80,000 to just over 15,000. A similar degree of ruthlessness had been applied in suppressing a native rebellion in German East Africa at the turn of the century. According to a Government spokesman in the Reichstag, 75,000 natives perished in the rebellion.

Nevertheless, although the introduction of modern weapons into economically and politically undeveloped regions of the world enormously increased the possibilities of mass murder and genocide, the greatest potential for mass killing remains with those nations having the most advanced forms of social organization. So far, the United States is the only state to have utilized the awful potential of the nuclear weapon. Germany is the only state systematically to have employed the most rationalized forms of administration with the sole purpose of extermination. The main victims, as we have said, were six million harmless non-belligerents: the Jews of Europe. In addition, many more millions of gypsies, Russians, Poles and other nationalities were deliberately massacred.

Anti-semitism is as old as Christianity. The early Christians, originally a Jewish sect, could not afford to extend toleration to the Jews, who challenged the fundamental basis of Christian belief by refusing to acknowledge the divinity of Christ. In the Middle Ages, persecution was aimed at conversion. Most of

the Jews of Spain managed to avoid massacre in the fifteenth century by hasty baptism. A racial dimension to the persecutions in Spain appeared when the Inquisition, sensing that these reluctant converts were insincere, started categorizing suspects on the basis of 'blood' *(limpienza)*. Possessing half or a quarter 'New Christian' (ie, convert) blood became enough to arouse suspicions leading to possible torture and death. Nineteenth-century anti-semites, who were no longer interested in converting the Jews, developed the racialist theory that Jews were socially harmful, corrupting the 'purity' of the nation. In the late nineteenth and early twentieth century, anti-semitism provided an international rallying-point for the Right, a counter-poise to the 'proletarian internationalism' of 'natural' allies, since most European countries had national claims against each other. The idea of a 'Jewish international' which manipulated all those forces tending to erode the boundaries of national states, such as Socialism and 'international capital', had a common appeal for Right-wing parties in practically every country. In Germany, where the Nazis came to power in 1933, anti-Jewish propaganda was able to draw on a tradition of Catholic and Lutheran polemic extending back to the Middle Ages. The Nazis used it skilfully, employing to the fullest advantage such recent technical innovations as radio and loudspeakers. Like most successful radicals, they believed their own propaganda, and once in power were able to reinforce their prejudices with spurious

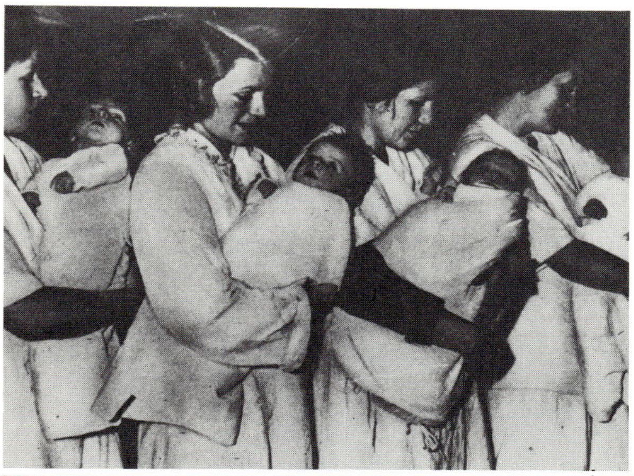

Far left
When the Nazis took over in Germany in 1933, their anti-Jewish propaganda was able to draw on a long tradition of Catholic and Lutheran polemic. Before long, they were forbidding any association between 'Aryans' and 'racially inferior' Jews. The placard this Hamburg woman was made to wear by Nazi storm troopers reads: 'I am the biggest swine in the place, and mix only with Jews'

Left
A wartime Nazi propaganda photograph purporting to show a Warsaw tram reserved for the use of the 500,000 Jews from all over Poland crowded into the ghetto. By September, 1942, the figure had fallen to less than 115,000 as the result of disease, starvation and deportation to Treblinka death camp

Left
'Pure Aryan' girls were encouraged to help in perpetuating the 'master race' by having babies by 'pure Aryan' men. They and their babies were looked after in every way and accommodated in special homes for unwed mothers

'scientific' evidence purporting to 'prove' the 'racial inferiority' of Jews to 'Aryans'.

The Nazis employed the full apparatus of the German state in their anti-Jewish policies. Lawyers and civil servants drafted decrees depriving Jews and, in some cases, non-Jews who had one Jewish grandparent, of their civil rights and property. The army, which after the outbreak of war in 1939 controlled vast areas of occupied territory in Eastern and Western Europe, participated in the mass killings of Jews or helped to transport them to death camps; the police helped to seek out Jews within the Greater Reich and the occupied territories; the Foreign Ministry negotiated with Germany's allies for the deportation of Jews from their territories; the judiciary co-operated by sentencing Jews to death

Using the full apparatus of the German state in their anti-Jewish policies, the Nazis organized the extermination of the Jews on an assembly line basis, setting up killing centres to make mass murder more efficient. The biggest was at Auschwitz, in Upper Silesia. The furnaces of its specially built crematoria consumed the bodies of 20,000 victims a day – and were kept working 24 hours a day

Born to Suffer
The killing of Jews, and the sequestration of their property was customary in Europe long before Hitler arrived on the scene

PRE NAZI PERSECUTION OF THE JEWS FROM 1096 to 1921

Year	France	Spain	Germany	Russia
1000	1096 – 1st Crusade estimated 10,000 killed		1096 – 1st Crusade estimated 5,000 killed. Worst individual massacre at Mainz, where death toll was 1,100	
1100				
1200	1236 – 3rd Crusade Pope Gregory VIX accused Crusaders of slaughtering 2,500 Jews		1298-9 The Rindfleisch massacres claimed 3,500 lives altogether	
1300	1320 – The Pastoureux (Shepherd's Movement) A popular religious movement predominant in S France, was responsible for deaths of about 700 Jews	1391-1492 100,000 Jews who refused to be converted to Catholicism were massacred.	1336-7 – Armleder Massacres – Bands of religious fanatics killed a total of 6,000 Jews 1348-50 – Jews were held responsible for the Black Death and 15,000 were burned. Worst example was at Mainz where	
1400		Worst individual year was 1490, when 70,000 Jews were slaughtered	6,000 were burnt	
1500				
1600				1648 – The Revolt against Polish rule in the Ukraine, led by Shmielniki, was responsible for the deaths of about 80,000 Jews
1700				
1800				1881 – Murder of Alexander II inspired anti-Jewish pogroms – hundreds were killed
1900				1903-6 – Persecution by 'The Black Hundreds', a right-wing anti-Semitic movement, resulted in a Jewish death toll of about 800. Worst individual example was at Odessa; 300 were killed 1917-21 – The right-wing Ukrainian National Army killed about 6,000 Jews General Denikin's white armies blamed Jews for Russian Revolution and slaughtered up to 60,000 Jews. Worst individual massacres: Fastov (death toll 1,500) in 1919 Tetiev (death toll 4,000) in 1921

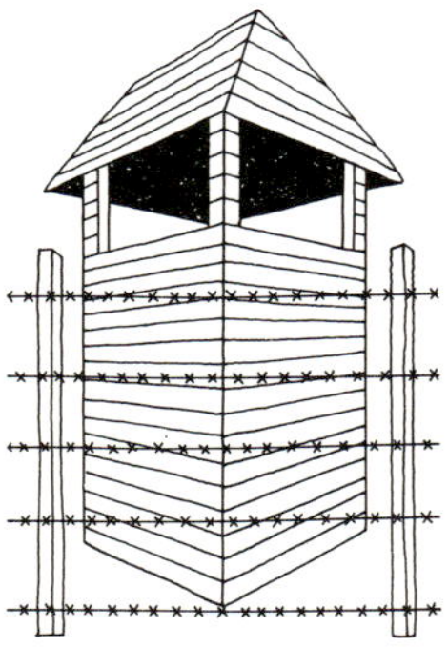

Stages of Evolution of a Nazi Death Camp

1 Acts of brutality instigated and provoked by the Nazi party – i.e. gang beatings of Jews in the street

2 Organized destruction of Jewish property – for instance 'Krystalnacht' in 1934, when Jewish shops and businesses had their windows smashed, and all Germany's major synagogues were burned down

3 Introduction of racial laws aimed at isolating and demoralizing Jews, with the intention of forcing them to emigrate

4 Pogroms (condoned acts of 'spontaneous' violence) by Nazi personnel in occupied territories

5 Beginnings of secret 'euthanasia programme' in mental hospitals for disposal of the insane, resulting in the deaths of at least 275,000 people

6 'Einzatzgruppen' activities (mobile killing operations) experimental use of gas vans, shooting squads, etc.

7 Setting up of concentration camps, the first of which was at Dachau, opened in 1933, for the large-scale internment of political enemies of the Reich

8 Establishment of death camps, with the sole purpose of 'finally dealing' with the Jewish question

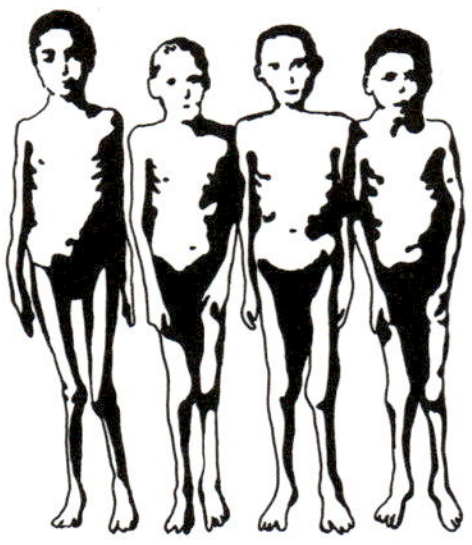

for such 'crimes' as having sexual intercourse with 'Aryans'; the medical profession participated in experiments in which live Jews were used as 'guinea-pigs'; private industry employed Jews as slave labour, working and starving them to death, and manufactured the gas used in the death camp gas chambers; the mass of small businessmen and ordinary citizens took advantage of their right as 'Aryans' to acquire expropriated Jewish property on extremely favourable terms. Hitler and the Nazi Party instituted these policies and provided the inspiration and authority for them, but they could never have been successfully achieved without the almost total collaboration of the German 'Establishment' at all levels. The mass murder of Europe's Jews got into its stride in 1941. The first executions were performed by special mobile killing units *(Einsatzgruppen)* attached to army divisions after Germany's attack on the Soviet Union in 1941. These units followed German army units into captured Soviet cities and towns, rounded up the Jews who, in Eastern Europe, were well-defined, and transported them outside the built-up areas. Here, the victims would be forced to dig special ditches, strip and hand over their valuables. Then they would be lined up along the edges of the ditches and shot. About a million and a half Jews, as well as many thousands of suspected Communist leaders, were executed in this manner. However, since the German occupation of western Russia and the Ukraine had placed about four million of the Soviet Union's 5 million Jews in Nazi hands, it soon became clear that the operations of the *Einsatzgruppen* were too limited in scope, besides being much too public and liable to demoralize the troops. It was decided to set up a number of killing centres, and these came into being in late 1941 and the spring of 1942. They brought together a number of separate developments: the concentration camps, first adopted by the Nazis in 1934 to isolate their political opponents; the technique of locking prisoners in vans and gassing them with exhaust fumes (carbon monoxide), used by the Nazis in Russia and Yugoslavia in 1941; gas chambers, first employed in Germany in 1939 to administer euthanasia to some 275,000 incurable mental patients, and large-scale crematoria to burn the bodies of the victims. By the summer of 1942 six killing centres were operating: Treblinka, Kulmhof, Auschwitz (Oswiecim), Sobibor, Belzec and Majdanek. By far the largest was Auschwitz in Upper Silesia, a combined concentration and death camp. It housed 67,000 inmates, and its gas chambers and specially built crematoria were able to dispose of 20,000 inmates a day. The killing centres worked quickly and efficiently, using modern assembly-line techniques. Within three years they had disposed of nearly three million Jews, as well as thousands of gypsies and vagrants classified as 'parasitical' social elements. Men, women and children would leave a cattletruck train in the morning, and by the evening of the same day they would have been murdered, and their clothes and valuables packed for shipment to Germany. The work of sorting clothes, gathering fuel for the ovens and disposing of the corpses was done by gangs of inmates organized into special squads *(Sonderkommandos)*. As in the 'ordinary' concentration camps, internal order was kept by exploiting national or racial animosities, awarding privileges to certain groups in exchange for obedience and power over other prisoners. The main privilege, of course, was life itself—a commodity to be rationed out to prisoners for a few weeks or months until, exhausted by work or illness, they were themselves ready to be 'selected' for the gas chambers.

At the Auschwitz rail-head, the transports of incoming prisoners were divided into two columns—

The Final Solution
It took the Nazis several years to fully organize the means by which they annihilated millions of people, including some six million Jews of a dozen different European nationalities

Exploiting Youth
Only about 17 percent of Nazi death camp guards were of German origin. The average age of a guard was 22

Trained in Cold Blood
The ultimate Nazi training camp was Schloss Hawtheim, near Linz, in Austria, originally a lunatic asylum. Here SS men were trained to kill without mercy and immunized against the horror of death and suffering. Anyone who showed any signs of weakness during the training period was taken away and shot

Right
Adolf Hitler with some of his aides at a giant Nazi rally in Nuremberg in 1937. Hitler and the Nazi Party could not have succeeded in their anti-Jewish policies without the virtually total support of all levels of the German 'Establishment'

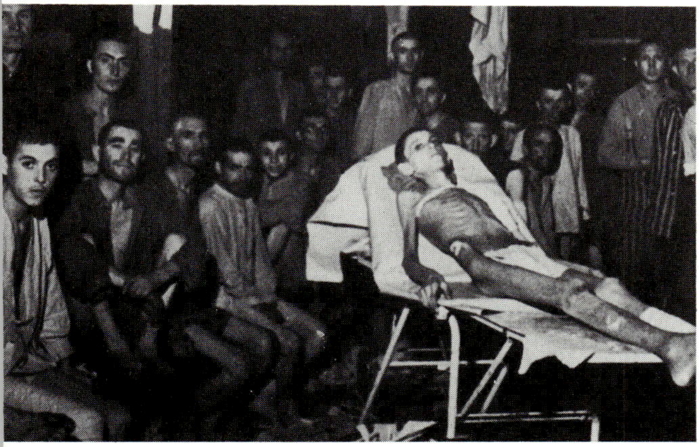

one for the concentration camp at Auschwitz, the other for the death camp and its gas chambers at Birkenau. Those selected for Birkenau were taken to the 'bath house', made to strip and forced to hand over rings and other valuables. The women had their heads shaved. The victims would then be taken to one of four gas chambers. They were usually under the impression that they were about to take a communal shower, but there would sometimes be disorderly scenes at the last minute, and they had to be pushed into the chambers by guards using rifle-butts. The doors were then locked and the gas (hydrogen cyanide) administered in pellet form through shafts in the ceiling. The gas was supplied under the commercial name *Zyklon-B* by a firm specializing in pest control. The victims of Zyklon-B took about 5-10 minutes to die depending on the climatic conditions. After the gas had been cleared by electric fans, the *Sonderkommandos* would find the bodies piled up in a pyramid, with the strongest men at the top. All constraints had been abandoned as the victims fought a last desperate struggle to reach the retreating band of air near the ceiling. In some of the other camps, where carbon monoxide was used, death might take up to three hours. A German professor who visited the death camps was known to place his ear to the wall of the gas chamber at the Belzec camp and remark that the screams of the dying sounded 'just like a synagogue'.

When news of the exterminations filtered out, Britain's then Prime Minister, Winston Churchill, wrote to his Foreign Secretary, Anthony Eden: 'There is no doubt that this is probably the greatest and most horrible crime ever committed in the whole history of the world, and it has been done with scientific machinery by nominally civilized men in the name of a great state and one of the leading races of Europe'. How were ordinary men and women brought to commit such a monstrous crime? In the early stages, soon after the Nazi seizure of power, the hate propaganda master-minded by Josef Goebbels played a vital part in alienating ordinary Germans from their Jewish fellow citizens. In countless newspaper articles and pamphlets, such as the notorious *Protocols of the Elders of Zion,* a forgery originating in Tsarist Russia, the Jews were portrayed as members of a vast global conspiracy whose aim was world rule and the destruction of the German nation. By the outbreak of war in 1939, the professed aim of deporting and 'resettling' the Jews in Eastern Europe had come to be regarded as a legitimate one, not only by the majority of the Germans, but by Germany's allies—Rumania, Bulgaria, Hungary and, to a lesser extent, Vichy France and Fascist Italy. The Jewish Councils through whom the Nazis operated in the ghettoes thoroughly acquiesced in this policy. They co-operated in registering the Jews within their jurisdiction, in supplying police for the ghettoes and, in many cases, in selecting candidates for deportation. Their actions were dictated by a mixture of motives and responses. In the beginning they may have been genuinely ignorant of what was happening and believed the tales of 'resettlement' in the East. In others, there was a wilful refusal to contemplate the 'impossible'. In yet other cases, there was the vain hope that, by co-operating in the destruction of the many, the few might be saved. Above all was the habit, ingrained in the traditional Jewish leadership, of co-operating with whoever happened to be in power—a policy which had worked reasonably well in the past. Few Jews seem to have been far-sighted enough to realize that it could not be made to work with the Nazis. By the time the majority had woken up to the danger (as in Warsaw in 1943), it was already far too late for them to save themselves.

Most of the Germans who carried out the Nazi genocide of the Jews were 'normal'. Although the Nazis found collaborators among those they conquered, some countries refused to give up their Jews, notably Denmark. Some 90 percent of Danish Jews were hidden or helped to escape to Sweden

As with deportation, which necessarily preceded extermination, this, too, was facilitated by propaganda. Many of the officers in the camps genuinely believed they were dealing with 'vermin', or at least with a category of beings not fully human. While there were some sadists and mentally deranged individuals among the killers, the majority were normal, regarding their jobs as an unpleasant and onerous duty in the service of the Reich. A large proportion of the camp personnel were policemen from the Kriminalpolizei (CID) seconded to 'euthanasia duty'—and then to the death camps in Poland.

Left
German soldiers pose near the body of a woman hanging from a gallows for a souvenir photograph. The film was found in a German house used by troops before they retreated

Below left
The emergency hospital set up in Buchenwald forced labour camp after it had been liberated by US troops at the end of World War II. The naked, emaciated young boy, a Hungarian Jew, has just had an operation

Badges of Suffering
These were the badges worn by different categories of prisoner at Dachau concentration camp. Dachau was used mainly for the internment of political and special surveillance inmates

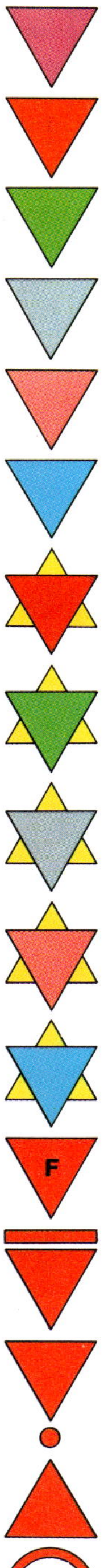

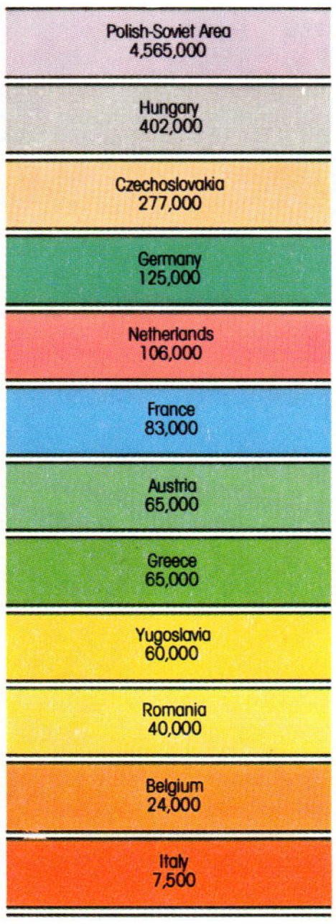

Nightmare Journey
From every country occupied by the Nazis issued trains filled with Jews destined for the death camps which had been set up in Poland

Secrecy was essential to the operation. The number of people who officially knew what was happening was severely restricted, though there were plenty of more or less accurate rumours. There were cases of SS men being ostracized on account of the contempt in which they were held. Senior officers evidently avoided talking about their work on grounds of secrecy and, perhaps, from shame. At the Nuremberg trials it emerged that during his three years as Auschwitz camp commander, Rudolf Hoess only once alluded to the killings in his wife's presence. Official secrecy, justified under war-time conditions, encouraged the wholesale co-operation of the German bureaucracy. The thousands of officials who helped in the operation—arranging train schedules or building contracts, or disposing of such items as the gold teeth removed from corpses—were prevented from acquiring any information beyond the bare minimum required for the execution of their tasks. No doubt the zeal with which these thousands of individual orders were carried out is evidence of the respect for authority and efficiency which marks the German character; but it should not be forgotten that the Nazis found willing collaborators among their allies and in the occupied countries, though not all, for there were some limitations on Nazi terror. In occupied Holland, it carried the day, because the Jews, concentrated in certain quarters of Amsterdam and other cities, were strategically vulnerable. In Denmark, however, the Prime Minister resigned rather than give up the Danish Jews. The Danish civil service, Jewish communal leaders and the bulk of Copenhagen's population combined to frustrate the Nazi deportations, and 90 percent of Danish Jews were hidden or were helped to escape to Sweden. In France, the Laval Government managed to avoid deporting some French Jews, though at the cost of sacrificing most of the Jewish refugees from Germany and Eastern Europe. Fascist Italy, while formally agreeing to Nazi demands, at first did much to frustrate them in practice. Many Jews were hidden, although, after the German occupation, many thousands were deported to share the fate of their co-religionists in Auschwitz.

It is probably impossible to work out a formula which would supply causal explanations for the varieties of mass killing mentioned earlier, as well as the many others which have been omitted for lack of space. However, a study of mass murder and liquidation reveals certain common threads or patterns.

Among peoples for whom warfare is part of the normal conditions of life, certain customs will usually develop which inhibit the destructiveness of conflict. However, a radical change in social and political organization may suddenly remove these internal checks and balances. Something like this seems to have happened at the time of the Mongol invasions. Suddenly, a people with limited intellectual and moral horizons, from an out-of-the-way part of the globe, found itself in control of much of the civilized world, without having yet acquired an outlook

Right
One of the gas chambers at Majdanek. Between 1942 and June, 1944, when the Nazis evacuated the camp, at least 360,000 prisoners had been killed, 200,000 of them Jews

Right
When it became clear that Germany was losing the war, the Nazis tried to destroy the evidence of their extermination programme. At Buchenwald they could not do so, having run out of coal with which to cremate their victims' bodies

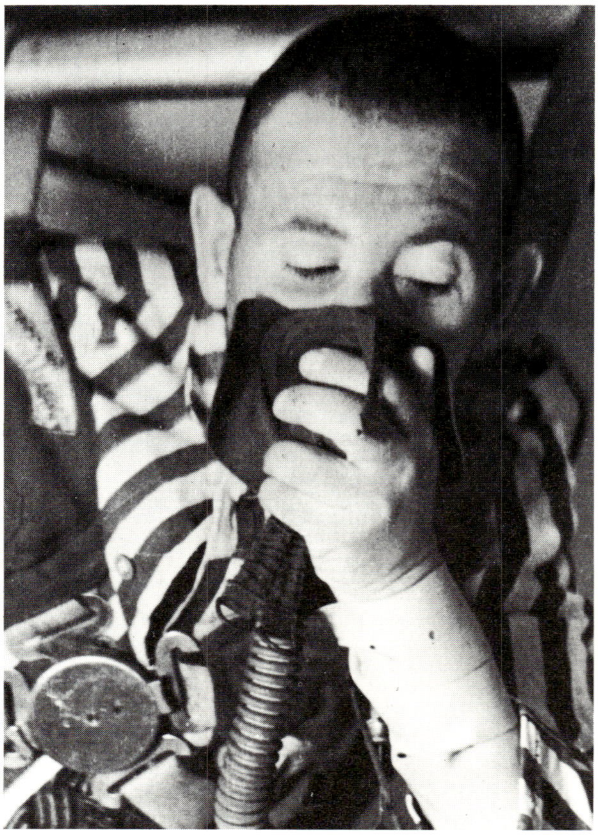

Far right
Nazi doctors put this Jew in a pressure chamber with a pilot's oxygen mask to hand. When the pressure rose, he grabbed the mask, only to find that there was no oxygen

Right
The Buchenwald crematoria as they were found by the liberating American Third Army, with charred remains still inside.

Choice of Evils
Suicide in Nazi labour camps was common among prisoners driven to desperation by starvation and exhaustion. One widely used method was self-electrocution by running into the electrified wire fences surrounding the camps. Another was hanging

commensurate with its responsibilities. For the first generation of Mongol conquerors, terror was not just a means of conquest and control, but also a result of their failure fully to understand the nature of the cultures they were bent on destroying. Imagining that their parochial Great Khan was the Lord of the Universe, appointed by God, they believed, in a simple-minded way, in their absolute right to destroy any living individuals or communities which seemed to stand in the way of his divine mission. Similarly, in more recent times, the parochialism of Europeans combined with their unprecedented military superiority and economic greed to facilitate the destruction of millions of people in the least developed regions of the world. The religious prejudice that heathens were unworthy of protection was reinforced by the racial prejudice that different or less rapid cultural development was evidence of intrinsic, biological inferiority. In parts of Africa and South America especially, the behaviour of the Europeans was no less barbaric and parochial than that of the Mongols in Europe and Asia. The first generations of conquerors rarely had any idea of the richness and complexity of the societies they were engaged in destroying.

Nevertheless, mass murder and liquidation are far from being confined to situations where there is a vast disparity of military strength between conquerors and conquered. Within living memory, terror and genocide have been practised on a barely imaginable scale by two great European nations, one of them a leader among the world's industrial powers. The holocausts in the Soviet Union and Germany drew on forces latent in European—and probably most other—societies, extending and amplifying them by means of centrally controlled bureaucratic machines. Stalinist persecution focused on the hidden 'enemy within'—a popular fantasy whose previous manifestations include the great witch-hunts and sporadic nineteenth-century attacks on freemasonry. The Nazis supplemented the medieval archetype of the Jew with pseudo-scientific notions purportedly derived from Darwinian evolutionary theory and anthropology. In both cases, the effect of this propaganda was to create an image of a society whose existence was threatened by enemies so demonic and so powerful, that they could be destroyed only if the régime acquired absolute power. Using propaganda to manipulate the subconscious fears of the masses, both Stalinism and Nazism were able to create killer squads from emotionally deprived, but otherwise normal individuals who sought self-fulfilment in total identification with the aims of the régime and obedience to its orders. The compartmentalized bureaucracy of the modern, centralized state lent itself admirably to this process, since the functionaries could be encouraged to direct all their energies towards furthering the 'cause', without having to bear any great responsibility. In Hannah Arendt's phrase, it is the 'banality of evil', rather than its monstrous proportions, that is revealed in the two greatest human catastrophes of the twentieth-century.

Starving to Death
The daily calorie intake required in order to perform manual labour is just under 5,000. Daily food rations for prisoners at Auschwitz contained between 1,300 and 1,700 calories, thus causing a high death rate

Left
General Eisenhower, Supreme Allied Commander, and a group of senior officers at Orhdurf camp, in Germany, where the bodies of Polish and Russian prisoners shot by the Germans lie sprawled where they fell

Below left
Aided by a freed political prisoner, US troops hook the body of a dead SS guard out of the moat surrounding Dachau camp. He had been killed by some prisoners

Factories of Death
This map indicates the locations of the six death camps constructed by the Nazis for the extermination of the Jews

After crushing and occupying Holland during World War II, the Germans deported more than 60,000 Jews to Auschwitz. A mere 1,052 survived. I was one of them

Above
The memorial on the site of Bergen-Belsen, one of a number of camps throughout the area of Hitler's Third Reich. Bergen-Belsen was opened in August, 1943, and liberated by British troops in April, 1945. They found 55,000 prisoners and 13,000 unburied corpses at the camp. During the following three days, a further 13,000 prisoners died

Wages of Sin
SS guards employed on gassing operations were given a 'bonus' for each individual operation they carried out. This consisted of one fifth of a litre of vodka; five cigarettes; 100 grammes of sausage; 100 grammes of bread

No Room for Disturbance
A minimum of 275,000 psychiatric patients were killed in German hospitals between 1939 and 1945 under the 'euthanasia' programme

Free from Retribution
Of the 9,000 guards who served at Auschwitz, barely ten percent were brought to trial, and only 2 percent of those convicted received sentences of more than five years in prison

Like my companions on the train of locked cattle trucks which brought us to Auschwitz on September 16, 1943, I did not know that it was a combined extermination and slave labour camp. We had heard rumours about the mass murder which was routine at Auschwitz and other camps, like Sobibor, but we did not believe them. The Nazis had said that we were being sent East to be 'resettled', which sounded plausible. We could not believe—indeed, most of us did not want to believe—that we were being sent East to be liquidated. That was why it never entered our heads to try to plan some kind of resistance. Even when the cattle trucks were unlocked, few of us had any real idea of what was happening at Auschwitz. It did not take long for us to find out.

As transport after transport of European Jews—men, women and children—arrived at the camp, they were divided up into two groups. The smaller group, making up between 20 and 25 percent of each cattle-truck trainload, consisted of 'healthy'-looking men. They were earmarked for slave labour. The others were destined for death by gassing soon after arrival. Not that more than a handful of the healthy ones were to be allowed to live longer than a few months. When overwork, malnutrition and disease made them useless for their tasks, they were also gassed and their bodies burned to ash in the crematoria of Auschwitz, whose chimneys belched smoke and flame day and night. The Germans had a term for this. They called it 'productive annihilation'.

Being a doctor, I was selected for life, and was herded, together with the rest of the group, into a shower room. So were the members of the second, larger group. But when their 'showers' were turned on, they emitted Zyklon B gas. Ours were genuine—water came out of them.

There was no forced labour at Sobibor. It was solely an extermination camp. Only a few men from each transport were spared almost immediate death. They were picked out to do the Germans' dirty work for them: extract the gold fillings from the teeth of the gassed corpses, wheel the corpses on carts to the ovens, dispose of the ashes. The Germans promised them a chance of survival, but these promises were not worth the breath they were uttered with. The Nazis wanted no witnesses. Sooner or later, those who spent their days moving corpses to the ovens themselves became corpses. So did their successors—and their successors and those after them.

Of the more than 34,000 Dutch Jews deported to Sobibor, 19 came back after the war, together with eleven other survivors. As a psychiatrist, I interviewed 15 of them. They told me that when they heard on arrival at Sobibor that all Jews sent there were murdered in the gas chambers within a very short time, except for those dealing with the corpses, they refused to believe it. Impossible, they declared. The other Jews in their transport must have been taken to the other side of the camp as slave labourers. This psychological defence mechanism did not function for all the Jews sent to Sobibor, however. When they were told what had happened to the others in their transport, they went into shock. The truth was too much for them, and they became psychologically paralyzed. Most died very soon afterwards.

Those who had reacted by denying the possibility of mass extermination at Sobibor could not maintain their illusions for long. They saw the unending stream of cattle trucks, the growing piles of clothes, shoes, battered suitcases, parcels of belongings. They could not blind themselves to the knowledge that men, women and children were being herded naked into the death centre 'shower rooms'. The dreadful facts forced themselves into their conscious minds, but they learned to live with them, in essence to find ways to adapt themselves to the horrors around them.

To these inmates of Sobibor death camp, their work became all-important. They immersed themselves in it, shutting out the knowledge that transports were arriving every day, bringing thousands of fellow Jews to their deaths by gassing. They could not allow themselves to react in any way when their comrades were sent to the death centre. They looked at what was going on all round them, but did not see it, because to have done so would have destroyed their mental balance. They could not afford to feel compassion. The only way they could keep going was to harden their hearts. After a time, this blinkered existence, this suppression of all feelings, this concentration on simply staying alive, turned them into robots, or, as one of the survivors told me, into animals—with only one instinct left, the instinct of self-preservation. They worked even harder, because this was their only passport to life in the charnel-house of Sobibor extermination camp.

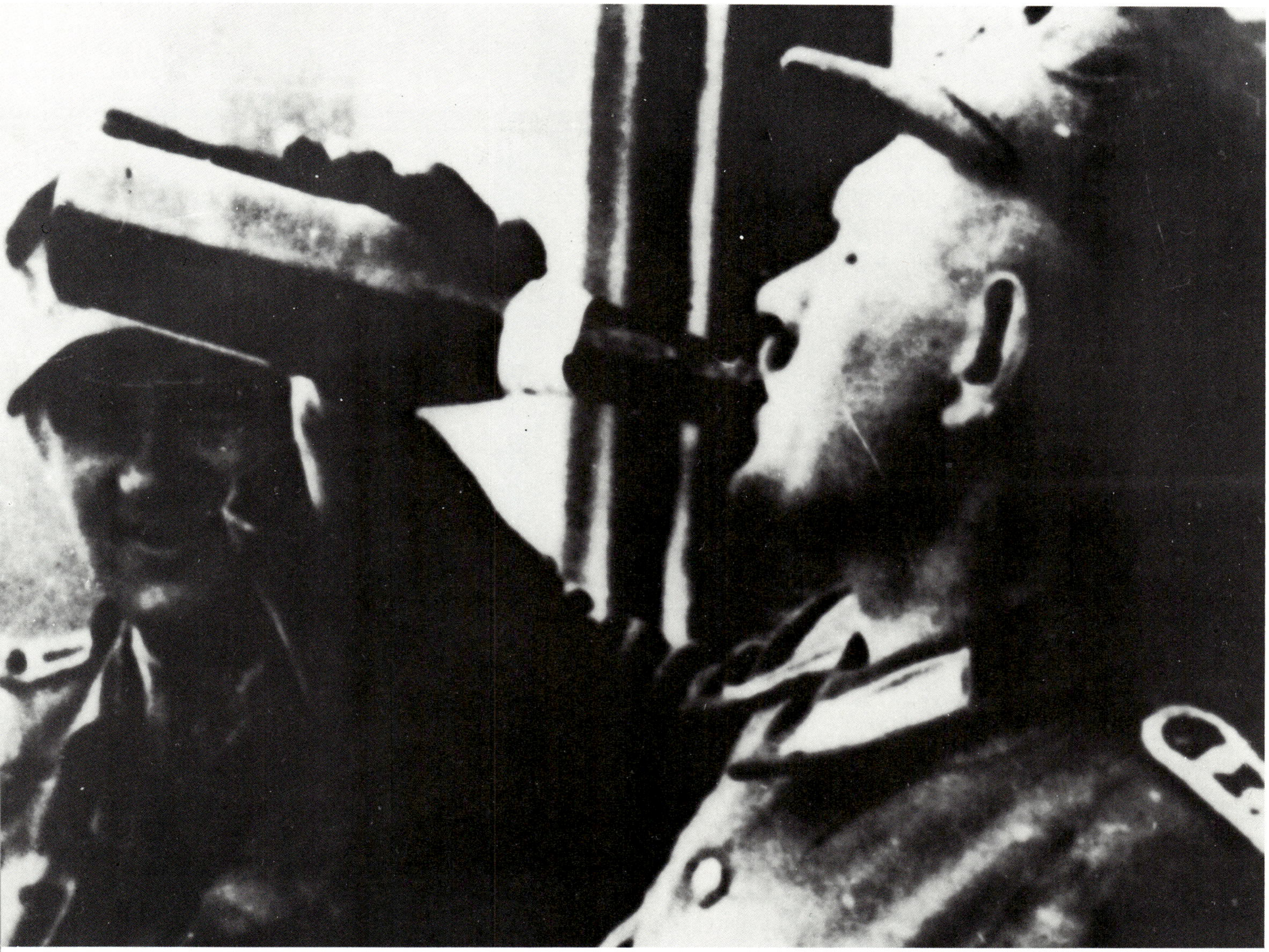

Did they feel guilty at having worked for the Germans, at having collaborated with them, as I did? I asked them. They did not answer directly. Some said: 'If we had refused, it would not have made any difference, because others would have worked for them instead. Even if nobody had collaborated, the Germans would have continued exterminating the Jews'. I could not then, and cannot now, accept this. In my view, everyone is responsible for his own deeds. Everyone wants to live, and if the only way to stay alive is to obey orders, however inhuman, then, stripped down to their core of egoism, following their instinct of self-preservation, people ultimately perhaps close their eyes and obey orders.

Many say that the Jews who worked for the Germans in the death camps are not to be condemned. They were forced to choose between life and death and, since life means hope, they had no alternative but to choose life. Their choice is understandable, but is it acceptable?

What about the Germans in the extermination camps? They were exceedingly productive. At Sobibor there were only 30 or 40 of them, assisted by 100 Ukrainians, but between them they murdered a quarter of a million Jews. The Germans and their Ukrainian helpers did not do the dirty work in the death centres. It was the Jews who had to do it—supervised and harassed by the Germans, masters of life and death. They lived a life of luxury they had never dreamt of, those Germans. They had servants—slaves, rather—to polish their boots, do their washing and clean up after them. They ordered tailor-made uniforms and suits, ate and drank whatever they liked, and went on leave with suitcases crammed with all sorts of things that were virtually unobtainable at that stage of the war by other Germans.

They had grown up in an authoritarian society. At home, the father had absolute power. So did the schools, the army, society. Those in command could do no wrong and must be obeyed absolutely, their orders carried out to the letter and unquestioningly. A subordinate did not question the orders he was given by his superior, nor did he feel responsible for them. This explains how Germans could come home from the camps and their daily job of killing, and play with their children, make love to their wives, go to concerts and parties, laugh and joke and sing sentimental songs. They believed the vicious doctrines of National Socialism, which proclaimed that the Germans were the master race and that Jews were sub-human, the cause of all the evil in the world, who must be exterminated.

The Germans were not predestined to embrace National Socialism—Nazism—because of their national character or by heredity, but because of their predilection for authoritarianism. This may partly explain the course of events in Europe during World War II, but it does not absolve the Germans of their guilt for the systematic and cold-blooded murder of millions of Jews.

Above
SS guard Erich Herman Bauer headed the gassing unit at Sobibor, where 250,000 Jews and Soviet war prisoners were murdered. He was sentenced to hard labour for life by a Berlin court in 1950. Sobibor ceased to operate in October, 1943, after an uprising by the Jewish inmates. Here, Bauer is enjoying a drink of champagne, after spending the day gassing Jews

The Link with Farben
Zyklon B, the gas the Nazis used to kill an estimated four million Polish Jews at Auschwitz and other extermination camps, was manufactured by the firm of Degesch (owned at the time by IG Farben Industrie). IG Farben made 300,000 Reichsmarks (then about £30,300) from the sale of the gas to concentration camps between the years 1941 to 1944. Situated near Auschwitz, IG Farben Industrie also made much use of Jewish slave labour. About 30,000 Auschwitz prisoners perished through forced labour at IG Farben in barely three years

Legions of the Dead

More people have died in war in the twentieth century than in any other. But while governments spend 60 percent more on the military than on medical services, technology has made war more dangerous for the civilian than for the soldier

Above
Red Army anti-tank riflemen at Stalingrad: an 'heroic' composition of the kind favoured by official Soviet artists. Of some 300,000 men of the German 6th Army besieged in the ruined city from 23 November 1942, only 91,000 survived to surrender on 31 January 1943 – and most later died in captivity

Right
'Some corner of a foreign field . . .' The graves of American war dead at Manila, Philippines, represent a tiny fraction of the estimated total of more than 100 million killed in war in the 20th century. Conventional eulogies of the 'glorious dead' ignore the fact that there is no international agency for recording war deaths

Death in war is the most terrible and at once the most human of all deaths. No other animal species can begin to compete with man in the alacrity with which he slaughters members of his own species. Today, improving the machines of death is a multi-billion dollar business: it is also probably the principal single area of government-financed research and development, absorbing between 25 and 50 percent of the scientific funds and personnel of several of the major industrial countries.

Death in war is both the most public and the most anonymous of deaths. War is given the greatest attention by the mass media and government and private agencies, but who are the *legions of the dead?* The tombs of the 'Unknown Soldiers', the endless war cemeteries throughout the world filled with identical gravestones, cry out against the faceless fate of death in battle.

It is estimated that some 25 million people have died in war since World War II alone, and that the total this century probably exceeds 100 million. Estimated is the operative word, for there is no international agency which records war deaths, and few governments keep accurate records of casualties, let alone publish them.

In little more than a century, technology has changed the nature of death in war in paradoxical ways. The Charge of the Light Brigade, during the Crimean War (1853-1856), which resulted in the deaths of 247 men and 497 horses out of a total of 673 mounted soldiers, was the result of close-range artillery fire. Also, conical bullets inflicted much more severe wounds than the older spherical bullets, and introduced a trend towards more devastating small arms fire. On the other hand, more men died of disease than were killed in battle, as Florence Nightingale's publicization of the plight of the sick and wounded of the Crimean War underlined. Indeed, this situation continued until after World War I. Many of those who died on the battlefield

Traffic of War
Accidents always occur in war, and the increased mechanization of armies has done much to add to the accident figures. During the quiet months in Vietnam, for example, traffic accidents often killed more US troops than did the enemy

Right
A French officer rallies his men for an assault on the Austrians at Solferino, 24 June 1859. Although victorious, Napoleon III was so horrified by the cost – nearly 20 percent of the 235,000 men engaged were killed – that he sought a truce with Austria

Bottom right
Henri Dunant (1828-1910), a witness of Solferino, gave the rest of his life to the prevention of such suffering, founding the Red Cross in 1864. Dunant laboured in poverty for nearly 50 years, but was recognized by the award of the first Nobel Prize for Peace in 1901

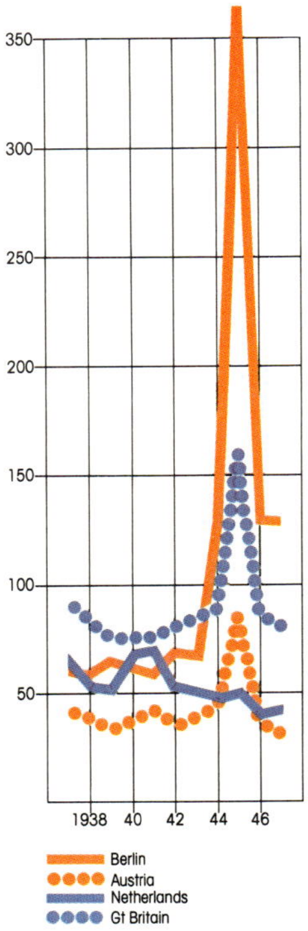

Death Claims the Youngest
Impact of World War II on infant mortality rates in selected countries, 1938-46 (deaths per 1000, under two years of age). The data for Berlin illustrate the effects on a city subjected to strategic bombing

Quick Treatment
In World War II, the time it took for treatment to reach wounded American soldiers was, on average, 10½ hours. In the Vietnam war, it had dropped to just below three hours

One Day's Loss
At the battle of Solferino in 1859, a total of nearly 40,000 French, Piedmontese and Austrian troops died on a single day

were not killed outright, but died from lack of care, while as many as 13 to 17 percent of those who survived long enough to be operated on in hospital died of infection. At the Battle of Solferino in 1859, 22,500 men of the Austrian army and 17,200 French and Piedmontese troops (a total of nearly 40,000) died in a single day. The slaughter was witnessed by a passing Swiss businessman, who found himself helping local farmers' wives to aid the wounded, since the armies themselves did little in this respect. Henri Dunant wrote a book about his experiences, which led to the establishment of the International Committee of the Red Cross and the introduction of the subsequent Geneva Conventions to improve the treatment of the sick and wounded in war, as well as of civilians and prisoners-of-war.

For the soldier on the battlefield, ironically, the increased firepower now available has made his life far less hazardous, and this has been a major factor in the reduced rate of battle casualties in modern wars. Yet this very same improvement in the machines of death has made the existence of civilians possibly more dangerous than at any other time

In spite of the tremendous increase in firepower since the 1850s and 1860s, battle losses at the rate of those suffered at Solferino have been extremely rare. At the height of World War I, the German army was losing 40,000 to 50,000 men a month. The Americans lost that number in ten years of fighting in Indochina. The reasons for this are many. They include changes in battle tactics, the replacement of manpower by firepower, and improved medical evacuation and treatment services. Thus, during World War II, the USA expended 1,100 kilogrammes (2,420 lb) of munitions for each enemy soldier killed. During the Korean war, this figure rose to 5,600 kg (12,320 lb), and during the Indochina war, to 17,800 kg (39,160 lb). At the same time, the rate of US battle deaths declined from 9.2 to 3.6 per thousand men between World War II and Vietnam.

If warfare has become 'safer' for the soldier on the battlefield, the great increase in firepower and the carrying capacity and range of the means of delivery has put civilian populations in quite a different situation. Although, to some extent, the notion of front lines remains (in the military acronym, FEBA – Forward Edge of the Battle Area), battle areas may range over thousands of square kilometres of territory. The massive use of area weapons – even excluding nuclear, chemical and biological weapons – can cause unprecedented disruption of the natural and man-made environments, with severe short-term and long-term effects for human, animal and plant populations.

Advances in the technology of death in war are largely responsible for many of the changes noted above. Armed men with hand weapons continued to be the primary factor in land war until the development of long-range magazine rifles and quick-firing artillery towards the end of the nineteenth century. So effective were these weapons that neither bayonet-armed infantry nor cavalry could cross the no-man's-land separating opposing forces without suffering unacceptably high casualties. The new weapons increased the width of the divide from some 200 metres – the range of the older muskets – to about 1,000. It took about 30 seconds to load a musket from the muzzle, about the same time it took the cavalry to cross 200 metres, but the more rapidly loaded breech-loading rifles, and the high-powered ammunition which soon followed, changed this situation forever.

If the musket was the mainstay of the eighteenth-century infantryman and the quick-loading rifle its equivalent in the nineteenth, then thereafter it would be the machine gun and trench tool that would come to dominate the battlefield. Tragically, the truth of this failed to penetrate the thinking of the general staffs until the corpses of fallen infantrymen lay wrapped around the barbed wire at the Somme and Verdun

Left
Although Baron Dominique-Jean Larrey (1766-1842), a military surgeon in the service of Napoleon I, was the pioneer of medical aid on the battlefield, his fame has been eclipsed by that of Florence Nightingale, who organized a nursing corps – seen here on the field of Inkerman, 5 November 1854 – for service during the Crimean War

Bottom left
Prussian cavalry charge French infantry at Rezonville, 16 August 1870, in the Franco-Prussian War. The repulse of cavalry by foot-soldiers armed with breech-loading, bolt-action rifles foreshadowed the demise of the 'arme blanche' in the face of the magazine rifle and machine gun, which came about by World War I

By the end of the century, a Polish banker, Ivan Bloch, was pointing out that, thenceforth, a spade would become as important to the soldier as his rifle. His words were ignored by many military men at the time—but they proved only too prophetic in the trench warfare of World War I.

Bloch also proved correct in his assessment that the outcome of war would, in future, be determined more by the capacity of industrial societies to pour out munitions and men, than by the cut and thrust of the sabre and lance. As the men in the front lines were forced to dig in, heavier munitions were brought to bear in ever greater numbers, and it was only the development of the tank and the aircraft which finally offered a vastly increased measure of battlefield mobility.

The introduction of compulsory military service and the enormous productive capacity made possible by the Industrial Revolution provided the means for battles on a vastly increased scale. During the Napoleonic period, a battle front might be 10 km (6 miles), with perhaps three to four cannon to a km. A hundred years later, battle fronts could exceed 100 km (62 miles), with 50 to 100 guns to a km. By World War II, battle lines in Central Europe exceeded 2,000 km (1,240 miles), and sometimes 200 to 300 guns to a km could be brought to bear. At the same time, the depth of battle lines increased. It was no longer a question of direct fire at specific targets, but rather the systematic blanketing of areas of territory, square kilometre by square kilometre, with lethal densities of ammunition.

These trends have continued since World War II. Fighting forces have become steadily more mechanized. The US Army calculates that the size of the battlefield on which a single armoured division would operate is 30-60 km (19-38 miles) in width and up to 100 km (62 miles) in depth. The firepower available to a Soviet mechanized rifle division increased 25 times between 1945 and 1968. Air power has become increasingly important, accounting for nearly 25 percent of the munitions expended by US forces in Korea and some 50 percent in Vietnam. The USA expended 26 times

Human Toll
At the peak of World War I, the German army were losing between 40 and 50 thousand men per month

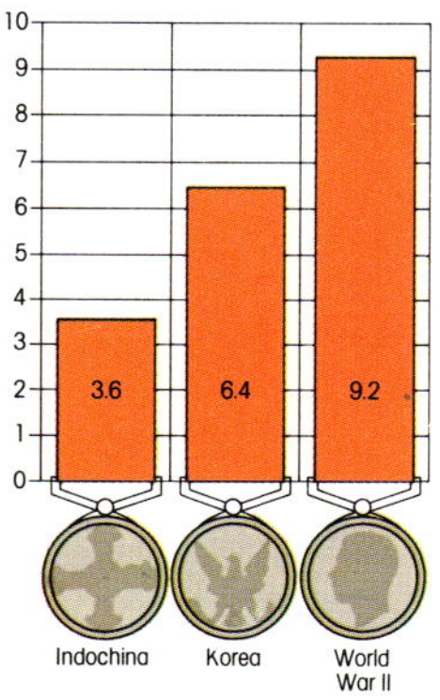

Battle Deaths Decline
In the three major wars involving US soldiers since 1939, the rate of deaths (per 1000 man-years) declined by almost two-thirds

Multiplied Devastation
It has been calculated that the effects of the atomic bombs on Hiroshima and Nagasaki were the equivalent of 1,000 tons of incendiary bombs

Twice Honoured
Only three men have won the Victoria Cross more than once – one having received the second award posthumously

Indirect Slaughter
At the end of the nineteenth century, small arms were responsible for around 90 percent of war casualties. By World War II, this figure had fallen nearer to 30 percent – mainly because of the increased use of high explosive shells and bombs

as much ammunition for each front-line combat soldier in the war in Vietnam as in World War II.

The trend from armed men to manned arms is reflected in the ratio of combat to support troops. This changing ratio explains in part the declining percentage of men in the armed forces who become casualties—an ever-diminishing proportion of them are actually doing the fighting. Changing technology is also reflected in casualty patterns. The nineteenth century was characterized by an increasing proportion of casualties from small arms fire, and a decreasing proportion from edged weapons. Small arms accounted for about 90 percent of the casualties by the end of the century. Again, by World War II, casualties from small arms had declined to about 30 percent, while nearly 70 percent were due to fragmentation weapons—mainly high-explosive shells and bombs.

One tactical nuclear weapon can wreak as much destruction in a second as 100 guns firing 18,000 high-explosive shells in half an hour. Nuclear bombs are mainly an incendiary weapon. The effect of the atomic bombs dropped on Japan in 1945 was the same as that of 1,000 tons of incendiary bombs

Large-scale area attacks along extended front lines of considerable depth require enormous quantities of munitions. An artillery officer, looking up the tables with which he is provided, might calculate that, to cover a target area of one square kilometre would require, say, 18,000 shells—some 30 minutes' firing by 100 guns. From this perspective it becomes a rational step to resort to a tactical nuclear weapon, or perhaps a dose of nerve gas, which can do the same job in an instant with far fewer logistical problems.

A tactical nuclear warhead of, say, 10 kilotons (that is, the equivalent in explosive power of 10,000 tons of TNT) might have a radius of effect, for military purposes, of perhaps 1,000 metres. In order to neutralize front lines several thousand kilometres long and 50 or more in depth, it might require several thousand tactical nuclear weapons. This is no doubt the explanation of the fact that there are more than 10,000 such weapons stationed in Europe alone.

Military strategists assume that, within a relatively short time of a nuclear attack, it would be possible to drive rapidly through the area in modern armoured vehicles. The *physical* damage from such an attack would not necessarily be greater than from a conventional attack with massed artillery and air power, although a conventional attack of such dimensions would take much more time. It is impossible to predict how severely the simultaneous use of many tactical nuclear weapons would affect the surrounding environment, but it is important to realize that conventional mass attacks, too, can cause severe, widespread and long-term damage to the environment.

Nuclear weapons are arguably more of an incendiary than a blast or radiation weapon. It has been calculated that the effect of the atomic bombs dropped on Hiroshima and Nagasaki was about the equivalent of 1,000 tons of incendiary bombs. Indeed, official estimates at the time showed that the fire-bomb raids on Tokyo and Dresden caused more casualties than the two A-bomb attacks. The A-bombs emitted about 50 percent of their energy as blast, 35 percent as heat and the rest as radiation. However, the thermal radiation from the heat was so intense that it caused direct burn casualties and secondary fires far from the centre of the explosion. The rather shallow flash-burns resulting from heat radiation might not look so dramatic as blast injuries, but, in the conditions of a mass attack, where medical facilities are limited or non-existent, may result in a higher death rate. Thus, of nearly 42,000 fairly serious burn cases reported among the survivors on the day after the Hiroshima A-bomb attack, 23.3 percent died subsequently. Of the 45,000 surviving blast casualties, 7.7 percent died, as did 15 percent of the 38,000 surviving radiation casualties.

The high incidence of 'flash-burns' from thermal radiation is peculiar to nuclear weapons. Conven-

Areas of War
During the Napoleonic period, an average battlefront would measure around ten kilometres, with between three or four cannons per kilometre. By World War II, battlefronts were over 2,000 kilometres and sometimes between 200 and 300 guns per kilometre were used

A Thing of the Past
There were more soldiers killed at Cannae than all the RAF personnel killed in both World Wars

Right
Fulfilling prophecies that in modern war the power of the spade might equal that of the rifle, the Western Front had, by late 1914, bogged down in trench lines from the Swiss border to the Channel. Not until the advent of the tank was the deadlock broken

Bottom right
An unknown soldier of World War I: one of an estimated 7.6 million killed in 1914-18. The 'war to end war' finally destroyed the myth of the 'glory' of battle: the literature that it inspired, much of it written by serving soldiers, emphasized the insane horror of war rather than patriotism, heroism or self-sacrifice—and expressed a profound contempt for political and military leaders

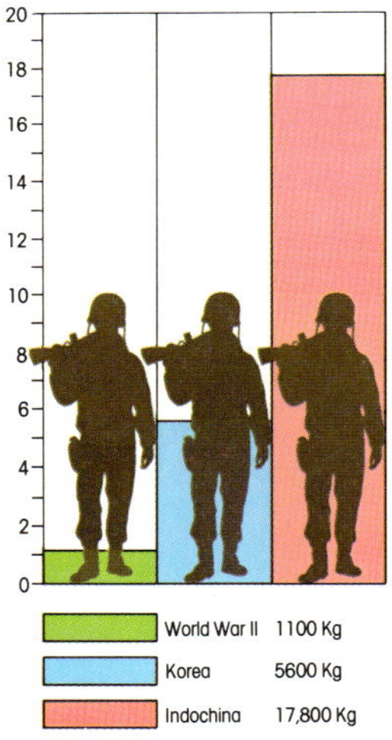

Munitions of Murder
Since World War II, the quantity of shells and small-arms ammunition expended by US forces for each enemy soldier killed rose dramatically from a low 1100 kg to almost 18000 kg

Speed Kills
In the 30 Years' War, which took place between 1618 and 1648, it took thirty years to kill over seven million people. Now that can be achieved in less than thirty hours

tional incendiary bombs cause 'flame-burns', due to actual contact with fire. In incendiary attacks, many victims are engulfed in fire. This causes high immediate mortality and fewer first-day survivors.

In recent years, new forms of incendiary weapon have been developed, producing a fireball which, like nuclear weapons, emits sufficient radiant energy to cause third-degree burns to people in the vicinity but not actually in contact with it. The USA has introduced small rockets of this kind to be fired by infantrymen and shells to be fired by tanks, thus turning any tank into a potential mobile flame-thrower. It is possible that fireball weapons of this kind may replace napalm bombs and flame-throwers, unless efforts at the United Nations to ban incendiary weapons are successful.

Nuclear war differs from conventional war because of the effects of ionising radiation. High doses of short-term radiation can kill living things, including human beings, extremely rapidly. Lesser doses may result in few ill effects until days, weeks or even years after exposure. For the soldier on the battlefield (not to speak of civilians), this is a particularly insidious aspect of the use of nuclear weapons. He may well be ordered to drive through a contaminated area, and do so without apparent ill effects. Only later will radiation sickness strike him down, although by then he will have completed his mission, so his commander might well regard him as expendable. Long-term radiation effects are even more problematic, since a great many radioactive isotopes of otherwise ordinary substances can spread through the environment, enter into food chains, and accumulate in the body, increasing the incidence of various forms of cancer and the frequency of genetic defects in babies. Much of this radiation is produced by fall-out, which can cover large areas. The radiation produced by the 160 one-

A 30 Year Chance
Alfred Nobel intended that his Peace Prize should be given only six times, once every five years, because he believed that if the world could not reform itself within 30 years 'reversion to barbarism will be inevitable'

Cost of Defence
Military spending around the world reached 400 billion dollars in 1976 – this works out at ten dollars for every man, woman and child alive

Left
A US Marine in Vietnam turns a flame-thrower on a Viet Cong memorial in honour of the dead. As part of the so-called 'pacification programme', entire villages suspected of giving shelter or aid to the Communist guerrillas were destroyed in this way and their inhabitants forcibly resettled elsewhere

Bottom left
Another way of destroying a Vietnamese village – or its inhabitants: a Douglas A-1 Skyraider drops phosphorous bombs. Phosphorous, which ignites spontaneously when exposed to air, and napalm (petrol thickened with aluminium salts) have been extensively used for burning off cover and as anti-personnel weapons since World War II

Casualties of War
Whereas in World War II most battle casualties occurred as a result of shell fragments, during the Vietnam War, most US soldiers were killed by small arms, a smaller percentage from shellfire, and an appreciable number from booby traps and mines

Top right
US commanders in Vietnam based their estimates of enemy dead on the 'body count' – but it was alleged that South Vietnamese civilians were often included in the totals along with dead Viet Cong guerrillas like these

Far top right
Although the bombing of North Vietnam by B-52 Stratofortresses aroused world-wide protest, only 6 percent of a total of 126,515 combat sorties in 1965-73 were made against North Vietnam, while 55 percent were against targets in South Vietnam

Right
Devastation in Cambodia (now Kampuchea) during the civil strife preceding the Communist takeover in 1975. It has been estimated that during the first two years of the Communist regime, some 2 million Cambodians were executed, died of disease or starvation, or perished as a result of economic policies involving the forcible resettlement of city dwellers in areas of agricultural potential

megaton missiles which can be launched by a single Polaris-carrying submarine, if detonated at ground level in order to maximize fall-out, could kill the entire population of Great Britain or West Germany, except for those in fall-out shelters. For this reason, even the tactical use of nuclear weapons in sparsely populated areas would be disastrous.

As knowledge of the effects of weapons increases, so does the ability to produce warheads 'tailor-made' to various missions. A recent example is the so-called 'neutron bomb'. This is a nuclear warhead designed to reduce blast and enhance the amount of short-term radiation in the form of neutrons. Since blast dissipates very rapidly from the point of explosion, a very large blast is required to cover an area of, say, one square kilometre (247 acres). An enhanced radiation weapon can produce lethal radiation over a large area, with a much smaller blast-damage zone. This radiation will kill not only human beings but also animals, plants and even micro-organisms in the soil, with far-reaching consequences for the fertility of the land. The military attraction of the 'neutron bomb' (actually, artillery shells and missiles) is said to be its ability to put tanks out of action by incapacitating the crews. However, to do this over a large area in Central Europe would require considerable numbers of neutron weapons, with irreparable environmental consequences.

Unpredictability reduces the military advantages of using biological weapons. Nerve gases are much more effective. It is almost impossible to provide protection against them, and they are rapid in their effects. One drop on the skin is enough to kill a person within a few minutes

Other weapons of mass destruction include chemical and biological weapons. Many disease vectors have been investigated for possible military use, but the spread of disease takes time and is rather unpredictable. This unpredictability reduces the military advantages of biological weapons, which is, perhaps, why the great powers were able to agree on the prohibition of these weapons and the destruction of stockpiles. The Convention entered

into force on March 26, 1975. Chemical weapons, on the other hand, continue to find advocates. There are various categories. Some are designed to be lethal, others incapacitating, and others merely harassing. Some remain active for only a short time, while others are more persistent. Chlorine and phosgene, which were used in World War I, are potentially lethal, but huge amounts are required in order to cover large areas with a sufficiently powerful concentration. Although their use aroused much concern in World War I, leading to the Geneva Protocol of 1925 which prohibited chemical and bacteriological weapons, they had rather low death rates. The so-called 'nerve gases' were developed during World War II, though they were not used. Large amounts of Tabun (military designation: GA; chemical name: ethyl NN-dimethylphosphoramidocyanidate) were produced. Today there are substantial stockpiles of GB (iso-propyl methylphosphonofluoridate) and VX (Ethyl S-2-diisopropylaminoethyl methylphosphonothiolate) nerve gases. These substances inhibit the transmission of acetylcholine between the synapses. A single drop on the skin, or the inhalation of a minute amount in the form of a finely dispersed aerosol, is sufficient to kill a person in a few minutes. It is very difficult, if not impracticable, to provide adequate protection against nerve gases, the use of which in addition to immediate military consequences, would also have dramatic—and undesirable—political and psychological consequences.

Harassing agents and herbicides were widely used by the USA in Vietnam. CS, popularly known as a 'tear gas', was a finely divided powder, which was pumped into tunnels or spread by a variety of means over open spaces. In a confined space it could be lethal, particularly to children and old or sick people. The USA procured nearly seven million kg of CS during the Vietnam war. Herbicides were used to defoliate trees and to destroy growing crops. More than 22,000 square kilometres (5,434,000 acres) were sprayed, of which almost a tenth was farmland. Spraying was discontinued after laboratory studies showed that dioxin, a contaminant in the chemicals used, produced birth defects. It is widely suspected that these chemicals, which are used for commercial purposes, cause liver cancer and other diseases.

In the absence of a chemical disarmament treaty, which has been awaited for some time, the USA has developed so-called 'binary chemical weapons'. In these, two relatively innocuous substances combine to produce a lethal nerve gas when a warhead detonates. A major function of these weapons is to ease the logistic and storage problems associated with nerve gases, thereby allaying public concern about storage sites, where leaks have been reported. In 1978, the USA announced that it would replace some of its stocks of chemical weapons because of such leaks, but the disposal of nerve gases also entails hazards.

Rapid battlefield evacuation techniques have vastly increased the chances of survival of troops wounded in battle. For United States soldiers in World War II, the average time between wounding and treatment was 10.5 hours. In Vietnam (1968) this time was cut to 2.8 hours

The prognosis for men wounded in battle has improved remarkably as a result of developments in military medicine and surgery. However, even more noteworthy, perhaps, is the introduction of rapid battlefield evacuation techniques.

By the end of the last century the efforts of the Red Cross had resulted in armies beginning to take on more responsibility for removing and caring for the wounded. Just the same, they might still have to wait until the end of the day before they could be piled into a horse-drawn ambulance. This waiting time was considerably reduced in World War I, when ambulance units, some of them run by voluntary organizations like the Quakers, became a regular feature of the battle zones. By World War II, not only motorized ambulances, but also aircraft, were being used to take the wounded to hospital. Recently there have been two major innovations in battlefield evacuation procedures. In Vietnam, the USA relied extensively on helicopters ('Dust Off') to remove the wounded directly from the battlefield—usually within 40 minutes, but sometimes in as little as 10. This was the spearhead of a highly efficient transport system

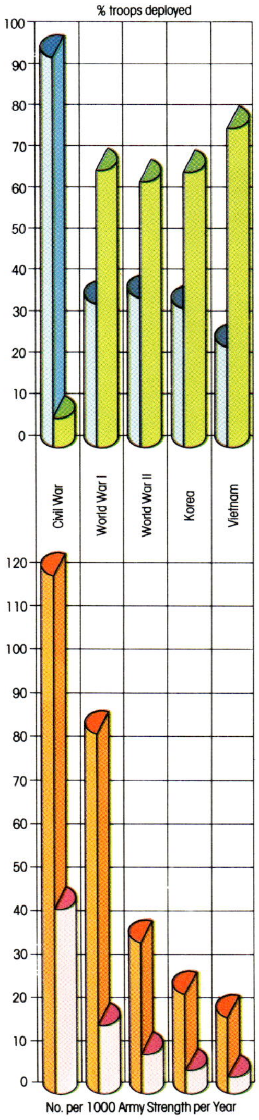

Armed Men to Manned Arms
The trend from armed men to manned arms is reflected in the ratio of combat to support troops. This changing ratio explains in part the declining number of casualties in terms of the number of men in the armed forces: it is evident that an ever-diminishing fraction are actually doing the fighting

Top left
Death of a jungle: a result of 'Operation Ranch Hand', the US Air Force's programme of defoliation and crop destruction in Vietnam by the spraying of herbicides. Initiated in 1962, such operations ceased in 1970 after investigation of their effect on human births

Left
This lunar landscape is a South Vietnamese forest cratered by US bombing. Damage to the environment apart, casualties caused by aerial bombardment in Vietnam were relatively low: it was estimated that each sortie by a B-52 Stratofortress (with up to 31,750 kg 70,000 lb, of conventional bombs) resulted in an average of only 0.7-3.4 deaths

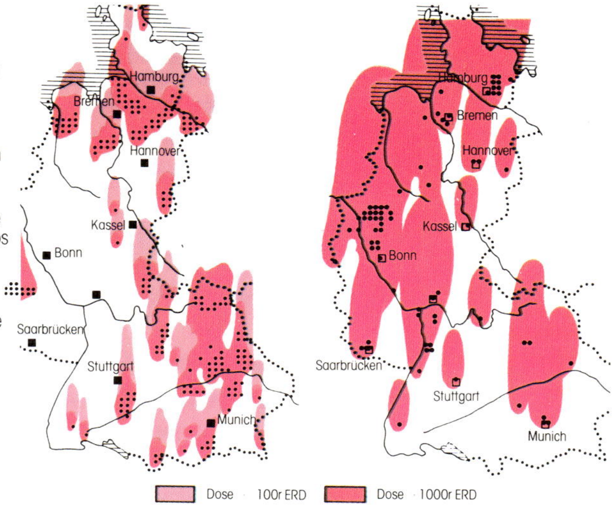

Right
Radiation deaths that could be expected from the blanket use of tactical or strategic weapons on West Germany. The lefthand diagram shows the radioactive contamination resulting from an attack with 800 20 kiloton bombs. The righthand diagram shows the effects of 76 2-megaton bombs

Far right
Children of South Vietnamese Air Force personnel fleeing the Communist entry into Saigon in April 1975 are carried aboard a US warship. The flow of refugees from Vietnam still continues, and many 'boat people' have died while attempting to sail to freedom

Right
Giving war another name cannot lessen its bitter inhumanity: Japan's attack on China in 1937 was designated the 'Sino-Japanese Incident' – but for this Chinese baby abandoned among the ruins of Shanghai after an air raid, it may as well be the end of the world

using specially equipped aircraft to fly patients all the way to the United States, if need be.

For US soldiers in World War II, the average time between wounding and treatment was 10.5 hours; in Korea, 6.3 hours; and in Vietnam (1968), 2.8 hours. Reducing this time-lag has had a dramatic effect on mortality rates. One study has shown that the death rate can be cut to 7 percent if patients are operated upon within eight hours. This rises to 14 percent within 12 hours, 22 percent within 24 hours, and 30 percent when a delay of 48 hours occurs. A different approach was adopted by Israel in 1973, when doctors in specially equipped rescue vehicles accompanied the troops into battle. Many doctors were lost as a consequence, but the medical results were impressive. Rapid evacuation has been matched by many improvements in military medicine and surgery. Penicillin and other drugs introduced during World War II greatly reduce wound infection. New surgical techniques, like delayed primary suture, also reduce wound mortality. It should be noted, however, that most wars since World War II have taken place in developing countries which do not have much in the way of medical facilities. For example, although the 'Viet Cong' was quite successful in providing primary medical care for troops and the civilian population, its technological standard was low – on a level with that prevailing at the time of the Civil War in the United States. Surgery was rarely possible within 48 hours, and it must be assumed that death rates exceeded 30 percent.

The number of soldiers killed in battle even in recent wars, can only be estimated within broad limits, since the relevant statistics are sketchy. Civilian casualties are even more of an unknown quantity and can only be guessed at. Some experts believe that as many as ten million people died in China's civil war

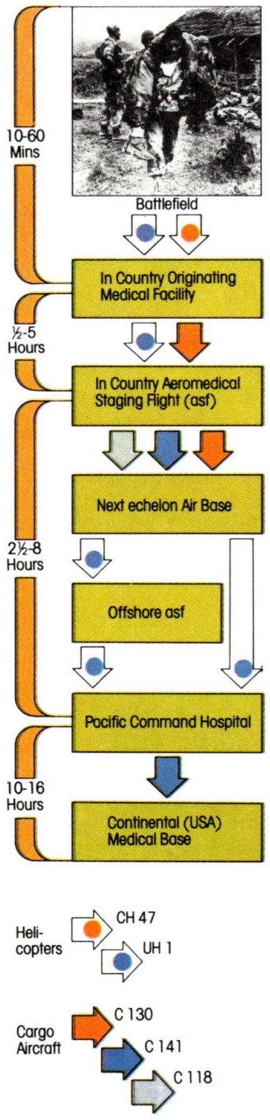

Evacuating the Wounded
As a result of the remarkably effective medical evacuation system in Vietnam, many US battle casualties who would have died on the battlefield in previous campaigns were saved in front-line medical facilities, and then extremely rapidly flown on to hospital bases offshore, or to medical bases in the US

Nobody knows with much accuracy how many soldiers have died in battle, even in recent wars. One reason is that, out of considerations of morale and national security, many governments are reticent about collecting and publishing such statistics. Another is that, in the heat of battle, no one has time to bother about statistics. Medical personnel are usually worked off their feet coping with casualties, and have no time to spare for form-filling. Only a very well-endowed army can maintain accurate statistics of its own and enemy losses. There are also technical medical reasons for the sparseness of accurate statistics. Usually, there are two categories of battle deaths: KIA (killed in action) and DOW (died of wounds). However, so rapid are modern evacuation methods, that many soldiers who would previously have been categorized as KIA arrive at the medical facility still living, even though they cannot be saved. The borderline between KIA and DOW is thus a nebulous one. The wounded may be sent on through a chain of hospitals, making it increasingly difficult to keep track of their fate. In some cases, initial problems, like haemorrhage and shock, may be overcome, but the patient may succumb weeks, months or even years later, as a result of infection, complications or cancers induced by the injury. Yet, after a certain time, late deaths may no longer be included in the statistics.

It is even more difficult to estimate enemy casualty rates. In Vietnam the US Command produced every week what were claimed to be precise 'body counts' of enemy casualties. However, these were almost meaningless, since the pilot of a B-52 flying at 10,000 metres (33,000 ft) has no means of knowing how many people are killed by the 25 tons of bombs he drops. Only in a few cases were follow-up counts

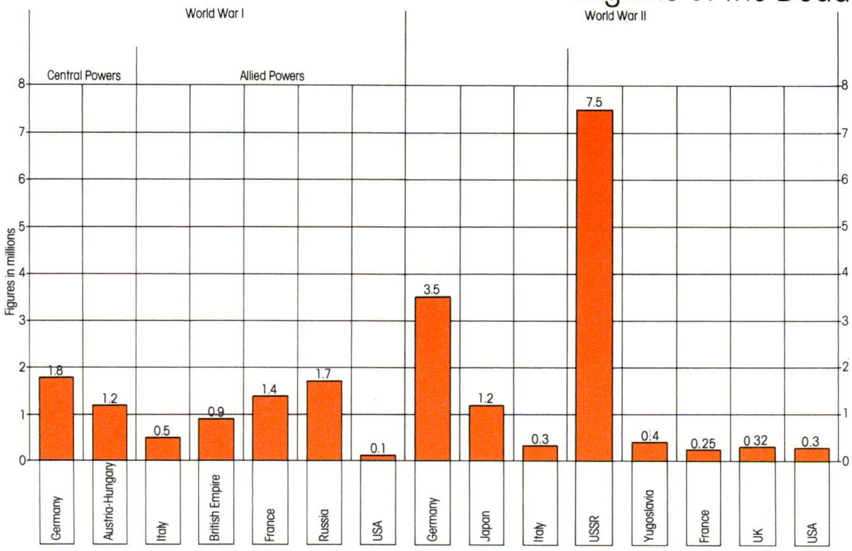

Ghost Armies
The total numbers of soldiers killed from each of the major participants in World War I and World War II, divided into Central and Allied Powers (WWI) and Axis and Allied Powers (WWII). Germany and Russia-USSR lost the most men in both world wars

Above left
US casualties in Vietnam await ambulance helicopters. All too often, the narrowing of the gap between wounding and hospitalization (to an average 2.8 hours) meant only that men died in hospital instead of in the field

Left
A wounded man receives plasma in the field in Vietnam. The proportion of deaths from small-arms fire rose from 32 percent in World War II and 33 percent in Korea to 51 percent in Vietnam, because of the increased use of automatic weapons firing lightweight, high-velocity ammunition

done on the ground. (They showed an average of 0.7 to 3.4 dead per B-52 per sortie, hardly an impressive figure.) In operations involving air and ground forces, both may report the same casualties, and extensive use of unobserved, indirect artillery fire makes it impossible to add up the dead. While there is no doubt that the huge quantities of munitions used in Indochina resulted in many casualties, there are good reasons for treating the official American figures of enemy casualties with hesitation, although they are the only figures available. According to these figures, nearly a million North Vietnamese and NLF troops died, compared with more than 200,000 South Vietnamese Government forces and more than 40,000 US troops. In addition, the USA lost a further 10,000 men from 'non-hostile' causes, such as disease, accidents and murder. This illustrates a further problem with casualty statistics—should these additional casualties be added to the total or not? It is undoubtedly the case that, of the nine million or so US soldiers who served in Vietnam, a number would have died, statistically speaking, even without the war. However, it is probable that the tropical climate and wartime conditions made death from disease and accident more likely.

Even less information is available about civilian casualties in recent wars. According to the most common estimates, about five percent of the casualties in World War I were civilians, and about 50 percent in World War II. In Korea, the proportion may have been even higher, yet in spite of the fact that the Korean War was a United Nations undertaking, there are no adequate statistics. Estimates range from less than one million civilian deaths to two, three or even four million.

In general, the number of civilian casualties in major wars, such as the civil war in China, the Algerian war or the wars in Indochina, can only be guessed at. But there are estimates that, in each case the number of civilians who died equals or exceeds the 500,000 to 600,000 civilians who died as a result of the mass area attacks on Germany or on Japan during World War II. The death rate in China is the greatest single source of uncertainty in postwar casualty estimates. Some people believe the civil war toll may have been as high as ten million. Even before that, authoritative estimates of civilian casualties in China in the war with Japan amount to 1.4 million—two or three times the civilian casualty toll in Japan or Germany.

There are other reasons for believing that, devastating though air attacks on cities are, the civilian population may fare worse if it is crushed between land armies. This is particularly true when

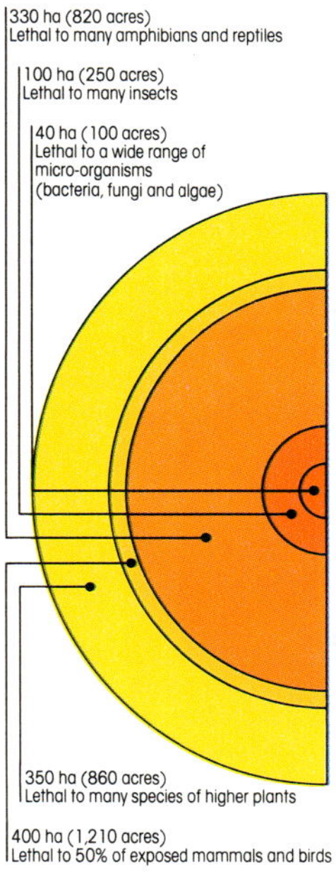

Enhanced Radiation Weapon
Neutron weapons maximize radiation and reduce blast effects, killing living organisms over a wide area, but causing more limited damage to property, ie buildings and weapons

the increase in population is taken into account. However, populations which decline as the result of war usually begin to increase within a few years, and affected countries experience a 'baby boom'. Thus, despite the views of Malthus—and some present-day cynics—war is not effective as a means of population control. Its effect is to increase the dependent part of the population (young children and invalids), and reduce the productive part (mainly men in the 15 to 40 age group). The consequence is that the increased burden of long-term debts and other social expenditures caused by fighting a war has to be shouldered by a population whose human resources have been depleted because of it.

War has always been accompanied by massacres and torture, sometimes as deliberate policy. Wars of independence have often been characterized by meaningless violence unleashed by the colonial peoples seeking freedom—not against the colonizers, but against each other

Torture, massacre and even, sometimes, extermination have accompanied most wars. In some cases, hatred and pent-up emotions give rise to a brutality which usually exists only in the imagination of diseased minds. In other cases, atrocities have been the result of deliberate policy. It is arguable that atrocities of a spontaneous kind are less frequent in modern combat than previously, simply because there is less direct contact between opposing forces. In civil wars, on the other hand, there is plenty of opportunity for contact—if not always between uniformed combatants, then between civilian supporters of one or other of the two sides. Franz Fanon, writing during the Algerian war,

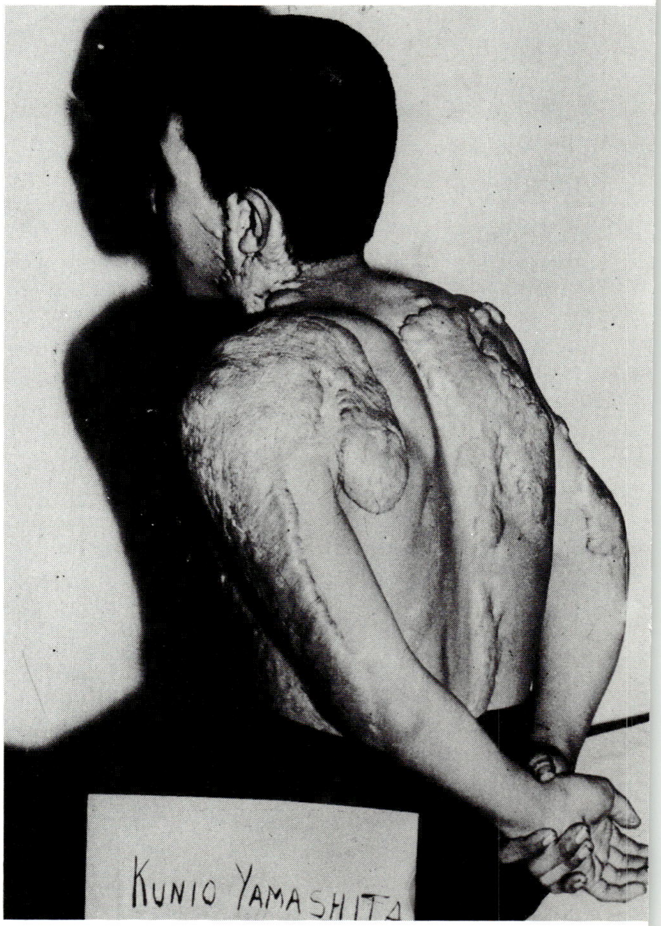

Above
Parodying James Montgomery Flagg's famous recruiting poster of World War I, a battered 'Uncle Sam' makes an anti-Vietnam War protest. War often results in a breakdown in the public's respect for authority

Right
A blast victim of the atomic bomb dropped on Hiroshima. Despite their horrifying appearance, blast injuries proved less deadly than heat radiation burns, which demanded more speedy medical attention

60 Second Holocaust
The one-kiloton Hiroshima A-bomb caused the deaths of 78,500 people in the space of sixty seconds, and more than double that number in the following decades

Halving a City
One out of every two people in Hiroshima at the time of the dropping of the world's first atom bomb perished: a total of about 240,000

these armies attempt to 'pacify' the civilian population by repression, the use of many as slave labour, deportation or deliberate extermination. The Soviet Union, Yugoslavia and Germany lost about 10 percent of their population during World War II, while Poland lost nearly 20 percent.

Of course, civilians do not die in war only as the result of direct hostile action. There are indirect deaths from disease, malnutrition and, if their homes are destroyed, from cold or heat. In the siege of Leningrad, in Holland and, more recently, in Biafra, hundreds of thousands of civilians died from starvation as a result of blockade. Low levels of nutrition contributed to the spread of epidemic diseases after World War I, which killed almost as many people as the war itself. In many cases, the stress of war decreases fertility, as well as increasing the number of non-medical abortions and infant deaths. Infant mortality rates are a sensitive indicator of a society's ability to provide for basic needs. During World War II, rationing was introduced in some countries. In Britain and Norway, for example, infant mortality rates decreased slightly, because of better nutrition, but elsewhere, infant mortality rates increased substantially. By the end of the war, the infant mortality rate in Berlin had risen to 359 per thousand—about three times the level of today's least developed countries, illustrating the total collapse of normal life-support systems.

More people have died as a result of war in this century than in any other. This holds true even if

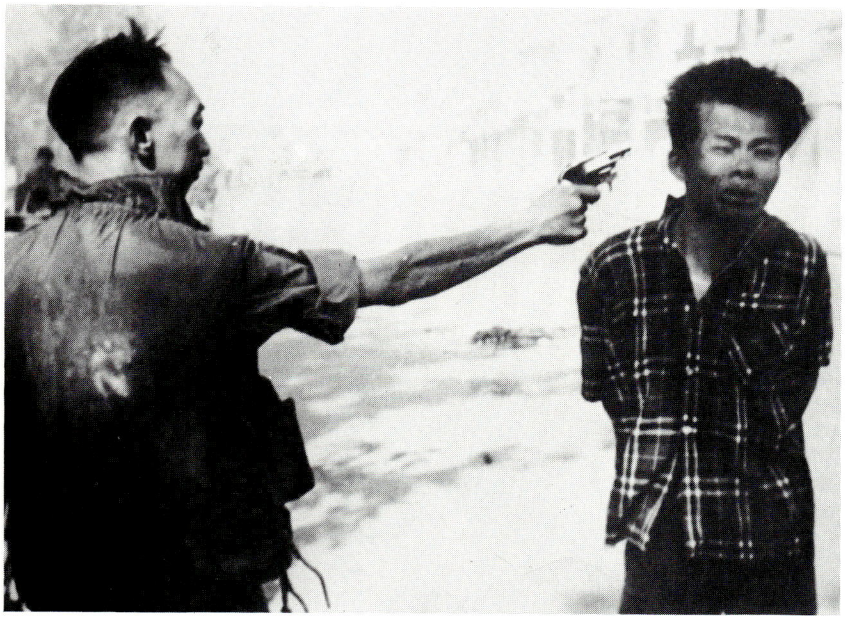

War	Years	Side for which data pertains	Disease mortality	Military mortality	Ratio
Napoleonic-Hait (San Domingo)	1802-1803	French	20,000 out of 30,000 French troops disabled by disease alone		
Napoleonic-Peninsular campaign	1808-1814	French	400,000	60,000	6.7:1
Crimean War	1854-1856	both	177,317	61,745	2.8:1
US Civil War	1861-1865		60%	40%	1.5:1
Boer War	1899-1920	British	14,200	7,785	2:1
Spanish-American War	1896	US	3,704	700	5:1
World War I	1917-1918	US	51,547	55,780	1:1
World War II	1941-1945	US	15,799	296,514 (75.2% were from battle casualties)	

commented on the meaningless violence unleashed by colonized peoples against one another, rather than against the colonizers. One reason for it may be the skilful way in which the colonial powers employed the policy of 'divide and rule', so that liberation armies are 'programmed', as it were, to kill each other, in the general climate of suspicion.

Battle conditions can create their own psychological tensions leading to a breakdown of normal discipline. The Mai Lai massacre in Vietnam is an example. The soldiers concerned are said to have been particularly nervous because so many of their fellows had become casualties from mines, booby-traps and sniper fire. Once wild shooting begins, it is very difficult for an individual to resist group pressures or the irrational command of an officer. A further factor is military training itself. In extreme cases, a deliberate effort is made to break down the individual's normal personality and replace it with a dehumanized 'killer' personality subordinate to a non-commissioned officer, for example. The resulting complex psychological effects may enable such soldiers to commit atrocities, but, at the same time, they produce a psychological burden equivalent to profound grief, which requires psychiatric treatment. It has been repeatedly reported that attempts are being made to produce assassins by means of such psychological techniques as drug treatment, and various 'Pavlovian'-type training sessions.

The Geneva Convention drawn up in 1864 as a direct result of Henri Dunant's moving account of the Battle of Solferino was the first step towards reducing human suffering in war. It was followed by others, which have been greatly expanded over the years, most recently by the adoption of two new protocols in 1977, which are now awaiting ratification by governments. The Conventions seek to alleviate the horrors of war and to eliminate some of its worst excesses by institutionalizing the role of medical units on the battlefield, drawing up guidelines for the treatment of prisoners-of-war, and trying to persuade combatants to respect civilians. Of course, drawing up rules on paper is one thing, and abiding by them in the heat of war is another. Nevertheless, there can be no doubt that the Geneva Conventions—and the public opinion behind them—do have a positive impact on the conduct of war. The 1977 protocols, one on international war and one on internal war, rule out the mass area bombing of inhabited areas, the destruction of crops, the bombing of dams and nuclear power stations, and the destruction of the environment.

It has been asserted that, if followed, these new rules would substantially affect the nature of war! Would that be bad? In the meantime, however, more sophisticated means of warfare are being developed and are proliferating rapidly. How many more will join the legions of the dead before the battle between the technologies of death and the technologies of life (medicine, agriculture and education) is fought out? And will the technologies of life win?

Above
Dramatic improvements in military medicine and surgery have changed the face of death in war. Prior to World War II, more soldiers died from disease and sickness than from combat wounds and other injurious effects of war

Top
South Vietnamese police chief Nguyen Ngoc Loan executes a Viet Cong officer captured during the 'Tet offensive' of early 1968. Pubiication of this picture aroused a world-wide storm of anti-war protest

Above left
The end of the 'paths of glory': the Ossuary of Solferino, where the skulls of some 7,000 of the soldiers who fell in the battle that inspired Henri Dunant to found the Red Cross are preserved

Costly Battle
The USA expended 26 times as much ammunition per front line combat soldier in Vietnam as in World War II

Tons of Tears
The USA produced nearly seven million tons of 'tear gas' during the Vietnam war

The End of Life

Despite our anxieties about the threat of natural catastrophe, the arrival of a lethal new disease or a nuclear war, nothing but the end of time is ever likely to bring death to all life

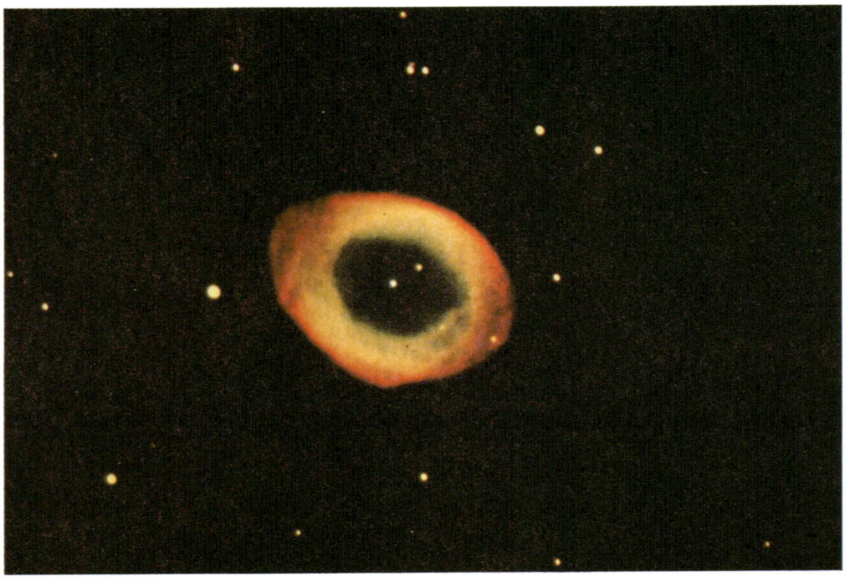

Above
The ring nebula in Lyra ('The Harp'), discovered some 2,400 years ago by the Greek astronomer, Eudoxus. Lyra contains Vega, which is the second brightest star in the entire Northern Hemisphere. There are about a hundred billion stars in our galaxy, the Milky Way, and a hundred billion in the universe. Many are thought to have planets which could support life

Right
Earth, which is some 4,600 million years old and has been inhabited by some form of life for at least two thirds of that time. Since all life on earth depends on the sun, it will come to an end when the sun dies – but this will not happen for another four billion years and, before then, man may succeed in escaping to another planet, there to continue perpetuating the human race

An Orgy of Destruction
At the end of its life the sun will not simply fade away like an exhausted log fire. Instead, it will expand until it has increased its volume 40 million times. Also, all the hydrogen in the core of the sun will be converted into helium, which itself will heat up to 200 million degrees F, and the fatal Helium Flash will occur. This will be the beginning of the explosion that will rip the surface of the sun apart and turn the fiery core of the star into a red giant

Death, as most of us see it, is the end of an individual's life – an individual human being or an individual animal, an individual man or an individual mouse. Untold hordes of men have died, and even greater hordes of mice, but every one of them died as a single being. Nevertheless, if we look beyond ourselves, broaden our perspective, we come to realize that, important though they are, individuals are not what ultimately matter. We should think about the death of all men, all mice – and, eventually, the end of all life as we know it.

It is possible to assert with some confidence that, in a developed society, a normally healthy man of 35 can reasonably expect to live another 35 years, and a woman of 35 slightly longer. But is it possible to say how long the human species will last? The answer is 'No', at least not with any certainty. Global annihilation may well be just around the corner. On the other hand, before our 35-year-old reaches the age of 50, we may well be able to promise him immortality.

The sun, the basis of all life on earth, *will* die. Of that there is no doubt. But perhaps we will escape to another, younger star before it does, there to start the ball rolling again. Indeed, there are those who think that some kind of inter-stellar seeding is responsible for the existence of life on earth and hence, for our existence. Comforting though this may be to some, it does not answer the more fundamental questions of who did the seeding and what happened to these inter-galactic farmers.

If we do manage to leapfrog across space, or to transfer some very primitive life forms to another fertile planet, where they could act as seeds, and if those seeds evolve and grow until, eventually, they, too, have to escape a dying sun, will we have achieved some kind of immortality? Will life in the end run out of places to run to, as the universe itself comes to an end in 15,000 million years time?

Above
As man extends his conquest of space, he will not only people other planets, but will also undoubtedly set up space colonies like that shown here, which was conceived in the course of a study in America. In this artist's impression, part of the colony is under construction. The louvres, shown being installed, are to reflect sunshine inside

Right
How a space habitat would look at night. In addition to living accommodation for thousands of people, it would also have areas set aside for agriculture. As crops are a great deal less sensitive to radiation than human beings, these areas would not need shielding against cosmic rays

Right centre
A space habitat which would accommodate 10,000 people. It would rotate, to provide them with gravity similar to that on earth, and would be shielded against cosmic rays and solar flares. The habitat would be 1.6 kilometres (a mile) in circumference. The large disc above the habitat is designed to radiate away its waste heat into the cold of outer space

End of the Earth
The earth is now around 4,600 million years old. It is estimated that in 1000 million years time, the sun's hydrogen fuel will run out, causing its middle to collapse and greatly increase in heat. This heat will kill all life on earth, while at the same time causing the outer layer of the sun to expand, engulfing the earth altogether after a few hundred thousand years, all the planets up to Mars within two or three hundred million years. It can therefore be reasonably assumed that the earth has reached late middle age

These questions are at one and the same time profoundly important and profoundly trivial. It would not matter at all if man, or even all life, ceased to exist tomorrow. Life is an aberrant reversal of some fundamental laws of physics. It has no real right to exist, interfering as it does with the pre-ordained slide into complete chaos. But exist it does, and if there are any characteristics that make man a unique form of life, they are curiosity and power. Curiosity forces us to contemplate futures that we may not be able to do anything about. Power enables us to attempt to direct ourselves into one future rather than another. In the short term, the direction we take is profoundly important. In the long term—the very long term—it is irrelevant.

There is no doubt that within a few billion years the sun will burn itself out. Whether man, or indeed life on earth, survives this catastrophe might seem a completely irrelevant problem: in terms of the fundamental laws of physics, life appears to be nothing more or less than a rather bizarre accident

If you go out into the fields, and count the number of mice of various ages, you will find that the number of each age drops steadily. The main cause of death is being eaten and, as there is an equal chance of being eaten at any age, the likelihood of a mouse surviving from one day to the next is the same no matter how old it is. The picture would be very different if you did an age count for men. At first, the number at each age drops very slowly, but then the decline becomes much steeper, and a large number die within quite a short age-span. Fish show the reverse pattern to man, dying in their millions while very young, but living for long periods if they can survive for a short time at the very beginning of their life.

Both fish and men are said to show age-related mortality—their chances of dying depend on how long they have been alive. In their natural habitat, where they live a normal life, mice do not show this link between age and death, for they are generally killed before they have the chance to die of old age. Nevertheless, bring some mice into a cosy laboratory, where there are no cats, owls or foxes, and you will find that they show roughly the same kind of mortality curve as man.

Nevertheless, the fact remains that men live for three-score years and ten, while mice, even in the laboratory, live for only some three years. Different animals have different life-spans, but still, death is programmed into life. Can we say that man is more

advanced than mice because he holds death at bay for longer? We could, but we would be foolish to do so, because larger animals generally live longer than smaller ones. It would be better to compare the mouse with something its own size—the bat.

The mouse is a generalist, it lives in a variety of places and will eat a variety of foods. The bat is a specialist, restricted in the places it can live and the foods it will eat. The mouse has many natural enemies which depend on it for food, and as a result suffers high mortality. The bat has few predators and enjoys very low mortality. The mouse compensates by breeding prodigiously, up to 45 young in a single year. The bat has only one young per year. The final outcome of the different evolution of mice and bats is a difference in their ability to stave off death. The mouse lives, at most, three years, while the bat can survive for 24. The obvious conclusion is that the bat has indeed found a way to keep death at bay, and if our current theories of death are correct, this must mean that it is able to keep its biochemical factories at work for longer. There are plans to compare the chemical machinery of mice and bats, and scientists predict that the bat's cellular mechanisms will prove to be the more accurate. These more faithful fabricators would accumulate errors more slowly, thereby delaying the inevitable error catastrophe that is death.

Can we find the means, through human selection, to increase man's maximum life-span? Should we be encouraging long-lived people to breed? Could medicine hold the answer to the riddle of man's immortality?

Consistent differences between species often mean that the differences are themselves the product of natural selection, which acts to produce organisms that are as perfectly suited as possible to a particular way of life. Maximum life-span would seem to be just such a difference. We can make great changes by doing some selection ourselves, to produce elk-hound and chihuahua from basic dog, for example, so is there any hope that we can select for longer life, and so delay death?

If there is, it is so slim as to be virtually non-existent, and for a variety of reasons. One is that death comes well after the time during which reproduction is possible. Natural selection has already seen to it that grandparents can be alive to lend parents a hand. Could we augment this by artificial selection, encouraging long-lived people to breed. The answer is 'No', because we would not know at the time of breeding who was going to live longer and who would have a shorter life-span. Nor

Above
Shown here is the trifid nebula in Sagittarius ('The Archer'). Like Lyra, which is also a constellation in the Northern Hemisphere, Sagittarius is mentioned by the fourth century BC Greek astronomer, Eudoxus. When a star begins to die, the burning helium at its core causes the gas 'atmosphere' of the star to expand to tremendous size, turning it into a 'red giant'. When all the helium has been exhausted, the star dies

The San Andreas Fault
This fault marks the boundary of the American and Pacific plates. At the present rate of movement, a person standing on one side of the plate could expect to see an object on the other side move 4 metres (13 feet) during his lifetime

Global Stability
In a cosmic context, the earth is in a reassuringly stable situation at present—there is little fluctuation in the movement of the earth or the sun, and there is unlikely to be any fluctuation for hundreds of millions of years

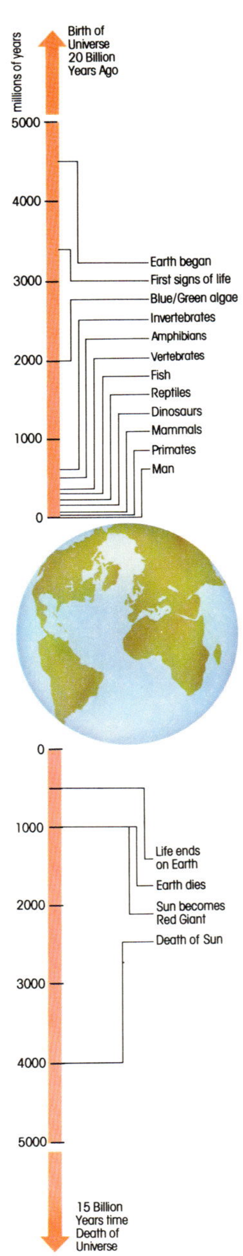

The Beginning and the End
This chart reveals something of the unimaginable time-span of the universe. The 35-billion year evolution of the cosmos embraces the 9 billion-year life of the sun, the 5.6 billion-year span of the earth and the 4 billion-year development of life on this planet. Scientists calculate that during the next 500 million years, the sun will begin the process of turning into a red giant – eventually dying in a brilliant solar explosion. Hundreds of millions of years before this cataclysmic event occurs, all life on earth will have perished, no longer able to resist the intense heat of the earth's atmosphere

could we do away with the children of those whose parents died young. Then again, we would have to choose between those who lived longest before finally dying, and those who were still spry till their last day. The problems are many, and it is clear that selection, natural or artificial, does not hold the power to delay death.

What about medicine? People often say that medicine has made the life of man longer. In a sense this is true, but it is not the whole truth. Reference has already been made to the biblical estimate for man's lifetime—three-score years and ten. Now, regardless of who actually wrote the Bible, it was obviously written well before the advent of modern medicine, yet it contains an estimate that remains true today. This is an estimate that must have been made by a very shrewd observer who ignored the very good chance that an infant would die young.

Modern medicine has not increased man's maximum life-span. What it has done is to enable more people to achieve the maximum possible. *Average* life-span has increased, from about 28 years in early Rome to about 70 nowadays, because nearly everyone in the developed world is able to enjoy his or her allotted span. The span itself is unaltered, however. Further proof of this comes from Chris McManus's careful study of Renaissance painters, who enjoyed a high standard of living because they had wealthy patrons. Their average life-span was 63 years, and the one woman about whom we have information, Sofonisba Anguissola, lived to the spectacular age of 97. Infant mortality, even among future painters, was no doubt very high, and it is this that has declined, thus giving an increase in average life-span.

Perhaps if we cured the diseases that bring death to old people, that would increase our life-span? It would, but not by very much. The discovery, overnight, of a complete cure for all forms of cancer would extend average life expectancy by only two years. This is because cancer is overwhelmingly a disease of the aged, who would still have heart disease and strokes to contend with.

The oft-quoted miracles of modern medicine, from organ transplants to vaccination, have had a dramatic effect on the life-span of the average man —an effect for which we are all grateful—but they have done nothing to stretch the maximum, and it is doubtful whether this can be achieved. Replacing single organs as they fail, with transplants or artificial organs, is no solution, because it is the whole fabric of the body that is falling apart. Nor is there any point in freezing for the future—cryonics. The chances that you would be thawed out, let alone rejuvenated and cured, are as close to nil as makes no difference.

The machinery of the body has a limited useful life, and the only hope for man's immortal soul would be to find another, healthy body to occupy. This has been tried in fiction, but not, to anyone's knowledge, in fact. Even the fictional transfer of an old man's mind to successive new bodies is not without its problems. So it rather looks as if we are stuck with our three-score years and ten.

One way out of the trap set by the ultimate decay of all cellular machinery would be to redesign the machinery. Selection among existing sets of machinery is not the answer, but perhaps we could manufacture a whole new set of cellular machines, which would not accumulate errors and so would

A Fresh Start
The worst possible nuclear holocaust would only destroy advanced forms of life – the process of evolution would then begin again from the thousands of forms of life in the sea, until it reached our present level of civilization

Far left and above
An island is born. Molten lava flows from Surtsey (far left), which began erupting from the seabed off the coast of Iceland in 1963 and continued to erupt until 1965. What Surtsey looks like from the air can be seen above. Volcanic eruptions, like earthquakes, spew enormous quantities of fine dust into the atmosphere. This acts as a screen, stopping some of the sun's energy from reaching the earth. When Krakatoa erupted in 1883, the temperature of the world dropped by two degrees Centigrade

Left
Vesuvius, near Naples, still an active volcano, with the excavated ruins of Pompeii in the foreground. Much of the town had been destroyed by an earthquake in AD 63, and rebuilding was still under way when Vesuvius erupted in AD 79, burying Pompeii under a mass of cinders and ashes

Far left
Surtsey was still erupting in 1965, when another volcanic island rose out of the sea not far away – Syrtlingur, or Little Surtsey. Here, a group of people on Surtsey watch as Syrtlingur begins to take shape. Volcanic eruptions frequently result in great destruction, and sometimes bring death to entire communities. This happened on the island of Martinique in 1902, when Mont Pelée erupted and wiped out the town of St Pierre

last much longer? This is the promise some people see in the new science of genetic engineering, or gene-splicing, but, again, they are likely to be disappointed, for genetic engineering will almost certainly be of no use at all in curing genetic diseases. An example will make clear why.

Genetic engineering, or gene-splicing, can do nothing to cure genetic diseases or to extend our longevity, although it does hold out hope of being able to help individuals by, for instance, making human insulin – the hormone so vital to diabetics

One of the classic simple genetic diseases is sickle-cell anaemia. This affects the haemoglobin in the blood, so that the sufferer cannot get enough oxygen to his tissues. Now, the disease of sickle cell is due to a single wrong amino acid in two of the four protein chains of the haemoglobin molecule. Instead of glutamine we have valine, and this in turn is caused by a single change in the gene that contains the instructions to build the protein chain. The instructions should, in the code of the geneticists, read $\begin{matrix}\text{CTT}\\\text{GAA}\end{matrix}$, which means glutamine. Instead, they read $\begin{matrix}\text{CAT}\\\text{GTA}\end{matrix}$, which means valine, and that simple change is enough to render the vital haemoglobin almost useless.

It would seem to be an easy matter to change the instructions back again, but there is only one such gene in each of the billions of haemoglobin-making cells produced by the body each day. The mistake would have to be corrected in a fair proportion of those cells to have any effect, and that is a tall order. A virus would have to take up the correct gene from normal cells – in itself no mean feat – and then a huge number of these viruses would have to be injected. The injected viruses would have to infect the cells that divide to produce the haemoglobin-making cells and persuade them to take up the new instructions. The odds against success are overwhelming, and because the right type of virus would be very like the 'cancer viruses', it is extremely unlikely that any authority would even consider allowing a trial of the technique.

Migrating to Survive
It has been estimated that by the time the earth has been engulfed by the sun, human technology will have advanced so far that we would have nothing to worry about – man would have the facilities to cope with the death of the earth by moving to another environment – ie a different planetary system

Above
Topped by its canopy of storm cloud, a tornado twists its way across the Oklahoma countryside, where it is unlikely to cause much damage. However, when a tornado hits a built-up area, often at 64 kilometres (40 miles) an hour, it can cause destruction and death

Right
Lava—molten rocks and other mineral matter—flows down the side of a volcano in Iceland. It has cooled from its original white heat, but is still fiercely hot

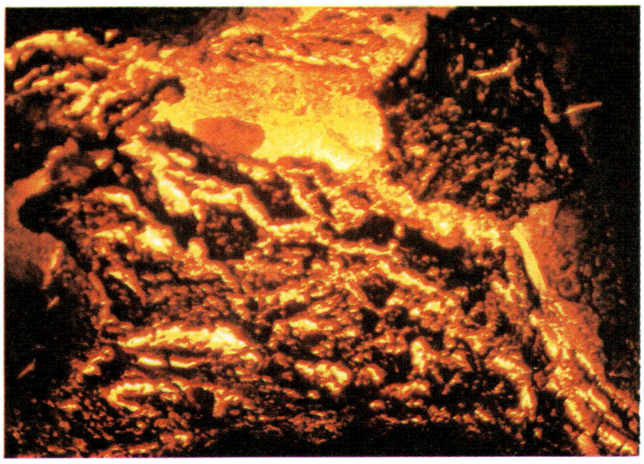

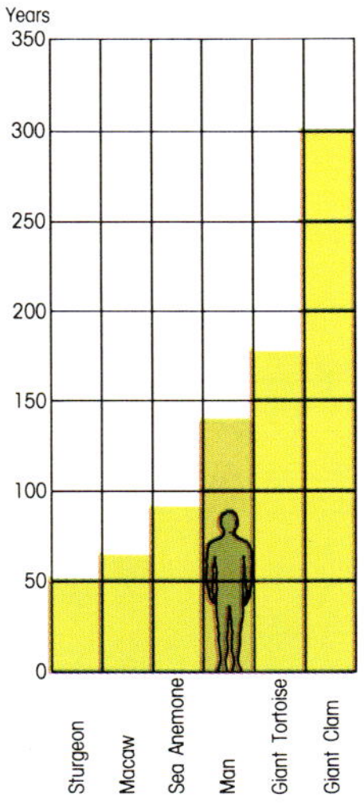

Heroes of Longevity
Examples of longevity of a variety of species, including man. Fierce controversy rages over the factors which apparently aid certain individuals to enjoy long life

Genetic engineering, tinkering with the body's cellular machinery, can subvert a set of machines to make a product for which they are not normally tooled up. Scientists in the USA have successfully engineered bacteria that will make human insulin, the hormone so vital for diabetics. They have even used a virus to transfer the genetic instructions for globin, part of the haemoglobin molecule that transports oxygen in the blood, from the cells of one mammal, a rabbit, to those of another, a monkey, which promptly began to make rabbit globin. Other successes will undoubtedly follow, yet it is extremely unlikely that the techniques of genetic engineering, now or in the foreseeable future, will be able to do anything about our longevity, despite the hope that gene-splicing holds for individuals.

Indeed, there are many who see genetic engineering not as a saviour, but as a catastrophe ranking with a nuclear holocaust as a threat to life. We simply do not know, these people say, what the effects will be, when (not if) some dreadful man-made bug escapes. They are right, of course. We don't know, but we can be fairly confident that no simple bug, even one created in the laboratory, could ever wipe us out completely. Vast numbers of people might

die, but this would leave fewer places in which the bug itself could survive, with the result that it would be less able to infect new hosts. We could hope that some natural resistance might be present among the world's 4.2 billion people, and that there would be some survivors. Civilization might collapse, but then it took only 10,000 years to arise in the first place, and could, given the right conditions, emerge like a phoenix from the ashes within a couple of hundred years or so.

Living organisms have been evolving on this planet for several billion years, and neither science fiction bugs nor even a nuclear war could put an absolute end to this process—although the latter would probably result in the extinction of Homo sapiens. A nuclear war would no doubt also produce some spectacular sunsets for many years afterwards

Even if every person were to die, it would not be the end. There has been life on earth for at least three billion years, expanding, multiplying and diversifying from a singular beginning to the kaleidoscope we see today, and if we lower our shield of anthropocentrism for just a moment, we shall see that no engine-red bug accidentally released can possibly destroy all life. (Or, rather, to be on the safe side, there is only an infinitesimal likelihood that such a bug could be produced in the first place, let alone escape and survive to destroy every living thing—including itself — from the

Centre and left
Geysers like this one (centre) at Westmaniland, in Iceland, are found in many volcanic regions, including North and South America, New Zealand and Japan. Basically, they are intermittent hot springs, which discharge a column of heated water and steam high into the air with great force at more or less regular intervals. Erupting volcanoes also discharge hot water and steam into the air, together with ash, cinders and dust, which are in fact solidified lava. At the same time, sheets of flame shoot skywards from the floor of the crater, as in this volcanic eruption in Iceland (left)

Above
Forked or chain lightning, a long electrical spark from a thunder-cloud to the ground. Sheet lightning is a flash from one cloud to another, or between two parts of the same cloud. Lightning occurs when the electrical charge stored in raindrops builds up so much that it overcomes the insulating effect of the surrounding air

organisms in the mile-deep trenches of the oceans, to those on mile-high mountain-tops.)

Just as genetic engineering poses no threat to life, despite the rather large threat it may pose to some forms of life such as ourselves, so, too, nuclear war is not a real threat. It is almost impossible to predict the likelihood of any nuclear act of aggression. There could be a war tomorrow, or never. You could come up with your own more or less informed guess of the chances of an out-and-out nuclear Armageddon, with all that overkill unleashed on a helpless planet, and you would be as correct as any expert. What you cannot guess—nor can the experts—is what it would do to life. Could a nuclear war be the ultimate death? For man, yes—especially if all the stockpiled weapons were deployed. Perhaps, also for all the complex forms of life that breed relatively slowly and depend on accurate instructions for their many and varied cellular factories. Those not killed by the blast would be killed by the radiation, which would spread much further than the physical danger, wreaking its ghastly havoc far and wide. But I am optimistic that some life, somewhere—perhaps simple organisms in the oceans—would survive to start the long haul once again. As consolation, we can be certain that whatever is left alive to see them will enjoy truly spectacular sunsets for a number of years after the blasts.

Thus, neither genetic engineering nor nuclear war poses a threat to life, even though they menace the advanced form of life that gave rise to them. Also, they are under our control, although political expediency may make it very difficult to exercise that control. There are other awesome forces that we cannot even dream of controlling, and these could well spell our end.

People who enjoy the sunny climate and good life of California are aware that they live in the world's most heavily populated potential disaster area. They also know that it is only a matter of time before that potential is realized. How many of them know, however, that the reason for this impending disaster is that half of California, the south-west half, is not really a part of North America at all. It is the edge of what geologists call the Pacific plate, and the San Andreas fault that slices its way through 700 miles of California is the visible boundary between the Pacific plate and the North American plate.

The two plates are sliding past one another as the Pacific plate rotates slowly anticlockwise. Northwards under the sea from Cape Mendocino, between San Francisco and Parkfield, and between San Bernadino and the Mexican border, the slide is a smooth harmless 'creep' of about five centimetres a year, a series of little tremors. But the slide is not safely smooth along the whole length of the fault. In the areas between Cape Mendocino and south San Francisco, and from Parkfield through Los Angeles

A Timeless End
The true way of defining the end of life is a state where time no longer exists. Time needs activity to measure it by, and without activity, there can be no time

A Negative Force
The 'black hole' theory is interesting in its idea of a negative, or 'dead' force. According to the theory, a 'black hole' is the outcome of the gravitational force of a star collapsing in on itself. This causes its mass to be squeezed inwards, leaving a dense ball of matter with an almost infinitely strong gravitational pull. The strength of this is such that it 'bends' the structure of the Universe, forming a kind of cosmic plughole. Any object falling into this plughole would be crushed completely and sucked with enormous force out of the universe—even light rays are sucked in, causing black holes to be invisible

Controllable Earthquakes
In some areas such as California, Turkey and Iran, earthquakes originate near the earth's surface, and may possibly be controlled with boreholes to release pressure. However, deeper-originating earthquakes in the regions of Alaska, Japan, Philippines, Indonesia, Greece, Chile and Peru cannot be controlled in any way: natural disaster in these regions is inevitable

to San Bernadino, the movement is much jerkier. Friction stops the easy slider, and tension energy builds up until it is sufficient to overcome the friction. Then the energy is released suddenly, and the result is a major earthquake, in which the plates may shift by as much as forty or fifty metres. The two earthquake zones around San Francisco and Los Angeles have been quiet for a long time. In 1906, an earthquake destroyed San Francisco, and in 1857 there was a major one in the Los Angeles area. Since then, the zones have been quiet. Far from being a comfort, however, this quiet period is a harbinger of disaster, for the strain has been accumulating during all that time.

There are a number of cities dotted around the world which are built on locations that will sooner or later be riven by massive earthquakes. Others are threatened by volcanoes. When the island of Krakatoa disappeared in a volcanic eruption almost a century ago, the world temperature dropped by two degrees Centigrade

Los Angeles rests uneasily on an area that has built up 120 years of irresistible force, and an earthquake that will shift the plates by at least six metres is inevitable. Perhaps it will be in 1982, when the planets of our solar system will be in grand alignment, and strange things might happen. Whenever the earthquake does come—as it must—the energy stored for all those years will be released in a disaster that will be, literally, earth-shattering. Millions of people could die, and there will be massive damage, but it will be a local disaster. Once it is over, the seismologists will be able to try a few new tricks to prevent it happening again. Some want to lubricate the rocks so that they will slip past one another more easily. Others want actually to trigger little earthquakes from time to time to prevent the massive build-up of power that menaces California at present. However, they can do nothing until the earth decides to release the pent-up energy that has been building up since 1857, for fear of unleashing the power themselves. Los Angeles is not the only city waiting for disaster. There are others in different parts of the world, and all they can do is wait. There are now very sophisticated ways of predicting earthquakes and volcanic eruptions, but the social consequences of being wrong can be as disastrous as letting the event occur without warning.

Earthquakes and eruptions can bring death to whole communities—witness the fall of Pompeii beneath Vesuvius, or the total destruction of St Pierre, in Martinique, levelled by the 1902 eruption of Mont Pelée. They can also have an insidious effect on the whole world, by triggering a change in the earth's climate.

Volcanoes and earthquakes are followed by quite astonishingly beautiful sunsets. This is because they eject vast quantities of fine dust into the atmosphere, and the dust reflects the colours of the sun when it rises and sets. The dust also acts as a kind of veil, blocking some of the sun's energy before it can reach the earth.

The entire island of Krakatoa vanished in an immense explosive eruption at 10.00 am on August 27, 1883, and tons of dust spewed out into the atmosphere. Five cubic miles of rock were ejected, and the average temperature around the globe dropped by some two degrees Centigrade. Another massive eruption would have the same effect today, and cold wet summers do seem to occur in years of greater volcanic activity. Our world, though, is in a much more precarious balance between hungry mouths and food to fill them than it was in the 1880s. Thus, a drop in average temperature, even if only of a couple of degrees, could mean disaster.

Global cooling—and we may be in the process of slipping from the abnormally high temperatures of the past few decades to the cooler conditions at the beginning of this century—has two main effects on agriculture. Directly, the growing season is shortened. Indirectly, and more worrying, rainfall tends to occur less over land, where it is needed, and more out at sea, where it is not. Both effects

Right
Repulse Bay, in Canada's North-West Territories. The ice begins to break up. There are only four months in the year when the main artery of the territories, the Mackenzie River, is free of ice. If the theory developed some 50 years ago by a Yugoslav astronomer is correct, and ice ages are linked with the orbit of the earth, the next ice age should begin in about 9,000 years' time. This might force man to move towards the equator and make life more uncertain, but it will not mean the end of man

Below
Aurora borealis in Canada, the result of solar flares, when millions of protons are discharged earthwards at great speed by the sun. They collide with the atoms and molecules of the air, causing them to emit light. It is this which is seen as the aurora borealis

decrease the amount of food we can grow. The decrease might not worry the growers, but a five percent decline in the North American wheat harvest can knock 30 percent off the amount available for countries that cannot grow enough to support themselves. The result, famine and widespread starvation—all because the average temperature has dropped a couple of degrees.

Dust in the upper reaches of the atmosphere, acting as a veil, could also trigger the next ice age. The conditions for an ice age are ludicrously simple. More snow must fall in the winter than will be lost the following summer. Once this happens, a vicious cycle begins: the extra snow reflects away heat, the temperature drops further, and this causes more snow to accumulate. Of course, a real ice age, like the one we emerged from some 10,000 years ago needs more than a little dust in the air or snow on the ground. The most important factor in the stately advance and retreat of the ice sheets is now known to be the path of the earth around the sun. This is not a perfect ellipse. There are three major imperfections in it, and these have a profound effect on average temperatures here on earth. The first is called precession. This is a wobble in the earth's axis of rotation, as it revolves, rather like a spinning top going too slowly to stay absolutely upright. The second is due to changes in the path of the earth around the sun, which can broaden from a more elliptical orbit to a more circular one and back again. This is called obliquity. Finally, there is a 'nodding' of the earth, which varies the tilt of the axis.

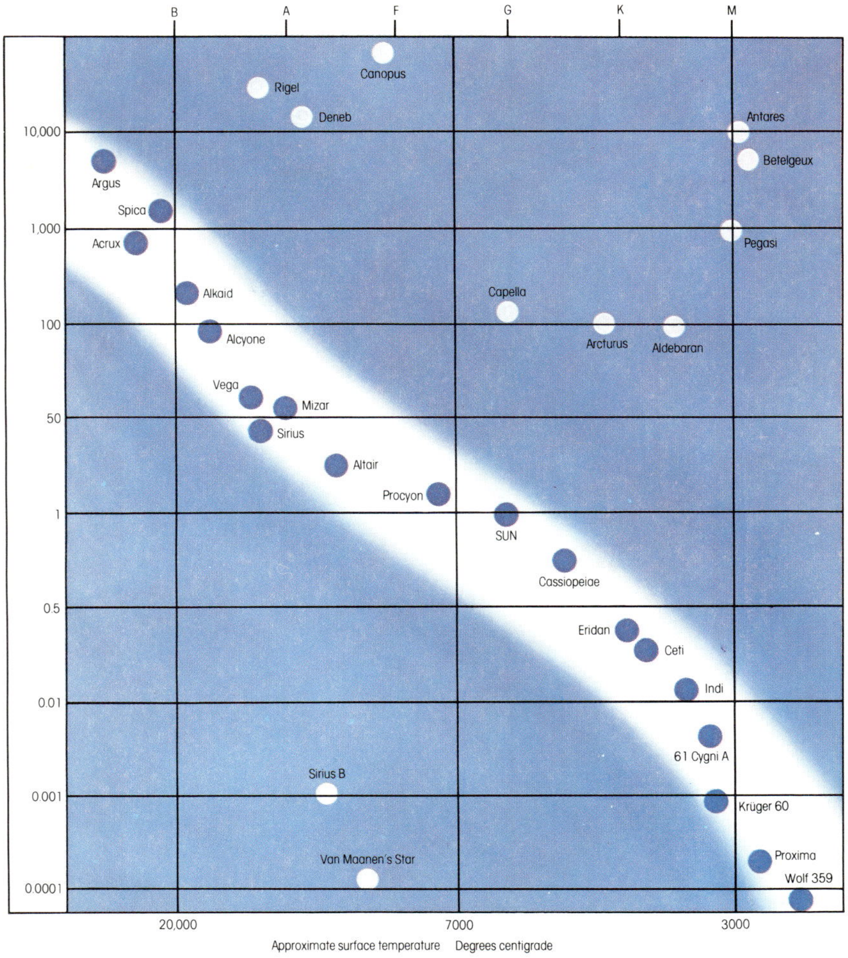

Star Death
The Hertzsprung-Russell diagram, illustrating the crucial relationship between a star's luminosity, and its spectral type and surface temperature. The great mass of stars lie along the well-defined band generally referred to as the main sequence. Very basically, this graph shows the evolutionary path most stars follow to their extinction. Supergiants occupy the uppermost section of the graph, giants lie to the right, white dwarfs to the lower left. This chart was first evolved in 1908

Left
With a huge splash, a mass of ice falls into the sea from the Hubbard Glacier at Disenchantment Bay, in Alaska. Geological evidence that the earth becomes covered with ice about every 250 million years has impelled a leading geophysicist to postulate the theory that this is the result of the solar system passing through the dust-filled spiral arms of the earth's galaxy, which it does every 250 million years in the course of its rotation around the centre of the galaxy

High Fuel Consumption
The larger a star is, the quicker it will burn itself out, because of the larger amount of energy it needs to compete with the ever-present pull of gravity

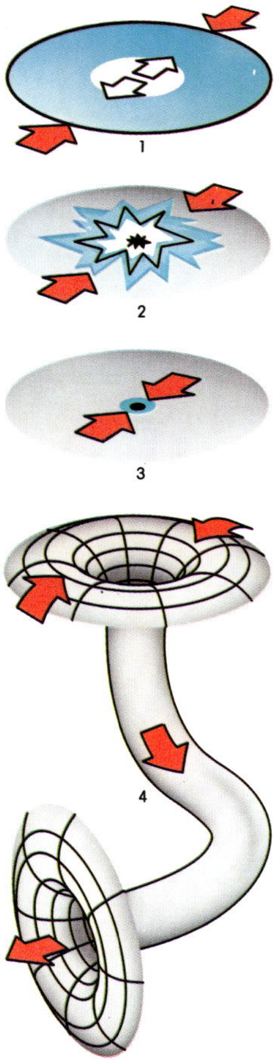

Birth of a Black Hole
A black hole is the result of the gravitational force of a star collapsing in on itself. This causes its mass to be pressed inwards leaving a dense ball of matter with a gravitational pull so strong, it forms a kind of 'plughole' in the universe

Above
Man sets foot on the moon for the first time. Buzz Aldrin, the pilot of America's Apollo 2 lunar module, walks across the dusty landscape of the moon in July, 1969. Whether or not a planet can support life depends on a number of factors, including its size and composition, as well as the size of its sun and the distance of the planet from it. The planet would have to have a temperature of between −80° and 100°C. About five percent of all known stars have planets which could support life

A Whimpering End
Spinning pulsars, or neutron stars, which are so dense that a cubic inch of their mass weighs 100 million tons, are believed to be the remains of stars that came to an end in supernova explosions. But so many have now been discovered that it seems unlikely supernova explosions caused them all. Many large stars may have ended their lives not with a bang, but with a whimper

Precession, 'nodding' and obliquity have predictable effects on the amount of energy that different latitudes receive from the sun in different seasons, and cause fluctuations in average temperature on a cyclical basis.

A Yugoslav physicist first posited the theory that ice ages are linked with the earth's orbit, although not everyone agrees with him. Another physicist thinks that major ice epochs occur when the solar system passes through the dust-filled arms of our own galaxy

There is very good evidence broadly linking the ice ages with the orbit of the earth. This theory was first postulated 50 years ago by a Yugoslav geophysicist, Milutin Milankovitch. If something, volcanic dust perhaps, were to trigger cooling at a time when the energy reaching the earth was at a low point in the cycle, a new ice age would be ushered in. If the imperfections are not 'right', there will not be a full-scale ice age, though there may still be severe cooling. The so-called Little Ice Age of the seventeenth to nineteenth centuries provides an excellent example of this phenomenon.

Sunspot activity was very low between 1645 and 1715, which implies that the sun was not quite as hot as usual, so there was not as much heat reaching the earth. There was also a lot of volcanic activity, with a resulting increase in the amount of dust in the atmosphere. The area covered by snow increased noticeably, and this, together with the volcanic dust, cooled the earth still further by reflecting heat away. Temperatures dropped, and with a succession of very severe winters, it looked as if another ice age was on the way. In 1730, however, temperatures started to rise again and the threatening ice age more or less went away. It was the earth's own orbit which prevented the Little Ice Age from growing into a major period of glaciation. The fact is that, at the moment, as in the eighteenth century, the relationship between earth and sun means that the Northern Hemisphere receives quite high amounts of sun in winter. This extra winter insolation was enough to overcome the temperature drop induced by the volcanic dust and slightly cooler sun. In another 8,000 to 10,000 years, however, the geometry of earth and sun will be very different. Winter insolation will be at a minimum, and if either condition favours a new ice age, it is extremely likely to occur. What is more, summer insolation will also be at a minimum, so, according to the Milankovitch theory, the next ice age—which should begin in about 9,000 years' time—will be more extensive and last for longer than the previous one.

Of course, not everyone believes that the Milankovitch theory is the whole story. Professor W. H. McCrea, of the University of Sussex, has

Above
Saturn, the second largest planet, which has a lower average density than water. Its rings form a thin disc round the planet. Of the 31 natural satellites, including the moon, nine (some say 10) are in orbit round Saturn. The largest, Titan, is the only one which is known to have an appreciable atmosphere

Left
A total eclipse of the sun in March, 1970. There is an eclipse of the sun whenever the moon passes between it and the earth, but it is not always total. There can be as many as five partial eclipses every year, but there are only about 65 total eclipses of the sun every century

Centre
Jupiter, the largest of the planets, of which there are nine, including the earth. Six of the planets have been known to man since prehistoric times, but one, Pluto, was not discovered until 1930. Neptune was discovered in 1846, and Uranus in 1781. The red eclipse in the photograph is called 'The Great Red Spot'. A group of hurricane-like thunderstorms, it has persisted through several centuries of observation

another, more dramatic, theory. He thinks that major ice epochs occur when the solar system passes through the dust-filled spiral arms of our own galaxy. The solar system rotates around the centre of the galaxy once every 500 million years, passing through an arm every 250 million years. The geological evidence is that the earth becomes covered with ice roughly every 250 million years. We came out of the Orion arm just over 10,000 years ago, when the previous ice age ended, and will not enter the other arm for at least another 100 million years, so perhaps the ice will not recur until then. On balance, though, Milankovitch is probably correct. We can therefore expect another ice age in less than 10,000 years' time, although we may be in for a truly spectacular glaciation in 100 million years as well, if Professor McCrea's theory also turns out to be correct.

Whenever the next ice age does come, it will inevitably bring death with it—but not the death of man. We are, one might almost say, a product of the ice, emerging from the cold, harsh challenge of the Paleolithic Age to become the creature we are today. The coming ice age might force us towards the equator, and make life more uncertain, but it will not mean the end of us. Nor, in fact, will it mean the end of all life. Indeed, it may spur a new leap of evolution, and our descendants might be lucky enough to see some truly spectacular new species, equipped to live along the margins of the ice wherever the opportunity presents itself.

When we contemplate the advance of the ice, whether in 10,000 or 100 million years from now, we are contemplating disaster on a very extended time scale. Perhaps we should also ask what will become of life in the cosmic future. Life depends on energy from our nearest star, the sun. Stars evolve, and the time must come when life on earth will no longer be possible. Although the sun's death is some 4,000 million years away, we can still contemplate the fate awaiting whatever survives on earth when that time comes.

The sun, like other stars, burns hydrogen to produce energy—millions of tonnes of it every second. There is enough hydrogen in the sun to last at least a billion years, possibly even five billion

Stars, like our sun, are the scene of a constant battle between two types of energy—gravity and radiation—and we can see the birth, life and death of a star in terms of this conflict. In the beginning, gravity is victorious, as it assembles our nascent star from a collapsing cloud of interstellar gas, mostly hydrogen, and other debris. As the cloud collapses under its own gravity, heat is released, and the cloud may glow visibly. When the temperature is high enough—a few million degrees

Ice Pollution
An idea of the continued pollution of the atmosphere can be gauged from a comparison between recent snowfalls near the polar icecap and undisturbed snows dating from before human civilization. Present-day snow contains 500 times more lead than that thousands of years ago

Big Bang
One accepted theory is that the universe was formed from the debris of a vast body of concentrated matter that exploded many millions of years ago. This is known as 'the big bang theory'

Cosmic Explosion
Some nebulae explode with a force equivalent to a million million million million hydrogen bombs

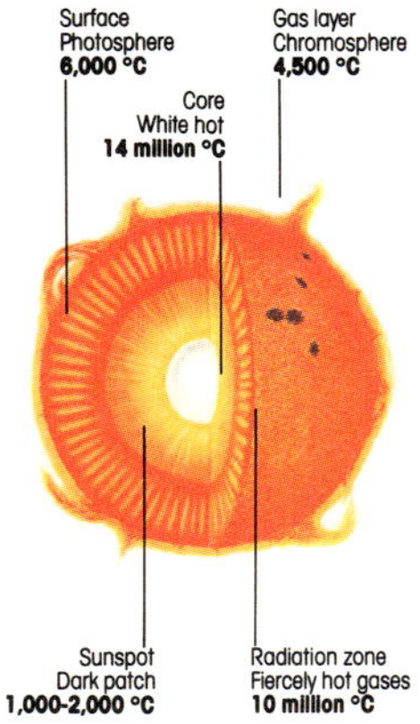

Solar Furnace
The sun is the fount of life on earth. Only the minutest fraction of one percent of the sun's tremendous outpouring of energy every second penetrates the earth's protective radiation belts and reaches the planet's surface. Nevertheless, this is all that is needed to sustain life here

Far right top
There are three types of galaxy—spiral (shown here), elliptical and irregular. The earth's own galaxy, the Milky Way, is spiral. The number of known galaxies runs into several billion, and there are undoubtedly many more which are beyond the range of even modern telescopes

Far right
An American thermo-nuclear device is detonated in the Pacific in 1952. By the time this photograph had been taken, the stem of the cloud had already penetrated deep into the stratosphere, a warning, if one were needed, of the awesome power contained within these devices. The fact that man holds his future in his own hand has never been more true

Right top
A typical mushroom cloud begins to form after the explosion of a nuclear device. If there were to be a nuclear war using all the weapons being stockpiled by various countries, it would almost certainly wipe out man. However, some other forms of life would survive

Right
Madagascar giant cockroach. It has been suggested by scientists that insects will outlive man and that the cockroach will outlive all other insects. There is also a suggestion that subjection to radiation by cosmic rays, produced either naturally or by some kind of man-made disaster, could result in giantism in some species of creatures

or so—nuclear fusion reactions begin. These burn up the hydrogen to form helium and release vast amounts of energy, as expressed in Einstein's celebrated equation, $E=mc^2$. The sun converts 4.5 million tonnes of mass to 4×10^{33} ergs of energy every second (4×10^{26} watts, or 4 million billion billion 100-watt light bulbs), and the energy released holds the star up against its own incredible gravity.

Despite the prodigious rate at which a star burns up hydrogen, there is enough in our own sun for at least a billion years. Even so, the time will come when the hydrogen that fuels nuclear fusion begins to run out. When this happens, gravity gains the upper hand, and the star contracts once more. As it does so, it gets hotter. Once the temperature reaches 120 million degrees, the helium produced by hydrogen fusion can burn. As it burns, it forms heavier elements and releases yet more energy, which can once again hold the star up against gravity. Because its core is hotter, the gas 'atmosphere' of the star expands enormously, and the star is now a red giant. It really is a giant, as large as the orbit of Saturn, or even Jupiter. If you know where to look for them, you can see some of these dying stars—Arcturus, Capella and Aldebaran are all red giants. When the helium at the core of a red giant is used up, the fires of fusion go out and the star dies. Death comes to a star either with a bang or a whimper. Sometimes, particularly if the giant is quite heavy and has a nearby companion star, the final stages of helium fusion burst all bounds. There is a huge explosion, which blasts the matter of the star out into space. At the same time, it may compress the core of the giant into a neutron star, as heavy as the sun, but as small as the earth. This huge explosion is of unimaginable force, and is called a super-nova. Astronomers have actually watched three red giants go out of control. There was Kepler's 'nova' in 1604, Tycho's star of 1572 and the outburst, witnessed by Chinese and Japanese astronomers in June, 1054, that produced the Crab Nebula. We would seem to be overdue for another super-nova and the astronomers are waiting impatiently to test their theories.

So much for going out with a bang. Our own sun, and I feel cheated by this, will go out with a whimper. It simply does not contain enough matter to sustain a super-nova explosion and will, when fusion is over, contract from a red giant to a white dwarf. The white dwarf will cool down very slowly as it dies, forming, in the end, a giant crystal of iron, covered with ice, perhaps, and surrounded by an atmosphere a few feet thick. Life, as we are able to imagine it, will have ended long before.

If man staves off death for about 2,000 million years, he will not be the same creature he is today. Life has developed from tiny bacteria and blue-green algae to its present state in about the same period of time. Whatever survives the ice, earthquakes, bugs, bombs and so on, will still have the problem of the red giant to contend with. The only answer then will be to escape to another planet circling another sun.

What are the chances of finding a new and hospitable home? A planet that can support life must have a temperature of between $-80°C$ and $100°C$, preferably for at least 100 million years. This will depend on the size of its sun and how far the planet is from it. A star with planets that could support life would have to be smaller than *class A0* but larger than *class K5* (see diagram p. 195). In theory, ten percent of all known stars would fit the bill. Different-sized stars have different-sized habitable zones. The star also has to be a single one, because the planets of binary stars often have wildly erratic orbits that would not be stable enough to sustain life. Since about half of all stars are binary stars, we are down to five percent of all stars, but the numbers are still, as we shall see, unimaginably large. Other factors which have to be taken into account include the size and composition of the planets within the habitable zone. Even if frozen Jupiter were closer to the sun, where earth now is, it would still not be suitable for life.

There are about 10^{11} (one hundred billion—100,000,000,000) stars in our galaxy, and about 10^{20} (a hundred billion billion — 100,000,000,000,000,000,000) in the universe. A very conservative estimate—by Harlow Shapley—puts the number of stars in the universe with planets that could support life at 10^9. A far more optimistic estimate—by Carl Sagan—postulates a much higher figure, perhaps as high as 10^{16} (ten billion billion — 10,000,000,000,000,000). Depending on which estimate one accepts, there are either a billion stars which could sustain life in our galaxy alone, or there is not even one. You pay your money and take your choice—although the odds may change in two billion years' time. If Sagan is

right, and there are hundreds of millions of planets out there eminently suitable for life, then they will surely be lived on. What in space will we do if we ever solve the problems of inter-stellar travel and set off across the void to a likely looking star, only to find it already occupied?

The universe is about 15 billion years old. It has much more than that still to go. It is absurd to imagine that we can even begin to contemplate what life will be like when the end of the universe approaches. Indeed, cosmologists are not even agreed on what the end will be. I rather like Paul Davies' model of a universe in which there are perpetual cycles of big bangs. After collapse, there is a big bang of matter, followed by a big bang of anti-matter, with the arrow of time reversed. This, in turn, is followed by another collapse and another big bang of matter, and so on *ad infinitum.* We can be confident that life will arise whenever conditions are suitable, regardless of how often that may be the case. Life is an aberration, and depends on an aberrant universe. Particular forms come and go. The blue green algae are still here, virtually unchanged, after 3 billion years. The dinosaurs came and went in a flash. Man himself has been around for a couple of million years at most, a rather special experiment in flexibility. If the experiment eventually fails, that's life. Something else will undoubtedly come along to take our place.

Facing the Facts

When we hear that someone near has died, we are often completely unprepared for the shock that inevitably accompanies this news. In the following pages we endeavour to give some guidance on coping with the process of dying and its aftermath

The Case for Abortion

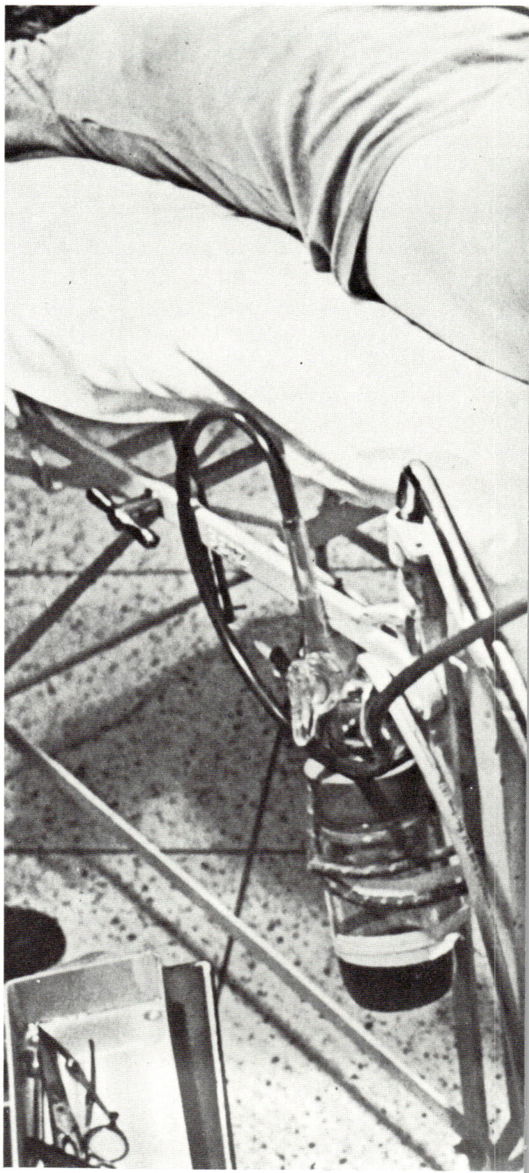

The untimely procured delivery of a foetus before it is viable, with intent to destroy it, is an induced abortion, euphemistically called a 'termination of pregnancy'

In practice, most abortions are performed within the first twelve weeks of pregnancy, through the vagina and neck of the womb (cervix), although they are uncommonly carried out after twenty weeks by an injection of a solution through the abdominal wall into the uterus to provoke labour and delivery. Occasionally, an abdominal operation—a hysterotomy—is used for a later abortion. This is similar to a caesarian operation, which is sometimes required for delivery later in pregnancy.

Abortion has been practised since the earliest recorded times. Instinctive feelings, morals, sociology, medical science and the law have been responsible in recent times for a change in attitudes to the practice of abortion. Religious beliefs, of greater importance in former times, are still a major factor for those opposed to the practice. Religious groups are largely responsible for the organization of the energetic and articulate anti-abortion pressure groups.

On the broadest level, the controversy between the pro and anti-abortionists is mainly concerned with the relief of suffering, as opposed to the sanctity of life.

In Britain abortion has been generally accepted under certain conditions and the law changed. In the detailed discussions about the stage of pregnancy after which it is not legally permissible to induce an abortion, there appears to be concern with the time at which the foetus can be said to possess a soul. 'The sanctity of life' is a religiously derived phrase used to support the view that, from the moment of conception, abortion is indefensible on moral and biological grounds. 'The apartheid of the unborn' is another phrase used to protest against the death of a 'human being' containing human genes.

Those supporting abortion put forward as their criterion for when the foetus becomes a human being the stage at which the developing foetus has the ability to live a separate existence from its mother and be a personality. They regard the destruction of the foetus, preferably well before this stage, as acceptable and think that abortion should be available on request to any woman who no longer wishes to continue with a pregnancy for a variety of reasons. They cite the presence in cancer cells of human

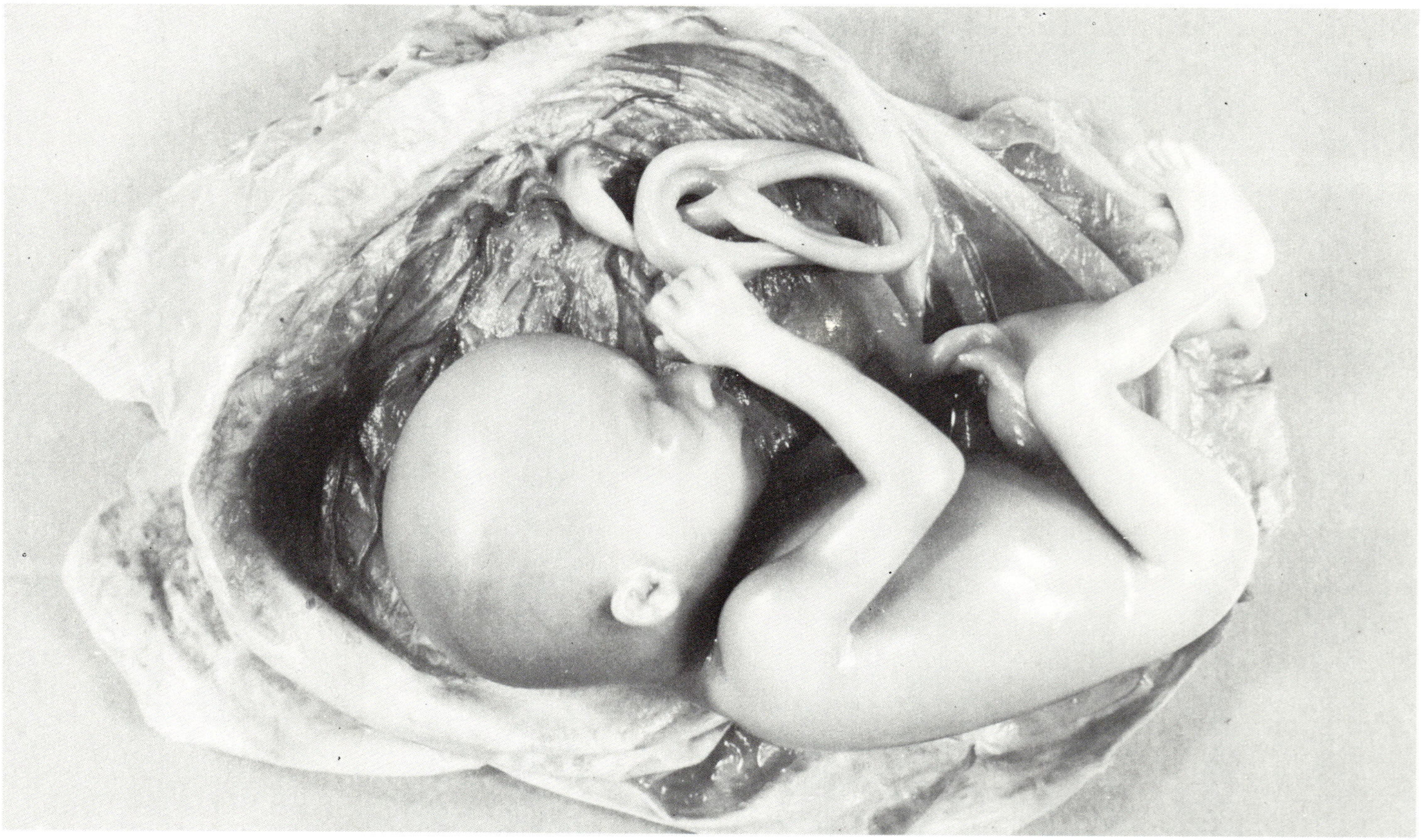

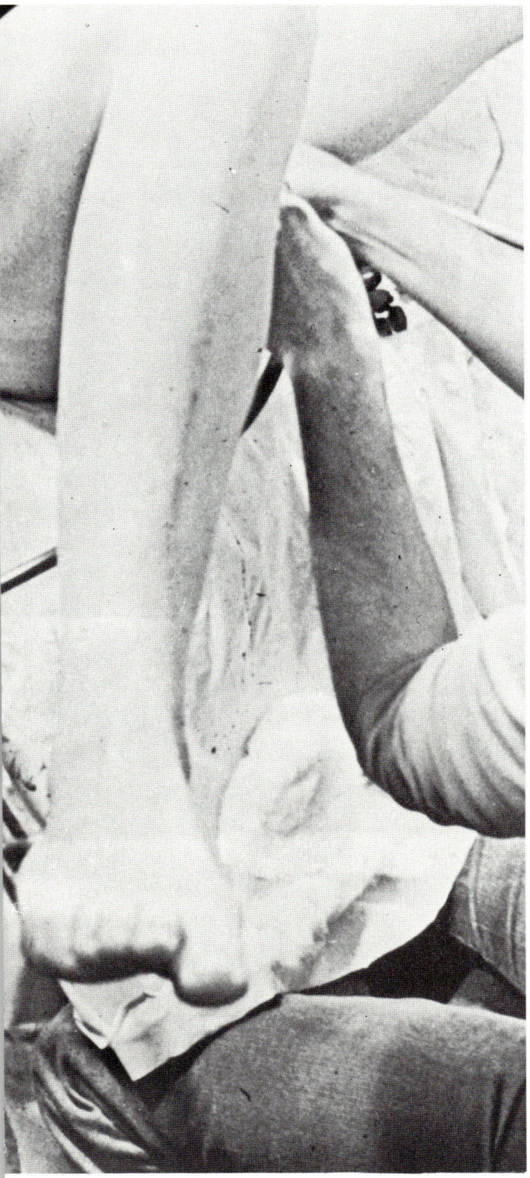

genes in order to falsify their 'human' significance in an early embryo.

When these arguments are extended to the practical aspects, the abortion protagonists cite examples where an unwanted pregnancy and the birth of the child has or would cause mental and physical ill health and hardship to the mother and her family, as well as to the unwanted child when born; contend that the ever-present demand for abortion requires a law allowing and controlling it to stop illegal abortionists flourishing and causing unnecessary disease and death to the mother; point out that there are already too many one-parent families (usually mother and child) and also that children with physical or mental handicaps are allowed to be born to the disadvantage of themselves, their parents and the resources of the community. Some believe that the law should allow abortion on demand, but most are prepared to accept 'conditions' as the compromise which allows the majority of these problems to be overcome.

The antagonist views legalized abortion as the thin end of the wedge, leading to contraceptive irresponsibility; the encouragement of promiscuity; the spread of venereal disease, and an acute shortage of children for adoption, thus causing further unhappiness to childless couples. They are concerned about the effects upon the medical, nursing and related professions, the lowering of the status of the speciality of gynecology, and the effects upon its recruitment in both quantity and quality. They consider that the disadvantages to society as a whole outweigh the relief of individual unhappiness or hardship.

The legal grounds for allowing abortion on health grounds, under the British Abortion Act 1967, are imprecise and can be widely interpreted: that 'the continuance of the pregnancy would involve risk to the life of the pregnant woman, or of injury to the physical or mental health of the pregnant woman or existing children of her family, greater than if the pregnancy were terminated; or that there is a substantial risk that if the child were born it would suffer from such physical or mental abnormalities as to be seriously handicapped'. Further to help to assess the possible risk to the mother's health, 'account may be taken of the pregnant woman's actual or reasonably foreseeable environment'.

In 1971, three out of four legal abortions were on the grounds of risk of injury to the mental or physical health of the mother; just over three in every 100 because of risk of injury to the physical or mental health of existing children; one in 50 because of risk to life, and one in 100 because the child would have been seriously handicapped.

In England and Wales, from a peak of 110,000 abortions in 1973, the numbers of resident women being aborted legally had fallen to 102,000 by the end of 1977. The fall has been more dramatic for non-residents. Since 1972, four out of five abortions have been carried out before the twelfth week of pregnancy. One in 100 occur after the twelfth week. Abortion deaths have continued to fall for the past 20 years, dramatically so since the peak years for legal abortions—1973/74. Convictions for illegal abortionists have diminished by 30 to one since 1976, and hospital admissions for septic (infected) abortions have declined by four to one since 1968.

Public opinion surveys in Britain in 1973 showed that more people believed either that the law should remain unchanged or that it should be made less restrictive than took the opposite view; the opinion among general medical practitioners was three to one in favour of liberal abortion laws.

The specially appointed Lane Committee, reporting to Parliament in 1974 on the working of the Abortion Act, was unanimous in its support and thought that the problems identified were not grounds for amending the Act in a restrictive way. They suggested that solutions should be sought by administrative and professional action and by better education of the public.

Since the inception of the British Abortion Act 1967, there have been five unsuccessful attempts to introduce parliamentary Bills aimed at increasing the restrictions contained in the abortion law currently in force.

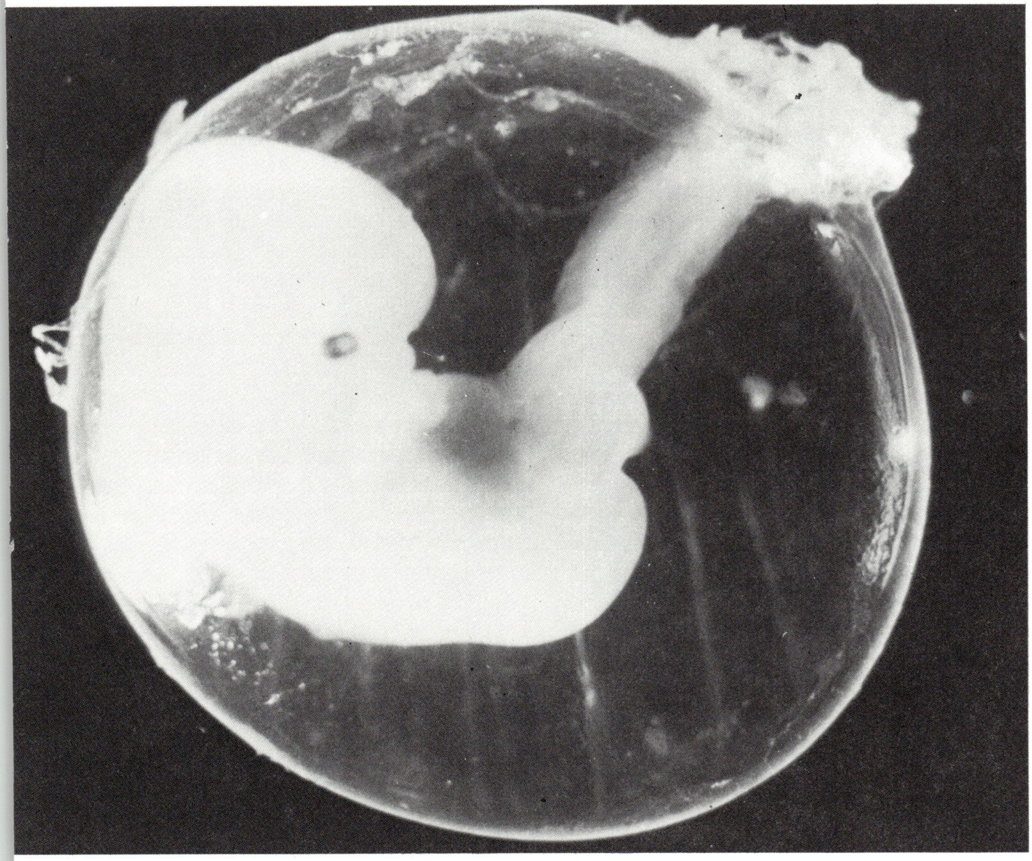

Care of the Dying

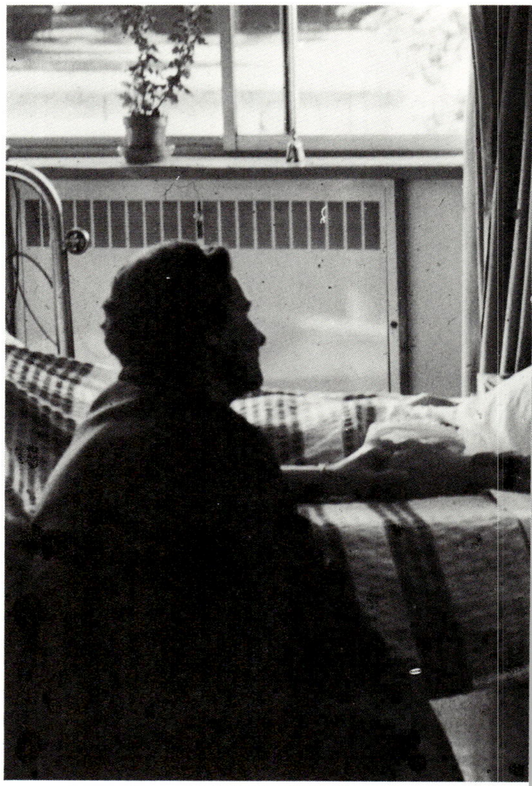

To many, dying may come easily, either as a sudden welcome release, or a gradual 'slipping away'. But very many others experience their deaths as a frightening and painful finale to an unfulfilled life. These people need special help

The time to die comes easily to many and, for them, the process of dying brings few problems. Death may be sudden, with little or no distress, or it may be as peaceful as it is gradual and take place in the care of a loving family. We should not forget how many still die in this manner. We cannot deny, however, that dying may be hard and long for some, especially among the elderly. These people and their families may need much help if this is to be a time when patients live 'until' they die, sure of their individual worth, and their families are enabled to live on afterwards, with this experience integrated for good into their lives. Nor must we forget that it is harder to leave a lonely life than a fulfilled one. Those who are out of touch with their families need special help from others.

Our concern for a particular patient changes into care for his dying when active treatment of all kinds becomes increasingly irrelevant to his needs. It is the time when we recognize that what we try to do for him should no longer be directed to his cure or rehabilitation—or even to the palliation of his disease—but primarily towards his comfort. It is the inability to do this which leads to inappropriate interventions and to what Florence Nightingale called 'the chattering hopes' of our friends. To accept the fact that our aim has changed is not therapeutic nihilism or the denial of all hope. Rather it can help us to work for positive control of symptoms and a new awareness of the patient as a person.

Care for someone who is dying should be concerned above all with the potential for living which the relief of distress may still make possible. Remarkable changes can be achieved by the understanding and skilled relief of the complex physical, emotional, social and spiritual components which make up the totality of terminal pain. During the past two decades, new knowledge of pain relief has greatly enhanced our capacity to help those who suffer pain at the end of life. What is known and practised in special centres such as pain clinics and hospices is becoming increasingly available throughout the whole field of hospital practice and home care.

Mental and physical distress are often closely interwoven. Emotional suffering is eased as physical problems are treated, and there are many drugs now available that can help reduce the mental burden to more manageable proportions, although it is having a listener that helps most of all. That is true even when it seems likely that communication is no longer possible. Very ill and elderly patients are often less confused than the hurried visitor supposes. We should face honestly the anxieties and depression of a deteriorating illness or the loss of faculties, and the humiliation and guilt aroused by dependence, weakness, incontinence and the sometimes desperate feelings of loneliness. Perseverance with the practical may be all that is needed, but I once asked a man who knew he was dying what he looked for above all in those who were caring for him. He said: 'For someone to look as if they are trying to understand me'. It is, indeed, impossible fully to understand another person, but I have never forgotten that he did not ask for success, only that someone should care enough to try.

It is from dying people themselves that we learn both the demands and the rewards of this time of life. The criteria of success are not to be found in what we do by our various activities, but in what the patient achieves in the face of his physical deterioration. Freed from the constant pressure of distress, dying can be a true part of life—full of courage, serenity and humour. It may well be the most important part of a lifetime, when a family is given a heritage of memories for comfort and future strength.

The first definition of the word 'care' in the dictionary is: 'A burdened state of mind arising from fear, doubt or concern'. We are dealing here with the heaviness of weakness, pain and parting. We sometimes forget this, as we apply the word to our own activities and concentrate on the *giving* of care, the alleviation of the burden. We need to remember, when we feel its weight, that it is only a pale reflection of the burden carried by those we are trying to help. Once we try to understand this and take our cues from each patient, the vexed question of whether or not to 'tell the truth' is far easier to answer. Much of the deception practised by professional staff and families alike would be found to be unnecessary, if only time were made for listening to what the patient has to say if given the opportunity. Most will reveal how much they already know, and whether they want or need to go further. Mental isolation is often the greatest suffering a patient has to bear, and many people are left alone with the very truth from which all around believe they are being protected. A recent survey showed that 'in practice, patients were better pleased and less troubled when the truth was more freely shared and they were not automatically shielded from the spoken verdict. Communication was fitted to individual readiness'.

It is important to say goodbye, perhaps indirectly during the course of the illness, directly at the moment of parting. Plate 1 shows the peace and companionship possible at the moment of death. This is the quiet dignity that comes from a natural process, not from a lethal injection. If a legal right to a quick way out were to be introduced, with it would come the difficulties of making an irrevocable decision, the second thoughts, the doubts, and the dangers of pressure being brought to bear upon the patient. This would bring new burdens rather than a new freedom to many of the most vulnerable members of our society.

To care also means 'to feel concern or interest, to take thought'. During the past two decades, much thought has been given to developing into 'efficient, loving care' the 'tender, loving care' given for years past by a few dedicated groups and individual doctors and nurses. One important contribution of the hospice movement has been the emphasis on the whole family as the focus of care—and

also as part of the caring team. Hospice home care programmes, enable many patients to stay in their homes. This support, with help for those in special need in their bereavement, is given in co-operation with the family doctor and any local services that can be involved.

For each of us, death is ahead, a mysterious and essentially lonely journey. Yet, if we are supported by those around us when the time comes, we may come to it with courage. This was illustrated by a series of pictures painted by a middle-aged woman when she was ill. They revealed with stunning clarity what those around her had observed of her change in attitude. She was finding her way through the place of which Ralph Harper wrote: 'We cannot know what is beyond the end of our days, but we can enter an order of things which can make us say: "I am not afraid" '.

Weakness of body and mind and the dependence of dying are not easy to accept or to see as achievements in a materialistic society, but life is made of receiving as well as giving, of simple being as well as of complex living. Many of us will reach our own truth only when we are no longer able to manipulate the people and things around us. Christians believe that this journey has been shared by God himself. A crucifix, damaged by bombs, gunshot and fire during the Warsaw Uprising, hangs on the wall of the rebuilt cathedral. It announces with stark simplicity that the incarnate God once died and this is what the sins and suffering of His children still do to Him. It is a witness to the faith that no one need travel this way alone, and that death is at the beginning of a journey that will lead to resurrection.

Time of Crisis

Grief appears to be one of the most potent causes of common neurosis and much unhappiness in family life, as well as some physical disorders. Yet the majority of symptoms should be treated by the family doctor if they are not to lead to major psychiatric breakdown

Many of us have suffered the loss of some relative or close friend, and no one can doubt that this is a powerful and all-prevailing experience. There are generally three stages: shock, realization and readjustment.

Each of these stages varies according to the individual's inherent personality, whether obsessional, immature, inadequate, hysterical, manic-depressive or, much more dramatic, schizophrenic or psychopathic. From the very outset, the severity of the reaction is very frequently related to feelings of guilt.

The first impact of news of the death of one who has been alive and active in the near vicinity is stunning, and all the physical features associated with shock can occur. To this is added the expression of grief as tears. It should be realized that tears are as important an expression of this powerful emotion as laughter is of amusement or pleasure, and flushing of the face of anger. To suppress tears is to suppress the emotion of grief. This leads to frustration and can only distort other emotions and functions, particularly alertness, clear thought, and general well-being. The patient may cry with or without sobbing, but cannot cry without tears. The stage of shock continues for several hours, possibly a day, and is gradually replaced by full realization.

With this stage comes the sensation of emptiness, because of the absence of the individual. Later, lonely feelings may lead the bereaved into emotional outbursts when associations recall the closeness of the relative, particularly noticeable during clearing up the personal effects and estate. This stage may last a considerable time, but runs almost imperceptibly into the next stage, which is readjustment.

This always occurs slowly, but may be delayed because of the intensity of the previous two stages. It is particularly prolonged if the patient has guilt feelings and the guilt is justified. Readjustment is mainly concerned with the life of the patient without the physical existence, but with the memory, of the relative concerned, the existence of a career and its progress, and the evolution of further personal relationships.

Observations in this field show that severe reactions occur particularly in three groups: where death has happened suddenly, either from natural causes, or from a road accident, a major catastrophe or in the peculiar circumstances of suicide; where death has occurred after long illness, and, perhaps most of all, where the death is that of a child.

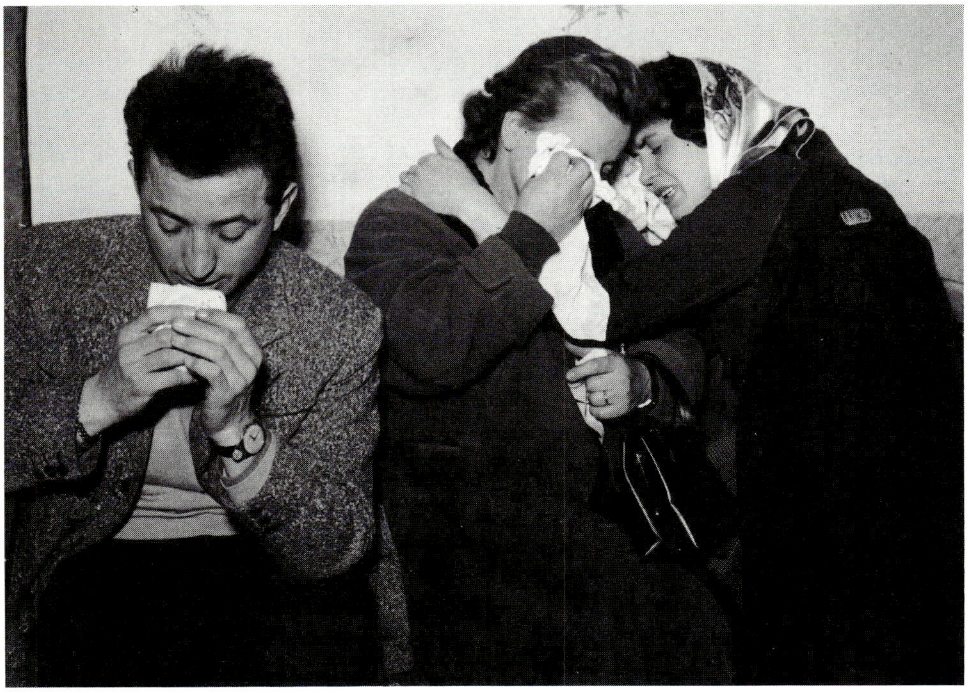

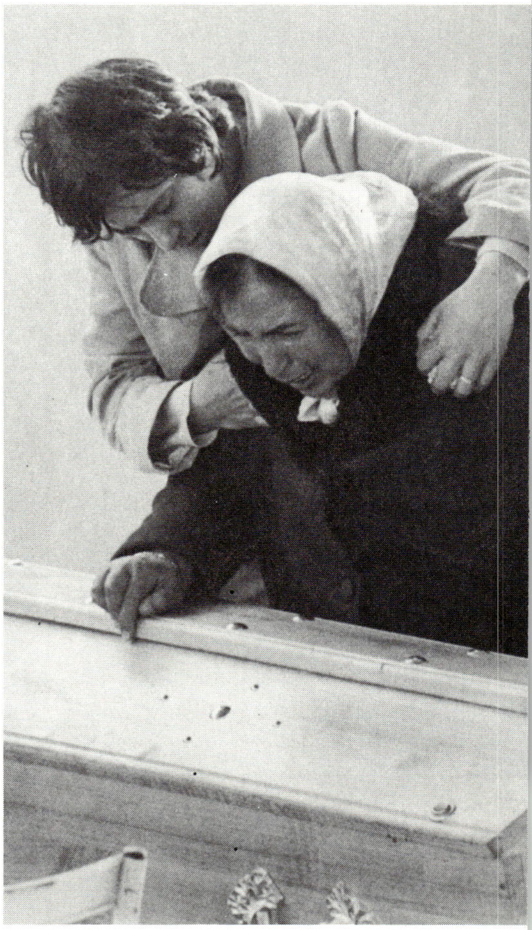

Depression and anxiety states are commonest in grief. They are expected and understood in the stage of shock, but the symptoms gradually worsen in the stage of realization. They are often under-estimated.

Grief reactions occurring after an interval of time are difficult to elucidate and appear to have a more prolonged effect. The psychosomatic signs associated with grief include rheumatoid arthritis, ulcerative colitis, asthma, anorexia nervosa, and neuro-dermatitis, and it is well to remember that these may be the presenting symptoms of grief. It is perhaps best to illustrate these with examples.

Miss A, aged 23, returned home as usual from her place of business at tea-time one day, and was told by a neighbour that her mother had died suddenly less than an hour before. Miss A gasped, ran upstairs to her room, shut and locked the door and refused to open it. She was not heard to be crying or sobbing, and this self-isolation worried her relatives more and more as time went by. By the middle of the next morning they felt they should get the help of a doctor.

The door was forced, and the girl was found lying face downwards on her bed. She was physically normal, but refused to answer questions and would only catch her breath as in dry sobbing. She would not let herself listen to advice or heed any entreaty. Eventually a consultant psychiatrist was called, and after some conversation a photograph of the mother was swiftly produced for her to see. This surprise broke the spell, and she became tearful, followed by a flood of words about her affection for her mother and how she had treated her badly. After reassurance and sedation, the girl improved. She talked freely about her mother, and then began to explain that, on the morning of the day her mother died, she had asked for a loan to enable her to get married. This had upset her mother, and they had had an argument, which had not been resolved when she left to go to work.

Miss A returned to work and carried on her normal activities but recovered only slowly. She attended the surgery frequently and repeated her story about her mother, finally admitting one day that the reason she had asked her mother for money to get married was that she had thought she was pregnant at the time, and would have to get married quickly. Once she had admitted this and had repeatedly been reassured, her anxieties were dispelled, and she gradually readjusted, now having no symptoms at all. This case illustrates the effect of immediate shock in a person with an hysterical personality. It also illustrates how important tears are as an expression of grief.

In general practice, it is clear that the immediate need for the bereaved person is to discharge the feelings of grief in tears, and the conduct of those concerned at the time—particularly the doctor or nurse—is contributory to the grief reaction. Care should be taken to talk to the relative in such a way as to facilitate the expression of this emotion. The bereaved person requires an opportunity to talk about the deceased, the illness, the suffering, the death. He (or she) should be encouraged to express his (or her) fears that there may have been pain or apprehension. The bereaved person should be reassured about these matters and told that the care which the deceased was given was the best in the circumstances. The physician, particularly the consultant, should have the mental and moral courage of his conviction, and discuss the problems of treatment freely.

The Reverend C. Pretty, writing in the *Nebraska State Journal,* described five needs of the bereaved: To fill the gap caused by the death; to actualize the loss and accept it emotionally; to express sorrow; to verbalize hostility and guilt; to establish new relationships.

It should be remembered that a brave face, dry eyes and perfect control are poor prognostic signs. These patients usually suffer great anxiety or depression at later stages. The bereaved should be given an opportunity for private grief, for oppression through lack of privacy is a particular aggravation in these highly-charged emotional states.

In the later stages, the best way to encourage realization is by reassuring the bereaved that the deceased would have liked him or her to continue to live a normal life. Something which they had planned to do together should be altered

only slightly to adjust for the void. Guilt feelings must be firmly allayed through each stage. In the readjustment stage, the continuance of the bereaved's original career and the development of further personal relationships are important, even including remarriage or the adoption of a child.

This subject seems to have received scant attention in print or in teaching. Most doctors become aware of the problem only when they are faced with it in practice. Occasionally, even the most experienced doctor cannot seem to face up to the incident. A great deal of work and care may have been taken over the patient, and it may be realized that these efforts have been truly appreciated by the relatives, but there has been a lack of explanation to the bereaved, and this absence of crucial mental support has allowed the neurosis to occur and actually develop.

I have purposely not mentioned the religious aspect, since it is clearly a very personal matter. It all knits together and, as Dr Cecily Saunders has said, it must be understood to be there. The doctor, the nurse, the medical auxiliary accept it, but we are not expected to give active support to these views.

To summarize, grief can give rise to a series of common neuroses, which may even precipitate attacks of psychosis and somatic disorders. Depressive illness is particularly common and everyone concerned with the occasion can help in simple ways to make things easier.

A Multitude of Faiths

Central to the doctrine of most religions is the concept of life after death. Yet the form this existence might take differs radically from one faith to another

The Protestant Conviction: A Tenet of Faith

In the crypt of St Leonard's Church in Hythe, Kent, hundreds of visitors come each summer to stare at 500 neatly shelved skulls and 8,000 femur bones, equally neatly stacked beside them. These human remains challenge healthy young European tourists with the unspoken certainty: 'As we are, so you will soon be'.

Faced with such solid evidence of the certainty of mortality, the imagination is hard put to it to picture these macabre exhibits as having been people who once lived, loved, laughed and cried like us. Is that it? Is the only certainty in life certain death, without even the privilege of joining such an august pile as these medieval compatriots, to gaze eyeless at posterity? The evidence is here, stacked in favour of mortality. 'When I die, I rot', said Bertrand Russell.

The Christian Church has all along said that this is neither the whole truth, nor the most important truth. Physical death does not necessarily mean non-existence. Not that this is a comfortable thought, because each person who dies will in some way be called to account for the way he lived. Man has freedom, man is accountable, and you cannot have one without the other. The New Testament warns: 'It is the lot of all men to die once, and after death comes judgement'. This Particular Judgement, as it is known, occurs immediately after death and so comes before, and is quite distinct from, the General Judgement, also known as the Last Judgement. This will be the occasion of God's final judgement on humanity as a whole. 'We must each of us have our lives laid open before the tribunal of Christ, where each must receive what is due to him for his conduct in the body, good or bad'. (2 Corinthians Chapter 4, verse 10).

If physical death is so decisive that it is like the end of an examination, when all the papers are collected in—and that is that—then the difficulty is going to be to find anyone who has been good enough to merit a pass mark. The failure rate is total. No one merits God's approval, except for one man. The Christian teaching is that, because one man—Jesus Christ—lived an absolutely unspoilt and perfect life, died and returned from the dead, and continues to live in His spirit, so all those who accept Him as God's son are enabled to live through His merit, not theirs. God was in Christ, saving the world from its self-inflicted destruction. The Protestant view emphasizes the necessity of accepting personally the offer made by God, if man is to avoid the consequences of his sinfulness. Salvation comes by having faith in Jesus Christ and thereby making a personal decision to accept him.

Hell is the worst that can ever happen to a person, which is to become alienated from God and from his true being. There is a great deal of teaching in the New

Testament about the death of the spirit of man, that which in him is divine, although comparatively little on the subject of physical death. Hell, in the teaching of the Church, is the place of separation from God. The way there is by living a life orientated to the glory of self, the way of sin. 'The wages of sin is death' does not mean that the sinner will immediately drop down dead, but that by sin, man hides himself from God.

Heaven is the best that can happen to a person. To unite himself with God means he finds his true being. This involves dying to self-glory, living to Christ, and so being where God is. The aim of the Christian is union with God. That is true life—heaven. Hell is separation—death.

The Bible and the tradition of the Protestant Church have emphasized the crucial importance of the resurrection event in Christ's life. The best evidence for the hereafter is based on the life-changing experience which comes in the here and now, which proves through faith that physical death is not the terminal state after which there is no further existence, but that, through Christ, eternal life is available.

The Jewish Position: Eternal Life

You will search the Jewish Bible in vain for any reference to life after death. In fact, biblical Hebrew has no word for 'after-life', while the Hebrew word generally translated as 'soul', *neshama*, is derived from the verb *nasham*, to breathe, and should properly be rendered as 'life'—that which causes the flesh to live. It has, in the Bible, no metaphysical connotation.

Biblical Judaism did not worry about these things. Man was created in the image of God, so that he should know to distinguish between good and evil, and God hopes that he will choose the good, by carrying out His will (though the option to do evil is open to him). His reward is that he is helping to build a good society.

Mark Anthony, the pagan, got it only half-right. The evil that men do does live after them, but so does the good. This thought is picturesquely expressed in medieval Jewish mysticism: every *mitzva*, good deed, that man does creates an angel, who ascends before the heavenly throne and pleads on his behalf—even though his body returns to the dust whence it came, his works live after him. *That* is his after-life, his contribution to the onward march of society. No contribution is too large, none too small to count, as one generation of Jews succeeds another.

To this day, it is the ambition of every pious Jew to leave behind him at least one son who will recite *kaddish* for him, the memorial prayer which glorifies God and his doings in this world.

It was only when Jewish society in the Land of Israel was disrupted by the intrusion of Imperial Rome and the future looked bleak, that the early rabbis turned inward and posited a soul immune to earthly power. This world, the rabbis concluded, is a valley of tears, and the life of the body a 'forecourt', a preparation, for the world to come. It was, incidentally, this strand in early rabbinism that Christianity took up and subsequently developed into religion.

Death, to the Jew, is still a calamity, even if an inevitable one. It is marked by *shiva*, seven days of deep mourning by the close family, when friends come to comfort, followed by 30 days of less stringent religious observance. For a whole year, as well as on every anniversary of the death, sons and brothers recite the *kaddish* and light candles, as well as giving charity in memory of the departed. A tombstone is erected, on which are inscribed the details of the departed life and death and the invocation (in Hebrew), 'May his (her) soul be bound up in the bond of eternal life'.

Among the rituals that have grown up around the passing of life—religious,

quasi-religious and plain superstitious—burial of the body is paramount, at least in Orthodox Judaism. The body must be encoffined and its resting-place marked; it must under no circumstances be cremated, lest its erstwhile occupant be missing at the Resurrection, at the End of Days However, some Jews, particularly those following the Reform and Liberal ritual and religious observances, do not reject cremation.

In any case, the true memorial to someone who dies is the life lived by his children. If they continue in the paths of Judaism which (it is to be presumed) he marked out, he lives on. This is the ambition of every Jew, even one whose attachment to Judaism may have been tenuous during his own lifetime.

As the psalmist put it: 'It is not the dead who praise the Lord, nor those who go down into silence; but we bless the Lord, from this time forth and evermore'.

The Catholic View: Miracle of the Resurrection

In many religions, death retains its terrifying quality for the mind, while being viewed as only a stage in the overall life of an individual, immortal spirit or soul encased in a body simply for convenience during its sojourn in the physical world. This is certainly paramount in the beliefs of Christianity, and is symbolized by the many ceremonies conducted by the Churches, particularly the Roman Catholic Church. In fact, the Bible and the teachings of Christ are replete with references to life after death, a fundamental part of Catholic doctrine. Even more crucial to Roman Catholicism is the miracle of the Resurrection, celebrated each year at Easter, when Christ, the son of God, overcame death, rising body and soul from the grave three days after His burial. In doing so, and thus mastering death, He demonstrated His godliness. The creation of life and, ultimately, the dominance of death is, Catholics believe, the province of God alone. In fact, on Ash Wednesday, the day marking the start of six weeks of fasting and penance leading up to Easter, Catholics are given an annual reminder of their humble origins and their bodies' mortality. Ashes of burnt palm leaves are blessed and then placed on each Catholic's forehead, accompanied by the words: 'Remember, man, that thou art dust and into dust thou shalt return'.

As with all other Christian religions, the belief in man's immortal soul is fundamental to Roman Catholicism. The Catholic Church believes that its rules, springing from Christ's teaching, will assist Catholics in maintaining the purity of that soul, and that its condition at death will govern its final destination. Many Catholics have their own, personal ideas of what heaven and hell are like, but nevertheless believe in their existence and that, unless a soul is in a state of purity at death, it cannot enter into the 'kingdom of heaven'. Depending on the gravity of the sin staining a soul at death, it will either enter purgatory and remain there for an indefinite period until purified enough to enter heaven, or 'for all eternity be damned in hell'. Even little children who die prematurely without the benefit of baptism are not eligible to enter heaven. Their souls

spend eternity in limbo, where, although there is none of the suffering in hell and purgatory, there is likewise none of the ecstasy of heaven.

It is with this in mind that the last rites, or last sacraments, are given to dying Catholics. The full rites include confession and extreme unction—a ceremony not unlike the anointing ritual of baptism—which prepare the soul for its entry into the next world. It is not uncommon for Catholics who are ill, but in no immediate danger of dying, to request these sacraments to help them fight their illness and speed recovery.

Even after death, the Roman Catholic Church has a special reverence for its 'souls departed'. Apart from prayers for the dead contained in the Church's liturgy, a special day, November 2, is set aside each year to pray for the 'repose of the souls of the faithful departed'. The altar is completely stripped of its decorative flowers, and the officiating priests are garbed in black.

Being human, people always feel pain at the death of someone dear to them. At the same time, Catholics believe that, if a person dies with a prospect of going to heaven, then death is a welcome release from the physical toil of earthly life, a relief from the agonies of the body which it is a privilege to endure in the name of Jesus Christ.

The Buddhist Solution: The Noble Eightfold Path

Buddha was 80 years old when he realized that his earthly end was near. It was precisely 45 years since he had attained 'perfect wisdom' and become Buddha, 'The Enlightened One'. Now, after dedicating himself to teaching and preaching, he prepared to leave his disciples and converts. On the evening of the full moon of May he had his bedding spread out between two trees and lay down on his right side, his head towards the north, according to an ancient custom. His mind remained perfectly clear as he said farewell to his disciples gathered around him. His last words were : 'Decay is inherent in all component things! Work out your own salvation with diligence'.

A Buddhist is not afraid of death. Philosophically he regards it as a natural and inevitable part of the continuing cycle of existence—'the cause of death is not disease, but birth'. Like a constantly revolving wheel, all beings pass from birth, through growth, to decay, death and rebirth with no fixed time-span. All things are changing and impermanent. The only certainty in life is the body's ultimate death. When the physical body dies, it becomes an empty shell. It is cremated in order to return it to the elements. The life-force within lives on to appear in a later life.

At rebirth, the individual's karma (actions or deeds) is carried over to the next life, with appropriate consequences. Karma, which can be understood as a law of cause and effect, is connected with a man's actions and thoughts during every hour of his life. Thus, a man's karma will affect the joy and misery he will experience in the next life. The consequences of this law prevail even after the death of the physical body. The Buddhist catechism formulates it as follows:

'If we have an excess of merit, we shall be well and happily born the next time. If an excess of demerit, our next birth will be wretched and full of suffering'.

A Buddhist does not believe in eternity in the Western sense. He conceives of existence as a path rising up a mountain of unimaginable heights. The nature of the path (its length, difficulty and so on) depends on where a man is standing at a given time, and on the progress he has made. Karma and rebirth are the means by which such progress can be achieved.

The philosophy of rebirth is complex. It is based on the belief that rebirth is caused by the tenacious desire to maintain a physical existence in the material world. The strong creative power of this force draws a being back into mundane life, where he is confronted with ignorance. This causes intense suffering, which can, however, be dispelled by the fact of his own sincere understanding of the Four Noble Truths. Expressed in these fundamental concepts is the belief that birth, death and life after death are miseries of evolutionary existence. Selfish desire, the root of misery, must be destroyed. Unsatisfied and ignorant cravings can be conquered by following the Noble Eightfold Path. The eight paths are: right belief, right attitude of mind, right speech, right conduct, right means of livelihood, right effort, right mind-control and self-discipline, and right meditation. An individual's true devotion to these Buddhist doctrines ultimately leads to emancipation from the suffering of earthly existence and rebirths. The final human goal is Nirvana (literally a 'blowing-out' of selfish desires). This enlightenment, perfect knowledge, is the ultimate transcendent state of freedom beyond birth and death. It is the total obliteration of everything that goes to make up the physical man. Nirvana is not a place, like a heavenly paradise, but the true detachment from the world that brings an end to rebirth and suffering.

Some of the ideas and practices of the

traditional, southern or Theravada school of Buddhism have been modified by believers in the Mahayana form. Their concept of the ideal Buddhist is someone who vows to prepare himself for enlightenment in order to serve and save other suffering mortals. Even when he is perfect in the necessary virtues of generosity, morality, patience, vigour, concentration and wisdom, and worthy to enter Nirvana, his love for humanity influences his desire to continue in his transmigratory existence in order to serve others.

In Japan, where Zen Buddhism has found its most popular form, the goal is 'Satori'—enlightenment through intense meditation. The purpose of meditation is actively to destroy the barriers of the mind and ultimately pass beyond the intellect to the actual experience of reality. The achievement of Satori is described as a breaking into the closed doors of the mind, so that the outside light can flood in.

If Zen is understood as the bridge between the world interpreted by the mind and the five senses, and the world of reality, then the true follower moves easily from the ever-changing world into undying life and back again. He knows that no one thing leads to salvation, but that each single aspect of the universe is equally valuable for what it is. Zen teachers warn their disciples not to seek enlightenment outside this world: 'The kingdom of Buddhism is in the world, within which we must seek enlightenment . . .'

The words of another Zen master summarize the aim of the meditative search. 'Whence comes birth? Whither goes death? He who knows this 'whence' and 'whether' is said to be a true Buddhist. But who is this that knows birth and death? Who is this that suffers births and deaths? If you would know who he is, dive down into the depths of your being, which no intellection can possibly reach; and when you know it, you know also that there is a place which neither birth nor death can touch'.

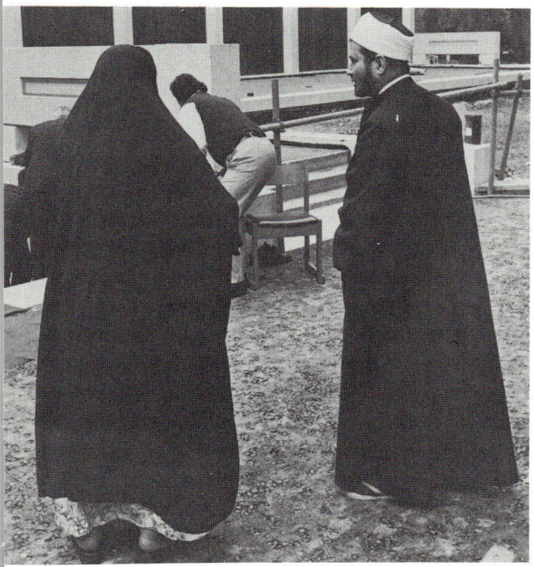

The Moslem Answer: Trial of the Grave

Moslem funeral rites stress the importance of the belief in life after death in the Islamic faith. The dying are gently moved into a position facing Mecca—the holy city. Once dead, the body is laid in a tomb with a high roof, allowing the deceased to sit upright for his forthcoming interrogation by the 'messengers of God'. These are the two angels (named Municar and Nakir) who visit the tomb after interment and question the deceased about his beliefs and deeds in life. A mourner, sometimes called the 'instructor' of the deceased, whispers correct responses to likely divine queries. The angels pronounce judgement in accordance with the result of the 'interview', and the deceased is either allowed into heaven or condemned to hell. This is commonly referred to as the 'trial of the grave'.

The resurrection of a man's body and soul is viewed by a Moslem as an inevitable element of the total order of the universe—the universe created by God, who is all-powerful, merciful and just. Man, since he is the 'noblest' of all God's creatures, has been endowed with a sense of responsibility, which must be used in the service of God and in obedience to Him. The Islamic faith teaches that pride is the cardinal sin, and genuine repentance of it restores a man to a state of freedom from sin and favour with God. Humility is one of the highest virtues sought by a Moslem. He must voluntarily subject his human arrogance—his gifts of reason and intellect—to the omnipotent power of God, which will be used for man's ultimate good.

The resurrection of men is necessary for God to mete out justice to good and evil alike. He can do this as easily as the dead earth is revived by rain. This act, the 'new creation', is referred to in the Koran as the 'great awakening'. Each person has a spiritual part of himself, a 'soul', which is taken by God, sometimes while he is asleep. A man survives the 'first death', just as a person does not cease to exist when he loses consciousness during sleep. Because his soul is snatched away by God, he retains his spiritual faculties beyond the grave.

As we have seen, the dead are consigned to heaven or hell. Paradise is described as a beautiful garden with springs and fountains, where believers are clothed in 'silk and brocade' and promised 'dark-eyed, wide-eyed' maidens. The most saintly are promised a glimpse of the radiance of God. The damned, on the other hand, are pictured as suspended in a state of agony, wishing for annihilation, 'dying but unable to die'. They are manacled, and pierced by swords, while burning in hell-fire. This torment never relents, as body skin is renewed periodically. It is this fate that serves to remind the believer of his duty to God.

The Dying Child

There has been a great change in the pattern, as well as in the relative numbers, of childhood deaths in the last 100 years and, indeed, in the last 50

The great infectious killing diseases such as diphtheria, whooping cough, scarlet fever and tuberculosis have largely disappeared, and their place has been taken by others. Of the approximately 1,900 deaths of children between the ages of 0 and 15 which occur in this country each year, 33 percent are caused by accidents, 16 percent by cancer and allied conditions, such as leukaemia, and 13 percent by congenital abnormalities. Advances in obstetric practice and improvement in the care of the newborn have meant that infant mortality has fallen from 149 per 1,000 live births in 1871 to 1888, to 17 in 1971 to 1975. It is, therefore, the firm expectation that children will live rather than die. Furthermore, changing social patterns and the development and acceptance of contraception have meant that the almost yearly pregnancies of the last century have given place to far smaller families. Furthermore, those children who are born are much more likely to have been carefully planned and, arguably, to carry a greater investment of time and effort on the part of their parents as far as their future is concerned.

It is this loss of potential and of the emotions involved in this potential which spell the great difference between the death of a child and that of an adult, however close and well loved. It means that the parents have not only to accept the loss of the child himself, but also of that part of themselves which they have invested in him. A child, far more than an adult, is dependent on the people around him. He becomes only too readily aware of anxiety and apprehension in his parents, and he quickly picks up non-verbal indicators of these feelings, even if they are not expressed directly. It is this which makes it impossible to consider the management of a dying child in isolation, and it means that the parents and other caring figures, such as doctors and nurses, may be almost as important during the course of his illness and, subsequently, of his death as the child himself.

A child's understanding and appreciation of death depends to a large extent on his age and stage of development. Children under the age of five do not usually regard death as final, generally seeing it as a sleep from which they may awake. At a later age, death may be thought of as a person or as an altered physical state. Because this is unknown and unfamiliar, it may seem frightening and may be associated with feelings of separation, abandonment and isolation. Adolescents develop an awareness of the inevitability of death. Not only does mortal illness represent a reduction of freedom and activity, but death may be seen as the final extinction of all his hopes of emerging as an individual. It is also sometimes regarded as a punishment for an adolescent's attempts at independence and gives rise to feelings of anger and guilt.

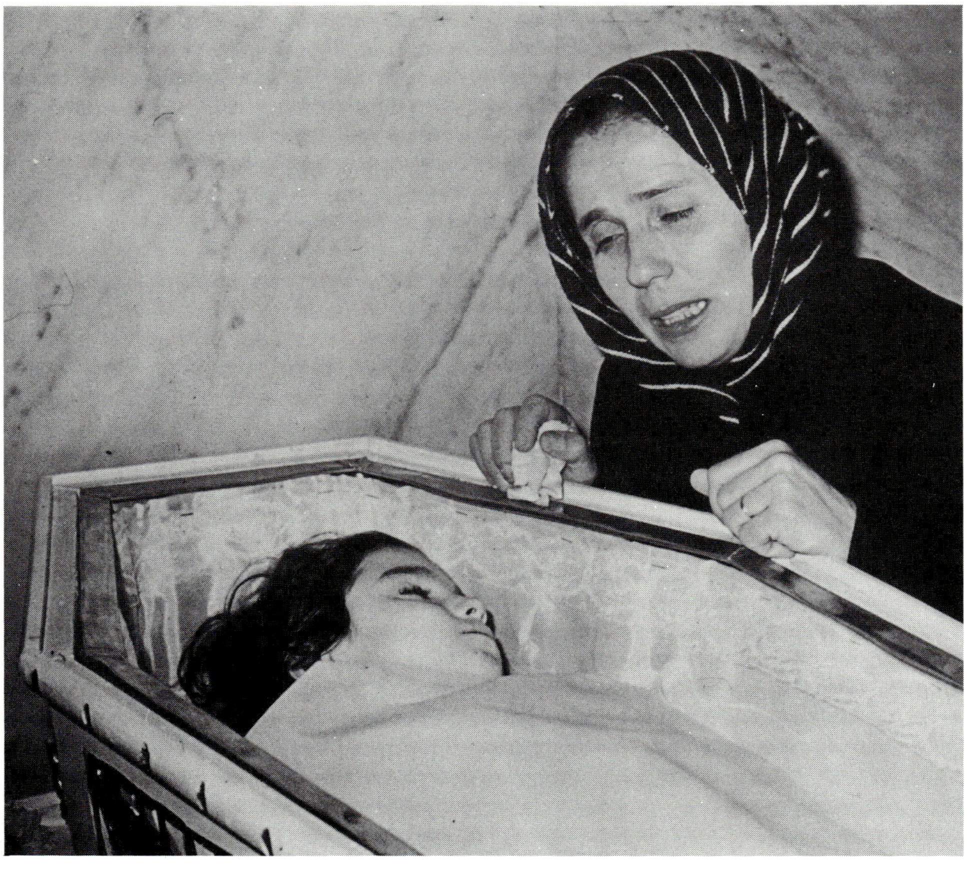

Everyone has to find some way of coping psychologically with an overwhelming threat, and the dying child (like the adult) is no exception. The most commonly used defence mechanism is that of denial, in which the reality of the serious illness and approaching death is not consciously considered at all. The child appears unaware of the severity of his illness, in spite of increasing weakness and other signs of deterioration. Other

children may become unusually cheerful, joking and laughing about their condition, trying in this way to lessen its importance. Some regress and become more infantile and dependent on those around them than their physical state warrants, as if by so doing they can enable caring adults to ward off the threat. Whenever there is mortal illness, there is almost always anger, and the question: 'Why should this happen to me?' is felt, if not asked. Sometimes this anger is shown quite openly, while in others, the child may feel that to express it is too dangerous, because he fears that if he does, there might be some retaliation. He is angry with his parents for allowing this disaster to happen, he is angry (as his parents may be) with doctors and nurses for not being able to cure him. If he feels it is not safe to express his anger, he may deal with it by splitting, that is to say, by making one person or group of people wholly good and another wholly bad. He may attack his parents, to their distress, and over-value the caring staff, because he fears that, if he is not good enough or grateful enough, they may cease to care for him. Parents, too, may have such feelings, and their distress may be increased by their fears of expressing dissatisfaction and rage. Caring staff, for their part, can find such feelings shown towards them very difficult to accept.

It is rarely necessary to 'tell' a child that he is going to die. Indeed, many who advocate this are actuated by their own anger at an intolerable situation, accompanied by an unconscious wish to punish the person who is the cause of it. A very distressed teenage girl demanded that her brother be told he was going to die, so that he would be forced to share her own rage and sorrow. Most older children are aware that they are dying, but their fears may not be so much of the actual death, as of the manner in which it will take place and the pain or suffering which may accompany it. The question on every child's lips: 'Am I going to die?' may really mean: 'Am I going to suffer?'

Often a child will convey his awareness of his approaching death in indirect ways, like the boy who said: 'It's strange to think of someone with cancer going to school, isn't it?' thus showing his realization that he would have no educational future. The important thing for those concerned with dying children is to be sensitive to what they really ask and why they ask it, and not to lie to them. Children, even more than adults, are sensitive to adult lies, and need to feel that they can completely trust those who care for them.

It is not easy for anyone, parents or caring staff, to look after a dying child. Not only must they tolerate the child's distress, but they must also tolerate their own feelings of anger, frustration and impotence to alter the course of events. Sometimes this leads to an effectual isolation and rejection of the child, as if those around him cannot bear to be close to him because of the strong feelings he arouses in them. When this happens, the child feels lost and abandoned and, sometimes, that he is being punished for being ill. If distress can be shared, if there can be acceptance of the inevitable so that some actual mourning can be done before the child dies, both his death and the parents' subsequent grief will be a great deal more tolerable to everyone concerned in the tragedy.

Euthanasia: For?

Considering that we all have to die one day, it is surprising that we do not make more effort to choose a time to suit ourselves, rather than leave such an important matter to chance, exhausted nature, or the decisions of others

There is an inertia in living, which tends to keep the life process going until the difficulties become insurmountable. Doctors know that most patients shy away from death and, however uncomfortable their life, would rather die tomorrow than today. Such is doctors' respect for this primitive urge that they have made an ethical principle out of it.

As a result, they are faced with a dilemma, which is now becoming extremely common. This is the problem of the very old. People do not start to age all at the same time, or all at the same rate. Different tissues of the body have their own times for getting old, so that muscles, bones and joints, the arteries and the heart, the eyes, hearing and the nervous system are not equally old at the same time. There are also wide differences between individuals. As life goes on into the seventies and the eighties, small incapacities and disabilities gradually accumulate. Life becomes more and more restricted, and even this restricted life becomes more and more difficult.

Nowadays, old people are no longer part of the nuclear family. Their children, with husbands or wives and children of their own, have no room for them in their homes, or in their lives. The world moves on with bewildering rapidity, and every new social change comes as an added strain. Then, perhaps, comes illness or an accident. The old person is taken to hospital and soon transferred to a geriatric ward. Here, he gets the best attention, and everything possible is done to put him right and make him able to look after himself again. Then he can go home, perhaps with yet another minor disability, or into an old people's home, or into a chronic ward where he can wait for death. These old people cling to life very tenaciously, and often gain a great deal of enjoyment and interest from a pitifully limited existence. Even then, however, as doctors who work in geriatric wards know well, about one in five of these patients will tell you—if you ask them—that they would very much like to be dead and done with it all, if only that were possible.

Since the Suicide Act of 1961, suicide in Britain has not been an offence under the law. However, it is a long-standing and persistent medical tradition to regard it as abnormal, usually the act of a mentally sick man. Indeed suicide is regarded as constituting strong *prima facie* evidence of mental illness. Doctors think it their duty to interrupt a suicide, however late before death, and then, after he has been resuscitated, to try to help the patient to solve his problems in other ways. Anyone who wishes to forestall well-meant rescue would do well to draw up a solemn declaration of his intention, and formally forbid anyone to interfere with it or lay hands on his person while alive.

I do not know that this has ever been done, but it seems to be lawful, and it might become an accepted practice. If it did, it would solve only a part of the problem. Patients who are very ill and confined to bed are helplessly in the hands of others and have no easy means of suicide. Those who wish to die could perhaps be helped by an amendment to the Suicide Act, releasing from the general prohibition against aiding and abetting a suicide the registered medical practitioner acting *bona fide* in his professional relationship. A doctor, who would never consider being an 'executioner', might find it easier, if the law allowed, to place the means of death within the reach of his patient, for him to use if he so wished of his own accord, neither encouraging nor preventing him.

This would still leave the cases of those who, without realizing what has happened to them, lapse into a demented state in which volitional acts are no longer possible. Their predicament would call for a change in the law, to give effect to a declaration made in advance, asking that in such a state they should be allowed to die as soon as possible. This was the substance of a Euthanasia Bill presented in the Lords in 1969 by Lord Raglan. It was defeated, although a substantial minority voted in favour.

The present state of affairs in law and in practice is a patent absurdity. In the long run, the human desire for comfort will find a way round the distresses and indignities of incurable illness or incapacity. Some time, man's need for freedom and self-determination will win against the forces that keep him in the servitude of a life sentence without remission or parole.

Euthanasia: Against?

The literal meaning of the word 'euthanasia' is 'dying well', so it could be used for any kind of medical practice designed to help people die in dignity and peace. However, it has come to bear the more restricted sense of the intentional killing by a doctor of a patient under certain specified conditions, the most important of which is the patient's free consent

Those who favour 'voluntary euthanasia' believe that, in a significant number of cases, the only way to ensure a peaceful and dignified death is for the doctor to take positive steps to end the patient's life. As English law now stands, this would constitute murder, so the debate about euthanasia has centred upon proposals to change the law.

It is important to distinguish euthanasia, so understood, from two practices with which it is sometimes confused. The first is that of allowing a patient who is suffering from a fatal illness to die in peace without being subjected to troublesome treatments which cannot restore him to health or significantly improve his condition. The second is the use of pain-killing drugs to control severe pain, even at the risk of shortening life. These are now generally accepted by the medical profession and although they call for great sensitivity and care on the part of all concerned, they raise no problems of moral principle. They are sometimes called 'passive' or 'indirect' euthanasia, but this language is misleading, because it obscures important moral distinctions. Nevertheless, there have been enough well-publicized cases of patients being kept alive unnecessarily to have caused a good deal of anxiety. It is likely that much of the demand for voluntary euthanasia would be satisfied if people could be sure that they, or their relatives and friends, would not be kept alive pointlessly or allowed to suffer unnecessary pain.

The debate about euthanasia turns on three issues. The first is one of fact—is there a significant number of cases in which the only effective way to control pain is to end the patient's life? The second is moral—are there circumstances in which it is morally permissible for a doctor intentionally to take life? The third concerns the role of legislation—would it be wise to change the law so as to permit voluntary euthanasia?

As to the question of fact, those who oppose euthanasia claim that, with improvements in drugs and in the education of doctors in their use, there are now very few cases in which severe pain and other distressing conditions cannot be adequately controlled. The growth of the hospice movement is evidence of this. Supporters of euthanasia contest this claim and challenge the basis for making it. It is not for doctors, but for the individual, to decide when life is no longer tolerable.

The moral case for euthanasia tends to take two different forms, a difference which has been reflected in proposals for legislation. In one form, the main emphasis is upon compassion. The appeal to compassion is directed to doctors and others who are in a position to make decisions about those who are terminally ill. The problem is regarded as essentially one of medical ethics, of what doctors should do, and should be allowed by law to do, in the case of patients suffering from a disease which is incurable, fatal and painful. Compassion, it is argued, requires that, in such cases, given the consent of the patient, the doctor should be ready and able to end his life.

The other appeals to a 'right to die' on the part of the patient who, it is recommended, should be able to sign in advance a request for euthanasia if he were to be found to be suffering from a serious physical illness liable to cause him severe distress or render him incapable of rational existence. The decision would be the patient's and the doctor would be acting as his agent. On this view, the individual has the moral right, and should be given the legal right, to decide whether, in certain circumstances, he will live or die, and to be medically assisted, if he chooses to die. It is evident that the first approach is much more restrictive than the second. Euthanasia would be available only in terminal cases. Also, given the patient's consent, the final decision would be entirely the doctor's. The second approach allows the patient to exercise his 'right to die' if he is suffering from an illness which is incurable, even if it is not thought to be fatal.

The moral case against euthanasia concentrates attention upon the role of the doctor who, whether out of compassion or in pursuance of the patient's 'right to die', would be called upon to kill the patient or assist in his suicide. How can he best show compassion for someone in distress: by killing him or assisting in his death, or by carefully accompanying him in his dying? There is, it is urged, a very strong presumption in the moral tradition of the West against the taking of innocent life. Both Christian and humanist influences have contributed to this tradition. The medical profession is deeply committed to this principle of 'the sanctity of life'. Although it is possible to conceive of exceptions in certain extreme situations, we ought to be very reluctant to sanction any departure from it. The recognition of an individual's 'right to die' would take too little account of the ties that bind people to one another, and would encourage the sick, the elderly and the helpless to regard themselves as dispensable. Moreover, if doctors were to be allowed by their professional ethics —and by the law—to kill, no matter how stringent the safeguards, public confidence in the profession would be weakened. So would the relationship of trust between the aged and infirm and all those who care for them.

The legal question cannot be separated from the moral one. Whether the law should be changed depends on whether changing it would remove greater evils than it would cause. Proponents of voluntary euthanasia believe that, by giving people freedom to decide, within certain limits, when and how they shall die, a change in the law would extend liberty and relieve distress without risk of serious countervailing evils. Its opponents believe that such a change would weaken respect for life, lessen public confidence in doctors and increase the stresses upon the aged and infirm and upon their families. They also argue that, however carefully a law might be drafted, it would be impossible in practice to avoid abuse, or to draw the line clearly between cases which the law considered justified and those which it did not.

How to Cope with Death: Some Practical Advice

Learning to cope effectively with a death in the family is a very demanding, if not actually shattering, experience. Not only are there a great many practical details to be taken care of when one feels least like doing anything, but there is also the weight of emotional pain and shock to be faced. The Golden Rule is—do not try to go it alone!

Get help from a friend, clergyman, doctor or anyone else you trust, and share your grief with them. You will appreciate their advice and assistance with the practical arrangements and feel supported by their genuine concern for your distress.

What to do First

If you are the one who discovers the body, ascertain that death has really occurred. See if breathing has stopped and whether any pulse or heartbeat can be observed. If the death appears to be from natural causes, telephone the deceased's doctor, or, if you do not know who he or she is, any local doctor. However, if you think that violence or an accident was involved do not touch the body or anything in the room, as this could interfere with vital evidence.

Getting the Right Forms

A doctor must issue a medical certificate stating the cause of death. He will usually give it to a relative, and it should be taken to the local registry office. Sometimes the doctor may post the certificate direct to the registrar. If the doctor states on the certificate that he has reported the death to the coroner, it cannot be registered until authorized by the coroner, and the body will be taken to the local mortuary. In this case, it is as well to keep in touch with the registrar, to know when the death can be registered.

There are a number of reasons for reporting a death to the coroner, who generally holds a post-mortem to establish the true cause of death. If he decides it was the result of natural causes, the family can take responsibility for the body and proceed with funeral arrangements. However, if death was caused unnaturally, by violence or an accident, there will be an inquest and you will be asked to attend. After the inquest, the coroner issues a certificate for cremation or an order for burial. If the death occurs in hospital, a relative will have to go there and deal with various formalities, as well as collecting the deceased's belongings. You may have to identify the body, and should be prepared to sign a form consenting to a post-mortem. The hospital authorities are very sympathetic and helpful. They will see to the necessary medical forms, so that you can arrange to have the body removed from the mortuary for the funeral.

Registering the Death

Normally, you will have to register the death within five days (in Scotland, eight days). You can find out at the post office or library which is the registry office covering the area in which the death occurred and the hours when it is open. You do not usually need to make an appointment. Take with you the medical certificate showing the cause of death, together with the medical card and government pension book—if available. The actual registration is fairly straightforward and should not be too distressing. The registrar will ask for various details, which he enters on a draft form. You should check that the information is correct, before the entry is made. You then sign the register, and the registrar adds his signature. Some of the information you are asked for is needed for statistical purposes only and will not appear in the register. Try to make sure, when you give the names of the deceased, that they match those on birth and marriage certificates, as this will prevent any queries about identity in connection with insurance and pension matters.

Once the death has been formally registered, you can obtain death certificates, which are certified copies of the entry. It is as well to note the number and date, in case you need further copies later on. The registrar can advise you about other types of certificate you may need for dealing with the affairs of the deceased and claiming benefits due from various sources. You should keep a record of the certificates obtained, the fees paid and where they are sent. Finally, the Registrar will give you a form known as a 'disposal certificate', which permits you to go ahead with burial or an application for disposal by cremation. (The details of registration and other procedures apply to England and Wales. In Scotland, the registration formalities are slightly different.)

Arranging the Funeral

Find out if the deceased left instructions regarding his or her funeral. Although not legally binding, they are usually followed, as a mark of respect. If the deceased has bequeathed his (or her) eyes, organs or whole body for medical purposes, Her Majesty's Inspector of Anatomy, or a medical school must be notified as soon as possible.

Contact an undertaker, who will take over the funeral arrangements. Discuss any special wishes of the deceased and his religious affiliation, if relevant. Let the undertaker know where and when you want the burial to take place, and if any particular clergyman has been asked to officiate. A non-religious ceremony is possible at most cemeteries and crematoria, and if this is what is required, you could contact the British Humanist Society. You might have to make special arrangements for burying someone of a different faith, so the local religious leader should be contacted first. Jews usually belong to a burial society, which will arrange the funeral. They are not usually cremated or embalmed, and there are no flowers at the cemetery.

It is very important to clarify financial details with the undertaker, and he should give you a very firm idea of the services to be provided for the cost quoted. It is best to find out whether additional expenses will be incurred. Discussions about money may seem out of place at a time of such emotional stress, but it is necessary if you are to avoid over-spending on a costly coffin and an elaborate funeral.

Cremation is permitted only when the medical cause of death is known, and several official forms have to be completed before cremation can take place. The undertaker will usually make the arrangements with the crematorium, and the costs should be far less than for a traditional burial.

Settling the Estate

Inform the deceased's employers and find out whether any pay is outstanding, and whether any insurance or pension monies are payable. You will almost certainly need a solicitor to handle all the financial details of the estate. If the deceased did not have one, contact your own or ask the local Citizens' Advice Bureau to recommend one. The solicitor will deal with the known assets, such as bank and savings accounts, stocks and shares and insurance policies. He will act on your behalf to establish how much more there is in the estate and will make sure after probate that the provisions of the will are carried out properly. There is particular need for a solicitor if the deceased has died intestate (without leaving a will), and he will advise the person appointed to take care of the financial affairs. A solicitor will tell you if the deceased was a tenant, and he can arrange for the rent or mortgage to be paid until his affairs are settled.

Remember to put in a claim for the death grant from the local office of the Department of Health and Social Security. This is intended to help towards funeral expenses. Also, find out if there are any unpaid pension or allowance payments to come. Finally, you will have to take care of the various other financial obligations. Notify hire purchase companies and the electricity, gas and telephone authorities of the death, if the agreements were in the deceased's name. Do not forget to contact the inspector of taxes to find out if any refund is due.

Clearing out the clothes and personal belongings of the deceased is a difficult task. You may find it too distressing to do and be tempted to leave everything just as it is. Resist the temptation, because it is far healthier to deal with the task as soon as possible. If you really cannot face handling the deceased's personal effects, ask someone else to do it for you.

Unless it is to be private, you will probably want to let friends and colleagues know when the funeral will take place. You can do this personally or through a sympathetic friend, and you may want to put an announcement in a local or national newspaper, specifying whether donations to a selected charity may be sent in lieu of flowers.

Coping with Grief

The funeral over, the financial affairs under control, you are suddenly faced with overwhelming and sometimes conflicting emotions that compound your grief. Bear in mind that, as has been said before: 'The shock of mortality never ceases to amaze and overwhelm the living'. You must accept the inevitability of death and not try to deny the reality of the situation. A loved one is dead, and you should not try to repress your feelings. Understanding grief is halfway to overcoming it, and it is very important to mourn, either within the rituals of your religion or on your own. 'Mourning is the process that guarantees that we happen to our grief, rather than having our grief happen to us'. Be prepared for shock to affect your outlook, but try not to be resentful of people who have not suffered your loss. You may even feel bitter that it has happened to you. Feelings of panic may overwhelm you if you were dependent on someone close. Instead of a planned life pattern, there seems an empty void and sense of loss. You cannot adjust to your loss by feeling sorry for yourself or withdrawing completely from the world. Try to realize that, the more you cut yourself off from people, the harder it is to return to the living and pick up the pieces.

Naturally, you will crave a certain amount of privacy, but be tolerant of the people who want to help you overcome your sorrow. It is just as uncomfortable for them to be with someone mourning grievously. Respond to messages of condolence and acknowledge that people care about your misery. Accept that you will probably suffer from some sort of guilt complex, perhaps because you are still alive, or because you feel that you did not do enough. Guilt is a normal reaction. It should not be bottled up or ignored. Be open to help from individuals or organizations. Ask for support and comfort from family, friends, doctor, minister, social worker, the Samaritans, the Salvation Army, the Citizens' Advice Bureau or organizations for the elderly. Eventually, you can come to terms with your grief and once again find joy in living.

Index

(Figures in italics indicate an illustration or caption in margin of text)

A

B

C

D

E

F

G

H

I

J

K

L

M

N

O

P

Q

R

S

T

U

V

W

Z

Picture Credits

The publisher wishes to thank the following organizations and individuals who have supplied photographs for this book. Photographs have been credited by page number; for reasons of space some references have been abbreviated as follows:

AP: Associated Press. EPL: Elisabeth Photo library.
NHPA: Natural History Photo Agency. NSP: Natural Science Photos.

Cover front: Ianthe Ruthven. Cover back: Space Frontier-NASA/Frank Spooner/Rex/P Morris. Prelims: Rex/EPL London/US Air Force. 10/11: Guys Hospital/Tate Gallery. 12/13: Biophoto. 14/15: Biophoto. 16/17: Biophoto/NHPA. 18/19: Bettman Archive/Mansell/Biophoto. 20/21: P Morris/Biophoto/Gerald Cubitt. 22/23: NSP/NHPA. 24/25: Ron Boardman/Bruce Coleman Ltd/NSP. 26/27: NSP/Bruce Coleman Ltd/ Michael Chinery/NSP. 28/29: John Topham/Bruce Coleman Ltd/NSP/ NHPA. 30/31: Ardea/Bruce Coleman Ltd. 32/33: Bruce Coleman Ltd/ Heather Angel-Biofotos/Gerald Cubitt. 34/35: Frank Spooner-Francolon-Gamma/Mary Evans/Bruce Coleman Ltd. 36/37: Museum of London/EPL London. 38/39: Popperfoto/Transworld/Keystone/EPL London/Mary Evans. 40/41: William MacQuitty/Robert Harding Associates/EPL London/Museum of Rouen-Michel Lerond/Museum of the American Indian, Heye Foundation/ 42/43: EPL London/Rex Features/Gerald Cubitt/William MacQuitty/Michael Holford. 44/45: EPL London/William MacQuitty/Keystone/Museum of Rouen-Michel Lerond. 46/47: EPL London/Douglas Dickens/William MacQuitty/Sheldon Crematoria Ltd. 48/49: John Hillelson Agency-Marc Riboud-Magnum/William MacQuitty/Museum of Liverpool/Douglas Dickens. 50/51: Orbis Library/Gerald Cubitt. 52/53: Mary Evans/Museo del Prado-AGE/City of Manchester Art Galleries. 54/55: Museum voor Schone Kunsten, Antwerp/Pinacoteca, Bologne/William MacQuitty. 56/57: Mary Evans/ Egyptian Museum, Turin/Victoria and Albert Museum/ATA Stockholm/ Spectrum. 58/59: Fogg Art Museum, Gray Collection Harvard University/ The National Trust-J Whittaker/Roger Violet. 60/61: Hermitage Museum/ Roger Violet. 62/63:L Robert Harding Associates/Ronald Sheridan/Museo del Prado-AGE. 64/65: EPL London/Ronald Sheridan/Museo del Prado-AGE. 66/67: Musei Capitolini, Rome/Louvre, Paris/National Gallery, London. 68/69: Louvre, Paris/Museo del Prado-AEG/Galerie Nationale, Oslo/Musee de Beaux Arts, Brussels/Tate Gallery. 70/71: Syndication International/ Robert Harding Associates/Ronald Sheridan/William MacQuitty/EPL London/Salamander/Gerald Cubitt/Robert Haas. 72/73: AP/Finler-Warner Seven Arts/Kobal-United Artists/Kobal-Warner Seven Arts/Finler-TCF. 74/75: Salamander. 76/77: Guys Hospital/Danish Tourist Board-Suckeborg Museum/Robert Hass (Courtesy of Dept of Morbid Anatomy, Kings' College Hospital)/Guys Hospital. 78/79: Ron Boardman/Salamander. 80/81: Salamander. 82/83: Rex Features Ltd/Salamander/Frank Spooner-Abbas-Gamma/Popperfoto. 84/85: Salamander. 86/87: Popperfoto. 88/89: Ron Boardman/Manchester Museum, University of Manchester/Gordon Museum, Guys Hospital. 90/91: John Harcup/Ron Boardman/Salamander/St Mary's Hospital Medical School/Michel Lerond-Museum of Rouen. 92/93: Mary Evans/Bodleian Library, Oxford. 94/95: Ron Boardman/Gerald Cubitt/John Harcup. 96/97: Mary Evans/Mansell/Ron Boardman. 98/99: NSP/John Harcup/St Mary's Hospital Medical School/EPL London/Ron Boardman. 100/101: EPL London/Ianthe Ruthven. 102/103: Rex. 104/105: Popperfoto/ EPL London. 106/107 Popperfoto/Rex/Industrial Accident Prevention Bureau, Sweden. 108/109: Rex/Popperfoto. 110/111: Rex/Salamander/Popperfoto. 112/113: Popperfoto. 114/115: Popperfoto. 116/117: Popperfoto/Colorific. 118/119: Mary Evans/Popperfoto. 120/121: Salamander/Mary Evans/Keystone. 122/123: Mary Evans/Keystone/Salamander. 124/125: Salamander/Kobal/ Michael Holford/Popperfoto. 126/127: Colorific/Popperfoto. 128/129: Colorific-Life/Robert Harding. 130/131: Popperfoto/Central Press/Rex. 132/133: Syndication International/Keystone/Museum of London. 134/135: Mary Evans/Mansell/London Express Features. 136/137: Keystone/Mary Evans. 138/139: AP/20th Century Fox/Colorific. 140/141: Popperfoto/EPL London. 142/143: Mary Evans. 144/145: Mary Evans/Popperfoto. 146/147: Mary Evans. 148/149: Rex/John Topham/EPL London/Popperfoto/Keystone/ Central Press. 150/151: Central Press/Popperfoto/Colorific/AP. 152/153: Popperfoto/Colorific. 154/155: Keystone/Colorific. 156/157: Mary Evans. 158/159: Salamander/Popperfoto/Keystone/Mary Evans. 160/161: Pictor International/Keystone. 162/163: Keystone. 164/165: South Dakota State Historical Society/Keystone. 166/167: Mary Evans/Keystone. 168/169: Colorific-Jaeger/AP/Keystone. 170/171: Mike Tregenza/Pictorial Parade/ Keystone. 172/173: EPL London/Mike Tregenza. 174/175: Novosti/William MacQuitty. 176/177: Mary Evans/Popperfoto. 178/179: Imperial War Museum/ US Defense Dept/Colorific. 180/181: Salamander/US Defense Dept/Rex/ A H Westing. 182/183: US Defense Dept/Keystone/Popperfoto. 184/185: Victoria and Albert Museum/Keystone/AP. 186/187: EPL London/NASA. 188/189: Salamander-NASA/EPL London. 190/191: Frank Lane/Spectrum. 192/193: Frank Lane/Spectrum. 194/195: Spectrum/Frank Lane. 196/197: AP/NASA. 198/199: UKAEA/Spectrum/Salamander-NASA/US Air Force. 200/201: Mike Abrahams. 202/203: Rex/Guys Hospital. 204/205: Cicely Saunders/Keystone. 206/207: Rex/Salamander. 208/209: EPL London/Rex. 210/211: Rex/EPL London. 212/213: EPL London/Rex. 214/215: Rex. 216/217: EPL London. 218/219: EPL London.